POLLINATORS
PREDATORS
& PARASITES

The ecological roles of insects in southern Africa

Clarke Scholtz • Jenny Scholtz • Hennie de Klerk

Published by Struik Nature
(an imprint of Penguin Random House South Africa (Pty) Ltd)
Reg. No. 1953/000441/07
The Estuaries, No. 4, Oxbow Crescent,
Century City, 7441 South Africa
PO Box 1144, Cape Town, 8000 South Africa

Visit **www.penguinrandomhouse.co.za**
and join the Struik Nature Club for
updates, news, events and special offers.

First published in 2021
1 3 5 7 9 10 8 6 4 2

Publisher: Pippa Parker
Managing editor: Roelien Theron
Editor: Marthina Mössmer
Project manager: Helen de Villiers
Designer: Janice Evans
Illustrator: André Olwage
Maps: Christian Deschodt
Proofreader and indexer: Emsie du Plessis

Reproduction by Studio Repro and
Hirt & Carter Cape (Pty) Ltd
Printed and bound in China by C&C Offset Printing Co., Ltd

FSC
www.fsc.org

MIX
Paper from
responsible sources
FSC® C018179

Print: 9781775845553
ePub: 9781775846321

Front cover Bee fly, one of a host of beautiful and
important pollinators in the region.

Back cover Representatives of ecologically important southern
African insects (left to right): a honey bee, regarded as the most
important pollinator on the planet.; wood-decomposing long-
horned beetle; parasitic wasp; pollinating butterfly.

Title page Sap-feeding bug (Hemiptera), one of many
important members of the group.

FOREWORD

Few people realise the immense importance of insects to the earth's wellbeing but books such as this are a timely reminder that without them life on earth would be very different to what it is now. Disturbing recent studies have reported alarming declines of insect populations worldwide with as many as half of the world's insect species so rapidly declining that one-third may already be threatened with extinction. Without rapid intervention to slow or reverse the situation, the environmental consequences are likely to be catastrophic.

This book reveals for the first time the importance of insects to southern Africa's natural environment: that 70% of the world-famous flora is entirely dependent on insects for pollination and that dung beetles bury in excess of 500 thousand tonnes of animal dung per day are among the staggering statistics.

The authors have taken the biological regions of southern Africa as the starting point of their narrative, outlining the major physical and biological characteristics of each region and then systematically relating the functions of each of the major ecological insect groups present; pollinators, predators, parasites, decomposers and others – and hence the title of the book. Furthermore, virtually every important species and its activities are illustrated in hundreds of exquisite photos accompanying the text.

The authors are eminently suitable to have handled the depth and breadth of the subject covered in hundreds of specific topics spread amongst thousands of scientific publications about insect biology; one a renowned professional academic entomologist, another a conservationist and the third a highly skilled photographer. They have produced a remarkable piece on the natural history of southern Africa's insect wealth that will stand as the reference on the topic for decades to come.

JOHAN VAN ZYL PHD, DSC (AGRIC)
Former Vice-Chancellor, University of Pretoria
Chairman of the Board, Sanlam Limited (former CEO)

Opposite (a) Pollinating adult butterfly whose larvae are herbivorous; **(b)** soil-living predatory antlion larva that has a free-living predatory adult; **(c)** leaf-feeding leaf beetle whose larvae also feed on leaves; **(d)** pollinating hover fly whose detritus-feeding larvae are aquatic.

CONTENTS

Acknowledgements 6
Preface 7
Introduction 8

Opposite (a) Pollinating wasp; **(b)** bark-gnawing beetle; **(c)** carnivorous firefly; **(d)** flower-feeding beetle; **(e)** predatory lacewing larva; **(f)** flower-visiting chafer beetle; **(g)** predatory dragonfly; **(h)** assassin bug.

ACKNOWLEDGEMENTS

Many family, friends and colleagues have contributed in various ways to the production of this book and without whose support it is unlikely it would have been completed.

A very special word of thanks is due to Johan van Zyl, a university colleague and friend who generously contributed to the publication costs of the book in order to make it more affordable for students.

The following people contributed in the form of taxon identifications, literature or information on the biology of certain insects, access to their properties or other aspects that were invaluable to producing the final product: Abdullahi Yusuf, Adrian Davis, Alan Burke, Alan Gardiner, Alberto Ballerio, Alex Nepomuceno, Alexandra J. Holland, Alfred F. Newton, André Coetzer, André Olwage, Andrew Davies, Andrew Forbes, Andrew Polaszek, Annelise Langman, Annette Bennet, Ansie Dippenaar, Antoine Marchal, Anton Scholtz, Arthur V. Evans, Ashley Kirk-Spriggs, Astri Leroy, Ben Fong, Beth Grobbelaar, Braam van Wyk, Brett Hurley, Bruce Blake, Bryan and Erica Church, Candice Owen, Carmen Jacobs, Caroline Chaboo, Catherine Sole, Charles Griffiths, Charles Haddad, Chia-Hua Lue, Chris Oosthuizen, Christian Deschodt, Christian Peeters, Christian Pirk, Christine Sydes, Colin Ralston, Connal Eardley, Corinna S. Bazelet, Dan Otte, Daniel de Klerk, Dave Rowe, David Herbert, Darren Pietersen, Dawid Jacobs, Denis Brothers, Deon Bakkes, Donald Quicke, Duncan MacFadyen, Elme Brand, Ernest Seamark, Ernst van Jaarsveld, Fabian Haas, Ferdy de Moor, Gavin Svenson, Gerhard Prinsloo, Gimo Daniel, Gunnar Mikalsen Kvifte, Gustav Venter, Hamish Robertson, Handré Basson, Hannelie Human, Hans Feijen, Helen James, Helene Badenhorst, Hermann Staude, I. Astrid Minnaar, Ian Engelbrecht, Ian Gaigher, Ian Millar, Ian Sharp, Ian Thomas, Ishtiag Hassan, Jackie Dabrowski, James Ding Johnson, James Harrison, Jan Myburgh, Jan Vlok, Jan-Andries Neethling, Janine Snyman, Jason Londt, Jason Sampson, Jenny Day, Jessica Badenhorst, Jeremy Midgley, Joe van Heerden, John Lawrence, John Manning, Jonathan Ball, Jonathan Colville, Joop Boomker, Joseph White, Karen A. Ober, Karien Labuschagne, Kera le Roux, Kerstin Junker, Kevin Cole, Kitty Stamhuis, Koziba Balisi, Krissie Clark, Leo Braack, Leon Lotz, Leslie Minter, Lizette Moolman, Louis du Preez, Louwtjie Snyman, Low de Vries, Lyle J. Buss, Lyndall Pereira, Lynette Rudman, Lynn Kimsey, Marco Alberto Bologna, Margaret Kieser, Margaret Thayer, Marieka Gryzenhout, Marietjie Oosthuizen, Mark Brown, Martin Kruger, Martin Villet, Maureen Coetzee, Meagan Mansell, Mervyn Mansell, Michelle Hamer, Michio Hori, Mick & Jayne McElwee, Mike Knight, Mike Picker, Mike Spies, Neal Evenhuis, Nelly Ndungu, Nico de Bruyn, Olivier Boilly, Oloff Paul, Pawel Jaloszynski, Peter Duelli, Peter Hawkes, Peter Schüle, Peter Slingsby, Phil Richardson, Philip G. Herbst, Piet Janse Van Rensburg, Piotr Naskrecki, Reinier Terblanche, Richard Dean, Richard Sehnal, Rina de Klerk, Robert Bryden, Robin Crewe, Robin Lyle, Roger Burks, Rolf Beutel, Ronald Cocks, Ruan Veldtman, Rudi van Aarde, Ruth Müller, Sarah Gess, Scott E. Brooks, Sébastien Rojkoff, Shane McEvey, Shannon Mitchell, Shaun Levick, Simon Van Noort, Sky Liu, Stephen D. Gaimari, Steve A. Marshall, Steve Johnson, Sue Dean, Sue Nicolson, Ted MacRae, Tharina Bird, Vaughn Swart, Vida van der Walt, Vincent Smith, Vivienne Uys, Warwick Tarboton, Werner Strümpher and Willem Augustyn-Goussard.

Besides the above, however, we are especially deeply indebted to a number of family and friends who have contributed in innumerable ways to the production of this book: Alberto Ballerio, André Coetzer, Anton Scholtz, Ashley Kirk-Spriggs, Braam van Wyk, Carmen Jacobs, Connal Eardley, Corey Bazelet, Dawid Jacobs, Hermann Staude, Ian Sharp, James Harrison, Jonathan Ball, John Manning, Mervyn Mansell, Mike Spies, Peter Hawkes, Rina de Klerk, Simon van Noort, Steve Johnson and Steve Marshall.

Besides collegial assistance and various contributions provided by Alberto Ballerio, André Olwage, Braam van Wyk, Hermann Staude, John Manning, Jonathan Ball, Mervyn Mansell, Steve Johnson and Steve Marshall, as mentioned above, we would like to pay special tribute to them for their steadfast and unwavering assistance up to the last minute by the provision of unpublished data, up-to-date information on various insect groups, and photographs or drawings when asked. They have undoubtedly contributed greatly to the finished product.

Also, the members of the Scarab Research Group in the Department of Zoology and Entomology at the University of Pretoria supported this project in numerous ways over many years – their names appear in the above list. Of these colleagues and students, Carmen Jacobs has been an absolute pillar of support in many different ways throughout the gestation of the book – we are extremely grateful to her.

The book benefited immensely from the dogged pursuit of perfection by the Struik Nature team of freelancers – Tina Mössmer, Helen de Villiers and Janice Evans, as well as Roelien Theron inhouse. Thanks to Pippa Parker for her highly efficient and pleasant guidance throughout. We are extremely grateful for all of their contributions to what we believe is a magnificent book.

Finally, two books on southern African insects have been the mainstay of much of the information we have used for this book and without which we would have made little progress. They are:

- Picker, M.D., Griffiths, C. & Weaving, A. 2002. *Field guide to insects of South Africa*. Cape Town, South Africa: Struik Publishers.
- Scholtz, C.H. & Holm, E. 2008. *Insects of southern Africa*. Pretoria, South Africa: Protea Book House.

CLARKE SCHOLTZ • JENNY SCHOLTZ • HENNIE DE KLERK

PREFACE

Insects are the dominant organisms in any terrestrial ecosystem and southern Africa has amongst the richest insect diversity of any equivalent area in the world. Furthermore, the percentage of endemic groups in the region is extraordinarily high. This diversity includes total species numbers but it also reflects the importance that insects fulfil as essential participants in most ecological processes. Yet, in spite of their significance in the region, the interesting stories about them have not been told in a generally accessible medium and the host of wonderful examples of their natural history have mostly remained hidden in research publications, and only revealed to other scientists with similar interests.

So, what we have tried to do in this book is to highlight and illustrate some of the interesting, often remarkable, aspects of insect life history in the different biomes and other regions where they occur, and to emphasise their environmental importance as ecosystem service providers, something never done before for southern African insects. Examples include virtually every type of insect behaviour known among most of the major groups, as well as between them and their environment, and they cover multiple aspects of the four main classes of insect behaviour: food acquisition, defence, reproduction and brood care, as well as the principal interactions between insects and their biological and physical environments. These comprise about 300 individual case studies and most of the phenomena and insects involved are illustrated in some of the more than 1,600 photographs that accompany the text. Furthermore, an illustrated guide to each of the 25 insect orders found in southern Africa is included, in which the diagnostic characters of each are provided.

The writing of the book has been a decade-long journey to accumulate the information and photographs that document the known, but also to discover and record novel phenomena and stories about insects, and we hope that by providing an intimate insight into the beauty and importance of a major component of the natural world it will help to emphasise the value of understanding and conserving it.

CLARKE SCHOLTZ ● JENNY SCHOLTZ ● HENNIE DE KLERK
October, 2020

'Southern Africa has amongst the richest insect diversity of any equivalent area in the world.'

A lacewing, *Italochrysa gigantea* (Chrysopidae), with dual ecological roles: a predatory adult and a parasitic larva.

INTRODUCTION

Southern Africa is world renowned for its abundant and diverse wildlife, wide variety of indigenous plants and breath-taking scenery. The region has some of the highest concentrations of large African mammals left on the continent and plant and animal endemicity on the subcontinent is exceptionally high, probably as a consequence of the wide range of landscape and vegetation types in the region that distinguish nine distinct biomes. These ecological regions are characterised by particular soils, vegetation structure and associated climate, which support distinctive combinations of plants and animals. The biomes grade across the subcontinent from tropical forest in the east to desert in the west, with vastly different environments in between. South Africa, as a result of its position on the continent, has the most varied topography and, consequently, the highest biological diversity in the region, which contributes to its being recognised as the fourth most biodiverse country in the world (after Brazil, Colombia and Indonesia).

But when biodiversity is discussed, it invariably refers to plant and higher vertebrate diversity, largely because most biodiversity scientists study plants and large animals, and because much less is known about the insect fauna. Accordingly, many readily accessible books have been written about southern African mammal and bird behaviour, while the complex behaviour of insects and the fascinating stories of their lives have remained hidden in hundreds of scientific publications. The stories reveal interactions between soil engineers and the landscape, pollinators and plants, insect predators and their prey, parasites and their hosts, and the sophisticated lives of social insects, as well as many other interesting aspects of their biology – presented here for the first time, featuring the most ecologically important and interesting insects in southern Africa.

Although larger vertebrates and plants generate the most interest, approximately 80% of all multicellular organisms are invertebrates, and of these about 75% are insects (**fig. 1**). In southern Africa, about 50,000 insect species have been named, but it is thought that this represents less than half of the actual number still to be discovered and described. In comparison, there are roughly 23,000 species of plant, about 860 species of bird, and only 354 mammal species in the region.

Furthermore, most insects go through four totally different developmental stages – egg, larva, pupa and adult – and the two feeding stages (larva and adult) usually feed on different food types, often in different habitats (e.g. butterflies feed on nectar from flowers, while their larvae feed on plant tissue, usually of quite different plants), so in ecological terms they could be considered completely different entities.

By virtue of insects' small size and short generation time, the numbers of some species are often very high, an aspect of their ecology that regularly brings certain species into conflict with humans. These so-called pest species compete for food, or spread human, domestic-livestock and pet diseases. However, pests represent only a tiny fraction of all insects; most are not in conflict with us, and many are highly beneficial to healthy natural and agricultural ecosystems and improve food production dramatically. When you consider that most plants and animals have a range of insects intimately associated with them, their immense ecological significance becomes apparent.

Every plant species has an array of different insect species dependent on each of its parts: some feed on specific organs – roots, leaves, flowers, fruits and seeds – but many others are beneficial, pollinating plants and thus leading to fertile seed and increased genetic fitness, which contribute to the astonishing plant species richness for which the region is famous.

Mammals and birds also have a wide range of associated insects: internal and external parasites; blood, fur and feather feeders; insects that feed on their dung; and in the end, specialists that consume every part of the remains of their bodies, leaving only bones.

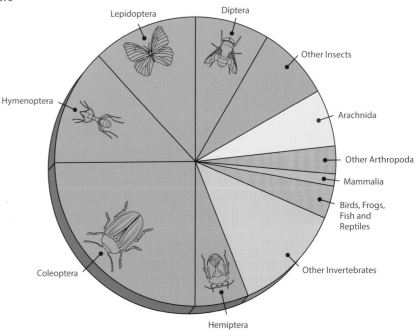

1 Insect numbers in relation to those of other animals and plants.

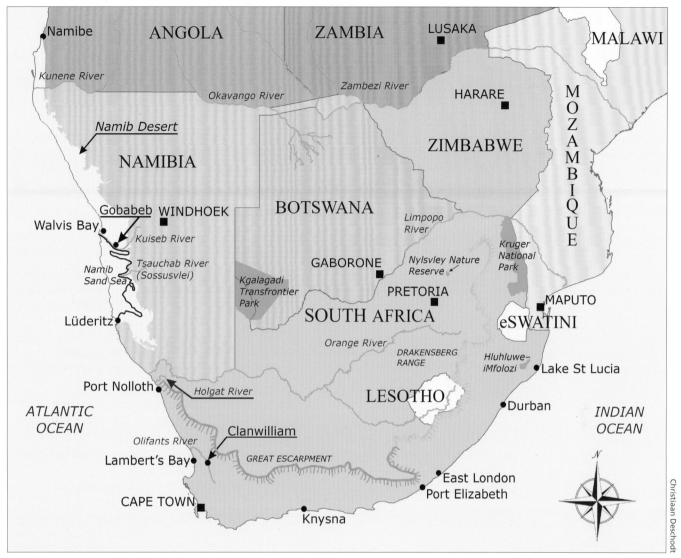

2 The southern African region, showing the countries, rivers and major cities, as well as towns and conservation areas mentioned in this book.

Not only do insects themselves eat, but they are also eaten, being the main food of numerous animals, including predatory insects, other invertebrates such as spiders and scorpions, as well as of many vertebrates. These include large numbers of bird and reptile species, all insectivorous bats, numerous small carnivorous mammals as well as some of the region's rarest and most unusual mammals – the pangolin and aardvark, which depend entirely on ants and termites for their survival. Furthermore, every insect species is potentially the host of other insects that parasitise it or feed on some stage of its life cycle. Insects are also part of the diet of carnivorous plants.

The activities of many insect species produce such large physical changes to their environment that these become suitable habitats for other animal and plant species. Some also recycle nutrients and are largely responsible for accelerating water penetration and much of the aeration of the soil, while pollinators determine plant establishment, maintenance and growth, and ultimately the plant composition of particular regions. This, in turn, largely determines the composition of insect communities that maintain the structure of the biomes.

It is little wonder, then, that insects have been dubbed 'the small things that make ecosystems function'. Life without them is unthinkable – natural ecosystems would gradually change; plants would die and their remains be left to accumulate, and in turn, birds and mammals dependent on the plants would also die and their remains be left to rot, leading to a massive build-up of organic matter that would start producing methane and other gases, making all life impossible.

To demonstrate the importance of insects, we have structured the book around the biomes. Within each biome, the insect fauna consists of suites with similar ecological roles (such as herbivores, pollinators, predators, parasites, soil engineers and so on). However, the species involved differ markedly across the biomes, as do their interactions with others and with their environment.

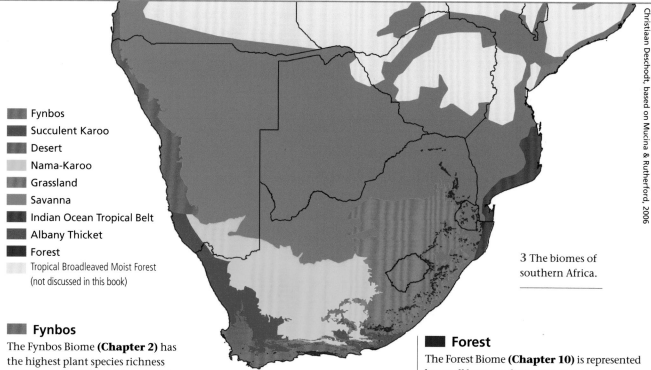

Legend:
- Fynbos
- Succulent Karoo
- Desert
- Nama-Karoo
- Grassland
- Savanna
- Indian Ocean Tropical Belt
- Albany Thicket
- Forest
- Tropical Broadleaved Moist Forest (not discussed in this book)

Christiaan Deschodt, based on Mucina & Rutherford, 2006

3 The biomes of southern Africa.

Fynbos

The Fynbos Biome **(Chapter 2)** has the highest plant species richness of all southern African biomes and counts amongst the most diverse plant regions in the world. It lies in the temperate winter-rainfall region in the southwestern part of the subcontinent.

Succulent Karoo

The Succulent Karoo Biome **(Chapter 3)** includes Namaqualand, which has the highest diversity of succulent plants in the world, making it the most species-rich semidesert on earth.

Desert

The Desert Biome **(Chapter 4)** is represented by the Namib Desert, most of which lies in Namibia. The desert's southern limits grade into the Succulent and Nama-Karoo biomes. Although the Namib has low species richness, its species endemicity is exceptionally high in most plant and animal groups. Many of them have remarkable adaptations to the extreme desert environment.

Nama-Karoo

The Nama-Karoo Biome **(Chapter 5)** is the third-largest biome in southern Africa (after Savanna and Grassland), occupying 19.5% of the land area. The major part of the Nama-Karoo is situated in South Africa, but it extends into southern Namibia. Despite being surrounded by six neighbouring biomes, with which it shares floral and faunal elements, it probably has the lowest species diversity of all.

Grassland

The Grassland Biome **(Chapter 6)** is found on the high central plateau of South Africa and Lesotho, and is the second-largest biome in the region (after Savanna). It covers 27.9% of the region's land area, representing by far the largest proportion of African highland grasslands.

Savanna

The Savanna Biome **(Chapter 7)** is located in the northeastern and northwestern areas of the subcontinent. It is the southern extension of Africa's (and South Africa's at 32.5% land area) largest biome and has the richest animal life.

Indian Ocean Tropical Belt

The Indian Ocean Tropical Belt Biome **(Chapter 8)** is a narrow eastern coastal strip consisting of fragmented remnants of Central and East African moist subtropical woodland intrusions stretching through Mozambique into South Africa.

Albany Thicket

The Albany Thicket Biome **(Chapter 9)** in the Eastern Cape of South Africa is an ancient vegetation type, which consists of plant forms intermediate between the Savanna, Nama-Karoo and eastern subtropical forest that surround it.

Forest

The Forest Biome **(Chapter 10)** is represented by small but very distinctive remnants of once more widespread Afromontane forests. Forest fragments are now restricted to areas that receive high summer and winter rainfall along the montane escarpment and the south and east coasts of South Africa.

Freshwater habitats

Freshwater habitats **(Chapter 11)** vary greatly: from low-altitude, large perennial or annual rivers to smaller, fast-flowing, cold mountain streams to pools formed after rain as well as thousands of artificial impoundments of various sizes across the region.

Caves

Caves **(Chapter 12)** in the region are mostly small dusty overhangs in the arid west while some in the higher-rainfall central and eastern regions are large and often house large bat populations with associated insect fauna.

Coastal zone

The Coastal zone **(Chapter 13)** consists of a narrow marine strip of rocks and stranded algae and sand that are regularly inundated by waves, as well as the bare inshore sandy beaches.

Urban environment

The Urban environment **(Chapter 14)** varies somewhat across the region but includes well-vegetated parks and gardens, human habitation and associated humans and pets as well as results of some of their activities: gardening and compost accumulations, and pet faeces.

This book covers the region south of the Kunene and Zambesi rivers and includes South Africa (which is the most intensively studied), Lesotho, eSwatini, Namibia, Botswana, Zimbabwe and Mozambique (fig. 2).

The biological richness of southern Africa can largely be attributed to the diverse ecoregions occurring in a relatively small but highly variable geographic space. These range from tropical eastern coastal plains and forest with high summer rainfall, through a rugged high mountain escarpment to a central highland grassland plateau, which grades eastwards and westwards into summer-rainfall savanna. Further west and southward the savanna becomes progressively drier, eventually grading into semidesert shrublands. The southwest coast and near interior have a winter-rainfall regime, which supports species-rich fynbos, but the rainfall diminishes northwards along the west coast, becoming progressively drier until the area eventually grades into the arid Namib Desert. Biome boundaries may be sharp, grading from one to the next over only a few metres, or very gradual, extending over several kilometres.

Nine biomes have been defined for southern Africa (figs 3, 4). Some are unique to the subcontinent and boast exceptionally high richness of endemic plants and animals, while others are part of more extensive African biomes.

In addition to the nine biomes listed here (see page opposite), we have included four smaller but equally important and characteristic bioregions that have distinctive insect faunas – freshwater habitats, the coastal zone, caves and the urban environment.

What we have tried to do is highlight and illustrate interesting and often remarkable aspects of insects' life history and behaviour within these biomes, and to emphasise their environmental importance as ecosystem service providers. As many insects interact with other arthropod groups in most habitats – competing for resources, or as prey of non-insect arthropod predators, or, in turn, preying on other arthropods – we have included sections on the major non-insect terrestrial arthropod groups in the biomes where they are most apparent, abundant or ecologically important. But, obviously, insects remain the primary focus!

Fynbos

Succulent Karoo

Desert

Nama-Karoo

Grassland

Savanna

Indian Ocean Tropical Belt

Albany Thicket

Forest

4 Each of the southern African biomes has its own group of insects involved in the functioning of the ecosystem.

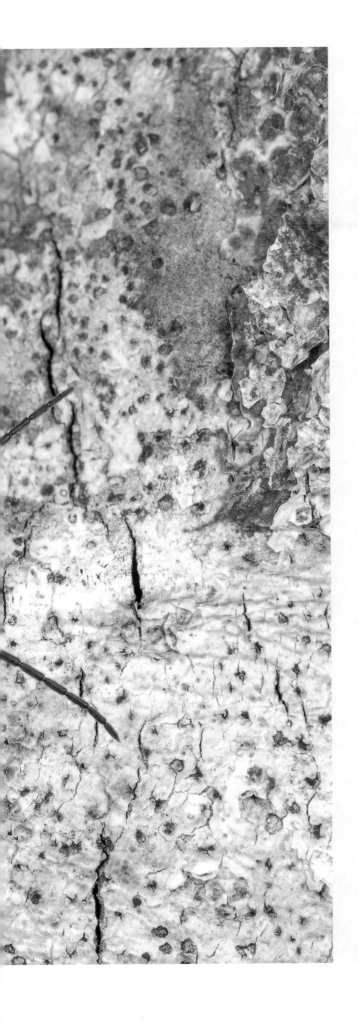

CHAPTER 1
INSECTS AND THEIR ECOLOGICAL ROLE

Insects are undoubtedly the most successful and important group of multi-celled organisms on earth – they belong to the oldest lineage of any major group, their diversity is unparalleled and their ecological significance immense. They owe their success to their flight capability, a largely impervious chitinous exoskeleton, and the process of metamorphosis. Virtually every species has obvious external structures that explain or predict its ecological adaptations – mainly body shape, leg morphology, the absence or presence of wings, and colour.

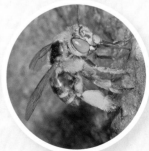

1.1 (pp. 12–13) Insects are the most species-rich group of multi-celled organisms and the order Coleoptera (beetles) contains the most described species. This carabid beetle, *Lebistina subcruciata* (Carabidae), can therefore be regarded as a typical representative of the class Insecta.

1.2 Some of the arthropods that share the phylum Arthropoda with the insects: **(a)** whip spider (Arachnida: Amblypygi); **(b)** crab (Crustacea); **(c)** centipede (Chilopoda); **(d)** millipede (Diplopoda).

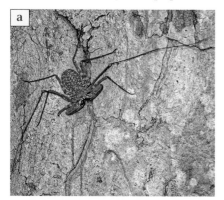

What is an insect?

Insects (fig. 1.1), along with all living things, are organised according to a classification system (see page opposite). They are members of the huge group of invertebrate animals (those without a spinal column) that specifically belong to the class Insecta, one of several in the phylum Arthropoda.

Other Arthropoda include spiders and their kin (class Arachnida), crabs and their relatives (class Crustacea), millipedes (class Diplopoda) and centipedes (class Chilopoda) (fig. 1.2). Other, more distantly related, invertebrate phyla include snails (phylum Mollusca), segmented worms (phylum Annelida) and velvet worms (phylum Onychophora) (fig. 1.3).

All Arthropoda have jointed appendages (from Greek *arthros*, 'joint', and *poda*, 'leg'), which have numerous specialist functions in many groups. Arthropods have a hard exoskeleton, called the cuticle, which is composed of chitin and largely determines the shape and rigidity of the body. It is made up of a series of specialised segments consisting of solid plates (sclerites), which are separated from each other by areas of thin flexible cuticle, forming joints and making movement possible.

1.3 Invertebrates distantly related to the phylum Arthropoda: **(a)** snail (phylum Mollusca); **(b)** planarian worm (phylum Platyhelminthes); **(c)** velvet worm (phylum Onychophora).

Michelle Hamer

This cuticle is one of the reasons for the great evolutionary success of insects and other arthropods. In addition to the rigid structure it provides, it affords protection from predators and disease, as well as from excessive moisture loss. However, the cuticle cannot grow with the animal and is therefore periodically shed in a process called moulting or ecdysis (see box, p. 39), during which the insect is especially vulnerable to predation.

The **class Arachnida** of the Arthropoda is very well represented in southern Africa, with members in the following orders discussed in this book: mites and ticks (Acari), whip spiders (Amblypygi), harvestmen (Opiliones), pseudoscorpions (Pseudoscorpiones), scorpions (Scorpiones), solifuges (Solifugae) and spiders (Araneae).

Arachnids are characterised by a body that consists of two parts: the head and thorax fused into a cephalothorax, and an abdomen. The cephalothorax bears the eyes, mouthparts and four pairs of legs (there are no antennae). The mouthparts consist of a pair of chelicerae for feeding (mandibles are absent), often a pair of venom glands for prey immobilisation and defence, and a pair of pedipalps. Prey is usually reduced to a pulp by the venom and chelicerae, and then the juice is sucked up. The pedipalps have a number of functions – as sense organs, for food manipulation, and during copulation.

The characteristics of millipedes, centipedes and one group of Crustacea, the terrestrial isopods, are discussed in various chapters.

Adults of the **class Insecta** of the Arthropoda are distinguished from other arthropods by a body consisting of three distinct parts – a head, thorax and abdomen (fig. 1.4). The head typically has two antennae, two compound eyes and a few simple eyes (ocelli), and mouthparts. There are always three pairs of legs and usually two pairs of wings attached to the thorax – insects are the only invertebrates capable of flight. The abdomen consists of 11 segments that are free of appendages, except reproductive (ovipositor) and terminal sensory (cerci) structures in some species.

Immatures are called nymphs or larvae depending on the type of metamorphosis.

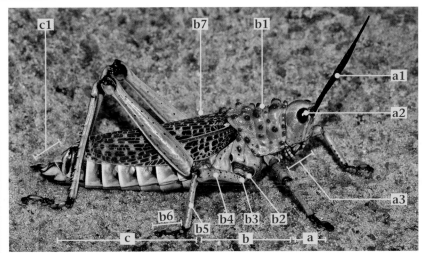

1.4 This grasshopper, a species of *Phymateus* (Pyrgomorphidae), is a typical insect and illustrates all the major external structures present in the class Insecta. (a) **Head**: (a1) antennae; (a2) compound eyes; (a3) mouthparts. (b) **Thorax**, bearing three pairs of five-segmented legs (one each on the pro-, meso- and metathorax) and two pairs of wings: (b1) pronotum (shield behind the head), part of the first thoracic segment; (b2) the purple basal coxa; (b3) trochanter; (b4) femur; (b5) tibia; (b6) tarsus, usually comprising five articles and a terminal pair of claws; (b7) parchment-like forewings on the mesothorax cover the folded membranous hind wings on the metathorax. (c) **Abdomen**, comprising a maximum of 11 segments, although fewer are usually visible; (c1) in the grasshopper female the ovipositor lobes are visible.

Insect names and classification

There are many more insect species than, for example, birds or mammals, and many of them are very small or poorly known; few, therefore, have common names. Common names are not always used exclusively for one group of insects and may often be misleading; insects are therefore usually referred to by their scientific names.

Scientific names

The starting point of scientific naming of all animals is taken as 1 January 1758, the publication date of the 10th edition of Carolus Linnaeus' *Systema Naturae*. Linnaeus introduced the binomial naming system for species – a genus name with a specific epithet, for example, *Homo sapiens*.

Most scientific names are derived from Latin or Greek, and usually refer to some characteristic of the animal, but the names can also be derived from place names or the names of people.

When a 'new' (undescribed) species is discovered, specimens are collected and taken to a taxonomist (a biologist who specialises in identifying, classifying and describing species) who describes it in writing, takes photographs or makes drawings, and gives it a unique name that has not been used before. The description

Changing names

Entomology, like all other life sciences, is a dynamic discipline that changes over time. With the recent, rapid development of molecular (DNA) analytical methods, there have been many important changes in our understanding of the evolutionary processes that affect insect relationships and classification. Some of these are profound, such as the close relationship between cockroaches and termites, long suspected but only recently confirmed; others are much less significant, for example, the many changes to insects' scientific names that have taken place as a consequence of deeper study. Whether great or small, all of these insights affect our understanding of insect natural history. In this book, we provide an up-to-date account of changes to the classification of southern African insect groups and use the latest scientific names as accepted by entomologists (the first major book to do so in over 30 years). We also present a large number of individual case studies that reflect some of the many changes that have occurred.

and name must then be published in a scientific journal for validation. Specimens of the species must be kept in a safe place such as a museum and clearly marked as the 'type' specimens of that species. However, with improved diagnostic technologies some names may change (see boxes, pp. 15, 18).

The classification system

In addition to the binomial species name, Linnaeus also introduced a hierarchical classification system for living organisms. This system starts with the 'big picture' of all known animals (living and extinct), and groups them from the most inclusive category – the animal kingdom – to the least – the species.

Main categories

Kingdom: The highest level at which living organisms are grouped is the kingdom, for example, the plant kingdom (Plantae) and the animal kingdom (Animalia).

Subkingdom: The animal kingdom is subdivided into subkingdoms, such as Invertebrata, which includes insects and all other animals without a backbone.

Phylum: Subkingdoms are further divided into phyla. Insects belong to the phylum Arthropoda, along with all other invertebrates that have an exoskeleton and jointed legs, such as crabs, spiders and centipedes.

Class: Phyla are divided into (usually five) classes. The class Insecta includes only arthropods that have six legs, Arachnida those with eight legs, and so on.

Order: The class Insecta is divided into 28 orders, of which 25 occur in southern Africa. All the insects in an order share a distinctive suite of characteristics that unite them. Examples of insect orders are flies (Diptera) and beetles (Coleoptera).

Family: An order may contain dozens of families. For example, the ladybird family Coccinellidae and the scarab beetle family Scarabaeidae are both in the beetle order Coleoptera.

Genus: A family may contain one or more genera (plural for 'genus'). For instance, *Scarabaeus*, *Pachysoma* and *Pachycnema* are genera in the scarab beetle family.

Species: A genus contains one or more species (a monotypic genus contains a single species). A species is a specific group of living organisms that interbreed

Insect orders

The 25 insect orders that occur in southern Africa are discussed and illustrated in the Appendix (pp. 410–425), which also gives references to the sections of the book in which members of each order are discussed.

and produce fertile offspring only with others of the same species. The sacred scarab, *Scarabaeus sacer*, and *Scarabaeus lamarcki* are dung beetles.

Sub- and super-categories

The main categories in the classification system can also be combined into larger groups such as superorder and superfamily (fig. 1.5) or divided further into smaller groups such as subclass, suborder, subfamily (fig. 1.6), tribe, subgenus (fig. 1.7) and subspecies. Different suffixes are used for the names of each level between superfamily and tribe; this makes it easier to recognise to which level the name refers (see table, p. 17).

Orders and families

Scientific order and family names (as well as those of suborders, superfamilies, subfamilies and tribes) can be transformed into nouns or adjectives and used as English words when referring to insects. In this way, beetles (Coleoptera), can be referred to as coleopterans; bugs (Hemiptera), as hemipterans; earwigs (Dermaptera), as dermapterans, and so on. Predatory ground beetles (family Carabidae) may be called carabids or carabid beetles; bladder grasshoppers (family Pneumoridae) can be referred to as pneumorids or pneumorid grasshoppers; and monkey beetles (family Scarabaeidae: tribe Hopliini) can be called hopliines or hopliine beetles.

Genus names

Genus and subgenus names always have an initial capital letter; subgenus names are always placed in brackets. Names at and below the level of genus are always italicised or underlined. Sometimes, only the genus name is given, followed by 'sp.' (species, singular) or 'spp.' (species, plural). For example, *Scarabaeus* sp. refers to a single unknown or unidentified species; *Scarabaeus* spp. refers to several species in the genus.

Species names

A species name always consists of two names: the genus and the specific epithet, *Scarabaeus lamarcki* (fig. 1.7a). The specific epithet is always in lower case.

Subspecies

Some species consist of more than one subspecies, for example, the dark opal butterfly, *Chrysoritis nigricans* (Lycaenidae), has three subspecies – *Chrysoritis nigricans nigricans*, *Chrysoritis nigricans zwartbergae* and *Chrysoritis nigricans rubrescens*. Although these three groups of butterflies have slight differences, they can still interbreed and produce fertile offspring, so they are considered to be a single species. Once the genus has been mentioned, it can be abbreviated to just its capital first letter, the species also just by the first letter but in lower case, and the subspecies name written out in full (e.g. *C. n. nigricans*).

Taxonomic classification of a scarab beetle

Here's an example of how the classification of a scarab beetle depends on subdivisions of the main taxonomic categories, suborder and superfamily (**fig. 1.5**) or divided further into smaller groups such as family, subfamily (**fig. 1.6**), tribe, genus, subgenus (**fig. 1.7**), species and subspecies.

1.5 Families of the superfamily Scarabaeoidea: **(a)** Lucanidae (*Nigidius bubalus*); **(b)** Trogidae (*Phoberus squamiger*); **(c)** Scarabaeidae (*Copris elphenor*).

1.6 Subfamilies of the family Scarabaeidae: **(a)** Melolonthinae (*Schizonycha* sp.); **(b)** Cetoniinae (*Anisorrhina flavomaculata*); **(c)** Scarabaeinae (*Proagoderus quadrituber*, male).

Category	Standard suffix	Example
Order		**Coleoptera**
Suborder		Polyphaga
Epifamily	-oidae	—
Superfamily	-oidea	Scarabaeoidea (fig 1.5)
Family	**-idae**	**Scarabaeidae** (fig 1.6)
Subfamily	-inae	Scarabaeinae
Tribe	-ini	Scarabaeini
Genus		***Scarabaeus*** (fig 1.7)
Subgenus		(*Kheper*)
Species		***lamarcki***
Subspecies		—

Taxonomic categories below class, with their standard suffixes (most commonly used in bold). The species used here is a scarab beetle, *Scarabaeus (Kheper) lamarcki*.

1.7 Subgenera of the dung beetle genus *Scarabaeus* (Scarabaeidae). The subgenera share a few minor but diagnostic morphological characteristics, as well as some biological attributes that typify them as members of a distinct group of species within the genus: **(a)** *Scarabaeus* subgenus *Kheper lamarcki*, with typical herbivore dung ball; **(b)** *Scarabaeus* subgenus *Scarabaeolus rubripennis*: members of the subgenus prefer carrion and bird or lizard faeces over herbivore dung; **(c)** *Scarabaeus* subgenus *Sceliages*: all species of the subgenus are obligate millipede feeders.

Acacias

A controversial botanical name change in the early 2000s has had far-reaching effects for African biologists. Research showed that different groups in the genus *Acacia* – which included the quintessential African thorn trees, Australian wattles, as well as plants from the Americas – were not descended from a common ancestor. This meant that the genus had to be split into several genera. Australian botanists, however, campaigned to reserve *Acacia* for the more than 900 Australian species, compared to fewer than half that number from Africa and other parts of the world. In 2005, the name change was officially adopted at the International Botanical Congress, and this decision was upheld at the next meeting in 2011. The African species were divided into two new genera, *Vachellia* and *Senegalia*, but many botanists from Africa and elsewhere disagree with the official decision. We have chosen to continue using *Acacia* and acacia as scientific and common names, respectively, for the African species.

Insect morphology

In order to understand the specific entomological language and terminology used in descriptions of insects, it is necessary to have some understanding of their morphology (shape and structure), especially of specific characteristics of the mouthparts, legs, wings and abdominal appendages. These parts are often easy to see and are the main structures that characterise the higher taxonomic levels such as order and family (fig. 1.8).

1.8 The exterior of an insect has numerous diagnostic morphological structures that can be used to identify or classify the insect in question. This stalk-eyed fly belongs to the order Diptera (two-winged insects with hind wings modified into halteres), family Diopsidae (eyes on stalks), and genus *Diopsis* (spines on the thorax, which are very variable among different groups).

Cuticle

The cuticle or exoskeleton is rigid and armour-like in most adult and some immature insects (fig. 1.9), but it may also be thin and flexible in immature stages.

The cuticle consists of three main layers:

- The endocuticle is the innermost layer and is soft, pliant and pale. It is secreted by the epidermis, which lies beneath it. The endocuticle forms the articular membrane present between joints and sclerites (plates). It also forms the integument (outer protective layer) of immature holometamorphic (see p. 41) insects, which usually only have hardened exocuticle on the head.
- The exocuticle hardens and darkens over a period after the insect has moulted, in a process called sclerotisation (fig. 1.10).
- The epicuticle is the outermost layer and consists of a waxy lipoprotein that makes the cuticle impermeable to water, helping to prevent desiccation. It also forms a barrier to microorganisms.

1.9 (right) The shed cuticle (exuviae) of a cicada nymph (Cicadidae), which formed the rigid exoskeleton of the immature insect, retains its shape after moulting.

1.10 (below) The cuticle is soft and pliant immediately after moulting, but hardens and darkens (sclerotises) quickly. This treehopper (Membracidae) has just moulted into the adult stage. Next to it is the dark sclerotised final-instar nymphal exuviae, as well as attendant ants that feed on the honeydew the bugs excrete.

The endocuticle and exocuticle together form the procuticle. Firm ridges and bars for muscle attachment are formed by the procuticle folding back on itself, and joints are formed by the articular membrane, which consists of endocuticle only. The protein resilin provides resilience of the exoskeleton, which allows the distortion necessary for such activities as flying and jumping.

Single cells of the epidermis may be modified into setae (hairs) or sensory receptors called sensilla, which protrude through the cuticle and sense much of the insect's tactile environment. They can be hair-like, feather-like, or plate-like scales. There might also be moveable spines and spurs on the legs. Some insects have sharp, hollow setae that are filled with venomous fluid for defence. The holes that form the spiracles, which permit gas exchange, are also modifications in the cuticle enabled by the epidermis. Glands in the cuticle produce species-specific olfactory substances.

Head

The head bears the eyes, antennae, mouthparts and brain (fig. 1.4). In most insects, the external structure of the head is simple, with the eyes, antennae and mouthparts visible and distinct (fig. 1.11). The mouthparts are attached at the front of the head capsule, which in most insects is unmodified; but in some it is highly modified, such as in most weevils (Curculionidae; fig. 1.11a), where it is elongated to form a highly variable rostrum with the mouthparts at the apex. The head capsule in some other groups bears various structures that are often sexually dimorphic and function in sexual selection (as in many dung beetles; fig. 1.11b). However, at the other end of the spectrum, the head capsule may be totally reduced, as in fly maggots, in which the only indication of a head is a pair of sclerotised mouth hooks (mandibles).

Eyes

The two relatively large compound eyes of adult insects and hemimetamorphic (see p. 40) nymphs usually lie dorsolaterally on the head, with three simple light-sensitive eyes (ocelli) typically arranged in a triangle between the compound eyes (fig. 1.12). Ocelli are not capable of vision and can only detect the difference between light and dark. The larvae of most holometamorphic (see p. 41) insects have simple eyes (stemmata) that are placed dorsolaterally. Stemmata can usually only be used to differentiate between light and dark, but in a few predatory groups, larvae are capable of acute vision (fig. 1.13).

1.11 In many insects the head is modified in some way. (**a**) It may be elongated to place the mouthparts deep inside a food source, as in this *Curculio* weevil (Curculionidae), which drills into green figs. (**b**) It may have sex-linked structures such as these antler-like horns in the male *Proagoderus rangifer* dung beetle (Scarabaeidae); the horns function exclusively in female attraction and mate selection.

1.12 All adult insects have ocelli (simple eyes) arranged in an inverted triangle between the compound eyes, as in this damselfly, *Phaon iridipennis* (Odonata: Zygoptera: Calopterygidae).

1.13 The simple eyes (stemmata) of holometamorphic insect larvae are usually small and used to distinguish between light and dark, but in some predatory larvae, the stemmata are large and vision is fairly acute, such as in the larva of this owlfly, *Ascalaphus bilineatus* (Neuroptera: Ascalaphidae).

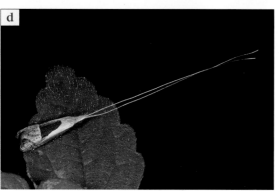

1.14 Antenna shape varies tremendously across insect families and is often diagnostic for a particular group. (**a**) Flabellate antennae in a male click beetle, *Tetralobus flabellicornis* (Elateridae); when at rest the flagellar elements are collapsed like the blades of a fan. (**b**) Moniliform antennae in a parasitic flat bark beetle (Passandridae). (**c**) Capitate antennae in the owlfly *Helcopteryx rhodiogramma* (Ascalaphidae). (**d**) Exceptionally long filiform antennae are characteristic of moths in the family Adelidae such as this *Ceromitia* sp. (**e**) Plumose antennae are common in male moths, such as *Laelia clarki* (Erebidae: Lymantriinae). (**f**) Lamellate antennae are characteristic of most scarab beetles, such as this *Scapanoclypeus* sp. (Scarabaeidae: Melolonthinae).

Antennae

Antennae are possibly the most important sensory organs in insects: they function largely through chemoreception (smell and taste) and mechanoreception (sound), but also through the detection of touch, air motion and heat. The antennae of adult insects vary greatly in size and shape and are placed medially, usually above the ocelli. In larvae, they are greatly reduced or absent. The antenna has three parts: the scape (base), the pedicel (stem) and the flagellum, which often consists of many elements known as flagellomeres. The scape and pedicel are usually undivided and unmodified. The flagellomeres, on the other hand, may be numerous and their shape and structure may be highly modified (fig. 1.14).

Mouthparts

Mouthparts (fig. 1.15) vary greatly in structure and function and are among the key characters used to distinguish between different insect orders. All insects feed in the larval or nymphal stage, and so do many in the adult stage; in adults that do not feed, the mouthparts are usually atrophied.

Mouthparts are formed from especially hardened cuticle and are situated on the lower surface at the front of the head. The most primitive mouthparts are those used for biting and chewing. In some large orders mouthparts have become very specialised, for example, in bugs, fleas, flies and moths and butterflies.

Mouthparts are divided into the following basic types, depending on the feeding method for which they are used (fig. 1.16):

- Mandibulate mouthparts are used for biting and chewing (see box opposite). These are the most primitive type and are found in most insect groups. Specific examples are crickets and grasshoppers (Orthoptera) and beetles (Coleoptera) (figs 1.16a, b).
- Suctorial mouthparts are used for piercing and sucking. They have stylets (needle-like projections) used to penetrate plant and animal tissue, and tubes for sucking up leaking fluids. Examples of insect groups with such mouthparts include all bugs (Hemiptera), some adult flies (Diptera; fig. 1.16c), and adult fleas (Siphonaptera).
- Siphoning and sucking mouthparts, such as the proboscis of butterflies and moths (fig. 1.16d).
- Hooked mouthparts used for ripping tissues, seen, for example, in some fly maggots.
- Filter-feeding mouthparts are used by insect stages living in water, for example, mayfly nymphs (Ephemeroptera) and caddisfly larvae (Trichoptera).

Mandibulate mouthparts

Mandibulate mouthparts (fig. 1.15) consist of the following:

- labrum (broad upper lip) that is hinged to the clypeus (the lower facial segment of the head);
- pair of strong, heavily sclerotised mandibles (jaws), one on each side of the mouth, with teeth along the inner margin for chewing food;
- pair of maxillae, also at the sides, each consisting of a galea, lacinia and sensory (maxillary) palp;
- labium (lower lip) comprised of two lobes, each consisting of a glossa and paraglossa, as well as short sensory (labial) palps on either side; and
- tongue-like hypopharynx.

The sensory maxillary palps and the labial palps are used for tasting and positioning food.

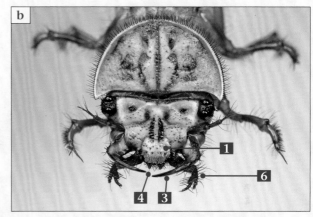

1.15 Mandibulate mouthparts are the most common type amongst adult and larval insects. Head and mouthparts of **(a)** an adult wasp, *Philanthus triangulum* (Crabronidae); **(b)** a larva of the tiger beetle *Manticora tibialis* (Carabidae: Cicindelinae). **(1)** clypeus; **(2)** labrum; **(3)** mandible; **(4)** labium; **(5)** labial palps; **(6)** maxillary palps.

1.16 Insect mouthparts are specific to a particular feeding mode and food type, and vary enormously. Many have functions other than feeding. **(a)** The chewing mouthparts of this weevil (Curculionidae) are small and located at the tip of the elongated head (rostrum). **(b)** This female long-horned beetle, *Mallodon downesi* (Cerambycidae), has huge mandibles with setal brushes on the inside. They probably have a reproductive rather than a feeding function. **(c)** The piercing/sucking mouthparts of this blood-feeding fly (Tabanidae) pierce animal tissue, and allow the fly to suck up leaking blood. **(d)** The butterfly *Catopsilia florella* (Pieridae) has siphoning (haustellate) mouthparts for sucking up thin fluids.

Many insects combine different feeding methods, and therefore have highly modified mouthparts. Bees and wasps (Hymenoptera) are good examples, as they have both biting and sucking mouthparts: biting is used for manipulating materials such as during nest building; while sucking is used to drink fluids during feeding. All mouthparts derive from the mandibulate type (see box, p. 21) and the terminology of the different parts is similar, although many of the parts are so modified that their ancestral state is unrecognisable.

In addition to their primary function of feeding, mouthparts, particularly mandibles, may also have secondary functions – either for advertising to other males or females, or (in males) for grasping and holding females during copulation.

Thorax

The thorax is usually box-like and situated between the head and abdomen (fig. 1.4). It consists of three segments: the prothorax (front segment), mesothorax (middle segment) and metathorax (hind segment). There is usually a pair of legs on each segment, and a pair of wings (when present) on both the meso- and metathorax. The meso- and metathorax usually also have a respiratory spiracle on either side. The thorax may be modified in various ways: it may be highly expanded or elongated or otherwise adapted into a variety of ornate structures and adorned with various knobs or spines.

Legs

In nymphs and adult insects, the legs consist of six segments: the short coxa that articulates with the thorax, the trochanter, the femur, the tibia, and the tarsus, which has five articles and terminates in a pair of claws (fig. 1.4). The femur and tibia are generally the longest of the leg segments and vary considerably depending on their function. Larvae often have fewer leg segments, or legs specially modified for their particular habits.

Besides their 'normal' ambulatory function, the legs of many insects are modified to perform particular functions (fig. 1.17). These include grasping (onto the substrate or another individual during mating), capturing prey (mainly front legs), jumping (especially hind legs), burrowing (mostly front legs), manipulating food (hind legs in dung beetles), and food gathering (pollen baskets in bees). They may be broadened and flattened to increase the 'flat' profile of cryptic species, as in certain bugs (Hemiptera). In some grasshoppers (Orthoptera: Ensifera), hearing organs are situated in the tibia of the forelegs.

1.17 Insect legs perform multiple functions besides the primary one of walking, particularly the first and last pair. (**a**) All grasshoppers have hind femurs enlarged with muscles that enable them to jump, as in this Thericleidae species. (**b**) The flattened forelegs in this planthopper, *Elasmoscelis* sp. (Hemiptera: Lophopidae), appear not to have any particular function other than camouflage, in combination with the body patterning. (**c**) Hangingflies, like this *Bittacus* sp. (Mecoptera: Bittacidae), usually hang from vegetation by their front and middle legs and dangle their prehensile hind legs to intercept and capture passing flying insects. (**d**) The forelegs of males, in particular, of the dung beetle *Pachylomera femoralis* (Scarabaeidae) are large and armed with spines, and used to 'hug' and squeeze opponents at dung sources. (**e**) The forelegs of mantidflies, such as this *Afromantispa tenella*, are raptorial and similar in shape and function to those of praying mantises (Mantodea). (**f**) The front tibiae of this male sweat bee, *Lipotriches* sp. (Halictidae), are possibly modified to soak up plant odours for use as a sex pheromone during mating.

Wings

Most adult insects have two pairs of wings but in some groups only one pair of wings can be seen, the second being reduced. However, the adults of several species are entirely wingless. Besides their primary function of flight, wings have many secondary functions such as camouflage and protection of vulnerable body parts.

There are various kinds of wings among insect groups in which type and shape are so significant that many of the orders are named after their particular type of wing (derivations are from Greek *ptera*, 'wings'). Some groups have both pairs of wings membranous but others have either the front or the hind wings modified.

Two pairs of fine and transparent membranous wings are present and are used in flight in the following orders:

- dragonflies (Odonata – 'toothed ones'), although the fastest flying insects with two pairs of membranous wings are not named for their wings, but for their mouthparts;
- lacewings, antlions and mantidflies (Neuroptera – 'veined wings') have wings with prominent veins (fig. 1.18a);
- moths and butterflies (Lepidoptera – 'scale wings') are characterised by wings covered in flattened scales (fig. 1.18b); and
- bees, wasps and ants (Hymenoptera – 'membrane wings') have two pairs of typical membranous wings (fig. 1.18f).

The following orders have either the front or hind wings modified in some way:

- in flies (Diptera – 'two wings'), only the forewings are membranous, the hind wings being reduced to club-shaped organs (halteres) that are used for balance and direction during flight (fig. 1.18c);
- the forewings of crickets and grasshoppers (Orthoptera – 'straight wings') are parchment-like (called tegmina; singular, tegmen; fig. 1.4); they protect the membranous hind wings and are not used in flight;
- the forewings of beetles (Coleoptera – 'sheath wings') are hard and protective (called elytra; singular, elytron); they cover the membranous hind wings and abdomen and are not used to power flight but are lifted to allow the hind wings to unfold in order to fly (fig. 1.18d);
- true bugs, such as aphids, cicadas and leafhoppers: the order Hemiptera ('half wings') and suborder Heteroptera ('different wings') have forewings that are partly hardened and partly membranous (fig. 1.18e); the forewings are used with the membranous hind wings in flight; and
- parasitic strepsipterans (Strepsiptera – 'twisted wings') have forewings modified into halteres and membranous hind wings.

1.18 Wings of insects vary greatly. **(a)** Membranous wings of the antlion *Macroleon quinquemaculatus* (Myrmeleontidae) have distinct veins. **(b)** In some butterflies and large moths, such as this *Epiphora mythimnia* (Saturniidae), the forewing overlaps the hind wing; the power stroke of the forewing pushes the hind wing down and they function in tandem. **(c)** Flies (Diptera) have membranous forewings and hind wings modified into balancing organs (halteres), seen in this Conopidae species. **(d)** The hardened, protective forewings (elytra) of beetles (Coleoptera) are lifted to allow the hind wings to unfold, as in this Chrysomelidae species launching itself into the air. **(e)** The bug *Boisea fulcrata* (Hemiptera: Rhopalidae) has forewings with the basal half toughened and the distal half membranous. **(f)** Wasps have both pairs membranous as in this *Bembix* species (Hymenoptera: Crabronidae).

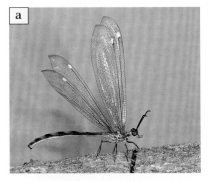

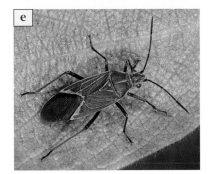

1.19 The abdomen seldom bears external structures other than those related to reproduction. (**a**) The sclerotised cerci (forceps) in earwigs (Dermaptera) at the end of the flexible abdomen, as in this male *Forficula senegalensis*, are mostly used to fold the large membranous hind wings under the small leathery forewings. Some species use them in prey capture. (**b**) The tails in this fishmoth (Zygentoma: Lepismatidae) are primitive sensory structures. (**c**) The extended sword-shaped ovipositor in this shield-backed katydid (Orthoptera: Ensifera: Tettigoniidae) is typical of most female katydids. (**d**) Male Odonata such as this dragonfly, *Paragomphus genei* (Gomphidae), have terminal abdominal claspers with which they hold females during copulation. (**e**) Many parasitic wasps (Hymenoptera) have long ovipositors for laying eggs on hosts deep inside a medium such as wood.

Abdomen

The abdomen consists of 11 segments, but fewer are usually visible in adult insects (fig. 1.4). It houses most of the visceral organs, including components of the digestive, excretory and reproductive systems; reproductive organs are located in the terminal segments while pairs of spiracles are usually found on segments one to eight, and the anus on the ninth segment.

In many adult insects no obvious appendages are visible on the abdomen; when present, they are part of the reproductive organs or have a sensory function (fig. 1.19). Adults of basal (primitive) insect orders such as bristletails (Archaeognatha), fishmoths (Zygentoma) and mayflies (Ephemeroptera) have long, thin, straight sensory 'tails' (cerci) attached to the last segment. In earwigs (Dermaptera), the cerci are robust and pincer-like, functioning as claspers during copulation, and are sometimes used for capturing prey. In some bees and wasps (Hymenoptera), the ovipositor is modified into a well-developed sting.

The 11 abdominal segments are usually distinctly demarcated in insect larvae and appendages are uncommon; exceptions are the terminal organs (urogomphi) present in some Coleoptera larvae, the prolegs and the often extravagant cuticular spines and setae (hairs) on many Lepidoptera larvae (fig. 1.20).

1.20 Larvae of certain primitive beetles, such as (**a**) this ground beetle (Carabidae), have terminal abdominal urogomphi, which have a tactile function. (**b**) Many Lepidoptera larvae have setae, tubercles or other structures growing from the abdomen, all of which have defensive functions such as this moth larva (Lasiocampidae) with long lateral hairs, probably cryptic, and rows of short, hollow, dorsal spines with a gland at the base of each that produces defensive chemicals.

Insect physiology

Insect physiology is very different from that of vertebrates. Understanding the basic physiological functions of insects gives us insight into their behaviour. This section discusses the insect's nervous system and the organs involved in gas exchange, circulation, digestion, excretion and reproduction.

Nervous system

Just as in other animals, the central nervous system (in conjunction with hormones) is responsible for regulating all physiological processes. It consists of a series of nerve centres (ganglia) linked by paired nerve cords, called connectives. The ganglia, which are the coordinating centres, coordinate impulses in the regions of the body where they are located.

There are two ganglia in an insect's head: the compound cerebral ganglion (or brain) and the suboesophageal ganglion. The suboesophageal ganglion, together with the thoracic and abdominal ganglia (the number of which varies between insects), form a chain that constitutes the ventral nerve cord, which lies on the floor of the body cavity running from front to back (fig. 1.21).

The compound cerebral ganglion is the principal nervous centre of the body, receiving and processing sensory input from the head and posterior ganglia, and, to some extent, controlling the activities of the rest of the nervous system. It is also the seat of many long-term organised behaviour patterns and regulates their modification by learning.

There are three major regions in the brain (fig. 1.22): the ocellar and optic lobes process visual input; the antennal lobes process input from chemoreceptors in the antennae ('smell'); and the bilobed tritocerebrum connects to the suboesophageal ganglion, which sends and receives sensory signals from the body.

Ventral nerve cord

The suboesophageal ganglion is the first ganglion in the ventral nerve cord (fig. 1.22). It is located in the head beneath the oesophagus. It is a compound ganglion that consists of the ganglia of the mandibular, maxillary and labial segments of the mouth, which regulate taste and feeding and innervate the salivary glands. The suboesophageal ganglion also has an excitatory influence on other body parts.

Typically, each segment of the thorax has a ganglion with five or six nerves that supply the muscles of the wings and legs, as well as the sensilla (sensory receptors) of the thoracic cuticle.

The abdominal ganglia are smaller than those of the thorax, with fewer peripheral nerves arising from them. They innervate the abdominal muscles and cuticle, heart, tracheal system, gut and reproductive organs. These ganglia regulate cuticular sensory receptors that receive mechanical, chemical or thermal stimuli from the insect's environment, as well as heartbeat, respiration, peristalsis of the gut, and stimulation of the reproductive organs.

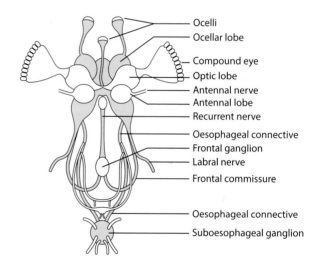

1.22 The insect brain is comprised of several lobes that process information received about light intensity (ocelli), vision (compound eyes), smell (antennae) and taste (mouthparts).

1.21 The nervous system of an insect runs along the floor of the body cavity. Nerves from each ganglion innervate the organs and tissues in the respective segments.

Gas exchange and respiration

Gas exchange and respiration in insects, as in vertebrates, involves taking up oxygen and getting rid of carbon dioxide. In insects, this function is performed by the tracheal system, which consists of a network of internal tubes (tracheae) and external 'breathing holes' (spiracles; fig. 1.23) through which air enters from the outside and carbon dioxide is expelled.

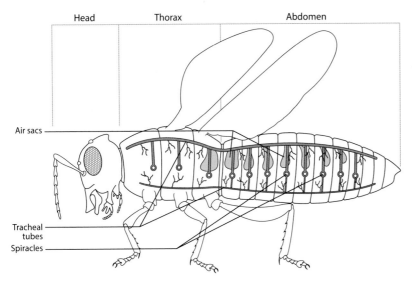

1.23 The spiracles and tracheal system are composed of tubes from the spiracles, which carry inhaled air to the tissues, and exhaled air back out of the spiracles.

1.24 Respiration in aquatic insects (**a**) is often through 'feathery' gills, such as on this mayfly nymph (Ephemeroptera: Leptophlebiidae), while in most terrestrial insects (**b**) it takes place via small circular openings in the body wall called spiracles, visible in this beetle larva (Scarabaeidae).

Spiracles

Spiracles are always paired, one on each side of the body, from a maximum of 10 functional pairs (one each on the meso- and metathorax, and eight on abdominal segments) to only a few pairs. Some insects have no spiracles, such as some aquatic immatures (fig. 1.24a; see 'Adaptations to aquatic life', p. 320) and endoparasites; in these, gases diffuse through the integument.

In most insects the spiracle opens into a chamber (atrium). In many terrestrial species (fig. 1.24b), the atrium contains filtering devices that restrict the entry of dust and parasites. Between the atrium and the trachea many insects have a valve with a closing mechanism, which helps to reduce water loss (see upper box opposite).

Tracheae

Tracheae are thin-walled tubes that branch into progressively finer tubes, forming a network eventually ending in permeable fluid-filled tracheoles. The tracheoles are microscopically narrow and cover internal organs and tissues, making close contact with, and sometimes even penetrating the cells. They are especially numerous in areas of high activity, where oxygen requirements are greater.

The tracheae are usually connected to adjacent spiracles on the same side of the body, as well as to tracheae on the opposite side, thus equalising pressure throughout the system. In some insects, parts of the tracheae dilate to form air sacs (see lower box opposite).

Gas exchange

In many small adult insects and larvae, the movement of air from the spiracles and through the tracheal system is by simple diffusion. In larger insects, diffusion is augmented by an abdominal pump-like ventilation action to move oxygen into, and carbon dioxide and water vapour out of, the tracheal system, in a process termed active ventilation.

Active ventilation is usually brought about by contracting the abdominal muscles, but leg and wing muscles and the movement of internal organs may also be used. Muscle contractions cause a localised drop in pressure in the body cavity, which results in the brief opening of some of the spiracles to draw in a gasp of air. In insects with many functional spiracles, a few pairs of anterior spiracles open at inspiration ('inhaling') and the posterior spiracles close; at expiration ('exhaling') the arrangement is reversed, so that there is a definite circulation of air in the tracheae. The process in insects with few spiracles is more complicated and is not discussed here.

Most large insects use a combination of active ventilation and diffusion: they start by ventilating actively, and then allow diffusion to move oxygen from the spiracles through the tracheae to the tracheoles, where gas exchange takes place. The oxygen concentration forms a gradient, from high concentrations at the spiracles, to low concentrations in the tissue.

In insects without spiracles, such as the nymphs and larvae of aquatic insects and endoparasites, air diffuses in and out of the body wall through a network of tracheae. In some aquatic nymphs, the network of tracheae is modified to form gills through which gases diffuse (fig. 1.25; see 'Adaptations to aquatic life', p. 320). Some endoparasites have posterior spiracles that extend to the body surface or tracheal trunks of the host, to which they attach.

1.25 Many aquatic insects breathe through external abdominal gills, the lateral white tufted organs seen in this dobsonfly larva, *Taeniochauloides ochraceopennis* (Megaloptera: Corydalidae).

Discontinuous gas exchange

Gas exchange in terrestrial insects allows oxygen to move inwards while carbon dioxide and water vapour move outwards. This creates a compromise between the need for oxygen at the risk of water loss. One way of guarding against the danger of water loss is to limit the number of open spiracles to the lowest possible level that activity demands.

Another method used by many insects is to exchange gases only at certain times and not continuously. The process is termed a discontinuous gas exchange cycle (DGC; see box, p. 148). A typical DGC starts with a closed-spiracle phase, during which little external gas exchange takes place. This is followed by a fluttering-spiracle phase, which is usually dominated by oxygen uptake by diffusion. The last phase is an open-spiracle phase, during which accumulated carbon dioxide escapes. The main function of the DGC is that it significantly lowers respiratory water loss rates, as the spiracles can be partly or completely closed for extended periods.

The functions of air sacs

In many insects, parts of the tracheae are dilated or enlarged to increase the reservoir of air. In some species, the dilations form air sacs, increasing the volume of air inspired and expired. The air sacs are usually found in the body cavity, but also occur in the thoracic appendages (legs and wings). Muscular movements of the abdomen, legs and wings draw air into the tracheae from the spiracles, expanding the sacs. When the insect 'exhales', the air sacs collapse.

Air sacs have additional functions in some insects:
- allowing the volume of internal organs to change during growth without changing the shape of the insect;
- reducing the weight of large insects;
- acting as resonance chambers to increase sound produced by stridulation in some Orthoptera (e.g. bladder grasshoppers, Pneumoridae; fig. 1.26; see 'Sound production in bladder grasshoppers', p. 115) and cicadas (Cicadidae; see 'Sound and breeding in cicadas', p. 275); and
- assisting flight by increasing buoyancy.

Jonathan Ball

1.26 The abdomen of this bloated bladder grasshopper male, *Bullacris intermedia* (Pneumoridae), is filled with air sacs, which are terminal dilations of respiratory tracheae. They function as a resonance chamber.

Circulatory system

The insect circulatory system (fig. 1.27) is based on haemolymph, a fluid equivalent to blood. Its main function is transportation, particularly of nutrients, hormones and waste products (see box opposite). Haemolymph is pumped through the insect body by a 'heart', but since the haemolymph of most insects (with a few exceptions) contains no haemoglobin with which to carry oxygen, the heart is not involved in respiration as it is in vertebrates.

The circulatory system is open – the haemolymph circulates freely around the internal organs in the body cavity (haemocoel). A single blood vessel extends along the dorsal side of the insect from the head to the abdomen. There is no closed pressurised network of blood vessels as there is in vertebrates.

Heart and aorta

The dorsal blood vessel runs along the midline of the body, just below the exoskeleton, and is suspended by connective tissue and thin muscles. The vessel is divided into two regions – a tubular posterior heart and a slender anterior aorta.

The heart lies in a tubular cavity in the abdomen. It is closed at the posterior end and is perforated by paired openings (ostia) in every segment. The ostia have one-way valves that allow haemolymph to flow into the heart from the haemocoel but prevent it from flowing back into the body cavity.

In the thorax, the dorsal blood vessel becomes narrower and has no ostia; this part is known as the aorta. The aorta extends through the thorax into the head and is open at the end. Haemolymph flows from the aorta into the haemocoel of the head.

Circulation

In the heart, the wall of the dorsal blood vessel is reinforced with muscle fibres that produce pulsed contractions under nervous control, starting at the posterior end. The resulting systolic (contraction) and diastolic (relaxed) peristaltic movement of the heart pushes the haemolymph forward along the blood vessel, from the abdomen towards the thorax and head. The haemolymph flows from the aorta into the head, and from there into the body cavity. Haemolymph pressure in the haemocoel forces blood to flow back into the heart through the ostia, setting up a circulatory system.

Insects can increase their haemolymph pressure by muscular contraction and compression of the body wall, or

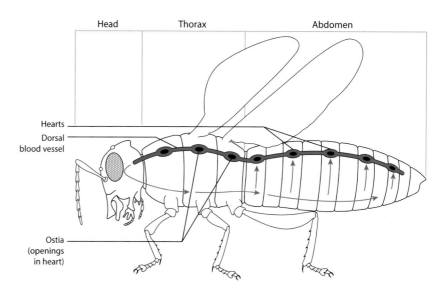

1.27 The circulatory system in insects is based on a simple tube with openings (ostia) at various intervals. The back portion is considered the 'heart', the front section the 'aorta'.

by swallowing air, which puts pressure on the haemocoel by dilating the alimentary canal. Some fast-flying insects have an additional heart in the thorax to increase the flow of haemolymph (and pressure) to their wings.

Although increased pressure is sometimes needed, normal haemolymph pressure in insects is generally very low (sometimes even lower than atmospheric pressure). One advantage of lower blood pressure is that it reduces the risk of bleeding. Some insects, however, use bleeding as a defensive strategy: under hydrostatic pressure, they force haemolymph through weak spots or pores in the cuticle (particularly at leg joints or between thoracic sclerites; fig. 1.28). This is termed reflex bleeding or auto-haemorrhaging and occurs in insects whose haemolymph contains malodorous or distasteful chemicals that serve as a deterrent against predators (see 'Armoured ground crickets', p. 213; box, p. 225).

1.28 Some insects, such as this foam locust, *Dictyophorus spumans* (Pyrgomorphidae), ooze haemolymph laced with repellent plant chemicals from between the thoracic sclerites to deter predators.

Functions of haemolymph and haematocytes

Haemolymph has the following functions:

- it forms the hydrostatic skeleton of the body by providing the internal pressure that supports the organs and helps retain body shape;
- it transports and disseminates nutrients, hormones and waste products;
- it provides hydrostatic pressure in the body during locomotion (including inflation of wings for flight), moulting, the protrusion of genitalia and defensive osmeteria in certain butterfly larvae, rolling and unrolling of the proboscis in butterflies and moths, and expelling faecal pellets; and
- it is an aqueous solution and is therefore an important water reservoir.

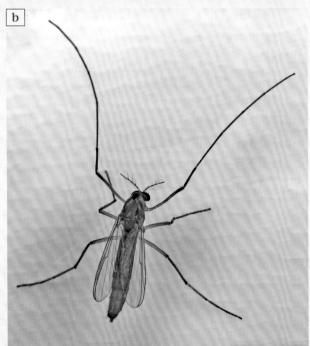

Haemolymph differs substantially from the blood of vertebrates. It is:

- rarely red – only a few insects such as the aquatic larval stages of some flies (Chironomidae) have oxygen-carrying haemoglobin in the haemolymph (fig. 1.29a; see 'Midges, gnats, bloodworms', p. 340);
- a single fluid, not divided into blood and lymph;
- usually clear and colourless, but may be pigmented yellow or green, depending on diet (figs 1.29b, c); and
- a watery plasma in which colourless haematocytes (cells) are suspended that are highly variable in size, shape, number and function.

Haematocytes within the haemolymph have the following functions:

- encapsulating and destroying endoparasites or other foreign bodies;
- mending injuries – especially the loss of limbs – by coagulating (clotting) with the plasma in some species, or by forming a plug of haemocytes in others;
- removing dead cells (as waste products) during moulting;
- supplying noxious chemicals that are used in defence; and
- preventing body tissues from freezing through the accumulation of 'antifreeze' compounds, thus allowing eggs and pupae of insects in cold regions to survive freezing temperatures.

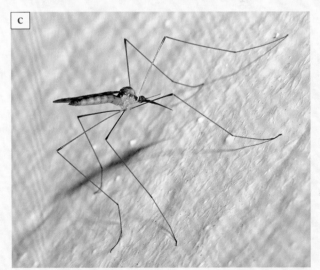

1.29 Insect blood (haemolymph) is usually colourless, but in some fly larvae such as those of (**a**) this bloodworm, *Chironomus formosipennis* (Diptera: Chironomidae), the haemolymph contains haemoglobin and appears red. (**b**) Other fly species may have adults with green haemolymph coloured by bile pigments and visible through the cuticle such as in this chironomid or (**c**), visible through the abdominal wall as in this crane fly (Diptera: Tipulidae).

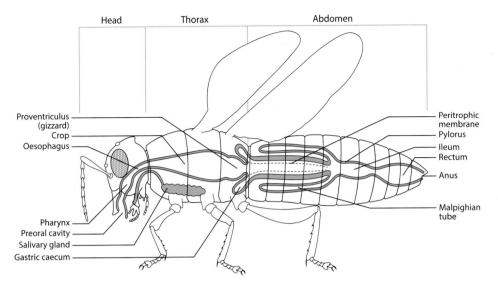

1.30 The digestive and excretory systems in insects are morphologically simple – the gut is for digestion while the Malpighian tubules remove most of the fluid waste.

1.31 Many insects use 'extra-alimentary' or 'extra-oral' digestion by injecting enzymes into their food; these digest the tissue and the resultant fluid is sucked up and absorbed directly in the midgut without further digestion; a seed bug, *Heegeria tangirica* (Alydidae), feeding on a dry, fallen seed.

Digestion

Insects feed on almost every organic substance found on earth, ranging from virtually pure liquid to solid wood, and everything in between. Insect digestive systems are therefore similarly varied; this adaptation to different diets can also be seen in the wide range of specialised mouthparts in different groups.

In the majority of insects, digestion takes place in the alimentary canal (fig. 1.30). Some adult insects do not feed and the alimentary canal is reduced or even absent – their nutrient requirements are provided by the 'fat body' (see page opposite).

For many insects, digestion starts even before the food has entered the mouth. These insects inject digestive enzymes into their prey or expel it onto their food, and partial digestion begins before the food is ingested. This is termed extra-oral, extra-alimentary or extra-intestinal digestion (fig. 1.31).

The alimentary canal (gut) of most insects consists of a simple tube that extends from the mouth to the anus. It is differentiated into three main regions: the foregut, midgut and hindgut, which are separated by sphincters (valves) controlling food and fluid movement between the regions. In many insects, these regions are subdivided into various functional parts. The fore- and hindgut have a cuticular lining, which is shed with the rest of the cuticle at moulting; the midgut is not moulted.

Insects have paired salivary glands and salivary reservoirs, usually located in the thorax, next to the foregut. Saliva plays an important role in the digestive process, as it mostly contains digestive enzymes; it is the primary digestive mechanism for insects without mandibles, which use extra-oral digestion and then suck up the fluid. Some insects have venomous saliva.

Generally, insects that feed on solid food have a wide, straight, short gut with strong muscles and a gizzard for grinding the food. As solid food is mostly readily available (e.g. plant leaves; fig. 1.32), these insects do not need storage areas. Insects that feed on blood, sap or nectar, on the other hand, usually have a long, narrow, convoluted gut to increase the absorption area, and a large storage capacity since their food supply is available intermittently.

Foregut

The foregut (stomodaeum) is involved in ingestion, storage, grinding and transport of food to the midgut, and consists of the pharynx, oesophagus, crop and, in some insects, the proventriculus (gizzard).

At the anterior end of the foregut, the mouthparts surround the preoral cavity. The cavity is often divided into a lower part or salivarium, into which the salivary glands empty saliva, and an upper area or cibarium, which forms part of the pharynx.

The pharynx has a series of muscles that are especially well developed in sucking insects, such as butterflies and moths (Lepidoptera) and bugs (Heteroptera), forming the pharyngeal (cibarial) pump, which is used to draw up fluids (fig. 1.33). In biting and chewing insects, the pharyngeal muscles help to move food from the mouthparts to the oesophagus.

The oesophagus is short and leads to a thin-walled crop, used for food storage in some insects. The crop is usually followed by a proventriculus (gizzard), which is modified in various ways in different insect groups. Its main function is to control the passage of food from the crop to the midgut. In many groups that feed on solids, such as cockroaches, termites and crickets, the proventriculus has well-developed plates or teeth to break up the food; it is greatly reduced in fluid feeders.

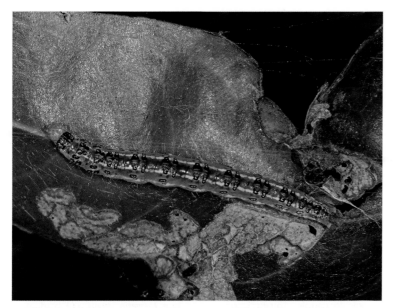

1.32 The food-filled alimentary canal is visible through the cuticle of some soft-bodied insects, as in this Lepidoptera larva (caterpillar).

1.33 Insects with long, thin, tubular mouthparts such as this butterfly, *Colotis subfasciatus* (Pieridae), suck up fluids using a well-developed pharyngeal pump.

Midgut

From the foregut, food passes to the midgut (mesenteron or stomach), where most digestion occurs. In many insects, the midgut is a simple tube with four, six or eight finger-shaped caeca (blind sacs) at the anterior end. The caeca secrete digestive enzymes and also shelter symbiotic bacteria (symbionts), which provide essential nutrients to insects with diets in which these are lacking. In some insects a peritrophic membrane is secreted to encapsulate the food passing through in order to protect the lining of the midgut.

Hindgut

Any material remaining after digestion has taken place, empties into the hindgut (proctodeum), together with uric acid from the Malpighian tubules (see 'Excretion', alongside). The hindgut consists of the pylorus, ileum and rectum. The pylorus forms a valve between the mid- and hindgut in some insects. The ileum is a simple tube that leads to the rectum in most insects. In some wood-feeding termites, however, it forms a pouch that houses symbiotic cellulose-digesting protozoa. Many dung beetles have a similar chamber in the ileum.

The rectum is an enlarged, thin-walled sac with six thickened rectal pads that are important in the reabsorption of water, salts and other useful substances from faeces and urine. Faecal pellets are eliminated through the anus.

The fat body

The fat body (*corpus adiposum*) is a storage organ often present in the larval and nymphal stages, as well as in adult insects that do not feed. The fat body is composed of white or yellow tissue formed of loose sheets or ribbons of cells suspended in haemolymph. It may occur as a peripheral layer beneath the cuticle or as a central layer around the gut, and stores fats, proteins and glycogen. In addition to its storage function, the fat body is intimately associated with insects' digestive processes and plays a central role in their metabolism. It also stores excretory materials.

Excretion

The Malpighian tubule system is the main excretory organ in insects (fig. 1.30). It consists of long, thin, branching tubes that arise from the gut at the junction of the mid- and hindgut. They are closed at the distal end and float freely in the haemolymph. Thin muscle layers encircle the tubules and produce writhing movements, ensuring maximum contact with haemolymph and improving the movement of fluid in the tubules. All insects except aphids (Hemiptera: Aphididae) have Malpighian tubules. The number of tubules present varies considerably between groups, from only two in scale insects (Hemiptera: Coccoidea) to about 250 in some Orthoptera.

Water, salts and nitrogenous waste products (see box, p. 32) pass into the Malpighian tubules from the haemolymph. The primary urine formed in the tubules is emptied into the hindgut, where it mixes with digested food. In the rectum, uric acid crystals precipitate from the urine and water and certain salts are reabsorbed. The Malpighian tubules and rectum are therefore both involved in the formation and excretion of urine and faeces, as well as in keeping the levels of water and salts in the body fluids stable (osmoregulation).

Ammonia is the primary end product of nitrogen metabolism, but is toxic except in extreme dilutions with water. Only aquatic insects or insects such as blow fly larvae that live in exceptionally moist environments excrete ammonia as their main waste product. Terrestrial insects cannot afford to excrete diluted ammonia, as this would mean the loss of large quantities of water. Uric acid is an alternative that is less toxic than ammonia and requires less water for excretion: it is insoluble and forms crystals that can be stored as a solid, nontoxic waste substance. There is a trade-off, however, because the conversion of ammonia to uric acid is energetically costly. Nearly half of the food energy a terrestrial insect consumes may be used to process metabolic wastes.

In aquatic insects, ammonia simply diffuses out of the body into the surrounding water and salts are conserved by the hindgut; faeces containing waste food are excreted via the anus. In terrestrial insects, uric acid is added to faeces in the hindgut,

water is extracted in the rectum, and almost-dry pellets (frass) are excreted.

In some species, uric acid is retained in the body and is excreted at the end of a particular life stage as meconium. In lacewings, antlions and mantidflies (Neuroptera), for example, the larval gut is fused and all waste products are voided at pupation (see 'Pit-building antlions', p. 349). In many lepidopteran larvae, as well as some mosquito larvae, uric acid is stored in epidermal cells and the fat body; at pupation it is transferred to the pupal Malpighian tubules, and is finally excreted with the meconium when the adult emerges. In 'white' butterflies (Pieridae), up to 80% of the uric acid produced in the larval and pupal tissues is stored and then deposited in the adult wing scales to provide white pigments (fig. 1.34a). In certain bugs (e.g. *Dysdercus* spp., Pyrrhocoridae; *Leptocoris* spp., Rhopalidae), uric acid accumulates in the epidermis and contributes to the white colour of the insect (fig. 1.34b).

1.34 Uric acid produced by the Malpighian tubules is one of the main excretory products in insects. In some species, instead of being excreted, it is diverted to (a) white wing scales, as in the butterfly *Pontia helice helice* (Pieridae); or (b) white epidermal pigments, as in this bug, *Leptocoris* sp. (Rhopalidae).

In a few insects, the Malpighian tubules are modified for functions other than excretion. In antlion and lacewing larvae (Neuroptera), they function as silk-producing organs for spinning the pupal cocoon (fig. 1.35; see 'Pit-building antlions', p. 349; 'Thread-winged lacewings', p. 350). In many female leaf beetles (Chrysomelidae), the tubules produce a sticky substance used to cover egg packets after laying; it hardens on contact with air to form an egg case (see 'Deadly leaf beetles and their parasitoids', p. 226).

1.35 In antlions and lacewings (Neuroptera), the Malpighian tubules are unusual: instead of having an excretory function, they produce the silk used to spin the pupal cocoon. This spherical cocoon belongs to a green lacewing (Chrysopidae).

Reproduction

Most insects are oviparous and reproduce by laying eggs after a male and a female have mated (fig. 1.36). During copulation, spermatozoa are transferred directly from the male to the female, and the eggs are fertilised inside the female before they are laid. Reproductive organs, particularly those of males, vary considerably between insects – so much so that they are often used by entomologists to identify species.

1.36 Reproduction in most insects involves copulation between a male and a female, and the transfer of sperm to the ovaries. Mating positions vary greatly among insects, as seen here: (a) the 'wheel' position is typical of Odonata, such as these damselflies, *Proischnura polychromatica* (Coenagrionidae); (b) bugs (Derbidae); (c) butterflies, *Azanus jesous jesous* (Lycaenidae); (d) flies (Muscidae); (e) tiger beetles, *Lophyra reliqua* (Carabidae: Cicindelinae); (f) long-horned beetles, *Philematium virens* (Cerambycidae); (g) moths, *Amata cerbera* (Erebidae: Arctiinae).

Female reproductive system

In most adult female insects, the internal reproductive organs are located in the terminal abdominal segments and consist of ovaries, oviducts, spermathecae and accessory glands (fig. 1.37).

There are usually two ovaries (one in dung beetles), each with a lateral oviduct. The two oviducts unite to form a common oviduct, leading into the vagina, which opens directly onto the ventral surface of the seventh, eighth or ninth segment of the abdomen. In some insects the vagina opens into a chamber, the bursa copulatrix, while in others the bursa copulatrix has a separate external opening.

An ovary (fig. 1.38) consists of a group of tubules called ovarioles, in which the eggs (oocytes) are produced. The number of ovarioles per ovary can vary from one (in dung beetles) to more than a thousand (in termites); most female insects, however, have about four to eight.

Spermathecae are tubes or sacs connected to the vagina, in which spermatozoa may be stored after mating. The female insect can use the spermathecae to control when fertilisation of her eggs occurs.

Various accessory glands secrete adhesive material to fasten the eggs to objects or to provide material that covers the egg mass with a protective coating (fig. 1.39). In some insects, the accessory glands may function as poison glands (e.g. in many Hymenoptera). In a few ovoviviparous insects, including louse and bat flies (Hippoboscidae; see 'Parasitic flies', p. 353) and tsetse flies (Glossinidae; see 'Tsetse flies as carriers of disease', p. 264), the accessory glands produce 'milk' that feeds larvae developing inside the body of the female.

The external genitalia of some female insects function as ovipositors (egg-laying tubes), and may be formed from appendages of abdominal segments 8 and 9 (termed appendicular ovipositors, fig. 1.40), or may consist of extendible posterior abdominal segments (termed substitutional ovipositors).

The appendicular ovipositor of certain parasitic wasps (Hymenoptera), especially those that parasitise wood-boring larvae deep inside wood, is many times longer than the body of the wasp (see 'Wood-boring long-horned beetles', p. 221). In other members of this order (some bees, ants and wasps), the ovipositor is modified as a poison-injecting sting, so the eggs are ejected from the vagina on the eighth abdominal segment at the base of the sting.

Substitutional ovipositors consist of a variable number of abdominal segments that are telescopic and can be extended as a slender, membranous tube called the pseudovipositor or oviscapt. In cycad weevils (*Antliarhinus* spp.; see 'Seed-feeding cycad weevils', p. 273), the tube is extended by many times the female's body length during oviposition.

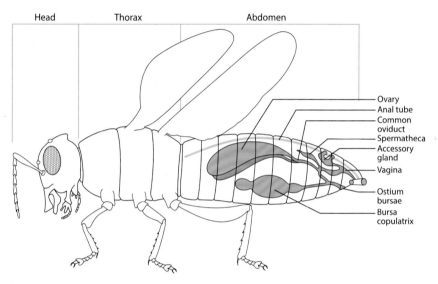

1.37 Position of reproductive organs of typical female insect relative to the digestive tract.

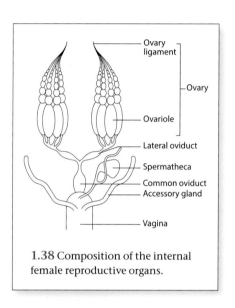

1.38 Composition of the internal female reproductive organs.

1.39 Many insects have accessory reproductive glands with various reproduction-related functions. In groups that produce an egg packet or ootheca, such as praying mantises (Mantodea), the oothecal compounds are secreted by the accessory glands.

1.40 Ovipositors such as that of this parasitic wasp (Braconidae), which parasitises wood-boring beetle larvae, are formed from appendages on the eighth and ninth abdominal segments and are termed 'appendicular appendages'.

Male reproductive system

In the internal male reproductive system (fig. 1.42), spermatozoa are produced in the testes, which are suspended in the body cavity by tracheae and the fat body. There are usually two testes, each with a lateral duct (vas deferens). A testis is made up of a group of sperm tubes containing spermatozoa at various stages of development.

A section of each vas deferens is usually enlarged to form a seminal vesicle in which sperm are stored. Accessory glands secrete seminal fluid into the vasa deferentia. The fluid forms the spermatophore (the package that surrounds the spermatozoa of many insects) and nourishes the spermatozoa.

The vasa deferentia eventually join to form a common median (or ejaculatory) duct (fig. 1.43) that opens on the male's eighth abdominal segment through the gonopore at the tip of the penis (or aedeagus). In most insects the often extensible, or eversible, penis is inserted into the female's vagina during copulation. The spermatozoa are either packaged in a spermatophore or are free in fluid. After mating, sperm are released from the spermatophores. In some groups, copulation does not take place; instead, a spermatophore is deposited on the ground by the male and picked up by the female – for example, in bristletails (Archaeognatha; see 'Bristletails: the oldest order', p. 286) and fish moths (Zygentoma; see 'Fishmoths', p. 347).

At each mating a large number of sperm are transferred to the spermatheca of the female, where they remain until the eggs are laid. This number may be sufficient to fertilise many eggs over a lifetime (e.g. in the honey bee; see 'The ubiquitous honey bee', p. 74). Most insects reproduce only once in their lifetime and may mate only a few times. Termites are an exception: the queen mates repeatedly with the king and lays thousands of eggs during a lifetime that may extend over several years.

The aedeagus is usually accompanied by lobes that function in clasping the female during copulation (fig. 1.41a). The most atypical copulatory 'clasping' (fig. 1.41b) occurs in the damselflies and dragonflies (Odonata; see 'Damselflies and dragonflies', p. 324), the males of which are unique in having two sets of genitalia. The primary genitalia are housed in the eighth or ninth abdominal segment, where a spermatophore is produced. The spermatophore is transferred to the secondary genitalia on the second or third segment, from which it is retrieved by the female during mating.

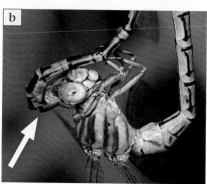

1.41 Males of many insect species have highly modified abdominal lobes that function as claspers for holding the female during copulation: (**a**) the antlion *Palparidius fascipennis* (Neuroptera: Myrmeleontidae); (**b**) all dragonfly males such as this *Crenigomphus hartmanni* (Odonata: Gomphidae) have claspers with which they hold the female behind the head during mating.

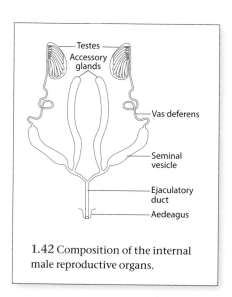

1.42 Composition of the internal male reproductive organs.

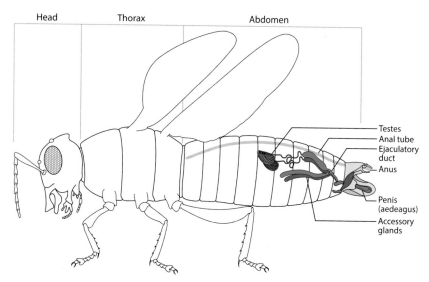

1.43 Position of reproductive organs in typical male insect.

Jonathan Ball

1.44 Many female insects mate with more than one male during a single reproductive event and it is usually the last male's sperm that fertilises the female. The males of some species produce large mating plugs to prevent another mating, as seen in this female mantidfly, a species of *Mantispa* (Neuroptera: Mantispidae). The plugs also have an additional function as a food supplement that is eaten by the female.

1.45 (a) A stink bug, *Glypsus conspicuus* (Heteroptera: Pentatomidae), laying eggs. **(b)** A female robber fly, *Ancylorhynchus crux* (Diptera: Asilidae), laying an egg mass in a hole in the soil. **(c)** A green locust, *Kraussaria* sp. (Orthoptera: Acrididae), laying eggs into a 'pod' (ootheca) produced simultaneously by reproductive accessory glands, with the tip of her abdomen pressed into the ground.

Some insect species have evolved traits to lessen the chances of a subsequent successful mating with another male. In some groups, the male remains in copulation with the female until she is fertilised (e.g. in Odonata). To prevent a female from mating again, male insects may produce a large, protein-rich 'mating plug' (spermatophyllax – see 'Armoured ground crickets', p. 213) that blocks the female genitalia, giving the eggs time to be fertilised by the male's sperm (fig. 1.44).

Eggs and fertilisation

In most insects, fertilisation occurs just before the eggs are deposited. As an egg leaves her oviduct (fig. 1.45), the female releases sperm from her spermatheca to fertilise it during its passage through the oviduct. A queen bee, for example, can choose to release sperm to fertilise the eggs, in which case they develop into diploid female bees, or she can withhold sperm and not fertilise the eggs; haploid males result (see 'The ubiquitous honey bee', p. 74). In some insects the eggs hatch while still inside the female and the larvae are 'born' (ovovivipary – see box, p. 38).

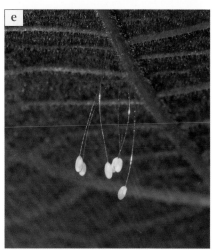

1.46 Insects developed various methods to protect their eggs against predation. **(a)** Ladybirds (Coleoptera: Coccinellidae) lay eggs in batches, **(b)** which all hatch at the same time, a strategy that prevents the first larvae from preying on their siblings. **(c)** Some bugs, such as this twig-wilter, *Homoeocerus nigricornis* (Hemiptera: Coreidae), guard their eggs until they hatch. **(d)** The eggs or 'nits' of parasitic lice are attached to the host's hair or feathers; these are the eggs of *Haematopinus suis* (Psocodea: Haematopinidae) on a warthog. **(e)** The stalks attached to green lacewing (Neuroptera: Chrysopidae) eggs decrease the chances of predation by siblings or ants. **(f)** This normally sap-feeding stink bug nymph, *Antestiopsis thunbergi* (Hemiptera: Pentatomidae), from an adjoining older egg batch, appears to be preying on a relative's eggs; bugs are known to deviate occasionally from their primary plant sap food source to acquire extra protein or minerals.

1.47 (a) Red leaf beetles (Chrysomelidae) and their **(b)** cluster of bright red eggs send a strong aposematic message to predators.

Eggs (fig. 1.46) are the most vulnerable stage of the insect life cycle. Eggs may be impregnated with defensive chemicals, for example, in ladybirds (Coleoptera: Coccinellidae; figs 1.46a, b), and in many bugs (Hemiptera). In some cases, they are guarded by the female until they hatch (fig. 1.46c).

The female can give them some protection against predators by choosing how and where to lay her eggs. They may be laid:

- singly, to lessen the chances of detection, as in stick insects (Phasmatodea; see 'Stick insects: the longest insects of the region', p. 215);
- in clusters (figs 1.46d–f), where 'safety in numbers' ensures better chances that at least some will survive, a strategy often used by butterflies and moths;
- in a protected environment, by being attached to stalks (fig. 1.46e) or in an egg case (ootheca), such as that produced by cockroaches (Blattoidea; see 'Breeding and parental care in cockroaches', p. 90) and praying mantises (Mantodea; fig. 1.39; see 'Praying mantises', p. 405); and
- at another extreme, the eggs are brightly coloured to advertise their unpalatability to would-be predators, for example, in some leaf beetles (Coleoptera: Chrysomelidae; fig. 1.47).

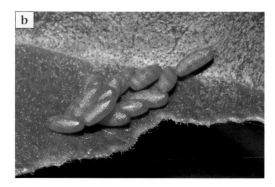

Most insects are oviparous – they lay eggs that develop and hatch outside the body. A few groups, however, are ovoviviparous – the eggs are fertilised and incubated internally by the female, and also hatch internally. The nymphs or larvae then emerge from the female. Examples are aphids and some cockroaches (see 'Breeding and parental care in cockroaches', p. 90).

This process is taken a step further in louse and bat flies (Hippoboscidae; see 'Parasitic flies', p. 353) and tsetse flies (Glossinidae; see 'Tsetse flies as carriers of disease', p. 264), in which a single egg is incubated in the mother's reproductive tract, where her accessory glands produce 'milk' that feeds the developing larva. The single mature larva is 'born' ready to pupate immediately.

Asexual reproduction

Some insects reproduce asexually by means of parthenogenesis, a process in which unmated females produce offspring from unfertilised eggs, either as a natural part of their life cycle or when environmental conditions demand it. Examples of parthenogenesis are found in aphids, all wasps, bees and ants (Hymenoptera). In honey bees, *Apis mellifera* (Hymenoptera), males develop from unfertilised eggs, whereas fertilised eggs develop into female offspring (see 'The ubiquitous honey bee', p. 74). Parthenogenesis is obligatory in some stick insect species (Phasmatodea) that have only females; males are completely absent.

In aphids (Hemiptera: Aphididae), asexual reproduction is seasonal (fig. 1.48). In spring, a flightless female gives birth to female nymphs without having mated. The nymphs mature quickly and reproduce asexually themselves, so the number of aphids on a

1.48 Asexual reproduction (parthenogenesis) is common in some insects. In most aphids, such as this *Macrosiphum rosae* (Aphididae), parthenogenesis is seasonal.

single plant multiplies quickly. Later in the season, winged females develop; they can fly to colonise other plants. In some species, females produce both female and male offspring in autumn to allow sexual reproduction (see 'Aphids and whiteflies', p. 374).

Hermaphrodites

Males and females are separate individuals in the vast majority of insect species, but there are rare examples of hermaphroditism, in which a single individual has both male and female sex organs. The hermaphrodite cottony cushion scale or Australian bug, *Icerya purchasi* (Hemiptera: Monophlebidae; fig. 1.49; see box, p. 377), is a cosmopolitan citrus pest.

1.49 The cottony cushion scale or Australian bug, *Icerya purchasi* (Monophlebidae), is one of the very few insect species that are hermaphrodites, with both male and female reproductive organs in the same individual.

Insect growth and development

Insects grow by the process of metamorphosis – the transformation in body form and habits of individuals, from the hatched egg through several larval or nymphal instars to the adult stage. There are three types of insect development, depending on the extent of transformation from hatchling to adult – ametamorphic with little change, hemimetamorphic with slight transformation, and holometamorphic with substantial transformation from egg to adult (see pp. 40, 41).

Moulting (see box opposite) is necessary while an insect is growing during the nymphal or larval stages, because the rigid cuticle cannot expand. The stages between moults during the immature stage are referred to as instars; the time between moults increases as the insect matures. Most insects have between three and nine instars, but some mayflies (Ephemeroptera) and stoneflies (Plecoptera) have as many as 30. Depending on the insect species, the entire life cycle can take from as little as five days up to several years without a rest phase, although the average time is probably about 30 days.

Insect growth would be impossible without the periodic shedding of the rigid exoskeleton, which cannot expand, and its replacement with a new, larger cuticle (fig. 1.50). This is accomplished through the process of moulting or ecdysis:

- Ecdysis is initiated and regulated by an increase in the hormone ecdysone.
- At the start of the process, enzymes secreted by glands in the epidermis dissolve the old procuticle, separating the old cuticle from the epidermis.
- Enzyme-containing moulting fluid is secreted into the space between the epidermis and the cuticle, but the enzymes remain inactive.
- A new procuticle and epicuticle are secreted by the epidermis. Once these layers have been formed, the enzymes in the moulting fluid are activated.
- The lower regions of the old cuticle are digested by the enzymes and are resorbed by the insect. The top layer of the old cuticle is resistant to the enzymes and is not digested.
- Finally, a layer of wax is deposited on the surface of the new cuticle.
- To free itself from the remains of the old cuticle (called exuviae), the insect stretches and makes crawling body movements, and the old exoskeleton splits open along predetermined ecdysal lines (exocuticle is absent in these areas). The exuviae often retain the shape of the insect.
- The cuticle of the newly emerged insect is soft and highly wrinkled, allowing a greater area for expansion. The insect expands the cuticle by swallowing air (or water, in the case of aquatic insects) and by moving its body.
- Once expansion is complete, pigmentation and sclerotisation (darkening and hardening of the cuticle) occur, which may take from a few hours to a few days.
- Additional layers are added to the endocuticle once moulting is completed.

Ecdysis occurs between the instars of ametamorphic insects that moult throughout their lives; between all the nymphal instars until the adult stage of hemimetamorphic insects; as well as between the larval instars, the pupal stage to the adult stage of holometamorphic groups. Wound healing and the regeneration of lost limbs also take place during moulting, and therefore cannot occur once the mature stage has been reached. The wax layer on the exocuticle continues to be produced, even after an insect reaches the adult stage (see 'Wax blooms', p. 139).

1.50 Insects grow in distinct stages, each of which is terminated by a moult (ecdysis) during which the cuticle splits open and a soft individual emerges. It may still need to expand, or if adult, to inflate its wings, after which it hardens and darkens (sclerotisation). (a) The shed cuticle (exuviae) may retain the exact shape of the insect prior to the moult, as shown by the nymphal exuviae of a hemimetamorphic cicada (Hemiptera: Cicadidae). (b) The final-instar hemimetamorphic katydid (Orthoptera: Tettigoniidae) moulting into the adult stage. (c) An adult hemimetamorphic twig-wilter (Coreidae) eclosing. (d) The second instar of a holometamorphic ladybird (Coccinellidae) larva moulting into the third instar. (e) A holometamorphic net-veined beetle (Lycidae) adult emerging from its pupal case. (f) A recently eclosed holometamorphic adult evening brown butterfly, *Melanitis leda helena* (Nymphalidae), near its pupal exuviae.

Ametamorphic development

Only the two most primitive insect orders – bristletails (Archaeognatha) and fishmoths or silverfish (Zygentoma) – are ametamorphic. The nymphs that hatch from the eggs resemble tiny adults and grow without change at each successive moult, until the sexually mature adult stage is reached. They then continue moulting throughout their life, although they do not increase in size (fig. 1.51).

Hemimetamorphic development

Hemimetamorphic insects undergo gradual or incomplete metamorphosis from an egg, through several instars as a nymph, and finally to the adult stage (fig. 1.52).

The nymphs of most hemimetamorphic orders resemble the adults, live in the same space and feed on the same food, therefore competing for these resources. Mayflies, dragonflies, damselflies (fig 1.53) and stoneflies, however, have aquatic immature stages and terrestrial adults. The nymphs do not resemble the adults, as they are adapted to an underwater life. Their diet also differs from that of the adult insects. These aquatic nymphs are sometimes referred to as naiads.

Hemimetamorphic nymphs have compound eyes and ocelli. In the early instars, the wings are small external pads, which grow larger during later moults, becoming functional only when the adult stage is reached. Depending on the species, the nymph stage may last from a few days to many years. The longest confirmed nymph stage is that of the periodical cicadas in the genus *Magicicada* (Hemiptera) of the eastern USA: one group of four species has a nymph stage of 13 years, while in three other species it is 17 years.

Hemimetamorphic orders
Ephemeroptera (mayflies)
Odonata (dragonflies and damselflies)
Plecoptera (stoneflies)
Blattodea (cockroaches and termites)
Mantodea (mantises)
Dermaptera (earwigs)
Embioptera (webspinners)
Orthoptera (grasshoppers and crickets)
Phasmatodea (stick insects)
Mantophasmatodea (heelwalkers)
Psocodea (lice)
Hemiptera (bugs)
Thysanoptera (thrips)

1.51 Ametamorphic development, in which there is negligible change other than size as individuals mature, occurs only in the two basal orders: (**a**) fishmoths (Zygentoma) and (**b**) bristletails (Archaeognatha).

1.52 In hemimetamorphic development, nymphs increasingly develop more mature characteristics after each moult, but otherwise remain similar in appearance throughout their development. Different instars of bug nymphs clustering together: (**a**) *Acanthocoris* sp. and (**b**) *Spilostethus pandurus* (Heteroptera).

1.53 The stages are morphologically dissimilar in hemimetamorphic insects that have aquatic nymphs and terrestrial adults: (**a**) the nymph and (**b**) the adult of the damselfly *Chlorolestes fasciatus* (Odonata: Lestidae).

1.54 In holometamorphic development, there are four completely different developmental stages in the life cycle, as shown here for the moth *Aurivillius fuscus* (Saturniidae): (**a**) adult; (**b**) hatched eggs (of another Saturniidae species); (**c**) first-instar larvae; (**d**) second-instar larvae; (**e**) fourth-instar larva; (**f**) fifth-instar larva; (**g**) nonfeeding prepupal stage that develops in the soil beneath the host plant; (**h**) pupa.

Holometamorphic development

Holometamorphic insects develop through four stages: starting life as an egg, hatching into a larva, which, after feeding and growth accompanied by several moults, develops into a pupal stage from which the adult eventually emerges (fig. 1.54). Each stage is morphologically distinct. The egg and pupa are nonfeeding developmental stages, whereas the larva always feeds and grows; there is no moulting in the adult stage.

The larva usually has a different food source from that of the adult, and often inhabits an entirely different environment, hence eliminating competition between them. A typical example is a butterfly whose larva (caterpillar) feeds on leaves, then enters the pupal stage, from which a nectar-feeding adult emerges.

The larva that hatches from the egg is one of various types (see box, p. 43), depending on the insect species. They mostly have true legs on the thorax, and sometimes rudimentary leg-like appendages (prolegs) on the abdomen (e.g. moth and butterfly larvae). Most have chewing mouthparts and simple eyes (stemmata). In species with winged adults, the larva hatches without wing rudiments, but these develop internally as the larva grows larger over several instars. With the exception of species that undergo hypermetamorphosis (see box, p. 42), the larval 'type' (figs 1.54c–g) remains the same during all the instars. Each larval instar may last for only a few days, although in certain species the final larval instar often lasts several years. For example, the larval stage of some large wood-boring insects, particularly long-horned beetles (Coleoptera: Cerambycidae), probably lasts as long as five years, mainly because of the poor nutritional quality of the dry wood on which they feed.

During the final instar, the larva forms a case or cocoon around itself and becomes a pupa or chrysalis, which is usually hard (fig. 1.54h). The pupal stage appears dormant, and is often used to pass the colder winter months, usually in a protected location such as in the ground, under bark or in plant tissue. During this time, however, changes take place within it; many larval organs break down and are resorbed, and new adult structures develop. These changes are mostly under the control of the moulting hormone ecdysone.

Prior to the final moult into the adult stage, the pupa starts to expand from inhaled air (or imbibed water in aquatic insects), until the pupal case splits along special weakened moult lines. In house flies (Muscidae), blow flies (Calliphoridae) and many other fly families, however, a sac on the head is inflated by haemolymph to split the puparium open and allow the adult to emerge.

The evolutionary success of the holometamorphic orders, which account for about 80% of all insect species, can be attributed largely to metamorphosis and the development of a pupal stage. These adaptations reduce competition between larvae and adults for food and living space, and make it possible for the insects to delay their development at certain stages when environmental conditions are unfavourable; this is a form of dormancy where any change or growth is arrested, and is termed 'diapause' or 'quiescence' (see p. 44).

Holometamorphic orders
Megaloptera (dobsonflies and alderflies)
Neuroptera (antlions and lacewings)
Coleoptera (beetles)
Strepsiptera (twisted-winged parasites)
Mecoptera (hangingflies)
Siphonaptera (fleas)
Diptera (flies)
Trichoptera (caddisflies)
Lepidoptera (butterflies and moths)
Hymenoptera (wasps, bees and ants)

Hypermetamorphosis

Hypermetamorphosis is an unusual type of larval development in which some or all of the larval instars have completely different forms (fig. 1.55). The phenomenon occurs in some predatory and parasitic holometamorphic insects. The larva's behaviour changes at the same time as its shape.

The first-instar larva is a small, active form with well-developed legs. The egg or the first-instar larva is laid in the vicinity of the host and the larva has to seek out its host. In other cases, the egg is laid in an area (e.g. on a flower) where the larva is likely to find a potential host – such as a bee, fly or spider – that will transport it to the nest, where it will prey on the brood or penetrate the host to become an internal parasite.

In beetles, this active first instar is known as a triungulin. Once on or in the host, the triungulin moults into a slightly less active form, called a caraboid (Carabidae-like) larva. It moults again into either a worm-like or grub-like form (see 'Blister beetle larvae: predators of locust eggs', p. 171). The active first instar is called a planidium or primary larva in hypermetamorphic wasps, flies and twisted-winged parasites.

Hypermetamorphic families
Neuroptera (Mantispidae)
Strepsiptera
Coleoptera (Meloidae, Staphylinidae, Ripiphoridae, Rhipiceridae, Passandridae)
Diptera (Acroceridae, Bombyliidae, Nemestrinidae)
Lepidoptera (Epipyropidae)
Hymenoptera (Perilampidae, Eucharitidae)

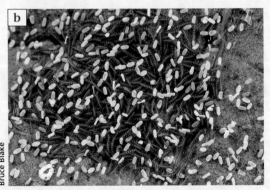

Bruce Blake

Bruce Blake

1.55 The larvae of a few groups of insects undergo substantial change during their development, termed hypermetamorphosis. (a) The long-legged, fast-moving triungulin larva of the CMR beetle, *Hycleus tricolor* (Coleoptera: Meloidae). (b) In this mantidfly species (Neuroptera: Mantispidae), the female has laid hundreds of tiny eggs, from which triungulin larvae emerge. (c) The triungulins disperse to find a spider egg packet, which they penetrate, and then moult into a sessile, short-legged individual that preys on the spider eggs.

Larval and pupal types

The larvae of holometamorphic insects are described using terms based on the number of legs present, the shape of the larva, and the presence or absence of a distinct head capsule (fig. 1.56).

The number of legs can be described as either:

- apodous (without legs);
- oligopodous (with a few legs); or
- polypodous (with many legs).

Shape is described by a term ending in -form:

- eruciform (caterpillar-like);
- scarabaeiform (grub-like);
- elateriform (wireworm-like);
- vermiform (maggot-like); or
- campodeiform (elongated, flattened, and active).

The absence of a head capsule is indicated by the term 'acephalic' (no term is used if a head capsule is present).

Pupae are classified according to whether appendages are loose (exarate), closely adhered to the body (obtect), or whether the pupa is encased in the exuviae of the last larval instar (coarctate) (fig. 1.57).

1.56 The larvae of holometamorphic insects are quite unlike the adults of the species, and different types of larvae occur in different groups. The types are described based on the number of legs present, the shape of the body, and whether a distinct head capsule is present or absent. (a) The blood-feeding parasitic maggot of the warthog fly, *Pachychoeromyia praegrandis* (Calliphoridae), is apodous and acephalic. (b) Most butterfly larvae, like this *Graphium* sp. (Papilionidae), are polypodous (with three pairs of 'true' thoracic legs, and several pairs of abdominal 'prolegs') and caterpillar-like. (c) Scarabaeidae beetle larvae are oligopodous and grub-like. (d) Many beetle and fly larvae are oligopodous and worm-like. (e) Leaf beetle larvae (Chrysomelidae) are typically oligopodous and caterpillar-like. (f) The larvae of ladybirds (Coleoptera: Coccinellidae) and (g) green lacewings (Neuroptera: Chrysopidae), like many other predatory larvae, are active and oligopodous, with an elongated, flattened body.

1.57 (a) The exarate pupa of a rhinoceros beetle (Scarabaeidae: Dynastinae). (b) The obtect pupa of a *Charaxes* sp. (Nymphalidae) butterfly; the larval exuviae with 'horns' characteristic of the genus are still attached. (c) The coarctate pupa of the parasitic fly *Gasterophilus intestinalis* (Oestridae); this pupal type is characteristic of the higher Diptera families.

Dormancy

During the developmental stage of the life cycle of insects there may be various periods of dormancy. These are known as diapause and quiescence.

Diapause is a form of dormancy that usually coincides with the physiological changes necessary for the progression from one stage of the life cycle to the next. It is fixed in the species, most often occurring during the egg and pupal stages (fig. 1.58). In most southern African insects, diapause takes place during the cold winter months (winter diapause or hibernation), which are unfavourable for insect survival. In regions of southern Africa where the summers are extremely hot and dry, diapause may occur in summer (summer diapause or aestivation).

Diapause is genetically determined and under hormonal control. It is usually set off by an environmental signal, most often the shortening or lengthening of days, as changes in day length correlate with seasons. Other triggers may be changes in temperature, food quality, moisture, pH, or certain chemicals. Diapause can last from days to months, but it can only be terminated when the 'correct' signal is received, irrespective of environmental conditions.

Quiescence is also a form of dormancy, but it differs from diapause. It is a direct result of unfavourable weather conditions: the insect arrests development when conditions become unsuitable, and as soon as conditions improve, quiescence ends and development continues. It may occur at any time during the developmental stages, or even after the insect has reached adulthood.

1.58 These large cocoons (25mm long), each housing a pupa, belong to a species of Lasiocampidae moth, the larvae of which have long sensory hairs and short urticating defensive spines. They are also aposematically coloured to ward off predators and live in groups, which results in many species pupating in close proximity to each other. When they pupate they incorporate urticating spines into the surrounding silk layers around the pupae, which continue to afford protection against predators. The pupae enter diapause and remain in this state over winter; adults emerge the following spring.

Jenny Scholtz

Ecological roles of insects

The vast numbers of diverse insect species and their vital ecological interactions with plants and animals result in their being the most important organisms in any ecosystem. They are the major soil engineers, herbivores, seed feeders and pollinators. Many exercise control over the population numbers of other insect species by preying on or parasitising them. They are essential decomposers of plant and animal remains and daily bury tonnes of dung, fertilising the soil in the process. Finally, they are the primary food source for numerous other animals, which could not exist without them. Simply put, ecosystems couldn't function without insects. Some insect groups have such a profound effect on biological or environmental elements that they are termed keystone species or ecosystem engineers (see box opposite); this section puts the role that insects play in ecosystem functioning into perspective.

Even though all of the biomes have representatives of most of the major insect groups, each has characteristic or unique species involved in broadly similar ecological associations that involve key processes in the ecological functioning of the biome.

Soil engineers

Some insects modify their physical environment to such an extent that they increase the resources available for plants or other insects and vertebrates. These effects are often so great that the term 'ecosystem engineers' was coined for such species. Many species modify soils by their activities but these are often barely noticeable. Dung beetles (see 'Dung beetle behaviour at a dung pat', p. 248), ants (see 'Ant biology and behaviour', p. 159) and termites modify soils by their activities to such an extent that nutrient levels improve dramatically, with resultant increased plant establishment and growth. Termites, however, are amongst the most important of these large-scale soil engineers and facilitators of vegetation change, and examples of their activities can be found in almost every biome.

Results of engineering activities vary from small-scale habitat effects, such as small holes in a substrate, to large-scale landscape changes brought about by extensive modification of soil, for example, by large termite mounds (see 'Termites as soil engineers', p. 199) and heuweltjies (fig. 1.59; see 'The heuweltjie termite', p. 104). Termites modify soil characteristics by changing the particle size of different soil layers, soil porosity, mineral distribution, water penetration, and nutrient levels. These changes often lead to the development of mosaics of different vegetation types, altering the landscape. Termite activities also provide cavities and tunnels in climatically stable and protected environments for secondary inhabitants.

1.59 Termite mounds built by *Microhodotermes viator* in Namaqualand result in large-scale soil modification, often resulting, after hundreds of years, in 'heuweltjies'.

Pollinators

Pollination is an essential part of the process through which plants produce seed. It involves the transfer of pollen grains from the male anther of a flower to the female stigma.

Some plants are self-pollinated: pollination may occur within a single flower, or between different flowers on the same plant. Many plants, however, depend on cross pollination – pollen from one plant is needed to pollinate the flowers of another plant. This occurs through various mechanisms, such as wind, water, gravity and animals; the most important of these are wind and insects.

Grasses and conifers are usually wind-pollinated as the pollen is light and can therefore easily be blown to receptive female plant parts. Many flowering plants, however, have pollen that is sticky and heavy, and therefore they need an agent (most often an insect) to carry it from one flower to another.

Insect pollinators, on which 70% of southern African plant species depend, are indispensable for maintaining plant life. Without pollinators, whole ecosystems would collapse. They are so important in sustaining balanced plant communities that they are amongst the most important keystone species in all biomes.

The pollen and nectar produced by plants are highly desired food sources for many insects, and consequently many species visit flowers (fig. 1.60). However, only a small percentage of flower visitors are considered efficient pollinators.

Keystone species and ecosystem engineers

Many animal species have a significant effect on their environment. Animals whose impact on their habitat or ecosystem is disproportionately large relative to their numbers are called keystone species (e.g. pollinators). Those that cause physical changes to living or nonliving materials through their activity, thereby creating or modifying habitats suitable for other inhabitants of the community, are termed ecosystem engineers (e.g. termites producing mounds).

The critical characteristic of an ecosystem engineer is that it must modulate or change the availability (quality, quantity or distribution) of physical resources used by other organisms. Keystone species, on the other hand, play a critical role in determining community structure; their removal leads to large changes in the species composition of the ecosystem (see box, p. 267). Ecosystem engineers may also be, and often are, keystone species.

1.60 Several lattice moths, *Arniocera erythropyga* (Lepidoptera: Thyrididae), on a flowering puzzle bush, *Ehretia rigida* (Boraginaceae). Although many moths are nocturnal pollinators, these are diurnal and fly slowly; their bright red and black colours keep predators at bay.

1.61 A pollen-covered honey bee, *Apis mellifera* (Apidae), one of the world's most important generalist pollinators.

In most cases, pollination is purely incidental during insect foraging visits to flowers, and most flowers have exposed nectar or pollen that is accessible to a wide variety of insects, including honey bees (fig. 1.61), which are generalist pollinators that are morphologically adapted to collect nectar and pollen from a great variety of plants rather than from only a few species.

In addition to such generalist pollination, specialised pollination systems have evolved between some plants and insects: such flowers have mechanisms that restrict access to their nectar to certain pollinators. This limits the exploitation of this physiologically expensive product, and also minimises possible damage to their reproductive organs by unspecialised flower visitors.

Specialised pollinators are found in most of the large holometamorphic orders, including lacewings (Neuroptera), beetles (Coleoptera), butterflies and moths (Lepidoptera), flies (Diptera), and wasps and bees (Hymenoptera), although the levels of specialisation are probably highest among flies, butterflies and moths (fig. 1.62).

1.62 A selection of typical flower-frequenting species and pollinators from the major orders: (**a**) spoon-winged lacewing, *Palmipenna pilicornis* (Neuroptera); (**b**) wasp (Hymenoptera); (**c**) *Aedes* sp. mosquito (Diptera) and *Herpetogramma phaeopteralis* (Lepidoptera) moth; (**d**) butterfly, *Physcaeneura panda* (Lepidoptera); (**e**) bee fly, *Australoechus* sp. (Diptera); (**f**) hopliine beetle (Coleoptera).

1.63 (left) The complex morphology of this *Alonsoa* sp. (Scrophulariaceae) flower restricts access to its floral oil (a substitute for nectar). It is pollinated only by *Rediviva* (Melittidae) bees that have long front legs and oil-absorbent tarsal pads. The flower visitor is *R. intermixta*.

1.64 (right) Bees have special organs for accumulating and transporting pollen. These are either on the hind legs in 'baskets' (corbiculae), or in less specialised areas of leg or body bristles as in this sweat bee, *Seladonia jucunda* (Halictidae).

Flowers may have various traits that make their rewards inaccessible to general pollinators: cryptic (camouflaged) colours, specialised structures such as long spurs with hidden nectar, perfume composed of unusual compounds, unpalatable nectar, or the secretion of oils instead of nectar (fig. 1.63).

Insects, in turn, have evolved various morphological traits that aid pollen and nectar collection. Morphological adaptations include pollen baskets on the hind legs of many bees (fig. 1.64), hairy pads on the forelegs of oil-collecting bees for soaking up oils, and in various flies, moths and butterflies, a tongue many times the length of the insect for probing exceptionally long, thin floral tubes.

Flower colour is one of the primary attractants used by insects to locate suitable plants. Those pollinated by insects are usually violet, blue or yellow, as insects see well at this end of the colour spectrum. Most insects (with the exception of some butterflies) do not see well in the red spectrum, so seldom pollinate red flowers – these are predominantly pollinated by birds. Some flowers even possess specialised markings, called nectar guides, which direct insects to the centre of the flower where the pollen and nectar are located. Nectar guides are often only visible in ultraviolet light – visible to insects, but not to the human eye.

Insects also have a well-developed sense of smell and are attracted by flowers that produce either sweet-smelling perfume or malodorous smells, depending on the pollinator. Brightly coloured flowers usually have little perfume and are pollinated by diurnal insects, whereas those pollinated at night are often white or dull-coloured but strongly scented.

The interactions between insects and plants have evolved over 100 million years and have resulted in some spectacular adaptations by the parties to each other. Some groups of plants – such as the orchid family (Orchidaceae) and the fig genus *Ficus* (Moraceae) – consist of hundreds of species, many of which depend on a single species of insect pollinator. Both flower and pollinator have an array of mechanisms or structures to facilitate pollination and to exclude thieves that 'steal' pollen, oil or nectar but do not pollinate. Specialised pollination systems are highly evolved in certain southern African biomes (see 'Pollinators', pp. 74, 106; 'Fig-pollinating wasps', p. 207).

Herbivores

The long and intimate association between herbivorous insects and flowering plants has persisted and increased over evolutionary time. We still see this direct dependence by recently evolved insects on plants – about half of all living insect species are herbivores. Yet, somewhat surprisingly, all of these species belong to only nine of the 28 insect orders – all webspinners (Embioptera) and stick insects (Phasmatodea), most crickets and grasshoppers (Orthoptera), free-living lice (Psocodea), most bugs (Hemiptera) and beetles (Coleoptera), and the larvae of butterflies and moths (Lepidoptera), some primitive wasps (Hymenoptera) and a few flies (Diptera) (figs 1.65–1.67).

The limited number of herbivorous orders suggests that feeding on plants involves problems that few major groups have overcome. These include:

- insect desiccation by exposure while feeding externally on plants;
- plants' protective structural armour, which inhibits insect attachment;
- tough plant tissues such as cellulose and lignin that are difficult to digest; and
- chemical deterrents in plant tissues.

1.65 Only nine of the 28 insect orders are entirely or mainly herbivorous. Four common orders with herbivorous species are: (**a**) stick insects (Phasmatodea); (**b**) crickets and grasshoppers (Orthoptera); (**c**) bugs (Hemiptera); (**d**) beetles (Coleoptera).

a

b

c

d

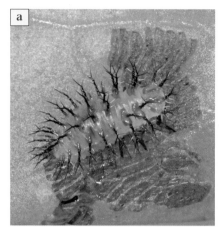

a

c

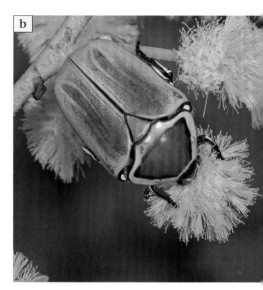

b

1.68 Feeding habits and food types vary greatly amongst herbivores: **(a)** a leaf beetle larva (Chrysomelidae) 'grazing' the upper epidermis cells of a leaf; **(b)** a savanna chafer beetle, *Dischista cincta* (Scarabaeidae: Cetoniinae), feeding on acacia flowers; **(c)** a seed-feeding bug, *Nariscus* sp. (Hemiptera: Alydidae), feeding on a fallen but still green seed.

1.66 Butterflies and moths (Lepidoptera) make up the largest order of almost exclusively herbivorous species, as in these larvae: **(a)** *Telchinia encedon* (Nymphalidae); **(b)** *Danaus chrysippus* (Nymphalidae); **(c)** *Rhanidophora* sp. (Erebidae); **(d)** *Aurivillius fuscus* (Saturniidae).

1.67 Despite the large size of the order, Hymenoptera (ants, bees and wasps) has very few herbivorous species; this sawfly larva (Tenthredinidae) is one.

Once these hurdles were surmounted by the early herbivorous insects, the huge diversity and biomass of plants available presented a new adaptive zone that stimulated rapid diversification in these groups. In spite of the potential obstacles that plants present to feeders, the mainly herbivorous insect orders contain amongst the highest numbers of species (e.g. Coleoptera); the immature and adult stages of some of these orders are almost exclusively plant-feeding (e.g. Lepidoptera).

Herbivory exerts strong selective pressure on plants by reducing their reproductive fitness. Seed feeders, specifically, play a significant role in regulating the composition of plant communities in each habitat. On the other hand, some specialised insect species aid in the dispersal and protection of live seeds.

Although such a large proportion of insects feeds on plants, the details of their feeding reveal that this habit is not nearly as simple as it appears. Some insects are generalist feeders, feeding on a wide range of different plant groups, while others are more restricted, feeding on a few plant species. Some are highly host-specific and feed only on a single plant species. Most species are restricted to feeding on particular plant parts – leaves, roots, flowers, fruit, seed or wood – where they chew on, suck from or bore into various tissues (fig. 1.68). Many feed externally, but others are small enough to complete a large part of their life cycle inside a leaf or tiny seed. These often induce plants to form galls in which the insects develop (see box opposite). There are also some specialist species that feed exclusively on fungi and lichens; although these are not related to plants at all, the insects that feed on them are grouped with herbivores. There are even insects that use the cellulose-digesting properties of certain fungi to break down the cellulose in their food.

The wide range of species that feed on plant remains are known as detritivores and are discussed in the following section.

How plant galls are formed

Galls are structural deformities produced by plants in response to attack by any of a host of different organisms and are found on a range of organs on many plant species (fig. 1.69). Galls are caused by viruses, bacteria, fungi (fig. 1.70), mites, nematodes and insects. The process of attack and consequent gall formation is probably the most specialised form of herbivory and has resulted in tightly co-evolved associations between plants and gall-forming organisms.

The galls may vary from a simple, localised swelling to highly complex structures in which whole organs are distorted. Some resemble normal plant parts such as berries or fruit; others take on bizarre forms, for example, fluffy balls with hairy tentacles.

Gall–insect interactions represent some of the most intimate relationships known between insects and their plant hosts. They are a form of physiological engineering of plant structures that results in a 'new' plant organ whose developmental control has been taken over by the attacking insect. Feeding on, or laying eggs in, the plant causes a wound-like stimulus; in response, the plant tissues produce defensive 'nutritive' cells on which the insect feeds.

The advantages of the gall accrue almost entirely to the attacking insect, which benefits by having a sheltered environment and a ready supply of high-quality food. The insect's encapsulation in the gall is a defensive reaction by the plant, which isolates the insect to keep it away from other organs and limits the extent of feeding damage.

For more details, see 'Gall-forming insects', p. 120; 'Moth galls on Bushveld trees', p. 233; 'Gall wasps', p. 381.

1.69 In spite of their common presence across all southern African regions, the insects involved in gall formation are mostly nameless. (**a**) A stem gall induced by a cecidomyiid fly on saltbush, *Salsola* sp. (**b**) A moth gall on the stem of a common wild currant, *Searsia pyroides*. (**c**) A bud gall caused by the fruit fly *Notomma galbanum* (Tephritidae) on a sickle bush, *Dichrostachys cinerea*. (**d**) A pea-sized gall induced in a few leaf cells of this red bushwillow, *Combretum erythrophyllum*, by a moth larva.

1.70 Some galls that are induced by organisms other than insects may be invaded by a variety of insects that feed on the tissues produced. (**a**) One common and widespread gall on flower buds of sweet thorn, *Acacia karroo*, is caused by the fungus *Ravenelia macowaniana*. (**b**) Moth larva (Noctuidae).

1.71 Damp, fungus-infected wood in high-rainfall forest results in detritus in the form of decomposing plant matter, which is an important food source for insects and other arthropods.

Decomposers and nutrient recyclers

The amount of dead plant material (detritus) in a specific biome depends entirely on the abundance of plants and the density of vegetation cover. It can range from virtually no detritus layer in deserts, to dead grass in grassland; grass and irregular patches of fallen tree remains in savannas, to multiple layers of whole fallen tree trunks, branches, twigs and leaves in the more or less permanently moist environment of forests (fig. 1.71).

Plant litter and wood are often abundant, but their low water content, hardness, low nitrogen levels and the presence of toxic plant chemicals make them less than ideal as a source of food. When fungi are present (e.g. in decayed litter) and are eaten with hard dry plant remains, they may contribute substantially to the overall nutritional content of the food. There are several advantages to feeding on decayed rather than fresh plant litter: fungal and bacterial decomposition enhance the levels of nitrogen and other nutrients; fungi growing in the decayed plant matter are themselves nutrient-rich; and toxic plant chemicals are often destroyed by decomposition.

Although a very wide range of insects and other invertebrates feeds on dead wood and litter, termites (Termitoidae) are undoubtedly the most important litter feeders in all biomes.

The classical view of termite feeding is that dry wood is their primary food source. In fact, termites feed on a range of plant matter – from living tissue at one end of the feeding gradient, through sound dead wood or grass and decaying, fungus-infested wood, to highly dispersed organic fragments in soil, at the other. Not only are termites important ecosystem engineers for the way they change the landscape with their activities, they also play a major role in returning nutrients to the soil by breaking down detritus. The interaction between fungi and termites in the decomposition of wood is exceptionally developed in the fungus-gardening termites (Macrotermitinae; see 'Fungus-feeding termites', p. 236).

Dung feeders

Dung is a general and loosely used term for the complex physical, chemical and microbial mix in excreted food remains, the nature of which is largely determined by the original food. Almost all dung is attractive to potential dung colonisers, whether it is produced by invertebrates or vertebrates, omnivores, carnivores or herbivores, but different types of dung attract different suites of insects.

Under natural conditions, the dung insect community is highly complex, often consisting of thousands of individuals of hundreds of species, most of which depend on the highly desirable and nutritious dung, but many predatory insects are also attracted to those feeding on the dung. In some agricultural systems, however, where pesticides are used indiscriminately to treat livestock for various parasites, dung-feeding insects may be scarce.

The most visible and well-known group of dung feeders in southern Africa are dung beetles (mostly Scarabaeidae: Scarabaeinae). Although they are a well-defined group of related beetles that feed mostly on mammalian herbivore dung, they have very wide dung preferences. Even the term 'herbivore dung' is not as simple as it appears – grazing and browsing mammals often produce very different dung types; ruminants (cattle, buffalo, antelope) produce fine-textured dung, whereas nonruminant (elephant, rhino, horses) dung is coarse. The dung may be plentiful or scarce, may be excreted in a mass or in pellet form, and could be the result of high-quality spring grass or poor-quality autumn graze (or something in between). The age of the dung is also important: some adult dung beetles feed on fresh dung, but prefer older dung for larval food. Whatever its origin, most dung is attractive to dung beetles and competition for the resource is often fierce (fig. 1.72).

In natural and agricultural ecosystems where large numbers of herbivores such as antelope and cattle are present, very large quantities of dung are produced each day; in southern Africa, cattle alone produce 500,000 tonnes per day! All of it is quickly buried by dung beetles. The ecological implications of this ecosystem service are immense: it prevents soil becoming covered by dung, keeps pestiferous flies from breeding and diseases from irrupting, and fertilises, aerates and loosens soil, allowing water to penetrate and generally improving conditions for plant growth.

Herbivore dung is abundant, especially on farms and in nature reserves, so the dominant dung fauna is usually cued into this particular resource. However, some dung beetles and other insects are preferentially attracted to carnivore and omnivore dung (fig. 1.73), which is generally much stronger-smelling than that produced by herbivores, and is often composed of soft tissue remains, but also contains hair or feathers. If the area is relatively undisturbed and predators and raptors are present, their dung (and in the case of owls, regurgitates or 'pellets') is a resource for these specialist dung feeders.

The high numbers of insects present at dung sources also provide a rich prey resource that is readily exploited by numerous vertebrate predators such as birds (hornbills, rollers), monitor lizards and mongooses.

Predators

Predatory insects are important regulators of the population numbers of numerous insect groups, as well as non-insect invertebrates such as mites. The important role that they play in controlling pest insect populations has long been recognised in crop production. Certain predatory species are commercially reared in large numbers for release against particular plant-feeding pests, the best known of such predatory species being ladybirds (Coleoptera: Coccinellidae), but many more fulfil similar functions in natural ecosystems.

It has been estimated that about a quarter of all insect species are predatory on other insects or small invertebrates (fig. 1.74). This is hardly surprising considering the large numbers of insects available as potential prey. There are possibly hundreds of insect families with members that are exclusively, primarily, or occasionally predatory. Some are predatory both as larvae and adults, others in only one of the two stages.

Some predators feed on just one species of prey; others prey on a few species, but most are generalist predators, taking any prey that comes their way. Predators are usually larger than their prey, and often occur in habitats where prey species are found in high numbers, making it easier to find, capture and consume the necessary amount of food. Most predators kill and eat their prey immediately, although there are some wasps that first attack and paralyse prey and then cache it for later use by their larvae.

Predatory insects usually have either biting-chewing or piercing-sucking mouthparts. Their methods for finding and capturing their prey fall into three broad categories:

1.72 To avoid the fierce competition at a dung source, one group of beetles has evolved the strategy of forming a ball of dung at the source, then rolling it away to bury it in a secure location where it can be fed on at leisure. This large species of *Scarabaeus* is rolling herbivore dung.

1.73 Flies are among the insects primarily attracted to dung. These calliphorid species are feeding on the dung fluids of primate dung, although their larvae feed on carrion. The larvae of other fly species breed and feed in dung and may compete with dung beetles for the resource.

1.74 It is estimated that a quarter of all insects are predatory. Members of many orders are predators, including (**a**) most ladybird (Coccinellidae) adults and larvae, such as this *Cheilomenes lunata* larva; (**b**) most adult and larval ground beetles (Carabidae), for example this adult *Lipostratia* sp.; (**c**) certain fly larvae, such as this larval hover fly (Syrphidae); (**d**) all adult robber flies, such as this *Promachus* sp. (Asilidae); (**e**) adult wasps that feed masticated caterpillars to their larvae, for example this *Polistes* sp. (Vespidae); (**f**) all damselfly and dragonfly adults and larvae (Odonata) – here the dragonfly *Notogomphus praetorius* is eating a smaller damselfly relative, *Platycypha caligata*.

- generalist, active hunting is used when the prey is slow-moving or sedentary, or when the predator runs or flies fast;
- sit-and-wait and ambush strategies are used when the predator is likely to be unobserved by the prey; and
- trapping is used by sedentary predators that prepare a pit into which the prey tumbles.

Predatory insects that hunt actively usually have large compound eyes with overlapping fields of vision, which allow them to perceive prey at a distance. Examples are dragonflies and damselflies (Odonata; see 'Damselflies and dragonflies', p. 324) and ground beetles (Carabidae; see 'Ground beetles', p. 127; 'Predatory ground beetles', p. 239). But not all active hunters rely on vision – many make use of their chemical senses to smell prey, while some use vibration senses with which they are able to perceive movements made by their prey. They usually have large, strong mouthparts, as well as legs adapted to seizing and holding onto prey. Those that fly are usually strong and often fast flyers, enabling them to hunt over large areas. Predators that hunt on the ground can usually move fast and run down their prey.

Predatory insects that use the sit-and-wait or ambush strategy usually first seek out a suitable place to wait for their prey to appear. They remain motionless on a plant or on the ground until the prey wanders within striking distance, then strike out and grab it.

They are often camouflaged or hidden, not only to increase the chance of prey capture, but also to reduce the chance of being preyed upon by other predatory species, since while remaining motionless in order to surprise their prey, they are easy prey for others. Mantises (Mantodea; see 'Praying mantises', p. 405) are good examples of this strategy.

The larvae of a few insect species excavate special pits, below which they lie in wait. When a prey animal tumbles down into the trap, it is overcome by the predator. This type includes the familiar pit-building antlions (Myrmeleontidae; see 'Pit-building antlions', p. 349) and ecologically similar wormlions (Diptera: Vermileonidae; see 'Pit-building wormlions', p. 351).

Parasites

The large size of most vertebrates makes it difficult for predatory insects to prey on them. There are a few exceptions – some large aquatic insects regularly capture small fish or amphibians, some ants prey on bird nestlings, and an extraordinary ground beetle eats frogs (see 'Frog-eating beetles', p. 310). However, most insects that use vertebrates as food are parasites. They usually feed on blood, the most common source of liquid food, but some use other liquids such as the lachrymal fluid in eyes. Insects also parasitise other insects, as parasitoids or hyperparasitoids. A few insects parasitise the prey or brood of other insects.

True parasites

Vertebrate parasites have a number of adaptations suited to a parasitic lifestyle, such as flattened bodies, special devices for grasping or clinging to the host's fur or feathers, and receptors to locate their hosts. In species that do not need to locate hosts over long distances, eyes, legs and wings may be greatly reduced or absent.

Many parasitic insects locate their hosts at a distance by responding to chemicals released by vertebrates during respiration, such as increased carbon dioxide levels (e.g. mosquitoes), or in vertebrate sweat or urine (e.g. tsetse flies). Once the parasite is closer to its target, visual stimuli as well as body heat and humidity may be tracked, and upon contact, especially when the parasite is host-specific, skin chemicals might be used to find an appropriate feeding site. Anticoagulants in parasite saliva facilitate blood feeding by preventing clotting.

True parasites, of which typical examples are head lice and fleas (see 'Head lice', p. 403; 'Fleas', p. 404) or elephant seal lice (see 'Parasitic elephant seal lice', p. 360) feed on blood, but they seldom kill their host (usually a bird or mammal).

Parasites may spend their entire life cycle on their host (continuous parasites, e.g. lice; fig. 1.75a), or part of their life cycle on the host, and part as free-living insects (transitory parasites, e.g. intestinal parasitic fly larvae; fig. 1.75b), or they visit the host only to feed (intermittent or temporary parasites, e.g. horse flies; fig. 1.75c). Parasites that feed continuously are most host-specific, and those that feed intermittently, least so.

Parasites that feed on the outside of the host are called ectoparasites (e.g. fleas and lice). The larvae of bot and blow flies feed inside the host and are called endoparasites (see 'Nasal bot flies', p. 193; 'Intestinal bot flies', p. 244). Although parasites depend on healthy hosts for their own survival, they are detrimental to the host to some degree, and do occasionally cause the death of the host, particularly when the parasite numbers are high.

Parasitoids

Parasitoids spend their entire larval stage feeding on the tissues of their host, which always dies as a result of the parasitism (fig. 1.76). (Technically infestation by a parasitoid is termed parasitoidism, but entomologists usually also refer to it as parasitism.)

Parasitoids are often tiny insects. The smallest known insect species (0.139mm long) and the smallest flying insect species (0.15mm long) are both parasitoids. They are called 'fairy flies', but are actually wasps (Hymenoptera: Mymaridae); the average size of members of the family is 0.5–1mm long, and all are insect egg parasitoids.

Not all parasitoids are small, though – at the other extreme, 50mm-long Pompilidae wasps parasitise large spiders, such as baboon and rain spiders (see 'Pollination by wasp deception', p. 83).

Most insect parasitoids are wasps in the families Ichneumonidae and Braconidae (see 'Parasitic wasps', p. 312) and flies in the Tachinidae (see 'Parasitoid flies', p. 311).

Adult parasitoids are free-living and lay their eggs on or in their hosts. The larvae are the parasitic stage and their feeding results in the death of the host. Virtually every insect and many arachnid species are parasitised during some stage of their development. Hosts may be at any of the immature stages, including eggs, larvae and pupae or, less often, adults. Parasitoids are usually fairly host-specific, although some species may be quite catholic in their choice of hosts.

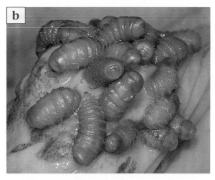

1.75 (a) The pig louse, *Haematopinus suis* (Psocodea), spends its entire life cycle living and feeding on the host. **(b)** *Gasterophilus intestinalis* (Diptera: Oestridae) spends the larval stage as an intestinal parasite of horses and zebras. **(c)** Horse fly (Diptera: Tabanidae) females feed on nectar but additionally need a protein-rich blood meal to develop their eggs before laying.

1.76 A *Theridion* spider parasitised by a pompilid wasp larva; an egg is laid on the spider and the larva consumes the still-living spider, killing it when it matures.

a

b

1.77 (a) *Quadrastichus gallicola* (Eulophidae), a wasp that forms galls on the leaves of coral trees, *Erythrina* spp., is parasitised by other wasp species in the same family, such as **(b)** this *Aprostocetus nitens*, in a process termed hyperparasitism.

1.78 Kleptoparasites feed on the brood and cached food in nests of other insects. Cuckoo wasps (Chrysididae), such as this *Chrysis* sp., parasitise the brood of other solitary wasp nests.

Hyperparasitoids

Parasitoids can themselves become the host of another level of parasitoid, the hyperparasitoid (fig. 1.77). The phenomenon occurs most commonly in wasps, where it has been recorded in many families (especially in the superfamilies Chalcidoidea and Ichneumonoidea). It is common for hyperparasitoids to parasitise parasitoid members of the same family. There are also a few hyperparasitoids amongst flies (Diptera: Bombyliidae and Conopidae) and beetles (Coleoptera: Ripiphoridae and Cleridae). As can be expected, most hyperparasitoids are extremely small.

Kleptoparasites

Kleptoparasites are sometimes called 'cuckoo parasites' because they parasitise the nests of another species, much like cuckoo birds do (fig. 1.78). Kleptoparasites may eat the eggs, larvae and food reserves in the host nest; an extreme example is the honey bee or paper wasp brood parasite *Oplostomus fuligineus* (Coleoptera: Scarabaeidae: Cetoniinae; see 'Invertebrate exploiters of honey bees', p. 77). Alternatively, they may lay their eggs on stored food in the nest or near the food; their eggs invariably hatch before those of the host, and the larvae eat the stored food, resulting in death or stunted growth of the host larvae. Examples of this type of kleptoparasite are the beetle *Eremostibes opacus* (Tenebrionidae), which feeds on the larval food of its relative *Parastizopus armaticeps* (see box, p. 236), and the dung beetle *Hammondantus psammophilus* that lives on food reserves in the nests of *Pachysoma* dung beetles (see 'Feeding adaptations in desert insects', p. 149).

Although there is some cost to the hosts of nest parasites, hosts often tolerate some parasites. Usually, the more intimate the association, the higher the level of tolerance exhibited by the host. There is often highly co-evolved behaviour between the parties, for example, between ants and lycaenid butterflies (see box, p. 97), and honey bees and the bee louse, *Braula coeca* (Diptera: Braulidae; see 'Invertebrate exploiters of honey bees', p. 77).

Carrion feeders

Carcasses are usually localised, widely spaced and irregularly present in any habitat. Because of the speed of decomposition processes, especially in summer, they are a highly ephemeral resource. Consequently, carrion feeders are tuned in to locate carcasses quickly, using mainly their sense of smell. A fast turnover of different waves of insects follows, either feeding on the carcass itself or attracted to it by the bounty provided by the primary carrion feeders to predatory insects. This turnover process usually proceeds in a fairly predictable sequence of events.

Insects that feed on carrion reduce the time it takes for animal remains to decompose, helping to control the build-up of disease-causing organisms. The shortened decomposition process returns nutrients to the ecosystem, either directly through the carrion feeders' faeces, or later, when the predators that feed on them disperse and die.

The range of species involved in the decomposition process depends on several factors: the size of the carcass, the biome, and local environmental conditions that affect the temperature to which the dead animal is exposed. The soil layer on which the carcass lies and its moisture level may determine how quickly the remains dry out.

In general, the larger a carcass, the higher the number of insects that are attracted to it. Insect remains may attract only ants (fig. 1.79a); a small reptile (fig. 1.79b), bird or mammal carcass may attract hundreds of individuals of a dozen insect species; while the carcass of a large

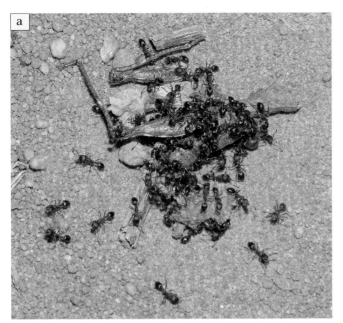

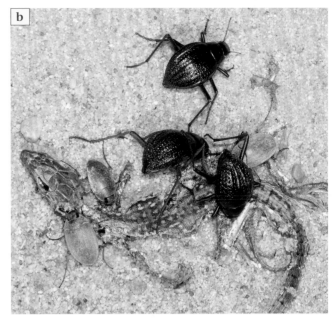

1.79 Carrion of all sizes attracts appropriately sized carrion feeders in numbers relative to the amount of food available. **(a)** Ants feeding on grasshopper remains. **(b)** Two different darkling beetle species (Tenebrionidae) scavenging on a dead lizard.

mammal is colonised by tens of thousands of insects of possibly hundreds of species.

A large carcass, however, is much more than just 'carrion' – it may consist of flesh, fluids, fatty exudates, stomach contents, skin and scales, feathers, hair, and horns – and each of these elements attracts a particular suite of insect species (see 'Carrion feeders', p. 250). Each of these, in turn, attracts a range of predators and parasites that attack them, resulting in a complex of interacting species.

Insects as food for other organisms

The diversity and abundance of insects in virtually every habitable terrestrial and aquatic environment make them a source of food for numerous organisms across the biological spectrum (fig. 1.80), including microorganisms such as bacteria and fungi, highly specialised carnivorous plants, and a multitude of insectivorous arthropods, reptiles, birds and mammals (including humans).

1.80 Insects are preyed on by various organisms across the biological spectrum. **(a)** A sundew plant, *Drosera* sp., consuming a bug captured by the plant's sticky glandular hairs. **(b)** A Knysna dwarf chameleon, *Bradypodion damarana*, swallowing a grasshopper. **(c)** An African hoopoe, *Upupa africana*, which specialises in extracting insects from soil or humus, holding the larva of a tenebrionid beetle in its beak.

CHAPTER 2
FYNBOS BIOME

The Fynbos Biome is situated at the southern tip of Africa and lies between the Atlantic Ocean in the west and the Indian Ocean in the southeast; inland the Cape Fold Mountains separate it from the Nama-Karoo Biome. It is bordered in the east by Albany Thicket and in the northwest by Namaqualand, a region of the Succulent Karoo. The Fynbos Biome covers only 6.7% of the South African land surface, but about a third of all plants in South Africa are found here – approximately 8,000 plant species – of which most are endemic. Many insect groups follow this trend, with several having co-evolved with the plants.

2.1 (pp. 56–57) A typical Fynbos summer landscape, with a mixture of fynbos plants in the foreground; the mountain in the background is capped with late afternoon mist being blown inland by the southeasterly wind.

Rina de Klerk

2.2 A valley recovering several years after a fire. Fires are a natural occurrence in the Fynbos and the plants need fire to clear the build-up of undergrowth and to release fire-dependent seeds from hard fruits.

2.3 Some of the endemic fynbos plants for which the biome is famous: (**a**) *Ceratandra atrata* (Orchidaceae); (**b**) *Syncarpha vestita* (Asteraceae); (**c**) *Elegia* sp. (Restionaceae); (**d**) *Dilatris ixioides* (Haemodoraceae); (**e**) *Berzelia abrotanoides* (Bruniaceae).

The high plant diversity within the Fynbos Biome is largely attributable to the complex mosaics of geological substrates on which different plant communities are established. The structure of these communities is maintained mostly by infrequent natural late summer and autumn fires, but regular, human-induced fires, particularly in spring, have devastating consequences for the vegetation and associated fauna.

Most of the region receives moderate to high winter rainfall, whereas summers are hot and dry. Strong, frequent summer winds blow dense fog inland, which precipitates on high-lying areas (fig. 2.1), where it is often the only source of water for summer-active fauna such as insects. Higher rainfall (above 300mm per year) encourages dense fynbos vegetation which is susceptible to fire, while lower rainfall (mostly below 200mm per year) favours succulence and wider interplant distances that do not support fire; in these regions fynbos is replaced by succulent karoo vegetation. Because of their high plant richness, endemicity and close geographical situation, the Fynbos and Succulent Karoo biomes are sometimes considered as representing a single plant region, called the Cape Floristic Region.

Although the vegetation types that comprise the Fynbos Biome are complex, they are broadly differentiated into three main types: fynbos, the largest, comprising 67% of the biome; renosterveld, covering 29%; and the small western strandveld.

The biome derives its name from the Dutch *fijn bosch*, meaning 'fine bush', referring to the small-leaved, evergreen, fire-prone plants that dominate the fynbos

Jonathan Ball

Jonathan Ball

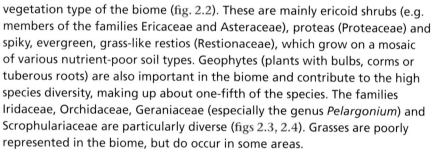

vegetation type of the biome (fig. 2.2). These are mainly ericoid shrubs (e.g. members of the families Ericaceae and Asteraceae), proteas (Proteaceae) and spiky, evergreen, grass-like restios (Restionaceae), which grow on a mosaic of various nutrient-poor soil types. Geophytes (plants with bulbs, corms or tuberous roots) are also important in the biome and contribute to the high species diversity, making up about one-fifth of the species. The families Iridaceae, Orchidaceae, Geraniaceae (especially the genus *Pelargonium*) and Scrophulariaceae are particularly diverse (figs 2.3, 2.4). Grasses are poorly represented in the biome, but do occur in some areas.

The insect fauna of the Fynbos Biome is characterised, as is to be expected, by high proportions of endemic groups that co-evolved with the fynbos vegetation. Many others represent ancient relict groups – these are remnants of once widespread taxa that were able to survive in refuge habitats for millions of years, as this part of the continent has remained climatically stable and escaped glaciation for the last 5–15 million years. Among them are summer-active stag beetles (*Colophon*), living on high mountain peaks that receive rainfall and snow in winter and moisture from fog in summer.

Many fynbos plants have evolved a strategy to avoid the effects of fire on plant reproduction and seed survival by making their seeds attractive to ants. The ants harvest and bury the seed in protected underground chambers that are rich in compost. In southern Africa, this strategy of seed dispersal by ants (myrmecochory) is found only in the Fynbos Biome. Another remarkable association between seeds and insects was discovered recently: the seeds of the restio *Ceratocaryum argenteum* chemically and physically mimic the dung pellets of antelope so perfectly that dung beetles are attracted to them, roll them away, and bury them in an underground burrow (a process called coleopterochory), where they abandon them after trying to eat them.

The Fynbos insect fauna is, in contrast to that of other biomes, not dominated by herbivorous species. Because they grow on nutrient-poor soils, fynbos plants have low nutritional values. The leaves are tough and woody, and contain high concentrations of plant chemicals that have herbivore-repellent or antifeeding properties. Nevertheless, various specialist herbivores have evolved in the region. Many have developed mechanisms to avoid repellent chemicals in leaves, or have switched to feeding on internal tissue instead.

2.4 Beautiful endemic fynbos flowers:
(**a**) *Watsonia meriana* (Iridaceae);
(**b**) *Disa uniflora* (Orchidaceae);
(**c**) *Erica* sp. (Ericaceae); (**d**) *Diastella* sp.
(Proteaceae); (**e**) *Gladiolus* sp. (Iridaceae);
(**f**) *Pelargonium* sp. (Geraniaceae).

Members of the large butterfly genus *Chrysoritis* (Lycaenidae), of which a large percentage are ecological specialists, feed on plants in their early larval stages, but later become intimately associated with ants that protect and feed them. Other endemic herbivores are restio grasshoppers in the genus *Betiscoides* (Lentulidae), adults and larvae of the restio beetle, *Pseudorupilia ruficollis* (Chrysomelidae, fig. 2.5), and larvae of various moths (figs 2.6–2.8). Those specialising on internal tissue feeding include endemic, restio-associated, sap-feeding bugs such as leafhoppers (Hemiptera: Cicadellidae). There are also some species that visit but do not feed at all (fig. 2.9).

The Fynbos Biome has an exceptional diversity of insects that are intimately involved with highly specialised pollination systems. These tend to be more specialised than in other regions: often a single group (or even just a single species) of pollinator is associated with many plant species belonging to diverse families. Amongst these are various beetle, fly, butterfly, moth, wasp and bee species.

Considering the dense fynbos vegetation and the consequent production and accumulation of litter, it would be surprising if there were not

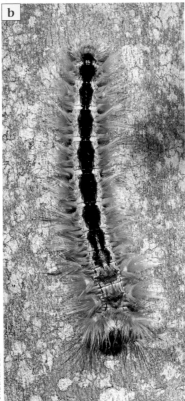

2.6 The moth *Eutricha bifascia* (Lasiocampidae) is a sexually dimorphic Fynbos endemic: **(a)** large female (top) and small male (bottom); **(b)** larvae grow up to 10cm long and are hairy, orange-red with a black and white dorsal pattern; they feed on *Erica* and *Passerina* (Thymelaeaceae).

2.5 The restio beetle, *Pseudorupilia ruficollis* (Chrysomelidae), a characteristic and curious member of the huge leaf beetle family; its typically swollen abdomen remains unexplained.

2.7 *Vegetia ducalis* (Saturniidae) is southern Africa's smallest emperor moth. This male, characterised by plumose antennae, has a wingspan of 50mm; females are slightly larger. One of their larger savanna relatives, *Imbrasia belina*, has a wingspan of 150mm.

2.8 *Argyrophora trofonia* (Geometridae), a Fynbos endemic whose larvae feed on *Erica* species.

2.9 The fruit chafer beetle *Trichostetha curlei* (Scarabaeidae: Cetoniinae). The beetles do not feed but use various flowers as mating platforms. Its close relative, the protea beetle, *T. fascicularis*, feeds on *Protea* flowers.

specialised detritus feeders in the biome. There are, indeed, and most belong to the Blattodea, amongst which the most important is the black-mound termite, *Amitermes hastatus*, which has adapted its feeding strategy to avoid the chemicals in plant tissues. It is the dominant termite species in the biome and feeds on well-rotted plants in which the defensive chemicals have already broken down. The termites are effective recyclers of the nutrients bound in plant tissues and improve the generally low-nutrient soils. Other detritus feeders in the Blattodea include some of southern Africa's most unusual cockroach species. The giant cockroach, *Aptera fusca* (Blaberidae), the largest species in southern Africa, is common; a recent discovery is the highly unusual Table Mountain leaproach, *Saltoblattella montistabularis* (Ectobiidae), which feeds on bird dung deposited on plants.

Fynbos predators include members of the typical predatory groups occurring in other biomes. One interesting group, the owlflies (Neuroptera: Ascalaphidae), has spectacular representatives in the biome. An unusual, but large group of atypical predators is the larval stage of the specialised butterfly genus *Thestor* (Lycaenidae), of which all the species are specialist predators of either scale insects (Hemiptera: Coccoidea) or ant brood in their early instars, after which they are fed and cared for by ants in their nests.

Fynbos endemics

The number of endemic or near-endemic insect groups in the Fynbos Biome is high and may be attributed to the high plant endemicity with which certain insect groups have co-evolved. These are either 'young' endemics, which have evolved from widespread groups over the past 15 million years as the fynbos has matured, or 'ancient' endemics, which are isolated remnants of groups that were once more common and widespread, and may have evolved from ancestors that lived in the area as long as 100 million years ago (mya).

Iconic mountain fynbos beetles

Stag beetles (Coleoptera: Scarabaeoidea: Lucanidae) are a fairly large, cosmopolitan family distantly related to dung beetles (Scarabaeidae). Lucanid males have large mandibles, which often have elaborate branch-like extensions growing from them, reminiscent of the antlers of male deer (stags). In most species, the mandibles of females are 'normal', small and without any extensions.

Stag beetles are mostly associated with forested areas in temperate regions and are therefore rare in southern Africa. There are only six genera in the region, of which the largest is *Colophon*. The genus

2.10 Typical high mountain habitat of certain *Colophon* (Lucanidae) beetle species.

is taxonomically unique, with no known close relatives. All the species in the genus are restricted to isolated patches of ericoid fynbos vegetation on cold, wet and wind-blown peaks (fig. 2.10) of the Cape Fold Mountains. It is thought to be an extremely ancient relict of an extinct early temperate Gondwanan lineage – a once widespread lowland forest group whose members were gradually forced into very small refuges on high mountains by changing environmental conditions caused by the northward drift of the continent and progressive warming of the area since the Pleistocene (the Ice Age, 2.5 million–12,000 years ago).

The 17 recognised *Colophon* species occur on isolated mountain peaks. They represent two distinct groups of related species, a western (fig. 2.11) and an eastern group (fig. 2.12; see box below). The western group includes one species on Table Mountain in Cape Town, and some on high peaks of the

Angelika Switala

2.11 *Colophon stokoei*, a member of the ancestral western lineage that split from the eastern lineage about 50 million years ago.

Evolution and speciation of *Colophon*

Angelika Switala and Clarke Scholtz of the University of Pretoria investigated the evolutionary origins of the genus *Colophon* and its species. To determine how much the species differed from each other genetically, as well as how old the genus was, they analysed the DNA of several genes of small numbers of each of the species, collected over several successive summer seasons. The DNA research suggests that *Colophon* experienced climatically driven allopatric (geographically separate) speciation.

The estimated time of origin of the genus was the mid-Cretaceous, about 85mya, a period when southern Africa was characterised by a warm, humid climate supporting extensive tropical and subtropical forests. It has been suggested that the genus evolved in areas currently lying in the Great Karoo and southern coastal flats of the Western Cape. Lucanidae usually inhabit woodlands or forested areas, where larvae feed on decaying wood, so it is possible that the Cretaceous forested environment was favourable for promoting the evolution of *Colophon*.

The study found that there was a clear split between two lineages: an older, ancestral and a younger, derived lineage. Species of the ancestral lineage currently inhabit mountains in the west of the genus's range and species of the derived lineage occur in the east. This split appears to have occurred during the early Palaeocene (63mya) to mid-Eocene (46mya). During the Palaeocene, arid conditions were present in the west of the continent and persisted well into the Eocene; the climate in the east was less arid.

Other species diverged during the early to mid-Miocene (21–15mya), when there was a gradual increase in aridity and temperature. This may well be when the beetles moved to the more hospitable climate provided by mountains. The cold Benguela upwelling system formed around 14mya, and is responsible for the southeasterly winds that bring cool moist air inland, creating dense orographic fog when it condenses against high mountain slopes. These conditions provided the ideal habitat for the beetles, and the mountains subsequently became a refuge for *Colophon*, with the most recent divergence of species occurring during the last 8 million years.

As time passed and the regional climates became even less suitable, *Colophon* populations became still more isolated, with most genetic lineages finally confined to specific mountains during the Pleistocene period (2.5 million to 12,000 years ago).

Angelika Switala

2.12 *Colophon primosi*, the most derived species, from the extreme east of the distribution range of the genus.

Hottentots-Holland range (above Stellenbosch and Somerset West), and the Hex River Mountains (near Worcester and Ceres). The species in the eastern group occur on peaks in the Langeberg (east of Montagu) and Swartberg (near Oudtshoorn).

The mandibles of male *Colophon* beetles (and often the front legs of, for example, *Colophon izardi*, fig. 2.13), vary considerably among the different species (fig. 2.14). There is also considerable mandible size variation amongst males of the same species. Many studies have shown that males of the same species in various beetle groups with large mandibles (and other head armature such as horns) have different mating strategies and

2.13 Front view of a male *Colophon izardi* showing the extreme modification of the front pair of legs.

reproductive success compared to individuals with smaller mandibles. (Females of most species of *Colophon* are quite similar.)

All *Colophon* species are wingless and have very localised distributions: they occur only on mountain peaks that receive evening and morning summer fog and have suitable patches of sandy soil where restios grow. Adults feed a little on fluids and soft, sugary food sources, while larvae live in and feed on organically enriched soil amongst restio tussocks and roots in isolated patches of sandy soil between rocks, in an association that has probably existed since the origin of the Restionaceae (about 70mya). Adults have a short life span, but larvae grow slowly over several years because of their low-nutrition diet and the cool conditions to which they are exposed.

Colophon is the only African insect group that is CITES-listed (Category III), because of the perceived rarity of the species and the astronomical sums that collectors are willing to pay for the beetles. Their remote distribution at high altitudes in largely inaccessible areas makes effective policing difficult, so in spite of legal protection, there is an established black-market trade in the beetles. Occasional, well-publicised arrests of foreign insect collectors found with *Colophon* in their possession have increased the interest in the genus.

Despite their apparent rarity, commercial value and status as highly endangered Cape endemics, there is very little scientific information about the species in the genus. A recent research project, however, investigated aspects of the biology of two co-occurring *Colophon* species on a high mountain peak in the Hex River Mountains (see box, p. 64).

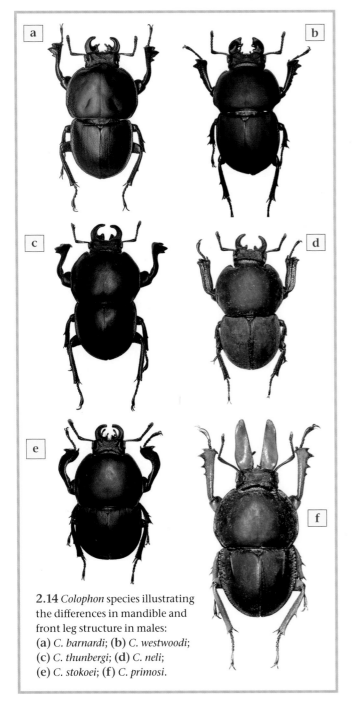

2.14 *Colophon* species illustrating the differences in mandible and front leg structure in males:
(**a**) *C. barnardi*; (**b**) *C. westwoodi*;
(**c**) *C. thunbergi*; (**d**) *C. neli*;
(**e**) *C. stokoei*; (**f**) *C. primosi*.

The biology of two co-occurring *Colophon* species

Three students from Bangor University, Wales, under the supervision of Clarke Scholtz from the University of Pretoria, spent three months during peak beetle activity living on a mountain where populations of *Colophon haughtoni* (fig. 2.15a) and *C. kawaii* (fig. 2.15b) occur. They studied various aspects of the species' ecology. This was the first-ever field study of the ecology of any *Colophon* species and the main aims of the project were to investigate the following:

- the size of the populations of both species;
- the weather conditions under which beetles were active;
- the specific habitats where beetles occurred;
- reproductive behaviour of both species;
- whether males fight for access to females; and
- whether large-mandible males win fights against small-mandible males.

All live beetles found were marked – either with nail varnish or by having tiny radio telemeters attached to them, so they could be traced and their movements followed. The results of this study both confirmed and refuted some assumptions about the beetles:

- Their populations are very small – a total of about 100 male *C. haughtoni*, 20 male *C. kawaii*, and only six females were found during daily searches over the three-month duration of the study.
- Adults live for about one month, with peak abundance during December.
- Beetles were mainly active at dusk and the weather parameters that had the greatest effect on their activity were ambient temperature and wind speed – not humidity as was previously assumed. No beetles were active after dark.
- They occupy very small areas of suitable restio habitat (less than 80m in diameter).
- Males do not fight for females.

Although males appeared to outnumber females in the populations, another reason for the apparently large bias toward higher male numbers in the populations was attributed to the fact that females remain well hidden in restio tussocks from where they secrete a male-attracting pheromone. Males wandered around, apparently searching for females, but distances covered were short (on average only 6.5m) and some remained stationary for several days at a time, presumably testing air currents for female pheromones; one male did not move from his position next to a tussock for 16 consecutive days. When a female secreted the sex pheromone, males converged on her and up to five males were found attempting to mate with her.

The mating attempts witnessed dispelled a previous assumption – that males fight for access to females and that large-mandible males enjoy higher mating success rates than small-mandible males. On the contrary, male–male encounters at a female were generally peaceful affairs with males clambering over each other without signs of aggression in their attempts to mate. Furthermore, females mated with several males over the course of a few days, and after mating, males started wandering again in a quest to find other females.

The study confirmed that these two *Colophon* species are, indeed, rare; that suitable habitat for their life cycle is sparse and fragmented; and that the beetles are very sedentary by nature, so would not easily venture far to locate other pockets of suitable habitat should their current habitat be destroyed. Since the study, an internet tower on a large concrete base covering much of the *Colophon* habitat has been illegally constructed. The effect on these two species is not yet known but serious consequences are predicted. In view of these results, as well as predictions that climate change will detrimentally affect conditions on mountain peaks in the Western Cape, both species should be considered highly endangered. To date, these are the only *Colophon* species that have been studied; nothing is known about the basic ecology of the other 15 species in the genus.

2.15 (a) *Colophon haughtoni* and (b) *C. kawaii* from the same site in the Hex River Mountains.

2.16 *Chrysoritis nigricans nigricans* (Lycaenidae) is a Fynbos endemic with an intimate association with *Crematogaster* ants.

2.17 *Thestor petra petra* (Lycaenidae) is a high-mountain Fynbos endemic whose larvae live in ant nests and are fed by the ants.

Rare fynbos butterflies

Fynbos is home to a large number of endemic butterflies, amongst which are some of the most threatened southern African insect species. More is probably known about butterflies than about most other insect groups in the region, because of the large network of butterfly enthusiasts who monitor species activity and abundance on a regular basis.

Most of the Fynbos endemics belong to the largest butterfly family, Lycaenidae. Although larvae of most butterfly species are herbivorous throughout their larval stage, many Lycaenidae have complex life cycles that involve feeding on plants during some stages of larval development, and depending on ants for the remaining stages. They are either predators of ant brood in ant nests (see 'Predatory butterfly larvae', p. 93), or are fed by the ants. These interdependent life cycles are often the reason for the threatened conservation status of many of the species, as the disruption of any of the essential interactions with other species may lead to population crashes or local extinction.

Two large southern African lycaenid genera are mainly endemic to the Fynbos Biome: coppers and opals, *Chrysoritis* (fig. 2.16), and skollies, *Thestor* (fig. 2.17). Several other species of Fynbos lycaenids are known or thought to be very rare and possibly threatened with extinction, for example, the Brenton blue, *Orachrysops niobe* (fig. 2.18, see box alongside).

There are 68 species and subspecies of *Chrysoritis* in southern Africa, all of which are endemic to the region; about half of these are found in the Fynbos and 10 of the species or subspecies are threatened. Adults are nectar feeders and larvae of all species feed on plants of various groups in their early stages and live in shelters with ants (mostly cocktail ants, *Crematogaster* spp., fig. 2.19) that feed them.

Thestor is represented by 34 species and subspecies in southern Africa, most of which are restricted to the

The Brenton blue butterfly

The Brenton blue, *Orachrysops niobe* (fig. 2.18), which has received substantial publicity, is named after the only locality from which it is currently known, Brenton-on-Sea. It was first collected near Knysna in 1858 and then only again 119 years later (in 1977) in nearby Nature's Valley by an avid butterfly collector and conservationist, Jonathan Ball. Since then, a breeding population that varies yearly between 50 and 280 adults (but averages about 100 individuals) has been found at Brenton-on-Sea, and the very small area (1.4ha) where the species is active was proclaimed a nature reserve in 2003 – the Brenton Blue Butterfly Reserve. This was achieved largely through the efforts of Ball and other members of the Lepidopterists' Society of Africa. Devastating fires in 2018 destroyed much of the local countryside, including the habitat of the butterfly. It has not been seen since and is feared extinct.

The Brenton blue, like many other lycaenids, has a complex life cycle and is dependent on at least two plant and one ant species. The first- and second-instar larvae feed on the young leaves of their host plant, the shrub *Indigofera erecta* (Fabaceae), growing in the shade of the candlewood tree, *Pterocelastrus tricuspidatus* (Celastraceae). The third- and fourth-instar larvae then move underground to feed on the host plant's roots, where they are attended by the ant species *Camponotus baynei*. Lepidoptera feeding on plant roots is a very rare phenomenon, known from only one other species.

2.18 The highly endangered Brenton blue butterfly, *Orachrysops niobe* (Lycaenidae).

Philip Herbst

2.19 *Crematogaster peringueyi* is one of the ant species associated with Lycaenidae butterfly larvae.

Fynbos Biome; five of the species or subspecies are under some form of conservation threat. All species live in very small colonies that occupy habitat patches under 100m in diameter. Some *Thestor* larvae are predatory on scale insects or ant brood (see 'Predatory butterfly larvae', p. 93) for the first three larval instars, after which they are fed by ants; others enter ant nests immediately after emerging from eggs laid by females near the nest of a specific ant species. Adults seem not to feed; they have not been observed to imbibe nectar or honeydew secreted by scale insects, aphids and the like (Hemiptera: Sternorrhyncha).

Insects and the effects of fire

Fire is a major component of the biome as it maintains the vegetation types in both fynbos and renosterveld; fynbos burns every 10–25 years and renosterveld every 3–5 years. The plants are generally high in flammable compounds. Without fire, the vegetation types deteriorate and forest and thicket elements start to grow. Such fynbos 'thicket' occurs in fire-sheltered habitats, such as deep ravines. Fire plays a lesser role in the western strandveld, largely as a result of the wider spacing and greater succulence of the plant communities, as well as dune formations that impede the spread of fire. Here, fires probably only occur at intervals of 50–200 years.

Fire removes older moribund plants, thus releasing nutrients into the nutrient-poor soils, as well as permitting sunlight and moisture to penetrate, allowing seeds to germinate and some plants to resprout. The majority of species, however, are killed by fire and have to regrow from seed. These plants are adapted to fire and retain their seeds in flowerheads that only release them after being burnt (serotiny). Many of these seeds are collected and buried by ants (myrmecochory); this protects them against the elements, as well as rodents.

Dung beetles are also involved in seed dispersal (coleopterochory), but, to date, are only known to collect those of one specific restio, *Ceratocaryum argenteum*.

Although the vegetation of the Fynbos Biome is adapted to fire, it is essential that fires are not too frequent and that they occur at the right time, which is late summer after seed setting. Human-induced fires in spring, when young plants have not yet set seed, and in summer, when harsh hot fires destroy seed, cause the elimination of species. Other threats include invasion by alien plant species and overgrazing, particularly shortly after fire.

Seed burial by ants

Fynbos is the only biome in southern Africa in which seeds are dispersed by ants in a mutualistic relationship between the plants and ants; about 15% of fynbos plants are dispersed in this way. This special mutualistic relationship is, however, under threat of collapse as a result of the invasive Argentine ant, *Linepithema humile* (see box opposite). Many ant species (Formicidae; see 'Ant biology and behaviour', p. 159 for detailed biology) collect and bury the seed of specific plants (figs 2.22–2.24) in an environment protected from fire and predators. This mutualism has co-evolved between seed-collecting ant species – such as *Anoplolepis custodiens* (fig. 2.20), *A. steingroeveri*, *Ocymyrmex cilliei*, *Pheidole capensis* (fig. 2.21) and *Tetramorium quadrispinosum* – and many characteristic and dominant fynbos plant families.

The benefit for the ant is that these ant plants produce seeds with an external food body called an elaiosome (literally, a 'fat body'). The elaiosomes (which are composed of fats, protein, sugars, starch and vitamins and are thought to mimic animal tissue) are very attractive to the carnivorous ants, which quickly collect the fallen seeds and carry them to their nests. There they eat the elaiosome and discard the

Philip Herbst

2.20 Workers and alates of the pugnacious ant, *Anoplolepis custodiens*, emerging from a nest. This important seed-collecting ant species harvests large seeds.

2.21 *Pheidole capensis*, another important seed-collecting species, gathers small seeds.

2.22 A pagoda bush, *Mimetes* sp. (Proteaceae), whose seeds are collected and buried by ants.

Jonathan Ball

2.23 Many pincushions, *Leucospermum* spp. (Proteaceae), depend on ants for seed dispersal.

2.24 Many *Aspalathus* species (Fabaceae), such as *A. cephalotes*, depend on ants to distribute their seed. The genus also includes rooibos tea, *A. linearis*.

Argentine ant invaders

The introduced Argentine ant, *Linepithema humile* (Hymenoptera: Formicidae: Dolichoderinae, fig. 2.25), has invaded large parts of the Western Cape, displacing many indigenous ant species. This has caused a serious disruption of the mutualism that exists between indigenous ants and fynbos plants.

The Argentine ant is aggressive towards other ant species, and is ranked amongst the world's 100 worst animal invaders. It is thought to have been introduced into South Africa with horse feed imported from South America during the Anglo-Boer War.

It is a tramp species that makes simple nests in superficial places such as in debris, under small stones or pieces of wood. Colonies are usually small, consisting of a few hundred workers and several queens (fig. 2.26), of which one, together with a few workers, may establish a new nest, hence their ability to spread quickly and easily, especially with the aid of humans. (Yet, there is evidence to suggest that all the ants over some very large areas, such as the 6,000km-long Mediterranean coast, may belong to a single supercolony.)

Indigenous seed-collecting ants and Argentine ants respond to elaiosome-bearing seeds in different ways. Whereas indigenous ants react quickly to seeds with elaiosomes and remove them from potential harm, Argentine ants may take days to find the seeds. Indigenous ants carry the seeds to their nest, remove the elaiosome and bury the seeds deep in the burrow where they are protected. Argentine ants may eat the elaiosome, but seldom carry the seeds to their nests, which are in any case so superficial as to offer the seeds no protection. Seeds in indigenous ant nests can survive fires; the protected seeds can germinate underground and seedlings grow. In areas where Argentine ants become established, seeds do not receive the necessary protection to ensure survival.

About 1,300 species in 78 genera, and five of the seven endemic families of Fynbos Biome plants are ant-associated. By displacing local seed-collecting ants, invasive Argentine ants pose a serious threat to the continued survival of many of these species, which could ultimately lead to the extinction of some of the most spectacular, rare and endemic myrmecochorous plants in the biome.

Philip Herbst

2.25 The Argentine ant, *Linepithema humile*, is an aggressive invader species that is displacing indigenous seed-collecting species in the Fynbos.

Philip Herbst

2.26 A young Argentine ant queen. *Linepithema humile* colonies spread easily with the aid of multiple young queens.

otherwise undamaged seed, either in a protected above-ground refuse dump, or in an underground refuse chamber. In both situations, the seeds are afforded protection against fire and rodents (which are also attracted by the extra nutrition offered by the elaiosomes). The elaiosome has no reproductive function and has evolved exclusively to attract ants with the necessary nesting behaviour.

Seed burial by beetles

Dung beetles are now known to collect and bury the seeds of a Cape endemic restio, *Ceratocaryum argenteum* (Restionaceae), which has evolved seeds that attract the beetles, both chemically and physically. This remarkable case was described by Jeremy Midgley and Joseph White from the University of Cape Town.

Ceratocaryum argenteum produces highly atypical seeds (nuts). The nuts are large and round; with a diameter of 10mm, they are the largest in the family. They do not possess an elaiosome for dispersal by ants, and instead of having the smooth black seed coat typical of large restio nuts, they have a rough brown outer covering.

The nuts emit a pungent scent – to humans, they smell like herbivore dung. Chemical analysis of volatile chemicals released by the nuts revealed that several of the compounds are well-known components of the scent of herbivore dung, and the quantity of volatiles emitted was 300 times greater than that of other restio seeds from the same area and well within the range of quantities of volatiles produced by antelope dung.

The area in which the plants grow is home to two antelope species: the eland, *Taurotragus oryx* (fig. 2.27), and the bontebok, *Damaliscus pygargus pygargus* (fig. 2.28), a Cape endemic. Both produce dung pellets to which dung beetles are attracted for food and reproduction.

Two species of dung beetle, *Epirinus flagellatus* (fig. 2.29) and *Scarabaeus spretus*, were readily

2.28 Bontebok, *Damaliscus pygargus*, are the smallest of the common antelope whose dung pellets are a mimicry model for the seeds of the restio *Ceratocaryum argenteum*.

Joseph D.M. White

2.29 A remarkable example of a plant bluffing an insect into dispersing and planting its seeds: a *Ceratocaryum argenteum* (Restionaceae) seed being rolled by the dung beetle *Epirinus flagellatus* prior to burial.

attracted to fresh nuts. They rolled away the nuts in typical ball-roller fashion – the spherical shape of the nuts facilitated rolling – then buried them (see box, p. 249; 'The famous Addo dung beetle', p. 279). After presumably attempting to feed on or oviposit in buried nuts, however, the beetles abandoned them, leaving them securely 'planted' in suitable moist, sandy soil, ideal for germination. The buried seeds showed no signs of damage; dung beetle mouthparts are specially adapted for feeding on particulate matter in dung fluids (see box, p. 124), so they are unlikely to damage the seeds in any way.

The researchers concluded that the size, shape, colour, texture and chemistry of the seed husk has evolved under pressure to be visually, tactilely and chemically attractive specifically to dung beetles for dependable and safe dispersal in a remarkable process they termed coleopterochory – seed dispersal by Coleoptera.

Black-mound termites as nutrient recyclers

Termites (Blattodea: Termitoidae) are undoubtedly one of the most important keystone groups in many terrestrial ecosystems. Different species occur across the region in several biomes. Feeding biology and nest structure differ among species and this affects the roles they play as nutrient recyclers in specific habitats. They are therefore discussed in several biomes – Fynbos, Succulent Karoo, Savanna, Grassland and Forest.

Of considerable ecological importance in the Fynbos Biome is the black-mound termite, *Amitermes hastatus* (Termitidae: Termitinae), and although their colonies

2.27 The dung pellets of eland, *Taurotragus oryx*, are the usual food of larger dung beetles in the area where coleopterochory occurs.

2.30 A mature, roughly 25-year-old mound of the black-mound termite, *Amitermes hastatus*, which is the most important recycler of nutrients in the nutrient-poor Fynbos soils. The mound contrasts strongly with the white sands on which it is built, a result of black termite faeces from a digested mix of plant tannins and soil.

are widespread in southern Africa, they are especially numerous in the Fynbos, where they are often the dominant termite species and are the most important nutrient recyclers in the biome. Fynbos soils are poor in organic matter, and the return of nutrients to the soil by termite activities leads to improved soil conditions.

Amitermes hastatus feeds on well-rotted, damp plant remains, not the dry litter and wood used by many related termite species. This is thought to be a mechanism to avoid the high concentrations of unpalatable chemicals in fresh fynbos plant remains.

Their oval mounds are always black and very hard – the mounds are most visible on white sandy soils, especially on mountain slopes (fig. 2.30). They are built using a digested and excreted mix of plant tannins and soil. Mound growth is very slow (see box alongside), and mounds vary in size, depending on the age of the colony. They range from a small conical dome a few centimetres high, to a large hemispherical or conical edifice about 60cm high, with a diameter of about 60cm. The colony is distributed through much of the mound, the base of which extends only 5–10cm below soil level.

Age of *Amitermes hastatus* mounds

Although fire is an integral process in the maintenance of healthy fynbos landscapes, its frequency has a major effect on the termite mounds and colonies within them. *Amitermes hastatus* colonies and mounds develop very slowly and only begin to mature after 4–5 years, when the mound is the size of a man's fist. At this time, the first batch of alates in the colony's life is produced; they are released after the first substantial rains in March or April. It may take up to a decade for a colony to reach full maturity. The lifetime of a mound is about 20–25 years – if spared from fire, which can completely destroy mounds as they burn easily. This is probably a consequence of the organic particles embedded in the building materials.

Under ideal and undisturbed conditions a founding king and queen may live for the full duration of the lifetime of the colony and mound. The human-induced fires that now frequently ravage the Fynbos are having a disastrous effect on the termites, resulting in incalculable negative long-term environmental consequences.

Young *A. hastatus* queens are initially white, but slowly turn brown over the years as a result of repeated licking by workers to acquire pheromones from her. The blind workers are only about 4mm long. Soldiers use both chemical and physical defences: they have large mandibles with which they can bite and a well-developed fontanelle on the head from which they release an irritating fluid into the resulting wounds (fig. 2.31).

The inner workings (fig. 2.32) of *A. hastatus* (then known as *A. atlanticus*) colonies in the Fynbos Biome were painstakingly studied over a 15-year period by S.H. 'Stacey' Skaife in Cape Town in the 1940s and early 1950s. In 1955, Skaife published his results in the book *Dwellers in darkness*, which remains, to this day, the most comprehensive account of termite social structure and colony founding. As all termites share a number of general, defining characteristics associated with sociality, Skaife's study of *A. hastatus* serves well as a background to the colony structure and feeding ecology of the species discussed in other biomes.

Social structure of a termite colony

All termites are truly social (eusocial) insects that live in colonies of various sizes, numbering from dozens to millions of individuals, and feed primarily on cellulose in one form or another. The more familiar species have above-ground mounds, which are characteristic of many parts of the African landscape (see 'The snouted harvester termite', p. 179 and 'The tall chimneys of fungus-growing termite mounds', p. 181; 'Termites as soil engineers', p. 199), but some have only subterranean nests (see 'The heuweltjie termite', p. 104 and 'The large harvester termite', p. 177).

The termite colony is made up of several morphologically and behaviourally different individuals, termed castes. Similar castes are also present in the social Hymenoptera, which include a few bee and wasp and all ant species, and similar terminology is used to describe them and their activities. However, the origin of the different Hymenoptera castes (see 'Ant castes and subcastes', p. 159) and their colony responsibilities are quite different from those of termites. Hymenoptera workers and soldiers are all sterile females, whereas in termites these castes are composed of both sterile males and females. Hymenoptera males die after mating, while in termites a single king will live alongside the queen for many years, and mating takes place regularly.

Termite families (see box, pp. 72, 73) differ in some respects regarding colony formation, caste structure and morphology, but there are general similarities.

The **queen and king**, of which there is usually only one pair, are the source of all the other colony members. The queen lays eggs from which first-instar larvae emerge; these then moult into second-instar larvae; further moults are followed by nymph stages, of which there may be several.

Workers are mostly blind, sterile males and females. As the name suggests, they are responsible for building, maintenance, food collecting and brood care in the colony, of which they make up about 95% of the inhabitants.

Soldiers are also (usually) blind and sterile, comprising (usually) both males and females (fig. 2.33), and make up the remaining 5% of the colony. They are responsible for the defence of the colony, mainly against their arch-enemies, ants.

2.31 Members of an *Amitermes hastatus* colony at a breached mound; soldiers rush to the breach to defend it, while workers follow to mend it.

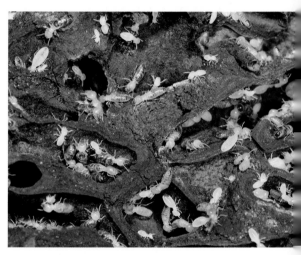

2.32 Section through an *Amitermes hastatus* mound showing the internal gallery structure and an assortment of colony members.

2.33 A mandibulate *Odontotermes* (Macrotermitinae) soldier; one of the two major soldier types in Termitoidae. They defend the colony by biting intruders.

Alates are a reproductive caste of winged males and females, which become kings and queens of new colonies. These reproductives differ from their brothers and sisters in the colony in several respects: they are generally larger than their nest mates, have good reserves of body fat, develop long functional wings that are shed after a short flight (fig. 2.34a), and have well-developed eyes. The wings and eyes are only needed for the few minutes that it takes them to fly from the nest, find a mate (fig. 2.34b) and dig a burrow; there they return to a life in the dark, where eyes are not needed and where wings would be a hindrance when crawling around in narrow galleries.

Ergatoids are short-winged secondary reproductives that develop from certain nymphs if the queen or king dies (fig. 2.35).

A **false worker** or pseudergate caste, a special nymph stage, is often present among some lower termites.

Colony founding in termites

Colony founding, in which a mated pair of reproductives (alates) establishes a new colony, is similar in most termite species. Alates are released from mature colonies in synchronised flights after the first substantial rains (autumn in winter-rainfall areas and spring in summer-rainfall areas). Mortality amongst alates is usually very high, with only a small fraction of those that leave the nest surviving to establish new colonies. Predation by birds, reptiles, amphibians, ants and a host of other opportunistic animals is the major cause of mortality, but hot, hard or dry ground that makes burrowing difficult also contributes to the low survival rate.

After the nuptial flight, a female sheds her wings and attracts males in a characteristic manner, bending her abdomen upwards and secreting an attractive pheromone (fig. 2.34a). Once a pair has formed, they run in tandem, the female leading with the male very close behind (fig. 2.34b). They then dig a shallow burrow in which they seal themselves and mate.

The female lays a few eggs that develop into the first brood of small, pale nymphs (termed nanitics), which assume some basic nest functions. During this phase, the reproductives depend mostly on their energy reserves, although they may eat some soil containing organic matter. When the first batch of nanitic nymphs die, the reproductives eat them and the queen then lays eggs that develop into adult workers, later followed by soldiers. Only years later, when the colony has grown substantially, does the queen lay eggs that develop into the first alates.

When more individuals are needed in the colony, the queen is fed special food by the workers, which stimulates her ovaries to lay the required number of eggs. The queen is fed virtually constantly and simultaneously produces a steady stream of eggs. Workers collect the eggs and place them in brood chambers, where they hatch into larvae and then develop into nymphs of different castes.

The development and control of castes and the numbers of each are determined by pheromones (see 'The large harvester termite ', p. 177), which are spread between nest mates during trophallaxis (exchange of liquid food) either orally or anally. During anal trophallaxis symbiotic gut fauna is also transferred between individuals (except in Macrotermitinae); it is particularly important that founders of new colonies have a healthy microbial gut fauna to transmit to new generations of immatures.

In higher termites, the development into one of the castes (worker, soldier or reproductive) is fixed at the first larval moult. The age of the colony determines whether reproductives are produced or not; they will only be produced after the colony is mature enough. There are two types of reproductive nymphs: those that give rise to primary reproductives (alates) or those that develop into secondary reproductives (ergatoids); these short-winged individuals behave like workers but are available as replacement reproductives should the king or queen die.

In lower termites, castes develop from late-stage nymphs (see 'The large harvester termite ', p. 177) or, in the case of replacement reproductives (i.e. if the king or queen dies), from pseudergates.

2.34 (a) This female *Hodotermes mossambicus* alate shed her wings soon after her dispersal flight. She is secreting an attractant pheromone in typical stance with her abdomen tip raised to better disseminate the pheromone. **(b)** The pheromones have enticed a winged *H. mossambicus* male even before he has shed his wings.

2.35 A large short-winged secondary reproductive (ergatoid) being attended by workers in an *Amitermes hastatus* colony.

The differences between termite families

Termites were previously placed in an order of their own, Isoptera, but they have long been considered to be closely related to cockroaches (see 'Cockroaches as essential detritivores', p. 88) – in fact, so closely that they are often termed 'social cockroaches'. This close relationship is now reflected in their shared classification as members of the order Blattodea. Besides several morphological and genetic similarities, primitive cockroaches and primitive termites both feed on wood. They have similar symbiotic, cellulose-digesting, flagellated gut protozoa, with which they live in a tightly evolved mutualistic relationship that enables them to utilise this otherwise intractable food source.

The presence of symbiotic gut protozoa (as well as gut bacteria that contribute to digestion) is the main reason for distinguishing between primitive (lower) termites and 'higher' termites. Most higher termites have no protozoa, only symbiotic gut bacteria that are involved in cellulose digestion. Macrotermitinae (fungus gardeners) have neither protozoa nor gut bacteria, but have a co-evolved relationship with external fungi that digest cellulose in special fungus gardens produced specifically for the purpose by the termites.

There are four lower termite families in southern Africa:

- Kalotermitidae (dry-wood termites, fig. 2.36);
- Termopsidae (damp-wood termites, fig. 2.37; see 'Damp-wood termites', p. 286);
- Hodotermitidae (harvester termites, fig. 2.38; see 'The heuweltjie termite', p. 104 and 'The large harvester termite', p. 177); and
- Rhinotermitidae (subterranean termites, figs 2.39–2.41).

2.37 *Porotermes planiceps*, one of only two extant members of the ancient damp-wood termite family Termopsidae in southern Africa.

2.38 Harvester termites, *Hodotermes mossambicus* (Hodotermitidae), with cut pieces of grass harvested nearby and dragged to the nest.

2.39 As their common name 'subterranean termites' suggests, Rhinotermitidae have mostly subterranean nests. This *Psammotermes* species from the arid west of southern Africa nests below ground in grass clumps or bushes.

Rina de Klerk

2.40 The tropical species of Rhinotermitidae, *Schedorhinotermes lamanianus*, nests at ground level in dead tree trunks and builds metres of clay-covered foraging runways up the trees to access suitable wood.

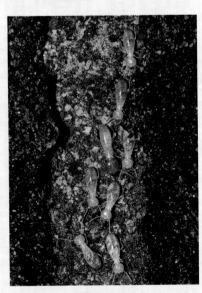

2.41 *Schedorhinotermes lamanianus* colony members exposed below a clay-covered runway.

2.36 *Bifiditermes*, a representative member of the dry-wood termite family Kalotermitidae.

Most lower termites do not have a worker caste; their functions are performed by nymphs and pseudergates.

The higher termites all belong to the very large family Termitidae, which is further divided into four subfamilies:

- Macrotermitinae (fungus growers, figs 2.42–2.45; see 'The tall chimneys of fungus-growing termite mounds', p. 181; 'Termites as soil engineers', p. 199): Some species have large and small workers; the larger workers are male and the smaller ones female. They perform different functions in the nest: the male workers are mostly builders and foragers, while the female workers are mainly responsible for nest maintenance and brood care. Soldiers are mostly female.
- Apicotermitinae: Commonly called soldierless termites, as they do not have a soldier caste.
- Termitinae (soil feeders; this chapter): In most species the soldiers are mostly female, although in *Amitermes hastatus* male and female soldiers occur in roughly equal numbers in the colony.
- Nasutitermitinae (snouted harvesters; see 'The snouted harvester termite', p. 179): *Trinervitermes* has large and small workers; the larger workers are female and the smaller ones male. Soldiers are mostly male.

Soldiers of many different forms are found amongst different termite species, although two major types predominate: those with large, exposed, mostly symmetrical mandibles are called mandibulate soldiers (e.g. Macrotermitinae; see 'Termites as soil engineers', p. 199); while those with an elongated, tube-like head capsule are termed nasutes (e.g. *Trinervitermes*; see 'The snouted harvester termite', p. 179). Mandibulate soldiers bite intruders, whereas nasutes spray a chemical cocktail of sticky and toxic substances from a special gland (fontanelle) on the head onto them. Many mandibulate soldiers combine physical and chemical defence (e.g. *Macrotermes* and *Amitermes*); some nasutes, though using mainly chemical defence, may also bite. There are also soldiers with specially modified heads (phragmotic head, e.g. in Kalotermitidae) that are used to plug tunnels when the colony is under threat.

2.43 *Odontotermes latericius* workers and soldier exposed in a nest in a tree trunk. Note the extreme dimorphism between the two castes.

2.44 An iconic African savanna structure: a 4m-tall *Macrotermes* (Macrotermitinae) mound in mopane veld in Botswana.

2.45 *Macrotermes* workers and soldier at a mound breach.

2.42 A typical Bushveld *Odontotermes latericius* (Macrotermitinae) nest mound showing multiple ventilation shafts.

Pollinators

As in all other biomes, insect pollinators are some of the most important keystone species in the Fynbos Biome. Amongst these are numerous generalist pollinators of which the honey bee, *Apis mellifera*, is the most important. There is, however, a high degree of specialisation of pollination systems in the biome. Some suites of plants have evolved morphologically to attract pollinators of only one, or a few, insect species. This phenomenon is not uncommon in the biome and is thought to have been a key driving force in the extensive speciation in the region. As a result, the Fynbos Biome is home to many good examples of these 'pollination syndromes'.

Insect pollination syndromes often occur among unrelated plant species that depend on the same group of insect pollinators. These syndromes are suites of similar flower characteristics (see box alongside) that are specially adapted to accommodate a particular group of pollinators, for example, red, erect flowers that attract butterflies specifically. The higher the level of specialisation, the more successful pollination will be (see bottom box, p. 82). Consequently, the fewer suitable pollinators available and the more specialised the association, the more likely the syndrome is to develop convergence among unrelated plant groups. This relationship can develop to such a degree that pollination of these plants is restricted to only one insect genus or species; this intimate ecological relationship is called a pollination guild. The insect group involved is not necessarily restricted to pollinating only those plants – under different conditions or at different times of the year, they may also pollinate other plants.

The ubiquitous honey bee

The honey bee, *Apis mellifera* (Hymenoptera: Apidae: Apinae), is undoubtedly the most important generalist pollinator in every terrestrial region. Honey bees are adapted to visit and pollinate a wide variety of flowers. They have been valued by humans for millennia as producers of honey and beeswax, and later in human history, also as crop pollinators.

Bees and their honey represent a rich and rewarding resource not only to humans, but also to a large number of animals that prey on adult bees or access and plunder their nests. There are various specialised vertebrate predators of adult bees (e.g. bee-eaters) and bee brood and wax (e.g. honey guides, honey badgers), as well as invertebrates that feed on adult bees, their brood, honey and pollen stores, or the wax they produce.

Specialised floral adaptations to attach pollen to pollinators

The most specialised plant–pollinator interactions (pollination guilds) are found in the plant families Orchidaceae, Iridaceae, Geraniaceae, Apocynaceae and Scrophulariaceae, with most occurring in the Orchidaceae.

Although most orchids are self-compatible, many have sophisticated floral adaptations to maximise cross pollination, as the transfer of pollen among flowers on the same plant can lead to reduction in plant fitness.

In most angiosperm families, pollen is powdery, but in the Orchidaceae and Apocynaceae, it is contained in cohesive compact masses of pollen known as pollinia (singular pollinium). One or two stipes (or, in some species, a caudicle) connect the pollinium to a viscidium (plural viscidia), a sticky disc. A pollinarium (plural pollinaria) is a pair of pollinia with two viscidia and the connecting parts (Orchidaceae), or a complete set of all the pollinia from a flower (Apocynaceae). The sticky viscidium attaches the pollinium to a pollinator.

Whereas loose, powdery pollen adheres most effectively to hairy parts of insects and mammals or the feathers of bird pollinators, the viscidia of orchid pollinaria stick to various smooth parts on the pollinator's body. In insects, these may be mouthparts, frons, eyes, thorax and legs. Most orchid pollinaria attach to the dorsal surface of the insect, but in some groups it is more precise. In *Disa racemosa*, for example, which is pollinated by carpenter bees, *Xylocopa* spp. (see 'Honey bees and carpenter bees', p. 393), only one pollinarium is attached at a time to a site on one of the bees' middle legs. Pollinaria of the Fynbos orchid *Satyrium stenopetalum* are attached to the proboscis of the moth *Agrotis segetum* (see 'Moth-pollinated succulents', p. 82), and those of the grassland orchid *Disa cooperi* to the proboscis of the moth *Basiothia schenki* (see 'The perfect proboscis size for an orchid-pollinating hawk moth', p. 185).

The precise placement of pollinaria on the bodies of pollinators is achieved, firstly, by specific olfactory and visual cues that attract only a particular guild of potential pollinators, and secondly, by the shape of the flower, which forces the pollinator to approach the scented or otherwise attractive area of the flower in a way that ensures contact between the viscidium and the precise target area on the pollinator.

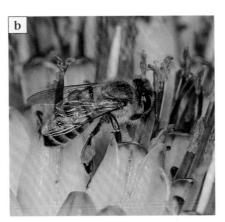

2.46 There are two honey bee subspecies in southern Africa: (**a**) the Cape honey bee, *Apis mellifera capensis*, and (**b**) the African honey bee, *A. m. scutellata*.

Apis mellifera was originally an Afro-European species, but its importance as a pollinator and honey producer has led to its being introduced into North and South America, Australia, New Zealand and parts of Asia. The species is divided into numerous subspecies based on morphology, genetics and behaviour. Two of the subspecies occur naturally in southern Africa: *Apis mellifera capensis* (fig. 2.46a) and *Apis mellifera scutellata* (fig. 2.46b). Prior to human intervention, *A. m. capensis* was restricted to the southwestern Cape, where it was hemmed in by the mountain ranges and Karoo to the north (see box, p. 76), while *A. m. scutellata* occurred throughout the other parts of the subregion.

Honey bee castes

A honey bee colony consists of various castes, as do their ant relatives (Hymenoptera: Formicidae; see 'Ant castes and subcastes', p. 159), some members of the related wasps (Hymenoptera: Vespidae: Polistinae; see 'Eusocial paper wasps', p. 389), and the unrelated termites (Blattodea: Termitoidae; see 'Social structure of a termite colony', p. 70). The castes in honey bees consist of a single large queen (fig. 2.47), hundreds to thousands of exclusively female workers, and a small number of males, called drones (fig. 2.48).

Workers are the smallest members of the swarm, but perform all hive functions (fig. 2.49; see box, p. 76) other than reproduction. Each worker is armed with a sting – the female egg-laying apparatus which, no longer used for that purpose, has become a weapon of defence. The sting is armed with recurved barbs so that when the bee stings an assailant, the sting remains in the victim and is pulled from the bee's abdomen, disembowelling her; she dies in the process.

Drones are larger and more robust than workers, and darker in colour. They are usually produced in spring prior to swarm splitting (fission) when young queens are also produced. A few of them will mate with a virgin queen on her nuptial flight; the rest are superfluous. These few are cared for by the workers who feed and groom them, but any surviving at the end of the season are banished from the hive – they die from exposure to the elements or from neglect.

The queen is similar in general shape to workers, but about twice the size. Her main purpose is laying eggs. She has control over the future gender of her progeny: fertilised eggs become female workers (the vast majority), and unfertilised eggs develop into drones (a small minority), which are only involved in reproduction. Since the eggs from which drones develop are unfertilised, they have only half the parental genetic material (only that from the female queen), and are haploid (with only 16 chromosomes). Females, on the other hand, are diploid (32 chromosomes), with two sets of genetic material, one set from the queen and one from a drone with which she has mated. This reproductive system, which occurs in all Hymenoptera, is termed haplodiploidy.

2.47 The honey bee queen (centre), here surrounded by attendant workers, is the mother of all the colony inhabitants. She has absolute control over colony composition.

2.48 Male honey bees or drones are the product of unfertilised eggs. They are fed and cared for by workers and their only function is for a few individuals to mate with virgin queens in spring. They are tolerated until autumn, and are then expelled from the colony.

Rearing a queen honey bee

The queen controls the colony composition by means of mandibular pheromones that she produces, which are distributed among colony members during trophallaxis (fig. 2.49) (liquid food exchange; see 'Communication among ants', p. 161). One of these pheromones suppresses the production of more queens. When the queen becomes too old to produce enough of the queen-suppressing pheromone, or the colony too large for all the workers to receive enough of it, workers build special large teacup-shaped queen cells and start to rear new queens. This usually happens in spring.

Queens can be reared from any female egg, but the queen larvae are fed a special glandular secretion throughout their development, so-called 'royal jelly', which is produced by young workers. The wax cells in which the queens develop are enlarged to accommodate their extra growth. The workers protect the developing queens from the old queen.

Usually, five to ten young queens are produced at a time. The first of these to emerge produces a special call, termed 'piping', to which her young sister queens (still encased in their cells) respond by 'quacking'. This response directs the first emergent queen to the younger queens, which she then kills.

When the new queen is ready to fly, she leaves the hive, flying high and producing a sex pheromone that attracts her brothers and drones from nearby swarms. During this nuptial flight the virgin queen will mate with 5–40 drones in quick succession. The mated

2.49 Worker honey bees are female and perform all colony duties, including defence, for which they are armed with a sting, the specially modified ovipositor no longer needed for egg-laying. Here two are exchanging oral food (trophallaxis), while attending to brood.

drone's genitalia are ripped from his abdomen by the mating process and he falls to the ground to die, his place in the mating sequence being taken over by another male who suffers the same consequence. After the nuptial flight, the queen never mates again, but stores all the sperm from each of these matings in a special abdominal chamber called a spermatheca. This store of sperm is large enough to fertilise eggs for the rest of her life.

The *capensis* problem among honey bees

An interesting phenomenon among Cape honey bees, *Apis mellifera capensis*, is that, in the absence of a queen, certain workers (called 'laying workers') can produce female (diploid) offspring without mating, by means of thelytokous parthenogenesis. Thelytoky occurs when two meiotic products in the eggs fuse, resulting in unfertilised diploid eggs with a full complement of 32 chromosomes. These develop into workers or queens, depending on the food that the larva receives. The mechanism is thought to have evolved in response to queen loss during nuptial flights in the very windy Cape region. As only one newly emerged queen survives in a colony (the first to emerge having killed her siblings), there is no immediate successor available if she dies soon after emerging. The quick response by laying workers to replace a queen ensures the survival of the colony. Death of the queen in an African honey bee (*A. mellifera scutellata*) colony, on the other hand, usually dooms the colony to extinction.

The so-called 'capensis problem' was created by commercial honey bee farmers moving Cape honey bees into areas historically occupied by African honey bees. This resulted in *A. m. capensis* worker bees from apiaries drifting into *A. m. scutellata* colonies. Unfortunately, *A. m. scutellata* queens are unable to pheromonally suppress *A. m. capensis* workers from laying eggs, and the laying workers continue to increase in number. This results in the breakdown of the social system in the colony, and as *A. m. scutellata* worker numbers diminish, normal activities cease and the colony eventually dies.

There is concern about the possible long-term conservation consequences of *A. m. capensis* destroying *A. m. scutellata*. Fortunately, it appears that the problem applies mainly to commercial beekeeping, where workers in apiaries readily drift between colonies, but that wild swarms, which are the mainstay of new genetic lines that ensure healthy regional bee populations, are largely unaffected.

Colony development

New colonies form in spring when the young queen leaves her natal colony, taking with her an often large percentage of the workers. The swarm then finds a temporary refuge, such as amongst vegetation on a branch, where they cluster for a few days while scouts search for a suitable permanent nest site. Once a nest site has been found, they move in and workers immediately begin to build combs (fig. 2.50) from wax produced by special abdominal wax glands. As soon as a few cells are completed, the queen begins to lay eggs. An egg is laid in each cell, and when the larvae hatch they remain in the cells and are fed by workers. After about 23 days, they pupate and the cell is capped by workers. The adults emerge from the pupal cells 10–12 days later.

The life of a worker bee

Workers perform all the main nest functions, and their specific activities and responsibilities are largely age-related – this is termed age-polyethism and works as follows:

- For the first three days after emergence from the pupa, the worker cleans cells from which other workers have emerged and caps pupal cells.
- For the next three days, she tends and feeds the older larvae (fig. 2.51).
- For the next week she feeds newly hatched young larvae with glandular secretions (royal jelly); however, the larvae receive this only for the first three days of their development, receiving a mixture of pollen and honey during the remainder of their 23-day development. The queen receives royal jelly throughout her life from workers of this age.
- From about the age of 10 days, the worker begins to undertake general nest-building and maintenance activities: she cleans the nest of debris and dead bees, builds combs out of wax from her now-functioning wax glands, receives pollen and nectar from field bees, packs the pollen into cells, and ripens the nectar. She does this by rolling regurgitated nectar on her tongue repeatedly and mixing it with saliva. As the nectar rolls, excess moisture evaporates until the water content drops from about 65% to 20%. At this point it becomes 'honey' and is placed in cells, which are capped with a thin wax layer. Her final nest activities constitute nest ventilation and guarding the entrance.
- About 18–25 days after emerging from her pupal cell, she becomes a field bee (fig. 2.52), collecting nectar and pollen until she dies – during a peak nectar-flow period this might be after a few days of relentless labour, but is more likely to be 15–40 days later. During a less frenetic period she might live as long as 140 days.

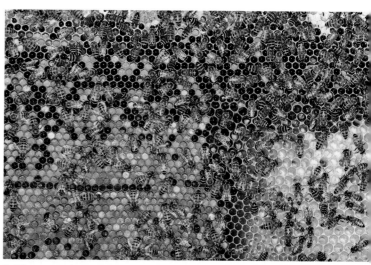

2.50 A typical wax comb in a honey bee nest: the yellowish cells on the left are filled with stored pollen; the dark cells in the centre contain honey; and the white brood cells on the right contain developing larvae.

2.51 Young worker honey bees attending to brood in nursery cells.

Invertebrate exploiters of honey bees

Adult bees, honey, bee brood and even wax are attractive and rewarding food sources. A number of invertebrates are specialised to either capture and overcome adult honey bees outside the nest, or to gain access to the nest, and feed on the brood, wax and harvested food supplies as kleptoparasites. Among them are species that live permanently inside the bee nest (termed inquilines).

Beewolves are a group of wasps of which the most common and widespread species is *Philanthus triangulum* (Hymenoptera: Crabronidae, fig. 2.53). It occurs throughout much of Europe and Africa and specialises in preying on honey bees. Other species of *Philanthus*, of which there are 13 in southern Africa, also prey on honey bees and solitary bees. *Philanthus triangulum* wasps are each capable of capturing up to 10 honey bees per day, which they capture on flowers

2.52 Once worker honey bees have become field bees, they spend the rest of their lives foraging for nectar and pollen. Pollen is placed in pollen baskets (corbiculae) on their hind legs for transport to the nest.

2.53 This beewolf, *Philanthus triangulum* (Crabronidae), is a specialist predator of honey bees outside the nest. The bees are stung and paralysed, then carried to the wasp's nest in the ground to feed her brood.

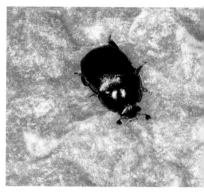

2.54 The small hive beetle, *Aethina tumida* (Nitidulidae), is a regular inhabitant and occasional pest of honey bee colonies in southern Africa.

or at the nest entrance. Victims are stung and paralysed; using its middle legs, the wasp then carries them to a burrow dug in friable sand. Burrow systems may be deep (up to 1m) and extensive, with up to 35 lateral tunnels radiating from a sloping main shaft and ending in a nest cell. Some are provisioned with several bees on which a single egg is laid; others are left empty, possibly as decoys for nest parasites such as Mutillidae and Chrysididae wasps.

The **small hive beetle**, *Aethina tumida* (Coleoptera: Nitidulidae, fig. 2.54), is dark brown or black, about 5mm long, and is a common inhabitant of honey bee nests in Africa, where it is an occasional pest of weak commercial hives. However, during the 1990s, beetles were accidentally introduced into the USA and more recently into Australia. They have quickly become one of the major hive pests, leading to huge colony losses in apiaries. When the beetles breed successfully in hives, stored nectar and honey ferment, possibly as a result of fungi carried by the beetles (which may form a component of their diet). The species is thought to have a more or less obligatory association with beehives, in which adults and larvae feed on brood, honey and pollen; however, adults feed and breed successfully in rotten fruit, and larvae can complete their life cycle on this resource, so it is probable that the beetles are specialised sap feeders (as are their relatives), with invasion of beehives being a secondary adaptation.

The **large hive beetle**, *Oplostomus fuligineus* (Scarabaeidae: Cetoniinae: Cremastocheilini, fig. 2.55), belongs to a specialised group that is specifically associated with social Hymenoptera, including honey bees, wasps and ants (see box, p. 99). *Oplostomus fuligineus* is a large, shiny black beetle, 20mm long, with mouthparts specially adapted to predation. The beetles are primarily predators of the brood of honey bees and paper wasps (Vespidae; see 'Eusocial paper wasps', p. 389), although they occasionally visit flowers

and feed on pollen. Their large size, smooth surface and hard exoskeleton make them a formidable adversary to bees and wasps and they mostly enter the nests and feed with impunity on brood and food reserves. Wasp nests are usually totally destroyed, but while a few beetles in a beehive may cause considerable damage, the swarm mostly survives. There is one record of about 750 beetles found in a commercial hive, a number obviously far in excess of that which a swarm could tolerate.

The **bee louse**, *Braula coeca* (Diptera: Braulidae, fig. 2.56), despite its common name, is actually a small, hairy, brown wingless fly (1.5mm long) and not a louse at all. It should also not be confused with the superficially similar varroa mite (see page opposite). It is found wherever honey bees occur and its entire life cycle is spent inside the host nest. Adults live on the bees (mostly on their heads, with a preference for that of the queen) and larvae live just beneath the wax capping on honey cells, where they make characteristic white tunnels as they feed on honey and pollen residues. The adults feed from a bee's mouthparts while two bees are exchanging liquid food (trophallaxis). They are tolerated by the bees and some studies suggest that the flies can even induce a bee to regurgitate food by stroking the upper edge of the bee's labrum; this induces the bee to extend its tongue with a drop of honey on it.

The **death's-head hawk moth**, *Acherontia atropos* (Sphingidae, fig. 2.57a), is an Old World moth species that occurs in Europe and Africa. It is notorious for entering beehives and stealing honey. Adults are among the largest members of the family, with a wingspan of up to 100mm. They have dark brown forewings with pale flecks and bands, while the hind wings and abdomen are bright yellow with black bands. A skull-like pattern on the thorax is the source of the popular name and the origin of many myths about the moths. The larvae, which grow to a length of more than 100mm, have a prominent spine on the caudal end (a characteristic of the family)

2.55 (right) The large hive beetle, *Oplostomus fuligineus* (Scarabaeidae: Cetoniinae: Cremastocheilini), is a rapacious predator of honey bee and social wasp nests.

2.56 (far right) The bee louse, *Braula coeca* (Diptera: Braulidae), a tolerated and obligatory inhabitant of honey bee nests, is actually a wingless fly. Here one is perching on the thorax of a worker.

2.57 The largest honey bee nest invader is (a) the death's-head hawk moth, *Acherontia atropos* (Lepidoptera: Sphingidae), which enters nests and feeds on honey with impunity; (b) the 'horn' at the posterior end of the hawk moth's larva is a family characteristic.

and are often brightly coloured in greens or purples and often banded in yellow (fig. 2.57b). They feed on a wide range of host plants in several families. Adults are capable of producing sound (squeaks) by a pulsed air stream. Although unproven, the squeaks may possibly startle a potential predator, giving the moth time to escape; alternatively, the squeaks are thought to be similar to the sounds produced by a queen bee that prompt workers in the colony to remain motionless, thus allowing the moth access to the colony's honey reserves.

Wax moths, *Galleria mellonella* (fig. 2.58) and *Achroia grisella* (Pyralidae), invade stored wax combs or weak swarms and lay eggs on the combs. Their larvae consume beeswax and both are considered pests by apiarists. Of the two species, *G. mellonella* is by far the worst: the larvae very quickly turn honeycombs into a mess covered in silk and faecal matter. Mature larvae leave the combs and pupate close to them. In beehives they add to the damage by tunnelling into the wooden hive or comb frames, substantially weakening them, in order to pupate.

Ants are probably honey bees' worst enemy. Food reserves and brood in bee nests are a very rewarding food source for ants. Their small size makes it easy for them to enter and rob nests with impunity. Ant attacks often lead to bees abandoning their nests. In the central parts of southern Africa, the brown house ant, *Pheidole megacephala*, and the pugnacious ant, *Anoplolepis custodiens* (see 'The pugnacious ant', p. 191), are amongst the worst bee parasites, while in the Fynbos Biome, the introduced Argentine ant, *Linepithema humile*, is the major parasite (see box, p. 67).

The **varroa mite**, *Varroa destructor* (Arachnida: Acari: Parasitiformes), is superficially similar to *Braula coeca*, but it is eight-legged (as are all adult mites; see 'Mites', p. 298), whereas the bee louse has six legs. *Varroa destructor* is indigenous to Asia, where its original host was the Asian honey bee, *Apis cerana*, but it successfully switched to *A. mellifera* around 1960. Subsequently, it has spread throughout much of the beekeeping world and has caused disastrous infestations

2.58 The larva of the greater wax moth, *Galleria mellonella* (Lepidoptera: Pyralidae), is one of the most destructive pests of unattended wax combs in weak colonies and in stored beehives in apiaries.

2.59 Pseudoscorpions (Arachnida: Pseudoscorpiones) similar to this (typically less than 1mm long) are occasionally found clinging to bees, which they use as transport from one site to another.

2.60 The rare peacock moraea, *Moraea villosa* (Iridaceae), is pollinated only by monkey beetles (Scarabaeidae: Melolonthinae: Hopliini).

2.61 *Pachycnema crassipes*, a monkey beetle that pollinates *Moraea villosa*.

2.62 Monkey beetles that pollinate *Ceratandra* orchids, *Lepithrix* sp.

of honey bee colonies. Adult mites suck the body fluids of adult bees, causing wounds and transmitting diseases, while the larvae develop on bee brood, which results in deformities and disease. It was first recorded in South Africa in 1997 and has since spread to all wild and commercial swarms throughout southern Africa. In Europe and the Americas, the mite has been a major cause of colony collapse, but fortunately both honey bee subspecies in southern Africa have apparently developed resistance to the mite.

The **bee scorpion** (fig. 2.59) is a member of a group of arachnids called pseudoscorpions (Arachnida: Pseudoscorpiones; see 'Pseudoscorpions', p. 307). They are mainly found amongst members of wild swarms as they are not tolerated by bees and need cracks and crevices in which to hide; suitable hideaways are more likely to be found in tree hollows and similar nest sites. These small predators use bees for transport (termed phoresis) between habitats, where they feed on mites and small insects such as bark lice (Psocodea) and beetle larvae.

Monkey beetles as pollinators

Some of the best-known examples of beetle pollination in southern Africa are among the monkey beetles (Scarabaeidae: Melolonthinae: Hopliini), which are pollinators of spring flowers in the Fynbos Biome (and Namaqualand; see more about 'Monkey beetles as pollinators', p. 109). Although they are usually associated with plants in the daisy family (Asteraceae), pollination of some species in the iris (Iridaceae) and orchid (Orchidaceae) families have been recorded.

Peter Goldblatt, Peter Bernhardt and John Manning documented an apparently co-evolved relationship between some Hopliini and flowers of the Iridaceae in a distinct pollination guild. They pollinate the rare and endangered species of the small 'peacock' group of the plant genus *Moraea* (fig. 2.60). The peacock moraeas have prominent iridescent, crescent-shaped spots on the outer tepals of the flower, reminiscent of the spots on male peacock feathers; this similarity was noted by Carolus Linnaeus's son as early as 1782. The spots on the tepals are thought to be guides that highlight the location of the food reward for pollinators.

The *Moraea* flowers are typically iris-like with three functional tubes or gullets on the upper side where the anthers and stigma are located. Nectaries are situated at the base of an inner tepal. The tube is just wide enough for the specific beetles to squeeze into, collect pollen, and then deposit it on the stigma. The iridescent floral guides lie on the outer tepals. Only hopliines (e.g. *Pachycnema crassipes*, fig. 2.61) visit and pollinate these *Moraea* flowers.

In another study, Kim Steiner of the South African National Biodiversity Institute (SANBI), found that the South African endemic orchid *Ceratandra grandiflora* was pollinated only by hopliines, mostly *Lepithrix hilaris* (fig. 2.62), but also *Heterochelus podagricus*. There is, however, no floral reward for the beetles attracted to *C. grandiflora* and it was found that the flowers' bright yellow and orange colours are the main attraction for hopliine beetles, chiefly males. They usually feed on bright yellow or orange flowers, often from the Asteraceae, and it appears that the orchid is a generalised food-source mimic that depends on its bright colour to attract them. The males spend extended periods on the flowers, during which they actively crawl around, pollinating them in the process. When females alight, mating takes place quickly. This suggests that the orchid is partially a food mimic, but that the beetles' attraction to the flowers is mainly for use as mating platforms (rendezvous pollination).

Long-tongued flies and long-tubed flowers

Although pollination by long-tongued flies has been recorded in India and California, it is most common in southern Africa. It occurs in several plant families, including Iridaceae, Geraniaceae (see box below, upper box, p. 82), Ericaceae, and Orchidaceae (see lower box, p. 82), especially in the Fynbos Biome, but also in Namaqualand and the Drakensberg. Long-tongued flies belong to two dipteran families, Nemestrinidae and Tabanidae.

Nemestrinidae is a small family with about 50 species in southern Africa. They are commonly called tangle-veined flies because the forewings have several distinct veins running parallel to the front wing margin. Adults of some species have reduced mouthparts and probably don't feed, but others feed on nectar. Nemestrinid larvae are endoparasites of grasshoppers, crickets and scarabaeid beetle larvae. The females lay thousands of tiny eggs (by comparison, a female house fly lays a maximum of about 500) spread over plants and the ground. These develop into tiny, active larvae that seek out an appropriate host.

Tabanidae (horse flies) is a large family with about 250 species in southern Africa. Its members are best known for the ability of gravid females to 'bite' in order to suck blood, on which they depend for the development of their eggs. Nongravid females and males feed on nectar and are often important pollinators of a wide range of plants. Some species spread various human and livestock diseases. Tabanid larvae live in decaying, often damp organic matter.

Moegistorhynchus longirostris (Nemestrinidae) is a large fly (wingspan about 40mm) and has the longest proboscis or rostrum (70mm long) of any insect relative to body size (fig. 2.63a). Some *Prosoeca* species (Nemestrinidae) in the region also have long proboscides; the flies are slightly smaller (wingspan about 35mm) and their mouthparts are shorter than those of *M. longirostris*, but they are, nevertheless, impressively long at about 40mm (figs 2.63b–d). Several species (adult wingspan 30–45mm) of the Afro-Oriental genus *Philoliche* (Tabanidae, fig. 2.64), including some southern African species, have long proboscides (40–50mm long) and are involved in specialised pollination guilds.

2.64 Unlike long-tongued flies (Nemestrinidae) that feed exclusively on nectar, this female needle-nosed fly, *Philoliche aethiopica* (Tabanidae), has mouthparts specially adapted for the dual purposes of feeding on nectar and piercing animal tissue to suck blood before laying eggs.

Correlation between floral tube and pollinator proboscis length

John Manning and Peter Goldblatt, associated with SANBI, found that a guild of 20 species of mainly Iridaceae and Geraniaceae (but also a few Orchidaceae) with very long floral tubes was pollinated exclusively by *Moegistorhynchus longirostris*. The flowers are mostly creamy-white or pink with red nectar guides and violet or red anthers and pollen, and produce copious quantities of nectar. The floral tube length varies between 50mm and 70mm, although some extend to 90mm. Similarly, the flies' mouthparts are usually between 40mm and 70mm long, but may be as long as 90mm.

Jonathan Ball

2.63 Long-tongued flies (Diptera: Nemestrinidae) are specialised pollinators of flowers with long, narrow tubes. Their fast, hovering flight is very energy-intensive. (**a**) *Moegistorhynchus longirostris* has the longest tongue of any insect; (**b**) resting *Prosoeca circumdata*; (**c**) *Prosoeca* sp. hovering and probing for nectar in a long-tubed flower; (**d**) *Prosoeca* sp. showing the elaborate proboscis structure.

SANBI research scientists John Manning and Peter Goldblatt also found that two *Prosoeca* species pollinate a large guild of 28 species in the plant families Iridaceae and Geraniaceae. The species are mostly visited and pollinated by one, but occasionally both, of the fly species. The flowers do not produce any noticeable scent.

The flowers of all of the species in the study have several morphological characteristics in common. All are purple to crimson with mostly white to cream nectar guides. The floral tube is straight or only slightly curved and very narrow (1.25–2.5mm diameter), with a length between 30mm and 70mm. The anthers and stamens are situated outside the mouth of the floral tube, where they would be brushed by the body of any insect attempting to reach the nectar at its base. However, most of the tubes fill to only about one-third from the base with nectar, so this rich resource is only available to pollinators with an extremely long proboscis.

2.65 *Drepanogynis albilinea* (Geometridae), one of the probable nocturnal pollinators of *Crassula fascicularis*.

2.66 The moth-pollinated *Crassula fascicularis* (Crassulaceae).

Moth-pollinated succulents

Several moth species from different families pollinate various fynbos plants at night. These include two *Drepanogynis* species (formerly *Axiodes*; Geometridae, fig. 2.65) that pollinate *Crassula fascicularis* (Crassulaceae, fig. 2.66), a small fynbos shrublet that grows on sandstone slopes in the Fynbos Biome.

Most *Crassula* species have small, unspecialised flowers that are typically pollinated by small flies or bees, but three Western Cape species are atypical, with long corolla tubes more suited to pollinators with long proboscides such as those of Lepidoptera. One of these species, *C. coccinea*, has red scentless flowers and belongs to a pollination guild that is pollinated by the butterfly *Aeropetes tulbaghia* (see 'The Table Mountain beauty butterfly', opposite). The two remaining species – *Crassula fascicularis* and *C. congesta* – have pale flowers, with a strong jasmine scent that is released at night.

Crassula fascicularis flowers are borne in tight clusters with the petal lobes recurved at right angles to form a settling platform on which pollinators alight. The anthers lie inside the narrow corolla, so that pollen is smeared onto a pollinator's proboscis as it is forced down the tube to reach the nectar. Both *Drepanogynis* species feed on nectar that is concentrated at the base of the corolla, about 16.3mm from the lip. They are able to reach the nectar with proboscides that are slightly longer than those of other insect species active at that time of night.

Another widespread moth, *Agrotis segetum* (Noctuidae), the larva of which is a common pest cutworm in the region, is the pollinator of the orchid *Satyrium stenopetalum*, which is also found on rocky, sandy or loamy soils in the biome.

Floral mimicry by some orchids

Many southern African Orchidaceae species have long-spurred or long-tubed flowers, but pollination of only a few has been documented. Species in the genera *Disa* (Western Cape and Drakensberg species) and *Brownleea* (Drakensberg) are pollinated by long-tongued flies. The flowers are white, pink or lilac with long spurs (10–70mm), have no discernible scent, and do not produce nectar. However, in spite of the absence of a floral reward, the flowers are regularly visited and pollinated by long-tongued nemestrinid and tabanid flies. Why?

The flowers of the *Disa* species are morphologically similar to nectar-producing flowers of other plant groups that attract both *Moegistorhynchus longirostris* and *Prosoeca rostrata*, so some form of floral mimicry seems to be involved. In one study, the nectar-producing species were more commonly visited than the orchids, so the latter were apparently visited more by mistake than by design – but for the orchids, this deception is necessary for successful pollination.

2.67 The Table Mountain beauty, *Aeropetes tulbaghia* (Nymphalidae: Satyrinae), is one of the few insects that pollinate red flowers.

Mike Spies

2.68 Red flowers pollinated by the Table Mountain beauty: (**a**) *Crassula coccinea* (Crassulaceae); (**b**) *Cyrtanthus elatus* (Amaryllidaceae), a localised endemic along forest margins and moist mountain slopes; (**c**) *Gladiolus saccatus* (Iridaceae).

The Table Mountain beauty butterfly

Plants bearing red flowers are common in southern Africa and it is generally assumed that they attract mainly nectar-feeding birds, of which southern Africa has many species. However, various reddish flowers are also known to attract butterflies. One of southern Africa's larger and more spectacular butterfly species is the Table Mountain beauty or mountain pride butterfly, *Aeropetes tulbaghia* (Nymphalidae, fig. 2.67), which feeds on the nectar of a large variety of flowers. It has been shown to be the only lepidopteran pollinator in southern Africa that is attracted to entirely red flowers, including some beautiful, very rare and range-restricted species in the Fynbos Biome.

Aeropetes tulbaghia is widespread along the cooler eastern highlands of southern Africa and is a fairly common and prominent member of the Fynbos butterfly fauna, which is generally poorer than in other parts of southern Africa. The sunbird fauna, which represents the most prominent group of nectar-feeding birds in the country, is also poorer in the Fynbos than in other parts of the region, so this may have provided the selective pressure on various plant species to attract butterflies as an alternative pollinator.

The plants known to be pollinated by *A. tulbaghia* all have morphologically similar red flowers, although they are unrelated. This pollination guild contains 20 species in eight genera and four families, including *Crassula coccinea* (Crassulaceae, fig. 2.68a) and species of *Brunsvigia, Cyrtanthus* (Amaryllidaceae, fig. 2.68b), *Gladiolus* (Iridaceae, fig. 2.68c) and *Disa* (Orchidaceae, fig. 2.4b).

Although the red colour of flowers in this guild is typical of bird pollination, the flowers' morphology prevents birds from feeding on them. Bird-pollinated flowers typically have a curved, horizontal tube with anthers arching over the top of the flower in a position that deposits pollen on the feeding bird's head. The *Aeropetes* guild flowers, on the other hand, have straight, narrow, erect floral tubes. The anthers are placed so they deposit pollen on the butterfly's proboscis, body or legs. The nectar is dilute and has a low viscosity compared to that of, for example, bee-pollinated plants. This enables the butterfly to suck up the nectar easily through its long, narrow proboscis. Other butterflies, of which there are several species of similar size and activity cycle to *A. tulbaghia*, ignore the red flowers as they are attracted to blue-white flowers. The *Aeropetes* pollinator guild of flowers thus excludes other potential pollinators by specialised morphology (birds) and red colour (other insects).

The advantages to the plants of having a single specialised pollinator are that they do not waste pollen collected by the wrong pollinators, neither do their stamens get clogged by pollen from other species. Furthermore, some of the plants that *A. tulbaghia* pollinates are rare in the communities in which they occur, so the bright red flowers clearly advertise their presence, making efficient location and successful pollination by the butterflies easier.

Pollination by wasp deception

'Wasp' is a general term for many groups of Hymenoptera with numerous diverse species; some are large and familiar flower visitors, others are minute seldom-seen parasites of all life stages of a wide range of insect species. Adults of all species feed on fluids, either of their host in parasitic species, or on nectar and various other plant exudates. Many nectar-feeding wasps pollinate the flowers they visit.

2.69 The spider-hunting wasp *Hemipepsis capensis* (Pompilidae) specialises in large spider prey.

2.70 A baboon spider, *Harpactira chrysogaster* (Arachnida: Theraphosidae), parasitised by the spider-hunting wasp *Hemipepsis capensis*. The wasp's egg is visible on the spider's abdomen.

2.71 *Hemipepsis* wasps (Pompilidae) are important pollinators of some fynbos flowers.

2.72 *Podalonia canescens* (Sphecidae) is a widespread caterpillar-hunting sand wasp that pollinates *Disa atricapilla* in the Fynbos. Pollen is visible on the head and body.

2.73 The insect with the longest front legs compared to body size: a female *Rediviva emdeorum* bee (Melittidae). Her front legs are adapted for harvesting oil deep inside tubular flowers. The yellow setae on the front tarsi soak up the oil, which is pressed by the yellow setal pads on the flexed middle legs in flight, then stored in transit in the hairy scopae on the hind legs. Body length about 15mm, leg length about 20mm.

2.74 A *Rediviva* oil-collecting bee (Melittidae) harvesting floral oil deep inside a *Diascia* flower. The hind leg with a yellow 'oil-pad' (scopa) for transporting the oil back to the nest is clearly visible.

The flowers of certain plants attract only male wasps that are deceived by the flowers' shape and smell. The wasps attempt to copulate with the flowers and in so doing the flowers are pollinated in a phenomenon termed 'pollination by sexual deception'. These flowers usually don't produce nectar, so there is no reward for the wasp (see box opposite).

The phenomenon is not as common in southern Africa as it is elsewhere, but has been recorded in the Apocynaceae, Hyacinthaceae and Orchidaceae, involving spider-hunting wasps of the family Pompilidae. One species of Sphecidae (mud-daubers or sand wasps), *Podalonia canescens*, pollinates Orchidaceae flowers in a similar way. Apocynaceae and Orchidaceae species pollinated by wasps share the ability to either glue or clip pollinia onto the hairless parts of wasp bodies.

Some of the largest Pompilidae species belong to the genus *Hemipepsis* (fig. 2.69) and fly with a characteristic loud rattling noise. They attack some of the region's largest spiders, for example, baboon spiders, *Harpactira* (Arachnida: Theraphosidae, fig. 2.70), and rain spiders, *Palystes* (Arachnida: Sparassidae). The females of some species will sting and paralyse a spider before dragging it to their nest and laying an egg in it; the wasp larva feeds and develops inside the paralysed spider. In other species, the wasp lays an egg on an active spider and the emergent larva then sucks the body fluids of the spider from the outside. Adults feed on nectar and are common flower visitors (fig. 2.71). *Podalonia canescens* (Sphecidae) females hunt on plants or in leaf litter for caterpillars (fig. 2.72) with which they provision their single-celled nests dug in the soil, placing a paralysed caterpillar in each cell.

Remarkable oil-collecting bees

The solitary bee genus *Rediviva* (Hymenoptera: Melittidae) is endemic to South Africa and comprises 25 species. Like all Melittidae, they nest in underground cavities excavated by the female. It is the only bee genus in the world in which the females of some species have evolved elongated forelegs.

Rediviva bees are about the size of honey bees, *Apis mellifera*. The females of some species have normally proportioned legs (e.g. *R. gigas*, *R. rufocincta*), but others have long to very long forelegs. For example, *R. longimanus* females have a body length of 14mm and forelegs of 19mm; *R. emdeorum* females have a body length of about 15mm, while their forelegs are 20mm long (fig. 2.73). The middle and hind legs in long-foreleged species are normal. Males have normal-length legs.

The females of all *Rediviva* species collect oil – not nectar – from oil-

Sexual deception by two *Disa* species

Although pollination by sexual deception is widespread amongst orchid species in other parts of the world, it has only been recorded a few times in southern Africa. Two closely related fynbos species, *Disa bivalvata* (fig. 2.75a) and *D. atricapilla* (fig. 2.75b), which are similar in many respects, were found to be pollinated by pompilid and sphecid wasps. The two orchid species have overlapping geographic ranges, where they occur together in similar habitats of seasonally wet seeps or swamps; they also have overlapping flowering times. In spite of their ecological overlap, hybrids between these two orchid species are rare, implying that their pollination systems are effective.

Both species are fragrant, although *D. bivalvata* is more so than *D. atricapilla*; the scent is produced mainly by the petals. Their flowers differ considerably in the shape, orientation and colour of the lateral sepals. The flowers of both species absorb ultraviolet light strongly, but in *D. atricapilla*, the back of the sepal is shiny in the visible and ultraviolet ranges, which is thought to mimic the shine from a pair of folded insect wings; this is lacking in *D. bivalvata*.

Disa atricapilla is pollinated by *Podalonia canescens* (Sphecidae) males, which exhibit typical mate-seeking behaviour when visiting the flowers. They patrol plants repeatedly, hover, inspect and probe the flower, particularly where the petals come together over the anthers – the site of maximum scent production, and where the flower's pollinaria are attached to the underside of the wasp (see box, p. 74). Wasps were recorded carrying 1–30 pollinaria, with an average of about 11. When foraging on other plant species, male wasps behave quite differently, landing on flowers and feeding for some time.

Disa bivalvata is pollinated by males of *Hemipepsis hilaris*. They behave in a similar way to *P. canescens* males, collecting pollinaria in the process; females of the species do not visit the flowers at all.

The evidence for the wasp behaviour at flowers being a result of deception lies in the following:
- mate-seeking behaviour by males;
- lack of any floral reward for the wasp;
- repeated visits to nonrewarding flowers (as seen by the large numbers of pollinaria carried by wasps); and
- absence of females visiting the flowers.

2.75 (a) *Disa bivalvata* (Orchidaceae) is pollinated by a *Hemipepsis* spider-hunting wasp. (b) *D. atricapilla*, a Fynbos endemic, is pollinated by the sand wasp *Podalonia canescens*.

secreting flowers (fig. 2.74) in the iris (Iridaceae), orchid (Orchidaceae) and foxglove (Scrophulariaceae) families. Various genera in these families are members of floral guilds adapted for pollination by particular *Rediviva* species, some of which are specialists on a single plant species, while others harvest oils from different plant groups within the same guild (see box, p. 86). About

140 species of plant in 14 genera are thought to be associated with *Rediviva* species. The bees' association with oil-producing plants has been well studied in South Africa, mainly by the botanist Kim Steiner (of the National Botanical Institute, now part of SANBI) and the late entomologist Vin Whitehead (of the former South African Museum, now the Iziko Museum).

The female bees have various morphological adaptations for collecting oil. They soak up the oil with pads of setae (hairs) on their foretarsi, which are inserted simultaneously into flowers, most of which have two floral spurs. (There is a strong correlation between bee foreleg length and floral spur length.) During flight, the oil is transferred from the oil-laden forelegs to the scopae (a dense covering of absorbent setae) on the hind legs (fig. 2.74), added to pollen and transported to the nest. The mixture of oil and pollen is used as larval food. Males have no scopae and feed on nectar from other plant species.

The relationship between oil bees and *Diascia* species

Diascia (Scrophulariaceae, fig. 2.76) is a southern African endemic plant genus with about 70 species, of which many are restricted to the Fynbos. Most species are low-growing annuals, often with brightly coloured flowers. The flowers have two characteristic spurs at the back, hence their popular name of twinspur.

Diascia flowers do not produce nectar: instead, the spurs contain oil that attracts long-legged *Rediviva* bees. There is a strong correlation between the length of the floral spur and that of the pollinating bee's foreleg – only these bees can access the oil. The flowers also have one or two translucent pouches or windows at the upper part of the corolla. By placing their head against these patches, pollinating bees assume the correct position to reach the oil in the spurs.

2.76 Species of twinspur, *Diascia* (Scrophulariaceae), that secrete floral oil at the end of deep tubes (spurs) have switched from attracting pollinators with nectar to providing oil to specialist long-legged bees in the genus *Rediviva*.

Herbivores

As a group, insect herbivores in the Fynbos are probably less well represented than in some other biomes. There are, nevertheless, various endemic groups that feed either externally (grasshoppers, caterpillars, leaf beetles) or on the internal sap and tissues (e.g. leafhoppers) of fynbos plants. There is a small group of insects specifically associated with the endemic Fynbos family Restionaceae; here we discuss the endemic grasshopper genus *Betiscoides* and the endemic sap-feeding restio leafhoppers *Cephalelus* and *Duospina*.

Secretive grasshoppers

Although grasshoppers (Orthoptera: Caelifera: Acridoidea) are one of the most important groups of herbivorous, mostly grass-feeding, insects (see 'Plague locusts', p. 165; 'Feeding in grasshoppers', p. 190), little has been written about the ecology of nonpest species, of which southern Africa has a very rich fauna (see 'Sound production in bladder grasshoppers', p. 115; 'Sound production in rain locusts', p. 117; 'Camouflage in toad and stone grasshoppers', p. 117). The small family Lentulidae, endemic to southern and East Africa (figs 2.77, 2.78), is one of about 10 grasshopper families. The family contains 150 species, of which about 100 occur in southern Africa, particularly in the Fynbos and Succulent Karoo biomes and in the grassland foothills of the Drakensberg.

All Lentulidae are wingless, and most are small grasshoppers with a strict association with particular plant species. Their small size and secretive habits of living deep inside their host plants mask the very high species richness in the family. The high species diversity can probably be attributed to speciation events stimulated by their lack of wings and consequent low dispersal abilities, as well as to their apparent association with particular plant species. American researcher Dan Otte is discovering tens of new species annually, particularly along the Drakensberg escarpment, but also in the Fynbos and Succulent Karoo biomes, so the true number of species in the group is in fact substantially higher than can currently be quoted.

The basic ecology and conservation status of two of the three species of the fynbos genus *Betiscoides* have been studied. The genus has a strict association with Restionaceae. Both *Betiscoides meridionalis* (fig. 2.79) and *B. parva* are morphologically extremely well adapted to the long leaf blades of restios. They are slender (15–42mm long) and wingless, and depend on their cryptic colours and tactic of dodging behind leaf blades to avoid threats. These grasshoppers seldom jump or leave the security of the plants on which they

2.77 A small, wingless grasshopper of the Lentulidae, a family that is highly diverse in the Fynbos Biome.

2.78 A mating pair of Lentulidae, illustrating the sexual dimorphism typical of the family.

Jonathan Ball

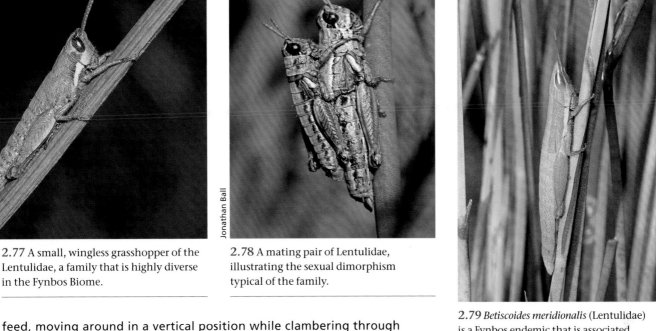

2.79 *Betiscoides meridionalis* (Lentulidae) is a Fynbos endemic that is associated with restios; the species is threatened by transformation of the biome.

Willem Augustyn

feed, moving around in a vertical position while clambering through the vegetation. Females descend to lay eggs in the damp soil in which the restios grow.

Betiscoides meridionalis is the larger of the two species, with males about 37.5mm and females 42.5mm long; *B. parva* males are 15mm and females about 18.5mm long. Males are more agile than females, and move greater cumulative distances, although usually less than a total of 15m per day; females seldom move more than 0.5m per day. Since the plants and their immediate vicinity have all the resources necessary for the grasshoppers to complete their life cycle, there is little pressure on them to move far – a factor that contributes to small populations being maintained in isolated fragments of undisturbed restio stands. On the other hand, populations are easily disturbed when their habitat is destroyed. Both species are threatened by increasing urbanisation, increased human-induced fire frequencies and invasion by nonindigenous plant species.

Restio leafhoppers

Restio leafhoppers (Hemiptera: Auchenorrhyncha: Cicadellidae: Ulopinae: Cephalelini) are probably members of an ancient Gondwanan lineage of leafhoppers that are exclusively associated with Restionaceae; species are known from South Africa, Australia and New Zealand. There are two genera in South Africa: *Cephalelus* (fig. 2.80), with 16 species, and *Duospina*, with three, and all occur only in the Fynbos.

The leafhoppers are 5–14mm long and their main distinguishing characteristic is their stick-like shape and extremely elongated head. Camouflage appears to be their main form of protection against predators: their brown colour and shape closely mimic the dry, sharp leaf sheaths at each node along the stems of restios. Unlike other leafhoppers, they are poor jumpers; additionally, all males are wingless, as are most females (96–97%). Interestingly, the proportion of winged females in the populations increases towards the end of summer, probably as a strategy to escape from fire or to colonise new growth after fires.

2.80 The Fynbos endemic restio leafhopper *Cephalelus uncinatus* (Cicadellidae: Ulopinae: Cephalelini) on its host plant *Hypodiscus aristatus* (Restionaceae). The extremely elongated head appears to increase the insect's general similarity to its host plant.

Detritivores

Woody fynbos plants are mostly evergreen, so detritus builds up fairly slowly. This slow build-up of plant matter is one of the reasons for the relatively long intervals between natural fires in the biome. The detritus that does collect contains plant chemical residues, and although high levels of plant chemicals deter many potential detritus feeders, endemic cockroaches and termites (see 'Social structure of a termite colony', p. 70) are important elements of the detritus fauna.

Cockroaches as essential detritivores

Most people are familiar with cockroaches and consider them loathsome and believe them to be associated with unhygienic conditions. However, this stereotype applies only to a handful of what are mostly cosmopolitan species, such as the German cockroach, *Blattella germanica* (fig. 2.81). Many species indigenous to the southern African region live far removed from humans and have interesting life styles.

Cockroaches (Blattodea: Blattoidae) represent one of the oldest surviving groups of modern insects. They and their early cockroach-like (roachoid) ancestors dominated the insect fauna for about 200 million years, but only a relatively small number (about 4,600 species) exist today. Early roachoids were among the most abundant insects of the Carboniferous (320mya) and were common into the Cretaceous (about 120mya), when the modern cockroach families evolved. Since then they have gradually declined in relative abundance compared to many other insect groups.

DNA studies have shown a close relationship between cockroaches (Blattoidae) and termites (Termitoidae; see 'Social structure of a termite colony', p. 70), which is now reflected in their classification in one order, Blattodea. Cockroaches mostly live as solitary individuals, although the adults and nymphs of the primitive cockroach *Cryptocercus* (Cryptocercidae) live in family groups for several years (see box opposite). By contrast, all termites are social insects living in colonies of hundreds or thousands of members and have four distinct castes that have different, well-defined duties (see 'Social structure of a termite colony', p. 70).

Although cockroaches are primarily found in association with plants and amongst plant litter, some species have adapted to life in deserts where they are capable of burrowing into the sand to avoid heat and dry conditions; a few unusual species are semiaquatic, with diving and swimming adaptations; others have adapted to life deep inside dark caves.

One of the main characteristics of cockroaches is that most species are omnivorous detritus feeders with the ability to digest cellulose. Omnivory has allowed some species to become synanthropic (associated with humans). They feed on a wide range of foodstuffs in and around the house, including refuse. This may lead to food contamination by mechanical transmission of various human pathogens, such as bacteria – a factor that fuels the widespread revulsion with which they are regarded.

Cockroaches have a high reproductive turnover, aided by the production of a leathery substance from the female's reproductive accessory glands that encases the eggs when they are laid to form the protective ootheca (fig. 2.82), and parental care of the offspring further enhances fecundity. In the relatively sheltered human environment, numbers may increase considerably after an infestation and populations may remain high without effective control measures. Even though cockroaches are mostly solitary insects, all species demonstrate some measure of gregariousness or tolerance of other conspecifics, and many live as family groups for extended periods.

2.81 The German cockroach, *Blattella germanica* (Blattodea: Ectobiidae), is the most common household cockroach in southern Africa.

2.82 Cockroach oothecae, deposited by the female inside the secure location of an old moth cocoon.

2.83 A female Madagascan hissing cockroach, *Gromphadorhina portentosa* (Blaberidae), one of few insects that 'hisses' by blowing air under pressure through its spiracles.

Cryptocercus (fig. 2.84) is a small genus of nine species, commonly known as wood-roaches. They are found in temperate forests of the USA and eastern Asia. Family groups of about 20 individuals live in burrows in rotten wood, on which they also feed. They are the most primitive living cockroaches and share several characteristics with primitive termites, hinting at a close phylogenetic link between them. One of the most important of these is the shared presence of cellulose-digesting flagellated protozoa in the gut: these two groups are the only insects known to have specific intestinal protozoans for digesting wood. Another characteristic is the long time that the cockroach adults and nymphs live together and the intimate association between them; this probably led to colonial living in termites.

Cryptocercus species live in family groups consisting of a male and female and their similar-aged offspring of one reproductive season. Although as many as 75 nymphs may emerge from up to four oothecae (egg cases) produced over a short period, mortality of especially the youngest nymphs reduces the number of colony members to about 20 over time. The freshly emerged nymphs (neonates) immediately start to congregate around the anal chamber of the parents where they imbibe liquid anal secretions infused with symbiotic gut protozoa. This process, termed anal trophallaxis, is the mechanism by which succeeding generations of cockroaches (and primitive termites) acquire the gut symbionts on which they depend for cellulose digestion.

The nymphs (of which there are probably five instars) continue to feed intermittently on parental anal fluids and faecal pellets for the first year of their lives; these are believed to supplement the nutritional content of their food since their own digestion mechanisms may take longer to become fully functional. Only from about the third instar are the nymphs capable of subsisting independently on their wood diet. Nymphs spend as much as 20% of their time grooming the adults, during which they probably acquire additional cuticular nutritional or pheromonal secretions. These factors may be part of the reason why a monogamous pair of parents and their offspring remain together for such an inordinately long time compared to almost all other insects (but similar to termites). Adults die at about the time that the nymphs mature and start to disperse (3–6 years).

2.84 *Cryptocercus wrighti* (Blattodea: Cryptocercidae), a primitive wood-eating cockroach from the southeastern USA, with subsocial behaviour and other characteristics shared with primitive termites (Blattodea: Termitoidae).

Cockroach families

Indigenous southern African cockroaches, of which there are about 200 known species, belong to four families: Corydiidae (formerly Polyphagidae), Ectobiidae (formerly Blattellidae), Blaberidae, and Blattidae.

The most common pest species in the region are all introduced. They are the German cockroach, *Blattella germanica* (Ectobiidae, fig. 2.81), the American cockroach, *Periplaneta americana* (although it is actually an African species; Blattidae), the Oriental cockroach, *Blatta orientalis* (also probably of African origin; Blattidae), and the Madeira cockroach, *Rhyparobia maderae* (formerly *Leucophaea maderae*, also of African origin; Blaberidae; see 'Cockroaches', p. 397).

The recent, growing interest in the micro-pet trade has also led to the introduction into South Africa of Madagascan hissing cockroaches (fig. 2.83), *Gromphadorhina portentosa* (Blaberidae). These are amongst the world's largest cockroaches (60–70mm long). They live in large family groups and hiss loudly when alarmed, but are gentle and easy to care for. There is concern in some quarters that escapees may eventually establish in the wild and start to compete with indigenous species.

The largest of the southern African species, the giant or Table Mountain cockroach, *Aptera fusca* (Blaberidae), is 30–40mm long and widespread in fynbos vegetation. In common with many other blaberids, *A. fusca* is strongly sexually dimorphic – males are smaller than females and winged (fig. 2.85a); females are wingless (fig. 2.85b). Another unusual cockroach known from Table Mountain is the Table Mountain leaproach, *Saltoblattella montistabularis* (Ectobiidae; see box, p. 91).

Breeding and parental care in cockroaches

Female cockroaches deposit eggs into an egg case (ootheca) from which the neonates emerge. If the ootheca is extruded externally before the eggs hatch (fig. 2.86), the process is considered to be oviparous; this occurs in all families except Blaberidae and in some species of Ectobiidae. In the exceptions, an ootheca with undeveloped embryos is extruded, then almost immediately retracted into a uterus or brood sac where the eggs continue to develop. Neonates then hatch internally from the eggs and emerge directly from the female – a process termed ovovivipary. Most cockroaches reproduce after mating, but parthenogenesis has also been recorded.

Parental care of some form is ubiquitous across the Blattoidae, and includes one or more of the following:

- preparing concealed 'nursery' burrows in which oothecae are deposited (in forest floor species);
- concealing oothecae with debris and faeces after gluing them to the substrate;
- carrying the ootheca (by the female) until it has hardened;
- retaining eggs in the female's brood sac or uterus until they hatch;
- protecting and providing the developing embryos with nutrients and water while they are still in the ootheca;
- feeding the neonates; and
- caring for nymphs until maturity.

Oviparous cockroaches may carry the ootheca externally for various lengths of time; they either drop it soon after extrusion (e.g. *Blatta orientalis*, *Periplaneta americana*), or carry it throughout embryonic development and drop it just before the eggs hatch. *Blattella germanica* neonates emerge from the ootheca while it is still attached to the female. If the ootheca remains attached to the female during embryonic development, water and (possibly) some nutrients are still passed from the female to the embryos. These oothecae are usually dark and strong, constructed from tanned proteinaceous materials produced by the female's accessory (or colleterial) reproductive glands.

In all Blaberidae (fig. 2.88) and a few Ectobiidae, the eggs develop inside the mother's body using yolk deposited at the earliest stages of embryogenesis, although water and (possibly) extra nutrients also pass from the mother to the embryos during their development. When the nymphs are ready to hatch, a thin, soft, pale ootheca is extruded from which they emerge (e.g. *Rhyparobia maderae*, *Gromphadorhina portentosa*).

The ootheca and eggs represent a large investment in energy and protein by the female (up to 50% of her body weight). To regain some nutrition, the female eats the ootheca, unviable eggs and egg shells after the neonates have hatched. In some species, the neonates consume the membranous oothecal lining as their first meal. The ootheca (fig. 2.89) typically has a dorsal keel (crista), which is a line of weakness formed by pressure of the ovipositor valves during its formation. The eggs lie in rows along the keel. Prior to emergence, the hatchlings inhale air and simultaneously exert pressure on the keel, which then opens to allow them to emerge.

Neonates are usually pale and lightly sclerotised, but most darken quickly. Those of some Blaberidae remain with the mother for at least the duration of the first instar, during which time she feeds them on anal secretions; others remain together in small family groups until the nymphs mature.

2.85 The giant cockroach, *Aptera fusca* (Blattodea: Blaberidae), is the largest indigenous cockroach in southern Africa and occurs in the Fynbos: **(a)** winged male; **(b)** wingless female.

2.86 Female Ectobiidae cockroach extruding an ootheca just before the hatchlings emerge.

The Table Mountain leaproach

One very unusual South African species has evolved specially adapted leg structures to facilitate jumping and landing after a jump, most probably as a defence strategy.

Saltoblattella montistabularis (Ectobiidae, fig. 2.87) was discovered on Table Mountain in the Fynbos Biome by Mike Picker of the University of Cape Town and colleagues as recently as 2010. (Subsequently, more undescribed species have been found further afield, including in Namaqualand.)

These small (7–9mm long) reddish-brown cockroaches are characterised by dramatically lengthened hind tibiae and femurs. The femurs are greatly enlarged to accommodate the muscles required for executing huge jumps – up to 48 times the insect's body length. The underside of the femur has a longitudinal groove into which the tibia is retracted to provide maximum flexion prior to a jump, and the euplantulae (pads under the tarsi) have special papillae that are thought to cushion the landing after a jump.

Table Mountain leaproaches live amongst vegetation, as do grasshoppers, to which they are ecologically similar; however, while grasshoppers are mainly herbivorous, the cockroaches are thought to feed mostly on bird faeces adhering to the plants on which they live.

2.87 The Table Mountain leaproach, *Saltoblattella montistabularis* (Blattodea: Ectobiidae), is a highly specialised cockroach endemic to the Fynbos Biome.

2.88 Female Blaberidae cockroaches are ovoviviparous: eggs hatch internally and females give birth to live young.

2.89 Cockroach ootheca (Blattodea: Ectobiidae) showing the keel along which the eggs lie; the keel opens under pressure when the hatchlings inhale, thus allowing them to emerge.

Cockroach defence mechanisms

Although cockroaches often live in sheltered places (amongst plant litter, under bark or other objects) that give them some protection from predators, most are fast-moving, agile insects that depend on speed to avoid attack; even flight-capable species run and hide rather than fly to escape.

Nymphs of the tropical African gregarious spotted cockroach, *Cartoblatta pulchra* (Blattidae, fig. 2.90), remain together in a tightly knit group throughout their development. These shiny black cockroaches produce noxious defensive secretions. Aggregation enhances the white and orange speckles that advertise their distastefulness to potential predators.

Some cockroach species have added sound to their defensive arsenal. The Madagascan hissing cockroach, *Gromphadorhina portentosa* (Blaberidae), is named for this defence mechanism, but it is also known in other (including some indigenous) species. The sound is produced by expelling air through specialised abdominal spiracles in a system unique to cockroaches among the Insecta.

2.90 Defence in numbers: an aggregation of nymphs of the tropical African spotted cockroach, *Cartoblatta pulchra* (Blattodea: Blattidae). Their bright colours warn would-be predators of the noxious repellent chemicals they produce.

Predators

Similar suites of predatory insects are found in the Fynbos as in other biomes, but there are some in the region that are highly unusual, including owlflies and predatory butterfly larvae.

Peculiar owlflies

The owlflies *Proctarrelabis capensis* (Neuroptera: Ascalaphidae, figs 2.91, 2.92) and *Nephoneura capensis* (fig. 2.93) are spectacular predatory Fynbos insects. There are about 60 described owlfly species known from southern Africa, but more await description. Although they are widespread across the region, individuals are seldom common.

Ascalaphidae adults often have hairy, mottled bodies and wings, with a wingspan of 45–80mm. They are characterised by very long clubbed antennae that are about as long as the forewing (fig. 2.94).

Their larvae are equally impressive; they are dorsoventrally flattened and often spectacularly

2.91 A female owlfly, *Proctarrelabis capensis* (Neuroptera: Ascalaphidae), a Fynbos endemic.

2.92 Mature *Proctarrelabis capensis* larva.

2.93 The owlfly *Nephoneura capensis*, another Fynbos endemic.

2.94 Beautiful owlflies from across southern Africa: **(a)** *Proctolyra hessei*; **(b)** *Helcopteryx rhodiogramma*; **(c)** *Melambrotus papio*; **(d)** *Strixomyia manselli*; **(e)** *Tmesibasis laceratus*; **(f)** *Imparomitis* sp.

sculptured with scalloped and hairy bodies that provide excellent camouflage against their resting background. Their massive mandibles are capable of opening up to 180° (fig. 2.92). They also have well-developed stemmata (simple eyes), which may allow better vision than the mere distinction between light and dark usually attributed to eyes of this type.

Both larval and adult Ascalaphidae are predators; most species are generalists, but the larvae of a few species appear to prefer certain prey.

Ascalaphidae adults are most active at dusk when they hawk prey on the wing, much like dragonflies (Odonata) do. When inactive, adults tend to use the same place to rest, which they often do over prolonged periods; they sit in a characteristic pose with the abdomen held up at a right angle to the thorax and the wings hanging down away from the body. They are occasionally attracted to lights in the early evening, but seldom remain there for long, flying off again almost immediately.

Females (fig. 2.95a) lay large batches of eggs (fig. 2.95b) in the appropriate habitat for larval life (e.g. on grass, branches, the underside of rocks), and larval body colour patterns closely match the background where they will spend their lives (figs 2.95d–f). Newly emerged larvae are mostly black and superficially look like bunches of ticks (fig. 2.95c), remaining clumped for the duration of the first instar, after which they disperse and start to feed.

Predatory butterfly larvae

The vast majority of Lepidoptera species have fairly simple larval feeding behaviour with most feeding on living plant tissues, while some atypical species feed on animal tissues, either as predators of sessile insects such as scale insects (Coccoidea), or on animal remains like fur, feathers or horns (see 'Final-stage carcass colonisers', p. 252) or wool and spiderwebs (see 'Clothes moths', p. 401; 'Household case-bearers', p. 401).

By contrast, most members of the Lycaenidae, one of the largest butterfly families (as in other parts of the world), have complex larval feeding biology: some species feed on plants but also have an intimate association with a particular ant species, living and feeding on ant brood in the ants' nest

2.95 Life cycle of the savanna owlfly *Ascalaphus bilineatus*: (**a**) an adult female after laying a batch of eggs; (**b**) eggs; (**c**) newly emerged first-instar larvae; (**d**) larvae remain clustered for much of their development; (**e**) a final-stage larva feeding on a syrphid fly; (**f**) a mature larva.

2.96 Southern Africa's smallest butterfly, *Oraidium barberae* (Lycaenidae); male wingspan about 10mm, female about 12mm.

2.97 Larvae of this *Thestor* species (Lycaenidae) are ant brood predators.

2.98 (a) Female woolly legs, *Lachnocnema bibulus* (Lycaenidae), preparing to lay eggs near scale insects on which the butterfly larvae prey; **(b)** *L. bibulus* larva with scale insect prey and attendant ants. The larva hides under a 'cloak' made with remains of its prey.

(myrmecophiles; see box, p. 99). Nearly half (47%) of all butterflies species in southern Africa belong to the Lycaenidae and it has been suggested that the high species diversity in the family is due to the complex feeding associations of the larvae. Lycaenidae are generally widespread in southern Africa but some are restricted to a particular biome, such as the Fynbos endemics (see 'Rare fynbos butterflies', p. 65).

Most Lycaenidae adults are small or medium-sized. The family includes the smallest butterfly species in the world: the western pygmy blue, *Brephidium exilis*, which is indigenous to North America. *Oraidium barberae* (fig. 2.96) is the smallest butterfly in southern Africa and the second-smallest in the world, and is one of the most widespread in the region.

Lycaenids are often brightly coloured in brilliant blue, violet, orange or red pigmentation, and sexes may differ greatly in colour. Many species have one to three pairs of delicate, hair-like tails on their hind wings which are usually associated with 'eyespots' on the under-surface of the wings (fig. 2.99). At rest, with the wings held upright, these spots and tails appear to be the head and antennae of the insect. This illusion is thought to divert predators from vital body parts, mainly the 'true' head. Specimens are often encountered with a wedge of wing in this area missing – the sign of a foiled bird attack.

Although the larvae of most species are primarily herbivores, about 75% of species either shelter in ant nests when not feeding on the host plant, or prey on ant stores or brood (kleptoparasites), or are fed by trophallaxis by the ants. Larvae may also be protected by ants while feeding on their host plant, which is usually close to the ant nest in which they shelter by day. In return for protection from predators and parasitoids and access to the ant nest, the lycaenid larvae provide the ants with appeasement substances produced by special 'honey' glands.

Many ant species have an intimate association with scale insects (Coccoidea; see 'Scale insects', p. 376), which they defend in return for the honeydew that they excrete. Some lycaenids, such as *Thestor* (fig. 2.97) and *Lachnocnema* (fig. 2.98a), have capitalised on this association by preying on the scale insects and simultaneously appeasing the attendant ants with their own secretions to mediate ant aggression. Some young *Thestor* larvae, such as *T. basutus*, feed on scale insects and then later switch to preying on the brood of the ants that attend the scale insects. The adults of *Lachnocnema*, which is a savanna genus closely related to *Thestor*, feed on honeydew secreted by scale insects. Their larvae live amongst the scale insects and their attendant ants (fig. 2.98b). They feed on the scale insects,

a

b

2.99 Lycaenidae species with prominent hairtails and eyespots:
(a) *Iolaus bowkeri*; (b) *Virachola dinochares*; (c) *Cigaritis namaqua*;
(d) *Hypolycaena philippus*; (e) *Axiocerses amanga*; (f) *Leptomyrina hirundo*; (g) *Lampides boeticus*.

Jonathan Ball

2.100 Lycaenidae species with ant-associated larvae that hide in ant nests: **(a)** *Aloeides apicalis*; **(b)** *Lepidochrysops plebeia*; **(c)** *Phasis thero*; **(d)** *A. damarensis*; **(e)** *Crudaria leroma*.

using specially modified forelegs to capture and hold their prey, but are ignored by the ants.

The association between lycaenids and ants (fig. 2.100) is an intimate and mostly obligatory dependence of the butterfly larvae on the ant species (figs 2.101, 2.102). It is based on a large measure of co-evolved tolerance of the larvae by the ants. To some extent, the butterfly larvae are chemically 'recognised' as ant larvae by the ants. This leads worker ants to feed them, or to ignore them when they prey on ant brood (see box opposite).

Although the butterfly larvae hide in the nest (fig. 2.103) and are mostly able to appease their host ants, they may still be subjected to attack by these or other ant species. This has exerted strong selection pressure on lycaenid larvae to develop defence mechanisms against ant bites:

- their cuticle is up to 20 times thicker than that of similar-sized larvae in other lepidopteran groups;
- they can retract their head under a sclerotised thoracic plate;
- various surface or extensible glands produce chemical appeasement substances that mediate ant attacks;
- some larvae have organs that produce sounds thought to mimic ant communication signals (see box opposite); and
- the larvae differ behaviourally from other members of the order: they move slowly and have a reduced 'thrashing response' (a common alarm signal in many Lepidoptera larvae), possibly because sudden movement may attract the attention of aggressive ants and provoke an attack.

In contrast to the larvae, freshly emerged adults of species that eclose (emerge) inside ant nests are not usually tolerated by the ants. To enable them to escape from the nest and avoid damage from ant attack, they may be covered in a layer of loose, slippery scales (known as eclosion wool) that become tangled in the ants' mouthparts and slip through their tarsi when they attempt to grasp the butterfly. These scales are shed when the adult inflates and spreads its wings in a protected position outside the nest.

Lycaenid communication with ants

Lycaenid larvae possess two highly specialised sets of organs that are used to manipulate ant behaviour: glands that produce chemical appeasement substances, and sound-producing organs that communicate mechanical signals. The chemicals and sounds influence ant behaviour by suppressing aggression, eliciting food, or exciting the ants into a defensive posture to stand guard over the larvae when threatened.

Glands

Most species have a median dorsal nectary organ or 'honey gland' on the seventh abdominal segment and a pair of dorsolateral eversible tentacle organs on either side of the eighth segment, while all known species have patches of small epidermal glands on various parts of the body.

The honey gland substance was initially thought to be similar to the honeydew produced by aphids, scale insects and other Hemiptera, but honeydew consists mainly of various sugars derived from the sap of the host plant, whereas honey gland secretions contain mainly amino acids.

The functions of the dorsolateral eversible organs are less clear. It has been suggested that they may produce substances that advertise to ants the presence of caterpillars with honeydew, or that they may deter over-persistent ants trying to obtain secretions from the honey gland, or produce a substance that mimics an ant alarm pheromone.

The epidermal glands are thought to produce volatile chemicals that mimic the brood pheromone of their host ants.

Sound organs

The larvae and pupae of various Lycaenidae species produce sound, apparently in concert with the chemical appeasement substances, as part of their adaptations to communicate with, and mediate attack from, ants.

Larval sound production appears to be widespread amongst lycaenid species, but is poorly studied. Where known, it is a slow drumming sound and communication with ants is probably by vibrations through the substrate, although there does appear to be an audible airborne component. It has been shown to be of similar pulse length and frequency to that of alarm drumming by their host ants.

Although it seems surprising that largely immobile Lepidoptera pupae can produce sound, the phenomenon is actually widespread among different families. All Lycaenidae pupae that have been examined have sound-producing organs and produce a sound when they wriggle after disturbance. Their stridulatory organs have the same basic structure as in many other insects that produce sound – they consist of a simple 'file' with numerous teeth, and a hardened plate, the scraper, which is drawn across the file to produce sound. In Lycaenidae pupae, the stridulatory organ is found between abdominal segments 4 and 5, 5 and 6, or 6 and 7. Pupae may produce one of three signals when they wriggle: a so-called primary signal (audible to humans) produced by all species; a secondary, lower-amplitude signal consisting of a set of clicks produced in bursts; and a tertiary signal which is only readily audible in large pupae. Sound production is thought to act primarily as a deterrent to predators and parasitoids. There is also some evidence to suggest that the calls may recruit ants.

2.101 *Anthene* sp. (Lycaenidae) larva attended by a *Myrmicaria natalensis* ant.

2.102 The relationship between some species of Lycaenidae larvae with ants is facultative rather than obligatory: (a) *Azanus moriqua* larva attended by a *Pheidole* sp. ant; (b) a freshly emerged adult *A. moriqua*.

2.103 The larvae of the southern African endemic Lycaenidae genus *Chrysoritis* hide in the nests of ants (*Crematogaster* spp.) where most are fed by their hosts: (**a**) *Chrysoritis chrysaor*, one of the more widespread species; (**b**) *C. thysbe*, a coastal Fynbos endemic; (**c**) *C. zonarius* from coastal Renosterveld; (**d**) *C. chrysantas*, an arid-adapted Karoo species; (**e**) *Chrysoritis* sp. larva from high-mountain fynbos; (**f**) *C. palmus* adult, a common lowland and montane Fynbos species.

Myrmecophiles: from benign to parasitic

Ant colonies are host to numerous insect species that live in their nests (termed myrmecophiles) with complex interactions that can be benign, parasitic or predatory in effect. Benign myrmecophiles present no threat to the ants and are simply ignored. Parasitic species chemically mimic ant brood and are fed by workers when they solicit food; they often provide the ants with 'appeasement' secretions of their own to gain acceptance. Predatory invaders chemically placate ants at the nest entrance so they can gain entrance and then continue to appease workers in the nest with desirable secretions while they prey on workers or brood.

Some benign myrmecophiles live in refuse in the nest, for example, various fishmoth species (Zygentoma; see 'Fishmoths', p. 347). Fairly large beetles breed in the accumulations of detritus of large ant species. These include all members (about 60 species in southern Africa) of the Cremastocheilini (Scarabaeidae: Cetoniinae, fig. 2.104) and the rare dung beetle species *Megaponerophilus megaponerae* (Scarabaeidae: Scarabaeinae, fig. 7.78f).

Cremastocheilini larvae are benign detritivores and are tolerated in the nest by ants, but the adult beetles prey on ant brood and are attacked. They depend on force to enter nests and are equipped with thick body armour, short retractile legs and

2.105 This *Lecanoderus* beetle (Cremastocheilini) has withdrawn all its appendages to protect itself against an ant attack.

special grooves into which the antennae can be withdrawn for protection against ant attack (fig. 2.105). Ant-nest beetles (Carabidae: Paussinae) are also ant brood predators (see box, p. 164).

Some of the most specialised myrmecophiles are parasites. Some members of the large beetle family Staphylinidae are ant parasites, but their relationships with ants are poorly studied in southern Africa. The ant-associated members of the butterfly family Lycaenidae have been studied in more detail. The interactions of different lycaenid species with their ant hosts grade from parasitism to simple predation.

2.104 While the larvae of ant-associated beetles (Scarabaeidae: Cetoniinae: Cremastocheilini) are tolerated detritus feeders in ant nest refuse, the predatory adults use force to enter and leave nests and have robust, strongly sculptured bodies and retractile legs: (a) *Chthonobius conspersus*; (b) *Lecanoderus* sp.; (c) *Anatonochilus platycephalus*; (d) *Arielina peringueyi*; (e) *Scaptobius capensis*; (f) *Coenochilus turbatus*.

CHAPTER 3
SUCCULENT KAROO BIOME

The Succulent Karoo is well known for its extravagant carpets of daisy flowers (fig. 3.1) that attract thousands of tourists each spring. Other plants also offer spectacular displays and closer observation reveals an astounding diversity of dwarf succulent shrubs, including mesembs ('vygies' – fig. 3.2), euphorbs and stone plants, as well as many geophytes from the iris, orchid and hyacinth families. Iconic quiver trees punctuate the landscape on hills and rocky outcrops (fig. 3.3). About 5,000 of the more than 6,000 plant species that grow here are succulents (fig. 3.4) and 26% of these are endemic to the biome. This enormous plant diversity makes it the richest semidesert in the world.

3.1 (pp. 100–101) A typical spring scene in large parts of the Succulent Karoo with mostly annual daisy species (Asteraceae) in full bloom. (Photo: Mike Spies)

3.2 (above) A selection of mesembs or 'vygies' (Aizoaceae), which are extremely diverse in the Succulent Karoo and comprise a large proportion of the plants in the region. They may be annuals or perennials, but all have succulent leaves and bright, shiny flowers: (a) landscape with different *Cheiridopsis* species; (b) *Cheiridopsis* sp.; (c) *Conophytum* sp.; (d) *Drosanthemum* sp.

The Succulent Karoo lies in a wide swathe of semidesert inland and north of the Fynbos Biome, with which it shares its greatest floristic affinity. It is bordered in the east by the Nama-Karoo Biome and in the north by the Namib Desert. Most of the coastal and near-interior parts of the biome have low winter rainfall, generally lower than 200mm (rarely above 250mm), supplemented by regular coastal fog. The more distant inland areas receive rain predominantly during winter, but also some in summer. The summers are mostly hot and dry, with temperatures often reaching 45°C. Unlike the sandy soil of the Fynbos Biome, soils in the Succulent Karoo are fertile. The variety of habitats and vegetation patterns in the biome are largely dependent on soil chemistry and fertility.

The high insect diversity and endemicity can largely be attributed to the localised radiation of certain groups and many species with specialised traits have evolved in step with the diverse plant groups with which they retain tight relationships. Furthermore, upwards of 75% of the plants in the biome are insect-pollinated, so it is hardly surprising that there is a wide array of insects involved in diverse pollination strategies. However, the species richness also extends to groups that are possibly only indirectly plant-associated.

Some examples of specialised pollinators are monkey beetles, bee flies, pollen wasps, and ribbon- and spoon-winged lacewings. There are also detritus- and dung-feeding beetles and several groups of herbivores with specialised traits. Herbivores include beautiful brush beetles, gall-forming beetles and flies, bladder, toad and stone grasshoppers, as well as long-horned grasshoppers. Many of these species are preyed upon by katydids, ground beetles, robber flies, heelwalkers, scorpions and solifuges.

Although the sparse vegetation results in a fairly low accumulation of detritus, there is a characteristic fauna of detritus feeders, which includes termites and a highly atypical group of detritus-feeding dung beetles.

3.3 The iconic quiver tree or kokerboom, *Aloidendron dichotomum*, which grows on rocky outcrops and hills in the Succulent Karoo and Nama-Karoo biomes.

3.4 Although the bright floral displays in spring suggest a benign environment, much of the year is extremely hot and dry, and perennial plants need special adaptations to survive. Succulence is one of these strategies: **(a)** *Pachypodium namaquanum* (Apocynaceae); **(b)** *Avonia* sp. (Portulacaceae); **(c)** *Larryleachia perlata* (Apocynaceae); **(d)** *Crassula columella* (Crassulaceae); **(e)** *Euphorbia* sp. (Euphorbiaceae); **(f)** *Hoodia* sp. (Apocynaceae).

3.5 The Gifberg near Vanrhynsdorp in central Namaqualand. The pale circles in the foreground are termite-induced heuweltjies.

Nutrient recyclers

Harvester termites have undoubtedly had a greater impact on the soils and vegetation of the Succulent Karoo biome than any other organism. As with most termite species, their role as soil engineers has significant ecological importance in the area.

The heuweltjie termite

An obvious and important aspect of the landscape of the southwestern Cape and Namaqualand is the presence of heuweltjies (Afrikaans, meaning 'little hills'). These are circular hills or mounds, up to 20m in diameter, with soil and vegetation that are noticeably different from that of adjacent areas (fig. 3.5). They have convincingly been shown to be the sites of ancient, as well as present-day activity of the harvester termite *Microhodotermes viator* (Blattodea: Termitoidae: Hodotermitidae). Although *M. viator* also occurs in the Nama-Karoo Biome, its activity there seldom results in heuweltjies.

Heuweltjies are formed during nesting and mound-building by *M. viator* and develop over many years as soil enriched with organic matter by the termites' feeding activities and excretory products is brought up from below the surface (see box, p. 106). When the colony dies, the mound weathers away, leaving the heuweltjie slightly raised in the middle and composed of subsurface soil particles and nutrient-rich soil, which results in more nutritious plants growing on them.

Most *M. viator* colonies are active below ground and the only above-ground signs of activity are those typical of the Hodotermitidae: foragers

3.6 Twigs collected in excess of immediate needs: signs of activity by heuweltjie termites, *Microhodotermes viator*.

3.7 *Microhodotermes viator* workers active at a foraging burrow.

that emerge under suitable weather conditions, piles of twigs and other plant debris surrounding an emergence hole, and small dumps of excavated soil (figs 3.6–3.8) (for detailed biology of the family, see 'The large harvester termite', p. 177).

Microhodotermes viator workers excavate tunnels upwards and outwards in small interconnected cells of activity over an area of many metres from a central nest, and push the excavated soil into small piles on the soil surface through numerous pencil-thickness holes. Directly above the nest, the soil dumps from tunnelling activity are usually closer together. Over years, these piles may coalesce into large heaps of soil from which a circular mound grows in the centre. The circles occur in regular, evenly spaced spatial patterns, which are thought to be maintained by foraging competition between the colonies. Over centuries the colonies die out but are again re-colonised (fig. 3.9).

3.8 Typical signs of *Microhodotermes viator* activity: soil mounds from foraging burrow excavation.

Jenny Scholtz

Mike Spies

3.9 An aerial photograph showing an active *Microhodotermes viator* mound in the foreground and inactive old mounds developing into heuweltjies in the distance.

Jenny Scholtz

3.10 The early stages of heuweltjie formation. *Microhodotermes viator* mounds on the Knersvlakte near Vanrhynsdorp in Namaqualand.

Soil improvement by *Microhodotermes viator*

Foraging *Microhodotermes* termites gather plant material, which they bury in their burrow system. Their tunnelling behaviour and the accumulation of decomposing organic matter create more well-drained soil with increased pH and soil nutrition compared to intermound areas. These lead to a build-up of calcium, magnesium and silica over time. As the heuweltjie ages, calcium carbonate is leached and forms a hard (petrocalcic) layer at a shallow depth in the centre of the heuweltjie. Water flowing off the centre toward the edges raises the pH there and dissolves silica which then re-precipitates and hardens. The result is a 'hard-pan' under each mound.

The top layer of soil on the heuweltjies differs in colour from that of surrounding areas, as a result of the changed chemistry and termite frass (excrement). The soil texture is also changed by termite activity, with finer soil particles and increased clay and silt being brought to the surface during mound-building. Nitrogen levels are invariably higher on the mounds than in intermound areas, as are levels of phosphorus and potassium. Micronutrient levels are also consistently higher on heuweltjies than in surrounding areas.

Heuweltjies have higher soil water content than surrounding areas. Increased infiltration is made possible by termite tunnels, while organic material in the soil acts as a sponge, retaining water. (In eroded areas where soils have a high clay content, however, heuweltjies are baked hard by the sun and become large mounds of very hard, bare earth.)

Secondary animal activity on the mounds further increases water penetration and aeration. The physical, chemical and nutrient improvements of the soil lead to changes in plant composition: plants on heuweltjies have a higher nitrogen content and better nutritional value and palatability. These plants attract herbivores such as whistling rats, *Parotomys brantsii*. The rats affect the soil and secondary vegetation significantly by burrowing and adding more nutrients in the form of dung. Their burrows attract additional inhabitants. Predators, including snakes and mongooses, and numerous other small animals, such as lizards and beetles, shelter within the burrows or modify the soil properties further by their activities.

Over time, the mounds change dramatically in appearance and biodiversity compared to the surrounding areas.

Many heuweltjies are the result of ancient termite activity and are more than 4,000 years old, with the majority thought to have been formed 20,000–30,000 years ago. In many areas, though, new heuweltjies are still being formed by current termite activity.

Sheep have been shown to feed preferentially on the heuweltjies and, even after years of crops being grown in the same area, wheat yields, for example, remain consistently higher on them than in surrounding areas.

Heuweltjies may cover up to 25% of the surface area in certain parts of the Succulent Karoo Biome. They are often very dense (fig. 3.5), with up to hundreds per square kilometre. The density and size of the mounds seem to vary in direct proportion to the amount of rain that falls in the region. In arid areas, there are 200–300/km², increasing to 300–500/km² in areas with higher rainfall. The area of a mound is about 90m² in the drier parts of their range and about 500m² at the wettest extreme.

Some researchers have queried the involvement of *M. viator* in the formation of heuweltjies and have suggested that bush-clumps or an extinct termite species similar to the large savanna mound-builder *Macrotermes* must have been responsible. However, *Microhodotermes viator* is capable of building huge mounds 1.5m high and 3m across in some areas, for example, on the Knersvlakte

near Vanrhynsdorp in Namaqualand (fig. 3.10). Once termite activity has ceased, and the mounds have eroded, what is left is a heuweltjie several metres across with all the attributes discussed on the previous pages.

Pollinators

Based on its plant diversity, the Succulent Karoo is the richest semidesert in the world. More than 75% of the 6,000 plant species that occur in the biome are pollinated by insects. Many of these are visited by specialised pollinators such as ribbon- and spoon-winged lacewings, monkey beetles, bee flies and pollen wasps.

Ribbon- and spoon-winged lacewings

The Nemopteridae (Neuroptera) are a small but charismatic family of lacewings characterised by extended hind wings – an innovation that is unique amongst insects. The family consists of two distinctive subfamilies: the larger, free-living ribbon- and spoon-winged lacewings (Nemopterinae, figs 3.11, 3.13, respectively) and the smaller, much more gracile cave-dwelling thread-winged lacewings (Crocinae, fig. 3.12) (see 'Thread-winged lacewings', p. 350).

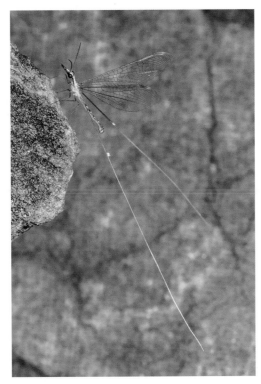

Southern Africa and the Succulent Karoo, in particular, are incredibly rich in Nemopterinae, especially diurnal species with extravagant hind wing morphology (see box, pp. 108–109; fig. 3.14). The 60-odd species in 12 genera represent about 60% of the global total; 94% of local species are endemic to the region. Members of eight genera are diurnal, the remainder nocturnal. Some species are fairly widespread, while others have very restricted ranges. Southern Namaqualand (Clanwilliam district) has seven endemic genera, a phenomenon ascribed to their evolutionary radiation in association with the high plant diversity of the area. In some regions, locals refer to them either as 'helikoptertjies' (little helicopters) or 'kruiwaentjies' (little wheelbarrows).

Many diurnal species have been seen feeding on flowers with an easily accessible 'landing platform', mainly smallish cup- or disc-shaped flowers that have readily available nectar or pollen. Most of the diurnal nemopterine species have a long rostrum and mouthparts elongated into a 'beak', which enable them to lick exposed nectar and pollen.

Diurnal nemopterines have been recorded to visit the flowers of plants in 12 families, all of which are also visited by other insects. The heavy pollen loads on the bodies of nemopterine lacewings, as well as extensive observations by Jonathan Ball, suggest that many are important generalist pollinators. Species of the diurnal genus *Palmipenna* visit numbers of different plant species in different families, depending on the flowers available where and when the insects are active. However, some species of *Halterina* appear to be more host-specific; *H. pulchella*, for example, has only been recorded to feed on *Serruria fasciflora* (Proteaceae).

Less is known about the feeding habits of so-called nocturnal nemopterines. Although they are characteristically attracted by lights – sometimes in vast numbers during spring and early summer in the Karoo – they are also often active during daylight hours. They appear to feed mainly on flowers of the Aizoaceae, particularly of the genus *Mesembryanthemum*. Many of the 'nocturnal' adults carry pollen on their thoraces, which could have been transferred during diurnal, crepuscular (during twilight) or nocturnal feeding. Some white mesembs, with which they are thought to be associated, remain open for a few hours after dark.

Jonathan Ball

3.13 An ovipositing spoon-winged lacewing, *Palmipenna palmulata*, with sand-encrusted egg at the tip of the abdomen.

Jonathan Ball

Jonathan Ball

Jonathan Ball

Jonathan Ball

Neuroptera specialist Jonathan Ball found that the hind wings of Nemopterinae have various striking forms with specialised functions. In southern African species, forewing length is 12–35mm and hind wing 13–77mm.

Aerodynamics

During flight, the hind wings are held away from the midline of the body, at a 25–40° angle from each other. The terminal portion of the wing is usually expanded and twisted – clockwise on the right wing and anticlockwise on the left wing and yields a structure that functions like the tail of an aeroplane. They usually fly fairly low over vegetation or soil, especially when the wind is strong or gusty. Flight speed is determined by the speed of movement of the forewings. In fast-flying species, the forewings are strengthened by increased numbers of individual cells.

Thermoregulation

Many diurnal taxa have a significant amount of dark pigmentation on both the fore- and hind wings, as well as on the thorax and abdomen. In spring, especially during cold fronts that commonly pass through the region at this time, the ability to warm the body is critical for flight. A number of species rest with their bodies and tips of the hind wings held close to some warm substrate (rocks, soil or dark plant detritus); the broadened areas then act like small 'solar panels', absorbing solar heat or that radiated from the warm environment. Large longitudinal veins in the wings transfer warmed haemolymph to the rest of the body.

In some *Palmipenna* and *Barbibucca* species, males have greater amounts of dark pigmentation on the body and wings than females. In one *Barbibucca* species from near the cold West Coast, males are darker and hairier than females; these characteristics also seem to differ between males, with the darkest and hairiest individuals warming and flying fastest and, consequently, having the best mating chances.

Semiosis (signalling)

Diurnal species are often seen synchronously ratcheting their hind wings up and down in an arc of 15–20°. There are brilliant white areas on the terminal portions of the wings immediately adjacent to darkly pigmented areas. It is suspected that the white portions reflect ultraviolet light, which is visible to insects, hence to their conspecifics.

An undescribed species from the Northern Cape is active amongst rocks in mid-summer when the surface temperature is over 45°C. Individuals often sit under shady rocky overhangs, where the only evidence of their presence is the rhythmical ratcheting of the tips of their hind wings. Small groups of *Palmipenna aeoleoptera* females are sometimes seen together on a rock, making rapid and jerky movements with their relatively large hind wings in what is thought to be mass signalling to attract males.

Predator avoidance

Adults are heavily preyed on by various vertebrates and invertebrates, including bats, birds, lizards, robber flies (Asilidae; see 'Robber flies', p. 128), predatory katydids (Tettigoniidae; see 'Predatory katydids', p. 126) and spiders (see 'Spiders', p. 304). Diurnal flying adults drop immediately into vegetation if threatened. It has been suggested that the extreme length of the hind wings and their expanded tips may make the insect's body appear much larger than it is, especially to robber flies.

The elongated hind wings also often merge exquisitely into the background, providing camouflage when the insects settle on or rest in grasses, restios, or blackened and detached dead leaves or twigs of Aizoaceae.

3.14 Nemopterinae have a diversity of hind wing shapes and functions: **(a)** *Halterina* sp.; **(b)** *H. pulchella*; **(c)** *Sicyoptera* sp.; **(d)** *Barbibucca* sp.; **(e)** *Palmipenna aeoleoptera*; **(f)** *Knersvlaktia nigroptera*; **(g)** *Nemia costalis*.

Mating appears to take place in a sheltered site on plants. Females have been seen laying eggs on rocks, dry vegetation and sandy soil (fig. 3.13). In two species (*Palmipenna aeoleoptera* and *P. palmulata*), females were noted to tap the tips of their abdomens into sandy soil before egg-laying: the thin-walled, ovoid eggs become encrusted with small sand grains and are laid on the shaded side of small rocks about 5cm above the soil surface. The sand grains appear to confer some degree of camouflage and also to lessen dehydration.

The larvae are carnivorous predators of smaller arthropods (see 'Thread-winged lacewings', p. 350). They feed like all Neuroptera larvae: they use their elongated and curved hollow mandibles to inject the prey with proteolytic enzymes that liquefy the body parts, then ingest their nonsolid meal. The larvae have a sealed hindgut and the solid components of their liquid diet are stored as a pale pellet (meconium), which is excreted at pupation – another family characteristic. Pupation is in a sand-encrusted, silken cocoon in the soil. Synchronised emergence of the adults occurs mainly in spring to coincide with the prolific spring flowering. In drought years, adult emergence can be suspended.

Monkey beetles as pollinators

There are claims that beetles – the largest insect order – may pollinate a large percentage of flowering plants, but other studies report that it rarely occurs. Although beetles were some of the first pollinators of plants, their contribution to successful pollination is questioned because of their generally destructive feeding habits in which they eat petals and pollen. Most flower-visiting beetles also lack suitable morphological specialisations for collecting pollen or reaching concealed nectar sources. Yet, evidence shows that certain beetles indeed play an important role in pollination.

Worldwide, the majority of studies on beetle pollination has recorded that bowl-shaped flowers are most often pollinated by beetles and that the flowers also function as mating platforms. Bee-pollinated plants have laterally orientated flowers with little or no landing platform, whereas beetle-pollinated species have flowers that face upwards to provide a broad landing platform (see 'Protea pollination by fruit chafer beetles', p. 184). Pollen is the major attraction for beetles and some pollination occurs at the cost of some of the flowers being eaten.

Some of the best-known examples of beetle pollination in southern Africa are those involving monkey beetles (Coleoptera: Scarabaeidae: Melolonthinae: Hopliini), which are important pollinators of spring-flowering plants in the Fynbos and Namaqualand. There are about 1,200 Hopliini species worldwide; about half of these are endemic to the winter-rainfall areas of the Fynbos and Namaqualand, where almost all species are associated with flowers. They use flowers for food or as platforms to assemble for mating (fig. 3.15). The early entomologist Louis Péringuey said of hopliines that 'on a bright day in the spring, no flower is without a tenant'. It is mostly unknown how specific hopliines are to a particular plant species or group of species (see box, p. 111) or whether they transport pollen from one flower to the stigmas of others. In certain cases, however, the beetles are important pollinators of some rare and endangered plants; for example, they are the only known pollinator of certain species of the Iridaceae (see 'Monkey beetles as pollinators', p. 80).

3.15 The Succulent Karoo is home to more monkey beetle species (Melolonthinae: Hopliini) than any other region in the world. All are associated with flowers, and many are important pollinators of various endemic plants: (**a**) *Anisonyx ursus*; (**b**) *Peritrichia* sp.; (**c**) *Clania coerulovittata*; (**d**) *Lepithrix* sp.; (**e**) *Scelophysa trimeni*; (**f**) *Heterochelus* sp.

Bee flies visiting beetle daisies

Bee flies (Diptera: Bombyliidae) are small to medium (2–20mm long), robust, often hairy flies (fig. 3.17). Many have a long, straight, protruding proboscis and are wasp- or bee-like, hence their common name. The family is very large, with about 1,000 species in southern Africa (which is three-quarters of the total number of African species). They are most common in the arid western parts of southern Africa, where they are regular flower visitors and important pollinators of some rare endemic plants. The larvae are predators or parasitoids of ground-breeding insect larvae, especially those of solitary wasps and bees.

Although the flies are often seen on flowers, they may just as often be seen sitting on the ground, either basking or if female, filling their 'sand chamber' with sand. This is a unique cavity at the apex of the abdomen which is surrounded by a thick fringe of setae (hairs). When the female presses her abdomen against the soil surface, special spines shovel fine sand grains into the chamber. After filling the chamber, she flies to locate a potential larval host burrow and then, in flight, ejects thin-walled sticky eggs through the sand chamber. A layer of sand adheres to the eggs as they are laid; this is thought to protect the eggs against desiccation. Females lay large numbers of eggs, with up to 3,000 recorded from certain species.

The emergent larva, termed a planidium (equivalent to the triungulin in Coleoptera; see 'Blister beetle larvae: predators of locust eggs', p. 171), is tiny, elongate, long-legged and fast-moving. It needs to locate a host nest before it can develop further. Once it has penetrated a host nest, the larva starts to feed. It moults twice during its development into a much larger, sessile, grub-like larva, a process termed hypermetamorphosis (see box, p. 42).

The beetle daisy, *Gorteria diffusa* (Asteraceae, fig. 3.18), is a common and well-known spring annual in Namaqualand, which is self-incompatible and therefore dependent on pollinators. The common name refers to the raised, insect-like structures at the base of the yellow-orange ray florets. During the 1940s, the English botanist John Hutchinson suggested that these spots may imitate beetles, although he observed that hopliines avoided the daisies. In fact, beetle daisies are pollinated by small bee flies, *Megapalpus nitidus* (fig. 3.18), which appear very similar to the dark spots when sitting on the flowers. The other bee fly species in the genus, *M. capensis*, is known to pollinate several species of *Pelargonium* (Geraniaceae) that also have dark spots similar to those on the beetle daisy.

These small dark bee flies are roughly the same size (4–5mm long) as the flower spots. They have a long proboscis (3–4mm long) relative to body size, which is extended forwards when the flies are at rest on flowers.

Flowers pollinated by monkey beetles

Monkey beetles (Hopliini) usually pollinate a particular type of flower: most are brightly coloured (yellow, orange, red or cream), are saucer-shaped, and often have dark 'beetle marks' at the base of tepals or petals. They usually have little scent.

There is little evidence to suggest that Hopliini are intimate, co-evolved pollinators of most of the plants on which they are regularly found, mainly daisies (Asteraceae) and mesembs (Aizoaceae). Nevertheless, some studies indicate that they are important pollinators of some flowers. Three different ecological groups or guilds of monkey beetles are associated with specific types of flowers, based mainly on flower colour:

- hairy, fast-flying species that are attracted to violet-blue or white flowers, where they feed on pollen and, possibly, nectar;
- hairy, fast-flying species that feed only on the pollen of red, yellow, orange or white flowers; and
- larger, relatively smooth species with pronounced sexual dimorphism that burrow deep into red, yellow or orange flowers where they feed on pollen, developing ovaries, stamens and ray florets.

The first group of beetles includes species of *Anisonyx* and *Peritrichia* (figs 3.16a, b, respectively). These are usually dark, densely hairy beetles without marked sexual dimorphism. They feed on pollen and probably also on the nectar of various unrelated blue-white flowers using their unusually long mouthparts. Their long, dense body hairs are often covered in pollen, which they undoubtedly spread from plant to plant. There is no evidence that they damage the host plant while feeding.

Members of the second group of beetles are often the most abundant, especially very active species of *Peritrichia* that fly quickly from flower to flower, much like bees (fig. 3.16b). They preferentially visit red, yellow, orange or white flowers where they feed on and collect pollen. There is no evidence that they imbibe nectar or damage the host plant while feeding.

Beetles in the third group belong to genera such as *Scelophysa, Heterochelus, Gymnoloma* (fig. 3.16c) and *Pachycnema*. They are characterised by extreme sexual dimorphism: males are usually bigger and more brightly coloured than females and have very large hind legs. They visit mainly red, yellow or orange flowers, which also attract various generalist pollinators such as bees, wasps, flies and butterflies. The beetles embed themselves deeply into the flower while feeding, leaving only their hind legs and the tip of the abdomen exposed. There is overt aggression between males on flowers. The enlarged hind legs have been shown to function as weapons in contests between males. In *Heterochelus sexlineatus* populations, for example, males outnumber females by almost 2:1, so male access to females is aggressively contested; the largest males with the largest legs invariably win the contest and the mating opportunity.

Jonathan Ball

3.16 Representatives of three pollinator groups of monkey beetles: (a) *Anisonyx ditus*; (b) *Peritrichia* sp.; (c) *Gymnoloma femorata*.

3.17 Bee flies (Bombyliidae) are important pollinators of endemic plants in the Succulent Karoo: (a) *Australoechus* sp.; (b) *Spogostylum* sp.; (c) *A. megaspilus*; (d) *Exoprosopa* sp.; (e, f) *Notolomatia* spp.; (g) *Exoprosopa* sp.; (h) *Bombylius* sp.; (i) *Bombomyia discoidea*; (j) *Gonarthrus* sp.

The flies have been shown to feed on the plants' nectar and pollen, and to transport pollen from one flower to another. Most of the heavy pollen load is carried on the head, which they rub against the stamens when probing for nectar.

The flowers are mostly visited by male flies, which land on the spots in a way that is similar to how they 'pounce' on females to copulate. The evidence suggests that the flower spots mimic resting flies and elicit attempted mating by males, which results in successful pollination. This might, however, not be the only reason why bee flies are attracted to flowers with dark spots (see box opposite).

3.18 A beetle daisy, *Gorteria diffusa*, with its actual pollinator: the bee fly *Megapalpus nitidus*.

Using flower spots to regulate body temperature

Gorteria diffusa, the so-called 'beetle daisy', is known to be pollinated by *Megapalpus* bee flies. Several plant species that often co-occur with *G. diffusa* have similar dark spots on their flowers. At least one species of *Dimorphotheca* (Asteraceae) and about nine *Pelargonium* species (Geraniaceae) – all with raised dark spots – are known to be pollinated by bee flies too, supporting the premise that the flies have placed evolutionary pressure on the development of specific floral patterns on unrelated plant lineages in the area.

A study of *M. capensis* (fig. 3.19a) pollinating *Pelargonium* flowers offers another possible reason for the relationship. *Pelargonium tricolor* is a small, sprawling shrublet endemic to the Klein Karoo, which sprouts after fire and may bear many flowers. The small flower has five petals varying from white to mauve; the two top petals always have a dark wine-red lower section and a black spot at the base (fig. 3.19b). The flowers have two phases: a 'hooded' phase when the flower is half open, with ripe anthers but unreceptive stigmas; and an 'open' phase when the flower is open, pollen has already been shed and the stigmas are receptive. The two phases exclude self-pollination, so pollinators are essential for seed set.

The dark spots on the petals have been discounted as sources of nectar or any other exudate that the flies might use. They are thought to act mainly as a visual attractant to the flies. Besides the possible connection to mating behaviour (see page opposite), an additional function has been suggested: that the flowers modify the microclimate to which the flies are exposed. This they do in the hooded phase when the lower pale petals reflect incidental heat onto the dark upper petals, which increases the temperature inside the flower. In the open phase, the dark raised area on which the fly sits when feeding is likely to absorb heat, and consequently, increase the fly's body temperature. Fly attraction to hooded flowers ensures contact with pollen, whereas flies visiting open flowers could result in pollen transfer to the stigmas.

The small flies are only active on sunny, windless days; they commonly shelter and aggregate in hooded flowers during inclement weather. This brings male and female flies together in an environmentally secure setting and also ensures that pollen is transferred from the ripe anthers to the bee flies.

It is therefore possible that *M. nitidus* is attracted to black spots on *Gorteria diffusa* not only because of sexual deception, but because the black spots may also help to increase the fly's body temperature.

3.19 (a) The bee fly *Megapalpus capensis* in the southern and Eastern Cape has an intimate relationship with (b) the flowers of *Pelargonium tricolor*.

Jan Vlok

Pollen wasps

There are about 300 southern African wasp species in the Vespidae (Hymenoptera). The family contains three characteristic subfamilies: paper wasps (Polistinae; see 'Eusocial paper wasps', p. 389), mason or potter wasps (Eumeninae; see 'Solitary potter wasps', p. 392) and pollen wasps (Masarinae, figs 3.20, 3.21).

There are six pollen wasp genera in southern Africa. Two are endemic to the region: *Priscomasaris*, with one Namibian species, *P. namibiensis*, and *Masarina*, with 13 species. The remaining four genera – *Ceramius*, *Jugurtia*, *Celonites* and *Quartinia* – are either widespread in Africa, or are fairly localised in southern Africa, North Africa, Eurasia and the Arabian peninsula. The wasps are mostly small (less than 10mm long), although species of *Ceramius* are 12–20mm long.

Almost all southern African Masarinae species are endemic. Most are found in the arid western part of the region, mainly in the Succulent Karoo, Fynbos, Nama-Karoo and Namibia. Many feed on the nectar and pollen of Asteraceae and Aizoaceae flowers.

Masarinae are bee-like in appearance and behaviour, and are solitary, although several females may nest close together. All species feed their larvae a mixture of pollen and nectar (unique among wasps) in individual cells within the nest. An egg is first laid in the cell, which is then provisioned with a pollen and nectar 'loaf', then sealed. Another characteristic that distinguishes pollen wasps from other Vespidae is the presence of an extraordinarily long tongue (except in *Priscomasaris*). The tongue varies from 20% to 110% of body length, with the largest range in *Quartinia*.

Pollen wasps were previously thought to be rare but in areas where they occur, they can in fact be abundant. They are easily misidentified because they are bee-like in appearance and are silent fliers. They do not hover over flowers but enter flowers directly and are alert and immediately leave when disturbed. Species that depend on water for the construction of their nesting burrows can be seen in numbers at water and in their nesting areas.

In areas of suitable habitat and flowers they may be abundant. Species that are dependent on water for the construction of their nesting burrows (see box opposite) can be seen in numbers at water and in their nesting areas.

3.21 Pollen wasps (Masarinae) showing characteristic behaviour: (a) a group of *Jugurtia* sp. imbibing water from a seep for nest building; (b) a mating pair of *Ceramius* sp., the males and females of which are monomorphic; (c) *Quartinia* sp. collecting nectar and pollen on a *Mesembryanthemum* flower.

3.20 A pollen wasp, *Masarina* sp., lining the entrance of its nest with clay pellets bonded with water from a nearby source.

Masarinae wasps, which feed on pollen and nectar in both the larval and adult stages, show considerable differences among the various genera in choice of nest location and the materials used in nest construction. Although mud or sand is used by all, the bonding material varies between groups: water, nectar or self-produced silk may be used.

Wasps that use water imbibe it from an open source by standing on the water surface or at the water's edge, and store it in their crop. At the nesting site, they regurgitate the water onto the soil surface and use their mouthparts to mix it into a small pellet. The pellet is then used as a building block. This process is repeated many times until the nest is complete.

Priscomasaris namibiensis imbibes water while standing on the water surface. A curved, tubular mud turret, which runs almost parallel to the ground over its length, leads to a subterranean burrow with a multicellular nest consisting of up to 13 cells.

Some *Ceramius* species imbibe water from the water surface, others take it from the water's edge. They construct (mostly) curved nest entrance turrets, but only some species build mud-walled brood cells in an underground shaft. The other species provision brood cells in individual soil cavities.

Jugurtia species, as far as is known, use water as a bonding liquid, although it is suspected that in desert areas nectar is probably used as an alternative. A low mud turret forms an entrance to the burrow, which is a vertical shaft with laterally radiating cells at the end.

Masarina species excavate near-horizontal burrows into vertical, firm soil banks. Some species use water as a bonding liquid, but the brood cells of some others suggest that nectar is used.

Nesting in *Celonites* species differs considerably from that in the other genera: some build earthen cells attached to rocks or plants above ground, while others nest in pre-existing burrows in the ground. One species, the Succulent Karoo endemic *C. latitarsis*, excavates a sloping shaft in dry sand. All species use nectar as a bonding liquid in nest and cell construction.

The smallest pollen wasps make up the largest genus, *Quartinia*. They have diverged completely from their relatives with regard to bonding material, switching to the more dependable but energetically expensive silk produced by their mandibular glands. The nests may be excavated in small pockets of sand held in rock crevices or against rocks or bushes, but most of the wasps studied used the sand-filled shells of terrestrial snails. Although the shells are seldom larger than about 2.5cm in diameter, they may house up to 20 brood cells of very small wasp species. The nest turret is a low vertical tube.

Herbivores

Herbivory in the Succulent Karoo is almost entirely restricted to softer herbaceous species and the foliage of woody plants. Orthoptera (grasshoppers and their relatives) are common and characteristic members of this biome, to which they are superbly adapted. Grass is mostly absent in the Succulent Karoo, so grasshoppers, despite their name, feed mainly on herbaceous and woody plants.

Sound production in bladder grasshoppers

Bladder grasshoppers (Orthoptera: Caelifera: Pneumoridae; see box, pp. 118–119) belong to a small, primitive, near-endemic South African family with nine genera and 17 species. Most species are endemic to eastern and western coastal South Africa, with the highest diversity along the West Coast and its near interior. Although most species appear to be generalist herbivores, some prefer particular plants.

3.22 A cryptic bush-inhabiting nymph of the bladder grasshopper *Bullacris serrata* (Pneumoridae).

Adults are large (50–60mm long), usually bright green grasshoppers (fig. 3.22) and are strongly sexually dimorphic. Males are larger than females and have a huge inflated abdomen that protrudes beyond the wings. The abdominal bloating is caused by large inflated air sacs (see lower box, p. 27).

Both males and females produce sound. In males, the sound is created by rubbing a row of teeth on the hind femur (the plectrum) against a file – a series of clearly visible ribs arranged in a crescent shape on the third abdominal segment (fig. 3.23). This is unusual among caeliferans, which usually produce sound by rubbing the hind femur on the edge of the leathery forewing (tegmen). Male bladder grasshoppers produce a very loud call (about 98dB at 1m) at relatively low frequencies (1.4–3.2kHz). The call is magnified by the inflated abdomen, which acts as an acoustic resonance chamber. A calling male can be heard up to 2km away at night (by humans). Pair formation is brought about through acoustic duetting over distances of about 50m when flying males approach flightless females; female calls are much softer. Males of different species produce different sounds, whereas female calls sound very similar. Sound production and hearing (see box below) are used exclusively for courtship.

Hearing in grasshoppers

Both male and female bladder grasshoppers (Orthoptera: Caelifera: Pneumoridae) have well-developed hearing organs on each of the visible abdominal segments (12 in total), but as they are not in the form of visible external ears as in most other caeliferans, the insects are considered atympanate.

Grasshoppers and locusts of the Acrididae and Pamphagidae (see 'Sound production in rain locusts', p. 117; 'Camouflage in toad and stone grasshoppers', p. 117) hear using tympanal sensory organs situated on either side of the first abdominal segment. The externally visible ear (fig. 3.24) consists of a thin membrane (3–5μm thick) backed by an air space in the adjacent trachea. Mechanoreceptors (chordotonal organs) that are connected to the membrane transform the mechanical energy of sound pulses into neural signals.

Pneumoridae lack the typical localised thinning of the cuticle that represents a tympanum (theirs is about 20μm thick, surrounded by cuticle 25μm thick), but they do have the same type of chordotonal organs and air-filled tracheal sacs as tympanate insects.

Although pneumorids lack an obvious external tympanum, their hearing is extremely acute. The first abdominal segment (A1) ear of the KwaZulu-Natal species *Bullacris membracioides* is the most sensitive of any orthopteran recorded. At frequencies of about 4kHz, a threshold sensitivity of 13dB sound pressure level has been recorded in inflated males and 20dB sound pressure level in virgin females.

The sensitivity of the pneumorid ear is well illustrated by comparing the number of sensory receptors (sensilla) in its chordotonal organ to those of a tympanate locust ear. The locust ear has about 80 sensilla, whereas there are nearly 2,000 in the pneumorid A1 ear. This is close to the number found in cicadas, which are thought to be the supreme sound production and hearing specialists among insects (see 'Sound and breeding in cicadas', p. 275). The chordotonal organs in the ears on abdominal segments 2–6 have about 11 sensilla each, so their sensitivity is markedly less than that of A1, but they still function effectively.

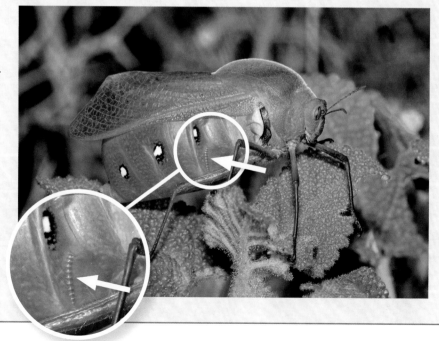

3.23 Bladder grasshoppers (Pneumoridae) such as this male *Bullacris intermedia* produce loud, characteristic night sounds in the Succulent Karoo. The sound is produced by the file on the third abdominal segment (exploded image) and resonated through the inflated abdomen.

Sound production in rain locusts

Rain locusts, *Lamarckiana* (Orthoptera: Caelifera: Pamphagidae; see box, pp. 118–119), are large grasshoppers with about 20 southern African species that occur across the northern half of the subcontinent. *Lamarckiana cucullata* from the arid west is the largest grasshopper in the region (about 100mm long).

They are strongly sexually dimorphic and often have characteristically flattened sword-shaped antennae. Males are winged, mostly slate-grey and lightly speckled, while females are squat, grey-brown and wingless (fig. 3.24). Males produce characteristic sounds by stridulating – rubbing the edge of the hind femur against the edge of the hind wing. The East African species *L. loboscelis* produces three bursts of song, lasting an average of 20, 10 and 6 seconds each, but they may sporadically be as long as 30, 15 and 10 seconds. *Lamarckiana* males sing from a perch in a bush or tree, where they may remain for days, calling at night while females in the vicinity are attracted closer. Since females have no wings and cannot presumably stridulate, it is not clear how an approaching female communicates her presence to a singing male.

3.24 *Lamarckiana* grasshoppers are highly sexually dimorphic: here, the winged male is grey, and the female is wingless and brown. Males produce loud night-time calls to attract females. She hears with the large tympanum visible on her first abdominal segment.

Camouflage in toad and stone grasshoppers

The arid areas of western southern Africa are home to some remarkably camouflaged ground-living grasshoppers. These include 16 species of toad grasshoppers in the genus *Batrachotetrix*, and the stone grasshopper, *Trachypetrella anderssonii* (Orthoptera: Caelifera: Pamphagidae; see box, pp. 118–119).

They live in bare stony habitats that typically have very little vegetation, amongst a range of pebbles of different geological origins (including shale, quartz and calcrete). They are superbly camouflaged, matching and blending with the colours and textures of the pebbles

3.25 Ground-living Succulent Karoo grasshoppers with substrate-specific camouflage: (**a**) *Batrachotetrix* sp.; (**b**) *Trachypetrella anderssonii*; (**c**) *Trachypetrella* sp. nymph; (**d–f**) various species of camouflaged Pamphagidae.

The differences between Caelifera and Ensifera

The Orthoptera – grasshoppers and their relatives – are divided into two distinctive suborders, Caelifera and Ensifera. Caelifera are known as 'short-horned grasshoppers' and have antennae shorter than their body length (for example, typical grasshoppers). Ensifera are called 'long-horned grasshoppers', and have antennae that are longer than their bodies (e.g. crickets; see 'Garden crickets and mole crickets', p. 383).

Several other distinct differences between the suborders are:

- In Caelifera, the ovipositor is a series of short blades (fig. 3.27), while in Ensifera it is an extended sword- or lance-shaped organ (fig. 3.28).
- Eggs are laid in clumps (pods) in Caelifera, singly in Ensifera.
- Sound is produced in caeliferans by rubbing the edge of the hind femur against the edge of the hind wing (tegmen, plural tegmina), termed femoro-tegminal stridulation. Ensifera produce sound by rubbing the edges of the tegmina together (tegminal stridulation).
- The ear (tympanum) in Caelifera is situated on the side of the abdomen (figs 3.24, 3.26; see box, p. 116) ; it is located on the foretibia in Ensifera.
- All Caelifera are plant feeders. Most Ensifera also feed on plants, but some specialised groups of Tettigoniidae are opportunistically omnivorous or cannibalistic (for example, armoured bush crickets; see 'Armoured ground crickets', p. 213) and a few are obligatory predators (for example, the short-winged predatory katydid; see 'Predatory katydids', p. 126).

3.27 A female grasshopper (Pamphagidae) illustrating the typical egg-laying behaviour of Caelifera: drilling deep into the soil with short ovipositor blades to lay a pod of eggs in a capsule. Her short antennae are also characteristic.

3.28 A selection of katydids, typical members of Ensifera, with long antennae and long, sword-shaped ovipositors with which eggs are mostly laid singly: (a) shield-backed katydid, *Arytropteris* sp.; (b) predatory *Clonia* sp.; (c) *Africariola longicauda*; (d) *Clonia* nymph.

3.26 The clearly visible tympanum (ear) on the first abdominal segment behind the knee of the middle leg of this female grasshopper (Pamphagidae) is a characteristic of Caelifera.

around them (fig. 3.25). They may be pinkish and smooth amongst similar-coloured quartz, whitish and rough amongst calcrete, or grey and smooth in areas with slate.

Batrachotetrix species (fig. 3.25a) are fairly widespread in the Succulent and Nama-Karoo biomes and southern Namibia. Female toad grasshoppers are considerably larger (about 30mm long) than males (20mm long). Males are always winged, while females may be winged or wingless. Colour amongst the species (and possibly even within species) varies according to the background in which they live.

The stone grasshopper *Trachypetrella anderssonii* is about 70mm long (figs 3.25b, c). Males and females have very reduced wings and are flightless. The species has a similar distribution to that of *Batrachotetrix*, and its colour and physiological adaptations to its environment also appear similar.

The areas in which they live are subject to very high summer temperatures, and therefore reproduction in both *Batrachotetrix* and *T. anderssonii* takes place in spring, enabling vulnerable egg and nymphal development to occur when environmental conditions are more moderate. Their food consists of foliage of various scrubby shrubs of apparently poor digestibility and low water content.

It has not yet been explained how these plump grasshoppers can sit virtually motionless for long

3.29 The herbivorous katydid genus *Brinckiella* is near-endemic to the Succulent Karoo. Most species are wingless and are therefore unable to produce sound like their relatives.

Jonathan Ball

Piotr Naskrecki

Jonathan Ball

3.30 A mature *Brinckiella wilsoni* female illustrating the total lack of wings and the well-developed ovipositor characteristic of the group.

periods against a hot background without overheating or dehydrating. This sedentary lifestyle appears to be mainly for reasons of defence; it has been determined experimentally that living against a matching background and remaining motionless are their major defence strategies against predators such as birds and baboons that hunt using sight.

Herbivorous katydids

Tettigoniidae (Orthoptera: Ensifera; see box above) is a large family comprising numerous subfamilies, several of which are characteristic of the Succulent Karoo biome. Most are herbivorous such as the bush and leaf katydids in the genus *Brinckiella* (Phaneropterinae) but the unusual predatory genus *Clonia* (Sagrinae; see 'Predatory katydids', p. 126) also occurs in this biome.

Tettigoniids are variable in colour and shape, but most are large and slender with long legs. Females have a sword-shaped, more or less straight ovipositor, which is often at least half the length of their body (fig. 3.28).

Brinckiella (figs 3.29, 3.30) consists of eight species, most of which are restricted to small localised areas in the Succulent Karoo. They are typical medium-sized (15–25mm long), greenish-yellow katydids, but are unusual in the Phaneropterinae because females, and sometimes males, are wingless (apterous).

Gall-forming insects

Gall-forming insects occur in all biomes (see box, p. 49), but their incidence is often higher in arid areas such as Namaqualand, where a high diversity of species has been recorded (see 'Moth galls on Bushveld trees', p. 233; 'Gall wasps', p. 381). Their close association with a specific host plant means that they can only occur within the distribution area of that plant species; in many cases, the gall-forming insect has a much smaller geographical distribution than the host plant.

Galls on *Galenia* species

Urodontus (Coleoptera: Anthribidae: Urodontinae) is a southern African beetle genus with about 20 species, most of which are seed feeders. However, some have switched to boring into and feeding inside the young stems of the host. Adult beetles emerge in late winter and early spring and females insert eggs into cracks in the bark of young stems. The larvae bore into the stem; this stimulates the plant to form a woody gall around the feeding larva (fig. 3.31a). The galls develop first by slight thickening (to about 5mm) and elongation (about 20mm) of the stem around the feeding larva, reaching maximum size within about two months. Final shape and size vary: some remain elongate (15mm wide and 25mm long); others are almost round (about 15mm in diameter). The beetles complete their development within 2–3 months. The young adults remain inside the gall cavity for about six months, emerging in late winter or early spring.

Galenia africana (Aizoaceae) is a pale green, woody shrub which grows to a height of about 1.5m; it occurs in drier areas of the Eastern Cape, Free State, Western Cape, Northern Cape and Namibia. It is a pioneer and often the only woody plant growing in severely degraded veld such as around livestock watering points and kraals; one of its common names is 'kraalbos'. It is one of the hosts of the gall-forming *Urodontus scholtzi*. The beetle also forms galls on *G. sarcophylla* (fig. 3.31b), which often grows adjacent to *G. africana* in undisturbed veld. Based on the numbers of galls per bush, *G. sarcophylla* appears to be the beetle's preferred host. The galls on *G. africana* are more inclined to remain elongate, while those on *G. sarcophylla* tend to be rounder.

Galls remain on the plants for several years after the beetles have emerged. The small emergence holes and feeding cavity inside the gall are favourite nesting sites for minute (2–3mm long) solitary *Afroheriades geminus* bees (Megachilidae: Megachilinae: Osmiini)

3.31 (a) The gall formed by *Urodontus scholtzi* (Anthribidae: Urodontinae) on *Galenia sarcophylla* (Aizoaceae), its preferred host; and (b) *U. scholtzi* inside the woody gall.

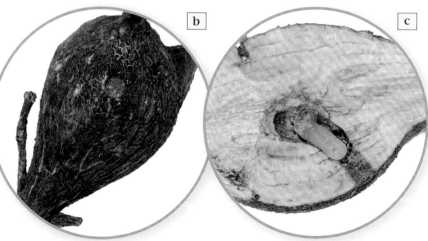

3.32 (a) The solitary bee *Afroheriades geminus* (Megachilidae), which nests in gall cavities; (b) the entrance to an *Afroheriades* bee nest plugged with resin; and (c) the larva of the bee *A. geminus* is a secondary inhabitant of gall cavities vacated by emergent beetles.

3.33 Galls on *Osteospermum sinuatum* (Asteraceae) caused by the fruit fly *Tylaspis crocea* (Tephritidae).

3.34 The gall-forming fruit fly *Tylaspis crocea* (Tephritidae).

(fig. 3.32a). The female bees become active in spring, and after mating, provision the nest with nectar and pollen, lay an egg next to the provisions, and then seal the entrance with resin (fig. 3.32b). The larva (fig. 3.32c) develops over the next several months and the young adult remains inside the nest until the following spring, when it emerges.

Galls on *Osteospermum* species

Bietou, *Osteospermum sinuatum*, and sandbietou or skaapbos, *O. oppositifolium* (Asteraceae) are widespread in the western parts of southern Africa. Both grow to a height of about 1m. They often occur in fairly dense stands over large, localised areas, especially where they are protected from browsing, such as along road verges. Their near absence on many farms in the region can be attributed to their palatability to livestock.

Galls appear to be fairly uncommon, but when present they develop in young terminal stem nodes (fig. 3.33); there are usually between two and five galls on adjacent twigs. They appear in July and develop

quickly to their maximum size within about a month. The gall is a round ball (15mm in diameter), green with a pinkish tinge, and often with a few stunted leaves emerging from the top.

The cause of the gall is the larva of the fruit fly *Tylaspis crocea* (Diptera: Tephritidae, fig. 3.34). The larva feeds inside an elongate chamber (5–8mm long with a diameter of about 1–2mm) and is a typical maggot – pale and translucent with only the mandibles sclerotised and no legs or other appendages. Prior to pupation, the larva chews a very small hole through the gall tissue to the outside, leaving only a thin layer of epidermis covering it. The twigs on which the galls develop die and the galls start to dry out at about the time that pupation takes place, towards the end of August. The pupa is encased inside a dark layer of larval moulted skins (puparium). As the gall dries out, the epidermis covering the emergence hole contracts, opening it and increasing the size of the hole to that necessary for the adult to emerge.

The emerging adult is very soft and fragile and only starts to inflate its wings once it has emerged. This it does on, or close to, the gall, requiring several hours to sclerotise before flying off. The flies appear to be rather weak and reluctant flyers, particularly females, which are bloated with eggs. It is quite likely that eggs are laid close to the emergence site, which may explain the clumping of galls.

Tylaspis crocea has multiple generations per year that seem to correlate with the host plants' response to rainfall: under dry conditions the plants lose their leaves, but they respond quickly to rain, with leaves appearing again within a few days. The young buds provide the necessary oviposition sites for the flies, but it is not known how well the life cycle of the fly is synchronised with that of its host.

Spectacular brush beetles

The jewel beetle family (Coleoptera: Buprestidae) consists of 11 subfamilies and has a total of about 90 genera and 1,500 species in southern Africa. The beetles vary in size from 1.5mm to 50mm. All species are diurnal, and most are brightly or metallically coloured. The larvae of most species tunnel in dead wood.

Some of the largest beetles in the Buprestidae belong to the small subfamily Julodinae, which has five genera and about 50 species in southern Africa. One common savanna species, *Sternocera orissa* (35–45mm long), feeds mostly on the foliage and flowers of acacias and the sickle bush, *Dichrostachys cinerea*. Julodinae are associated with a wide variety of plants, although some species appear to have specific preferences for the foliage of certain plants, amongst them species of *Lycium* (Solanaceae).

Jonathan Ball

3.35 Brush beetles (Buprestidae: Julodinae): (a) *Julodis chevrolatii*; (b) *J. viridipes*; (c) *J. sulcicollis*; (d) *Neojulodis tomentosa*; (e) *J. humeralis*; (f) *J. mitifica*.

The spectacularly colourful and bristly brush beetles are species of *Julodis* and *Neojulodis* (fig. 3.35). The richest *Julodis* fauna is found in the Succulent Karoo, although species also occur in the Nama-Karoo and the Namib Desert. Females lay their large eggs (about 5mm in diameter) in the soil at the base of plants. Emergent larvae remain in the soil where they feed on roots. The beetles' life cycles appear to be largely rain-dependent and may be several years long, with development interrupted by extended periods of quiescence. As a result, adults emerge irregularly, or only in localised areas after sufficient rain has fallen.

Detritivores

The Succulent Karoo is home to two unusual groups of flightless dung beetles: the detritus-feeding genus *Pachysoma* (fig. 3.36) and primitive tunnelling dung beetles that are associated with rock hyraxes or dassies.

Detritus-feeding dung beetles

Pachysoma (Coleoptera: Scarabaeidae: Scarabaeinae: Scarabaeini) is a small genus with 13 species of large flightless dung beetles (15–35mm long). They occur along the West Coast from Cape Town to the Kuiseb River.

Flightlessness is widespread amongst some dung beetle tribes (see 'Hyrax-associated dung beetles', p. 125;

'The earliest dung beetles', p. 290), but in the Scarabaeini only *Pachysoma* and some desert species in East and North Africa have lost the ability to fly. Loss of flight is common in desert beetles and is thought to be an adaptation to conserve energy and water in hot, dry habitats.

The species of *Pachysoma*, possibly more than any other insect group, illustrate the effect that ancient rivers had on isolation and speciation in southwestern Africa (see box opposite). Five *Pachysoma* species occur between Cape Town and the Orange River; two further species are found close to the Orange River, but on opposite sides; and the remaining six species occur in the transition zone between the Succulent Karoo and the Namib Desert or in the desert itself (see 'Specialist dung beetles', p. 150).

Although *Pachysoma* species are distributed across three biomes (Fynbos, Succulent Karoo and Desert), the regions have certain topographical features in common that are more important to the beetles' ecology than vegetation types (on which biomes are based). The important shared landscape and climate conditions are: a sandy substrate, regular coastal fogs that provide free water to plants and animals, and dry dung pellets from small mammals such as rodents or hares (or sheep) or sufficient plant detritus for food.

Foraging
The biology of *Pachysoma* is unique amongst dung beetles. They belong to one of the most typical groups of ball-rolling dung beetles (Scarabaeinae: Scarabaeini),

3.36 *Pachysoma* beetles forage by (a) dragging a dung pellet, as demonstrated by *P. striatum*, or (b) dragging detritus brushed together with their leg brushes, as shown by *P. glentoni*.

Jonathan Ball

Effect of ancient rivers on *Pachysoma* speciation

The thirteen species of *Pachysoma* are all flightless and are found along the West Coast from Cape Town to the Kuiseb River. Phylogenetic studies by Catherine Sole show that the most basal (primitive) species occur in the south, while the most derived (advanced) species are found in the Namib Desert in the north. This indicates that winglessness evolved in the ancestral species in the south and that populations became isolated and speciated as they advanced northwards over the last 3 million years.

Population isolation probably occurred on patches of alluvial sand along major ancient water courses (fig. 3.37). When the ancient rivers were perennial, they prevented beetles from crossing; when river courses dried, beetles were able to cross and move farther north. This process created isolated beetle populations and led to their speciation. The following rivers (see map on p. 9) are believed to have played a role in *Pachysoma* speciation:

- the Jakkals River near Lambert's Bay (now minor);
- the Olifants River in central Namaqualand (still a significant perennial river);
- the Buffels River, west of Springbok (non-perennial);
- the Holgat River (nonperennial), between Port Nolloth and the Orange River, served as one of the courses of the Orange, which changed beds several times in response to topographic changes in ancient times;
- the permanently dry Koichab River, east of Lüderitz, permanently impeded by sand dunes that prevent it from reaching the sea, was a centre of speciation of the most advanced *Pachysoma* species.

3.37 *Pachysoma* species (Scarabaeidae: Scarabaeinae: Scarabaeini) evolved close to large rivers over the last 3 million years: (a) *P. glentoni*, from a very small area on alluvial sands along the annual Jakkals River; (b) *P. endroedyi*, from a small area just north of the Olifants River; (c) *P. striatum*, a fairly common species that occurs between the Olifants and Buffels rivers; (d) *P. gariepinum* occurs from the Buffels River to the northern banks of the Orange River; (e) *P. denticolle*, one of two deep-sand species from the Namib dune sea that lies to the north of the Koichab River.

Feeding in *Pachysoma glentoni*

Pachysoma glentoni (fig. 3.37a) is a large species of dung beetle (35mm long) that occurs in a relatively small area near Lambert's Bay in the Western Cape. The area is sandy and most plants are succulent shrubs. *Pachysoma glentoni* feeds exclusively on detritus. The beetles seem to be selective when collecting plant fragments; they may choose items such as fallen flower petals that have a higher nutritional value than leaves and twigs.

Although detritus may appear to be a rather unrewarding food source, the items collected by *P. glentoni* are actually considerably more nutritious than expected. The ratio of carbon to nitrogen (C/N ratio) provides a good index of the poorer carbon (C) content against the more nutritious nitrogen (N) content of plant matter: the lower the C/N ratio, the more nutritious the plant matter. Analysis showed that the C/N ratio of the litter consumed by *P. glentoni* was about 35.

Compared to European forest litter (C/N ratio: 45) and the straw of various grain crops (C/N ratio: 40–184), the detritus is of high nutritional quality. In addition, *P. glentoni* assimilates about 60% of the ingested detritus, which is considerably better than the average of about 20% assimilated by many other terrestrial detritivores.

Pachysoma glentoni is able to use dry plant remains as a food source because its well-developed mandibles are adapted to cutting, breaking and grinding large plant pieces into edible fragments – a complete change from the mouthparts of its ancestors, which fed on tiny particles suspended in dung fluids. Its digestive system has undergone an equally radical change from one that digested very small, highly nutritious organic particles, to one capable of overcoming the hurdles of digesting relatively large chunks of plant remains.

but share none of the behavioural characteristics of their ball-rolling relatives (see box, p. 249; 'The famous Addo dung beetle', p. 279). Other Scarabaeini roll a single ball of moist herbivore dung backwards to a suitable site, then dig a burrow and bury it. *Pachysoma* species collect dry dung pellets or plant fragments, which they drag forwards to an already excavated burrow. They repeat the process until there is enough material in the burrow. *Pachysoma* larvae are free-living in this accumulation of dry food, whereas all other Scarabaeini larvae live inside the ball of dung buried by their parents.

Some *Pachysoma* species feed on dung pellets only, others on dung pellets and detritus, and three species collect only detritus. Detritus specialists have dense brushes on their hind tarsi and tibiae, with which they comb detritus together into clumps. The higher the percentage of plant detritus in their food, the bushier are the brushes. A glance at their hind tarsi gives one a good idea of their feeding preferences.

After locating suitable food, *Pachysoma* beetles dig a food-holding chamber, usually within about 1m of the main food source, but often as far as 10m away. They then begin to forage, either by clutching pellets in their hind tarsi (fig. 3.36a), or brushing detritus together into bunches which they grasp with the long setae on their hind legs (fig. 3.36b). They drag the food behind them to the burrow. As they have to make several trips to collect enough food, they must be able to find the burrow again. They navigate using polarised light (see box, p. 151), which is visible to the beetles even on partly cloudy days when the sun is obscured.

Once the beetle has amassed a satisfactory amount of food, it deepens the burrow and constructs a second chamber below the first. The food is then moved to this feeding or nesting chamber and the burrow entrance is back-filled with sand. The beetle, whether male or female, returns to the feeding chamber and begins to feed. Unlike their relatives, which feed by filtering tiny suspended particles out of fluid using brushes on their mouthparts, *Pachysoma* species have strong mandibles with which they crush dry dung particles or plant fragments (see box above).

Breeding and larval development

Once a male is ready for breeding, he sits at the entrance to a burrow provisioned with enough food for larval development and secretes an attractant pheromone. When a female responds, she enters the burrow, after which the male closes the entrance and mating takes place. He leaves a few days later. The female then lays an egg in the accumulation of dung pellets or detritus, after which she also abandons the nest.

Morphologically, the larvae are different from dung-beetle larvae that develop inside a ball. *Pachysoma* larvae live in a loose accumulation of dry food in a sandy chamber that is well supplied with oxygen. They have small spiracles that allow sufficient intake of air, but exclude sand from entering the respiratory system. By comparison, Scarabaeini larvae that develop inside a ball of dung where oxygen supply is limited (but sand particles are not a problem), have large spiracles for adequate respiration.

Hyrax-associated dung beetles

The earliest ancestors of dung beetles (Scarabaeidae: Scarabaeinae) diverged into two lineages, one that gave rise to 'tunnelling' groups (Dichotomiini) and another (Canthonini) from which all 'rollers' evolved (see box, p. 249; 'The earliest dung beetles', p. 290). These ancestors lived in Africa about 60 million years ago, and their descendants dispersed around the world from there. However, relicts of these ancient lineages still live in southern Africa. These species are all small and wingless, which suggests that they have lived in stable and food-rich environments for millennia. Some of the most basal (primitive) rollers live in forest remnants in the east of the subcontinent, whereas the most primitive tunnellers occur in the Succulent Karoo in the west.

The tunnellers are confined to isolated rocky outcrops that are inhabited by rock hyraxes (dassies), *Procavia capensis* (fig. 3.38), in the Richtersveld of South Africa and the Fish River Canyon in southern Namibia. They live in what appears to be a very hostile environment, which is dry and very hot in summer. The rocky habitat seems less than ideal for beetles that require moist soil in which to bury the dung destined for larval food. Yet, their association with hyraxes has provided them with a suitable environment for millennia.

Rock hyraxes live in groups of various sizes in rocky regions with some woody plants – the rocks afford protection, and the plants provide food. They have a wide tolerance to plant chemicals and can eat plants that are poisonous to most other herbivores. They defecate in communal latrines (middens), where a thick layer of dung at various stages of decomposition accumulates over time. The dung beetles feed on fresh dung pellets which they drag to burrows dug in the soil nearby. There they feed on and breed in, the collected dung.

3.38 Rock hyraxes, *Procavia capensis*, live in small colonies in rocky habitats. Their communal middens are a dependable dung source for various small dung beetles in the arid west of southern Africa.

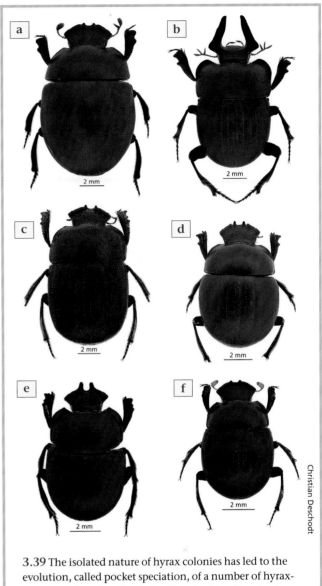

Christian Deschodt

3.39 The isolated nature of hyrax colonies has led to the evolution, called pocket speciation, of a number of hyrax-associated dung beetle species (Scarabaeidae: Scarabaeinae: Byrrhidiini): (**a**) *Byrrhidium convexum*; (**b**) *Dicranocara deschodti*; (**c**) *Versicorpus erongoense*; (**d**) *Drogo stalsi*; (**e**) *Namakwanus irishi*; (**f**) *Namaphilus endroedyi*.

The isolation of hyrax-inhabited outcrops in the arid west has led to speciation amongst the dung beetles: there are 14 species in six genera (e.g. *Namakwanus*, *Byrrhidium*, *Dicranocara*). They vary in size from 4.5–10.5mm, although most species are under 8mm in length (fig. 3.39). Given their highly localised occurrence in isolated habitats, more species will no doubt be discovered.

Predators

Insect predators in the biome include predatory katydids, ground beetles, robber flies and many species of heelwalkers (Mantophasmatodea). Two arachnid groups – scorpions and solifuges ('sunspiders') – are also important predators.

Predatory katydids

Although most katydids (Orthoptera: Ensifera: Tettigoniidae; see box, pp. 118–119) are herbivorous, some, such as the armoured bush crickets of the subfamily Hetrodinae (fig. 3.40) (see 'Armoured ground crickets', p. 213) are opportunistically omnivorous or cannibalistic, while all members of the Saginae are predatory.

Saginae are aggressive and voracious predators. They use their fore- and middle legs, which are armed with spines, to capture and hold prey encountered while they clamber around in bushes. They are unselective about their prey and eat almost any invertebrates they can overpower.

Species of the predatory katydid genus *Clonia* are concentrated in southern and East Africa (figs 3.28b, d). Five species have been described from southern Africa, of which the short-winged *C. melanoptera* is unique to the Succulent Karoo, although several undescribed species, especially from the Succulent Karoo, are known to exist. They are the largest katydids in the region, with *C. melanoptera* females reaching a total body length of about 100mm (fig. 3.41). The related savanna species, *C. wahlbergi*, is about two-thirds the size. *Clonia melanoptera* is green with silver and red patches on the body and has short wings; *C. wahlbergi* is mostly green and has fully developed wings.

Heelwalkers

Insects in the order Mantophasmatodea were described for the first time in 2001. The name of the order is a concatenation of 'manto' from Mantodea (praying mantises) and 'phasma' from Phasmatodea (stick insects), as the insects superficially share characteristics with members of these two orders. One of their unique

3.40 Although armoured bush crickets such as *Hetrodes pupus* (Tettigoniidae: Hetrodinae) are primarily herbivorous, they often cannibalise injured individuals and occasionally turn predatory.

3.41 This short-winged predatory katydid, *Clonia melanoptera* (Tettigoniidae: Saginae), is a voracious predator of smaller arthropods.

3.42 A heelwalker, *Karoophasma botterkloofense* (Mantophasmatodea), illustrating the reason for its common name: the lifted left front leg showing the 'heel' folded back.

features is that the terminal tarsal segments fold up, giving them the appearance of walking on their 'heels' – leading to their common name, heelwalkers (fig. 3.42). Almost all of the extant members of this small, ancient order are southern African: there is one Tanzanian species, but all others are known from Namibia and South Africa. There are two modern families with 12 genera and 18 species, as well as several species known from Baltic amber fossils (44 mya). Although these predatory insects have been found in the Fynbos, Succulent Karoo, Savanna and Nama-Karoo biomes, they are most common in the Succulent Karoo.

Heelwalkers live in bushes where their grey-green body colours match the plant background. They crawl slowly amongst the vegetation where they prey voraciously on the small insects they encounter. Prey is captured and held in the front and middle legs, in a manner similar to the Saginae (see page opposite).

The heelwalker seasonal activity cycle begins after the onset of autumn rains in winter-rainfall areas, and, although undocumented, probably after the first spring rains in the rest of the country. Nymphs emerge from egg pods laid in the soil during the previous season, and moult five times (six instars are the norm) over a period of about two months, reaching adulthood towards the end of the rainy season. All species are wingless and females are approximately twice the size of males (10–20mm long). Both sexes produce sound by drumming the abdomen against the substrate – usually twigs in bushes.

Ground beetles

The tyrant ground beetle, *Anthia maxillosa* (fig. 3.43) (Coleoptera: Carabidae: Anthiinae), is the largest terrestrial insect predator in the Succulent Karoo, where it may be particularly visible running around hunting among the sparse vegetation, especially in summer. All members of the family are aggressive predators both as larvae and adults.

Anthia, a sizeable African genus, contains the largest ground beetles (35–55mm long) on the continent. About 20 species are known from southern Africa, including some previously placed in the genus *Thermophilum*. Among the largest species are *A. thoracica* (45–55mm long), mainly from the eastern parts of the region (see 'Predatory ground beetles', p. 239), and the slightly smaller *A. maxillosa* (40–45mm long), from the west.

Defensive chemicals produced by Carabidae

Most ground beetles (Carabidae), besides some tiger beetles (Cicindelinae), have an armoury of defensive chemicals, produced in special glands in the eighth or ninth abdominal segment. The glands are bilobed, with a larger defensive chemical reservoir and a smaller synergist-producing lobe. Threat to the beetle causes contraction of the glands and mixes the chemicals from the two lobes. A tube leads from the glands to a 'nozzle' with a 'one-way valve' at the margin of the eighth abdominal tergite. Both are under muscular control and the nozzle can be orientated to spray in the direction of the threat, while the valve prevents the chemicals from exploding inwards. The entire glandular system including the secretory, storage and expulsion systems is lined with chitin, probably to protect the beetle from poisoning itself.

The beetles can spray the secretions in almost any direction and up to about 35cm away. If a hind leg is touched, the beetle can spray in an arc of about 25°; if a front leg is touched the beetles attempt to bite and spray in an arc of 50°, and if attacked from above, the secretion is sprayed all around the beetle in a radius of about 20cm.

The defensive chemicals that are produced by Anthiinae are composed primarily of formic acid, but acetic, tiglic and angelic acids, as well as isovaleraldehyde are also present as minor components.

Formic acid is the major component of the defensive chemicals in about half of Carabidae species, and is thought to be the basal defensive chemical. It is a strong, biologically common chemical irritant and cytotoxin that easily penetrates mucous membranes or blisters sensitive areas of skin (also used by ants; see box, p. 162). Reports of severe skin burns, as well as blindness, caused by the beetles have been reported in chickens, cats, dogs, cattle, horses and even a child. In a recent case reported from a farm near Pretoria, dogs, horses, calves and adult cattle suffered severe eye problems (even blindness) where these beetles were particularly abundant.

Some carabid groups have deviated from producing mainly formic acid for defence. For example, bombardier beetles (Brachininae) eject a concoction of near-boiling hydrogen peroxide and hydroquinones, while ant-nest beetles (Paussinae) expel quinones in an audible report that is produced as the chemicals explode outwards in a puff of vapour. The quinones stain human skin brown if a beetle is handled.

Jenny Scholtz

3.43 A tyrant ground beetle, *Anthia maxillosa* (Carabidae), one of the largest terrestrial insect predators in the Succulent Karoo.

All Anthiinae are strongly sexually dimorphic, particularly in mandible size. The mandibles are huge in males of some species – between one-quarter and one-third of the body length of the individual. They are often also asymmetrical, with the left mandible more curved than the right (distinctly so in *A. maxillosa*). In addition to using their large mandibles to capture prey, the males use them to hold the female during mating. Like many other carabids (fig. 3.44; see box, p. 127), Anthiinae readily spray defensive chemicals when cornered, often with apparent unerring accuracy toward the face and eyes of the unsuspecting predator or inexperienced beetle enthusiast. This ability has led to one of their local vernacular names of 'oogpisters'.

To advertise to potential predators that they are not to be trifled with, most are coloured in warning colours, a mechanism called aposematism (see box, pp. 240–241). They are either all-black and very visible against the sandy substrate on which they live (*A. maxillosa*, fig. 3.43), mostly black but with large yellow patches on the thorax (*A. thoracica*), or predominantly black but with a reddish pronotum and white spots on the elytra (the ten-spotted ground beetle, *A. decemguttata*, of the southern and southwestern Cape, fig. 3.44a).

Robber flies

Robber flies (Diptera: Asilidae) are characteristic, often hairy, elongate flies that vary from small (4mm) to very large (body length 65mm). Southern Africa has a very rich fauna of about 500 species (fig. 3.45). They are active, fast-flying predators that mostly capture their prey in flight and overpower them with their bristly legs and robust proboscis. A characteristic of many species is a bristly comb on the face (termed a mystax), which protects the head, mouthparts and eyes from damage by struggling captured prey.

Some robber flies are opportunistic predators that capture a variety of prey organisms, although many species are specialists, feeding on a certain group of insects, such as grasshoppers, monkey and dung beetles, bees and wasps, or other flies. For example, *Hoplistomerus nobilis* feeds exclusively on small dung beetles, which are captured when they arrive at dung; *Lasiocnemis lugens* preys on spiders, which it snatches out of the web; *Synolcus dubius* preys on bugs, mainly seed or ground bugs in the family Lygaeidae.

3.44 Ground beetles (Carabidae) from the arid west of southern Africa: (**a**) *Anthia decemguttata*; (**b**) *Graphipterus hessei*; (**c**) *Cypholoba alstoni*; (**d**) *G. velox*; (**e**) *C. semisuturata*; (**f**) *G. fasciatus*.

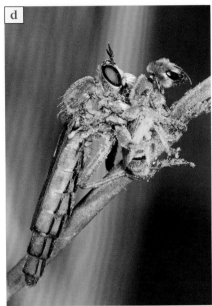

Jonathan Ball

3.45 Robber flies (Asilidae), the largest family of predatory flies, are exceptionally well represented in the Succulent Karoo: **(a)** *Gibbasilus* sp.; **(b)** *Neolophonotus* sp.; **(c)** *N. bimaculatus*; **(d)** *Microstylum* sp.; **(e)** *Acnephalomyia* sp.; **(f)** *Storthyngomerus* sp.

Robber fly larvae have a typical maggot-like appearance and mostly live in soil or leaf litter. Some feed on detritus, some on locust or grasshopper egg pods, and others are predatory.

Scorpions

Although scorpions are not insects (Arachnida: Scorpiones; see 'What is an insect', p. 14), they are often encountered in the field, particularly in hotter western regions of southern Africa such as the Succulent Karoo. There are three scorpion families in southern Africa: Buthidae, Hormuridae and Scorpionidae, containing nine genera and about 100 species. They vary in length from about 2.5cm (*Uroplectes* spp.) to about 21cm (males of *Hadogenes troglodytes*, figs 3.46a, b).

Many scorpions live under rocks or logs or in rock crevices, while species of *Opistophthalmus* (fig. 3.46c) dig deep burrows. Most species are nocturnal, although one species found in the Succulent Karoo, *Parabuthus villosus* (fig. 3.46d), also hunts by day. All species sting to subdue prey and to defend themselves.

Scorpions have a short cephalothorax that bears a pair of large median eyes and two to five pairs of small lateral eyes, a pair of small chelicerae, a pair of large pedipalps (pincers) and eight legs. The abdomen consists of a pre-abdomen with five visible segments, and a long slender post-abdomen with seven pronounced segments forming the tail and ending in a bulbous stinging apparatus that injects venom into prey. The first abdominal segment carries a pair of comb-like structures (pectines) on its ventral surface; they are sensitive to vibrations, chemicals, humidity and temperature.

Members of the Hormuridae and Scorpionidae have large pedipalps (pincers), thin tails (very thin in some *Hadogenes* spp.) and relatively mild venom. Buthidae, by contrast, have smaller pedipalps and noticeably thick tails, with potent venom. Some *Parabuthus* species are among the most venomous species in the region – they are large, robust scorpions and all should be considered as potentially life-threatening, although only a few human fatalities are recorded in southern Africa each year. Their stings are extremely painful, and children and pets are at most risk of fatal stings.

Most scorpions actively hunt their prey, but some sit and wait for potential prey at their burrow entrances. Prey is usually detected by sensors on the pedipalps or

Ian Engelbrecht

3.46 Scorpions are common nocturnal predators in southern Africa. **(a)** The flat rock scorpion, *Hadogenes troglodytes* (Hormuridae), hides in rock cracks in arid savanna regions and is the longest scorpion in southern Africa. **(b)** The Karoo species *Uroplectes carinatus* (Buthidae) is active on sand and gravel, resting by day under various shelters. **(c)** *Opistophthalmus glabrifrons* (Scorpionidae) is a burrowing eastern savanna species. **(d)** The diurnal *Parabuthus villosus* (Buthidae) occurs in the arid west.

through the pectines which pick up vibrations through the substrate (even insects active below the soil surface). The greatly enlarged pedipalps form a pair of pincers for capturing and holding prey, which is stung and then covered with digestive juices, slowly torn apart with the chelicerae, and sucked up.

A male scorpion detects a female through the pheromones that she secretes. Once he has located a female, the pair begins an elaborate courtship 'dance'. The male and female face each other with pedipalps and tail held high, and they move around in circles. The genital opening of both males and females is on the ventral side of the first abdominal segment. At some stage during the dance, the male grabs the female's pedipalps with his, and they move backwards and forwards and from side to side until the male has found a suitable site to place a spermatophore (packet of sperm). He then deposits it and manoeuvres the female over it. The spermatophore is equipped with a special lever – when the female's genital opening touches it, pressure on the lever releases the sperm into the female.

The female broods the eggs internally; in some species, this may take up to 18 months. She then gives birth to well-developed nymphs, which are carried around on her back for up to four weeks until after their first moult, after which they begin to disperse. Some species are sexually mature at six months, but others take six years to reach maturity; some species can live for as long as 30 years.

One unusual aspect of scorpion biology is that all species fluoresce, producing a blue-green shine when exposed to ultraviolet light. The physiological and chemical mechanisms of how the fluorescence is produced are known, but there is little consensus among scorpion biologists on its specific function.

Solifuges

Although solifuges (Arachnida: Solifugae; see 'What is an insect', p. 14) appear spider-like in many respects (and have popular names such as 'sunspiders'), they lack two of the main defining characters of spiders: venom and silk glands (see 'Spiders', p. 304). There are six solifuge families in southern Africa, with 240 species; this is about 20% of the world total (fig. 3.47). They are most abundant in hot, arid areas and about 70% of the species are found in the western and northern parts of the subcontinent.

Solifuges are elongate eight-legged arachnids that are usually fast-moving, and vary in size from small to moderately large (10–150mm with spread legs). Diurnal species are mostly very hairy and grey or black and white. When running fast across the hot soil surface, they look like a seed blowing in the wind. Nocturnal species are usually yellowish-brown and less hairy.

All solifuges have characteristic large projecting mouthparts (chelicerae) and what appears to be an extra pair of front legs, which are in fact the pedipalps. The pedipalps have a sensory function, like the antennae in insects, but are also used for feeding, fighting and walking. During locomotion, the pedipalps are held forward, just off the ground to detect obstacles and potential prey. The tips have retractable adhesive organs that help the solifuge to climb smooth surfaces. The true front legs are often thinner and smaller than the other three pairs, and they also have a sensory function (and may lack tarsi). The back three pairs of legs are used for running. On the underside of the last pair of legs are fan-shaped sensory organs called racquet organs (malleoli); although their precise function is not known, it is thought that they may function as vibration sensors to detect possible prey, potential predators, or mates.

The huge chelicerae are not only used to capture, kill and eat prey but also serve as tools for digging and during mating. The scissor-like chelicera consists of two toothed parts – an immobile top 'jaw' and a strongly muscled and highly mobile bottom 'jaw'. The bottom jaw moves past the top in a shearing motion, exerting considerable force. Although solifuges are capable of inflicting a painful 'bite' if carelessly handled, they are harmless as they do not have venom.

Solifuges are mostly generalist predators eating any prey they can overpower, but their main prey is other arthropods; however, large individuals are capable of overwhelming and killing small vertebrates such as lizards. There are even records of certain species feeding on dead birds whose feathers they cut off before feeding on the carcass. Some of their colloquial names ('haarskeerders', hair cutters; 'baardskeerders', beard cutters) refer to them occasionally cutting hair from sleeping humans for nesting material.

After mating, the female lays eggs in a burrow and guards them during the two-week incubation period. When the young hatch, they remain more or less immobile for another two weeks, after which they moult and become active, leaving the nest to fend for themselves. There are nine nymph stages until adulthood is reached after about 12 months.

3.47 Solifuges or sun spiders (Solifugae) are widespread in southern Africa, but are most common in the arid west: (**a**) *Solpugiba* sp. (Solpugidae); (**b**) *Solpugema* sp. (Solpugidae); (**c**) Solpugidae species; (**d**) *Blossia* sp. (Daesiidae); (**e**) *Chelypus* sp. (Hexisopodidae); (**f**) *Zeira monteiri* (Solpugidae).

CHAPTER 4
DESERT BIOME

The Namib Desert is a vast area along the west coast of southern Africa – it stretches from the Richtersveld (which forms the northern part of the Succulent Karoo Biome and straddles the Orange River) through Namibia and into southern Angola. The barren mountains in the south give way to a massive 34,000km^2 dune field (fig. 4.1), the focus of this chapter. This 'sand sea' is a 100km-wide expanse of parallel sand dunes, interspersed with wide dune valleys. It extends for 600km from the Orange River northwards to the Kuiseb River, where the dunes are abruptly terminated (fig. 4.2). The Kuiseb flows periodically and prevents dunes from 'migrating' onto the gravel plains to the north of the river.

Jonathan Ball

4.2 The Kuiseb River is the boundary between the dune sea and the gravel plains to the north. Occasional flows in the river prevent the dunes from migrating across.

Dune formation has been taking place since the Miocene, about 15 million years ago. Sand deposited by the Orange River at its mouth is blown inland in a northeastern direction, initially as small but ever-growing, moving sand dunes. These travelling dunes are called barchan dunes – they are crescent-shaped with the two leading edges facing downwind (fig. 4.3). Wind pushes the sand up the growing upwind side, where it flows over the crest down the slip face, lifting the crest until it reaches the maximum angle of sand repose (32°). The dune 'migrates' when sand blown over the crest flows down the other side in avalanches. The dunes in the southern Namib have been shown to migrate at 25–60m per year, while those at the northern extreme of the Namib, in southern Angola, move about 100m per year. The dunes eventually coalesce into ridges that extend for hundreds of kilometres. Barchan dunes are thought to have carried with them various insect populations over time, separating populations and leading to speciation.

The central dune field is composed of long, linear (seif) dunes that are orientated roughly north–south.

Some of these dunes are up to 300m high and are among the highest sand dunes in the world (fig. 4.4). They are separated by interdune valleys or plains, which can vary from 100m to 3km wide. Dunes have a base and windward and leeward sides; these differ from each other in sand particle size (coarser particles near the base and finer grains higher up), compaction and organic content. The plains are more homogeneous, with a sandy-gravel substrate. The colour of the sand varies: white coastal sands become progressively redder further inland. This is biologically important, as it affects the heating, cooling and water evaporation rates in the dunes – white dunes reflect more light and therefore provide a less severe environment.

In spite of its barren, mostly vegetationless dunes, high levels of solar radiation and strong winds, the Namib is considered a cool coastal desert with a mild, warm-temperate to tropical climate. The conditions in continental deserts such as the Sahara are much harsher. The Namib, particularly inland, has hot summers with temperatures frequently rising over 40°C, and warm to hot winters without freezing temperatures (seldom below 3°C). Rainfall is low (less than 70mm per year) and falls mostly in late summer, but the dependable advective fog caused by the moist air above the cold off-shore Benguela current is an alternative source of water. It is blown inland by onshore winds and condenses over the warm sand. Droplets that form on plants, stones and sand are a source of water for plants and animals, many of which have developed strategies for collecting or using it. The fog, which can reach up to 50km inland, forms mainly at night (as many as 120 nights per year) and lasts about three hours; but can linger until about 09h00 the following day. Fog occurs most frequently between August and December.

When 20mm or more rain falls (the minimum necessary for seed germination), the dunes and interdune valleys may be covered with annual grasses, which grow quickly, set seed and then die.

4.3 A typical crescent-shaped barchan dune creeping slowly northwards behind its leading edges. These moving dunes carry dune insects that populate new regions and eventually evolve into new species.

4.4 Some of the highest dunes in the world occur around Sossusvlei. They may be up to 300m tall.

They are soon uprooted and fragmented by wind action and much of their biomass is quickly incorporated into detritus 'pads' against the dunes (fig. 4.5). The pads consist mainly of plant remains such as leaf fragments and seeds, but arthropod remains, feathers and bird and reptile faeces may occasionally make up an important component. Strong, mainly easterly winds blow the detritus into the dune fields. Most of it accumulates on the slip faces of leeward dune slopes, from where the detritus pads, mixed with sand, slide to the dune base in avalanches. The sand-covered pads are protected from the elements and 'stored' until changing wind patterns eventually expose them. They might be covered, uncovered and added to repeatedly by regularly changing wind patterns over long periods. The detritus is therefore periodically available to detritus feeders, which include many endemic insects in a range of taxonomic groups. The high numbers of detritus-feeding creatures in the Namib can largely be attributed to the dependable availability of this wind-blown resource.

Strong daytime winds blowing detritus over the sand often elicit frenzied activity in diurnal and nocturnal beetles and fishmoths. Buried insects can detect the wind-induced substrate noise caused by swirling and sliding sand particles. This brings the insects, especially beetles, to the surface in large numbers. The wind promotes activity for two reasons: it brings or exposes food, and it reduces the extreme surface temperatures considerably, making activity possible.

Permanent vegetation in the Namib consists of isolated clumps of a few spiky grass species, such as *Stipagrostis sabulicola* and *Cladoraphis spinosa* (fig. 4.6), and the succulent cushion-plant *Trianthema hereroensis* (Aizoaceae), which survive on coastal fog. The spiny nara melon, *Acanthosicyos horridus* (Cucurbitaceae, fig. 4.49), is common along the sandy banks of the Kuiseb River and the nearby dunes, as well as in other areas where underground water may rise to near the surface. These plant species stabilise sand at dune bases and wind-blown detritus collects around them. Plants also provide shade and therefore cooler sand. This creates a reliable thermal refuge for many arthropod and reptile species.

Although the Namib Desert appears to be a hostile environment, its insect life is incredibly diverse and is possibly the most specialised of any

4.5 Dark clumps of detritus in the lee of a dune. These fragments of organic matter blown in from the adjoining plains comprise the bottom rung of the food chain in the mostly vegetationless dunes.

4.6 Clumps of perennial and annual grasses that flushed after rain are the main forage for seasonally migrating animals such as this young gemsbok, *Oryx gazella*.

region in southern Africa. Endemicity at species level is almost 100% and is thought to be a result of the heterogeneity of the dune habitats and the strong abiotic environmental factors to which the species are exposed. Most species have some special adaptation to move in or on the sand, to avoid excessive direct heat, or to acquire water. About 100 species of large insects are known from the Namib interior, a very small number compared to any other southern African biome, but the high level of endemicity makes the Namib ecosystem unique. In comparison, the seasonally dry lower Kuiseb River bed (the northern boundary of the dune sea) has about 700 insect species, but almost all are nonendemic; some have a distribution that includes the arid savanna of the distant Kalahari.

About half of the dune insect fauna is in the Coleoptera, of which 70% are darkling beetles (Tenebrionidae) – it is amongst these that some of the most interesting adaptations to living in the desert are found. Diptera (flies) and Hymenoptera (wasps, bees and ants) account for 5–10% of the fauna each, while the remainder includes representatives of about five other orders. Members of the dune habitat that depend mainly on wind-blown detritus have developed many adaptations to feeding on detritus and living in a sand habitat (psammophilous). Although the Namib ecosystem is largely based on a detritus food chain, annual grasses and a few perennial plants enhance herbivore and pollinator numbers and activity.

Tenebrionid beetle diversity

Tenebrionidae are amongst the most common and noticeable insects in the Namib (fig. 4.8). Many have special adaptations to desert life and the family has therefore been the subject of more studies than any other insect group in the biome.

Tenebrionidae is one of the larger beetle families, with about 3,000 species in 200 genera in southern Africa. Morphological variation amongst its members is possibly the most extreme of any beetle family. Yet, somewhat surprisingly, most species feed on generally similar types of food: detritus, dry seeds and wood (although some species feed on germinating seeds and roots). The common name for the family is darkling beetles, based on the nocturnal habits of some species, although many desert species are adapted for diurnal activity.

Several familiar cosmopolitan tenebrionid species are reared for study in laboratory experiments, and for feeding pet fish, birds and reptiles, while some are pests of stored food products. The well-known meal worms of the pet trade are the larvae of *Tenebrio molitor*. A few species of *Tribolium* (*T. castaneum*, *T. confusum*, *T. destructor*), known as flour beetles, are serious grain

and meal pests. Species of *Gonocephalum* and *Somaticus* endemic to southern Africa are pests of germinating cereal crop seeds and are called false wireworms – to distinguish them from wireworms (Elateridae), which are similar in appearance and habitat occurrence.

Adult tenebrionid beetles can be 1.5–65mm long and are most often black; they can also be mottled or patterned in black, brown, yellow and white, or have bright metallic colours (fig. 4.9). Body shapes vary from flat to oval, globose, tubular or saucer-shaped. The body surface can be smooth, sculptured, hairy (setose), wax-coated or covered in dirt and fungal strands. Wings are often absent, especially in species in the arid western parts of southern Africa. Legs may be robust,

4.8 Tenebrionidae species from the Namib Desert, illustrating the morphological diversity of this large family in a relatively small geographical area: (a) *Stenocara* sp. 1; (b) *Stenocara* sp. 2; (c) *Rhammatodes kalaharicus*; (d) *Physadesmia* sp.; (e) *Stips* sp.; (f) *Pachynotelus comma*.

4.9 Tenebrionidae species from across southern Africa, illustrating the wide diversity in the family: (a) *Derosphaerius anthracinus*; (b) *Asthenochirus plicatulus*; (c) *Cryptochile* sp.; (d) *Herpiscius spinolae*; (e) *Strongylium* sp.; (f) *Anomalipus* sp.

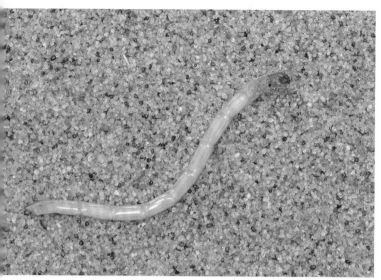

4.10 A typical tenebrionid larva.

long to very long and clearly visible, or very short and mostly hidden beneath the body.

The adults may be diurnal or nocturnal, and slow- to fast- or very fast-moving. Some produce defensive secretions. Most are solitary, but one western group has subsocial nesting and brood care, and its nests are parasitised by a related species (see 'Subsocial beetles and their nest parasites', p. 234). One southern African group is known colloquially as 'toktokkies' because they tap on the ground as a form of sexual communication (see box below).

Larvae across the family are superficially quite similar in appearance (fig. 4.10). They are slender and well sclerotised; most are yellow-brown with a darker head and thorax, well-developed legs and a strongly segmented body. They usually live underground, in litter, or in decomposing wood.

Tapping toktokkies

The production of sound by percussion in insects is probably best known in the southern African toktokkies (Tenebrionidae: Molurini, fig. 4.11). These beetles have the habit of tapping the abdomen on the ground several times in quick succession to attract a mate, 'listening', then tapping again. A finger tapped on the ground near a tapping beetle elicits intense excitement from the beetle, which happily attempts to copulate with the sound-producing finger!

This form of communication is one of the simplest known in insects. It is widespread in the Tenebrionidae worldwide, but particularly amongst flightless African members of the tribe Molurini. The southern African genera *Psammodes*, *Dichtha* and *Moluris* are the most well-known toktokkies.

Psammodes striatus communicates by tapping its abdomen on the ground – the resultant substrate vibrations are effective over a distance of about 50cm. The taps are produced in trains of 4–20 taps by both males and females. Crudely mimicked human taps also elicit a reaction, but are quickly ignored when the taps are identified as bogus. A study found that the apparently simple communication system used by *P. striatus* is a highly efficient means of attracting mates: it is at least ten times more energetically efficient than walking to find mates. Males are the most active of the sexes, drumming repeatedly; females only tap in response to male sounds. Although taps by other males are identified and noticed, they are ignored by the male; when he identifies taps from a receptive female, however, he responds vigorously, running in the direction of the taps, tapping repeatedly at short intervals, until they find each other.

4.11 Three typical toktokkies (Tenebrionidae): (a) *Phanerotomea* sp.; (b) *Psammodes retrospinosus*; (c) *Psammodes ponderosus*.

Morphological adaptations of desert insects

Most Namib insect species have some noticeable, even remarkable, morphological adaptation to their desert habitat, either to enable ease of movement in or on the sand, or to avoid excessive heat, or both.

Flightless beetles

The evolution of flight during the Carboniferous period (350 million years ago) was probably the main reason why insects became the most successful group of animals on earth. It provided them with exceptional mobility with which they could escape their surface-restricted predators, reach the nutritious flowers and fruit of tall trees, disperse to more suitable habitats, and locate mates more readily. We now know that more than 99% of modern insects evolved from a winged ancestor.

If having wings led to such evolutionary success, why would any insect relinquish the obvious advantages that flight confers? As evolution works on the principle of selection of those traits of an organism that are better adapted to their environment and therefore more likely to produce offspring, it follows that something about the environment must favour the loss of wings. Flightless insects occur in several diverse habitats – deserts, forests, islands and high mountains. These may appear to be very different, but they all have one aspect in common: ecological stability over millennia. Insects in cold, stable environments such as mountains and islands need to conserve energy for living and reproducing; if this can be achieved by not flying, loss of flight ensues.

In deserts, the main selective pressure is to acquire water and limit desiccation. Beetles are already well adapted to restrict body water loss. They have hard, shell-like front wings (elytra) that cover the hind wings and abdomen, which houses most of the visceral organs. Their respiratory openings (spiracles) are located on the sides of the abdomen and open under the elytra. A considerable amount of body water is lost during respiration, so the air trapped under the elytra becomes saturated with water vapour. However, when a beetle lifts its elytra (fig. 4.12), which it needs to do in order to fly, the saturated air quickly dissipates and the exhaled water vapour is lost. When beetles become flightless, their hind wings degenerate and the space beneath the elytra (the subelytral cavity) increases in volume. Because they no longer need to lift the elytra to fly, a permanently saturated atmosphere can be maintained in the subelytral cavity; this conserves water. The abdomen can also expand upwards into the additional space in the subelytral cavity; this allows the insect to eat more food, an advantage if it has a low-quality diet such as detritus. Female insects also have extra room for more eggs to develop. These changes make flightless insects more likely to produce offspring, thus favouring their survival in desert conditions.

All tenebrionid species in the Namib are flightless, with reduced hind wings and sealed elytra, as are most other dune beetle species, including weevils (Curculionidae, fig. 4.13) and some dung beetles (Scarabaeidae; see 'Specialist dung beetles', p. 150). Flightless weevils are common all over the world, so their presence in the desert is not surprising, but flightless dung beetles (and their relatives) are very unusual. Fewer than 10% of southern African species are flightless. They are found only in stable physical environments such as deserts (see 'Keratin beetles of the Kalahari', p. 253), forests (see 'The famous Addo dung beetle', p. 279; 'Detritus-feeding dung beetles', p. 122) and mountain peaks (see 'Iconic mountain fynbos beetles', p. 61).

Wax blooms

The environment in which insects live is often reflected in the properties of the cuticle, which forms the exoskeleton: its colour (see box, p. 141), hardness, the chemical composition of its layers, and especially the surface of the epicuticle.

The cuticle consists of three layers: the endocuticle (which lies directly above the epidermis), the exocuticle, and the outermost epicuticle.

4.12 (left) When a beetle, such as the savanna species *Hycleus tricolor* (Meloidae), lifts its elytra in flight, respiratory water is lost to the environment.

4.13 (right) A Namib weevil (Curculionidae) displays the typical highly convex shape of a wingless beetle.

4.14 Different colours and patterns of wax bloom in Namib Tenebrionidae species: **(a–d)** *Zophosis* sp.; **(e, f)** unidentified species.

The epicuticle is made of a waxy lipoprotein, which makes the cuticle largely impermeable to water loss. The main function of the wax is to reduce cuticular water loss, one of the main sources of insect body water loss (see 'Limiting evaporative water loss', p. 148), but it also plays a role in increased reflectance of solar radiation, protection against ultraviolet light, microorganisms, predators and abrasion. It may also carry pheromones that are used in chemical communication.

About half of the diurnal Namib tenebrionids have a thick cuticle, which produces wax from special dermal gland pores that open onto the epicuticle surface. The wax is extruded in a powdery or filamentous form; the individual filaments collapse and coalesce into a mat that covers part or most of the cuticle in a 'wax bloom' (fig. 4.14). The wax bloom is produced continuously and may be completely replaced within eight hours. Beetles can be induced to produce wax by exposing them to low humidity and high temperature, or to stop producing wax by raising the humidity and lowering the temperature. The wax colour varies tremendously among (and even within) species, and can be blue, brown, pink, red, white or yellow.

Various studies of desert beetles, including those of the Namib, have provided strong support for the role of wax blooms in water balance and thermoregulation. The waxy mat and the boundary layer of air between the cuticle surface and the underside of the wax layer limit the diffusion and evaporation of cuticular water vapour.

Temperature increases and humidity decreases from the coast to inland areas of the Namib. There is a parallel increase in the number of diurnal tenebrionid species with a wax bloom from west to east. In some species, the degree of wax cover is much higher for individuals in inland areas than in coastal areas. For example, flat desert beetles, *Onymacris plana* (fig. 4.15), occurring inland have a bluish appearance caused by a coating of wax over most of the body, while coastal populations lack the bloom.

Cauricara phalangium is a wax-covered tenebrionid species that lives in gravelly interdune plains. In an experiment, the rate of water loss of wax-covered and wax-denuded individuals of *C. phalangium* was compared. The wax-covered beetles were found to lose considerably less water than those without wax.

Wax blooms also help with thermoregulation. Beetles with a pale wax covering warm up more slowly and remain active for longer than dark beetles, as the lighter colour reflects more solar radiation. In *C. phalangium*, the reflective properties of the white wax on the dorsal surface are 100 times more effective than areas of black cuticle without wax.

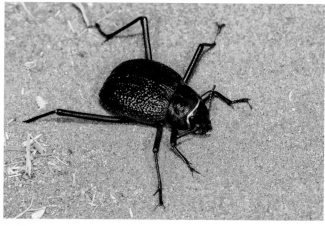

4.15 *Onymacris plana* (Tenebrionidae) with faint wax bloom.

Wax colour and crypsis in frantic beetles

Frantic beetles in the genus *Zophosis* display wax colours that seem to play a role in camouflage and predator avoidance.

Some species have populations with different wax colours; for example, *Z. dorsata* beetles that live on quartz gravel in the central Namib have a white bloom, while those further north, on red sand, have a pink-red bloom. In this case, the colours seem to be substrate-specific and might help them to blend in with their environment.

Zophosis fairmairei beetles have interrupted patches of yellow-brown dorsal wax bloom (figs 4.16a, b). They are most active during strong winds, when they run around amongst drifting sand and pieces of detritus. The cryptic effect is quite remarkable and probably helps them to avoid predators, such as fast-moving, sand-diving dune lizards, *Meroles* spp. (fig. 4.16c), which are often active at the same time and under similar conditions.

  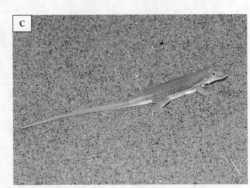

4.16 (a) *Zophosis fairmairei* (Tenebrionidae) with full wax bloom, and (b) with wax abraded. (c) This dune lizard, *Meroles cuneirostris*, is a major predator of dune insects.

Colour and thermoregulation

Most dune beetles are black. This led the early desert ecology researcher William J. Hamilton III to formulate the 'black desert beetle paradox' – why would diurnal beetles in a hot environment be black, a colour that would absorb heat and make them even hotter?

Furthermore, some species closely related to black ones have white elytra (fig. 4.17). The most obvious explanation for the development of white elytra would be that white reflects light and heat, so white beetles would have a thermal advantage over those that are black. Although some early researchers came to this conclusion, subsequent studies have found little support for this hypothesis, suggesting that white beetles are cryptic or aposematic rather than merely thermally advantaged.

One comprehensive study compared the thermal biology of two similarly sized diurnal *Onymacris* species (Tenebrionidae) that occur in the same area – the black head-stander or fog-basking beetle, *O. unguicularis* (fig. 4.26), and the black-and-white desert beetle, *O. bicolor*, which is white above and black below. Both are active at temperatures of 20–45°C, with their lethal upper limit at about 48°C. Results showed that black *O. unguicularis* beetles absorbed more direct heat because of their black elytra, whereas *O. bicolor* individuals absorbed more reflected radiation from

Chantelle Bosch

4.17 Namib beetles such as this *Stenocara eburnea* (Tenebrionidae) are often white, which is thought to give them a thermal advantage over black beetles.

below because of their black ventral surface. Yet, they both cooled equally fast by convective heat loss in even very slight surface wind. The answer to the black desert beetle paradox is that wind has the greatest overall effect on body temperature, completely overriding the effect of body colour (see 'Warming up and cooling down', p. 144).

All species of *Pachysoma* (Scarabaeidae) are black, except the widespread Namib dune beetle *P. denticolle* (fig. 4.20a). The majority of *P. denticolle* individuals have a black pronotum and orange elytra, although some coastal individuals are all black. The reason for black beetles occurring on the coast could be that strong cool winds are more common along the coast, negating the requirement for colour adaptations needed for other functions. However, the species'

The effect of wind on communication in dunes

Many ultra-psammophilous Namib beetles spend up to 18 hours per day buried in soft dune sand without any form of a structured tunnel, and are effectively isolated from potential mates, food, and even from the sand surface. Only a few individuals may be active at one time over their activity cycle – nocturnal species may be active all night, but diurnal species are usually only active during thermally favourable periods of the day. However, most of the species living beneath the sand surface respond to strong wind blowing across the dunes, irrespective of whether it is during their normal activity period or not. Many individuals come to the surface when the wind blows. For example, for nocturnal species of *Lepidochora* (Tenebrionidae, fig. 4.18), strong winds at any time of the day may elicit frenzied activity of up to hundreds of individuals. The windy conditions not only carry the promise of fresh detritus blowing in, but create opportunities for socialising with conspecifics. It has been suggested that one of the species, *L. argentogrisea*, is actually a gregarious species, and that wind is the factor that heightens social activity, probably enhancing reproductive effectiveness.

Strong wind, particularly during daytime, reduces the near-surface sand temperature to below the thermal maximum of most dune species, whether they are diurnal or nocturnal, thus maximising activity during favourable conditions.

Various studies have been done to determine whether wind actually generates substrate-borne vibrations that can be perceived by buried beetles, whether they can sense and identify noises made by other beetles moving on the surface above, and whether beetles on the surface can distinguish sounds made by buried beetles. Results have shown that some *Lepidochora* species can clearly perceive wind sounds; *Onymacris laeviceps* can recognise the sound of beetles walking above them; and *O. plana* males can locate buried females (fig. 4.19).

4.18 This species of *Lepidochora* is one of several flying saucer tenebrionids in the Namib.

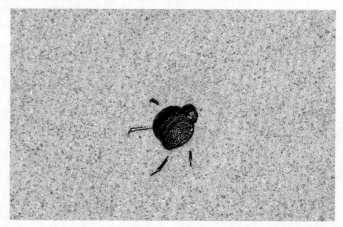

4.19 A male *Onymacris plana* (Tenebrionidae) diving into the sand to locate a buried female. Its broad elytra distinguish it from the female.

orange elytra remain unexplained, and it has been claimed that *P. denticolle* mimics *Scarabaeus rubripennis* (both Scarabaeidae, fig. 4.20b). At least two other, considerably larger, Namib *Scarabaeus* species are also black and orange (see 'Ball-rolling dung beetles', p. 151), so it is more likely that some factor of the physical environment has actually selected for this specific colour combination.

One of the main results of these studies is that wind is the major factor in temperature control in desert beetles, but its importance extends far beyond that.

4.20 (a) *Pachysoma denticolle* (Scarabaeidae) is the only bicoloured species in the genus, as well as being the smallest. **(b)** *Scarabaeus rubripennis* (Scarabaeidae) has similar colouring to *P. denticolle*.

Wind not only provides the detritus that is the main food source for a majority of insects, but also facilitates communication amongst insects buried in the sand (see box opposite).

Environmental pressure on leg structure

The loose and often hot sand in the Namib has put pressure on some insects to adapt their leg structure to compensate either for the loose sand on which they walk, or to enable them to stretch their legs to raise their bodies as far as possible above the hot sand.

Most of the diurnal insects active during the hottest time of the day have somewhat extended legs; this includes many of the Tenebrionidae and the terrestrial ant species *Ocymyrmex robustior* (see 'Thermal tolerance in the Namib ant', p. 145) and *Camponotus detritus* (see 'The Namib detritus ant', p. 153).

Some insects have setal brushes or expanded lobes on their tarsi that provide an increased surface area for walking on loose sand. The predatory dune cricket, *Comicus calcaris* (Schizodactylidae, fig. 4.21; see box below) has 'sand shoes': four-segmented enlarged tarsi, somewhat like the toes of a gecko. They live mainly on very loose dune sand where they spend most of the day in burrows and come out at night to prey on other small invertebrates. Their specialised tarsi enhance their digging ability, facilitate walking on loose sand, and enable them to land on soft sand without sinking after a long leap.

Some of the diurnal tenebrionids have extraordinarily long legs: *Cauricara phalangium*, one of the wax-covered species, 'stilts' during extremely hot conditions (see 'Leg-stilting as a thermoregulatory strategy', p. 145). Even some of the very small beetles, such as the wax-covered *Zophosis fairmairei*, stilt when

---

Predatory dune crickets

Schizodactylus and *Comicus* are the only genera in the dune or splay-footed cricket family, Schizodactylidae (Orthoptera: Ensifera). All species are predatory. *Schizodactylus* (seven species) occurs in Asia and *Comicus* (eight species) in Africa. *Comicus* species are wingless, while those of *Schizodactylus* are capable of flight. All except the Namib dune species, *C. calcaris* (fig. 4.21), live on firm sand.

Most *Comicus* species are known from the arid western parts of southern Africa, from Namaqualand to southern Angola. One species has been recorded from the central Free State, and another has a typical Kalahari savanna distribution across Namibia and Botswana into northern South Africa.

All *Comicus* species are pale, yellowish-brown crickets, about 10–20mm long, with exceptionally long antennae (five times their body length). The hind femora are as long as the body and the tibiae are characteristically swollen, with six flat spines at the distal end. The tarsi consist of four segments, each of which has long sideways-projecting lobes; these are more pronounced on the hind tarsi. The tibial spines and tarsal lobes increase the surface area of the feet and function as 'sand shoes', permitting the crickets to make jumps of up to several metres at a time.

The crickets are nocturnal and lie in small depressions in the sand with their antennae outstretched, waiting for approaching insect prey. When prey arrives, they pounce on it, and hold it down with their foretarsi while consuming it.

Most Ensifera produce sound by rubbing a file on the hind femur against pegs on the forewing, and have hearing organs (tympana) on their foretibiae. *Comicus* crickets produce sound by rubbing a ridge on the hind femur against a row of pegs on the side of the abdomen, but they do not have tympana. Their swollen tibiae, however, contain complex vibration-sensitive organs that are possibly adapted for sensing surface vibrations produced by individuals drumming during mate attraction, and for sensing approaching prey or predators.

4.21 The predatory dune cricket, *Comicus calcaris* (Schizodactylidae), has highly modified legs: muscular hind femurs allow it to make prodigious defensive jumps, its swollen tibiae contain vibration-sensitive organs, and its four-segmented tarsi have an increased surface area to enable it to run and jump on loose sand.

sand temperatures are above 45°C. Though this raises them only 2–3mm above the sand surface, it is sufficient to lift them into the wind path, which reduces their body temperature.

The Namib species of *Pachysoma* (see 'Specialist dung beetles', p. 150) have long bristles on their hind tibiae and tarsi. The main function of these setal brushes is to help the beetles to collect and hold dry dung pellets (e.g. *P. denticolle* and *P. rodriguesi*) or for brushing detritus into a 'basket' so it can be transported (*P. rotundigenum*).

Behavioural adaptations to desert conditions

Namib insect species come into contact with sand at some stage of their daily activity and seasonal developmental cycle, so high daily sand temperatures are a critical limiting factor for most. Summer dune surface temperatures may exceed 70°C, but are usually below 65°C. For most insects, dune surface activity is limited to about two hours in the morning and three hours in the afternoon, when temperatures are between 20°C and 45°C.

Subsurface temperatures decrease rapidly up to about 20cm below the surface, where they remain constant around 30°C. Insects therefore have to retreat to a minimum depth of 20cm to avoid overheating.

Relative humidity at the soil surface varies between 100% during foggy nights to a midday low of less than 10%, but 10cm below the surface the relative humidity remains at 25–45%. Dune insects can effectively reduce their evaporative water loss by remaining in this moderate environment while above-ground conditions are too harsh for activity.

Desert insects have evolved a range of strategies to minimise their exposure to dangerously high temperatures and desiccating conditions. These include behavioural changes that affect thermoregulation, as well as methods of obtaining water or minimising water loss.

Mobile diurnal insects use behavioural strategies to deal with high desert temperatures. They move fast and have the ability to seek out moderate microhabitats for shelter, and complement this by burrowing, squatting, stilting or climbing. Some turn light-coloured body surfaces toward the sun to attain and then maintain a maximum body temperature of about 40°C (often close to the lethal maximum) for several hours each day. Sedentary insects, on the other hand, tolerate and remain 'active' at a very wide range of daily temperatures.

Desert insects obtain water by drinking from fog droplets that have condensed on plants or sand ridges,
or by extracting moisture from detritus. Fog may occur too irregularly to fulfil all species' complete water requirements, making other mechanisms necessary, such as metabolising body fat. Insects that spend a large part of their life cycle underground or covered by detritus have specialised adaptations to acquire water, such as absorbing water from subsaturated air.

Warming up and cooling down

The flat desert beetle, *Onymacris plana* (Tenebrionidae, fig. 4.22), is a large, black, highly sexually dimorphic species with long legs. Females are typically elongate (15–20mm long), whereas males have a greatly expanded abdomen and elytra, making them appear almost round (up to 25mm in diameter) when viewed from above.

4.22 A male flat desert beetle, *Onymacris plana*, showing its distinctive profile. The flat body and long legs enable it to run fast, dive and 'swim' in loose sand when threatened.

The beetles' activity is largely controlled by their ability to warm up in the morning and late afternoon when the sun's rays are low and heat energy is transmitted through the elytra to the abdomen. However, the elytra and subelytral cavity block most of the energy from direct rays when the sun is high overhead. This is made possible by a remarkably textured elytral surface and the presence of an air-filled subelytral cavity.

Onymacris plana beetles are capable of running very fast even across the soft sand of the leeward dune slopes, and can dive readily into the sand when physically threatened or when they start to overheat. They become active an hour or two after sunrise (07h00–08h00), remain active until late morning (10h00–11h00), then dive into soft sand, where they remain until it becomes cool enough for activity again by late afternoon.

How the flat desert beetle uses solar energy

Most of the incoming solar energy in the Namib has wavelengths in the range of 300–2,500 nanometres (nm). This range includes ultraviolet, visible and infrared radiation. Light in the visible spectrum (visible to human eyes) has wavelengths from about 380–740nm (violet to red); ultraviolet light has short wavelengths of 10–380nm; and infrared radiation has long wavelengths in the region of 800–1,000nm. Wavelengths between 700nm and 740nm at the end of the visible spectrum are known as near-infrared (NIR) radiation. Infrared and NIR radiation are experienced as heat.

When the sun is directly overhead at midday, with relatively short atmospheric travel distances and thin air, about 50% of the incoming solar radiation in the Namib is NIR radiation. At low sun angles, in the early morning and late afternoon, light travels farther and penetrates denser air masses,

so 60% of the energy that reaches the surface is contained in wavelengths longer than 700nm.

The flat desert beetle, *Onymacris plana*, uses NIR radiation to warm up in the morning and late afternoon. At these times, a major proportion of the incident radiant energy is in the NIR range, and about 20% of that striking the beetle is transmitted through the elytra and subelytral cavity to reach the abdomen and warm the beetle, while 74% is absorbed by the elytra.

At higher sun angles during the day, there is less energy in the NIR range. About 80% is absorbed by the elytra, and only 14% of the incident energy passes through to the abdomen. Although this may raise the surface temperature of the elytra to above 60°C, much of the heat is lost through wind cooling. The air layer in the subelytral cavity further insulates the abdomen from the hot elytra.

Leg-stilting as a thermoregulatory strategy

The long-legged interdune beetle *Cauricara phalangium* (Tenebrionidae) is pear-shaped and smaller than *Onymacris plana*. It is restricted to the harsh plains habitat, where the uniformly grey-white stony gravel reduces the range of available air temperatures suitable for activity. The beetles survive the extreme conditions by being active mainly during winter, for shorter periods during the day, and by using behaviour to increase or decrease their body temperature.

Because of their small body size, the beetles' body temperature remains close to the air temperature. They can only become active when the air temperature about 1cm above the ground reaches 34°C, which enables them to achieve an optimal body temperature of about 36°C. They increase their temperature by 'squatting' with bent legs and body pressed to the warming ground, perpendicular to light coming from the sun.

They remain active until their body temperature reaches 40–42°C, after which they begin to demonstrate temperature-reducing behaviour. The first step is to find the largest available rock and to clamber onto it; the top of the rock is a few degrees cooler than the soil surface and provides a temporary thermal refuge. As their body temperature further increases, they begin to 'stilt', stretching their legs until they stand on the tips of their tarsi and point their slender wax-coated abdomen towards the sun. This decreases the surface area exposed to the sun and increases reflectivity. At its peak of tolerance (40–42°C), the beetle's body temperature may be 10°C cooler than that of the ground surface.

Thermal tolerance in the Namib ant

The Namib ant, *Ocymyrmex robustior* (=*O. barbiger*, Hymenoptera: Formicidae: Myrmicinae, fig. 4.23a), is a small species that preys actively on heat-stressed arthropods during hot times of the day (fig. 4.23b). To do this, workers must forage at temperatures that are close to their own lethal threshold.

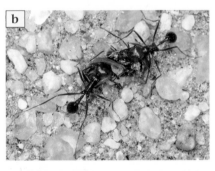

4.23 (a) The Namib ant, *Ocymyrmex robustior*, (b) preys on heat-stressed arthropods. (c) When close to its thermal maximum, the ant climbs onto raised objects for a short time to escape the hot surface. It remains here until its body has cooled a few degrees.

In a hot environment, a small organism has the disadvantage of heating up quickly to the temperature of its immediate environment; conversely, it also loses heat quickly in a suitable thermal refuge. The Namib ants take advantage of quick and efficient heat exchange to survive high soil temperatures of up to 67°C, which are far in excess of their lethal maximum (about 50°C). They climb onto objects such as sticks and stones that are raised about 10–20mm above the ground (fig. 4.23c); these thermal refuges are a few degrees cooler than the soil surface. There is usually also an air current at this height, which lowers the ant's body temperature even further. Under very hot conditions, they might climb as high as 100mm up a grass stalk or into a bush. The ants increase the rate of heat loss in these thermal refuges by maintaining a grip with some limbs and vigorously flailing the others about to disturb the boundary layer of air in contact with their bodies. A few seconds in a thermal refuge lowers the ant's body temperature to optimal operational temperatures.

At soil temperatures below 51°C, workers spend about 93% of their foraging time on the soil surface. As the soil temperature increases, their rest periods in thermal refuges become more frequent and longer. They pause for 5–6 seconds in thermal refuges at soil temperatures near 48°C, but when soil temperatures reach 58°C, they rest for more than 10 seconds. At the limit of their surface-temperature tolerance (up to 67°C), they may remain on thermal refuges for up to 85 seconds.

Thermal refuges of antlion larvae

The larvae of the antlion *Cueta trivirgata* (Myrmeleontidae: Neuroptera) (fig. 4.24a) live in pits in the sand, where they lie in wait for their prey (fig. 4.24b). Stout digging plates on their abdomen enable them to dig quickly in hot, hard soil. Two-thirds of the diet of third-instar larvae consists of Namib ants, *Ocymyrmex robustior*; other prey includes Mutillidae wasps and Anthicidae beetles.

Although the antlion pits lie in sand in barren areas that are directly exposed to sun for 10–12 hours per day, the structure and shape of the pits ameliorate thermal conditions inside them. The pits of third-instar larvae are about 28mm deep and 55mm in diameter at the top; the bigger and deeper the pit, the more buffered it is against changes in environmental temperatures, remaining cooler during the day and warmer at night. During daytime, the pit temperature is always lower than that of the surrounding soil, and the trend is reversed at night. At midday, the pit temperature is 15°C cooler than the surrounding soil; later in the afternoon this difference becomes smaller, but the pit remains cooler.

The antlions also use behaviour to deal with temperature changes: during the early part of the day when the sun is rising, they move to the cool, eastern side of the pit to lessen the effects of increasing temperature; after a midday retreat into cooler sand below, they return to the eastern face of the pit in the late afternoon to obtain maximum warmth from the sinking sun.

Cueta trivirgata antlions can tolerate a very wide range of soil and body temperatures. They remain vigilant – attentively watching for prey – in their pits at sand temperatures from 13°C to 63°C by day or night. At lower temperatures, vigilance decreases; for example, at 15°C, only 60% of antlions are still vigilant. At temperatures below 13°C, the antlions remain in their pits but cease vigilance. At higher temperatures, the antlions become more active: at 45°C, for example, 80% are vigilant. As soil temperatures increase to 50–55°C, about 50% of the antlions remain vigilant, although their critical maximum body temperature is about 53°C. *Ocymyrmex robustior* ants – the antlions' favoured prey – are most active in this temperature range, so the antlions expose themselves to near-lethal temperatures to increase their chances of obtaining food.

When soil temperatures go above 55°C, the antlion larvae burrow deeper into the soil below their pits to escape the heat. The average depth of this retreat is about 62mm, at which the soil temperature is around 53°C, but some are as deep as 120mm.

4.24 (a) *Cueta trivirgata* larva. (b) Although the pits of the antlion *C. trivirgata* are dug in exposed locations, their depth and shape protect the antlions from temperature extremes.

Rina de Klerk

The fog-basking beetle

The detritus-feeding fog-basking beetle, *Onymacris unguicularis* (Tenebrionidae), is most active during the warmest part of the day, usually when the soil temperature is around 50°C. These diurnal beetles remain buried in the sand of dune slip faces at night, but when coastal fog drifts into the desert (fig. 4.25), they crawl out of the cool sand and climb to the dune crest. Here they adopt a head-down position, facing into the incoming fog. As the fog condenses on the beetle's legs and body, water trickles down to the head and mouthparts (fig. 4.26). Beetles usually drink about 12% of their body weight during a fog, but some may drink as much as 34% of their total body weight.

The fog-stand beetle

The fog-stand beetle, *Stenocara gracilipes* (Tenebrionidae, fig. 4.27), collects water in a similar way to *Onymacris unguicularis*. It stands with its head down and its body held at a 45° angle into the wind, and spreads its hard, bumpy elytra. Minute water droplets stick to the bumps – which are hydrophilic – and provide a surface for other droplets to attach. The droplets grow up to 5mm in diameter, after which they roll into waxy hydrophobic troughs surrounding the bumps and then down the inclined back towards the mouthparts.

Fog-catching trenches

Flying saucer beetles have short legs and most of the dorsal part of the body is covered by the pronotum and elytra. Their flattened and rounded shape helps them to 'swim' quickly through the loose sand on dunes.

Three nocturnal species, *Lepidochora discoidalis*, *L. porti* and *L. kahani* (Tenebrionidae, fig. 4.28), dig fog-catching trenches on mornings when fog drifts in off the ocean. The beetle bulldozes a shallow trench that is as wide and deep as its body and up to a metre long, pushing up two parallel sand ridges on either side of the trench. The trench is perpendicular to the wind bearing the incoming fog. Water condenses on the ridges and beetles return along them, drinking water from the wet sand and flattening the ridges as they move along. They may drink as much as 14% of their body weight.

4.26 *Onymacris unguicularis* in head-down position, drinking from the film of condensed fog covering its body.

4.27 *Stenocara gracilipes*, another of the beetles that drink water from fog condensed on their body.

4.28 One of the *Lepidochora* species that dig fog-catching trenches during early misty mornings.

4.29 The fishmoth *Ctenolepisma terebrans* is able to absorb water from subsaturated air at a relative humidity below 50%.

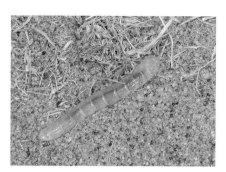

4.30 The larvae of some larger tenebrionid species can also absorb water from sub-saturated air.

4.31 *Eurychora* species have a dorsal covering of wax and hairs to which soil particles adhere; these limit desiccation and protect the cuticle from ultraviolet radiation.

Absorbing water from air

Fishmoths (Zygentoma; see 'Fishmoths', p. 347) are common and abundant in and around the bases of perennial plants and in detritus cushions. The common species *Ctenolepisma terebrans* (fig. 4.29) is active above the surface during mornings and evenings as well as during strong detritus-bearing winds. It was experimentally found to be able to absorb water from air with a minimum relative humidity threshold of 45–47.5%. This is substantially lower than the 60% minimum relative humidity recorded for *C. longicaudata* from the Eastern Cape and KwaZulu-Natal, which is already remarkably low. Although the precise mechanism for absorbing water from subsaturated air is still undetermined, it is known to be located in the rectum of the fishmoth.

The larvae of some of the common larger tenebrionid species in the Namib (fig. 4.30), such as those of the flat desert beetle, *Onymacris plana*, and the similar species *O. marginipennis*, develop entirely underground, where they feed on buried detritus. Development takes 8–10 months in *O. plana* and 4–5 months in *O. marginipennis*. The larvae can absorb water from air with a relative humidity above 83%, but moisture levels below the soil surface do not normally rise above a relative humidity of 50%. At a depth of 20cm it is 31–35%, and 80cm below the surface it remains relatively constant at 48–50%. It is assumed that the beetle larvae must visit the surface or near-surface frequently to absorb water, especially during fog (water obtained from metabolised fat would be the only alternative source). The mechanism for absorbing water seems to be rectal, as in fishmoths.

Limiting evaporative water loss

In desert beetles, discontinuous gas exchange cycles and the subelytral cavity (see 'Flightless beetles', p. 139) help to minimise respiratory water loss. Cuticular evaporative loss, however, increases with temperature and beetles have developed various adaptations to minimise this.

Respiration beneath the sand

The late Gideon Louw and Sue Nicolson (then at the University of Cape Town, currently at the University of Pretoria) studied and compared respiratory patterns and carbon dioxide production of the fog-basking beetle, *Onymacris unguicularis* (fig. 4.26), buried beneath 5cm of soft slip-face sand, with that of beetles that were left exposed. Their study found that resting insects respire in bouts of discontinuous gas exchange cycles (DGCs; see upper box, p. 27), a mechanism thought to be a water-saving adaptation, especially in flightless desert beetles with fused elytra (see 'Flightless beetles', p. 139).

The DGCs are characterised by the repetition of three major periods:
- a 'flutter' period during which the spiracles open and close;
- an 'open' period when the spiracles are fully open and the exchange of oxygen and carbon dioxide takes place; and
- a 'closed' period during which the spiracles are tightly shut.

Measurement of the intermittent bursts of carbon dioxide released by resting sand-covered beetles and resting uncovered beetles demonstrated that covered beetles respired normally and in a pattern broadly similar to that of exposed beetles. The only difference was that they opened their spiracles less frequently than did exposed beetles, sometimes keeping them closed for as long as 60 minutes. This suggests that long periods of apnoea under the sand minimise respiratory water loss.

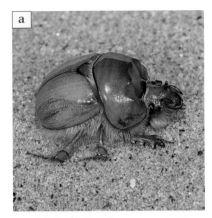

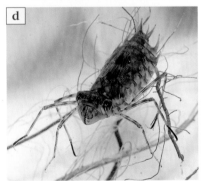

The wax layers (see 'Wax blooms', p. 139) produced by many desert beetles under very hot conditions develop in direct response to heat to minimise cuticular water loss. Some beetles, such as species of *Eurychora* (Tenebrionidae), have long stout hairs and waxy filaments on the upper body surface to which soil particles adhere (fig. 4.31). The soil covering protects the cuticle from desiccation and ultraviolet rays. Many ultra-psammophilous Namib tenebrionids spend up to 18 hours per day submerged in soft sand to escape temperature extremes and water loss (see box opposite).

Feeding adaptations in desert insects

Food is seldom plentiful in the desert, but occasionally natural events may create short periods of plenty for insects. These include detritus carried into dune fields by periodic strong winds, the effects of rainfall on desert flora and fauna, and dung deposited by large mammal herbivores. The insects that respond to these short-lived flushes of food often have morphological and behavioural adaptations that help them to use food resources quickly and effectively (fig. 32a).

Detritus is a dependable food source that is blown into dune areas by wind. Some tenebrionid beetles, such as *Zophosis fairmairei* (see box, p. 141) and *Lepidochora argentogrisea* (see box, p. 142), respond to strong wind as an indicator of a fresh detritus supply. Despite its name, the common detritus ant, *Camponotus detritus* (see 'The Namib detritus ant', p. 153), feeds mainly on honeydew produced by aphids and scale insects that live on perennial plants, and may occasionally eat small pieces of dry animal matter when available; it uses plant detritus only during nest construction.

Rain is a rare event in the Namib. The average annual rainfall is 10mm, but it can range from 5mm in the west to 85mm in the eastern parts of the desert. Rain is often limited to a small geographic area. After a rain shower, annual plants may germinate from seed, grow and flower rapidly; perennial plants may produce a flush of leaves and flowers. These provide food for flower-frequenting insects (fig. 4.32), such as bees and wasps, as well as herbivores, from small moth larvae (see box, p. 152) to large mammals, such as gemsbok.

Ephemeral pools formed after a downpour attract a range of aquatic insects, such as the wandering glider dragonfly, *Pantala flavescens* (fig. 4.32c, d). Namaqua sandgrouse (fig. 4.33) and the iconic gemsbok are examples of nomadic animals that travel across the desert to reach such water sources.

Rain also triggers the rapid emergence of insects that have remained buried in the sand in a quiescent state for years. The sudden increase in available prey attracts predators, such as spiders (fig. 4.34), scorpions (fig. 4.35), birds (fig. 4.36) and mammalian insectivores. Dung and carrion feeders benefit in turn.

The dung beetle fauna of the Namib is relatively rich in spite of the harsh environment and the dearth of fresh herbivore dung on which most dung

4.32 Rain in the Namib triggers the emergence of members of the rain fauna. Rain-water pools and flushing and flowering dune plants attract nomadic animals. **(a)** The fungus-feeding dor beetle (Bolboceratidae) is active for only a few days after rain; **(b)** a flower-frequenting wasp (Scoliidae); **(c)** the globe skimmer or wandering glider, *Pantala flavescens*; **(d)** *P. flavescens* nymphs develop rapidly in ephemeral pools, taking just 20 days to reach adulthood.

4.33 One of the rain-dependent birds of the arid western parts of southern Africa, the Namaqua sandgrouse, *Pterocles namaqua*, arrives in flocks to drink water at ephemeral pools.

4.34 The white lady spider, *Leucorchestris arenicola* (Sparassidae), a formidable nocturnal predator of insects and other arthropods.

4.35 Scorpions, such as this *Opistophthalmus adustus* (Scorpionidae), often emerge at night in large numbers after rain and roam the dunes in search of prey.

4.37 Lesser dung flies (Sphaeroceridae) ride and perch on foraging dung beetles to access moist dung exposed by the feeding beetle.

4.36 Secretary birds, *Sagittarius serpentarius*, are among the large predators attracted to the abundance of arthropods and reptiles active after rain.

4.38 *Pachysoma rotundigenum* collects only detritus for food and larval development.

4.39 *Pachysoma denticolle* dragging a gemsbok dung pellet in typical fashion.

beetles feed and in which they breed. There are several endemic species of the flightless west coast genus *Pachysoma* (see below), a few endemic or near-endemic winged species of widespread genera such as *Scarabaeus*, and a strict dune endemic with no known close living relatives, the monotypic (only one species in the genus) and kleptoparasitic *Hammondantus psammophilus* (see 'Small kleptoparasitic beetles', p. 152).

Lesser dung flies (Sphaeroceridae, fig. 4.37) are also attracted to dung. They perch on dung beetles making forays to and from the dung; the dung beetle exposes inner, moister dung, in which the flies lay eggs. Winged dung beetles also carry mites that prey on dung fly eggs.

Specialist dung beetles

There are 13 species in the flightless dung beetle genus *Pachysoma* (Coleoptera: Scarabaeidae: Scarabaeinae: Scarabaeini). They occur along the West Coast from Cape Town to the Kuiseb River. Five species occur in Namaqualand south of the Orange River in South Africa (see 'Detritus-feeding dung beetles', p. 122); two further species are found close to the Orange River, but on opposite sides; and the remaining six species are restricted to the Namib dune sea. *Pachysoma* species do not feed on wet herbivore dung like their close living relatives, but eat detritus (*P. rotundigenum*, fig. 4.38) or dry dung pellets produced by rodents, hares and the occasional gemsbok passing through in search of annual grasses (*P. denticolle*, fig. 4.39; *P. rodriguesi*, fig. 4.40).

4.40 *Pachysoma rodriguesi*, the largest of the Namib species, is a gemsbok dung pellet specialist.

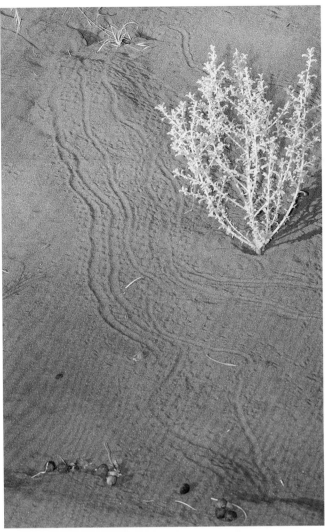

4.41 Signs of repeated foraging trips by a *Pachysoma denticolle* beetle from its burrow to a source of gemsbok dung pellets about 5m away. The beetles navigate using polarised light as a directional cue.

Although they belong to the group of ball-rolling dung beetles (see box, p. 249), the nature of their desert food does not allow them to form and roll balls. Instead, *Pachysoma* beetles hold dry dung pellets or plant fragments with their hind tarsi and drag them forwards to an already excavated burrow. They have to do this repeatedly to collect enough food on the barren dunes. They are able to navigate precisely between the food source and the burrow (fig. 4.41) using polarised sunlight (see box below).

Ball-rolling dung beetles

Two large, winged, ball-rolling dung beetles (Scarabaeidae: Scarabaeinae: Scarabaeini) that are found in the Namib have larger distribution ranges that lie outside the desert: *Scarabaeus proximus* also occurs in Namaqualand, and *S. costatus* in the Kalahari. Both species have two colour morphs: they are either completely black, or black and orange.

Until quite recently, these beetles were thought to belong to a separate genus, *Drepanopodus*, based on their atypical colour patterns and specialised legs. However, phylogenetic studies have revealed that the leg attributes on which the definition of the genus was based (the number of tarsal claws and the shape of the tibial teeth) are characteristics that have probably evolved in a sandy environment. In other words, they are merely slightly atypical species of the large, variable genus *Scarabaeus*.

Scarabaeus proximus and *S. costatus* are active by day on dunes of the southern dune sea. They are very fast-moving, nervous beetles, flying off when approached. However, they appear to follow a person

Polarised light is used by some insects

Polarised light is light that vibrates in only one direction (in a single plane) such as up-and-down, while light waves emitted directly by the sun vibrate in all directions (more than one plane), such as up-and-down *and* left-and-right.
Light from the sun is scattered by gas and water vapour molecules when it passes through the atmosphere. Upon impact with a water or gas molecule, the photon (light ray) from the sun is scattered at right angles to the direction that it was coming from, and is polarised either vertically or horizontally, that is, in one plane. The amount of light scattered depends on the size of the molecule and the wavelength of the light.

Human eyes are unable to detect polarised light because the longer wavelengths such as red, orange and yellow (which humans detect easily) are not scattered very effectively, whereas the shorter blue wavelengths are. The compound eyes of insects, on the other hand, have a greater sensitivity to shorter wavelengths, and this may explain why some insects are able to detect polarised light, which is used in navigation and orientation.

Some insects, for example bees, ants and dung beetles, can determine the position of the sun, moon or stars by analysing the pattern of polarisation in even a small patch of clear sky (such as on a cloudy day). This ability enables insects that forage for long periods far from their nests to find the nest again, even though environmental conditions may change (such as the partial blocking out of the sun by clouds).

Communal nest caterpillars

The caterpillar of an unidentified moth species (Lasiocampidae, fig. 4.42a) feeds on the leaves of a perennial *Hermannia* species (Malvaceae). The shrubs grow in deep sand on dunes where they flush and flower after rain. The colourful caterpillars are remarkable in that a number (probably all the progeny of one female that have emerged from a batch of eggs) remain together and spin a communal nest, which varies from fist- to football-sized, consisting of an outer envelope and inner galleries (fig. 4.42b).

Interspersed in the silk are faecal pellets excreted by the spinning larvae; the caterpillars appear only to defecate in the nest, leaving no tell-tale frass pellets lying under the bushes. This may be an additional defensive strategy, as many parasitic wasps use the volatile chemicals evaporating from fresh frass as a cue to locate their caterpillar host.

The silk nest also functions as a thermal refuge for the caterpillars by day; the larvae are nocturnal and leave the nest to feed, retreating into the nest at daybreak.

The caterpillars' bright colours may indicate distastefulness. The *Hermannia* shrubs are mostly avoided by gemsbok, so they may contain noxious chemicals that are sequestered by the caterpillars. The bright aposematic colours may protect the larvae when foliage becomes depleted on the host plant, and the caterpillars are forced to migrate across the sand to nearby shrubs.

4.42 (a) This beautiful caterpillar (Lepidoptera: Lasiocampidae) is brightly coloured, probably as a warning of noxiousness to potential predators. **(b)** It lives in a communal silk nest with its siblings.

4.43 The small ball-rolling *Scarabaeus rubripennis* feeds on carrion or dung, especially that of birds and reptiles. Here, one has collected a bird dropping and is digging a burrow in which to bury it. It is accompanied by lesser dung flies.

walking on the dunes, landing at regular intervals a few metres away, running or flying short distances, stopping when the person does, and then following again. This has led to the appealing (but untested) hypothesis that they follow large animals such as gemsbok on the dunes in anticipation of a meal of fresh dung, a very rare commodity in this environment.

Scarabaeus rubripennis is also predominantly orange and is one of the smallest *Scarabaeus* species (fig.4.43). It occurs in the deep Namib and is a near-endemic species, as it has occasionally been found at some distance from the sand sea. *Scarabaeus rubripennis* feeds on carrion (small dead vertebrates such as lizards and rodents), as well as on the faeces of small predators, including lizards, foxes and jackals, which it rolls backwards in typical ball-rolling fashion.

Small kleptoparasitic beetles

Hammondantus psammophilus (Scarabaeidae: Scarabaeinae: Scarabaeini) is a very small dung beetle (5–6mm long) with an orange pronotum and pale yellow-brown, semitranslucent elytra (fig. 4.44). It is fast-flying and bee-like in behaviour, and has clawless tarsi.

The beetles have overcome the difficulty of finding sufficient food and running the risk of exposure to predators (fig. 4.45) and the elements while foraging: they home in on large, easily visible *Pachysoma* beetles and their burrows, parasitising their food supplies.

4.44 The endemic dung beetle *Hammondantus psammophilus* is a kleptoparasite of *Pachysoma* nests.

4.45 (above) Although one of the advantages of kleptoparasitic behaviour is decreased exposure to predators while foraging, specialised predators such as this robber fly, a species of *Anasillomos* (Asilidae), still pose a risk.

4.46 (right) A foraging group of *Camponotus detritus* ants, consisting of major and minor workers.

4.47 *Camponotus detritus* workers scavenging the remains of a spider.

4.48 Competition amongst neighbouring *Camponotus detritus* colonies for scarce resources is fierce, and captured neighbours are ruthlessly attacked, dismembered and eaten.

Hammondantus psammophilus enters the unattended *Pachysoma* nest while the host is travelling between its burrow and the food source. Several *H. psammophilus* individuals may enter the same burrow, where they feed on the host's food reserves. They may also breed in the *Pachysoma* nests, but nothing is known about this aspect of their biology. Their kleptoparasitic habit explains why they lack tarsal claws: they do not need to collect and manipulate food, so the claws have been 'lost' during evolution.

The Namib detritus ant

The endemic black-and-yellow Namib detritus ant, *Camponotus detritus* (Hymenoptera: Formicidae: Formicinae, fig. 4.46) is a conspicuous member of the desert insect fauna.

Camponotus has more than 1,000 species worldwide; about 70 species are known from southern Africa. Workers are polymorphic, with a range of workers from small (minor) to large (major) (see 'Ant biology and behaviour', p. 159). *Camponotus detritus* workers are 7–16mm long. Most foraging is done by minor workers, but major workers often assist them in retrieving large food items. Like many ant species, *C. detritus* is omnivorous, opportunistically preying on invertebrates and scavenging when they have the chance (fig. 4.47), but their main source of food is honeydew, produced by various scale and aphid species (see 'The pugnacious ant', p. 191; box, pp. 218–219) that live on the perennial grasses *Stipagrostis* and *Cladoraphis spinosa* and on *Trianthema hereroensis* (Aizoaceae). Their nests are excavated among the roots of these plants. The roots provide a structure that enables the ants to live in the unstable dune sand. The location also ensures that they are close to their main food source.

Unlike many other *Camponotus* species, *C. detritus* does not store food and does not have a replete (honey pot) caste (see 'The pugnacious ant', p. 191). This implies that food is readily available year-round, and that food items brought to the nest are consumed immediately. The honeydew-producing bugs maintain high populations during most of the year, owing to the relatively mild climate of the Namib, and the ameliorating effects of feeding high above the ground on the sap of perennial plants. *Camponotus detritus* is the only honeydew-feeding species in a large part of its distribution area in the central Namib; it therefore has almost exclusive access to this rich and dependable food source. However, competition for the resource between colonies is fierce (fig. 4.48).

Camponotus detritus is active over a wide range of environmental temperatures (5–54°C), and although it is diurnal, workers may be present all night on bug-infested plants. Surface activity takes place throughout the daylight hours. Ant activity starts when the morning temperature reaches about 10°C, peaks when temperatures are between 25°C and 38°C, and ceases when soil temperatures exceed 56°C. The ants have long legs and raise their bodies high above the hot sand. The steep thermal gradient above the sand allows their body to remain about 10°C cooler than the soil temperature. They also escape high temperatures by climbing onto plants. Their predominantly liquid diet helps them to counteract the dehydrating effects of high ambient temperatures.

Workers are often seen carrying plant detritus, leading to the mistaken assumption that detritus is a food item. In fact, the ants use detritus to line their nests, which are a relatively simple series of tunnels and chambers seldom deeper than 40cm. A colony may consist of up to four separate nests. These multi-nest colonies have some disadvantages, such as the time spent walking between nests and the risks associated with being in the open. The most significant benefit of the multi-nest system is that if one nest is disturbed or destroyed, surviving colony members can quickly be moved to another. The chances of this happening are high in the unstable soft sand in which the nests are built.

Iconic Namib plants and their associated insects

No report on the insects of the Namib would be complete without mentioning the welwitschia, *Welwitschia mirabilis*, and the nara, *Acanthosicyos horridus*, as well as the near-obligate insect species associated with them.

The nara melon and the nara cricket

The nara melon, *Acanthosicyos horridus* (fig. 4.49), is a remarkable and atypical species of the cucumber family (Cucurbitaceae). It has melon-like, spiny fruit that have been harvested and eaten by indigenous people in the region for centuries. The leafless spiny perennial shrubs have long stems up to about 1m tall, which grow into densely tangled thickets that may cover areas of up to 1,500m². They grow on dunes where their long tap roots reach into underground water. The species occurs along coastal southwestern Africa from Port Nolloth in South Africa to Mossâmedes in southern Angola.

The nara cricket, *Acanthoproctus diadematus* (Orthoptera: Tettigoniidae: Hetrodinae, fig. 4.50), is a Namib endemic that is strictly associated with the spiny nara bushes on which it feeds. Hetrodinae are commonly known as armoured bush or ground crickets, because the common species have heavy, defensive spines on the thorax (e.g. *Acanthoplus discoidalis*; see 'Armoured ground crickets', p. 213). *Acanthoproctus diadematus* is spineless and depends on the virtually impenetrable *Acanthosicyos* thickets to protect it from predators. Nara crickets only leave the safety of their prickly cover to move between bushes. They also appear to have lost the ability to eject repellent body fluids used by their relatives as a secondary defence mechanism.

4.49 The nara plant, *Acanthosicyos horridus*, a thorny inhabitant of dunes overlying shallow subsurface water sources, is the host plant of certain endemic insects.

4.50 The endemic nara cricket, *Acanthoproctus diadematus*, has an obligatory association with the nara plant.

Rina de Klerk

4.51 Iconic living fossils of the Namib, *Welwitschia mirabilis* plants have two continuously growing ribbon-like leaves that may reach 4m in length. The leaf tips split and fray into narrow sections. Many of the plants are more than 1,000 years old.

The welwitschia and its bug

Welwitschia mirabilis (fig. 4.51) is the only surviving member of an ancient cone-bearing plant lineage and is placed in its own family, Welwitschiaceae, in the gymnosperm order Gnetales. The order contains only two other extant genera: the species-rich *Ephedra* from North America, Europe and Asia, and the equally speciose tropical genus *Gnetum*, which occurs in South America, Southeast Asia and tropical Africa.

Welwitschia mirabilis is endemic to the Namib Desert and occurs in fragmented populations from the Kuiseb River northwards to the Nicolau River in southern Angola, always within about 100km of the coast. The largest population, with thousands of plants, is found east of Swakopmund, and there are other small populations scattered throughout the region. The plants grow mostly in dry water courses where sporadic flow after rain increases subsurface water, which supplements the water the plants obtain from fog. The species is dioecious, meaning that male and female cones are produced on separate plants.

The insect long known to be associated with *Welwitschia* is the bug *Probergrothius angolensis* (Hemiptera: Pyrrhocoridae, fig. 4.52), not *P. sexpunctatus* as claimed in most references. In spite of its well-known association with *Welwitschia*, very little is known about

the bug or about its true relationship with its host. Various apocryphal 'records' have been perpetuated about the bug's obligatory relationship with its host, and about it being the plant's principal pollinator; others claim the bug is also associated with baobabs, *Adansonia digitata*, in various parts of Africa. In the most recent general study of the Pyrrhocoridae of Africa, the only species recorded to be associated with the baobab (as well as many other plant species) is the East African *P. confusus*. There are no confirmed records of *P. angolensis* on any plant species other than *Welwitschia* in the study, so it appears likely that it actually does have an obligatory association with *Welwitschia*.

Pyrrhocorids are mainly seed feeders, and since *P. angolensis* bugs are most often found on female rather than male *Welwitschia* cones (fig. 4.52b), or beneath female plants where fallen seeds often lie thickly, the likelihood of it also being a seed feeder is strengthened. These findings would seem to discount the possibility of the bug being a pollinator – certainly of it being the principal pollinator – since female plants do not produce pollen. Other, more typical general pollinators, such as honey bees and various fly species, regularly frequent male and female cones – bees feed on or collect pollen, and flies feed on sticky exudates from the cones – so they are the more probable pollinators.

Jonathan Ball

4.52 (a) Mating welwitschia bugs, *Probergrothius angolensis* (Pyrrhocoridae), are obligate sap feeders on *Welwitschia* cones. **(b)** *P. angolensis* adults and nymphs on *Welwitschia* cones.

CHAPTER 5

NAMA-KAROO BIOME

The Nama-Karoo is a large inland area of wide plains and mountains situated on the central plateau of the western half of southern Africa. The region is characteristically dry and becomes progressively more arid as one travels westwards (figs 5.1, 5.2). It is the second-largest biome in the region and is surrounded by six other biomes: Desert to the northwest, Succulent Karoo to the west and southwest, Fynbos to the south, Albany Thicket to the southeast, Grassland to the east and Savanna to the north. Although some of these biomes are rich in endemics, local endemism in the Nama-Karoo is low and the fauna and flora are largely composed of intrusions from these neighbouring areas.

5.1 (pp. 156–157) The Nama-Karoo becomes more arid towards the west. (Photo: Rina de Klerk)
5.2 (above) The vast semi-arid plains and mountains of the Nama-Karoo.

Rainfall in the Nama-Karoo Biome occurs across a steep gradient, with higher rainfall (520mm average per year) in the east (fig. 5.3), to about one-fifth of that (100mm average per year) in the west (fig. 5.4). However, years with below-average rainfall occur periodically, leading to droughts, which are often severe. The northern interior and eastern parts have mainly summer rain (fig. 5.5), but bimodal spring and autumn peaks are common features. The western areas experience a winter rainfall maximum. Summers are usually hot and winters cold, with frost common.

The soils of the semi-arid regions in southern Africa are characterised by high inorganic nutrient status and low organic matter content. They are generally alkaline with relatively high potassium and phosphorus and low nitrogen status. The low organic matter content results in poor water infiltration, which, with the correspondingly low nitrogen, causes poor plant germination, establishment and growth. The actions of various animals, including insects such as harvester ants and termites, and some of their predators (e.g. the aardvark, *Orycteropus afer*), concentrate organic matter in patches, or contribute to the movement of organic matter underground.

The flora is composed mainly of dwarf shrubs interspersed with grass; in areas of overgrazing by livestock and game, grass decreases and shrubs increase. Overgrazing also increases the spread of mainly unpalatable species such as driedoring, *Rhigozum trichotomum* (Bignoniaceae), bitterbos, *Chrysocoma ciliata* (Asteraceae), and the sweet thorn tree, *Acacia karroo* (Fabaceae), which is common in riverbeds.

Extensive sheep (and, more recently, game) farming is the agricultural mainstay of the region. At least two of the endemic insect species discussed on the pages that follow have special adaptations to compensate for the irregular and unpredictable weather patterns, and are considered to be livestock competitors.

The insect fauna of the Nama-Karoo Biome, like other indigenous animals and plants in the biome, is largely made up of elements intruding from one of the adjacent biomes. Interestingly, some of the herbivorous insects of the region are typical 'outbreak' species that occur in low numbers in a particular area for several years – then some environmental cue triggers a dramatic increase in their population numbers with devastating consequences

Rina de Klerk

5.3 The Karoo landscape after rain, which is more plentiful in the eastern part of the region.

5.4 A dry Karoo landscape, typical of the arid western region of the biome.

5.5 In the summer-rainfall regions of the Karoo the plains are covered in grass after good rains.

for the local flora. Two of the most extensively studied of these species are the Karoo moth, *Loxostege frustalis*, although it is not restricted to the Nama-Karoo Biome, and the brown or Karoo locust, *Locustana pardalina*. The moth is considered a pest as its larvae compete with sheep for foliage of Karoo bushes (mostly *Pentzia incana*, Asteraceae). The Karoo locust is one of southern Africa's main migratory insect species.

The irregular build-up of high population numbers of certain Karoo insect species has been attributed to the occurrence of periodically favourable weather conditions, as well as to 'release' from their predators and parasites. This happens when the predator and parasite populations themselves are suppressed by environmental or biotic factors to such an extent that their effect on their prey is lessened – this permits the prey population, in turn, to irrupt.

Loxostege frustalis populations are kept low at times by a host of parasitic wasps, while those of *Locustana pardalina* are kept in check by several egg pathogens under wet conditions, or by the larvae of various Meloidae beetles that prey specifically on locust eggs.

Finally, no southern African region is without insects that function as ecosystem engineers, and this is also true for the Nama-Karoo Biome, although, in addition to the ubiquitous termites that usually fulfil that role, the harvester ant, *Messor capensis*, also has a major effect on soils and vegetation in the region.

Ant biology and behaviour

It is useful to have an understanding of general ant biology before looking at the role of the harvester ant, *Messor capensis*, in the Nama-Karoo Biome. This general background information is also relevant to ant case studies discussed in other chapters.

All ants belong to one very large hymenopteran family, Formicidae; seven morphologically and behaviourally distinct subfamilies are found in southern Africa. Characteristic species of the Myrmicinae are discussed here and elsewhere (see 'The woven-leaf nests of weaver ants', p. 260) and three other subfamilies are discussed in various biomes: the very large subfamily Ponerinae (see 'Matabele

ants: specialist termite predators', p. 243) and Formicinae (see 'The pugnacious ant', p. 191), and the smaller Dolichoderinae (see box, p. 67). The remainder of ant species found in southern Africa are placed in Dorylinae, Leptanillinae and Pseudomyrmecinae. Ponerinae, Dorylinae and Leptanillinae are termed 'primitive' or 'lower' ants, while the other subfamilies constitute the 'higher' ants.

Ant castes and subcastes

All ant species are eusocial, living in colonies that vary from a few hundred to many thousands of interacting and cooperating individuals. Colonies are dominated by females, as in all social Hymenoptera. In most species, a colony consists of a single egg-laying queen, numerous female workers that perform all the colony functions other than egg-laying, and a few males, which take no part in colony activities. Queens and workers are wingless, although winged females and males (alates) are produced at certain times of the year – these mate and the fertilised females (foundresses) start new colonies.

Although ant colonies consist of the same three principal castes as do other social Hymenoptera (queens, males and workers), subcastes also occur frequently. Caste determination is based on various factors (see box, p. 161); some of the more typical castes and subcastes and their functions are explained below.

Males (aners) are usually permanently winged, but die after mating. They vary considerably in size, depending on the species. The males of the frequently encountered, widespread red ant, *Dorylus helvolus* (Dorylinae, fig. 5.6), are exceptionally large (many times larger than the females); they are often attracted to light at night.

Queens (gynes) are initially winged but their wings are shed when the new colony is established; from then on they remain cloistered in the nest (termed claustral founding).

Ergatogynes (ergatoid queens) are a queen subcaste that is anatomically intermediate between a queen and a worker, and is considered 'worker-like' in many respects, particularly size, but, additionally, they have ocelli and large eyes (which are mostly smaller or absent in workers, fig. 5.7). Ergatoid queens occur in colonies of primitive ants such as Ponerinae (e.g. the Matabele

5.6 (left) A winged *Dorylus helvolus* (Dorylinae) male or aner. *Dorylus helvolus* is one of the few ant species in which males are considerably larger than females.

5.7 (right) 'Worker-like' queens are called ergatogyne or ergatoid queens. These ergatogyne queens of the Matabele ant, *Megaponera analis* (Ponerinae), are distinguishable from workers by their large eyes, which are mostly absent in workers.

ant, *Megaponera analis*; see 'Matabele ants: specialist termite predators', p. 243), in which foundresses commonly forage outside the nest during colony founding, not being nest-bound as are the gynes.

Gamergates are queens that are anatomically indistinguishable from workers. They are found in various groups of Ponerinae, of which southern African examples are *Ophthalmopone berthoudi* (fig. 5.8) and *Bothroponera kruegeri*.

Workers (ergates) are sterile females. The worker caste is sometimes divided into minor, media (rarely) and major subcastes, based principally on size. When major workers function mainly in defence, they are called soldiers. The large-headed workers in *Messor capensis* and in some *Pheidole* species (fig. 5.9) are erroneously called 'soldiers', but their only function is actually to carry and mill the seed that forms a major part of the species' diet.

Repletes ('honey pots') are a special worker subcaste. They are usually large workers that are selected by their sisters early on in their adult development while their integument is still soft and elastic (so-called 'callow' adults). They are used as storage vessels for sugar solutions and sometimes, water, when their crop may be overfilled to such an extent that it extends into the abdomen causing expansion there; movement by the recipient becomes difficult, and in extreme cases, impossible (see 'The pugnacious ant', p. 191).

Ant colony establishment

Colony establishment in ants is divided into three main stages: the founding, ergonomic and reproductive stages.

Most commonly, the colony-founding stage starts with the nuptial flight (fig. 5.10) when a virgin queen departs her maternal nest, mates with one or several males, finds a suitable location to begin the process of excavating a burrow, sheds her wings and starts nest construction and egg-laying. Males die after mating. The founding female does not feed and draws on reserves stored in her fat body and from degenerating wing muscle tissue while cloistered in the nest cavity (a claustral system). The first adults to emerge are special small (nanitic) workers that take over nest-building and maintenance activities from the queen, who thereafter confines herself to egg-laying.

A short while later, normal workers are produced and the colony then develops into the ergonomic stage, during which colony growth and development are the main functions.

After some period that is more or less fixed for different species, the colony reaches the reproductive stage of development. This is when new queens and males are produced, which then start the process over again (fig. 5.11).

5.8 A gamergate of *Ophthalmopone berthoudi* (Ponerinae) with termite prey. A gamergate is a queen morphologically indistinguishable from workers.

5.9 These *Pheidole* workers are dimorphic: some have small heads and others have large heads. Winged reproductives (alates) are also visible.

5.10 (a) The first stage in potential new colony establishment: the departure of alates from the parent nest in preparation for the nuptial flight of *Anoplolepis custodiens*. (b) Males of the ant species *A. steingroeveri* swamping a female while attempting to mate with her after her nuptial flight.

Caste determination in ants

Ants, like all Hymenoptera, have a haplodiploid sex determination system: all males are derived from unfertilised eggs and are thus haploid, and all females are derived from fertilised eggs and are thus diploid. The conditions that determine whether a diploid egg will develop into a queen or worker are complex and variable, but are overwhelmingly dominated by environmental and physiological, rather than genetic factors. Some of these factors are:

- **Larval nutrition** – Larvae that receive a disproportionate amount of food during early development grow larger and faster and are destined to become queens or major workers.
- **Temperature** – Larvae reared at temperatures closest to optimal for growth tend to become queens.
- **Winter chilling** – In species where the queen and her intra-ovarian eggs are exposed to cold winter temperatures, it is more likely that they will develop into queens in an apparent mechanism for timing the emergence of queens in spring.
- **Caste self-inhibition** – The presence of a queen and soldiers in a colony may inhibit development of, respectively, more queens and soldiers.
- **Egg size** – Larger eggs, which have more yolk than smaller eggs, are inclined to develop into queens as opposed to workers.
- **Queen age** – Young queens lay smaller eggs, particularly at nest-founding, which develop into nanitic (abnormally small) workers that begin colony activities, while later eggs are larger and produce normal-sized workers.

5.11 A mature *Lepisiota* colony, with a large queen, workers with brood, and alates. The alates indicate that the colony has reached the reproductive stage of colony development.

5.12 The invasive Argentine ant species, *Linepithema humile*, can rapidly establish new colonies by having multiple queens. One of these queens and a few workers abscond from the parent colony to form a separate colony.

In most species, colony-founding is mainly claustral. However, colonies may also originate by 'budding' or 'fission'. This happens when a group of workers, accompanied by one or more queens (usually ergatoid queens), separates from the main nest and starts a new nest-founding process, for example as in Argentine ants, *Linepithema humile* (Dolichoderinae, fig. 5.12).

Communication among ants

Modes of communication in ants are extremely diverse. They tap on the surface of their nests and tunnels or the substrate on which they are active, stridulate, stroke, grasp, nudge and antennate (stroke with antennae) each other, streak chemical drops while dragging the abdomen, produce clouds of chemical vapour, as well as exchange chemically laden liquid food (trophallaxis, fig. 5.13a). Individually, or in combination, some or several of these forms of communication may elicit responses from simple recognition to recruitment and alarm.

Several other groups of insects have evolved chemicals that largely mimic certain ant communication pheromones (fig. 5.13b), which they then use to gain entrance to, and live in, ant nests. These invaders, termed myrmecophiles, vary in the type of responses they elicit from ants.

5.13 Trophallaxis is the most important process amongst ants (and other social insects) by which chemical information is communicated between members of a colony. (a) *Pheidole megacephala* carrying a droplet of honeydew harvested from aphids to share with a co-worker by trophallaxis. (b) Individuals of *Polyrhachis schistacea* exchange liquid food laden with communication chemicals soon after harvesting honeydew from bugs.

Philip Herbst

Exocrine glands and communication in ants

In ants, the mandibular glands are situated on the head, adjacent to the mandibles, and the secretions that the glands produce apparently function almost exclusively in alarm and defence, either independently, or in combination with those produced by other glands (fig. 5.14).

The metapleural gland is situated in the metathorax just above the articulation of the hind coxa, and the secretions ooze passively from the leg joint and are groomed off by the legs and applied to the body. The gland is thought to function primarily as a producer of powerful antiseptic substances that protect the ant's body surface and nest against microorganisms and one that probably contributed largely to the evolutionary and ecological success of the group; its function as a producer of antibiotics may have permitted ants to nest in damp situations such as underground, in litter and under rocks and logs where microorganisms such as fungi normally flourish. The gland is thought to have been present ancestrally in all ant species and castes, but has been secondarily lost in some ants, mainly in the Formicinae and Myrmicinae (e.g. in *Polyrhachis* and *Oecophylla*; see 'The woven-leaf nests of weaver ants', p. 260), as well as in males of many other groups. If present in males, it is smaller than in workers in which, in turn, it is smaller than in queens.

Dufour's gland, which is situated at the tip of the abdomen and opens at the base of the sting, produces a very wide range of different chemicals across the subfamilies, but most are thought to function in alarm and recruitment behaviour, as well as in sexual attraction.

The poison gland empties the compounds it secretes into a large poison sac. These compounds consist largely of formic acid in the Formicinae, and of various proteinaceous venoms, particularly in the more primitive groups (e.g. Ponerinae and Dorylinae). The venoms are neurotoxic or histolytic, quickly paralysing prey (and causing painful stings in humans), and are principally used for overpowering prey (fig. 5.15) and in defence. However, some constituents of the secretions may act as recruitment substances, for eliciting alarm, or as defensive repellents. The acid or venoms are secreted or sprayed through an opening called an acidopore.

The pygidial gland opens at the seventh abdominal tergite and is present in all subfamilies except the Formicinae. It produces substances that function in recruitment and sexual attraction, as well as alarm pheromones and defensive repellents. The Matabele ant, *Megaponera analis* (see 'Matabele ants: specialist termite predators', p. 243), and the African stink ant, *Paltothyreus tarsatus*, produce very strong foetid-smelling secretions from it when threatened.

The group of glands treated as 'sternal' glands consists of a large diversity of secretory organs with different origins; the greatest variety is found in the Ponerinae (e.g. *Megaponera analis*). The compounds function mainly in orientation trails and nest-mate recruitment.

5.14 Communication glands common to most ants: (1) the mandibular glands occur adjacent to the mandibles; (2) the metapleural gland lies in the metathorax just above the hind coxa, its secretions oozing passively from the leg joint; (3) Dufour's, poison, pygidial and sternal glands are located in the abdomen. (4) The 'waist' (petiole) is the second segment of the abdomen; it acts as a hinge, allowing a great deal of abdominal flexibility for squirting defensive gland substances forwards from the tip of the abdomen.

5.15 Prey, consisting of any small animal that can be overwhelmed, may be taken back to the nest for food. It is finely masticated and the resultant soup imbibed and spread around the colony by trophallaxis. Here *Hagensia havilandi* is carrying a Tenebrionidae larva that is still alive.

Chemical communication

Chemical communication using pheromones appears to be central in the organisation of ant societies (as it is in many other insect groups) and it is thought that 10–20 different chemical signals may play a role. And, just as complex as the chemical signals, are the numerous exocrine glands that produce them (see box opposite). Amongst these are six key gland complexes that are present in most ant species and perform a variety of functions. They are the mandibular glands in the head, metapleural glands on the metathorax, and four glands on the abdomen: Dufour's, poison, pygidial, and sternal glands. The metapleural gland is a characteristic of all ants (although secondarily lost in some higher ants) and its presence is one of the main characters that typify the family as a whole. No equivalent gland is found among other insects.

Acoustical communication

Although weakly developed compared to chemical communication, sound in the form of vibrational signals is produced by drumming and by stridulation. Vibrational signals are mostly used in conjunction with chemical signals. The main functions of sound signals are for alarm and recruitment.

Drumming is produced by the worker ant striking the substrate with her mandibles and gaster (abdomen), while rocking the body back and forth. Stridulation, which produces chirps that are often quite audible to the human ear, is a more sophisticated form of communication than drumming, and is made possible by the ant lowering and raising her gaster, which causes a file of dense ridges in the middle of the fourth abdominal segment to rub against a scraper (plectrum) on the border of the preceding abdominal segment. The sounds produced are mostly monotonous chirps with little obvious meaning, although chirps produced by workers buried under soil during tunnel and nest construction apparently signify distress, as they are regularly freed by co-workers.

Tactile communication

Touch has been shown to have several communicative functions in ants, but apparently only conveys limited information. One of its commonest forms is displayed by antennation (stroking with antennae) of one individual by another, during which the active participant receives rather than conveys information (it is smelling its nest-mate, not informing it). However, it has been shown to be important in recruitment behaviour, in which one worker ant approaches another and antennates her and strokes her with her forelegs – the recruiter then turns and runs off, depositing an odour trail as she goes, which is followed by the recruited worker (see box alongside). In some species, the leading ant needs the touch of the follower before continuing.

The most important mode of tactile communication is during trophallaxis when individuals share liquid food. This is initiated by a food-soliciting individual antennating or tapping a food-bearer with the forelegs, which causes the one being tapped to turn towards the antennator. If the tapping is continued on the mouthparts of the food-bearing worker, it regurgitates food. This simple mechanical process is also used by some myrmecophilous nest parasites, such as ant-nest beetles (Carabidae: Paussinae; see box, p. 164), to obtain food from their hosts. Once the process is under way there is a consistent interplay of antennae between the donor and recipient.

Recruitment and foraging trails

Among ants, recruitment serves to bring nest-mates together where work is required for food retrieval, nest location and construction, and colony defence. Depending on the species, combinations of touch, sound and chemical cues are used.

Odour trails laid by pheromones are used by many species, particularly during foraging, but they only help the foraging workers to remain on the trail – not to determine the direction of the food source or nest; this they do by following the direction taken by outgoing or returning food-laden nest-mates. The workers continue to reinforce the trail pheromone as they walk on it.

A large number of ground-nesting species of Formicinae and Dolichoderinae lay 'trunk trails' (fig. 5.16) during foraging. These are tree-like in structure, starting with a single, broad path (the trunk) that splits first into branches then into twigs. Workers continue to clear them of vegetation and debris and those using the trail reinforce the pheromone trail odour as they forage.

5.16 A semipermanent 'trunk trail' leading out from the ant nest to areas of dependable forage. These are kept clean of debris and reinforced with trail pheromone odours by walking ants.

Some insect groups are specialised predators of ant brood (see box, p. 99). Among them are the so-called ant-nest beetles, members of the huge predatory beetle family Carabidae (see 'Predatory ground beetles', p. 239), of which all species of the tribe Paussini, subfamily Paussinae, are ant-associated in both adult and larval stages (fig. 5.17). Both stages have various morphological and behavioural adaptations for their predatory lifestyle.

Adult paussines are mostly smooth, flattened, uniformly reddish-brown beetles. Their most distinctive characteristic is their unusual antennae – and not only do they appear unusual, they have atypical and highly specialised functions. The beetle uses its antennae to find and follow the trail pheromone of the appropriate host ant. When the beetle approaches the nest and ants emerge, the beetle proffers its antennae, which are eagerly antennated, then licked by the ants. The ants also lick various other parts of the beetle's body that have tufts of setae (bristles) covered in antennal secretions deposited while beetles groom themselves. The beetle is then dragged by its antennae into the ants' nest, where it integrates into the colony and begins to consume adult ants and brood.

If male and female beetles are present simultaneously in the colony, mating takes place, eggs are laid, and eventually larvae emerge. These are also highly modified; in some species, the terminal abdominal segments are fused into a cup-shaped structure into which glandular secretions are discharged. The secretions are highly attractive to the ants and suppress aggressive behaviour. Ants that have fed on the secretions tolerate the paussine larva, even though it preys on ant brood.

Adult paussines, in common with most Carabidae, have abdominal glands that produce specific defensive chemical compounds, which are mainly used in defence against vertebrate predators and not against ants. In paussines these compounds are mostly benzoquinones. These are explosively secreted in a visible puff with an audible report that results from the mixing, immediately prior to the secretion from the defensive gland, of an active ingredient and synergist that results in the reaction. The chemicals produce a reddish-brown stain on human skin.

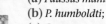

5.17 Ant-nest beetles (Carabidae) are highly specialised predators of ants and ant brood. Their antennae contain glands that produce appeasing secretions.
(a) *Paussus manicanus*;
(b) *P. humboldti*;
(c) *Cerapterus* sp.;
(d) *P. natalensis*;
(e) *P. vanrooni*;
(f) *P. cylindricornis*.

Necrophoresis: corpse removal by ants

Although recognition of the state of dead nest-mates is not strictly a form of communication, the identification of dead nest-mates based on chemical cues and their removal from the nest is a stereotypical behaviour pattern common to most ant species. And, since hygiene inside ant nests is kept to high levels by meticulous cleaning behaviour in which workers remove dead nest-mates and other decomposing matter, recognition that a nest-mate is dead is essential.

Oleic acid, a common chemical product of decomposing insect corpses, is the main recognition cue that results in corpse removal. This has been tested in simple experiments in which small pieces of paper are immersed in oleic acid and placed near an ant nest; these are treated in the same way as corpses of dead nest-mates, whereas chemically cleaned ant corpses are treated as carrion and consumed. Live ants covered in oleic acid are removed from the nest by other colony members, only to wander back and be ejected repeatedly until the chemical wears off.

Harvester ants as nutrient recyclers

The harvester ant, *Messor capensis* (Hymenoptera: Formicidae: Myrmicinae, fig. 5.18), is one of about 100 species in the genus *Messor*, which is distributed across arid areas of Africa, southern Europe and western Asia. The ants are appropriately named 'harvester ants', as they feed almost entirely on seeds (fig. 5.19), occasionally supplemented with arthropod remains. The genus was named after Messor, a minor Roman harvest god. Although *M. capensis* occurs throughout southern Africa, it is a dominant member of the soil insect community in the semi-arid southwestern parts of the region, particularly in the Nama-Karoo and Namaqualand.

Messor capensis are large ants (4–12mm long), and like most *Messor* species, are polymorphic, with a range of workers from small (minor) to large (major) (fig. 5.20). The larger the workers are, the more disproportionately large (allometric) their heads and mandibles become; the largest workers can carry and crush the husks of large or hard seed. All workers have a basket-like set of bristles (psammophore) beneath the head, which is used to carry sand from the nest.

The burrowing and foraging activities of *M. capensis* have important effects on the physical and chemical properties of the poor soils in the Nama-Karoo; they lead to improved water infiltration rates and increased plant nutrient status, and correspondingly higher germination rates and productivity of some plant species. These aspects of the effects of *M. capensis* activity were intensively studied by Richard Dean during the 1990s at the well-known Tierberg Karoo Research Centre near Prince Albert in the southern Karoo (see box, pp. 166–167).

5.18 Foraging harvester ants, *Messor capensis*.

5.19 (a, b) *Messor capensis* workers carrying seeds of Karoo plants, some of which they will deposit intact in their burrows where they will eventually germinate.

Jenny Scholtz

5.20 *Messor capensis* workers with harvested food, including a dead beetle, massing at a nest entrance. Big-headed major and small-headed minor workers are clearly visible.

Herbivores

In spite of the generally dry conditions of the Nama-Karoo, favourable weather conditions for grass and shrub growth occur every few years. These may lead to dramatic increases in the populations of 'outbreak' herbivorous species. These are species whose populations remain depressed for years until suitable conditions occur – then they quickly build up to large numbers of individuals. Outbreak species include the brown locust and the Karoo caterpillar; both species can reach such high numbers under optimal conditions that they defoliate vegetation and outcompete livestock and wild game, sometimes leading to financial distress for farmers in the region. Both groups, however, provide an abundant food source for local predators.

Plague locusts

Grasshoppers and locusts (Orthoptera: Acrididae) are among the most important indigenous herbivores in natural open-land ecosystems such as grasslands (see 'Feeding in grasshoppers', p. 190) and savannas (see box, pp. 212–213), but also in regions such as the Nama-Karoo. Although there is no taxonomic difference between grasshoppers and locusts – smaller ones are termed grasshoppers and larger ones, locusts – the latter term is often used for large species whose populations build up to plague proportions.

Several plague locust species occur in southern Africa, some permanently, others as irregular visitors from elsewhere on the continent. Those occurring in southern Africa belong to two subfamilies of Acrididae: Cyrtacanthacridinae and Oedipodinae.

The effects of *Messor capensis* on soil and plant growth

The harvester ant, *Messor capensis*, is the major seed predator in large parts of the Karoo and Namaqualand. At the Tierberg site, these ants were recorded to remove about 11kg of seed per hectare per year of about 19 plant species. This was estimated to represent about 32.5% of the plants' annual seed production. The seeds are stored in the nest mounds above ground, as well as in underground chambers. Soils from nest mounds were found to contain significantly more viable seeds than soils of intermound spaces; experiments confirmed that significantly more seedlings germinated on undisturbed mounds (although, see aardvark activity, page opposite).

The nest mounds of a *M. capensis* colony are composed of organic matter and excavated soil (fig. 5.21); they are constructed around the entrances to their nests of which there may be several a few metres apart. The mounds are most conspicuous when above-ground ant activity is high after rain and are typically conical or elongate, and can be up to 0.42m high, 1.6m wide and 3.0m long (really large for ants!). The ants add soil in thin layers (5–10mm) in bursts after rain, which probably reflect underground tunnelling activity. Over longer periods of reduced activity, they continue to dump waste seed husks and other plant material on the mound, which may add up to 1.5kg of plant matter per nest during the succeeding 30-odd days after

the rain; although some of this is blown away by wind, sufficient matter remains to substantially increase the organic content of the soil there.

Mound densities vary according to soil type, being clumped on loamy plains and more dispersed on sandier soils. At one site, colonies were at a mean density of about 8 colonies per hectare on the plains, whereas in 1km × 5m transects across the study area, the numbers of nests varied from 2–23 per hectare, with a mean of 9.6 per hectare.

Messor capensis nest mounds are not static, however, with new mounds being built around replacement entrances after rain or disturbance by aardvarks, so in this way the effect on soils is far greater than just in the immediate vicinity of nests. Founding queens select new sites some distance from their maternal nest, with the result that colonies are spread widely over a region.

The ants' tunnelling and foraging activities affect soils and plant growth in various important ways. The major physical change to the soils of the nest mounds is reflected in drier mound than intermound soils over time; 30 days after rain, mound and intermound soil moisture did not differ, but 55 days thereafter, intermound soils had a higher moisture content. The studies showed that mound soils absorb more water more rapidly (water infiltrates better) than intermound soils, but that they also dry out faster, possibly as a result of less compaction and higher organic content. The chemical properties of mound and intermound

Cyrtacanthacridinae

Members of the Cyrtacanthacridinae are large locusts characterised by a well-developed spine (prosternal process) between the front and middle legs; the common, widespread garden locust, *Acanthacris ruficornis* (fig. 5.23), is a typical member of the Cyrtacanthacridinae.

The plague locusts in the Cyrtacanthacridinae are among the most destructive of all locusts. Two species reach southern Africa occasionally. The red locust, *Nomadacris septemfasciata*, breeds in seasonally flooded depressions in central southern Africa (Zambia, Tanzania, Malawi and Mozambique), then invades southwards. The desert locust, *Schistocerca gregaria*, is represented

5.23 The garden locust, *Acanthacris ruficornis* (Acrididae: Cyrtacanthacridinae), is a familiar urban species. Some of its relatives are plague locust species.

5.24 *Schistocerca gregaria flaviventris* (Cyrtacanthacridinae) is the southern African subspecies of the devastating North African plague locust.

5.25 A common nonplague Karoo locust species (Acrididae: Oedipodinae).

soils also differed significantly, with mound soils containing about 50% more phosphorus, potassium and nitrogen, as well as organic matter, than did intermound soils. Sodium and pH were similar in both soil types.

Amongst the five dominant woody plant species growing on mound soils, three had higher nitrogen levels in their leaves (4.8–9.2mg/g greater) than those growing on intermound soils. Furthermore, two mound species had longer internode distances than those growing off mounds, suggesting better growth, and six of nine species sampled had significantly higher seed production than the same species growing in intermound spaces; the other three species also inclined towards higher seed production.

Mounds disturbed by the ant-foraging activity of aardvarks introduces an extra dimension to the dynamics of ants and their effect on the ecosystem; aardvarks (fig. 5.22) are major predators of ants and termites and are common in the Karoo. They often dig into the nests of *M. capensis*, which are extensively damaged but usually not destroyed, and the seed stores are frequently distributed with the mound soil over a larger area. Many of the seeds become buried and remain to germinate when conditions are favourable. Some seeds may also be ingested by the aardvarks while feeding on the ants and these are dispersed to nutrient-rich sites with their faeces. Consequently, aardvark activity provides more and improved germination sites for some Karoo plants and their ant-feeding activity may inadvertently disperse seeds of several Karoo shrubs over a wide area.

5.21 A *Messor capensis* nest mound consisting of excavated soil particles, seed husks and other organic debris.

5.22 An aardvark, *Orycteropus afer*, one of the major predators of *Messor capensis* nests.

in southern Africa by the subspecies *S. gregaria flaviventris* (fig. 5.24), which swarms periodically in the Kalahari savanna and areas adjacent to the Namib Desert; it occasionally reaches sufficient numbers to be considered a pest, but is of minor importance.

Oedipodinae

Oedipodinae are more difficult to characterise, although most species of this subfamily, as implied by the common name, band-winged grasshoppers, have a dark band crossing the hind wing somewhere between the middle and outer margin (fig. 5.25), and in many the basal part of the wing is coloured.

The Oedipodinae include the southern African endemic brown locust, *Locustana pardalina* (fig. 5.26), and the subspecies of the African migratory locust, *Locusta migratoria migratorioides* (fig. 5.27).

Locusta migratoria has a huge distribution area, which covers most of Africa, but also Asia, Australia and even New Zealand; it occurred in Europe in historical times. Its outbreak area is the Niger flood plain in West Africa and swarm invasions stretch across the continent, occasionally reaching down to southern Africa as far south as the major grain-producing areas of the South African Highveld. They breed en route and form new generations of swarms as they travel. Interestingly, though, this

5.26 The brown locust is southern Africa's most important plague locust species.

5.27 Subspecies *Locusta migratoria migratorioides* is permanently present in the region but does not form swarms here.

Morphological and physiological differences between *solitaire* and *gregaria* phases in the brown locust, *Locustana pardalina*	
***Solitaire* phase**	***Gregaria* phase**
Adults smaller, female larger than male	Adults large and sexes of equal size
Colours cryptic, matching background	Colours contrasting in black, red and orange
Hind legs larger in proportion to body length	Hind legs smaller in proportion to body length
Lower metabolic rate	Higher metabolic rate
Respiration and body temperature lower	Respiration and body temperature higher
Poor night vision	Good night vision

species is permanently present in southern Africa, but only in the solitary phase. Several attributes contribute to its widespread distribution and pest status:

- The locusts are large and fly strongly, at 15–20km per hour with the wind and are capable of flying nonstop for 5–130km per day.
- A single swarm may encompass an area from one to several hundred square kilometres, with each square kilometre consisting of 40–80 million individual locusts.
- The locusts eat more than their own body weight each day and one million of them are capable of consuming one tonne of food per day.

Needless to say, very little green vegetation is left after the swarms leave an area.

The southern African endemic *Locustana pardalina* builds up to plague proportions in the Karoo and then invades northwards into much of central southern Africa, including Namibia, Botswana and Zimbabwe, although its spread is currently controlled by various government agencies, particularly in South Africa.

Swarm formation in plague locusts

Plague locusts may be present in three different, distinctive phases: a *solitaire* (solitary) phase; a gregarious (swarm) phase, termed *gregaria*; and an intermediate (transitional) *transiens* phase.

Swarm formation in locusts requires a series of complex morphological, physiological and behavioural changes (see box opposite) in members of the population. These are brought about by genetic as well as environmental effects.

Under 'normal' (nonswarm) conditions, the locusts live as solitary individuals, behaving in a way similar to typical field grasshoppers and locusts. Under favourable climatic and edaphic (soil) conditions, and when there has been a build-up of egg pods in a particular region, swarms may start to form. The denser the numbers of recently emerged nymphs (hoppers) are, the more *gregaria*-like they become.

It has been suggested that swarms result from the build-up of solitary forms during the previous season, as well as periodic input from gregarious females. Because solitary females lay more diapause (see 'Dormancy', p. 44) eggs than gregarious females, and because this increases with advancing female age and decreasing day length, it results in a build-up of egg numbers before the onset of winter.

Solitary females are selective in their choice of oviposition sites, whereas gregarious females lay eggs in large egg beds up to several square kilometres in extent; when some females in a swarm begin to lay, this signals to the swarm that conditions are suitable for egg-laying and all the females ready to oviposit start to congregate and lay eggs. Densities of up to 540 egg pods/ha have been found. During such years, egg pods may be heavily parasitised by blister beetle larvae (Meloidae; see 'Blister beetle larvae: predators of locust eggs', p. 171).

The genetic basis to the phase phenomenon (which is first manifested in the eggs) and its inheritance in *L. pardalina* are determined by the female; a *solitaire* female × a *gregaria* male produces *solitaire* offspring, while a *gregaria* female × a *solitaire* male yields *gregaria* progeny. The morphological and physiological differences are illustrated in the table above, but there are also behavioural differences between them. The physiological differences are mainly a result of the higher metabolic rate of *gregaria* compared to *solitaire*.

Effect of climate on locust swarm formation

The Nama-Karoo Biome has a pronounced climate gradient, with moist conditions in the east and arid conditions in the west. *Locustana pardalina* is well adapted to this highly variable climate. Eggs are usually laid in dry soil, often in shaded situations (such as under bushes) and it is in this stage that most of the specialised adaptations to desert life are found.

Females can lay five or six egg pods at roughly weekly intervals, each containing 40–50 eggs. The eggs require a maximum of 45 days in dry soil before they will respond to rainfall, but they may remain viable in dry soil for long periods. Whether the eggs begin to

Locusts display significant behavioural differences during their distinctive life phases. These range from a total absence of contact in *solitaire* nymphs to close contact between *gregaria* individuals of all ages and stages.

The cryptically coloured *solitaire* nymphs disperse after hatching, and after a 3–4-week development period, finally moult into adults. After a 2-week sexual maturation period, the adults (which remain throughout in roughly the same area) start to breed. Most of the eggs laid will enter a period of diapause (resting stage of fixed duration – see 'Dormancy', p. 44), only hatching about a year later.

The black and red or black and orange-striped *gregaria* nymphs (a vernacular name is 'rooibaadjies' or red jackets), on the other hand, cluster in tight groups (hopper 'bands'), remaining in close contact even while moving over considerable distances, which they do daily. From afar they appear as rivers of reddish water flowing over the ground (figs 5.28, 5.29). After five nymphal instars, but occasionally four in males, they reach adulthood in about 6 weeks, and sexual maturity in a further 4–5 weeks (figs 5.30, 5.31). During short stops while migrating, the females lay eggs, which mostly start to develop immediately, without entering diapause.

Solitaire fly little but when they do, it is for short distances of about 2m; *gregaria* fly high and may continue flying for many hours during which they cover long distances.

5.28 Rivers of red: bands of migrating brown locust 'hoppers' (nymphs) crossing a road.

Jenny Scholtz

5.29 Brown locust hoppers marching inexorably on.

Piotr Naskrecki

5.30 Swarming adult brown locusts in a sorghum field.

Piotr Naskrecki

5.31 A brown locust swarm on the move.

Piotr Naskrecki

develop (the incubation period is 10–20 days), or enter quiescence (see 'Dormancy', p. 44) or diapause depends on endogenous factors and on rainfall: 15–25mm of rain over a period of a day or two is required for incubation.

- Nondiapause eggs may start to develop, then enter a quiescent state and suspend development under dry conditions until adequate moisture is again available for development. The eggs slowly lose moisture under dry conditions, but are capable of absorbing water from light rain, even when it is insufficient to promote hatching.

- Quiescent eggs have 76% of the water content of those ready to hatch and they only die when their water content drops to below 40%. They can intermittently return to the quiescent state during bouts of moist/dry conditions.

- Eggs already in diapause enter an even deeper state of diapause when exposed to wet conditions. It is broken only by an unknown combination of endogenous and environmental factors. Furthermore, from any batch of diapause eggs that hatch, about 5% will not do so and they enter even deeper diapause, lasting 1–15 months, which is only broken some time later.

Because of these adaptations, viable eggs can accumulate in the soil until conditions are suitable for hatching , when a mass emergence results.

Locust swarms build up mostly in the eastern parts of the biome and studies have shown that these correlate with climate events (see box above). During years of high rainfall, three successive generations may occur over summer (September–April), and a fourth over winter. Swarms tend to occur in mid- to late summer (January–March) after populations have grown sufficiently.

The Karoo caterpillar

The Karoo caterpillar, *Loxostege frustalis* (Lepidoptera: Crambidae, fig. 5.32), is a widespread moth in southern and East Africa. It is notorious in the Karoo because of its sporadic population irruptions, when voracious larval feeding leads to the complete defoliation of many of the Karoo shrubs that livestock depend on for food. Although *L. frustalis* is polyphagous and feeds on as many as 20 plant species in four families, ankerkaroo, *Pentzia incana*, and vaalkaroo, *P. globosa* (Asteraceae), are apparently the preferred hosts.

The handsome moths are small, with a wingspan of about 20mm. The wings are dark brown, usually with two distinct white spots. The wing margin is black with white streaks running inwards and the fringe of marginal hairs is dark brown. The larvae vary from greenish through grey to black.

Adults and larvae may be active from spring throughout the summer to autumn, although activity and, especially, high population numbers, are dependent on rainfall. Peak adult activity is usually in February and March and millions of moths may be attracted at night to house, street and other lights.

The females lay eggs, either singly or in small batches, on the underside of leaves of the host plant. The emergent larvae then feed on the plant, constructing a silken web over the leaves as they feed (fig. 5.33); in large numbers they quickly defoliate the plants and the web-covered plants are repellent to domestic stock and game animals.

Mature larvae climb down the plant and spin a tough silken cocoon in the soil at its base and here they may remain for up to three years, waiting for favourable conditions for emergence. The cocoon structure is thought to be the factor that contributes most to larval survival for long periods, which may include very hot or very cold conditions, and even occasional flooding.

5.32 The moth of the Karoo caterpillar, *Loxostege frustalis* (Crambidae).

Jenny Scholtz

5.33 A shrub covered in webs spun by feeding Karoo caterpillars.

The Karoo caterpillar, *Loxostege frustalis*, is parasitised by *Macrocentris maraisi* wasps (Hymenoptera: Braconidae). Apparently attracted primarily by odours released by leaves of the host plant damaged by feeding caterpillars, the wasps target mature, but still feeding, larvae, in which they lay eggs. The developing parasitoid larva then exercises one of three developmental options:

- It may develop rapidly in the host, killing it in the process, then pupate and emerge within a few weeks.
- Depending on the developmental stage of the host, the first-instar parasitoid may enter a nonfeeding phase simultaneously with one in which the host enters diapause, which may last for up to three years. When the resting phase is ended by some environmental cue, the parasitoid

larva develops quickly, consuming the still-living host. It then pupates in the host's larval case and the adult emerges shortly thereafter.

- The mature larva may consume its host and then enter a rest phase in the host's silk cocoon, which may last for up to three years. Some environmental cue then initiates the final stages of development, the larva pupates and the adult emerges.

Macrocentris maraisi has clearly adapted superbly to the host's complex life cycle to ensure synchronous development with it in order to be able to utilise host larvae as soon as they become available during irregular and sporadic emergences. This ability to track the host's largely indeterminate emergence and population build-up has ensured its success as a highly efficient parasitoid of *L. frustalis*.

Populations in non-outbreak years are thought to be kept in check by adverse environmental conditions, but also by a range of tiny parasitic wasps (Hymenoptera: Chalcididae, Braconidae and Ichneumonidae) and parasitic flies (Diptera: Tachinidae), which may kill 40–50% of the *L. frustalis* larvae. The most important of these is *Macrocentris maraisi* (Braconidae); its complex and interesting biology is very intimately tied to that of its host (see box above).

Predators

The irregular episodes of favourable weather conditions that sustain populations of herbivorous species also provide food for the next trophic level, the predatory guild. Among the specialists in the region are predators of the abundant prey provided by common or outbreak species; examples are blister beetle larval predators of locust eggs and those that specialise on ant brood.

Blister beetle larvae: predators of locust eggs

The blister beetles (Coleoptera: Meloidae) form a large family of plant-associated species; in southern Africa about 350 species are known from about 35 genera (fig. 5.34). Adults of many of the species have modified mouthparts for feeding on nectar, while others feed on the flowers themselves or on foliage. Larvae of most species, however, are predators of the brood of ants, solitary wasps and solitary bees (see box, p. 395) and a number – including the large CMR beetle, *Hycleus tricolor* – are important predators of Acrididae locust egg

pods, including those of plague locusts, and during an outbreak numbers build up significantly (fig. 5.35).

All meloid larvae pass through a complex developmental process termed hypermetamorphosis (see box, p. 42), in which the different instars change in morphology and behaviour at each moult.

Meloidae usually lay their eggs close to where the emergent tiny mobile first-instar larvae (triungulins) are able to quickly locate a suitable host (fig. 5.36), but this remains a hazardous process for them and mortality among the larvae is very high. In compensation, females usually lay large numbers of eggs to increase the chances of at least some surviving.

Southern African meloids fall into different groups as far as larval hosts are concerned:

- In species that prey on solitary wasp or bee brood, the female meloid lays eggs on flowers where the emergent triungulins attach to the wasp or bee and are transported to the nest, where they feed on the host's brood.
- Females of species that prey on ant brood seem to lay eggs randomly; the triungulins of some find and attach to ant-eating predatory beetles (Coleoptera: Carabidae) that carry them to ant nests, where they climb off and enter the nest to feed on the ant brood (see box, p. 173).
- In species that prey on grasshopper and locust egg pods (e.g. *Hycleus tricolor*), the female beetle lays eggs close to the egg pod site; the emergent triungulins locate them by smell, burrow down and feed on them.

All species of Meloidae produce the strong blistering agent (hence the common family name) cantharidin, which is created in a complex metabolic process in the larval stage

5.34 A selection of Meloidae from the arid western parts of southern Africa: **(a)** *Hycleus dentatus*; **(b)** *H. deserticolus*; **(c)** *Ceroctis capensis*; **(d)** *Iselma pallidipennis*; **(e)** *H. scalaris*; **(f)** *Meloe angulatus*.

of all meloids (see box, p. 225). This is unlike the process in ground beetles (see 'Ground beetles', p. 127), in which only adults produce defensive chemicals in special abdominal glands. Also, Meloidae 'leak' toxic haemolymph from body joints (reflex bleeding or auto-haemorrhaging), whereas Carabidae spray the chemicals. The defensive compounds are, moreover, chemically quite different.

Adult *Hycleus tricolor* beetles are large (about 50mm long), and black with broad yellow or red bands, colours that advertise their toxicity (fig. 5.37; see box, pp. 240–241). The vernacular name, CMR beetle, refers to the black-and-yellow banded tunics of the Cape Mounted Rifles (CMR), a battalion of mounted soldiers in the Cape Colony more than 100 years ago.

A *Hycleus* female digs a hole in the hard, dry soil of the locusts' breeding area, deep enough for her abdomen to fit into, then backs into it and lays 20–30 eggs in batches (stuck together in a mass by an adhesive substance) (fig. 5.36). She then scrapes soil into the hole

5.35 (left) *Hycleus tricolor* populations build up significantly during a brown locust outbreak because their larvae are predatory on locust egg pods.

5.36 (right) A female *Hycleus tricolor* laying eggs in a hole that she has dug near locust egg pods.

5.37 A gravid female *Hycleus tricolor* (Coleoptera: Meloidae), her abdomen swollen with eggs and cantharidin. The combination of black and yellow colours on the beetle serve as warning of its noxious nature.

and stamps it with her feet. The process is repeated several times.

Three to four weeks later the eggs hatch and the highly mobile, tiny first-instar triungulins burrow to the surface and then spread out in search of grasshopper egg pods on which they prey during a complex hypermetamorphic development cycle.

The triungulin larva has well-developed eyes and other sensory organs, as well as long legs that enable it to run around above ground and search for locust eggs, which it locates mainly by scent. Once eggs are found, the triungulin burrows into the ground, penetrates the egg pod and starts to feed. After consuming two eggs, it moults into a second-instar, caraboid (Carabidae-like) larva, which has a long and somewhat flattened body and much shorter legs than those of the triungulin. In the third and fourth instars, the larva becomes grub-like, termed scarabaeiform (Scarabaeidae-like). These four larval stages are all predatory and feed on the eggs in the pod.

If weather conditions deteriorate (become too hot and dry or too cold) the fourth scarabaeiform larval stage leaves the egg pod and burrows deeper into the soil, where it forms a sessile, legless, coarctate larva or pseudopupa in an earthen cell near the prey remains. Should weather conditions improve, it moults again, producing an active scolytoid larva, which continues to feed. A short while after this, it moults again into a pupa. After a period that is determined by soil moisture conditions, it emerges as an adult.

Ant brood predators

In southern Africa, triungulins (first-instar larvae) of a few genera of Meloidae (e.g. *Cyaneolytta*, fig. 5.38), whose larvae prey on ant brood, appear to have a unique obligatory phoretic (transport) association with another beetle species, the predatory *Anthia* (Coleoptera: Carabidae, fig. 5.39).

The meloid adults apparently lay eggs randomly, and the louse-like triungulins (fig. 5.40) find and attach firmly to the large predatory *Anthia* beetles. It has been speculated that the larvae cue into the defensive glandular secretion, formic acid, that *Anthia* beetles produce (see 'Ground beetles', p. 127), which is chemically similar to that secreted by ants (hence the name 'formic', from ants).

Clinging to the *Anthia* beetle, the triungulin is carried directly to an ant nest when the carabid locates one. While the *Anthia* is preying on surface-active ants, the triungulin detaches and enters the nest, becoming a myrmecophile (see boxes, pp. 99, 164) and completing its hypermetamorphic development while feeding on the ant brood.

5.38 *Cyaneolytta depressicornis* (Meloidae) larvae depend on *Anthia* beetles (Carabidae) for transport and have a predatory association with ants.

Mervyn Mansell

5.39 (above) *Anthia thoracica* feeding on *Pheidole* ants at their nest.

5.40 (left) A *Cyaneolytta* triungulin removed from an *Anthia* beetle.

CHAPTER 6

GRASSLAND BIOME

The Grassland Biome is largely confined to the high central plateau (Highveld) and Drakensberg Mountain Range (fig. 6.1) of southern Africa where, as the name suggests, grasses make up the dominant vegetation type (fig. 6.2), although sheltered koppies, valleys and mountain gorges are often covered by woody vegetation. The area is subject to severe winter frosts and veld fires are common and regular in the dry season; these two external factors maintain the grassland by preventing large shrubs and trees from growing. Most rain falls in summer. The biome covers about 27% of South Africa, making it the largest biome after that of the Savanna.

6.1 (pp. 174–175) The Drakensberg range forms the majestic spine of the high central Grassland Biome of southern Africa.
(Photo: Rina de Klerk)

Although there are no clear regions of plant endemism in the grasslands, plant endemicity is, nevertheless, quite high. This extends to various grass species and herbs, especially those with rhizomes (e.g. *Chlorophytum cooperi*, fig. 6.3a) and bulbs (e.g. *Crinum bulbispermum*, fig. 6.3b), although the highest endemicity (at about 67%) is found amongst the orchids (e.g. *Satyrium longicauda*, fig. 6.3c). Many of these plants survive as underground structures during winter, and then flush and flower in spring, especially after fire. Some of these species have interesting associations with insects.

Insect endemism in the grasslands is generally poorly studied, although it is fairly well established that many of the high mountain grassland insect species are restricted to certain habitats and are quite possibly endemic. However, there is little evidence to suggest that insect pollinators in the grasslands are narrow endemics (specific to a particular habitat restricted to this biome only). Although many of the highly endemic grassland fire-adapted plants are intimately associated with particular insect pollinators, they depend on generalist (as opposed to specialist) flower visitors. In this way they differ from plants in the Fynbos Biome, which often have specialist pollinators. However, some pollinators, although not restricted to the region, are nevertheless significant there. Among them are spider-hunting wasps, some moths, various beetles and a bug.

The overwhelming dominance of grasses over other plant groups in the grasslands determines that the majority of herbivores belong to generalist plant-feeding groups, but feeding predominantly on grasses. There are many, but most belong to the following groups: termites, grasshoppers and their relatives, stick insects and moth larvae. Amongst the specialised Lepidoptera are also species that feed on the foliage of various fire-adapted grassland bulb plants in the hyacinth (Hyacinthaceae) and amaryllis families (Amaryllidaceae), while certain weevils are typical borers in underground bulbs.

Several species in the region are important soil engineers and play a vital role in soil and nutrient turnover, leading to successive plant community changes, as well as aeration of and water penetration into the soil. Three termite species are soil engineers with macro-scale regional effects, and are also important prey for birds and mammal carnivores. Lichen-feeding bagworms are moth larvae that loosen quartz crystals while feeding on rock faces, and thus contribute to soil formation. Although this occurs on a much smaller scale than termite activity, the results are nevertheless significant.

Amongst insect predators, the pugnacious ant, *Anoplolepis custodiens*, is dominant and a significant predator of various invertebrates, of which termites are the most important. It is also one of the principal prey species of various specialised mammal carnivores.

An interesting group of parasitic flies has a close association with some of the ungulates endemic to the grasslands: these are the bot flies, the larvae of which inhabit the nasal cavities of their mammalian hosts.

Rina de Klerk

6.2 Most of the Grassland Biome consists of vast grassy plains.

6.3 Fire-adapted bulb and rhizome plants are common in grassland, and flush in spring, especially after winter fires: **(a)** grass lilies, *Chlorophytum cooperi* (Anthericaceae); **(b)** river lilies, *Crinum bulbispermum* (Amaryllidaceae); **(c)** orchids, *Satyrium longicauda* (Orchidaceae).

Nutrient recyclers

The soils of large parts of the arid Karoo, grassland and savanna regions of southern Africa are nutrient-poor. The intervention of organisms that break down cellulose in dead plants returns nutrients to the soil and benefits plants. Termites are without doubt the most important of these across all regions, especially in the Grassland Biome. Three major termite groups dominate in grasslands: the large harvester, snouted harvester and lesser fungus-growing termites. Each has a specific habitat and role in the decomposition process, which contributes significantly to overall soil improvement. Large numbers of a small bagworm species feed on lichens growing on sandstone; they not only break down the relatively intractable lichen tissues, but their feeding also causes erosion of the sandstone itself, actually forming sand.

The large harvester termite

Harvester termites (Blattodea: Termitoidae: Hodotermitidae) are represented in southern Africa by two species: *Hodotermes mossambicus* and *Microhodotermes viator*. *Hodotermes mossambicus* is widespread in the grasslands, but also extends southwards into the adjoining Nama-Karoo Biome and northwards through the Savanna Biome to Ethiopia. The endemic *M. viator* occurs mainly in the drier southwestern areas of southern Africa (see 'The heuweltjie termite', p. 104). These two species are known as large harvester termites to distinguish them from the unrelated and behaviourally different snouted harvester termite, *Trinervitermes trinervoides* (Termitidae; see 'The snouted harvester termite', p. 179).

Hodotermitidae are amongst the 'primitive' termites (see box, pp. 72–73). They build underground nests (fig. 6.4a, see box, p. 179) and their network of underground tunnels and cavities greatly improves soil aeration and water penetration. They differ from most other termite groups in having adult workers and soldiers that are able to survive above ground – at night under hot (mostly summer) conditions or by day in cooler weather. This is made possible by various characteristics: they have well-developed eyes (as do the Termopsidae; see 'Damp-wood termites', p. 286), and their bodies are sclerotised (pigmented, fig. 6.4b) to protect them from ultraviolet radiation; other termites are blind and unsclerotised.

Both large harvester termite species collect mainly dry forage, always above ground. Their ability to survive periods of exposure to direct sun gives workers the opportunity to forage during the day, allowing them to

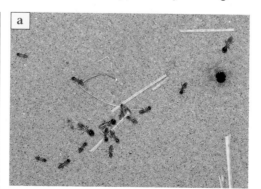

6.4 Harvester termites, *Hodotermes mossambicus*, are among the major consumers of dry grass in grasslands, where they compete with livestock and game animals for grazing. Their nests are underground, a possible consequence of regular winter fires, and workers are sclerotised to enable them to forage above ground in daylight. **(a)** Workers dragging grass stalks towards the nest entrance; **(b)** a sclerotised worker detaching a piece of grass.

compete successfully for a food resource that is actively sought by several co-occurring termite species, such as *T. trinervoides*, which are strictly nocturnal (see 'The snouted harvester termite', p. 179).

Colony structure and pheromones

The colony structure, castes and division of labour in *Hodotermes mossambicus* are somewhat different from those of other termites (see 'Social structure of a termite colony', p. 70). It has two larval and four nymphal instars. Colonies are made up of 75–92% of larvae and nymphs, the bulk of which are last-instar nymphs. Soldiers comprise only 0.4–3.5% of colony members, while 7–25% are adult workers.

The last-instar nymphs make up the majority of colony members and perform virtually all of the housekeeping activities, including constructing hive shelves; feeding larvae, other nymphs, adult workers, soldiers, and the reproductive pair; and also dispensing the pheromones that regulate caste determination.

The adult workers are the main above-ground foragers and also excavate the below-ground tunnels and chambers, although if many such workers are killed, the large nymphs assume foraging responsibilities. Soldiers are mainly active in defence of the open foraging holes and of foraging workers leaving and returning to the hole.

New colonies are established when winged male and female reproductives (alates, fig. 6.5) emerge from their natal colony after rain in summer (see 'Social structure of a termite colony', p. 70).

Caste determination is complex, but is largely regulated by pheromones. Under 'normal' nest conditions, when appropriate numbers of different castes are present to perform essential colony activities, the reproductive pair produces pheromones that 'ooze' through the cuticle. These pheromones are then licked up by the attending nymphs and circulated amongst other colony members during trophallaxis, and fed to the larvae and smaller nymphs. The pheromones, coupled with the type of food, ensure that the larvae and nymphs mature into the desired castes needed to maintain a healthy balance of caste members for the colony's needs.

Soldiers and workers also produce and secrete pheromones in their faeces, which are highly attractive to the nymphs and are eaten by them. The soldiers produce a soldier-inhibiting pheromone and workers a worker-inhibiting pheromone that regulate soldier and worker numbers, respectively. As soldiers and workers are the only castes that spend time above ground, their mortality rate from predation is higher than that of other members of the colony. When their numbers become depleted and, consequently, the amount of inhibiting pheromone is insufficient to suppress rearing of the necessary replacements of either of those castes, then additional soldiers or workers are inevitably produced from developing nymphs.

Foraging

Hodotermes mossambicus may forage by day or night, depending mainly on soil surface temperature. They feed on dry grass, which they cut and drag to the nest. During daylight (and when the moon is bright at night), they navigate between the nest holes and a food resource using the sun (or moon) as a reference point. Under dark conditions, foraging termites depend on pheromone trails to orientate.

When termites emerge from nest holes during the day, they mark the area around the hole with pheromone secreted from a gland on the underside of the abdomen (the sternal gland), then move in widening loops away from the hole without marking until they encounter suitable food, usually within 2m. To return to the nest, they walk in a straight line with the antennae held off the ground using the sun as their orientation cue, until 5–10cm from the nest when they tilt their antennae towards the ground and chemically locate the hole. After dropping the food at the nest hole they return to the food source (also in a straight line) laying a chemical trail on the ground as they do so, which serves as a route marker to the food source for other workers to follow, thus forming a foraging path between the food source and hole.

In the dark, emerging foragers also perform exploratory widening loops, but in this case they continuously lay a chemical trail on the ground. If food is encountered, the returning forager lays a direct chemical trail from the food source to the hole, which is then reinforced by successive foraging events.

6.5 A *Hodotermes mossambicus* alate that has just emerged from an underground nest after spring rain.

The pieces of food dropped at the nest hole are collected and dragged down by other workers. The large nymphs ingest and apparently partially digest food before distributing it to other colony members, and by withholding food from adult workers the latter are induced to forage.

Nest defence

Defence of exposed above-ground workers in *H. mossambicus* is unlike that in other termites. In most termite species the soldiers are the main means of anti-predator defence, and their morphology and behaviour are specially adapted for defence against their principal predators, ants. However, although *H. mossambicus* soldiers have large mandibles, they are not as aggressive as those of other termite species. Furthermore, the relatively low numbers of soldiers in a colony make their availability and effectiveness as a defence mechanism rather tenuous, which necessitates further defence mechanisms, including predator avoidance.

Predator avoidance in *H. mossambicus* differs depending on the predator; vertebrates such as lizards, birds and small mammal carnivores cause the workers to retreat to the foraging hole and to block it with a soil plug. An attack by invertebrates such as spiders or ants, however, leads to several soldiers plugging the hole with their heads (fig. 6.6); and then, if the threat persists, they block the hole with soil, cease using it and move foraging activity some distance away where new holes are opened and where foraging resumes. By continually opening and closing foraging exits over the often very large area that the colony may be spread, the predictability and availability of foraging workers in a particular area are obscured.

6.6 *Hodotermes mossambicus* soldiers have large heads and mandibles. However, their mandibles are not used in defence and they do not usually bite intruders. Instead, when defending a colony, several individuals put their heads together in order to block a breach in the mound.

Hodotermes mossambicus nest structure

The totally subterranean nests of large harvester termites (*Hodotermes mossambicus*) are huge complexes of separate interconnected 'hives', often stretching over kilometres, and as deep as 6m underground. The hives are round, up to about 60cm in diameter, and consist of clay shelves constructed from termite faeces. These serve as a depository for brood and food reserves. The hives are linked to a complex system of tunnels that lead to hundreds or thousands of above-ground foraging openings, which, with the small mounds of displaced soil or excess forage around them, are the only signs above ground of the colony's presence. The foraging openings are also connected to many superficial temporary food storage cavities. *Hodotermes mossambicus* feeds mostly on dry grass, but virtually any source of available cellulose will be taken. This species prefers to colonise bare ground, so under conditions of overgrazing on farms the situation is exacerbated still further by the termites consuming large quantities of potential livestock graze.

The snouted harvester termite

Snouted harvester termites, *Trinervitermes trinervoides* (Blattodea: Termitoidae: Termitidae: Nasutitermitinae, fig. 6.7), are also harvesters and also feed on cut dry grass, but their appearance, nests and biology are quite different from those of the Hodotermitidae. They are nocturnal grass harvesters and their characteristic low, rounded, dome-shaped mounds are the only signs of their presence. The mounds vary from less than a football in size to up to 1m high (fig. 6.9).

Trinervitermes trinervoides is one of the most common (fig. 6.10) and widespread

6.7 *Trinervitermes trinervoides* is one of the most common grassland termite species: (**a**) workers; (**b**) characteristic nasute (long-snouted) soldiers rushing to defend a breach in the mound.

Improvement of soil quality by *Trinervitermes trinervoides*

Trinervitermes trinervoides mounds, whether occupied or abandoned, cause localised disturbance of the soil on and in the immediate vicinity of mounds, resulting in changes to the soil chemistry. These changes usually bring about soil improvement which leads to colonisation by species such as red grass, *Themeda triandra*, a dominant climax grass in natural grassland and a highly palatable and nutritious food source for domestic and wild grazers. Because *T. trinervoides* mounds have a limited lifespan of 10–20 years, grassland areas have large numbers (although densities vary considerably over the species' distribution range) of both active and inactive mounds in various stages of weathering. Studies in the Free State recorded about 2.5 living mounds per hectare of grassland and up to ten times more unoccupied mounds of various ages and stages. Mound turnover was about 10% per year and the termites turn over an estimated 350kg of soil/hectare/year in this area.

The occupied mounds lack surface vegetation, but plant colonisation increases over time near and on abandoned mounds as they erode and weather away. Soils on eroded mounds, and up to 0.5m from mound edges, have a lower pH and higher concentrations of the elements magnesium, calcium, nitrogen and potassium, resulting in increased soil fertility. This is reflected by increased plant growth and higher protein and nitrogen levels in the grasses, improving palatability and nutritional value for herbivores (fig. 6.8). An additional but undesirable consequence for veld management is that grazers preferentially feed on the grasses in these localised areas, which leads to over-use of the patches, resulting in trampling and eventually, erosion.

6.9 *Trinervitermes trinervoides* builds dome-shaped mounds: (**a**) a characteristic living nest mound; (**b**) a mound soon after the colony had died of old age.

6.10 Severe winter frosts kill above-ground grass growth, seen here amongst *Trinervitermes trinervoides* termite mounds.

Jenny Scholtz

6.8 Stages of decay and nutrient recycling by *Trinervitermes trinervoides* mounds: (**a**) living mound; (**b**) dead mound invaded by couch grass, *Cynodon dactylon*; (**c**) eroded mound surrounded by grass and weedy pioneers; (**d**) complete change in vegetation after succession by palatable grasses on the nutrient-rich soil remaining after decay of a mound.

Low de Fries

6.11 An aardwolf, *Proteles cristata*, is one of the specialist mammal species that feeds almost exclusively on *Trinervitermes trinervoides*.

termite species in southern Africa and is arguably one of the most important keystone species in several biomes, especially in the Grassland and Nama-Karoo biomes and the Kalahari region of the Savanna Biome. It is a major herbivore, competing successfully with grazing livestock and game. However, its mound-building and foraging behaviour significantly increase the quality of the soil (see box opposite), and it is also the principal food item of several insectivores, including some of Africa's rarest and most unusual mammals: the aardvark, *Orycteropus afer*, the aardwolf, *Proteles cristata* (fig. 6.11), and ground pangolin, *Smutsia temminckii*.

The tall chimneys of fungus-growing termite mounds

The lesser fungus-growing termite, *Odontotermes transvaalensis* (Blattodea: Termitoidae: Termitidae), is found in arid grasslands in the northwestern areas of southern Africa and beyond to East Africa, and builds very characteristic tall clay chimneys (fig. 6.12) connected to an underground nest system. The chimneys are not inhabited by the termites, nor are they haphazard piles of earth that result from nest excavation; they are in fact a complex system of ventilation passages and air spaces associated with nest respiration (box, p. 182). The ventilation shafts greatly improve soil aeration and water penetration, and are also favoured climatically controlled refuges for a host of other small animals.

In mound-building termites, the mechanisms of nest ventilation differ somewhat between colonies of different species, depending to a large extent on the architecture of the mound, and whether it is a 'closed' or an 'open' ventilation system.

In an 'open' ventilation system, the mounds have holes into which fresh air can stream and from which gases can be expelled by the warm temperatures generated by colony and fungus metabolism or sucked out under wind pressure, while in a 'closed' ventilation system there are no holes in the mound surface and gases diffuse through it between the interior and exterior walls of the mound. An open ventilation system is used by *Odontotermes* species such as the moist savanna *O. latericius* and the eastern arid grassland species *O. transvaalensis*, while *Macrotermes* species use a closed ventilation system (see box, p. 204).

Odontotermes nests are usually deep underground, possibly as deep as 2m, and those of *O. transvaalensis* are characterised by conspicuous, often slender and very tall (1–2m high), above-ground chimneys, around the base of which are numerous small holes that are the openings of air passages to the colony. Warm air, heated by the metabolic processes of the termites and their symbiotic fungi (see 'Fungus-feeding termites', p. 236), can readily be felt rising from the chimneys. The warm air is in large part responsible for the appeal that the vents have for assorted animals: small and large reptiles, from geckos to monitor lizards, as well as rodents and small carnivores such as mongooses, are regular inhabitants of the vents. *Odontotermes badius*, one of the common savanna species, seldom has distinct chimneys, but is characterised by a partially raised above-ground clay dome (fig. 6.13). To produce the clay they use for chimney construction, *Odontotermes* workers regurgitate water held in the crop onto suitable clay soil, then mix it to the correct consistency using their mandibles (fig. 6.14).

6.12 Certain *Odontotermes* species produce characteristic clay chimneys, which are connected to an extensive underground nest system. The arid grassland species *O. transvaalensis* builds the tallest chimneys, either as (**a**) single columns; or (**b**) multiple chimneys.

6.13 The savanna species *Odontotermes badius* occasionally builds low chimneys on top of a large, low nest mound.

6.14 *Odontotermes* workers producing and manipulating clay during feeding and nest construction.

6.15 *Odontotermes* workers coating plant remains on the ground with a clay covering, under which most foraging takes place.

6.16 Fungus-gardening *Odontotermes* termites culture symbiotic *Termitomyces* fungi to digest cellulose in the plant matter they collect. After rain, the fungi may produce mushrooms that emerge from the mound; they are often the only sign of the below-ground termite nest.

Nest ventilation in *Odontotermes transvaalensis*

The mechanism of ventilation in the nest of the lesser fungus-growing termite, *O. transvaalensis*, was studied in North West Province by J. Scott Turner of the University of Bophuthatswana (now University of North West, Mafikeng Campus).

The chimney tube opens into a large subterranean air space called the gallery, which is separated from the colony and fungus gardens by a partition of porous soil. The structure of the mound and chimney suggests that ventilation is by induced flow (a Venturi mechanism), which requires that there be at least two openings to the area to be ventilated – one at ground level, the other raised some distance above the ground. Because of boundary layer effects, the variation in the speed of wind flowing past the two holes induces a negative hydrostatic pressure difference between the two openings, which draws air into the lower opening (into the nest), and out of the higher vent (through the chimney).

However, two other mechanisms also contribute to ventilation under certain conditions:

- When ambient air is still, warmed colony gases diffuse by convection into the chimney, from which they drift into the still air.
- During gusty wind episodes, outside air might be forced into the chimney, reversing the normal pattern of induced flow, or it might become tidal, pulsing one way, then the other.

The study also showed that although the metabolic activity of the termites and fungi raised the temperature in the chimneys by 2–3°C above the surrounding soil temperature (and 10–12°C above cool ambient temperatures), and that this heat was dissipated during ventilation, the air flow induced by ventilation actually had little effect on colony temperature. The deep, below-ground situation of the colony apparently ensures that it is sufficiently thermally buffered from temperature extremes.

Odontotermes termites feed mostly on grasses and dry wood, which they coat with clay (fig. 6.15) to form a protective cover against predators and ultraviolet light, and under which they feed. Chewed wood is egested onto 'combs' and then inoculated with spores of the fungus *Termitomyces* (see 'Fungus-feeding termites', p. 236); the fungus grows over the combs and digests the cellulose and lignin. It also produces nodules (asexual fruiting bodies), which the termites consume to inoculate new combs. The termites use fragments of old combs as food. After rain, the fungus produces sexual fruiting bodies (mushrooms) above ground (fig. 6.16).

Lichen-feeding bagworms

Bagworms (Lepidoptera: Tineoidea: Psychidae) are moths that belong to the same superfamily as clothes moths and case-bearers (Tineidae; see 'Clothes moths', p. 401 and 'Household case-bearers', p. 401), with about 30 species occurring across various biomes in southern Africa. The larvae live permanently in 'bags' that are constructed with silk and material from their habitat – the material used is often diagnostic in species identification (see 'Bagworms feeding on wattle trees', p. 227).

6.17 A rock buttress of the renowned colourful Clarens Sandstone in the eastern Free State.

Jayne McElwee

6.18 An important micro-ecosystem engineer, the bagworm *Penestoglossa* (Lepidoptera: Psychidae) degrades the sandstone by loosening quartz crystals while feeding on algae between them.

Although bagworms usually feed on leaves of grasses, shrubs or trees, they have been recorded feeding on endolithic lichens covering a rock formation known as Clarens Sandstone in the Rooiberg Mountain Range, which is among the foothills of the Maluti Mountains in the Free State, near the Lesotho border. This is one of the rock formations that contributes to the renowned golden, ochre and orange-hued, deeply eroded sandstone colours for which the Golden Gate Highlands National Park in the area is famous (fig. 6.17).

Endolithic lichens cover extensive areas of Clarens Sandstone, and it was discovered in a study by Dirk Wessels of the University of Limpopo that these are the food for, and habitat of, the larvae of a probably undescribed *Penestoglossa* species. The larvae live inside bags comprised of an outer shell of quartz crystals held together by silk threads (fig. 6.18), while the inner cavity is silk-lined with openings at both ends – the anterior one through which the larva protrudes while feeding, the posterior through which faecal pellets are ejected. The bags of mature larvae are about 2cm long. Larvae first appear in late summer and feed throughout the winter and into summer, maturing in December. Pupation takes place in sheltered situations on rocky outcrops, or beneath stones that lie scattered about.

The larvae retrieve the quartz crystals that they use for bag construction from amongst the lichens. The larvae loosen the crystals by dissolving the cementing material of the sandstone. The bags of final-instar larvae consist of about 96% quartz crystals and about 4% silk. The larvae feed unselectively on the lichens, and faecal analysis revealed the presence of algal cells, fungal hyphae, lichen fragments, lichen spores and quartz crystals. A large proportion of the algal cells and hyphae remain intact, indicating a somewhat inefficient digestive system. The inclusion of quartz crystals in the larval diet is thought to improve digestibility by crushing some of the more intractable algal and fungal cells, a system somewhat analogous to the bird gizzard. This would contribute to digestion by crushing lichen cells whose contents would then leak into the bagworm gut.

The feeding process detaches lichens from the rocks and loosens quartz crystals from the base, increasing the effects of weathering on the sandstone. Considering that there are as many as two bagworms per square metre on the sandstone and that the Clarens Sandstone formation constitutes about 10% of the sandstones in the area, researchers have calculated that the bagworms could erode as much as 4.4kg of quartz crystals per hectare per year, and contribute a minimum of about 200g of organic matter for the same area over the same time period. They extrapolated their findings to the roughly 12,000-hectare area where Clarens Sandstone is abundant, and where it has almost 100% endolithic lichen cover, and arrived at a figure of about 5,000kg of quartz and more than 250kg of organic matter added to the soils in the region per year.

This is an example, albeit on a micro scale, of an insect–lichen association that contributes to soil formation, soil nutrient input and lichen dispersal. The bagworm can therefore be classified as a typical ecosystem engineer.

Pollinators

Insect pollination is essential and virtually universal across plant groups in southern Africa, including those of the Grassland Biome with its own assemblage of insects that play a significant role in pollination. The plants comprise milkweeds, proteas, orchids, hyacinths and lilies; their pollinators range widely across insect groups from bugs, beetles and moths to wasps. Each has a unique and intimate relationship with its plant host.

Unusual pollinating bugs

Although bugs (Hemiptera) form the largest order of hemimetamorphic insects, and most are associated with plants, very few species appear to be involved in intimate pollination relationships. However, an exception has been recorded in an upland grassland assemblage in KwaZulu-Natal, where *Aspilocoryphus fasciativentris*

6.19 (a) A bug similar to the main pollinator of *Xysmalobium gerrardii*. **(b)** *Xysmalobium* (Apocynaceae) is pollinated by *Aspilocoryphus fasciativentris* (Hemiptera: Lygaeidae).

6.20 Grassland *Protea* species that are pollinated by chafer beetles (Scarabaeidae: Cetoniinae): **(a)** *P. caffra*; **(b)** *P. dracomontana*.

(Hemiptera: Lygaeidae, fig. 6.19a), about which little is otherwise known, has been shown to be the main pollinator of the milkweed *Xysmalobium gerrardii* (Apocynaceae, fig. 6.19b). Lygaeidae is a very large and diverse family of bugs, many of which feed on seeds, hence their popular name of seed bugs.

Xysmalobium gerrardii is visited by several different groups of insects and is, consequently, considered to be part of a generalist pollination system. *Aspilocoryphus fasciativentris* is one of those visitors and it carries numerous pollinaria (see box, p. 74) on various parts of its body and actively flies between flowers. Its population numbers, numbers of pollinaria carried, and flower-visiting activity indicated that it was probably the most important of the potential pollinators at the time of the study.

Protea pollination by fruit chafer beetles

Beetles (Coleoptera) are not generally considered to be efficient pollinators. It is well known in southern Africa that *Protea* (Proteaceae) flowers are mostly bird-pollinated, but are also frequently visited by a host of insects, including beetles (such as the protea beetle, *Trichostetha fascicularis*, Scarabaeidae: Cetoniinae). It was not absolutely clear whether any of the beetles pollinated the plants. However, a recent study has provided well-supported evidence that at least some *Protea* species are undoubtedly beetle-pollinated.

A study of four low-growing *Protea* species (known as grassland or savanna sugarbushes) along the eastern escarpment of southern Africa by Steve Johnson of the University of KwaZulu-Natal found that the flowers were highly attractive to a wide diversity of insect species. Representatives of many of the major groups visited them, including ants, bees (honey bees and solitary bees), beetles, butterflies and flies, although the majority were beetles, including several cetoniine species.

Flowers of the four species, *Protea caffra* (fig. 6.20a), *P. dracomontana* (fig. 6.20b), *P. simplex* and *P. welwitschii*, share several characteristics:
- large, bowl-shaped inflorescences with open bracts suitable as landing platforms for insects;
- small, flexible florets producing exposed pollen and dilute nectar; and
- a strong, fruity scent.

Flower colour appears to be relatively unimportant, since the four species have variably coloured flowers; xylose is the main sugar in the nectar.

The cetoniine species that visited the flowers (dependent on locality) were *Atrichelaphinis tigrina* (fig. 6.21a), *Trichostetha fascicularis* (fig. 6.21b), *Cyrtothyrea marginalis* (fig. 6.21c), *Leucocelis haemorrhoidalis* (=*L. amethystina*, fig. 6.21d), *Mecynorrhina passerinii* and *Phoxomela umbrosa*. Surprisingly, *A. tigrina* was shown to be the principal pollinator, not the protea beetle, *T. fascicularis*, nor the others recorded on flowers.

Atrichelaphinis tigrina has been demonstrated to pollinate flowers of a wide range of species in different families, including Proteaceae. It occurs in grassland or savanna areas of northeastern and eastern southern Africa, from Port Elizabeth in the Eastern Cape to the Soutpansberg in the north. A generalist flower feeder, it visits a large variety of species across its distribution range.

Atrichelaphinis tigrina beetles show a distinct preference for low- over higher-growing flowers. They eat large quantities of pollen and drink nectar accumulated in the flower base in a head-down position, or by licking petals and styles. They also use flowers as mating platforms and burrow into the inflorescences at night. Pollination occurs when the pollen that adheres to the hairs on the underside of the body and legs is dispersed over the inflorescence of the plant on which the beetle is feeding, or it is carried to another plant or flower.

6.21 (a) *Atrichelaphinis tigrina* (Cetoniinae) is the main pollinator of certain grassland proteas. Other Cetoniinae species are common visitors to *Protea* flowers, but contribute little to pollination. **(b)** The protea beetle, *Trichostetha fascicularis*, is a common flower visitor. Research has shown that it does not pollinate *Protea* flowers; neither do **(c)** *Cyrtothyrea marginalis* or **(d)** *Leucocelis haemorrhoidalis*.

The nectar pools in *Protea* flowers are placed at a distance from the pollen and stigmas, which correspond to the size of the pollinators and their mouthparts, so that the pollen is deposited on the insects' bodies while they feed on nectar. In the four species mentioned here, these distances suit insects that are 17–35mm long. The cetoniines recorded were 8–23mm long, and *A. tigrina* had an average length of 15mm.

The perfect proboscis size for an orchid-pollinating hawk moth

The hawk moths (Lepidoptera: Sphingidae) are considered to be typical nectar feeders and are assumed to be important pollinators of a wide range of plants, including orchids (see box, p. 74). The first study on orchid-pollinating hawk moths in South Africa was done in 1954, and involved the pollination of the highland grassland ghost orchid, *Habenaria epipactidea*.

Forty years later, Steve Johnson of the University of KwaZulu-Natal showed that the hawk moth *Basiothia schenki* (figs 6.22a, b) pollinates the orchid *Disa cooperi* (fig. 6.22c) in montane grasslands in the Drakensberg foothills. *Disa cooperi* produces inflorescences that are taller than the surrounding grasses and bear about 50 white flowers, each with a pink spur and sepals and a broad, greenish, scent-producing lip. In the study, the spur length of the *D. cooperi* flowers averaged about 42mm, while the proboscis length of the *B. schenki* moths averaged about 43mm. The moths visited the flowers for a short period at dusk and probed flowers on the same and adjacent plants. During this process, pollinaria attached to the base of the proboscis. Another

Hermann Staude

Hermann Staude

6.22 (a) The hawk moth *Basiothia schenki* (Sphingidae), of which **(b)** is the larva, is the main pollinator of **(c)** *Disa cooperi* (Orchidaceae). **(d)** Another hawk moth, *Agrius convolvuli*, feeds on nectar of *D. cooperi* flowers at the same time as *B. schenki*, but does not pollinate the flowers.

hawk moth species, the cosmopolitan convolvulus hawk, *Agrius convolvuli* (fig. 6.22d), was active at the same time as *B. schenki*. It has a much longer proboscis that enables it to reach and feed on the nectar, but it did not collect pollen from the flowers, so could be ruled out as a pollinator. *Basiothia schenki*, on the other hand, with a proboscis that fits perfectly into the spur and collects pollinaria, is undoubtedly a co-evolved pollinator.

Nocturnal pollinating moths

Diaphone (Lepidoptera: Noctuidae) is a small genus of colourful moths (fig. 6.23) with equally colourful larvae. Adult *Diaphone eumela* moths pollinate *Drimia macrantha* (Hyacinthaceae) in KwaZulu-Natal and its larvae feed on the same plant.

A study of the pollination of *D. macrantha* by Steve Johnson demonstrated that the greenish-cream, strongly perfumed flowers opened at dusk and closed at dawn. Each inflorescence carries about 20 flowers, which open over a period of about one week; each flower opens only once, after which it dries out.

Diaphone eumela was recorded to visit flowers on-and-off for much of the night, feeding on nectar and picking up sticky pollen that attaches to its abdomen. While flying amongst the plants and feeding, female moths stopped periodically to lay eggs on unopened buds on the inflorescence. Larvae (fig. 6.24) emerging from these eggs then fed on the buds, moving from bud to bud and eventually eating the developing fruits from the first flowers to be pollinated. However, in the population of plants studied, only about 6% of the fruits were destroyed by larval feeding, so the net benefit to the plant of advertising its flowers' presence to attract specific moths, even though their larvae might destroy some fruit, is obviously greater than the resultant fruit loss, and overall, outweighs the negative effects.

6.23 Two common grassland *Diaphone* moths (Noctuidae): **(a)** *D. eumela*, which pollinates *Drimia macrantha* (Asparagaceae); **(b)** *D. mossambicensis*.

6.24 **(a)** Aposematic *Diaphone eumela* larva feeding on the foliage and buds of *Drimia macrantha*, which is pollinated by the adult moths. The plants contain cardiac glycoside toxins, which are sequestered by the larvae for defensive purposes. **(b)** *Diaphone mossambicensis* larva on a grass leaf; they feed on *Ledebouria floribunda* (Asparagaceae).

Spider-hunting wasps as pollinators

The large black pompilid wasps, *Hemipepsis* (Hymenoptera: Pompilidae, fig. 6.25), are nectar feeders as adults. Their common name 'spider-hunting wasps' refers to the female's behaviour of hunting spiders, which she paralyses and takes to her nest (usually a hole in the ground) and upon which she then lays her eggs. The emerging larvae feed on the paralysed live spiders. Various *Hemipepsis* species have specialised pollination relationships with a range of plants.

6.25 The spider-hunting wasp *Hemipepsis capensis*, which is a specialist pollinator of the rare orchid *Disa sankeyi*.

6.26 (a) Spider-hunting wasps, *Hemipepsis* spp. (Pompilidae), are pollinators of various herbaceous grassland plants, including (b) *Pachycarpus* (Apocynaceae).

Orchids

Disa sankeyi (Orchidaceae) is a rare grassland endemic, known from only a few sites in the Drakensberg. The plants are low-growing, 15–20cm high, and well hidden amongst grasses. They produce inflorescences of about 50 yellow-green flowers flecked with purple, which emit a very strong, sweet, cinnamon-like fragrance. The flowers are visited and pollinated only by male and female *Hemipepsis* spider-hunting wasps of two species, *H. capensis* and *H. hilaris*, and it appears that the strong floral scent is the main attraction. Nectar is present in the form of a small drop in a shallow depression at the spur entrance. The wasp grasps adjoining flowers while drinking the nectar. This causes up to 15 pollinaria to stick to its front tarsi, which are then spread across the inflorescence as the wasp moves about feeding.

The combination of low-growing plants, dull floral colour, the position of the nectar and strong fragrance composed of many volatile compounds, of which some are clearly highly attractive to these wasps (although others quite probably repel nonspecialist visitors), has led to an intimate association between the participants in this system.

Milkweeds

Several *Hemipepsis* species (fig. 6.26a) were recorded to be the pollinators of two KwaZulu-Natal grassland species of the milkweed genus *Pachycarpus* (Apocynaceae, fig. 6.26b), which comprises about 20 species in southern Africa.

Both *Pachycarpus* species are genetically self-incompatible. They have open flowers that produce copious amounts of exposed, concentrated nectar – from which it can be deduced that they have a generalist pollination system. However, they are visited and pollinated exclusively by *Hemipepsis* wasps. *Pachycarpus asperifolius* is pollinated by two species, *H. capensis* and *H. dedjas* (or *H. gestroi*), which are large wasps (more than 20mm long). *Pachycarpus grandiflorus* is pollinated by three (large to small) species, *H. capensis*, *H. errabunda* and *H. hilaris*, of which *H. capensis* appears to be the most important. As in the example of pollination in *Disa* above, certain volatile compounds in the *Pachycarpus* floral nectar appear to specifically attract the pompilids while at the same time repelling other nectar feeders such as honey bees.

In a bizarre twist of a specialised pollination relationship – which is usually mutualistic in that both parties benefit from the interaction – another *Pachycarpus* species, *P. appendiculatus*, widespread in rocky grasslands in eastern parts of southern Africa, detaches the palps of its only pollinator, *H. dedjas*, during pollination. Both the wasp's maxillary and labial palps may become detached while it feeds, and it is common to find wasps with segments (from one to all) of each palp removed. These become trapped by various parts of the flower's complex floral armature. The palps are important sensory organs used by insects to locate and test quality of food so their loss is likely to affect future food location and feeding. In spite of this, pollination success as a result of the interaction was found to be high. However, the actual cost of the disfiguration to the wasp has not been ascertained.

Pineapple lilies

Hemipepsis capensis, *H. errabunda* and *H. hilaris* have also been found to be the major pollinators of two pineapple lily species, *Eucomis autumnalis* and *E. comosa* (Hyacinthaceae, fig. 6.27). Both plant species are widespread across the eastern half of southern Africa, where they occur in dense, damp grasslands in wetlands.

Unlike the situation in the orchid and milkweeds discussed earlier, these flowers are visited by a wide range of insects, including honey bees and various other Hymenoptera, beetles and flies. However, in spite of the diversity of flower feeders visiting the flowers, the *Hemipepsis* wasps were the major pollinators in one study and scent is apparently the key floral attractant.

6.27 *Eucomis* (Hyacinthaceae) is pollinated by three species of spider-hunting wasps, *Hemipepsis* spp., but also honey bees, other Hymenoptera, beetles and flies.

Herbivores

'Grass feeding' would appear to be a rather unspecialised form of herbivory, but since there is little known about the precise details of the actual feeding habits of most insect species, it is quite likely that many grassland species may have specific associations with certain grasses. On the other hand, the fire-adapted grassland geophytes (bulb plants) appear to have rather narrow associations with specific herbivores, which include foliage and bulb feeders. As the Grassland Biome is among those most threatened by transformation, it is very likely that many of the endemic insects will become increasingly rare and also threatened.

Insects living amongst grasses are often grass-like in appearance – cryptically slender and green-brown in colour. This includes grass feeders (figs 6.28a–c) but also extends to their insect predators (fig. 6.28d).

The dominant foliage-feeding insect group in grasslands is Orthoptera, specifically the grasshopper family (Acrididae), but stick insects (Phasmatodea; see 'Stick insects: the longest insects in the region', p. 215) and caterpillars (Lepidoptera) are also common (figs 6.29, 6.30). Lepidoptera larvae are among the most abundant herbivores of bulb plant leaves and fruit. The lily borer, *Brithys crini* (Noctuidae; see 'Lily borer moths', p. 371), is a common borer in the leaves, stems and bulbs of Amaryllidaceae species. Other common bulb borers are the larvae of various lily weevils, such as *Brachycerus ornatus* (Coleoptera: Curculionidae, fig. 6.31; see 'Red-spotted lily weevils', p. 370).

6.28 Many grassland insects blend into their background by being slender and grass-like in appearance, and coloured in cryptic greens and browns. These include grass feeders such as (**a**) stick insects (Phasmatodea) and (**b, c**) grasshoppers (Orthoptera), but also insect predators such as (**d**) praying mantises (Mantodea).

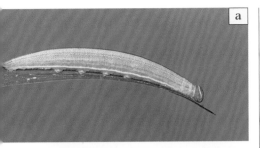

6.29 Many lepidopteran larvae are grass feeders. Some have special adaptations to break down the tough plant epidermis and to digest cellulose. **(a)** The larva of the butterfly *Gegenes niso niso* (Hesperiidae) has a more strongly developed head capsule and mouthpart muscles than relatives that do not eat grass. The larvae of the moths **(b)** *Ceryx fulvescens* and **(c)** *Epitoxis amazoula* (Erebidae) feed on decaying grass in wet habitats. Hatchlings imbibe organically enriched water to obtain the microorganisms required to digest cellulose.

6.30 Common grassland larvae and their moths: **(a)** *Regima ornata* larva (Notodontidae); **(b)** *R. ornata* adult; **(c)** *Psalis africana* larva (Erebidae); **(d)** *P. africana* adult.

6.31 (left) Many of the bulb plants contain toxic defensive chemicals that deter generalist feeders, but not specialists, which often sequester the toxins for their own defensive purposes. They are typically brightly coloured to advertise their distastefulness to potential predators, as in this lily weevil, *Brachycerus ornatus* (Curculionidae).

6.32 (above left) Because of the frequency of natural fires in grasslands, many endemic insects have adaptations during a particular stage of the life cycle to avoid immolation. One method is to lay eggs in the soil, where they overwinter and are protected against fire: **(a)** a katydid, *Conocephalus caudalis* (Orthoptera: Tettigoniidae), with an exceptionally long ovipositor; **(b)** a mantis (Mantodea) burying her egg-filled ootheca out of harm's way; in other regions, mantids attach oothecae to above-ground objects.

6.33 Some of the many species of grass-feeding grasshoppers (Acrididae: **a–d**) common in the biome. Most are cryptically coloured and typically slender to blend in with a background of grasses.

Most of the grass feeders are morphologically cryptic, while those feeding on the (often toxic) bulb plants are usually brightly coloured to warn potential herbivores.

Many of the grassland species have behavioural adaptations at some stage of their life cycle to avoid fires – these include feeding on bulbs below the ground surface, or laying eggs or pupating in the soil, where they spend that stage protected from frost and secure against late winter fires (fig. 6.32).

Feeding in grasshoppers

The grasshopper family (Acrididae) belongs to the suborder of short-horned grasshoppers (Orthoptera: Caelifera; see box, pp. 118–119) and has about 400 species in southern Africa (fig. 6.33).

Orthopterans are hemimetamorphic insects (see 'Hemimetamorphic development', p. 40). Most adult females dig holes near the food plant with their ovipositor and lay batches of eggs in pods, after which the hole is covered with soil and litter. The eggs are usually laid in summer and develop partially before they enter diapause for the winter (see 'Dormancy', p. 44). The nymphs emerge in spring and then pass through about five or six instars (depending on species) before reaching the adult stage. In some species swarming occurs when numbers are high (see 'Plague locusts', p. 165).

Acridids are equipped with short, stout antennae and the ovipositor of the female is also short and usually concealed, while the abdomen of the male often turns up at the rear end. The first segment of the abdomen is fused with the thorax and usually houses a tympanal organ on each side, used for hearing. In most species, sound is produced by rubbing pegs situated on the femur of the hind legs, against a strengthened vein in the forewing (see 'Sound production in bladder grasshoppers', p. 115; 'Sound production in rain locusts', p. 117).

The forewings (tegmina) are long and leathery and serve to protect the long, membranous hind wings that power flight in most species. The hind pair of legs is usually particularly long and powerful, enabling the insect to jump long distances. The strong leg muscles power the jump, but propulsion is enabled by a crescent-shaped organ, comprised of elastic fibres, that is located in the knee of the hind leg, which is able to store energy in preparation for the jump.

Although most grasshoppers in the Grassland Biome are generalist herbivores, grass makes up the bulk of the diet of most species, and in some studies they have been found to consume more grass matter than large mammal herbivores (see box, pp. 212–213). Some species, however, eat mainly forbs (herbaceous plants that are not grasses).

All orthopterans have chewing mouthparts, but those that eat mainly grasses have larger mandibles and mandibular adductor muscles, and subsequently larger heads than those that eat mainly forbs. Furthermore, the mandibles have different adaptations to these food types. The mandibles of both types are asymmetrical, and the left mandible, the lower part of which has a cutting edge used to cut food into pieces for consumption, overlaps the right when the mouthparts are closed. The cutting edge differs between the two feeding types: in grasshoppers that feed mainly on grasses, it resembles a smooth knife blade, while in those that feed on forbs it is serrated. The serrated mandible punches pieces of leaf before the insect devours them, while the smooth edge is used (assisted by strong muscles) to chew through tough grass fibres. Since grasses are generally lower in nutrient value than forbs, they need to be ground more finely in order to extract nutrients.

Grass-feeding grasshoppers also frequently have elongate heads; presumably a form of crypsis, in which they match the shape of the grasses (fig. 6.34), making them less easily observed by predators. Other forms of predator avoidance are the use of the large hind legs to jump, while some species include a short flight with brightly coloured wing flashes (that startle the predators), after which they close their wings and cryptically 'disappear' into the grass. Other species use aposematism (see box, pp. 240–241), in which they advertise their toxicity to would-be predators with the warning colours of black, red or yellow.

Insect predators that prey on grasshoppers include praying mantises (Mantodea, fig. 6.35; see 'Praying mantises', p. 405), which prey on eggs, nymphs and small adults, while Meloidae (e.g. *Hycleus tricolor*) larvae are specialist predators on grasshopper eggs (see 'Blister beetle larvae: predators of locust eggs', p. 171). Other predators include various carnivorous insects from different orders, as well as various reptiles, birds and mammals.

6.34 The cryptic elongated body and head of grass-living grasshoppers are clearly visible in this mating pair of *Acrida acuminata* (Acrididae). The female is larger than the male.

Predators

Prey for the major insect predators in the Grassland Biome largely consists of the abundant termites, but also includes herbivorous insects such as grasshoppers and their eggs. As in many other regions, ants are the chief insect predators. Pugnacious ants mainly inhabit hard and sparsely vegetated soils. As termite populations increase, so does bare ground, as a result of their foraging activities. This, in turn, creates favourable conditions for the ants, thus creating a cycle of predator–prey dependence.

The pugnacious ant

The pugnacious ant, *Anoplolepis custodiens* (Hymenoptera: Formicidae: Formicinae), is one of the most widespread and common ant species across a large part of southern Africa. It nests most commonly in hard and sparsely vegetated soils (fig. 6.36), such as those found in much of the Grassland and Nama-Karoo biomes (see 'Ant biology and behaviour', p. 159). Their populations increase greatly in disturbed soils, particularly those compacted by animal trampling, farm implements or vehicles along rural dirt roads. Rural children know all about pugnacious ants, which are often abundant and swarm readily over bare feet, biting and 'stinging'. However, Formicinae ants do not have a developed sting (although some primitive subfamilies do; see 'Matabele ants: specialist termite predators', p. 243).

6.35 A praying mantis, *Miomantis* sp. (Mantodea), a grassland insect predator.

A characteristic of all formicine ants is, at the tip of the abdomen, a specialised glandular opening fringed by hairs, called an acidopore. This is the external opening of a large venom gland that produces copious quantities of formic acid (see box, p. 162), which some formicine ants (e.g. *Camponotus*; see 'The Namib detritus ant', p. 153) are capable of spraying. However, pugnacious ants have a different strategy when threatened: they rear up on their middle and hind legs, curl the abdomen underneath the body and bite the offender while simultaneously spraying formic acid from the acidopore into the bite wound (see 'The woven-leaf nests of weaver ants', p. 260), producing a burning sensation similar to that of a sting.

Feeding

Like most other ants, pugnacious ants are predatory when prey is available, but feed mostly on sugary secretions, such as honeydew from sap-feeding bugs (Hemiptera) and nectar from floral and extrafloral nectaries (fig. 6.37a). Their protein requirements are satisfied by their preying on various invertebrates (fig. 6.37b), or even small, weakened vertebrates, which many recruited individuals overrun and bite into small pieces to be carried back to the nest.

6.36 The pugnacious ant, *Anoplolepis custodiens* (Formicidae: Formicinae), is one of the most widespread and common southern African ant species, but it is particularly abundant in degraded grasslands. This is an active colony with a surrounding mound of soil.

Anoplolepis custodiens is one of the most common predators of other insects (particularly termites) in many regions because of the abundance of the colonies and the large numbers of individuals in each colony. In turn, their abundance results in their being an important prey item for specialised social insect predators such as the aardvark and pangolin at certain times of the year.

They do not accumulate food reserves in the nest but have a 'honey pot' or 'replete' caste of workers in which surplus food is stored, either as liquid honeydew or nectar or, in winter, converted into oenocytes (white milky fat masses). Such individuals have a greatly distended abdomen and a 330% increase in body weight.

Pugnacious ant colonies are fairly small but their density, based on the amount of food available in an area, might be high. As with all Hymenoptera, only females make up a colony; males are only produced for reproductive purposes. Each colony consists of 500–800 workers, in three discrete size classes: minor (3.5–5.0mm long), media (5.3–7.0mm) and major (average 9.2mm). Minor workers dominate (about 62% of colony members), media comprise about 33% of the workers, and major workers about 5%. However, the percentages change depending on the nature of the available food; when honeydew is plentiful, minor and media worker numbers increase but when insect prey is readily available, more major workers are reared.

Minor and, to a lesser extent, media workers, forage exclusively for honeydew and nectar, and care for the brood. Major workers, on the other hand, dig burrows, serve as soldiers in nest defence, and are the only ones that hunt actively for prey.

Colonies

Colonies are founded according to the typical claustral system (see 'Ant biology and behaviour', p. 159), where a mated female starts a colony, first by digging a small, shallow burrow in which she lays a few small eggs. She then feeds the hatched and developing larvae on regurgitated food from body fat reserves. The larvae develop into small workers, which start to enlarge the nest and perform other colony functions. When they begin to forage, the queen starts to lay normal-sized eggs and the stage is set for the development of a colony.

Each colony has from one to a few queens, which are replaced, roughly yearly, after exhausting themselves during bouts of egg-laying. Eggs and brood are only present in the nest when weather conditions and availability of food permit, and includes the brood of male and female alates (reproductive individuals, fig. 6.38a) that emerge after rain. Usually many more male than female alates are produced. After flight and landing on the ground, each female becomes 'balled' by many males, several of which eventually mate with her. Mated females then return to their natal or another nest (fig. 6.38b), or start digging a burrow as the basis of a new colony; they are easily identifiable by the presence of wing articulation stubs on the thorax. Alate males, however, die shortly after the nuptial flight, and any that try to return to their natal nest, or enter another, are killed by the workers.

Nests

Pugnacious ant nests consist of an underground maze of tunnels, some interrupted at regular intervals by brood chambers, each with brood of different ages (fig. 6.38c). Eggs are located in the deepest chambers, then successively older brood, with pupae in the uppermost chambers. Nests are permanently occupied and the tunnels and chambers are lined and reinforced with a white substance, thought to be superfluous cuticular wax from workers. The lining strengthens soil binding in already hard soil. It is assumed that nesting in hard soil ensures that tunnels and chambers are strong enough for repletes and overwintering clusters of hibernating workers to be able to hang from the walls without their collapsing. If nests are damaged and collapse, the ants abandon, rather than trying to repair them, since they lack the ability to bind loose soil particles together or extricate themselves from even a thin covering of loose sand.

6.37 *Anoplolepis custodiens* ants feed primarily on (a) honeydew and nectar from extrafloral nectaries, but supplement their protein intake by (b) preying on arthropods.

6.38 (a) *Anoplolepis custodiens* alates amongst their sisters, preparing to abscond to start a new colony. (b) A de-winged and mated female searching for her maternal nest to return to or a neighbouring nest to enter. (c) Inside an *A. custodiens* colony; major and minor workers are visible amongst the brood.

Parasites

The southern African grasslands are home to several endemic herbivorous ungulates, as well as farmed livestock. These are host to a group of highly specialised parasitic flies known as bot and warble flies, which either infest nasal cavities of their host (nasal bots), the alimentary canal (alimentary bots), or burrow under the skin (warbles).

Nasal bot flies

Flies in the Oestridae (Diptera) have a complex life cycle and their larvae are internal, blood-feeding parasites of mammals, including humans. The phenomenon of maggots living and feeding in the tissue of a living host is termed myiasis. The flies are generally called bot flies, but depending on the biology of the species, some are termed warble flies, and those that inhabit nasal cavities are called nasal bot flies.

Amongst the Oestridae are some common livestock pests, such as the nasal bot fly or nasal worm of sheep and goats *Oestrus ovis* (fig. 6.39), the horse bot fly, *Gasterophilus intestinalis* (see 'Intestinal bot flies' p. 244), and the ox warble fly, *Hypoderma bovis*. The human bot fly, *Dermatobia hominis* of Central and South America, is the only oestrid known to routinely attack humans, but several members of the blow fly family, Calliphoridae (e.g. the tropical African mango/putsi/tumbu fly) also do so.

Most African mammals (see 'Intestinal bot flies', p. 244) are hosts of one or more bot or warble flies. The parasites fall into three general categories: nasal bots, alimentary bots, and warbles. As suggested by the names, nasal bots develop in the nasal cavities of their hosts, alimentary bots in the stomach or intestine, while warbles are the visible lumps formed by the maggots living and feeding directly under the host's skin.

The grasslands of the central plateaus of southern Africa are the original biome of two endemic antelope species: the black wildebeest, *Connochaetes gnou* (fig. 6.40) and the blesbok, *Damaliscus pygargus phillipsi*. They and their relatives – the hartebeest, *Alcelaphus buselaphus*, and the blue wildebeest, *C. taurinus* – belong to the tribe Alcelaphini and all share a related group of parasitic Oestridae flies, whose larvae live in the nasal cavities of their hosts. The bot flies *Gedoelstia cristata* and *G. hassleri* are widespread across Africa and both are nasal parasites only of Alcelaphini species. In southern Africa, *G. cristata* has been recorded from both blue and black wildebeest, as well as from hartebeest, and *G. hassleri* has also been found in blesbok.

The life cycles of bot flies are complex. Flies deposit first-instar larvae (known as larvipory) directly into the host's eye, from where they enter a vein and are then transported into the animal's cardiovascular system; it is there that they spend the early part of their development. From there they migrate up the trachea to the nasal cavity and moult into the second instar, where they remain, feeding on blood, until maturity. Mature larvae are discharged (fig. 6.41a) by the antelope 'sneezing', after which they pupate (fig. 6.41b) in the soil. The characteristic head-shaking and snorting so typical of alcelaphine antelopes is thought to be in reaction to flies (fig. 6.41c) buzzing around their heads and the irritation caused by the nasal infestation.

6.39 (above) The bot fly *Oestrus ovis* (Diptera: Oestridae); its larvae are nasal bots of sheep and goats.

6.40 (right) Black wildebeest, *Connochaetes gnou*, are parasitised by nasal bots in the genus *Gedoelstia* (Oestridae). This black wildebeest is attempting to reach the nasal bots in its nose with its tongue. Most African mammals are hosts of one or more bot fly species.

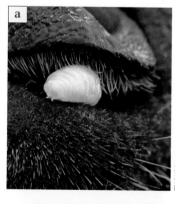

6.41 (a) A mature bot, *Gedoelstia* sp. (Oestridae), leaving the nasal cavity of a dead wildebeest. (b) The mature bot just before pupating. The black spots are its terminal spiracles, the only functional pair, through which the larva breathes while attached to the host's sinus tissues. (c) The adult fly.

CHAPTER 7
SAVANNA BIOME

The African savanna regions are renowned for their diverse and spectacular large mammal fauna, which is richer than on any other continent, but also for their wide landscape vistas and beautiful trees (fig. 7.1). Consequently, many of the continent's largest nature reserves (see box, p. 202) and other conservation areas have been proclaimed in these regions. Savanna insect diversity is also spectacularly rich; this is due to the presence of many, widely heterogeneous habitats across the savanna region, and also the high diversity of plants and animals with which many of the insects are associated.

7.1 (pp. 194–195) Wild syringa, *Burkea africana*, a characteristic and common Bushveld tree, growing between typical Bushveld grasses on sandy soil.

Rudi van Aarde

7.2 An aerial view of an eastern southern African savanna with a wide variety of trees, including baobabs, and shrubs interspersed with open glades.

7.3 A fever tree, *Acacia xanthophloea*, possibly the tree species most typically associated with the Lowveld. Historically, it was linked to areas in which malaria was prevalent – hence its common name.

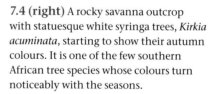

7.4 (right) A rocky savanna outcrop with statuesque white syringa trees, *Kirkia acuminata*, starting to show their autumn colours. It is one of the few southern African tree species whose colours turn noticeably with the seasons.

The Savanna Biome is the largest African and southern African biome and covers about one-third of South Africa, as well as large parts of neighbouring countries.

In South Africa, most of it lies in the northeast, north and northwest of the country. The biome is divided into ecoregions, which are variously defined by different authors. We have used four broad ecoregions based on differences in climate and vegetation: Lowveld, Mopane Woodland, Central Bushveld and Kalahari. Despite large differences in climate, soils, plant composition and associated fauna across the biome, there are sufficient shared characteristics among the subregions to justify the biome being considered a single large representative entity.

Most rain falls in summer but rainfall decreases from east to west. In a similar way, soils grade from higher clay content in the east to deep sands in the west. The vegetation reflects these two environmental factors: it grades from highly diverse, moist, tropical Lowveld in the east with 80–100 plant species per hectare, through Bushveld (with which it shares a similar diversity of plants and animals), to the drier open acacia veld of the Kalahari in the west, where there are only 20–30 plant species per hectare. Adjacent to, and intruding into the Lowveld and Bushveld in the northeastern parts of South Africa

and continuing into other parts of southern Africa north of the border, lies a swathe of a virtual monoculture of mopane, *Colophospermum mopane*, vegetation.

The **Lowveld** lies east of the Drakensberg escarpment in South Africa at altitudes lower than 1,000m above sea level and extends into southern Mozambique and eastern Zimbabwe. It is a hot to warm, largely frost-free subtropical environment with summer rainfall (about 600mm per year).

The **Bushveld** is situated in South Africa north of the Magaliesberg range, between the Lowveld in the east and the Kalahari in the west, at altitudes of 750–1,400m above sea level. Within South Africa, much of it falls in Limpopo province, but some also lies in North West province, extending northwards into central and northeastern Botswana and adjacent areas of Namibia and Zimbabwe. It is also a warm to hot region and rainfall varies greatly from east (600mm per year) to west (350mm per year), and occasional frosts occur in winter.

The distinction between Lowveld and Bushveld is somewhat blurred, with both being subtropical and having a high diversity of plants and animals, but the Lowveld is defined by large broad-leaved and thorn trees interspersed with patches of grass, while in the Bushveld there is often little distinction between tall shrubs and small trees, which results in the characteristic 'bushiness' that defines it; overgrazed areas tend to give way to dense bush, usually due to proliferation of sickle bush, *Dichrostachys cinerea*.

The flora of the Lowveld and Bushveld is characterised by a vast diversity of large, beautiful trees (fig. 7.2), often growing in dense, forest-like pockets, but sometimes standing out as solitary majestic specimens. In the Lowveld, these include wild teak, *Pterocarpus angolensis*, several species of fig trees, *Ficus* spp., and green-trunked fever trees, *Acacia xanthophloea* (fig. 7.3). In the Bushveld, one sees statuesque baobabs, *Adansonia digitata*, and beautiful wild syringas *Burkea africana* (fig. 7.1); numerous *Combretum* species are common, including leadwood, *C. imberbe*, as are various other trees, such as white syringa, *Kirkia acuminata* (fig. 7.4).

A probable consequence of the favourable climate and corresponding vegetation of this subtropical area is that there are more insect species here than in any of the other southern African biomes. Not only are there more species, but many of the largest and otherwise most spectacular insects occur here.

The most typical landscape elements of this region are, undoubtedly, the huge, castle-like mounds built by *Macrotermes* termites, which are so quintessentially associated with African savannas (fig. 7.5). The termites' nutrient recycling behaviour plays an important role in the ecology of the region.

Other noteworthy insect representatives are huge stick insects (Phasmatodea); the largest wood-boring beetles (Coleoptera: Cerambycidae); bagworms (Lepidoptera: Psychidae), a collective name for a wide range of moth larvae that construct portable shelters out of grass stems, sticks or the thorns of their host plant; and the commonly encountered processionary caterpillars (Lepidoptera: Notodontidae) walking 'nose to tail' in columns metres long. Amongst the multitudes of flower-frequenting insects are two groups of brightly coloured, slow-flying herbivorous beetles (Coleoptera: Lycidae and Meloidae) and their similarly coloured mimics that often aggregate on flowering plants; their bright colours advertise distastefulness, while their mimics benefit equally from their pretence.

Many of the tree species have one or more characteristic insect species associated with them in an often intimate relationship. One of these associations is a consequence of the high numbers of *Ficus* species in the region, resulting in equally high numbers of specialised pollinating fig wasps. Another is a group of insects whose activities have inspired the colloquial name of one of the common Bushveld trees, the weeping wattle, *Peltophorum africanum*, derived from the copious quantities of liquid that 'weeps' from the host tree, the product of excess fluids excreted by sap-feeding spittle bugs (Cercopidae). A variety of the woody plant species are hosts to galls induced by a wide range of insect species.

Predators include some of the largest and most ferocious beetles (Coleoptera: Carabidae), and the large and formidable predatory Matabele ants, *Megaponera analis*.

All members of the diverse and rich mammal fauna are hosts of numerous parasites such as ticks and fly larvae (including the continent's largest fly, *Gyrostigma rhinocerotis*, whose larvae are intestinal parasites of rhinos), while the abundant herbivores produce vast quantities of dung that support southern Africa's richest dung beetle fauna. The presence of an abundant predatory guild of small to large vertebrate predators enables a rich carrion fauna to exist.

Mopane Woodland occurs in the north of South Africa, largely in northeastern Limpopo province, but is only a small part of this huge deciduous woodland type, which extends into Botswana, Zimbabwe, Zambia and parts of Namibia. As suggested by the name, it is dominated by mopane trees, *Colophospermum mopane* (fig. 7.6).

7.5 A large *Macrotermes* termite mound; the mounds and their inhabitants are amongst the most characteristic and important elements of African savannas.

7.6 Mopane Woodland is mostly a monoculture of *Colophospermum mopane* trees, which are the habitat for a number of ecologically important endemic insect species.

These trees fall into one of two size classes, depending on the soil type on which they grow: 'cathedral' mopane veld grows on sandy soils forming high, moderately closed savanna dominated by 10–15m-tall mopane trees, whereas 'shrub' mopane, growing on clay soils, consists of multi-stemmed shrubs 1–2m tall. Rainfall is moderate in the region (400–500mm per year) and frosts are rare.

Since the region is composed more or less of a mopane monoculture, the resultant low species richness has a considerable effect on insect richness, with significantly lower insect (and other animal) diversity than neighbouring Lowveld and Bushveld. Some local insects, such as the mopane 'worm', *Imbrasia belina* (Lepidoptera: Saturniidae), are undoubtedly keystone species in the region. They, together with elephants, play an important role in ecosystem functioning: elephants feed on and trample trees, opening up the woodland and making it possible for other plant species to grow, while the mopane caterpillars regularly defoliate trees, allowing more light to penetrate, as well as stimulating a new flush of palatable leaves for large herbivores.

The bug *Retroacizzia mopani*, a localised endemic, capitalises on the virtually unlimited supply of food and is usually also present in large numbers on mopane leaves; their sugary secretions enhance the palatability of late season leaves for browsers. Another important insect group, albeit one that is not restricted to Mopane Woodland, is common and well known in the region. This is a group of a few species of small, stingless bees (Hymenoptera: Apidae: Meliponini), colloquially known as 'mopane bees'.

The **Kalahari** is the westernmost savanna subregion in South Africa, lying mainly in Northern Cape province. However, as with the other savanna subregions, the proportion of Kalahari within South Africa is considerably smaller than that lying outside the country, where it covers most of Botswana, large parts of Namibia, as well as parts of western Zimbabwe and Zambia. It is an arid parkland of grasses, where umbrella thorn, *Acacia tortilis*, and other *Acacia* species grow interspersed with grasses (fig. 7.7); in the far west, the dominant trees are camel thorn, *A. erioloba* (fig. 7.8), and grey camel thorn, *A. haematoxylon*, which grow on deep red Kalahari sands.

This is a hot, low-rainfall (200–300mm per year) area with cold winter nights during which temperatures often drop to below freezing. Although the diversity of both fauna and flora is considerably lower than in moister savanna regions, many species are unique to the area. Rain falls during irregular late-summer thunderstorms, but sufficient precipitation creates favourable conditions (though often of short duration) for insect activity, and sporadic irruptions of certain insect species lead to populations with vast numbers of individuals.

There are several characteristic or unusual insect species representative of 'rain fauna' in the Kalahari,

7.7 Although the Kalahari is generally considered to be a desert, with all the associated connotations of aridity, sparse vegetation and poor animal diversity, its biota is far more complex than these descriptions suggest. This aerial view shows the diverse landscape: beautiful acacia trees, grassy plains, dunes and ancient river valleys, all of which support a rich fauna.

7.8 Camel thorn trees, *Acacia erioloba*, undoubtedly one of the most iconic Kalahari trees, with which several bird and insect species are intimately associated.

with a suite of special behavioural and physiological adaptations that permit them to quickly exploit favourable environmental conditions, as well as another set that enables them to survive the long unfavourable periods in between:

- The leaf-feeding *Sparrmannia flava* is a large 'furry' beetle that sometimes arrives in large numbers at lights at night.
- The detritivorous beetle *Parastizopus armaticeps* is one of only a few beetle species with subsocial behaviour and fairly advanced brood care.
- Large predatory antlions (Neuroptera: Palparinae) have black-and-white mottled adults that often fly clumsily to lights at night.
- Keratin beetles, *Omorgus* spp., are common on keratin sources, such as skin, hair, scales and feathers, that remain at carcasses after predators have fed.
- The armoured ground cricket or 'koringkriek' *Acanthoplus discoidalis* (Tettigoniidae: Hetrodinae), is a large, wingless, spiny long-horned cricket, often occurring in large numbers on grass, bushes and trees; when they cross roads during local migrations, they occasionally get squashed in hundreds by vehicles.

7.9 A 4m-tall *Macrotermes* mound, showing its impressive size relative to the trees growing around it, and also the volume of soil transported from below ground to form the mound.

7.10 **(a)** Dead termite mounds serve as habitat and refuge for numerous animal species, including dwarf mongooses as seen here. **(b)** The dwarf mongoose is the smallest in the family Viverridae.

Besides members of the rain fauna, there are several insect species with permanent specialised associations with Kalahari plants. These include various ant species with an intimate relationship with the specially thickened thorns of one of the dominant Kalahari trees, *Acacia erioloba*. One of southern Africa's best-known migratory butterfly species, the brown-veined white, *Belenois aurota*, although not restricted to the Kalahari, breeds on the shepherd's tree, *Boscia albitrunca*, which is common there.

Finally, this is also the region where surviving members of southern Africa's oldest human inhabitants, the Bushman (San) people, who have lived in the Kalahari for millennia, have specialised associations with certain insects, among them, poison-arrow beetles (Chrysomelidae) and the Kalahari silk moth, *Gonometa postica*. Poison-arrow beetles, as their name implies, are highly toxic leaf-feeding species used to poison hunting arrows. *Gonometa postica* produces large, white, spiny pupal cocoons, which are used to make ankle rattles that are worn during ritual dances.

Termites as soil engineers

Not only are the tall spires of *Macrotermes* mounds (fig. 7.9) a significant component of the savanna landscape, but feeding and mound-building profoundly affect decomposition processes and soil fertility in the biome, enhancing plant establishment and growth. Such plants are more attractive to and nutritious for animals feeding on them. Termite mounds, both living and dead, provide a safe and climatically moderated environment and are inhabited by numerous other animals (fig. 7.10). However, the spires are not just empty edifices; they are used by the termites to regulate the temperature and ventilation inside the mound cavity, which facilitates breeding by a mutualistic fungus species that populates 'fungus gardens' which are carefully cultivated by the termites (see 'Fungus-feeding termites', p. 236).

Termites in African savannas have been recorded to consume as much as 55% of available surface plant litter, moving 1–1.5 tonnes/hectare of litter to their nests per year. The termites themselves constitute 70–110kg/hectare of biomass, while mammal herbivore biomass in the savannas has been estimated to be only around 10–80kg/hectare. In addition, the termites move tonnes of soil during their feeding and mound-building activities, and the transport of deeper soils to the surface extensively modify whole soil layers to such an extent that in certain regions these are identifiable as special termite-developed geological horizons.

Development of a termite mound

Macrotermes are large fungus-growing termites that build impressive conical clay mounds, which are an integral and characteristic aspect of the African savanna landscape. These are home to the colonies of millions of both male and female individuals (fig. 7.11), each the offspring of a single king and queen (for details on the social structure of termites see 'Black-mound termites as nutrient recyclers', p. 68). In southern Africa the species that build the tallest mounds are *M. michaelseni* and *M. natalensis*.

Macrotermes species are amongst the largest termites – a *M. natalensis* queen is a huge, bloated, egg-laden (physogastric) individual (fig. 7.12) and may reach a length of 15cm; the king is one-third her size. The royal pair are not normally seen, as they live in a cavity deep inside the mound. The soldiers, which appear when the mound is breached, have large sclerotised heads and massive mandibles and are half as long as the king. The millions

7.11 (left) *Macrotermes* workers and soldiers at the entrance of a disturbed above-ground foraging burrow.

7.12 (below) A large, bloated, egg-laying *Macrotermes* queen, mother of all colony inhabitants, is surrounded by her attendant worker and soldier offspring.

of workers are pale, lightly sclerotised, blind individuals only about 3mm long – they live inside the dark chambers of the mound and under clay foraging tunnels.

A 3m-tall mound may consist of as much as 3–5 tonnes of soil, carried particle by particle by these tiny insects, the base being continually widened as the tower is built higher (see box opposite). The building process is undertaken by workers, who collect clay from as deep as 1.5m below the soil surface (where the moisture content is often higher) and mix it with saliva in their mouth. They then collect sand grains in their mandibles, place them in position, and squirt the wet clay around them; after this they knead the particles with their head and mouthparts.

The mounds of *M. michaelseni* and *M. natalensis* in southern Africa can be up to 4m tall with bases 20m in diameter; there can be up to 73 living *Macrotermes* mounds per square kilometre (fig. 7.13). In central Africa, mounds can be much taller (9m), with wider bases (30m) and they are also more abundant (200–700 mounds/km²). The larger the mound, the older it is, and estimates of the age of large living mounds put them at up to 100 years old. One partially occupied *Macrotermes* mound (3m tall, with a base about 15m in diameter), however, excavated by archaeologists in Zimbabwe, was calculated to be about 700 years old. It is unlikely that the mound had been continuously occupied for all of that time by a single colony of termites, and it is more likely that it had been re-occupied several times over that period, possibly also by *Odontotermes* (see 'The tall chimneys of fungus-growing termite mounds', p. 181), which often seem to colonise *Macrotermes* mounds.

A survey of termite mounds built by five mound-building genera in the Kruger National Park (KNP) determined that only about half of the mounds that dot the countryside are occupied by termites at any

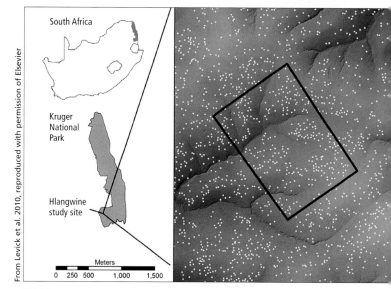

From Levick et al. 2010, reproduced with permission of Elsevier

South Africa

Kruger National Park

Hlangwine study site

Meters
0   250 500   1,000   1,500

7.13 A satellite image of *Macrotermes* mounds in the Kruger National Park shows a landscape of several hundred living and dead mounds.

one time. The other half of the mounds, although abandoned by termites, are secondarily colonised by ants and various other insects, as well as by reptiles such as snakes and monitor lizards, and a host of small mammals, including rodents, shrews and mongooses. The labyrinth of tunnels and numerous small to large cavities provide shelter and refuge in an equitable micro-environment for many years.

Mound effects on vegetation and landscape

The distinctive tall mounds, either living or abandoned, have characteristic vegetation patches associated with them, often supporting flora quite different from that in surrounding areas. The mounds consist of finer soils

The rise and premature fall of a *Macrotermes* mound

The only well-documented age of a large termite mound in southern Africa is that of a *Macrotermes natalensis* mound built inside a shed on an abandoned mine on the Wild Coast of eastern South Africa. Its growth and development were monitored by an ecotourism enterprise that was using some of the abandoned mine's facilities. Over a period of a mere 27 years it grew from the first tiny pile of sand into a huge mound with seven turrets, the tallest of which was 4m high (fig.7.14). The soil displacement was estimated to be 20–30 tonnes. At the end of the 27-year period, the Eastern Cape Department of Conservation took over the old mine buildings and decided to demolish the mound to make place for vehicle parking. The mound had become a significant tourist attraction in the area, but appeals to save the mound by the owners of the ecotourism enterprise and scores of visitors, including many foreigners, fell on deaf ears. The Department of Conservation went ahead and demolished the mound, but the doorways of the shed were too small to allow vehicle access – so the shed was never used and the mound was destroyed unnecessarily.

Strandloper

7.14 It has been speculated that large termite mounds take decades to build; this mound with seven turrets, the tallest of which was 4m high, was constructed over 27 years in eastern coastal southern Africa.

Jenny Scholtz

7.15 The origin of a termite island in the seasonally flooded Okavango Delta of northern Botswana. A large tree and surrounding bushes have grown on the drier and nutrient-rich mound soil, attracting roosting birds. Seeds in their droppings germinate and extend the vegetation matrix. Browsing mammals feed on the plants and trample the mound margins, progressively increasing the island's size and form.

7.16 Animal paths joining strings of termite islands in the Okavango Delta of Botswana. The islands provide food sources and dry refuges for animals.

Rudi van Aarde

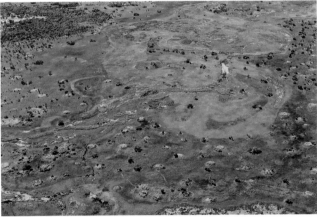

Rudi van Aarde

7.17 An aerial view of termite islands (the yellow circles in the foreground) on the flood plains of the Okavango Delta of Botswana. The islands may coalesce or become trampled by large mammals walking between them (paths are visible) to form depressions that collect water. Over years, this dynamic process results in changes in vegetation, animal densities and flood levels.

and have more nitrogen and phosphorus than adjacent areas, so they are essentially nutrient hotspots in often nutrient-poor soils, hence the distinctly different vegetation type on mounds.

In many savanna areas of Zimbabwe, Zambia and Mozambique (and to a lesser extent, the Lowveld of South Africa), the large mounds increase in size over time, forming huge 'termite hills' that tower above the surrounding areas, creating 'islands' of distinctive vegetation (fig. 7.15). The 'hills' in open areas are usually colonised by the palatable grass species *Cenchrus ciliaris*, while the even more palatable grass *Panicum maximum* grows on those that are more wooded; these grasses, together with palatable foliage on trees, attract a host of herbivores (fig. 7.16).

The 'hills' are started by partial weathering of the exterior of a mound during the rainy season (fig. 7.17) and increasing plant growth around the base. The soil

As a consequence (mainly) of the large mammal diversity, the Savanna Biome is home to some of southern Africa's largest and oldest nature reserves and other conservation areas, including (among many others) the Kruger National Park (KNP) in the Lowveld of South Africa, and the Kgalagadi Transfrontier Park, which straddles the border between South Africa and Botswana in the Kalahari ecoregion. Intensive entomological studies have been done in both of these huge game parks, as well as in some others, including the small Bushveld Nylsvley Nature Reserve in Limpopo province.

Among the insect groups that have been studied in the KNP are: dung beetles and the effects of their dung-feeding and -burying activities on soils; carrion feeders and the speed of decomposition processes; pollination of dominant tree species; and the effects of termites on the landscape. There have also been attempts to quantify the biomass of some guilds of insects to obtain a measure of their availability and importance as food for numerous insectivores, as well as crude estimates of the numbers of insect species in the KNP (see sidebar) as a proportion of total numbers in southern Africa. Many of these studies were undertaken, or facilitated, by Leo Braack (currently at the University of Pretoria) over the 30 years that he was the research scientist responsible for invertebrates.

The studies in the Kgalagadi Transfrontier Park largely involved research into the various ways that certain insects have adapted to their hot and dry environment.

Studies at Nylsvley Nature Reserve formed part of the South African Savanna Ecosystem Project undertaken in the 1970s and 1980s. These included determining the ecological importance of various insect groups in the system, one of which focused on the amount consumed by herbivorous insects, and then compared it to that of large herbivores – with totally unexpected results.

Savanna insect species as percentage of southern Africa's total number

The estimated total numbers of insect species per country or region, or worldwide, have long been contentious because of their huge numbers, often small size, and the difficulty of sampling comprehensively (since their activity may fluctuate over short time spans from hours to days, and they may occur in a wide variety of habitats). In spite of these limitations, there have been numerous attempts, using different approaches, to estimate insect species numbers worldwide. An estimate of the number in southern Africa yielded a figure of about 45,000 known species, which was thought to represent about half of the species actually occurring in the region. A roughly similar approach to estimate the number of species in the Kruger National Park (KNP) concluded that about half of the insect species thought to occur in southern Africa could be expected in the KNP. Although these figures are very crude approximations of species numbers, they do give an idea of the incredible richness of the insect fauna of the KNP and Lowveld and hint at their apparent value in ecosystem functioning and maintenance.

---

eroded off the mound over time is deposited around the base of the mound. Over several years, this forms a low hummock, with the mound situated at the apex. This is followed by successive invasions of the same or other termite species, with new mounds constructed on, or adjacent to, the hummock, followed by their eventual extinction and the gradual collapse of their mound; often the only signs of a past 'island' are the mature trees that remain (fig. 7.18). This is repeated many times over, over many years, and leads to a gradually increasing hill, until some reach heights of 8m and a basal diameter of up to 30m.

Indeed, the upward transport of tonnes of subsurface soil by the collective activities of millions of colonies over millennia has resulted in a recognisable geological formation. In Malawi, for example, a soil horizon 5m thick

7.18 A mature termite island with a copse of trees in a seasonally partially inundated flood plain in northern Zambia.

Alan Gardiner

and spread over an area of 8,800 square kilometres was formed by the activity of *Macrotermes falciger*, which has been active since about 100,000 years ago. The clay and sand formation is the result of about 44 million cubic

7.19 Termite mounds covering a grassy plain in the distance. Over time, termites move so much soil that they change the sand and clay horizons, creating distinctive, recognisable geological formations.

Alan Gardiner

From islands to pans

The dense cover and abundant browse on 'termite islands' attract numerous mammals, particularly browsers, which then place the islands under disproportionate pressure, opening up the habitat and trampling the soils. This ultimately leads to erosion.

The early stages of this process lead to the formation of pans at the base of hills. These hold water after rain, attracting mammals that come to drink and wallow, which increases the size and depth of the pans and leads to more erosion around the hill bases. Eventually, the hills are destroyed by trampling, wallowing and feeding mammals, and are entirely transformed into large pans.

So, over many years, what starts out as a single termite mound, grows over time into a densely vegetated island in a sea of grass. It is then attractive to a host of animals as a source of food and protective cover, which then ultimately leads to its extinction and conversion into a pan that holds water into the dry season.

metres of subsoil having been transported to the surface by termite activity. In Zambia (fig. 7.19), vast numbers of *Cubitermes* termites have had a similar effect on the soil.

A study in central Zimbabwe comparing vegetated *Macrotermes* mounds with adjacent woodland areas showed that the mounds supported twice as many tree species, and that these were taller on average than those on the nonmound areas. Furthermore, the woody vegetation was denser on mounds than in surrounding areas and attracted more birds and mammals. Large browsing mammals, including black rhino, elephant, kudu, eland and impala, browsed more on trees on mounds than those off them. A similar study in the KNP yielded comparable results.

Trampling and manuring by large mammals further develop (or destroy, see box above) the structure of the hill. This then becomes a feedback loop, as megaherbivores such as elephants preferentially feed on the more nutritious plants growing on the islands, but their destructive feeding habits cause branches and leaves to be broken and dropped. These, in turn, serve as food for the termite occupants, which then re-incorporate the nutrients back into the soil where it is again available to plants.

Termite islands are of particular importance in floodplain areas associated with large river systems that are seasonally or regularly inundated by rising floodwaters, and where fires are a common occurrence during the dry season. Areas favoured by termites have soils with a high clay content, used in mound construction, or have a high ground-water table (e.g. in seasonal pans and drainage lines). Such islands have been described in the Okavango Delta

in Botswana and the Gorongosa-Cheringoma plain in Mozambique, and their importance as significant modifiers of large areas in seasonally flooded savanna has been well documented.

Termite nest ventilation

Large *Macrotermes* colonies may consist of as many as 2 million individual termites in a massive structure. Inside the mound, the termites largely control the microclimate and collectively function as a single superorganism. This requires oxygen in sufficient quantities to drive the metabolism of the individuals, and an efficient ventilation system to clear the colony of carbon dioxide and methane produced by their metabolism. How this happens is complex, but depends to a large degree on the architecture of the mound: some termites (e.g. *Odontotermes transvaalensis*) build mounds that use 'open' ventilation systems (see box, p. 182), while those of *Macrotermes* are suited to 'closed' ventilation systems.

Mounds built by the different species of *Macrotermes* vary in size and shape – from conical and spire- to dome-shaped – even within a species, but they are all completely sealed externally ('closed system') in southern African species.

The effect that mound structure and architecture have on mound ventilation as a model for a closed ventilation system has been studied in considerable

Ventilation of termite mounds is essential for the wellbeing of the colony, and is driven by complex interactions between mound architecture, external wind forces and convection of metabolically warmed nest gases. It is dependent largely on variation in wind speed (gusts) and direction, which result in tidal, as opposed to circulatory, air movement in the mound.

The exposed clay mound and its large base warm up in sunlight and radiate heat that warms the air currents around the mound. These intercept wind blowing across the mound, causing disturbed air movements near the mound that ebb and flow.

The wind forces exert their strongest effect on the sub-surface air ducts through the porous mound surface by driving air down into the nest and, via the lateral connectives, into the chimney (the effects of strong winds are modulated in the lateral connectives before reaching the nest or chimney). Warm air rising from the colony mixes with this fresh air in the middle of the chimney as it drifts upwards; it then moves outwards through the lateral connectives back to the sub-surface ducts. As the wind changes velocity near the mound, tidal gusting, followed by a lull, leads to thorough mixing of the gases in the conduits, then sucks out the mixed air. Relative humidity inside the mounds remains at about 90%, and temperature is kept within a narrow range of 25–30°C, irrespective of external seasonal changes.

Rina de Klerk

7.20 A large *Macrotermes michaelseni* mound in Mopane Woodland in the northern Kruger National Park. The bare mound rises from a huge, partially vegetated base formed by recolonisation and expansion by successive colonies over decades. Although the exterior of the mound appears impermeable, it is porous, to enable colony respiration.

The reproductives and the nursery galleries, with attendant workers, are found in the bottom half of the nest, while the top half consists of an array of chambers containing fungus combs, which make up the fungus gardens (see 'Fungus-feeding termites', p. 236).

One of the remarkable aspects of the colony is how the termites determine the 'correct' height of their mound. This is thought to work as follows: the balance between rising metabolic gases and fresh air in the middle of the chimney provides the termites with a measure of which state is starting to dominate, and since they are exceptionally attuned to changes in carbon dioxide, oxygen and humidity, they can respond by opening or blocking holes in the mound surface where building activities are taking place. As the colony grows and metabolic waste gases start to dominate, they add to the height of the spire to maintain the long-term equilibrium of the colony environment.

detail in *M. michaelseni* mounds (fig. 7.20) in mopane savanna in northern Namibia, where the termites create tall mounds with a conical base and a somewhat pointed spire (see box above).

The internal mound structure of *M. michaelseni* comprises the nest and fungus gardens, a spherical space 1.5–2.0m in diameter, of which roughly half lies in the mound base, the other half below ground level, with a network of tunnels above and below the nest. These merge above the gallery and form the uninhabited chimney that extends upwards into the spire. The chimney is surrounded by a network of tunnels, termed lateral connectives, which open into a number of vertical ducts that lie just below the mound surface. The surface consists of a porous soil layer 1–3cm thick.

Pollinators

Pollination of woody savanna plants differs somewhat from that in other biomes – generalist pollinators such as beetles and honey bees pollinate most dominant plants. Fig trees, on the other hand, have an intimate, complex and specific relationship with specialised wasp pollinators.

Pollination in the Kruger National Park (KNP)

The interactions of insects with the flowers of the 27 dominant woody plant species (mostly trees) upon which many of the large charismatic browsers, such as

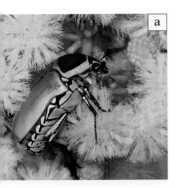

7.21 Flowers of the dominant savanna trees are visited by large numbers of insects of diverse groups, of which about 40% are beetles, mainly fruit chafers (Scarabaeidae: Cetoniinae); they also comprise the bulk of the pollinators: (**a**) *Dischista cincta*; (**b**) *Anoplocheilus figuratus*; (**c**) *Mausoleopsis amabilis*; (**d**) *Pachnoda picturata*; (**e**) *Anisorrhina umbonata*; (**f**) *Rhabdotis semipunctata*.

elephant, rhino and giraffe, as well as antelopes and many other animals depend for food, were the focus of a study in the KNP. Many of the wide diversity of insects that were attracted to the flowers contributed little to pollination, but there was a large suite of others that apparently contributed to some extent. What was clear, however, was that pollination (as in all other biomes) was important for seed set and ultimately for plant species survival.

Flowers of most of the studied plant species were visited by very large numbers of insects, which included beetles (Coleoptera), flies (Diptera), wasps and bees (Hymenoptera), and butterflies and moths (Lepidoptera). Many of these were merely floral visitors, attracted by the bounty of nutritious floral tissue, pollen or nectar; only 35 species that visited flowers were found to be transporting pollen between flowers and could be considered to contribute to active pollination of the plants.

The flower visitors were dominated by Coleoptera, which comprised about 40% of the total number of species. These included a variety of families, but fruit chafers (Scarabaeidae: Cetoniinae) comprised the majority (17%) of beetles visiting flowers and made up 29% of the pollinators (figs 7.21, 7.22). The high percentage of beetle pollinators is a somewhat surprising result, and of particular significance in the savanna, since beetles are usually thought of as being destructive feeders rather than important pollinators (but see 'Monkey beetles as pollinators', pp. 80, 109; 'Protea pollination by fruit chafer beetles', p. 184). However, many plants are adapted to tolerate some measure of flower destruction in return for pollination services.

Hymenoptera comprised a small number of floral visitors (0.7% of the total), but a disproportionate 14% of pollinator species. The most important of these was the honey bee, *Apis mellifera* (see 'The ubiquitous honey bee', p. 74 for detailed biology), but large carpenter

7.22 Many fruit chafer species (Scarabaeidae: Cetoniinae) feed mainly on ripe fruit and fluids oozing from wounds in tree bark (**a**); (**b**) *Cheirolasia burkei*; (**c**) *Dicronorrhina derbyana*.

a

b

7.23 Although honey bees (**a**) and solitary bees such as carpenter bees (**b**) account for a small percentage of visitors to flowers, they represent a disproportionate percentage of effective pollinators.

a

b

7.24 Flies are also important pollinators, especially during the early part of the season. Two characteristic species are (**a**) the red-headed fly, *Bromophila caffra* (Diptera: Platystomatidae), and (**b**) *Notolomatia* sp. (Bombyliidae).

bees, *Xylocopa*, were also important (see 'Honey bees and carpenter bees', p. 393). *Apis mellifera*, as in most other regions, is probably the most important general pollinator, as it is widely catholic in flower choice and is active all year long (fig. 7.23).

Diptera (fig. 7.24) were also common flower visitors, accounting for about 4% of the total, and were considered to be important pollinators, particularly during the early part of the season before most beetles and solitary bees become active. Two of the common – and very characteristic – flies to visit flowers were the red-headed fly, *Bromophila caffra* (Platystomatidae), and a long-tongued fly, *Philoliche* (Tabanidae; see 'Long-tongued flies and long-tubed flowers', p. 81); *Philoliche* females also suck mammal blood before laying eggs.

Butterflies (e.g. Hesperiidae, Lycaenidae, Nymphalidae, Papilionidae, Pieridae, fig. 7.25) and moths (e.g. Zygaenidae, fig. 7.26) were also prominent flower visitors (4% of the total), although Lepidoptera were considered to be of low importance as pollinators. No night observations were made during the study, so no nocturnal moths were observed, but these are likely to be common and to increase the recorded importance of Lepidoptera.

a

b

c

d

e

f

7.25 Butterflies are common flower visitors at savanna plants, although only a few species appear to be important pollinators. Among these are: (**a**) *Leucochitonea levubu* (Hesperiidae: Pyrginae); (**b**) *Spialia mafa mafa* (Hesperiidae: Pyrginae); (**c**) *Leptomyrina gorgias gorgias* (Lycaenidae: Lycaeninae); (**d**) *Colotis evagore antigone* (Pieridae); (**e**) *Stygionympha wichgrafi* (Nymphalidae: Satyrinae); (**f**) *Acraea natalica* (Nymphalidae: Heliconiinae).

7.26 Although moths are amongst the most important nocturnal flower visitors, little is known about their value as pollinators. Certain diurnal species are commonly attracted to flowers, but they appear to be of low importance as pollinators. **(a)** *Uresiphita* sp. (Crambidae); **(b)** *Palpita vitrealis* (Crambidae); **(c)** Scythirididae; **(d)** *Erastria leucicolor* (Geometridae); **(e)** *Zutulba namaqua* (Zygaenidae); **(f)** *Utetheisa pulchella* (Erebidae).

Fig-pollinating wasps

Fig wasps (Hymenoptera: Agaonidae) are obligatory specialist pollinators and have a well-established intimacy with fig trees, *Ficus* (fig. 7.27); it can be assumed that each of the more than 750 fig species worldwide is pollinated by fig wasps. There are 19 fig species in the KNP, and although the details of the associations between them and their pollinating wasps have not been studied there, enough is known about fig wasp biology to assume their importance.

Each fig species has a single co-evolved pollinator in the form of tiny, fragile, short-lived winged female and wingless male wasps. The plant and pollinator are totally interdependent, locked into a relationship that has resulted in extreme specialisation in both species; for example, there are guarding scales on the fig ostiole (a tiny, bract-lined opening at the apex of the fruit) that allow only a fig wasp of the correct size and shape to enter, and the wasp responds only to the volatile chemicals of its host fig (see box, pp. 208–209).

The fig 'fruit' is actually an inflorescence called a syconium, which is a hollow receptacle that bears many minute flowers on the inner surface (figs 7.28, 7.29). There is often an open space (lumen) in the centre. Flower numbers may vary from hundreds to thousands in a single syconium. There are two kinds of flowers: male and female. The syconium may contain both kinds of flowers (monoecious), or it may have only male flowers on a 'male' plant and only female flowers on a 'female' plant (dioecious or gynodioecious).

7.27 A large red-leaved fig, *Ficus ingens*.

7.28 'Fruits' of the common cluster fig, *Ficus sycomorus*; the fig 'fruit' is actually an inflorescence (syconium), which contains numerous tiny flowers.

7.29 Pollination of fig flowers by minute obligate specialist wasps is legendary. The fig flowers are borne on the inside of the syconium and these are pollinated by species-specific wasps. The fig wasps are, in turn, parasitised by a host of specialised wasp parasitoids. Numerous interacting individuals are visible in this opened syconium.

a

b

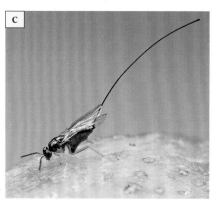

c

7.30 The obligate pollinator wasp life cycle is complex, and male and female wasps differ completely in appearance and function, as seen in these wasps associated with the broom cluster fig, *Ficus sur*: **(a)** *Ceratosolen capensis* (Agaonidae) female; **(b)** *C. capensis* male. Some parasitic species have an exceptionally long ovipositor with which they penetrate the syconium wall to reach the host wasp, **(c)** seen here in the parasitoid *Apocrypta guineensis* (Pteromalidae).

Fig wasp life cycle

Fig pollination is the special preserve of wasps, with each wasp species holding the key to just one corresponding fig species (fig. 7.31). The first flowers to mature in the fig 'fruit' are female and this is the stage when fertilised, pollen-bearing female wasps (one to a few) enter them.

The fruit is completely closed to the outside except for the ostiole, which is partly blocked by the tightly packed bracts between which the fertilised and pollen-bearing wasp must wriggle to gain access to the flowers. Although she is morphologically well adapted to do so, having a flattened and elongate head and thorax, and special rows of backward-pointing teeth on the mandible that prevent her slipping backwards, she does not get through unscathed: in most cases her antennae and wings are torn off in the process; these losses, however, do not affect her pollination or egg-laying ability. Once inside, she pollinates hundreds of tiny, single-ovule florets, and lays an egg in each of many ovaries by inserting her ovipositor down the style. She then dies. The larvae developing in the ovules cause galls in which the tissues surrounding them swell with sequestered nutritious fluids on which the larvae feed.

Male flowers only mature 3–20 weeks after the female flowers, coinciding with the maturation of the immatures of the pollinating wasp species. About one month after oviposition, wingless male wasps emerge from their natal ovule. They cut holes through the sides of the floral ovary in which mature females (often their sisters) are still incarcerated, and using their telescopic genitalia, mate with them. In certain species, males then drag the females out of their natal galls by their antennae in order to prevent them from mating again, as only females still lodged in their galls are attractive to males. In some other species, females may mate several times with different males. After mating, some males cut a communal escape tunnel through the wall of the fruit through which they escape.

Fertilised, winged females emerge from the galls and either collect pollen passively on their hairy bodies, or pack it into special pollen-storing recesses on the body, and then escape from the fruit via one of the tunnels cut by the males. After the male flowers have finished flowering, the fig ripens.

The female then flies to another tree (either monoecious 'female' trees or dioecious trees) with green fruits that have florets at the receptive stage for pollination. She is attracted by special, species-specific volatile chemicals. Once inside she pollinates some flowers and lays eggs in others. These develop into the next generation of wasps. For the wasp and figs to survive, there must be at least one fig tree of the right species with fruit at the appropriate stage of development within flying distance of the tiny wasps.

In most southern African fig species, the flowers on a single plant open synchronously but the different plants in a specific region flower asynchronously. This ensures that there are flowers of a particular species receptive for pollination and wasp development for most of the year. Fruit also ripen synchronously by changing colour and smell, which attracts a wide range of vertebrates (mammals, birds and even some lizards) that eat them; most of these do not damage the seeds inside the fruit but distribute them widely.

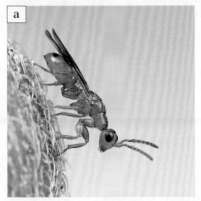

7.31 Wasps associated with the common wild fig, *Ficus thonningii*: **(a–c)** *Sycophila* spp. (Eurytomidae); **(d–e)** females of gall-forming *Lachaisea* spp. (Pteromalidae).

Besides the obligate pollinating species, numerous other equally tiny, non-pollinating wasp species (3–30 species in a single fig species) are associated with developing figs. Whereas the pollinating wasps associate with only one fig species, the nonpollinators may be more catholic in their associations. Some are parasitoids of the pollinating wasp larvae (fig. 7.30), fig seeds, or both; others have as yet ill-defined associations. The nonpollinators usually have long ovipositors with which they pierce the fig wall to lay eggs on the pollinator larvae or seeds.

Tiny stingless mopane bees

Mopane bees (fig. 7.32a) are social stingless bees (Hymenoptera: Apidae: Apinae: Meliponini) named for their presence in areas where mopane trees, *Colophospermum mopane*, are common. They are an important member of the guild of generalist pollinators in these areas. The stingless bees in southern Africa, of which there are about eight species in five genera (*Cleptotrigona*, *Hypotrigona*, *Liotrigona*, *Meliponula* and *Plebeina*) are restricted to the tropical eastern and northern parts of the region.

They are mostly small black bees that, depending on the species, either nest in secluded locations in hollows in tree trunks or in cavities in the ground. They are often attracted in considerable, irritating, numbers to people who are active outdoors on hot, sweaty days. Rural people plunder the nests for the sought-after honey the bees produce and the pollen they store, although only small quantities are yielded.

Stingless bees share some similarities with their distant cousin, the true honey bee, *Apis mellifera* (see 'The ubiquitous honey bee', p. 74); both groups nest in a variety of natural cavities in trees or the ground, make honey in perennial nests founded by a swarm of sterile female workers and a queen, and colonies occasionally produce males. However, there are also substantial differences between them:

- stingless bees, as their name suggests, cannot sting;
- the colony is not cooled by evaporating water from collected nectar;
- workers do not build their nests with pure wax;
- males feed themselves at flowers and may even perform some colony tasks such as feeding the larvae and cleaning the nest;
- stingless bee colonies cannot migrate; and
- gravid (egg-bearing) queens cannot fly.

Colony founding and mating are also slightly different. A new stingless bee colony is founded by a virgin queen and a swarm of workers absconding from their natal nest. Swarming is infrequent, however, possibly because unoccupied cavities of the proper dimensions may be rare in any area. There is also some indication that arboreal species prefer certain tree species for nesting sites. The ground-nesting species often use cavities in active or abandoned termite nests. The queen produces a pheromone that is highly attractive to male bees. Hundreds of males may converge on the site; the queen, however, mates with only one, unlike honey bee queens who usually mate with several or even many males.

Brood is produced in a similar manner to most solitary bees; an egg is placed on top of a food mass in a cell, then the cell is sealed. Honey and pollen are stored in separate 'pots'. Brood cells are round or ovoid and food storage containers are small to large spheres (fig. 7.32b).

Nests are constructed with cerumen, a mixture of wax produced by a dorsal gland and plant resin. The resin is collected fresh from preferred host plants, attached to the corbiculae (pollen baskets) as with pollen, and then stored in resin deposits in the nest until needed. Wax from the wax glands

Nelly Ndungu

Temperature control and ventilation in stingless bee nests

The nest of the stingless bee is enclosed in a virtually water- and airtight cavity, accessed by a small nest entrance and long entrance tube – features that are effective in reducing water loss and buffering against outside ambient temperature variation.

The depth at which soil-nesting species establish nests apparently enables them to achieve a stable nest temperature even when soil surface temperatures are high; *Plebeina hildebrandti* colonies are able to maintain a nest temperature of about 32°C, despite soil surface temperatures higher than 60°C. Tree-nesting species, because of their generally shaded nest positions and the insulating properties of the surrounding wood, experience more moderate ambient temperatures. The temperature in *Hypotrigona gribodoi* nests is maintained at about 35°C, irrespective of outside ambient temperature.

However, the airtight nature of the nesting cavity and its single entrance tube also create difficulties in regulating the concentration of respiratory gases in the nest. The entrance tube is the only route for fresh air to enter and stale air to exit the nest, so this requires special 'respiratory' behaviour on the part of the colony inhabitants. Both ground and tree nests have similar problems with the build-up of stale air from bee respiration and brood metabolism.

Both types of nests were recorded to 'breathe' in a manner similar to that of a mammal. This colonial breathing is not the result, however, of synchronised individual bee breathing but rather by bees fanning their wings. Their fanning expels stale air, and creates a corresponding small drop in pressure inside the nest cavity, which results in the passive entry of fresh air from outside.

In soil-nesting *P. hildebrandti*, breathing pulses were more frequent and inspired air volumes smaller during daytime than at night. The smaller volumes inspired by day are probably a response to the hot outside air and are programmed to prevent the nest from heating up.

The breathing frequencies and volume of expired air of tree-nesting *H. gribodoi* were much higher than those of *P. hildebrandti*, suggesting that the more moderate environment of their nests allows for more regular and deeper breaths.

7.32 Stingless social bees are a characteristic element of many savanna areas.
(a) *Hypotrigona ruspolii* (Apidae: Apinae: Meliponini) worker imbibing fluid.
(b) Inside a *Hypotrigona* nest: top half is old brood, below that and to the left of centre, new brood; the brown mass to the right are honey 'pots' and the yellow structures in the left bottom corner are pollen 'pots'.
(c) *H. ruspolii* workers leaving their nest in a tree trunk through the tubular wax entrance.

is stored in wax deposits. Consequently, there is always a ready supply of building materials when they are needed. Cerumen is much more pliable than the pure wax used for cell building by honey bees.

The stingless bee nest is virtually water- and airtight. The only access to the nest is through a narrow tube (fig. 7.32c). Although the virtually sealed nest is well protected from invaders, air ventilation and drainage of excess water built up by condensation need special respiratory adaptations by the colony, and, in ground-nesting species, special drains constructed to lead water away from the nest are necessary. Workers of arboreal species imbibe excess water droplets in the nest, then carry and eject them outside. The bees defend the nest, mostly against ants, by placing sticky resin droplets near or in the entrance, or by blocking the entrance with large resin balls.

Robin Crewe of the University of Pretoria and his collaborators studied ventilation (see box opposite) in the nests of two species: the arboreal *Hypotrigona gribodoi* (=*Trigona gribodoi*) and the ground-nesting *Plebeina hildebrandti* (=*Trigona denoiti*).

Hypotrigona gribodoi workers are 2–3mm long and colonies consist of 500–800 individuals. They appear to nest preferentially in certain tree species in different regions: in KwaZulu-Natal they have been recorded to prefer cavities in dead wood of tamboti trees, *Spirostachys africana*, whereas in Limpopo province they use red bushwillow trees, *Combretum apiculatum*. In Uganda, they have been recorded to nest not only in cavities in trees, but also in clay walls and pipes. They have a single narrow nest entrance tube (4–7mm in diameter and 20–200mm long) that extends only to the edge of the nest cavity.

Plebeina hildebrandti worker bees are 3.3–5.2mm long and colonies number 3,000–10,000 individuals. Nests in KwaZulu-Natal were located about 650mm below ground level in cavities that appeared to be abandoned termite nests. In Uganda, they have been found in living termite mounds, with the bee nest placed close to the core of the termite colony. A single, sticky resinous tube that projects a few centimetres above the ground provides the only access to the nest. A similar tube extends from the bottom of the nest, but acts as a drain for excess water that builds up in the nest from condensation.

Herbivores

The Savanna Biome is renowned for its grazing and browsing mammal herbivores. Few people would consider that insect herbivores actually surpass the mammals in ecological importance – but it has been shown that they consume more plant tissue than the mammals, and convert more consumed energy into biomass. Moth and butterfly larvae and crickets and grasshoppers are the dominant consumers of woody plant and grass foliage, respectively, while beetles are the most important flower feeders and consumers of both live and dead wood.

Insect and mammal feeding compared

Nylsvley Nature Reserve in Limpopo province lies within the Bushveld, where it forms part of a vegetation unit also sometimes referred to as 'Central Sandy Bushveld'. The sandy plains support various grass species and tall, deciduous silver clusterleaf, *Terminalia sericea*, and wild syringa, *Burkea africana*, trees growing in deep sandy soils, interspersed by smaller patches of loamy soils with *Acacia* trees. Low-lying areas along the Nyl River in the reserve are a declared Ramsar wetland site, well known for its high bird diversity.

Detailed studies of local savanna ecosystem processes in the reserve during the 1970s and 1980s included studies of archaeology, soils, climate and energy flow through the entire system. The research was part of an international biomes programme under the auspices of the South African Savanna Ecosystem Project. As a result, Nylsvley is one of the most intensively studied areas in South Africa.

Insects were included in various studies, but the main entomological projects concerned Lepidoptera as primary consumers of broad-leaved foliage, and Orthoptera as primary consumers of grasses (see box, pp. 212–213). The results give a good idea of the importance of insects versus large herbivores (fig. 7.33) in energy terms – first as consumers of photosynthetic energy, and then its conversion into secondary producer biomass available for the next trophic level. These are some of the only studies in southern Africa that actually provide empirical data on the importance of insects in energy flow in an ecosystem; presumably similar results could be expected in the other biomes.

7.33 Impala, *Aepyceros melampus*, one of the savanna mammal herbivores rivalled by grasshoppers in terms of grass consumption.

Rina de Klerk

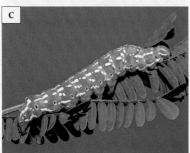

Ian Sharpe

Ian Sharpe

7.34 The dominant herbivores of woody foliage in the central savanna Bushveld are the larvae of two Lepidoptera species: (**a**) larva of the pallid emperor, *Cirina forda* (Saturniidae); (**b**) adult *C. forda*; (**c**) larva of the sundowner moth, *Sphingomorpha chlorea* (Erebidae); (**d**) adult *S. chlorea*.

A study was conducted of moth caterpillars (as the dominant arboreal herbivores) and of grasshoppers (as their grass-feeding equivalent) to determine their consumption of foliage compared with that of large mammalian browsers and grazers – with interesting results.

Larvae of the pallid emperor moth, *Cirina forda* (Saturniidae) (fig. 7.34a), were usually present in low numbers on trees of their preferred host (the dominant *Burkea africana*) for about six weeks during a first generation in October–November and again in still lower numbers during a second generation in February–March. However, roughly each alternate year, populations increased significantly and these irruptions led to extensive

defoliation of the trees. Less commonly, roughly each fourth year, larvae of the sundowner moth, *Sphingomorpha chlorea* (Erebidae) (fig. 7.34c), which also feed on *B. africana* at Nylsvley, irrupted, often at the same time as *C. forda*, leading to large areas of complete defoliation.

Foliage consumption in outbreak and non-outbreak years was determined and compared: in non-outbreak years, the moths were found to consume about 22kg/hectare/year; during a mild outbreak, 98kg/hectare/year; and during a large outbreak about 124kg/hectare/year.

Annual browse consumed by large mammalian browsers (mainly kudu and impala) was 61kg/hectare/year, less than during a mild caterpillar outbreak and only half that of the caterpillars during a severe outbreak year. Averaged over

a four-year 'cycle', annual consumption by caterpillars was substantially more than that by antelope. Keep in mind that foliage consumption was only calculated for these two caterpillar species; the numerous others not studied would undoubtedly have substantially increased the total amount consumed.

Secondary animal tissue production by the caterpillars was about 5kg/hectare/year, while that of mammalian herbivores was equivalent to 1.3kg/hectare/year, about a quarter of the biomass of the caterpillars. So, not only did the insects consume much more leaf matter (photosynthetic energy) than the mammalian browsers, but substantially more of it was converted into biomass available to the next trophic level.

Grasshoppers (fig. 7.35) were found to be the major primary consumers of grass in the Nylsvley system and consumed more grass than naturally occurring grazing antelope and cattle at the recommended agricultural stocking rate for this area. Grasshoppers consumed 388kg/hectare/year and converted 44kg/hectare/year into secondary productivity, while cattle consumed 182kg/hectare/year and produced 38kg/hectare/year of biomass from the grass eaten.

These results show that insects are more important than the mammals in the same consumer guilds in terms of the energy flow processes in this system, as they consume more photosynthetic energy and convert more of it into secondary producer biomass than do mammals. However, they appeared not to compete directly; caterpillars were most abundant on tree species (*Burkea africana*, *Terminalia sericea*) that

7.36 Armoured ground crickets (Orthoptera: Tettigoniidae: Hetrodinae) are large, often spiny, aggressive crickets; most groups are endemic to southern Africa, especially drier areas of the region: **(a)** *Hetrodes pupus* (west to south coast and near-coastal areas); **(b)** *Acanthoproctus cervinus* (widespread in the Nama-Karoo).

Armoured ground crickets

Crickets commonly referred to as armoured ground crickets or koringkrieks (fig. 7.36) are present mainly in the western parts of southern Africa, while *Acanthoplus discoidalis* (Orthoptera: Tettigoniidae: Hetrodinae) (fig. 7.37) is common right across the drier savanna regions of South Africa, Botswana and Namibia (see 'The nara melon and the nara cricket', p. 154). *Acanthoplus discoidalis* is a typical 'outbreak' species whose populations periodically build up to huge numbers. Because of their diurnal activity, large size, spiny appearance and the repulsive fluids they secrete when alarmed, they are a very obvious and characteristic element of this area.

Their primary food source is grass seeds and they mature in late summer when grasses set seed. Their preference for grass seeds has led them into competition with humans, since they sometimes switch from feeding on indigenous grasses to cultivated species, such as pearl millet and sorghum, which are staple human food items in arid areas. *Acanthoplus discoidalis* is considered the most important insect pest of these crops and huge losses are often suffered as a result of their feeding.

Though nominally herbivores (figs 7.37a, b), *A. discoidalis* adults need extra protein for breeding, and they will feed on carrion or prey on any injured conspecifics (fig. 7.37c) or other animals incapable of escaping or defending themselves. They have been known to attack nestlings

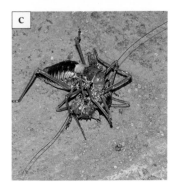

7.37 (a) The armoured ground cricket, *Acanthoplus discoidalis*, builds up into **(b)** large swarms under optimal weather conditions; as their principal food, grass seeds, becomes depleted and their nutritional requirements for extra protein increase, they turn to **(c)** cannibalism of injured conspecifics and have even been recorded to eat nestlings of **(d)** red-billed quelea, *Quelea quelea*.

7.35 Grasshoppers, such as this widespread African savanna species, *Acanthoxia gladiator* (Orthoptera: Acrididae), are the major consumers of grass in the central savanna Bushveld, consuming substantially more than antelope and cattle.

were little browsed by mammals, and grasshoppers preferred grasses (e.g. *Eragrostis pallens*) that were mostly shunned by mammal grazers. Fresh green grass flushing in spring after a winter fire, however, was equally attractive to both grasshoppers and mammals, leading to direct competition for a relatively scarce resource.

Avoiding sperm competition in *Acanthoplus discoidalis*

Males of the armoured ground cricket, *Acanthoplus discoidalis*, produce a huge sperm ampulla and spermatophyllax (a 'mating plug'), accounting for about 20% of the male's live weight (fig. 7.38a). The spermatophyllax prevents other males from mating with the female while sperm is being released into her reproductive system. This is, in effect, a mechanism to avoid sperm competition with other males.

Mating takes place late at night, after several hours of courtship initiated at sunset by males stridulating consistently. Mating lasts 40–50 minutes, after which the females are abandoned and they begin to consume the spermatophyllax (fig. 7.38b). This takes several hours and lasts well into daylight. Soon after this they lay eggs in pods in the soil. Females mate again as soon as two days after oviposition, but the mean is about seven days later; the cycle is repeated twice on average. Males are ready to mate again three to four days after a mating. Interestingly, males have a clear preference for virgin females, which they judge on size, as they are significantly smaller than females that have mated previously.

Jenny Scholtz

Jenny Scholtz

7.38 (a) During mating, male *Acanthoplus discoidalis* produce huge 'mating plugs' consisting of a sperm ampulla and spermatophyllax that 'block' the female's reproductive organs; **(b)** this prevents the female from mating again until she is fertilised, but also provides extra nutrition for the female, who consumes the plug.

of the red-billed quelea (fig. 7.37d), a seed-eating bird that usually nests in large aggregations, as well as to decimate huge numbers of mature mopane worms, *Imbrasia belina*, during an irruption of the caterpillars.

The *A. discoidalis* life cycle is well synchronised with average summer rainfall events of the western savanna regions, but as 'average' years only happen irregularly, population irruptions are sporadic. During a year suitable for emergence and development, eggs hatch in early summer (November), about 3–4 weeks after a substantial amount of rain has fallen (a minimum of about 60mm in less than three weeks). The nymphs then undergo six instars, maturing in February–March. The adults are active until about May, when mating takes place (see box above).

Eggs are laid in packages in the ground and enter a dormant stage for about six months, until the first substantial rainfall of the next summer, making this stage the longest and most vulnerable of the life stages. In order to survive the long periods of heat and desiccation during summer and the intense cold of winter, the egg has a thick, relatively impermeable chorion (shell) and eggs are clustered together in a pod – a hard rectangular soil pellet with eggs firmly cemented inside. Eggs may lie dormant for as long as three years. The mortality of eggs and nymphs remains high during unfavourable conditions, but once the crickets have matured, they are fairly well protected against the elements and predators.

The adults are very mobile, climbing into trees and shrubs to avoid hot soil surface temperatures. They are physically well protected by their armoured and spiny exoskeleton and large mandibles, with which they bite readily when attacked. Males also stridulate actively when attacked by lifting the pronotum and rubbing the greatly reduced wing buds together, producing a low buzzing sound that acts as a deterrent to some predators. However, stridulation is primarily a mechanism for males to attract females during courtship, so only males stridulate.

These physical and behavioural defences are backed up by chemical defence. The crickets squirt toxic green haemolymph for up to 30cm from between their leg joints or from behind the head (auto-haemorrhaging or reflex bleeding). They try to bite their attacker when attacked from the front or side, or ooze haemolymph from various pores to coat the body when attacked from above. The final act of defence is to regurgitate the stomach contents onto the attacker. The haemolymph has been shown to be extremely distasteful to naïve predators, as well as having a repellent effect. Predators learn to associate the smell and taste of haemolymph and regurgitated stomach contents, as well as stridulation sounds, with the crickets and consequently avoid them. Only a few animals, including bat-eared foxes, jackals and kori bustards (fig. 7.39), eat them on occasion.

7.39 *Acanthoplus discoidalis* produces noxious defensive secretions that deter all but the hardiest predators, such as this kori bustard, *Ardeotis kori*.

7.40 Stick insects (Phasmatodea) are stick-like in many respects: (**a & b**) their shape and colour blend with the background, and legs and other appendages resemble twigs. (**c**) Legs often detach when grabbed by a predator. (**d**) Their eggs are dropped to the ground and look like seeds.

There is, however, a downside to crickets coating themselves with haemolymph – the smell is highly attractive to other individuals, who apparently associate the smell with injured conspecifics, which are attacked and eaten. Consequently, crickets that survive a predator attack after auto-haemorrhaging will quickly clean themselves of the fluid; if they don't, they will be attacked by other crickets.

When population numbers increase dramatically, the crickets often embark on directional and local 'migrations', possibly in search of better food. This may involve crossing roads, where large numbers may be squashed by passing vehicles. The dead and injured crickets then attract others who feed on them, which often culminates in a slippery mess of insect pieces and body fluids covering the stretch of road.

Stick insects: the longest insects of the region

The stick insect *Bactrododema reyi* (Phasmatodea: Diapheromeridae) is the longest insect in southern Africa, with a length of 25cm. Stick insects, as the name suggests, are stick-like in every aspect – they are thin, with twig-like appendages, have colour patterns that mimic their host plant, and lay eggs that mimic seeds (fig. 7.40). Furthermore, they have slow swaying motion like a twig in a breeze that further camouflages them. Although these characteristics suggest that they are a rather dull group of insects, they actually have a suite of interesting biological attributes.

All stick insects eat either grasses or leaves of woody plants. In southern Africa they rarely become very numerous, unlike in Australia where several species are considered pests.

Females are always longer than males – in *B. reyi* it is the females that reach 25cm, with males seldom longer than 11cm. However, in many species males are entirely absent and reproduction is solely by parthenogenetic production of female eggs.

The process of egg-laying and the eggs themselves are exclusive to stick insects. There are a few species that stick their eggs to the host plant tissue, or deposit them in cracks in the host plant bark. Females of most species, however, merely drop their eggs to the ground or, at most, flick them away; the eggs of these species are patterned like seeds, which they undoubtedly mimic.

In the simplest form of brood care, the females of most insects lay their eggs on or close to a larval food source to enable the delicate hatchlings to start feeding without having to undertake a hazardous journey to find food. Stick insects have evolved a different strategy: their eggs are attractive to ants. The eggs are quickly removed from the soil surface by ants and buried in an environment safe from potential desiccation, predation, parasitism, physical damage and fire.

The eggs of many of the species that are dropped to the ground have a 'cap' (capitulum), very similar in appearance and chemistry to the elaiosome on seeds of many plants (see 'Seed burial by ants', p. 66); both are composed of fatty acids. It has been shown that eggs with a capitulum and seeds with an elaiosome are equally attractive to ants, which rapidly collect them and carry them to their nests where the capitulum is eaten off and the undamaged egg is left unharmed. Many of the ant species that behave in this way regularly abandon their nests, leaving the eggs behind where they eventually hatch. Although freshly hatched stick insects are extremely delicate, they are capable of emerging through soil of up to 10cm deep, although the highest survival rate is by emergence through less than 6cm of soil.

Another biological attribute of stick insects is that they can shed limbs if these are seized by a predator. The limbs snap off at a special hinge at the leg base (trochanter) in a process called autotomy, as in lizards casting their tail when grabbed. Autotomy is fairly common among insects, but once a limb is lost, it usually does not re-grow. Immature stick insects are an exception; at the moult following leg-shedding, the terminal joint of the leg (tarsus) grows again, and at successive moults the succeeding joints follow. However, since at least five moults are necessary to replace most of a leg, these seldom regenerate fully. Stick insects may therefore sometimes have some incompletely re-grown legs.

The sugary lerps of mopane psyllids

Mopane psyllids, *Retroacizzia mopani* (Heteroptera: Psyllidae), are tiny sap-feeding insects characterised by the sugary, crystalline shells with which they cover themselves, called 'lerps' (fig. 7.41). Lerps are composed mainly of plant fluids that have passed through the insect's digestive system and are excreted as honeydew, which then hardens to form the cover. The main function of the lerp is to protect the tiny, fragile insect against desiccation, and it possibly plays some part in protection against predators and parasitoids as well.

Mopane psyllids are most active in early winter, just before the leaves on the host plants (fig. 7.6) start to drop off (senesce). Females lay up to about 500 eggs in several spiral batches on the leaves. Each egg is attached to the leaf by a basal pedicel stuck to the leaf.

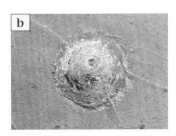

7.41 Sap-feeding mopane psyllids (Hemiptera: Psyllidae) (**a**) cover themselves in cone-shaped 'lerps' (**b**), formed from excreted sugary plant sap, that protect them against desiccation. (**c**) Large numbers of lerps increase the palatability of mopane leaves for browsers.

The tiny nymphs that emerge from the eggs wander off on the leaf but quickly attach to nearby veins by piercing the phloem tissue on which they feed. Then, using their mouthpart stylets embedded in the leaf as a pivot, they start to construct lerps over themselves by slowly rotating around this point while secreting a pale brown liquid from the anus onto the leaf surface; the liquid quickly hardens. They continue this action until they have constructed a simple dome-shaped cover. In some Australian species, the lerps have a more complex architecture – some are cone-, valve- or bivalve-shaped; others resemble intricately woven baskets and fans.

Incidence of lerps on mopane leaves and numbers per leaf vary from year to year, but in a study in Limpopo province as many as 95% of leaves carried at least some, with an average of about 40 per leaf.

The sugary lerps attract honeydew-feeding arboreal ants such as *Crematogaster* species, but are also very attractive to monkeys and baboons, various bird species, as well as rural children who lick them off the leaves.

Browsing wild antelope and livestock appear to select mopane leaves encrusted with lerps. Senescing leaves are fairly high in tannins that reduce palatability for browsers; this is offset by the improved palatability of leaves covered in sugary lerps. Livestock farmers in the mopane woodland areas are well aware of the importance of the lerps for their livestock in the winter months, as mopane leaves are often the only remaining fodder at that time, but are shunned unless sweetened by lerps.

Spittle bugs on the weeping wattle

Spittle bugs, in common with most of their relatives (Hemiptera: Auchenorrhyncha), feed on plant sap and produce excessive amounts of waste fluid while doing so (fig. 7.42). This excreted fluid may be concentrated and sugary, or liquid and frothy. Concentrated fluid is called 'honeydew' and is typically produced by aphids (Aphididae) and scale insects (Coccoidea; see 'Scale insects', p. 376), whereas the liquid, frothy exudate is known as 'spittle', and is produced by members of the families Aphrophoridae and Cercopidae (about 70 species in southern Africa). Honeydew is attractive to a wide range of insects such as ants (see box, pp. 218–219), flies, bees and wasps, which imbibe the sugary fluids, while spittle is not.

Ptyelus grossos (Hemiptera: Aphrophoridae) (fig. 7.42d) is the spittle bug responsible for the common name 'weeping wattle' given to the indigenous tree *Peltophorum africanum*; the name is derived from the liquid that drips from the feeding bugs. But what is the reason for the production of excessive fluid in these insects?

When their mouthparts pierce the phloem vessels in the plant, the sap, which is under pressure in the vessels, is forced into the insects' gut. In order to avoid exploding under the pressure, the insects have a more or less 'through-flow' alimentary canal, modified so that the bulk of the liquid bypasses the midgut and flows straight to the hindgut from which it is excreted. The insects are able to do this because the hindgut is folded back alongside, and wrapped around the foregut, and most of the ingested fluid passes directly from the fore- to the hindgut by way of a 'filtration chamber'; the tiny fraction that passes into the midgut is digested.

Only spittle bug nymphs produce the foamy liquid with which they surround themselves. This is done by blowing air through their spiracles, which open into a special chamber made up by flaps of cuticle that arise from the dorsal plates (terga) of the abdomen, and mixing it with the excreted liquids and a waxy secretion from special anal glands. The froth is produced by the flexible abdomen being whipped and rotated back and forth to stir the mixture. The main function of the wax is to coat the air bubbles to prevent them from bursting.

Nymphs, either singly or in groups, live in the foam from the time of their emergence from the egg until their final moult into adulthood, when they become free-living. The main functions of the foam are preventing desiccation and protection against parasites and predators; it is claimed to have an unpleasant, bitter taste to humans – and probably possible predators too!

Ptyelus grossos is one of the largest (wingspan of up to 35mm) and most widespread species in the family in southern Africa. Individuals are grey with large yellowish blotches on their wings. They feed on a variety of indigenous trees in addition to *Peltophorum africanum*; these include *Acacia*, *Searsia* (formerly *Rhus*), *Lonchocarpus* and *Strychnos*. They also feed on nonindigenous trees, including *Tipuana* (a favourite food plant) and occasionally *Eucalyptus*. A smaller red-and-black species of spittle bug, *Locris arithmetica*, is common on lush grass such as kikuyu in urban areas of the eastern parts of the subcontinent.

7.42 Cercopidae and Aphrophoridae (Hemiptera: Auchenorrhyncha), are known as spittle bugs but only nymphs produce spittle. (**a**) An adult spittle bug; (**b**) nymph producing excreted foamy plant sap while it feeds; (**c**) the foamy excess dripping from the host tree and giving rise to the common name of 'rain trees'; (**d**) *Ptyelus grossos* (Aphrophoridae).

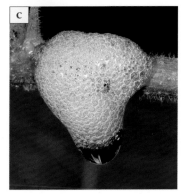

Some ant species that have a preference for feeding on nectar or honeydew (see 'The Namib detritus ant', p. 153 and 'The pugnacious ant', p. 191) have been found to have associations with *Acacia* trees – either for the nectar produced by extrafloral nectaries, or for the honeydew produced by other insects living on the trees. Ants have also been found living in the broadened bases of the thorns of some *Acacia* trees (figs 7.43, 7.44). This association is well known in *Acacia* species in Central America and East Africa, but the details of such associations in southern Africa have not been published.

In Central America, most *Acacia* species are largely protected against herbivory by various chemicals contained in the leaves and other organs. However, a few species without such chemicals are protected by aggressive ants, with which they have an intimate co-evolved relationship. The ants live in the bases of the thickened thorns and obtain food in the form of nectar from extrafloral nectaries on the plant, and in return, protect the plants against insect and mammal herbivores by preying on herbivores such as caterpillars, and stinging and biting mammals that try to feed on the foliage.

In East Africa, ants have an association with *A. drepanolobium* (fig. 7.45), which is a common and widespread species in the region and is characterised by thorns with very swollen, bulbous bases. After the ants have chewed holes into the thorn bases, a whistling sound is produced when the wind blows, so the trees are known as 'whistling thorns'. At least four ant species are associated with them – three *Crematogaster* and one *Tetraponera* species. The ants vary in their association with the trees and with each other, and the different species compete aggressively among each other for exclusive use of a particular tree. Some *Crematogaster* species trim the foliage on their host tree to lessen the chances of it touching neighbouring trees, which might allow an attack from 'foreign' ant fauna. The *Tetraponera* ants, which do not feed on nectar produced by extrafloral nectaries, destroy the nectar glands on their host tree to discourage nectar-feeding ants from establishing on it. However, none of the species is entirely dependent on the whistling thorns and they also use other plants and various natural cavities for nesting sites.

7.43 Several *Crematogaster* ant species are associated with African acacias: (**a**) feeding on nectar secreted by extrafloral nectaries on *Acacia* twigs; (**b**) attending honeydew-producing scale insects feeding on tree sap; (**c**) living in cavities inside thickened thorns, especially of camel thorn, *A. erioloba* (**d**).

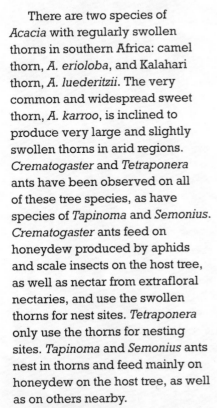

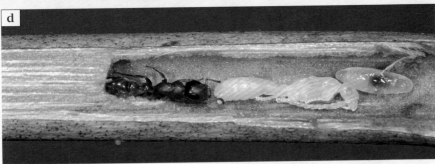

7.44 **(a)** Sweet thorn, *Acacia karroo*, occasionally has thickened thorns, especially in arid areas; **(b–d)** they are inhabited by slender ants such as these *Tetraponera* species.

There are two species of *Acacia* with regularly swollen thorns in southern Africa: camel thorn, *A. erioloba*, and Kalahari thorn, *A. luederitzii*. The very common and widespread sweet thorn, *A. karroo*, is inclined to produce very large and slightly swollen thorns in arid regions. *Crematogaster* and *Tetraponera* ants have been observed on all of these tree species, as have species of *Tapinoma* and *Semonius*. *Crematogaster* ants feed on honeydew produced by aphids and scale insects on the host tree, as well as nectar from extrafloral nectaries, and use the swollen thorns for nest sites. *Tetraponera* only use the thorns for nesting sites. *Tapinoma* and *Semonius* ants nest in thorns and feed mainly on honeydew on the host tree, as well as on others nearby.

It is thought that the ants protect the trees in the same way as Central American ants. *Tetraponera* species use their potent sting to discourage herbivores. *Crematogaster* species, on the other hand, do not sting. Instead, individuals of the very large colonies swarm over insect herbivores attempting to feed on the acacia foliage, killing and dismembering them and blanketing the nose and mouth of vertebrates; this is claimed to repulse even large mammals such as giraffes and elephants.

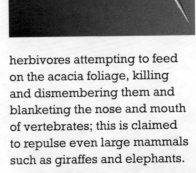

Ben Fong

Ben Fong

7.45 **(a)** An East African *Acacia drepanolobium* with swollen thorn bases. **(b)** *Crematogaster* ants make holes in them, inside which they nest. The trees are known as 'whistling thorns' because wind blowing over the holes produces a whistling sound.

Temperature control in *Sparrmannia flava*

The abundance in a hot part of the country of *Sparrmannia flava* beetles with their furry covering has long intrigued entomologists. When it was recorded that the beetles in the Kalahari are actually most active around 03h00–04h00, the coldest part of the day, researchers decided to investigate the beetles' body temperature in relation to their activity and the ambient temperature to determine why this was the case.

Steven Chown and Clarke Scholtz found that there were two peaks of adult activity: an early evening peak, just after dark and until about 22h00, and then another in the early hours of the morning. The adults that were active during the first period were mostly sexually immature and had not accumulated large fat reserves, whereas those that flew in the early morning hours were mature and fat.

Sexually mature *Sparrmannia flava* adults are, to a large extent, able to control their own body temperature (endothermy). This is done by the energetically expensive process of vibration and contraction of the flight muscles in the thorax prior to flight, which takes place at body temperatures of about 38°C. The dense fur pile covering the thorax insulates it and allows the temperature to build up quickly. During flight, however, the flight muscles generate extra heat under the fur, warming the thoracic blood – to prevent overheating, it is pumped into the bare abdomen, which then sheds heat to the cool atmosphere by conductance. The thoracic fur also keeps the flight muscles warm while the beetles are feeding and relatively inactive, which enables them to fly immediately if they are threatened.

During the early evening activity period, young adults are forced to fly at relatively high ambient temperatures because they have not yet had sufficient time to build up the fat reserves necessary to fuel sustained flight and feeding activity at the low early morning temperatures of the early morning activity period. Overheating is still a possible consequence of flying at this time, so these beetles are both energetically and thermally stressed.

Older adults switch their activity to the cool early morning flight period. The reason for this strategy appears to be because of predator pressure – most nocturnal predators set off to forage as soon as it gets dark and beetles emerging from the soil or alighting on the soil to lay eggs are very vulnerable to predation. However, by late night most predators have fed or returned to their burrows or dens, so beetles active during that time are less exposed to predation. On the other hand, this is the coldest period of the day and insects active at this time need to burn large amounts of energy to fuel activity – but this is not a problem for a beetle with a good supply of body fat and a dense furry coat to keep it warm; hence this fascinating strategy.

7.46 **(a)** The dense, long mane of hairs that covers the head and thorax of the woolly chafer, *Sparrmannia flava* (Scarabaeidae: Melolonthinae), provides insulation against cold early morning temperatures when the beetles are most active. **(b)** Their larvae are also unusual amongst chafer beetles, as they feed on the dung of antelopes, such as **(c)** springbok, instead of on plant roots.

Dung feeding in woolly chafer beetle larvae

The woolly chafer, *Sparrmannia flava* (Coleoptera: Scarabaeidae: Melolonthinae), is a fairly large (20–25mm long) brown beetle with a furry mane of long cream hairs around the head and thorax (fig. 7.46a). They are often attracted in quite large numbers to lights, buzzing loudly in flight.

The genus *Sparrmannia* consists of 24 named species, many of which occur in the Kalahari, and *S. flava* adults are fairly typical members of the group known collectively as leaf chafers (see 'Chafer beetles', p. 369), feeding at night on *Acacia* leaves. The biology of *S. flava* larvae (fig. 7.46b), however, is very unusual compared to that of other leaf chafers – they feed on antelope dung, while their relatives feed mostly on plant roots and are known as white grubs (see 'White grubs', p. 384).

It appears that females seek out the dung middens of species such as springbok (fig. 7.46c), *Antidorcas marsupialis*, where they lay their eggs. The larvae emerge at night and crawl, sometimes covering several metres, to the nearest dung fragment (young larvae) or pellet (larger larvae) and once it is located, burrow down into the soil dragging the fragment or pellet with them, and begin feeding. Each larva does this repeatedly until mature, after which it pupates in a soil cell in an underground chamber. The adult emerges from the pupa at night, burrows to the soil surface and becomes active.

Adults spend daylight hours buried in the soil and emerge nightly (see box opposite) to feed on leaves. Within days, they accumulate large quantities of body fat, and the females develop ovaries full of eggs. This makes them very desirable prey items for a host of small predators: at night their activity makes them vulnerable to small owls, foxes and jackals, and by day they are excavated from their burrows by mongooses and suricates. They are particularly vulnerable when emerging from the soil in early evening, when females alight to lay eggs, and also when males and females burrow back into the soil after night-time activity.

Wood-boring long-horned beetles

The wood-boring beetles of the large family Cerambycidae (fig. 7.47) are probably amongst the most important insect decomposers of wood. They occur commonly in southern Africa and other warm parts of the world. There are about 800 species in southern Africa, with the highest diversity occurring in the savanna regions.

Members of the family vary greatly in size (3–100mm); some are amongst the largest and heaviest beetles in southern Africa, whereas others are very small and delicate. All species have a distinct head, with large mandibles and characteristic antennae that are as long as or longer than the body. All have broadly similar biology.

Depending on the species, females oviposit on freshly cut, damaged or decaying wood, in cracks or under bark. In a few species, females remove a ring of bark from a twig of the appropriate thickness and lay an egg on the part beyond the ring; the ringbarking cuts off the flow of sap and kills the twig, in which the larva then develops.

Emergent larvae of large species bore into stems and thick branches, while small species bore into twigs; everything in between is used by species of the relevant size. Much of the feeding takes place just below the bark, but larvae often tunnel deep into the phloem and xylem layers. In some groups digestion of cellulose is aided by intestinal symbiotic yeasts, protozoa or bacteria. In spite of the presence of cellulose-digesting symbionts, larval development is slow because of the low nutritional quality of wood.

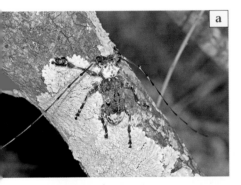

7.47 Cerambycidae are wood-boring beetles with a very high diversity in savanna regions: (**a**) *Lasiopezus longimanus*; (**b**) *Nitakeris nigricornis*; (**c**) *Macrotoma palmata*; (**d**) *Phyllocnema gueinzii*; (**e**) *Merioneda africana*.

7.48 (right) (a) A typical wood-boring cerambycid larva. **(b)** Parasitoids of wood-boring beetles have exceptionally long ovipositors, which, although appearing flimsy, are capable of penetrating several centimetres of hard wood.

Larvae are elongate, fleshy white grubs with a retracted head and protruding mandibles (fig. 7.48a). The legs are often reduced but movement in the tunnels is facilitated by coverings of spines or robust setae (bristles). Tunnelling larvae are able to avoid competition and damage caused by chewing neighbours by sensing their presence from the vibrations they cause while chewing. The downside is that parasitic wasps (fig. 7.48b) that specialise on wood-boring larvae are also able to sense the vibrations – this provides them with information on the precise location of the larvae. They then drill their (often exceptionally long) ovipositors into the wood and lay an egg on the wood-boring larva. The parasitic larva then consumes its wood-boring host over time, but before the host dies, it is programmed by the parasitoid to chew an emergence hole from the wood, just as it would if it reached larval maturity. This enables the rather feeble adult wasp to escape from incarceration.

Cerambycid larvae also often fall prey to the larvae of Cleridae, a specialist beetle family. The larvae pursue their wood-boring prey inside their tunnels. Similar to their prey, Cleridae are diverse in southern Africa (fig. 7.49).

Cerambycid larval development is relatively slow because of the low nutritional quality of their food, and the larger the species, the longer its larval development. Some of the region's largest species may spend as long as five years in the larval stage inside the wood before pupating – and the pupal stage may last from weeks to months, depending on the size of the species. The adult emerges from the pupa through an emergence hole chewed by the mature larva. Adults of some species feed and others do not. Their life span is generally short, less than a month. They die after mating and laying eggs.

7.49 (left and below) The larvae of savanna Cleridae are predators of wood-boring beetles (Cerambycidae): **(a)** *Gyponyx* sp.; **(b)** *Phloiocopus consobrinus*; **(c)** *Eucymatodera cingulata*; **(d)** *Tenerus variabilis*; **(e)** *Diplocladus louvelii*; **(f)** *G. signifer*.

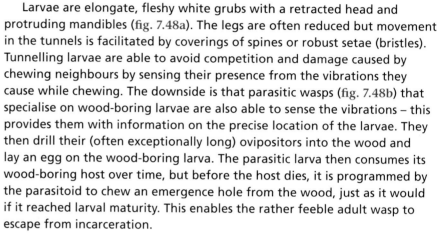

7.50 Meloidae are diverse, mostly aposematically coloured beetles: (**a**) *Epicauta velata*; (**b**) *Zonitoschema* sp.; (**c**) *Hycleus stahli*; (**d**) *H. lugens*; (**e**) *H. surcoufi*; (**f**) *H. villosus*; (**g**) *Actenodia chrysomelina*.

Toxic body fluids in blister and net-veined beetles

Blister beetles are members of the fairly large beetle family Meloidae, with about 35 genera and 350 species in southern Africa (fig. 7.50). Net-veined beetles belong to the Lycidae, of which about 50 species occur in southern Africa. Both families have toxic body fluids that are synthesised metabolically. To advertise to potential predators that they are noxious, adults of some species are brightly coloured in typical aposematic colours (see box, pp. 240–241). Although members of these families are fairly common throughout southern Africa, some of the largest species occur in the savanna, where they are characteristic herbivores, often congregating in large numbers on flowering plants. Meloid larvae are predators of solitary bee brood and grasshopper egg pods (see 'Blister beetle larvae', p. 171), while those of Lycidae feed on fungi.

Members of the Meloidae are known as blister beetles, as contact with their toxic body fluids results in blistering. They produce cantharidin as a defensive chemical (see box, p. 225). Adults of the various species vary greatly in size (5–50mm long) and in colour, including uniform yellow, brown, red, grey, blue and green, or typical aposematic colours of black with yellow or red spots, stripes or distinct, wide, transverse bands.

Lycidae are commonly known as net-winged or net-veined beetles because of the network of visible longitudinal and cross ridges on the elytra (fig. 7.51). Virtually all species in the region are black and orange. Females of some species are slender and elongate, while the males have broadly expanded elytra. Their head is greatly reduced and hidden from above by an expanded pronotum. They have tiny mouthparts with which they lick up nectar in flowers. Larvae feed on fungi in protected situations, such as under bark and in leaf litter. Lycids are also thought to contain cantharidin, but the mechanism for its production is unknown.

Adults of both families fly slowly as if secure in their invincibility. They are the models in mimicry complexes: a wide range of insect species in many orders mimic their appearance for the possible protection from predators that this might confer. These include wasps, moths, flies and other beetles of several families (fig. 7.52).

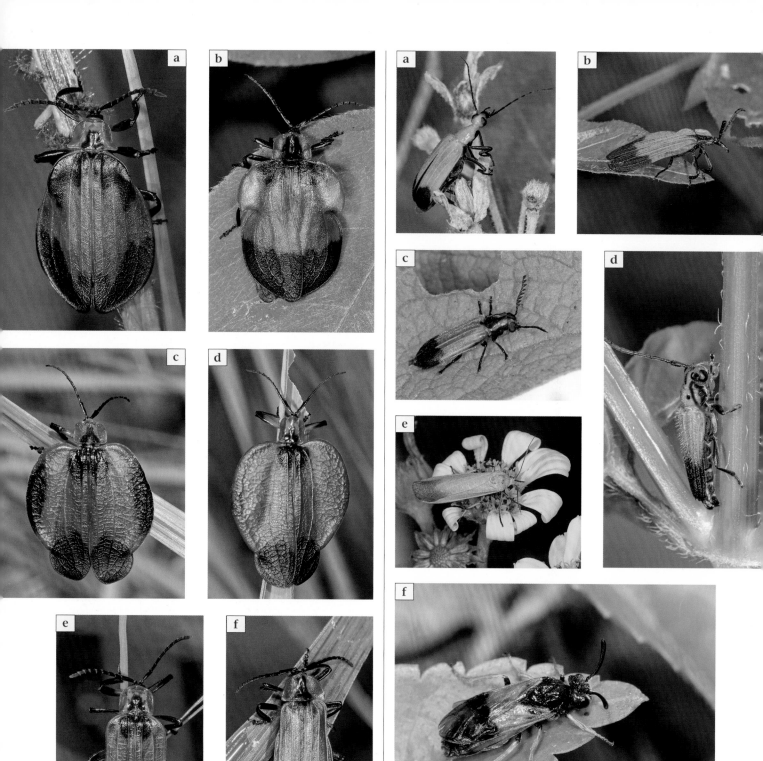

7.51 Colour patterns across species in *Lycus* (Coleoptera: Lycidae) are very similar, mostly orange and black, although their morphology varies considerably between species, and even between sexes: **(a)** *L. rostratus*; **(b)** *L. humerosis*; **(c)** *L. trabeatus* male; **(d)** *L. trabeatus* male; **(e)** *L. trabeatus* female; **(f)** *L. trabeatus* female.

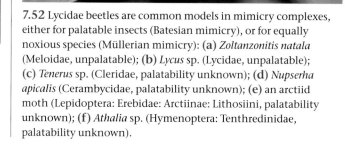

7.52 Lycidae beetles are common models in mimicry complexes, either for palatable insects (Batesian mimicry), or for equally noxious species (Müllerian mimicry): **(a)** *Zoltanzonitis natala* (Meloidae, unpalatable); **(b)** *Lycus* sp. (Lycidae, unpalatable); **(c)** *Tenerus* sp. (Cleridae, palatability unknown); **(d)** *Nupserha apicalis* (Cerambycidae, palatability unknown); **(e)** an arctiid moth (Lepidoptera: Erebidae: Arctiinae: Lithosiini, palatability unknown); **(f)** *Athalia* sp. (Hymenoptera: Tenthredinidae, palatability unknown).

The production of cantharidin in Meloidae

Adult meloid beetles (unlike their predatory larvae) feed on plants in exposed situations and fly slowly, often congregating in large numbers on flowering plants – apparently unconcerned for their safety, thanks to their ability to produce a potent defence toxin, boldly advertised by their coloration. Many other insect groups mimic meloid colour patterns and some of these may be found amongst the aggregations on flowers where their similarity to the noxious models also affords them some protection from predators.

All stages of the meloid life cycle contain cantharidin, which is metabolically synthesised in the larval stage, with quantities increasing during growth. The prepupal and pupal stages have high, but static quantities. Freshly emerged adults of both sexes have similar amounts of the substance. However, in males, the quantity of cantharidin increases dramatically – it may comprise 20% of the dry weight of the male. In unmated females, body cantharidin content decreases at an inversely proportional rate to that of the male, until large quantities are passed from the male to the female as a nuptial gift during copulation (fig. 7.53). Females then lay large numbers of eggs that are infused and coated with cantharidin.

Although the site of cantharidin biosynthesis is not known, it has been shown that in meloid larvae, most of the cantharidin is contained in the alimentary canal. Disturbed larvae produce a milky, cantharidin-rich fluid from the mouth, which spreads and covers the body. In adult males, the toxin is accumulated in the reproductive accessory glands, which sequester it from the haemolymph using a system that functions as a 'cantharidin kidney'. Disturbed adults ooze cantharidin-laden haemolymph from their leg joints in a process called reflex bleeding. This is the first line of defence for the beetle when threatened, as the haemolymph is repellent to vertebrates and causes blistering on sensitive skin. Ingestion of a beetle leads to vomiting and blistering in the mouth and throat of a predator.

For centuries, various meloid species, notably the European 'Spanish fly', *Lytta vesicatoria*, have been thought to have aphrodisiac or other medicinal properties. The Asian *Mylabris phalerata* has been used for more than 2,000 years in China and is still used in folk medicine – in topical application for piles and ulcers, and systemically for rabies, as an anticancer agent and as an abortifacient. In southern Africa, crushed *Hycleus tricolor* beetles are used by traditional healers to make 'seletsa', which is administered as an aphrodisiac, to induce abortion or to 'clean the blood', but fatalities are common.

Poisoning in humans usually results from the ingestion of an aphrodisiac dose. As little as 1mg/kg of body weight of the user is sufficient to cause death, usually from renal failure, but severe damage to the gastrointestinal tract may also occur. There is no known antidote to cantharidin poisoning.

Besides the putative medicinal properties claimed in traditional medicine, cantharidin has several scientifically proven medicinal uses in dermatological applications. It is regularly used in modern paediatric dermatology to cure warts and *molluscum contagiosum*, a common viral disease in children. Under experimental conditions, cantharidin has also been shown to act as a vasoconstrictor and, although too toxic to administer systemically, has been considered for possible future development of drugs for the treatment of heart failure.

7.53 Cantharidin synthesis takes place mostly in Meloidae larvae. During adult development it decreases in females, but continues to increase in males. During copulation, males provide females with a large 'gift' of cantharidin, as in these *Hycleus tricolor*, with which the eggs are infused, beginning a new cycle of cantharidin production and replenishment.

7.54 Leaf beetles (Chrysomelidae) feed on leaves and may sequester toxic plant chemicals for their own defence. (**a**) Species of the genus *Polyclada* (e.g. *P. bohemani*) contain such high levels of toxins that Kalahari hunter-gatherers used the pupae to poison arrows. (**b**) The larvae of *Lebistina* beetles (Carabidae) parasitise the leaf beetle pupae and concentrate the toxins still further, making them even more desirable for arrow poison.

Deadly leaf beetles and their parasitoids

Chrysomelidae adults and larvae feed on the leaves of certain plants, hence their common name of leaf beetles. Many species feed on plants that contain toxic compounds, which both larvae and adults may then sequester during feeding. They display warning colours to advertise their distastefulness to potential predators.

Diamphidia and *Polyclada* larvae (Chrysomelidae: Galerucinae, fig. 7.54) feed on corkwood, *Commiphora* (Burseraceae), and marula, *Sclerocarya birrea* (Anacardiaceae), respectively. Members of these plant families produce white or yellow latex that may have irritating properties. In turn, the sequestered plant toxins are taken up and concentrated further by parasitoids in the ground beetle genus *Lebistina* (Carabidae, fig. 7.54b), which not only parasitise their chrysomelid hosts, but may also mimic them closely in colour, general morphology and even defensive chemistry. The sequestered plant toxins from crushed chrysomelid and carabid pupae were used by Bushman people in the Kalahari to poison the shafts of their hunting arrows (see box alongside).

Diamphidia and *Polyclada* females lay eggs in clumps on the host plant, then cover them with a layer of sticky, chemical-impregnated green faeces. Although soft at first, the covering soon darkens and hardens. When the larvae emerge, they immediately start to feed and pack faecal pellets on their back. After maturing, the larvae climb down off the host plant and pupate in the soil. Here they may be attacked by the carabid parasitoids. The carabid larvae attach themselves externally to the chrysomelid pupae, one larva per host, feeding until the host dies and the parasitoid matures. The carabid larva then pupates in the soil and eventually the adult emerges.

Bushman arrow poison

The Bushman (or San) people of the Kalahari, who until fairly recently lived as hunter-gatherers (fig. 7.55), traditionally poisoned their hunting arrows with the body fluids of toxic insects, harvested from two beetle groups – leaf-eating Chrysomelidae and their specialist Carabidae parasitoids.

The toxic chemical produced by *Diamphidia* pupae – the main ingredient of Bushman arrow poison – was found to be a novel protein, diamphotoxin, which is a slow-paralysing agent capable of killing large antelope within a few hours. The precise mixture of poison compounds varies according to availability in different regions of the Kalahari, but in northern Botswana and Namibia, the poison is prepared by macerating four or five pupae, weighing about 0.2g each, together with a knife-point of baked and powdered seedpod of the tree *Swartzia madagascariensis* (Caesalpiniaceae) moistened by saliva produced while chewing acacia bark. (The seedpods are known to be slightly toxic to fish and small mammals, and apparently have some insect-repellent and insecticidal properties, but whether these contribute in any way to the toxicity of the poison is doubtful.) The mixture, sufficient for about 10–12 arrows, is applied sparingly to the sinew binding on the shaft immediately behind the barbs and allowed to air-dry. The arrows retain their lethal potency for about a year.

7.55 George Scholtz (left), Fred Rowe-Rowe (centre) and a G/wi hunter examining arrows and beetle pupae in the Botswana Kalahari in the late 1950s.

Dave Rowe

7.56 Bagworm (Lepidoptera: Psychidae) larvae live in 'bags' or portable shelters, which they construct from a variety of species-specific materials arranged in characteristic patterns: (a) thorns of sweet thorn, *Acacia karroo*; (b) twigs; (c) pebbles; (d) short pieces of grass stems; (e) grass leaves; (f) grass stems harvested after a veld fire; (g) grass seed husks.

Bagworms feeding on wattle trees

Members of the moth family Psychidae are called bagworms because the larvae and adult females live in 'bags'; the adult males are mostly nondescript brown or grey free-living moths. This is a relatively small and poorly studied family in southern Africa, with about 30 known species, but it is very likely that more species await discovery.

The many different types of bags they construct and the wide range of building materials they use are well known, as these familiar structures are found attached to plants across the region. The bags range in size from about 10mm to about 60mm long and may be composed of sand grains (see 'Lichen-feeding bagworms', p. 182), pebbles, grass stalks, twigs or thorns, depending on their host plant or the ready availability of suitable building materials (fig. 7.56).

One endemic species that has been well studied is the wattle bagworm, *Chaliopsis junodi* (=*Kotochalia junodi*), and the biology of all species in the family is probably similar. *Chaliopsis junodi* is an African species whose natural food plant is *Acacia*, but Australian wattle (also an *Acacia* species) has been grown commercially in South Africa for at least the past 100 years, and the bagworm has successfully switched host plants from indigenous acacias to wattles, to the extent that it is now considered a pest of wattle.

Chaliopsis junodi larvae develop inside cases of twigs and leaves they cut from the host plant and tie together with silk (fig. 7.57). The bag is started by the young larva biting off leaf fragments and binding these into a collar behind its head. They add to the collar and develop the bag around themselves as

7.57 The wattle bagworm, *Chaliopsis junodi*, an indigenous acacia-feeding species, has switched to feeding on exotic wattles (which are also acacias): (a) larval bag; (b) adult female inside an opened bag. Female bagworms remain underdeveloped, without wings, legs or mouthparts. They never leave the larval bag, and mate, lay eggs and die inside it.

they grow, incorporating larger and larger building materials from their immediate environment; this makes the case well camouflaged, protecting the larva from predation.

The case has a hole at both ends with the head, thorax and legs exposed and protruded from the bag while the larva is feeding and moving; waste material is discarded through the posterior opening. While feeding, the larva attaches to the host plant with a silken anchor so that if threatened it can retreat into the bag without falling off the plant. Larval development lasts all summer, at the end of which the larva firmly attaches the bag to a twig. It spins an inner silk lining, which closes the bag, and pupates within.

Male larvae develop and pupate inside their bag and emerge as fairly normal winged adults, except that they have only a thin covering of scales and totally reduced mouthparts and therefore cannot feed. They fly fast and erratically.

Female larvae also develop into adult moths inside the bag, but have no wings, legs, antennae or mouthparts – they are little more than an immobile larviform (larva-like) cylinder full of eggs. The phenomenon of an underdeveloped female breeding is termed paedogenesis. They remain inside the case and emit a pheromone to attract the flying males, who mate with them by using an extensible abdomen that they insert into the bag. The males die after mating.

Once the eggs have been fertilised, the female dies and disintegrates, allowing the eggs to hatch and the young to escape from the bag. They climb onto surrounding branches to which they attach with silken threads or onto other exposed structures where they spin a silk thread that aids in their wind dispersal to suitable feeding sites where they start the cycle anew.

Mopane worms

The mopane 'worm' is the larva of the emperor moth *Imbrasia belina* (Lepidoptera: Saturniidae) and is well known throughout the subcontinent by local human inhabitants as a desirable food source (fig. 7.58a). There are regular population outbreaks of the species, which lead to almost total defoliation of the host tree *Colophospermum mopane* by the larvae, making them an important keystone species in Mopane Woodland. They also feed on a range of other trees in the savanna, but seldom undergo explosive outbreaks on those.

The emperor moths are large (fig. 7.58b), with a wingspan of 120mm, and range in colour from green and brown to red, but all have a large eyespot on each hind wing. Males have feathery antennae (used to detect pheromones from the female moths), while those of the females are unfeathered.

The (sometimes) large egg clusters are laid on the leaves of the host plant and the larvae (fig. 7.58c), which hatch in summer, go through five instars, the final of which is most desirable for harvesting as human food (see box opposite). Larvae in the first three larval instars are brown and particularly vulnerable to predation by insects, birds and mammals. Eggs and larvae are also heavily parasitised by flies of the Tachinidae and various wasps, particularly members of the Braconidae, Ichneumonidae and Chalcididae. The mature larvae are speckled in black, white, green and yellow, but have a few black or reddish spines covered in hairs that provide some protection against predation.

Mature larvae descend to the ground and burrow into the soil where they pupate. The pupal stage lasts for six to seven months through winter. The adult moths emerge the following summer (November–December), the female moths already bearing eggs. The adult moths do not feed and live for only three or four days, during which they locate each other, mate, lay eggs and then die.

7.58 (a) Harvested larvae being cooked for human consumption. (b) The emperor moth *Imbrasia belina* (Saturniidae) of which the (c) mopane 'worm' is the larva.

Jan Myburg

Mopane worms are a valued food source in rural southern Africa. Mature larvae are handpicked from trees, and the hind part of the caterpillar is pinched to rupture the innards, which are then squeezed out and discarded. The larvae are then laid out in the sun to dry. Dried mopane worms are eaten just as they are as a snack, or are rehydrated and fried until they are crunchy, or boiled with vegetables and served with maize porridge to provide a tasty, nutritious meal. A study in Angola determined that a 100g serving (20–30 larvae) of another edible *Imbrasia* species (*I. ertii*) provided 26% of the human daily requirement of protein, 5% calcium, 55% phosphorus, 58% magnesium, 11% iron and 70% copper. The caterpillars are also very efficient at converting leaves into protein: 3kg of mopane leaves yield 1kg of mopane worms, while cattle require 10kg of feed to produce 1kg of meat!

Traditionally, mopane worms were harvested and eaten by local inhabitants, but they have become more widely popular and are now viewed as a profitable commercial enterprise. However, their seasonal and erratic occurrence makes it difficult to know when and where there will be an outbreak of significance for the harvesters. Generally, where outbreaks occur, the land owners charge the harvesters a fee for entry, and the caterpillars are then picked, bagged and sent for processing. There is a danger of overharvesting, with consequently fewer mopane worms the following year.

Mopane worms may defoliate up to 90% of Mopane Woodland at times, and come into conflict with farmers who rely on the leaves as browse for their livestock and wild game herbivores, but the caterpillar stages are short and the trees quickly flush again after an outbreak, providing fresh new leaves for the browsers. Mopane worms are harvested for human consumption during outbreak years (see box above).

Processionary caterpillars

Processionary caterpillars are the larval stage of the moth *Anaphe reticulata* (Lepidoptera: Notodontidae: Thaumatopoeinae), also known as the bagnest moth, because larvae pupate individually in a communal silken 'bag', which may be as large as a soccer ball and contain 600 pupae. The species is widespread across tropical Africa and mature caterpillars are fairly often seen in the Lowveld, with regular reports from tourists in the KNP of encounters with caterpillar processions stretching right across the road (fig. 7.59).

Two distantly related species with similar behaviour are the European oak processionary, *Thaumatopoea processionea*, and the pine processionary, *T. pityocampa*, which are serious pests of their host plants.

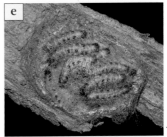
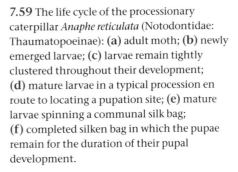

7.59 The life cycle of the processionary caterpillar *Anaphe reticulata* (Notodontidae: Thaumatopoeinae): (**a**) adult moth; (**b**) newly emerged larvae; (**c**) larvae remain tightly clustered throughout their development; (**d**) mature larvae in a typical procession en route to locating a pupation site; (**e**) mature larvae spinning a communal silk bag; (**f**) completed silken bag in which the pupae remain for the duration of their pupal development.

Ian Sharpe

Ian Sharpe

Ian Sharpe

The larvae also produce urticating hairs that get blown around and often cause severe irritation in sensitive people.

During the 20th century there was a rather ambitious proposal to harvest bagnests across Africa and exploit the silk commercially, but besides the logistical problems of finding isolated bags over tens of thousands of square kilometres and transporting them to Europe, the problem of the intensely urticating larval hairs bound into the silk was overlooked!

Females may lay large batches of about 300 eggs on their preferred host trees, which in southern Africa are wild pear, *Dombeya*, and horn pod, *Diplorhynchus*; elsewhere, species of sweetberry (*Bridelia*), karee (*Searsia*, formerly *Rhus*) and raisin bush (*Grewia*) have been recorded.

The larvae from a batch of eggs remain together in tight clusters throughout their lives, and close batches may merge, maintained by contact through long hairs (setae) on the caterpillars. Only when food is depleted or mature larvae descend from the tree to find a suitable pupation site, does the habit of clustering change to one of moving in single file, head to tail.

The processions are kept together by a secreted abdominal pheromone. Experiments have shown that abdominal secretions smeared on a piece of wood will be followed by caterpillars. The famous early 20th-century French entomologist Jean Henri Fabre attached larvae of the European pine processionary head to tail in a circle close to food, but they chose to follow each other rather than deviate to the food, round and round for a week before they died of exhaustion!

7.60 Life cycle of the migratory brown-veined white butterfly, *Belenois aurota* (Pieridae): (**a**) the shepherd's tree, *Boscia albitrunca*, the preferred larval host tree in the Kalahari; (**b**) mating adults; (**c**) egg cluster; (**d, e**) developing larvae; (**f**) pupa; (**g**) adults feeding on nectar.

Millions of migratory butterflies

Belenois aurota (Lepidoptera: Pieridae) is one of southern Africa's commonest and most widespread butterfly species (fig. 7.60) with a distribution that extends throughout Africa. Their preferred larval host species, the shepherd's tree, *Boscia albitrunca*, is common in the Kalahari and this is where populations build up and most migrations begin.

The duration of the immature stages is fairly short: egg – 8 days; five larval instars – 28 days; pupa – 14 days. During favourable seasons local populations build up quickly and in mid-summer make up the first wave of the periodic migrations, which result in beautiful, white, fluttering 'clouds'. Other individuals may join the migration along the way, sometimes resulting in enormous numbers – it is estimated that there are up to five million butterflies over a 5km front per day, on occasion reaching 1km above the ground, and sometimes these migrations continue day after day for up to two months. Because of their abundance, larvae and adults are a major food item for various insectivores, including many bird species.

The timing of the migration is dependent on weather conditions, but usually occurs from mid-November to mid-February. The butterflies fly in a northeasterly direction from sunrise to dusk, flying over and not around obstacles and thus never deviating from their course. They stop from time to time to suck nectar from flowers and to lay eggs, and are common around puddles after rain, where they drink water, and on soil dampened by urine, where they suck up minerals. When darkness falls they settle en masse on plants. They move from the arid western areas across South Africa to KwaZulu-Natal and Mozambique, and onwards over the Mozambique Channel, where many die at sea.

Although this behaviour is referred to as a migration, it is not actually a true migration but rather an emigration, since the butterflies move in only one direction; they never return to their place of origin. True migration only occurs in regions with extreme differences in summer and winter conditions, where, for example, populations migrate to a warmer climate to overwinter, and return to their breeding region the following spring.

Kalahari silk moths

The Kalahari silk moth, *Gonometa postica* (Lepidoptera: Lasiocampidae), is one of two *Gonometa* species with irruptive populations; the other is known as the mopane silk moth, *G. rufobrunnea*, as its preferred host plant is the mopane tree, *Colophospermum mopane* (fig. 7.61). The cocoons of both species are harvested for their silk in some southern African countries, as the silk is tough and of a sufficiently high quality for weaving into fabric (see box, p. 232).

Alan Gardiner

Alan Gardiner

Carmen Jacobs

7.61 Indigenous southern African silk moths in the genus *Gonometa* (Lasiocampidae): (**a**) *G. postica* (Kalahari) adult; (**b**) *G. postica* larva on an acacia twig; (**c**) *G. postica* cocoon; (**d**) *G. rufobrunnea* (mopane savanna) larva on a mopane branch; (**e**) *G. rufobrunnea* pupal cocoon; (**f**) ceremonial Bushman ankle rattles made from *G. postica* cocoons.

Gonometa postica is a large moth, with striking hairy caterpillars. The larvae and cocoons are large and visible. During irruption years, there are often immense numbers on various *Acacia* species, including camel thorn, *A. erioloba*, grey camel thorn, *A. haematoxylon*, black thorn, *A. mellifera*, and umbrella thorn, *A. tortilis*; of these, *A. erioloba* appears to be the preferred host. The larvae have also been found feeding on wild syringa, *Burkea africana*, species of *Brachystegia*, and even the exotic invader mesquite, *Prosopis glandulosa*.

The nocturnal adults are cryptically coloured, resting on branches during the day. The female moth is brown with grey flecks and is much larger (forewing 39–45mm) and bulkier than her darker male partner (forewing 20–22mm); and she flies clumsily – this is because she emerges from the pupa with a fully developed batch of about 200 eggs. The males fly strongly so they can locate females with which to mate. Once mating has taken place, the female searches for a large host tree with sufficient foliage for the larvae, and lays her straw-coloured oval eggs in clusters. Both adults die after mating and egg-laying have taken place.

Larvae are also cryptically coloured and nocturnal to reduce predation. In spite of this, the early and mid-instar stage larvae are heavily preyed on by a multitude of animals. They mature within 50–60 days, growing up to 20cm long. The mature caterpillars are grey and hairy, with long white and black hairs that hide rows of reddish, hollow spines on the back. At the base of each spine is a cell containing venom, which is ejected when pressure is applied to the spine. The venom is strongly urticating (on humans) and probably acts as an effective defence mechanism against some predators since predation is low in the final instar. When they spin their silk pupal cocoons, they incorporate some of the urticating spines into its external surface; these continue to provide some protection for the pupa. Many mature larvae move away from the host plant before pupating, so cocoons are often found on nonhost plant species some distance away. This dispersing behaviour is thought to decrease accumulations on the host plant and consequent visibility.

In addition to the incorporated defensive urticating spines, the surface of the cocoon is uniformly covered with a layer of (mainly) calcium oxalate crystals, which makes the outer wall of the cocoon very hard and is responsible for its white colour. The cocoons of female pupae are significantly harder than those of males. The combination of urticating spines, hardness and calcium oxalate crystals appears to afford good protection against most vertebrate predators. During drought years, however, the cocoon defences fail to repel herbivorous mammals such as springbok and livestock, which have been known to eat large numbers of the cocoons – with fatal results. The silk from which the cocoons are spun

Commercial use of wild silk

The pupal cocoons of the large moth *Gonometa postica* (Lasiocampidae) are constructed from high-quality silk, which is slightly coarser than the silk produced by the commercial silkworm, *Bombyx mori*, but finer than the silk of other wild silk moth species. It has a natural gold colour and dyes well (fig. 7.62).

The empty cocoons, from which the adults have already emerged, are collected by local people in some rural areas in Namibia, Botswana and northwestern South Africa. The hard, calciferous cocoons are then 'degummed' by placing them in a bath of sodium hydroxide (caustic soda). This strong alkali dissolves the calcium oxalate layer, as well as the urticating setae found in the walls of the cocoons. Once the hard outer layer has dissolved, the cocoons are put out to dry, and then the silk is carded and spun on spinning wheels to make yarn.

The practice is sustainable at present because mostly empty cocoons are collected; however, this silk is of slightly poorer quality than that from occupied cocoons. Collecting cocoons with live pupae places extensive pressure on natural populations. Little is known about the effects of climate and predation on the species or about the factors causing sporadic irruptions in certain years. It is therefore crucial that a better understanding of the ecology of the species be obtained before the populations are permanently affected.

Carmen Jacobs

7.62 A skein of *Gonometa* silk produced from veld-harvested cocoons.

Ian Sharpe

7.63 Moth-induced galls on silver cluster-leaf, *Terminalia sericea*: **(a)** terminal axial gall and **(b)** stem gall, both caused by larvae of *Microcolona pantomima* (Lepidoptera: Elachistidae); **(c)** living gall and **(d)** old gall caused by larvae of *Cecidothyrus pexa* (Lepidoptera: Thyrididae); **(e)** adult *C. pexa*.

Ian Sharpe

Hermann Staude

Moth galls on Bushveld trees

Certain plants are particularly susceptible to galling, some by many individuals of the same insect species, or by several different insect species; if the plant is host to several species it is termed a superhost. In southern Africa, members of the widespread savanna plant family Combretaceae are considered superhosts, especially silver clusterleaf, *Terminalia sericea*, and some species of bushwillow, *Combretum*.

Terminalia sericea is a small to medium-sized tree with silvery-green leaves. It is one of the tree species that characterise the vegetation of deep Bushveld soils, but occurs across most of the savanna region. It is host to several gall-forming moths, including *Microcolona pantomima* and *Cecidothyrus pexa* (fig. 7.63; see box, p. 234), of which the former produces two completely different gall forms. All of these galls are hard, woody structures that remain on the tree for years, and are especially noticeable in winter when the trees are bare.

Combretum trees are characterised by their four-winged fruit, which vary in size from about 20 × 20mm to 80 × 80mm (fig. 7.64a). Many of the species grow into large, beautiful trees and include some of the most iconic Bushveld species, such as the leadwood, *C. imberbe*.

The moth *Pauroptila galenitis* (Lepidoptera: Elachistidae) has been recorded to gall the fruits of the velvet bushwillow, *C. molle*. Instead of developing the characteristic four-winged shape, these galled fruits deform into a solid, woody, elongate structure,

is totally indigestible and unravels in the gut, eventually blocking the rumen and leading to death from starvation, unless the entangled silk mats are surgically removed.

Cocoons take years to decompose and may remain on trees long after the moths have emerged, leading to accumulations of cocoons from several generations. Kalahari Bushman people collect the cocoons, fill them with small stones, attach them to a cord and use them as ankle rattles during ceremonial dances (fig. 7.61f).

Numerous insect parasitoids are known to attack the pupae; these are mainly Tachinidae flies, but also small wasps belonging to the Braconidae, Eurytomidae (which are often hyperparasitoids of the Braconidae parasitoids) and Chalcididae. The parasitoids lay their eggs on or in a mature larva before it starts spinning its cocoon. The fly larva chews an escape hole for the adult to escape prior to pupating itself, while the adult wasps chew holes in the cocoons upon emergence. Cocoons are often found with these parasitoid emergence holes, and the species involved can usually be identified by differences in the emergence holes.

Perhaps the most characteristic galls on *Terminalia sericea* trees are those caused by the small moth *Microcolona pantomima* (Lepidoptera: Elachistidae). The silvery-black moths, with a wingspan of 12–15mm, are seldom seen. They live for a few days in early summer after emerging from the galls, which remain very noticeable for a long time. The species forms two types of gall: bare elongate galls on branches 6–15mm in diameter, or round axial galls at the tips of thin twigs. The elongate stem galls are 10–27mm wide and 27–58mm long, while the round axial galls are 6–20mm in diameter; in the latter the growing tip dies and the stunted leaves on fresh galls remain attached for some time. The galls are solid except for small cavities in which the larvae develop; each gall contains one to six larvae. Although the two gall forms yield moths of different sizes and colour patterns, they are considered to be the same species – one of the few records of a single species causing two structurally different galls and producing adults of two distinctive size and colour forms.

Another moth, the gall-forming *Cecidothyrus pexa* (Lepidoptera: Thyrididae) has two generations per summer: October–January and February–June. The galls are spindle-shaped and develop at the growing tip of a twig after eggs have been laid in October. The fully developed gall is about 80mm long and about 20mm broad at its thickest point. There is always only one larva per gall; it hollows out the gall, leaving only a thin-walled shell. Various insectivorous birds have learned of their presence and break the galls open to consume the larvae. Once mature, the larva chews an emergence hole for the adult moth, empties the gall of accumulated faeces, and pupates. The adult moth of the first generation emerges in January, mates and lays eggs in February. The larva of the second generation remains in the gall until the following spring when pupation takes place and the adult emerges.

7.64 (a) These winged fruits are characteristic of a *Combretum* species; (b) a pea-sized leaf gall induced by a moth larva on the leaf margin of a red bushwillow, *Combretum apiculatum*.

measuring 8 × 17mm, without wings. Moths lay their eggs on young fruit into which the emergent larvae tunnel (one per fruit). Larval development proceeds over the summer, after which the larvae spin a tough silken cocoon inside the gall. Pupation takes place the following spring and adults emerge about 10 days later.

Another, as yet unidentified, very small moth was also recently recorded to make round, fluffy, pea-sized galls (fig. 7.64b) on the leaf edges of red bushwillow, *C. apiculatum*. Although the galls are fairly common and very characteristic, nothing is known of the moth's identity or biology.

Detritivores

The relatively low rainfall of the western parts of the Savanna Biome creates conditions in which nutritious detritus seldom accumulates in sufficient quantities to maintain a diverse detritus-feeding fauna. One specialist that has adapted its feeding and breeding to use the available detritus is a highly specialised subsocial beetle, one of very few worldwide.

Subsocial beetles and their nest parasites

Parastizopus armaticeps (Coleoptera: Tenebrionidae: Opatrini: Stizopina, fig. 7.65) is one of many tenebrionid beetles that has adapted to life in an arid environment (see 'Tenebrionid beetle diversity', p. 136). It is unusual, however, in that it is subsocial, with sex-based division of parental labour to prepare and provision a nest for the brood. This is comparatively rare amongst solitary insect species. *Parastizopus armaticeps* lives in an intimate association with its distant relative *Eremostibes opacus* (also in subtribe Stizopina), which is a tolerated nest parasite in the *P. armaticeps* burrows; the biology and relationships of these beetles were studied in the Kalahari by Anne Rasa and her students at the University of Bonn (see boxes, opposite and p. 236).

Parastizopus armaticeps has a fairly widespread distribution across the Kalahari, where the beetles live on stable sand dunes. In summer, they are active at night, by day retreating into stable, long-lasting burrows, which they have dug themselves. Here they congregate with members of their own species, as well as with members of the kleptoparasitic *Eremostibes opacus*; they also breed during this time (see box alongside). During winter they congregate with various other tenebrionid species in abandoned rodent burrows or other holes, in what are thought to be defensive aggregations, as the beetles produce defensive chemicals.

Parastizopus armaticeps is closely associated with one plant species, the pioneer legume *Lebeckia linearifolia*, which is high in protein but not very plentiful and whose fallen leaves and twigs (detritus) constitute the majority of the beetles' diet. They collect the detritus and carry it back to the nest for food for themselves and their larvae; it is this detritus that is parasitised by *E. opacus* adults and larvae (see box, p. 236).

a

b

7.65 (a) The subsocial beetle *Parastizopus armaticeps* (Tenebrionidae) carrying a long piece of detritus back to its burrow for larval food. (b) *Gonopus tibialis*, one of several tenebrionids with repellent chemicals; these beetles share nonbreeding burrows in defensive aggregations with *Parastizopus*.

Breeding in *Parastizopus armaticeps*

Males of this tenebrionid beetle usually set about digging breeding burrows after rain. Females may initially help, but after a while they switch to foraging, while the males continue extending and deepening the burrow. Females drop the forage (detritus) at the burrow entrance and the males drag it into the burrow and place it in a breeding cavity. When enough food has been accumulated, the female lays an egg in the burrow. Once the larva emerges, the female continues to collect food for the fast-growing larva.

The research done by Anne Rasa and her students found that breeding females emerge to forage just after sunset when soil surface temperatures are high (about 30°C) and relative humidity (RH) is low (5–10%). Nonbreeding females and males emerge 30–40 minutes later, when the surface temperature has dropped to 21–24°C and RH has increased to 20%. The increased risk of desiccation for breeding females is apparently offset by the competitive advantage of earlier activity for an obviously limited resource – forage of higher protein composition – needed for larval food.

Burrows are about 30cm long and slope downwards, with the end of the burrow 12cm below the surface. These beetles only breed after rainfall of at least 10mm, which triggers reproduction in certain individuals. This is also the minimum amount necessary to maintain an atmosphere of saturated air in the underground burrows for long enough to ensure successful breeding – an average of 23 days, after which the system dries out quickly. The egg and larval stages are dependent on high humidity for successful development, which, at 23 days, is remarkably fast for a detritivore. Rapid desiccation of the sand is therefore a major limiting factor for their development.

The mature larva spins a silken cocoon in which it pupates; the cocoon increases the vulnerable pupa's resistance to desiccation. When this occurs the parents back-fill the burrow and remain with the developing pupa until the young adult emerges after 11–12 days. Breeding pairs produce two adult offspring in most summers, and they live about two years; a female's lifetime fecundity is thus very low compared to most other insect species (see 'The famous Addo dung beetle', p. 279).

Eremostibes opacus is a distant relative of the detritivorous beetle *Parastizopus armaticeps*, and lives and breeds in its nests. The association between these two species is very close, with most *P. armaticeps* nests inhabited by the parasite. *Eremostibes opacus* produces defensive chemicals very similar to those of its host when threatened; it is thought to mimic the host chemically, primarily to gain access to the host's burrow and food stores.

Male *P. armaticeps* usually guard the burrow entrances and attempt to block them with their body, or they grapple with any 'intruder' and try to expel it. If the individual is a conspecific female, the male identifies her as such by smell after some grappling; when the appropriate odour is recognised, the female is admitted. *Eremostibes opacus* adults are considerably smaller than *P. armaticeps* and enter the host's breeding burrows either while they are unattended by the male or by deceiving them by the production of odours that are chemically very similar to the host's.

Once inside, the kleptoparasitic adults feed on the accumulated detritus in the food or breeding chamber, mating takes place, and eggs are laid under the host's provisions. The parasite larvae live and feed under the provisions at the soil/detritus interface. Breeding burrows excavated in the Kalahari contained an average of one to four *E. opacus* beetles, but sometimes as many as 15 were found in a burrow. After breeding, the parasites usually leave the host burrow.

Research shows that the presence of adult and larval *E. opacus* in *P. armaticeps* nests leads to a decrease in the amount of food available for the host larvae, resulting in their undernourishment and, ultimately, to the development of smaller than normal adults with a reduced probability of breeding. When these small adults manage to breed, they produce fewer offspring. Excessive numbers of the parasite in breeding burrows causes the host parents to abandon the burrow, at substantial cost not only to their own reproductive effort, but also to that of the parasite. It is therefore in the parasite's best interests to avoid overpopulation of the host's burrow.

How did the relationship between *P. armaticeps* and *E. opacus* evolve? The two species are related and have narrowly overlapping ecological requirements with respect to seasonal activity, habitat, food and temperature preferences. The close congruence in defensive chemicals is thought to have been the overriding factor leading to the kleptoparasitic association – the similarity between host and parasite is exploited mostly to the parasite's own advantage. Nevertheless, there are also significant ecological advantages for the host: increased humidity in shared burrows and improved defence by aggregating.

Fungus feeders

In the African savannas, there is an intimate relationship between fungus-feeding insects and fungi that live in an obligatory association. The insects are fungus-growing termites and the fungi are specialist cellulose-digesting species. Without their cellulose-digesting fungi, these mound-building termites would be unable to consume the large quantities of wood for which they are renowned.

Fungus-feeding termites

One of the defining characters of *Macrotermes* and other fungus-gardening termites (*Pseudacanthotermes, Odontotermes, Ancistrotermes, Allodontermes* and *Microtermes*) is how they digest wood, their principal food source, which consists largely of intractable cellulose and lignin.

Termites, as evidenced by their modern classification in the order Blattodea, are essentially social cockroaches (see 'Detritivores', p. 88). Primitive termites and primitive cockroaches both have specialised protozoan gut symbionts that digest cellulose (see 'Hindgut', p. 31). Higher termites (Termitidae) have evolved a more advanced process for feeding on wood (for the difference between primitive and higher termites, see box, pp. 72–73).

Fungus-gardening termites (Termitidae: Macrotermitinae) have lost the ancestral gut symbionts and have switched to culturing cellulose-digesting fungi (*Termitomyces* spp., fig. 7.66) on special 'fungus gardens' in nest chambers; the symbiotic relationship assists with the breakdown of the wood upon which they feed. This specific feeding phenomenon is termed extra-alimentary digestion, since digestion of food takes place outside of the body of the feeder.

Macrotermes chew on the source of wood and swallow small amounts, which are not digested but begin to ferment in the gut where they are mixed with fungal spores. Back in the nest, the faeces, which are composed

7.66 Clumps of *Termitomyces* mushrooms break through the soil surface after rain. The fungus is cultivated below ground by members of the fungus-gardening termite subfamily Macrotermitinae (Termitidae) on combs of wood chewed by the termites.

of the fermented wood paste and fungal spores, are added to a 'comb' of spongy, cardboard-like material in special chambers. The temperature in the chambers where the combs are cultivated is maintained at a reasonably constant 29–32°C. The fungus develops on the combs in this 'fungus garden' and in the process breaks down the cellulose into a paste suitable for termite food.

Small white nodules (reproductive bodies containing asexual spores) appear abundantly on the fungus and are fed to the king, queen and young termites, while the soldiers and workers feed on the comb itself after the fungus has reduced it into a digestible format. This process leads to about 80% of the digestion of the original cellulose collected by the termites.

A question that arises is why pathogenic fungi don't overrun the combs, as they are cultured in a moist and warm environment also perfectly suited for undesirable species. The answer lies in yet another remarkable process that is involved in the intimate associations between the termites and fungi: a special bacterium has also evolved as one of the participants in the food and feeding web. The bacterium produces an antifungal chemical, bacillaene, that suppresses general fungi. *Termitomyces* is resistant to bacillaene and thus a pure culture of the food fungus is maintained.

After rain the fungus may produce above-ground fruiting bodies (mushrooms) (figs 7.66, 6.16) that release millions of sexual spores.

Predators

Some of the largest and most spectacular insect predators are found in the Savanna Biome. These include giant lacewings with wingspans sometimes larger than some of the bats that compete with them, hawking insect prey on the wing. Their ferocious soil-living larvae are capable of capturing prey many times larger than themselves. Giant

ground and tiger beetles patrol the soil surface in search of prey, which they grasp and crush in large mandibles. Matabele ants rustle through the undergrowth in search of the termites on which they prey.

In response to the onslaught of such predators, many savanna insects have evolved special defensive mechanisms. Some insects use contrasting colours to advertise their unpalatability, and either produce defensive chemicals or sequester toxins from the plants on which they feed.

Giant lacewings and their antlion larvae

The largest and most striking lacewings are in the subfamily Palparinae (Neuroptera: Myrmeleontidae, fig. 7.67). Of the world total of 124 species, 89 are found in Africa. There are 44 species in southern Africa, of which 25 occur in arid and semiarid areas extending from the Nama-Karoo through Namaqualand (Succulent Karoo) to the Kalahari (Savanna) and Namibia. Local endemism is high.

Adults vary in size from the smallest, appropriately named *Pamares parvus* (Latin for 'small') with a wingspan of 45mm, to the largest, *Palpares immensus*, which has a wingspan of 155mm. All species have wings blotched with black and grey patterns that afford them superb camouflage when resting on plants by day. They are nocturnal and readily attracted to lights.

Like the adults, the antlion larvae are particularly striking, ranging from dark purple to black and white with red and green patterning (fig. 7.68). This coloration reflects the habits of the larvae, and their adaptation to camouflage and temperature regulation in the hot sand environments in which they live.

Palparine larvae – some species are 30mm long – are all free-living in loose sand and don't build pits like some other antlion species do (see 'Thermal refuges of antlion larvae', p. 146 and 'Pit-building antlions', p. 349). The vast sandy areas of southern Africa have been especially conducive to their diversification and proliferation, which has contributed to making southern Africa the main global centre of palparine distribution. All are voracious predators that are an important component of the predator guild in the areas they inhabit.

Most palparine larvae live in deep sand and migrate to the surface in the late afternoon and evening when sand temperatures cool. They lie just below the surface with only the head and spread jaws exposed (fig. 7.69), and are alerted by vibrations from approaching prey. The six simple eye (stemmata) facets set on a prominent tubercle play a role in directing the jaw strike towards prey. Once the prey is secured by the tips and intermeshing teeth of the sickle-shaped mandibles, the larva moves backwards to subdue the prey and avoid injury to itself. Proteolytic enzymes are injected into the prey through the composite

7.67 Adult giant lacewings (Neuroptera: Myrmeleontidae: Palparinae) are important elements of the predatory insect guild: (**a**) *Palparellus pulchellus*; (**b**) *Palparellus nyassanus*; (**c**) *Palpares caffer*; (**d**) *Palparidius capicola*; (**e**) *Lachlathetes moestus*; (**f**) *Palpares immensus*.

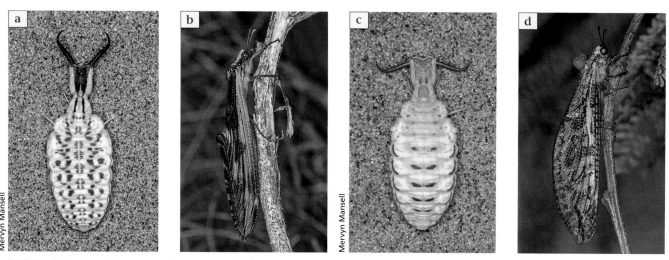

Mervyn Mansell

Mervyn Mansell

7.68 The Palparinae (Neuroptera: Myrmeleontidae) larvae of the southern African arid savanna regions are the largest and most spectacular antlions in the world: (**a**) *Golafrus oneili* larva and (**b**) adult; (**c**) *Annulares annulatus* larva and (**d**) adult.

Mervyn Mansell

7.69 This *Palpares inclemens* larva, like all Palparinae (Neuroptera: Myrmeleontidae) larvae, is free-living in loose sand, where it lies buried with only the spread mandibles and stemmata (simple eyes) protruding, waiting for approaching prey.

mandibles and maxillae that slot together to form a salivary canal (as in all Neuroptera larvae). The enzymes then digest the internal tissue of the prey, and the resulting fluid is drawn back into the alimentary canal. Prey consists mostly of surface-dwelling arthropods, with records of a gecko and even a small adder being attacked, although this invariably leads to the death of the larva, as it is unable to retract its jaws from the soft tissues of vertebrates.

Predatory ground beetles

The insects of the terrestrial predatory guild are mainly large ferocious predatory beetles (Coleoptera: Carabidae, fig. 7.70), which prey on any other invertebrate they can overpower. Almost all Carabidae adults and larvae are predators. The family is divided into more than 30 distinct subfamilies of which some have familiar southern African members (fig. 7.71). Members of the largest groups are generally referred to as ground beetles, but others have more specific common names that allude to some aspect of their biology; examples are ant-nest beetles (Paussinae) and bombardier beetles (Brachininae). Bombardier beetles are named for their habit of squirting noxious chemicals towards a predator ... or careless insect collector (see 'Ground beetles', p. 127). In fact, many members of the Carabidae are capable of doing so and often have colours to warn potential predators of their toxicity: they are either black with yellow or white spots, black and red, or are brightly metallically coloured. This phenomenon is referred to as aposematism (see box, pp. 240–241).

7.70 The largest predatory beetle family is Carabidae. These savanna species are 30–60mm long: **(a)** *Anthia* (formerly *Thermophilum*) *omoplatum*; **(b)** *A.* (formerly *Thermophilum*) *massilicata*; **(c)** *Calosoma senegalense*; **(d)** *Cypholoba tenuicollis aenigma*.

7.71 Most Carabidae beetles produce noxious defensive compounds from special abdominal glands. To advertise their unpalatability, many species are aposematically coloured. These smaller species are 10–30mm long: **(a)** *Rhysotrachelus quadrimaculatus*; **(b)** *Thyreopterus flavosignatus*; **(c)** *Stereostoma* sp.; **(d)** *Pheropsophus fastigiatus*; **(e)** *Bradybaenus opulentus*; **(f)** *Lebistina caffer*.

In order to defend themselves against the onslaught of so many predators, insects have evolved a very wide range of defensive strategies. These vary from simply hiding in protected environments, to primary lines of defence such as assuming colours and forms that assist them in blending with their immediate environment (crypsis); evolving protective morphological structures, such as spines, scales and saltatorial hind legs; or certain defensive behaviours, often combined with the evolution of a wide range of defensive chemicals. Ground beetles (Coleoptera: Carabidae) are amongst the groups with well-developed chemical defence mechanisms.

A defence mechanism used by many insects is crypsis (camouflage): the insect adopts strategies that make it difficult for a potential predator to distinguish it from its background (fig. 7.72).

Aposematism is the antithesis of crypsis, but is also a primary defence mechanism: the animal displays itself or otherwise 'advertises' its unsuitability as prey to potential predators (fig. 7.73), warning them that it is protected by other, secondary defensive systems, such as venom in snakes, stings in wasps and bees, or the noxious or toxic body chemicals in some frogs and many insect species.

Although many reptiles and amphibians (and a few mammals, e.g. skunks) are brightly or contrastingly coloured and noxious or toxic, the phenomenon is particularly widespread among insects and many striking examples can

7.72 Crypsis, the most basic and most common form of insect defence, is widespread across the orders. (**a**) The primary defence of this bark katydid, *Cymatomera denticollis* (Orthoptera: Tettigoniidae), is crypsis, but its secondary defence involves (**b**) flashing bright body colours when threatened. (**c**) Similarly, the moth *Amyops ingens* (Lepidoptera: Notodontidae) has black and white cryptic forewing patterns, but responds with (**d**) bright underbody flash colours when threatened.

be found across the orders. The most common colours involved are black, yellow and red (or combinations of these); usually, the brighter and more conspicuous the insect, the more toxic it is. A naïve predator experiences a bad taste or sensation when it tries to eat brightly coloured prey; it associates the unpleasant experience with the bright coloration, and in future avoids anything with those colours.

Aposematically coloured insects usually contrast distinctly against the background or their habitat, and often move slowly and with jerky movements as if confident of their safety.

Most members of the Carabidae produce, and readily spray, defensive secretions when cornered. Many are also brightly coloured and run with typical jerky movements. The abundance of these beetles and the potency of their secretions have granted the juveniles of the co-occurring Bushveld lizard, *Heliobolus lugubris*, the adaptive advantage of mimicking the beetles by displaying similar colour patterns and jerky movements (fig. 7.74). Predators with experience of the beetles' defensive secretions would hesitate to attack anything with similar colour patterns and movement, thus giving the lizards time to escape into cover.

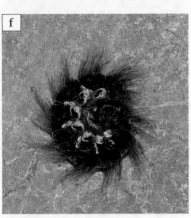

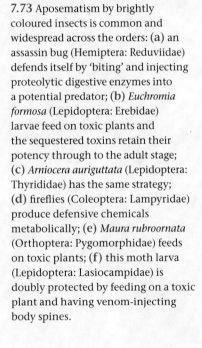

7.73 Aposematism by brightly coloured insects is common and widespread across the orders: (**a**) an assassin bug (Hemiptera: Reduviidae) defends itself by 'biting' and injecting proteolytic digestive enzymes into a potential predator; (**b**) *Euchromia formosa* (Lepidoptera: Erebidae) larvae feed on toxic plants and the sequestered toxins retain their potency through to the adult stage; (**c**) *Arniocera auriguttata* (Lepidoptera: Thyrididae) has the same strategy; (**d**) fireflies (Coleoptera: Lampyridae) produce defensive chemicals metabolically; (**e**) *Maura rubroornata* (Orthoptera: Pygomorphidae) feeds on toxic plants; (**f**) this moth larva (Lepidoptera: Lasiocampidae) is doubly protected by feeding on a toxic plant and having venom-injecting body spines.

7.74 (left) The immature stages of the Bushveld lizard, *Heliobolus lugubris*, mimic co-occurring *Anthia* (Carabidae) beetles in general colour patterns and jerky movements, characteristics that are thought to provide protection against certain predators.

7.75 An *Anthia* (Carabidae) larva: a large, free-ranging predator of surface-dwelling invertebrates.

7.76 Monster tiger beetles such as this *Manticora tibialis* (Carabidae: Cicindelinae) are amongst the largest insect predators: (**a**) a free-ranging, hunting adult and (**b**) the burrow-inhabiting 'sit-and-wait' larva.

The beetles may be active by day or night, may be capable of flight or wingless, and vary considerably in size. Some of the region's largest (up to 50mm long) belong to the Anthiinae (*Anthia*, including *Thermophilum*), of which the most common species occur in the Savanna Biome. All have prominent, forward-projecting mandibles and are large, wingless, diurnal insects with black and red, yellow or white dorsal markings. Adults are long-legged, fast-running and voracious predators of any prey they can overpower. Larvae are mostly nocturnal, but are also free-living and fast-moving, aggressive predators (fig. 7.75).

Another large Carabidae subfamily is the Cicindelinae, commonly known as tiger beetles (for detailed biology, see 'Ferocious tiger beetle larvae', p. 363). Most are colourful, long-legged diurnal beetles that have huge protruding mandibles and are fast runners and flyers. By contrast, the world's largest 'monster' tiger beetles, species of *Manticora* (40–50mm long), are dark brown to black and flightless; this African genus is widespread across the subcontinent and several species occur in savanna regions. Unlike most of their cousins in the Carabidae, *Manticora* species do not produce defensive chemicals (few Cicindelinae do) and rely mostly on speed to avoid danger. However, they are equally ferocious predators in both adult and larval stages (fig. 7.76). Again,

Invertebrate biomass as food for predators

Many predatory insects, as well as reptiles, fish, birds and mammals, feed largely or only on invertebrates. The populations of many of these predatory groups are high in the relatively pristine savanna ecosystem of the Kruger National Park (KNP). Many feed on a wide variety of prey, but others are insectivores, feeding mostly on insects, and some only on those of a specific ecological guild, or those restricted to a particular habitat.

Some of the endemic fish species prey on aquatic invertebrates, of which insects make up a large proportion; lizards, some snakes and frogs feed mostly on terrestrial invertebrates; bats (of which there are 39 species in the KNP) feed almost exclusively on nocturnal flying insects; and aardvarks and pangolins (fig. 7.77) feed exclusively on ants (in summer) and termites (in winter).

An estimate of the biomass of invertebrates of just one habitat stratum in the KNP – the tree canopy layer – yielded a figure of about 2,400kg/km², roughly the same as that for medium and large mammalian herbivores combined. Considering that this figure reflects mainly herbivorous insects and their invertebrate (mostly spider) predators, in one relatively small habitat type, we can expect the rich terrestrial and below-ground invertebrate fauna to increase the total biomass substantially. There can be little doubt that invertebrates have immense ecosystem-scale importance and that they contribute very significantly to maintaining the rich diversity of insectivores in the KNP.

Darren Pietersen

7.77 One of Africa's rarest and most unusual mammals, the pangolin, *Smutsia temminckii*, is a highly specialised insectivore that eats only termites and ants.

unlike their relatives, the larvae are sit-and-wait predators, living in vertical tunnels from which they launch themselves to capture approaching prey. Adults have large eyes and good eyesight, while larvae are unusual amongst holometamorphic insect larvae in having large stemmata (simple eyes) with which they can see well.

Matabele ants: specialist termite predators

Matabele ants, *Megaponera analis* (formerly *M. foetens*), are formidable and aggressive members of the primitive subfamily Ponerinae (Hymenoptera: Formicidae; for more on ants see 'Ant biology and behaviour', p. 159). They are specialist termite predators and have various morphological and behavioural adaptations for this way of life. Yet, in spite of their aggressive behaviour, the ants tolerate various nest inhabitants including dung beetles and fishmoths.

Their common name is based on the behaviour of their raiding parties, which are made up of fierce, orderly groups of workers that erupt from nests to seek out and attack termites; this is reminiscent of the regiments of early 19th-century Matabele warriors who carved a swathe of destruction across southern Africa from Zululand to western Zimbabwe. The warriors banged on their ox-hide shields with their spears as they travelled on raiding parties; the ants stridulate audibly when alarmed. In addition to stridulating, the ants produce a strong, offensive smell (the origin of the outdated specific name 'foetens') and readily inflict a painful sting when threatened. Although *M. analis*

is widespread in Africa, in southern Africa they are confined to the eastern and northeastern tropical and subtropical Lowveld parts of the savanna. Various aspects of African *Megaponera* biology have been studied by Martin Villet of Rhodes University and Robin Crewe and other members of the Social Insects Research Group at the University of Pretoria.

The ants nest in holes underground, which may extend down to 70cm below the surface, but also under logs or rocks, in old termite mounds (often of their prey species) and at the base of trees. A colony consists of a single worker-like (ergatoid) queen and 250–2,000 female workers, who vary substantially in size and morphology (fig. 7.78). Small workers (7–9mm long) are shiny black and have mandibles without teeth, while large workers (15–16mm long) are covered in grey setae and have toothed mandibles. The presence of workers of different sizes in a ponerine species is unusual, and in *M. analis* it has been attributed to its specialisation as a termite predator.

Species of *Macrotermes* (see 'Termites as soil engineers', p. 199) and *Odontotermes* (see 'The tall chimneys of fungus-growing termite mounds', p. 181) are their preferred prey. The termites are located by ant scouts that usually work alone. They move slowly, searching amongst leaf litter and under wood while palpating their antennae. The scouts locate active termite foraging galleries by cueing in to chemicals produced by termite saliva during the construction of the fresh clay sheeting that covers the galleries (see 'Development of a termite mound', p. 199); older sheeting soon loses its attractiveness.

7.78 Matabele ants, *Megaponera analis* (Ponerinae), are specialist termite predators. (**a**) Workers on a raid with as many termites as they can carry. (**b**) Central collection point from which they carry the prey back to the nest after the raid. (**c**) The termite soldiers resist the attack fiercely. (**d**) The start of a periodic nest migration in which pupal brood is carried to the new nest by workers, accompanied by (**e**) alates, which will soon depart to establish a new nest. (**f**) Obligatory nest inhabitants (myrmecophiles) join the exodus, including these unusual *Megaponerophilus megaponerae* (Scarabaeidae: Scarabaeinae) beetles, which breed in refuse in the ants' nest.

After locating prey, either at a termite nest or in the foraging galleries, the scout quickly returns to the ant nest, laying a pheromone trail as it goes by allowing droplets of poison gland chemicals to flow out from the end of the sting. In the nest, it recruits a group of workers of both sizes and together they form an orderly raiding column and follow the trail back to the termites.

Raiding parties vary considerably in size, with records of 20–850 workers embarking on a raid. There is usually only one raiding party out hunting at a time, at a distance of about 35–100m from the ant nest. Most raids take place during cooler morning and afternoon periods, but occasionally at night.

Trail-following and termite attack are mediated by two different chemical compound mixes from the poison gland and mandibular gland (see box, p. 162). The trail pheromone from the poison gland leads the raiding party to the termite nest, where the column splits up – some ants invade the termite nest, and others go directly to the termite foraging area also located by the scout. Once the clay sheeting over a termite foraging gallery or the termite nest has been located, it is the responsibility of large workers to break it open, while they also produce mandibular gland secretions to attract other workers to elicit digging behaviour at the breach.

Small workers enter the termite nests and foraging galleries at these breaches and capture termite workers, which they drag out to be killed by the larger workers. A large worker ant grabs a termite with special hooked tarsi on its forelegs and pulls it back between its legs and under its abdomen, where it can sting the termite. Dead termites are then eviscerated individually by the large workers, which hold them on the ground with their foretarsi, grasp the anal region in their mandibles, and pull out the gut, which they discard. The ants eat only eviscerated termites.

Soldier termites, which have large mandibles, are confronted head-on. The ant proffers its pointed and hardened abdomen through under its thorax and between its legs to the termite soldier, which snaps its mandibles shut over the tip of the ant abdomen, but the hard, scimitar-shaped abdomen slips free while the termite soldier's mandibles stay locked. The ant then stings the soldier on the mouthparts and paralysis occurs within a few seconds.

Raids usually last 13–20 minutes, but depending on termite resistance to the attack, might be as brief as 2 minutes, or last as long as an hour. Sometimes a worker will pick up as many termite bodies as it can manage (large workers carry 6 or 7 termites, small workers 1–3) and return to the nest alone. More usually, however, at some signal the attack ceases and the ant workers withdraw from the termite nest, stridulate aggressively, collect the prey, and return to their own nest.

Parasites

Savanna mammals provide a large resource for another level of consumers: blood-feeding parasites. These may live in or on the host. Among them are bot fly larvae, which are endoparasites that live either in the host's nasal cavities, beneath its skin or in its intestines. The most important ectoparasites of savanna mammals are ticks, which may transmit disease-causing microorganisms to their host while feeding.

Intestinal bot flies

The larvae of all species of bot flies (Diptera: Oestridae) are internal mammal parasites. They are found in the nasal cavities (nasal bots; see 'Nasal bot flies', p. 193), intestines (intestinal bots) or subcutaneous tissues (warbles) of their hosts. Adults do not feed and are short-lived.

Certain members of the subfamily Gasterophilinae are intestinal parasites of large herbivores: *Gasterophilus* species in equids (horses and zebras; *G. intestinalis* is a cosmopolitan horse parasite, fig. 7.79), *Cobboldia* species in elephants, and *Gyrostigma rhinocerotis* in rhinos. The rhinoceros bot fly is Africa's largest fly and is intimately associated with both African rhino species. Today the rhinos and their bot flies are threatened species (see box opposite).

7.79 (a) Larvae of the bot fly *Gasterophilus intestinalis* (Diptera: Oestridae) are intestinal parasites of equids such as (b) the plains zebra, *Equus quagga*.

The plight of the rhinoceros fly

As recently as 2006, David Barraclough, a Diptera expert at the University of KwaZulu-Natal, Durban, wrote an article celebrating the reprieve from extinction of Africa's largest fly, the rhinoceros bot fly, *Gyrostigma rhinocerotis*. This upbeat article was a response to the increasing numbers of its hosts – white rhinos, *Ceratotherium simum*, and black rhinos, *Diceros bicornis* – in southern Africa (fig. 7.80). In the early 20th century, African rhinos were driven to the brink of extinction, but their conservation success story in South Africa was remarkable: numbers in reserves and game farms soared from a handful of animals to about 15,000 white and 3,500 black rhinos in 2006.

However, about a year after this article was published, the demand for rhino horn in some East Asian countries led to a dramatic escalation in rhino poaching, unparalleled by any period in the past. The situation in South Africa remains bleak: poaching continues and rhino numbers are declining annually.

The rhino conservation crisis is, of course, not only about saving rhinos, but also about the fauna that has an obligatory association with them. One of the most impressive is *Gyrostigma rhinocerotis*, which, according to the early French explorer Adulphe Delegorgue, occurs in 'bushel-fulls' in the stomach of the black rhino. There are three larval instars, all of which suck blood from the stomach lining of the host.

The large adult flies are about 40mm long and have a wingspan of about 70mm. They are black with orange head and legs and buzz audibly in flight. Superficially, they resemble the large and fairly common spider-hunting wasps (Hymenoptera: Pompilidae). However, they are seldom seen, even in areas where rhinos may be relatively common. The flies have reduced mouthparts and probably don't feed, so their main function, breeding, must take place within a few days of emergence.

The adult flies have two activity peaks per year, early summer (October–December) and early autumn (March–May). Females lay hundreds of tiny eggs, mainly on the head of the rhino. It is not known how the 2mm-long larvae that emerge from these eggs find their way into the rhino's stomach, but it has been speculated that they wriggle to the rhino's nose and mouth and from there into the oesophagus and then down into the stomach. They attach to the stomach wall with mouth-hooks, and suck blood. They are elongate and surrounded by bands of spines. They moult twice (three larval instars) and the 40mm-long, finger-thick, last-instar larvae leave via the rhino's anus. They drop to the ground and quickly burrow into the soil where they pupate into a cigar-shaped black pupa, from which the adult flies emerge about six weeks later.

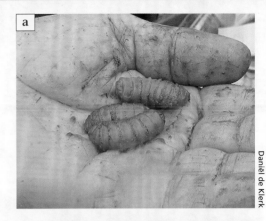

7.80 (a) Larvae of Africa's largest fly species, *Gyrostigma rhinocerotis* (Diptera: Oestridae), are intestinal parasites of black and **(b)** white rhinos, *Ceratotherium simum*. It has been suggested that the **(c)** adult fly is a mimic of **(d)** the spider-hunting wasp *Hemipepsis* (Pompilidae).

The life of ticks

Ticks and mites are not insects but form part of another arthropod class, the arachnids (Arachnida: Acari: Ixodida; see 'What is an insect?', p. 14). There are an estimated 2,500 mite species and about 115 tick species in southern Africa. Ticks are usually easily visible, whereas most mites are tiny and seldom seen unless specifically sought. All ticks feed on the blood of terrestrial vertebrates, including humans, while mites are very diverse in their biology (see 'Mites', p. 298).

Besides their nuisance value of sucking blood with corresponding allergic reactions and infection from bites, ticks are the vectors of a wide range of serious (even fatal) human, wildlife and domestic animal diseases. They transmit more potentially disease-causing microorganisms than any other arthropod group, and are second only to mosquitoes in terms of their importance as vectors of human and domestic animal diseases. The organisms that they transmit include bacteria, rickettsiae, protozoa, viruses and helminths (see box, p. 248). While feeding, some species produce toxic saliva that paralyses the host, and unless the tick is removed, the animal may die of secondary complications such as dehydration or exposure to the elements.

Ticks in southern Africa fall into three families: the more typical and common Ixodidae (hard ticks); the rarer, more specialised Argasidae (soft ticks); and the Nuttalliellidae, which is represented by a single rare species. Most species will suck the blood of a wide range of hosts, but some are quite host-specific or even prefer a particular part of the host's anatomy. Ticks are more prevalent in the Savanna Biome, particularly in the warmer eastern parts, because of the abundance of large mammal species.

The tick life cycle consists of an egg (usually the product of mating between a male and a female; parthenogenesis is rare), one larval stage and one (Ixodidae) or several (Argasidae) nymphal stages, followed, finally, by the adult tick. The duration of the life cycle may vary from a few weeks to many years, depending on food availability. Argasids, particularly, are capable of living without a blood meal for years.

Ixodidae

Ixodidae are typically oval or round and mostly have the mouthparts extended forwards. These consist of two palps with a hardened, calcified hypostome with terminal cutting blades between them; the hypostome is the part that is inserted into the host, where it is held in place by barbs that prevent it from slipping out. Some species continue to force their mouthparts into the host while feeding, until the entire tick becomes tightly embedded in host tissue; this often results in secondary infections.

Male and female hard ticks are different in appearance. Fully engorged females, which may imbibe 1–5ml of blood, become a large, often grey, leathery bag of blood and developing eggs. Males are usually smaller and have a distinct, hard shield behind the head that covers much of the body.

Fed mature females drop from the host and then lay thousands (a record of nearly 23,000 is known) of tiny eggs in a secure site at the base of a bush or rock. Tiny red six-legged larvae emerge from the eggs. These 'pepper ticks' will be familiar to people who spend time in the veld and will have been attacked by large numbers of them at once.

Ticks may spend long periods on an appropriate perch, such as a grass blade, waiting for a potential host to pass (termed questing), grasping with their middle and hind legs while holding and waving their front legs about in the air. The front legs have a special, complex sensory organ, called Haller's organ, in the tarsus behind the terminal claws, which is roughly equivalent in function to antennae in insects. It is sensitive to vibration, humidity, temperature, infrared radiation, odours and exhaled carbon dioxide from an approaching host, and also has a reproductive function, as it is used for tracing attractant pheromones between the sexes.

Hard ticks (fig. 7.81) fall into one of three general classes with respect to their life cycle: they are classified as either one-, two- or three-host ticks, depending on whether they need one, two or three different individual hosts to complete their life cycle.

- In one-host ticks, the ticks feed on the same host through all stages of development and the adult stage.
- In two-host ticks, the six-legged larvae feed on a host, then drop off, moult into eight-legged nymphs, and proceed to find a new host on which they then remain.
- In three-host ticks, the first two stages are the same as in two-host ticks, but after moulting into the adult stage, drop from the host and need to find a new host.
- The hosts may be of the same or different species. Host preference may change between the different stages, necessitating a change in host-selection behaviour; they may, for example, switch from feeding on a rodent, reptile or bird to a large mammal.

Argasidae

Soft ticks (tampans) are oval to egg-shaped and leathery, and their mouthparts are not visible from above (fig. 7.82). They are less common and less well known than their hard tick relatives. This is mainly because of their smaller numbers, more restricted distribution, specialised habitats and secretive habits. Most species

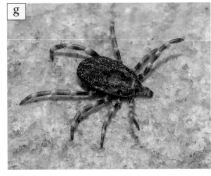

7.81 Hard ticks (Arachnida: Acari: Ixodida: Ixodidae) are common in savanna and transmit diseases to humans and domestic animals: **(a)** adult male rhinoceros tick, *Dermacentor rhinocerinus*; **(b)** adult female *D. rhinocerinus* before feeding; **(c)** 'questing' *Rhipicephalus* tick; **(d)** red-legged ticks, *R. evertsi evertsi*, on their preferred host, zebra; **(e)** bont ticks, *Amblyomma hebraeum*, whose immature stages readily attack and bite humans; **(f)** *Rhipicephalus* sp.; **(g)** bont-legged ticks, *Hyalomma rufipes*, attack a wide range of hosts and are an occasional vector of serious human diseases.

7.82 Soft ticks or 'tampans', *Ornithodoros* sp. (Ixodida: Argasidae), remain attached only for as long as it takes to become engorged, after which they detach and bury themselves in the soil, where they may remain for years before an appropriate host ventures by and they can feed again.

do not live on their hosts except when feeding, which takes place quickly (15–30 minutes) and mostly at night. When not feeding, they live in the host's burrow or nest or in other sheltered situations, such as the permanently shaded sand beneath trees in arid areas.

One of their major ecological characteristics is their ability to live for very long periods without food. Adults of the fowl or poultry tampan, *Argas*, can live for up to three years without a blood meal. Each of the four or five nymph stages of *Ornithodoros* species, which attack poultry, domestic pigs, warthogs and humans, can live for two years without a meal, and adults for four to five years. *Ornithodoros porcinus* transmits the virus that causes swine fever in domestic pigs (when in contact with warthogs, which are reservoirs of the virus). *Ornithodoros moubata* transmits *Borellia duttoni*, the causative organism of human relapsing fever.

Major tick-borne diseases

Hard ticks are major vectors of serious diseases of humans and domestic animals.

The **African blue tick**, *Rhipicephalus decoloratus*, and **Asian blue tick**, *R. microplus*, are one-host ticks with a wide variety of hosts, including cattle, antelope and equids. They transmit *Babesia bovis* and *B. bigemina*, which cause bovine babesiosis ('redwater'), as well as *Anaplasma marginale*, the causative organism of anaplasmosis ('gall sickness') in cattle.

The **bont-legged tick**, *Hyalomma rufipes*, is a two-host tick that attacks a wide range of hosts, including ground-nesting birds, hares, various large wild mammals and most farm animals. Its major effect on host health is that the long mouthparts of feeding ticks cause tissue damage that attracts blow flies, and may become infected with bacteria. However, the tick is also an occasional vector of *Rickettsia conorii*, which causes 'spotted' tick-bite fever, and the Crimean–Congo haemorrhagic fever virus in humans.

The **bont tick**, *Amblyomma hebraeum*, is a three-host tick of small antelope, guineafowl, hares, cattle and humans. It transmits *Ehrlichia ruminantum*, which causes heartwater disease in cattle, and *Rickettsia africana*, which causes tick-bite fever in humans. Most ticks that attack and bite humans are members of this species.

The **brown ear tick**, *Rhipicephalus appendiculatus*, is a three-host tick of hares, antelope and cattle. As the name suggests, the ticks prefer to feed on the outer ear. They may become so abundant on a host's ears that certain game species, such as eland, introduced from areas free of brown ear ticks onto game farms that have the ticks, may have their ears totally destroyed and die as a result of secondary infections.

The **Karoo paralysis tick**, *Ixodes rubicundus*, is a three-host tick whose larvae and nymphs feed on elephant shrews, red rock hares and caracal. Adults feed on sheep, goats, dogs, caracal and certain antelope species. While feeding, female ticks produce a salivary toxin that causes paralysis of some hosts: if removed, the animal recovers; if not, it may die of secondary complications.

The **yellow dog tick**, *Haemaphysalis elliptica*, is a three-host tick of dogs, cats and large wild carnivores; the immature stages feed on rodents. It transmits *Babesia rossi*, which causes canine babesiosis ('biliary') in dogs.

Dung feeders

With the large numbers of mammals, especially herbivores, living in the savanna, it is not surprising that there is a correspondingly rich and abundant dung fauna. The thousands of tonnes of dung excreted by mammals every day are an ephemeral and desirable resource for dung insects, among which are many dung beetle species. These vary in size from tiny to large and partition the resource by feeding and breeding on different parts of the dung source (see box opposite). Fly larvae also compete for a share of the resource; they attract a host of predatory insect species, resulting in dung pats becoming small ecosystems.

Dung beetle behaviour at a dung pat

The Kruger National Park (KNP) is home to one of the largest concentrations of large mammals in Africa. These include major dung producers such as elephants (current population about 13,000) and buffalo (about 30,000), as well as tens of thousands of individuals of many other herbivorous species. A single elephant produces about 150kg of dung per day, and a buffalo about 40kg. In one day, KNP elephants and buffaloes yield 5,150 tonnes of dung! What happens to it?

In summer, most of it is buried within hours by the many dung beetle species (Scarabaeidae: Scarabaeinae) active at this time of the year. During the cool, dry winter months, dung beetle populations are greatly reduced and much of the dung dries out quickly, after which it is rapidly colonised and buried by termites. Much of the energy tied up in the cellulose that is produced by photosynthesis in plants is passed undigested into the herbivore's dung, where it is subsequently broken down by the dung beetles into small particles suitable for the final release of nutrients into the soil by microbes.

One rough count in about 25kg of elephant dung in the KNP yielded 7,000 individual dung beetles of approximately 120 species, but this is substantially less impressive than the 16,000 dung beetles attracted over two hours to 1.5 litres of elephant dung in an East African savanna experiment!

The richest southern African dung beetle fauna is found in the Savanna Biome (particularly in the KNP), where about 250 species have been recorded. Although most feed on any form of herbivore dung, many have a preference for either the fine dung of ruminants such as buffalo and antelope, whose four stomachs to a very large extent fragment and digest the food eaten, or the much coarser dung of monogastric animals such as zebra, rhinos and elephants. Another adaptation to lessen the fierce competition between different dung beetle species is their very specific behaviour at the dung pat (see box opposite). Variations in activity peaks (particular time of day or night) also greatly reduce competition.

Rollers, dwellers, tunnellers and nest parasites

Dung beetles (fig. 7.83) feed on herbivore dung in both the adult and larval stages. Adults consume tiny fragments of dung, bacteria and fungi suspended in a soup of organic matter in the liquid component of fresh dung (but see box, p. 124), while larvae chew the partially digested cellulose fibres that the mammal excretes. In all species, the adults provide a cache of food in which the larvae live and feed – the manner in which they do this forms the basis of a behavioural classification of the species. Consequently, dung beetles are classified either as rollers (telecoprids), tunnellers (paracoprids), dwellers (endocoprids), or nest parasites (kleptocoprids). A majority (about 75%) of southern African species are tunnellers, followed by rollers (15%), with dwellers and nest parasites at about 5% each.

Rollers are probably the most familiar group to most people because of their above-ground activity. They form a ball at the dung source, then roll it some distance away and bury it. If the ball is a food ball, a single beetle rolls it away and buries it; but a brood ball involves both male and female, where it may be rolled by the male, with the female hanging precariously onto it or following behind; by the male and female together; or, rarely, by the female alone (see 'The famous Addo dung beetle', p. 279).

Tunnellers dig down into the ground immediately after arriving at a dung source, and begin to drag chunks of dung into an underground chamber. Once sufficient dung is accumulated, brood balls are formed by the adults. Mating takes place and the female lays an egg in a small cavity at the top of each brood ball. The larvae then feed down into the ball. Depending on the species, the balls may be coated in clay or left bare. In some species, the balls are abandoned by the parents, whereas in others, the female may remain in the nest until the offspring emerge.

Dwellers are usually small species that live inside a dung source, where the brood balls are formed, eggs are laid and the larvae develop.

Nest parasites are small species that parasitise the brood balls formed by other, larger dung beetle species. As they are smaller than their hosts, their eggs hatch faster and their larvae feed on the dung provisioned by the host. The host larvae usually die.

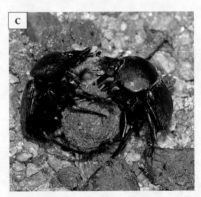

7.83 Herbivore dung is produced in large quantities in savanna regions, where it provides food for a host of dung beetle (Scarabaeidae: Scarabaeinae) species: (**a**) the dung-burying strategy of large *Pachylomera femoralis* varies between rolling and tunnelling, depending on competition pressure at the source; (**b**) *Garreta wahlbergi* scavenge on the margins of a large dung source; (**c**) *Kheper nigroaeneus* fighting over a food ball; (**d**) *Kheper* sp. (right), an obligatory herbivore dung roller, and *Chalconotus convexus*, a facultative dung or carrion feeder; (**e**) large male *Copris elphenor*, a tunneller.

Jenny Scholtz

7.84 Dung feeders other than dung beetles: (**a**) sepsid fly (Diptera: Sepsidae); (**b**) *Orthellia rhingaeiformis* (Diptera: Muscidae); (**c**) *Dolicaon lathrobioides* (Coleoptera: Staphylinidae); (**d**) lesser dung flies, *Ceroptera* sp. (Diptera: Sphaeroceridae), riding between dung sources on a dung beetle; (**e**) the final stages of dung decomposition by termites.

Insect communities in a dung pad

A detailed study on insect communities, undertaken near Pretoria by Gary Bernon of the Australian Dung Beetle Research Unit (DBRU, based in Pretoria), recorded between 700 and 1,500 individual beetles in single fresh cattle dung pads in summer. These belonged to 161 species, of which 42% were true dung beetles (Scarabaeidae: Scarabaeinae), 35% small dung beetles (Scarabaeidae: Aphodiinae), 9% water scavenger beetles (Hydrophilidae), 9% rove beetles (Staphylinidae) and 5% hister beetles (Histeridae). The Scarabaeinae, Aphodiinae and Hydrophilidae were probably all feeding on the dung itself, as were possibly some of the Staphylinidae. The other Staphylinidae and the Histeridae would have made up the bulk of the predatory guild that fed on the many fly maggots and mites.

Similar studies on cattle dung by Adrian Davis (then with the DBRU, currently at the University of Pretoria) in KwaZulu-Natal recorded 72 dung beetle species (up to 1,200 individuals), 100 Staphylinidae species, 21 Histeridae species and 13 Hydrophilidae species.

Other insects at dung

A host of insect species other than dung beetles may arrive quickly and compete with dung beetles for the resource (fig. 7.84). The morphologically and behaviourally similar but unrelated group of dung-feeding water scavenger beetles (Coleoptera: Hydrophilidae) are attracted to fresh dung. Small black ant-like flies that wave their wings at rest (Diptera: Sepsidae) and large bright green muscids and house flies (Muscidae) may also be present. Many predatory insects are also drawn to the dung – not for the dung, but to prey on the dung beetles, fly larvae and other insects in and around the dung. These are most commonly hister beetles (Histeridae) and rove beetles (Staphylinidae).

These other beetle species, dung beetles and fly maggots often co-exist in and feed on the dung (see box above), but if dung beetles colonise the dung first, they usually exclude flies mechanically by their tunnelling activity.

The dung beetles also provide transport from one dung source to another for many small dung-feeding flies and thousands of tiny flightless mites, some of which feed on the dung, whilst others are predatory on fly eggs in the dung. Ants are also usually present, waiting around the periphery of the dung for beetles to tunnel into it and open up passageways for them to access and feed on fly eggs and maggots. Finally, when most of the moist and nutritious dung has been fed on, removed, or buried, the dry scraps that remain are colonised by termites, which feed on the cellulose and lignin that were unusable to the earlier colonists.

Carrion feeders

The large numbers of antelope in the savannas support a correspondingly large guild of mammal predators and scavengers, and dead animals or prey remains left by mammal predators are quickly located and invaded by insects (see box, p. 254). Blow flies are the first wave of a fairly predictable succession of insects that invade animal remains. They are followed by predatory beetles that feed on the maggots. As the remains start to dry out, a fresh wave of consumers arrives. Flies and beetles feed on fats oozing from the skeletal parts and on the rich broth composed of body fluids and decomposing insects below the carcass. Finally, the last remains of tendons, skin, hair, hooves and horns are colonised by specialist keratin-feeding beetles and moths.

Blow flies: the first carcass colonisers

Flies are the first colonisers at carcasses. Metallic green and blue blow flies (Diptera: Calliphoridae, fig. 7.85) arrive very soon after the death of an animal and lay eggs in natural orifices (mouth, nose, anus) or wounds. The first species to arrive at a carcass is usually the greenbottle blow fly, *Lucilia sericata*, which lays 200–300 eggs that look like clusters of tiny rice grains. At large carcasses, the bluebottle blow fly, *Chrysomya marginalis*, also arrives early, and its larvae may become dominant. It is followed a few hours later by the copper-tailed blow fly, *C. chloropyga*, and a day or two later by the banded blow fly, *C. albiceps*. *Chrysomya* species lay 100–400 eggs and incubation takes 12–16 hours, depending on the particular species and air temperature; in cool weather it could take up to three days.

The emerging larvae are mostly white legless maggots, elongated and broadest at the end of the abdomen, which is blunt and flattened. The mouth is equipped with a pair of hooks that function as jaws. A pair of spiracles is located at the posterior end that protrudes from the fluids around the feeding maggot; this enables the maggot to breathe while feeding continuously. Feeding is facilitated by digestive enzymes in the maggots' excreta that break down proteins in the carcass, as well as mechanical grinding by the mouth hooks. Digestion takes place outside the bodies of the maggots, forming a broth that is sucked up; it also creates a liquid environment through which they can easily wriggle.

The larvae moult three times before pupation begins; *Lucilia sericata* larvae reach maturity about 90 hours (3.75 days) and *Chrysomya* species about five days after oviposition if air temperatures are high; in cold weather it may take up to three weeks. The maggots then seek out a suitable spot in which to pupate and bury themselves in the soil – either below or away from the carcass. The pupae resemble elongated oval capsules with a tough brown or black skin and are called puparia, as they are covered by the moulted skin of the last larval instar. The pupal stage lasts 7–10 days in summer, after which the adult fly emerges; larvae that reach full size in autumn may spend the winter either in the soil or as puparia.

Lucilia sericata, Chrysomya marginalis and *C. chloropyga* larvae are considered to be primary carrion feeders, while *C. albiceps* is both a carrion feeder and a predator of other maggot species. The flies often lay more eggs on the carcass than it can support, and since carrion is a highly ephemeral and often limited resource, there is intense competition for food and space among the feeding maggots. *Chrysomya albiceps* usually oviposits one or two days after the initial wave of blow flies and its larvae readily resort to predation of other maggots and even cannibalism, should the carcass become depleted before they have completed development. *Chrysomya albiceps* is also unique in that it is the only blow fly species in Africa whose larvae have characteristic outgrowths from the cuticle, which makes them easily recognisable – they are also called 'hairy maggots' (fig. 7.85b).

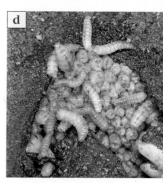

Steve Marshall

7.85 Flies associated with fresh carrion: (**a**) adult *Chrysomya albiceps* (Diptera: Calliphoridae); (**b**) *C. albiceps* larvae; (**c**) adult *C. marginalis* (Calliphoridae); (**d**) *C. marginalis* larvae; (**e**) *Calliphora croceipalpis* (top) and *Lucilia sericata* (bottom) (Calliphoridae); (**f**) house flies, *Musca domestica* (Muscidae), feed on carrion fluids, but do not usually breed in carcasses.

Other insects at the carcass

Soon after the fly larvae have hatched, the first wave of predators starts to arrive, attracted by the abundance of maggots. Most of them are beetles in the Histeridae and Staphylinidae, which are then followed by other species (fig. 7.86).

By the time the calliphorid fly maggots begin to pupate, the body fluids oozing from the carcass have usually formed a rich broth of decomposing tissue, insect faeces and the remains of dead insects under the carcass. This attracts another wave of small flies, including some from the house fly family (Muscidae), which lay eggs in the broth. Parasitic wasps that specialise on fly pupae also usually arrive at this stage.

Insects not typically associated with carrion might well be attracted because of a particular attribute of the carcass. Some dung beetles might be attracted to the carrion itself, for example, the large purple *Chalconotus convexus* (fig. 7.83d) and various *Onthophagus* species. If the dead animal was a herbivore, the gut content could attract various other dung-feeding dung beetle species.

As the carcass begins to dry out and the body fats turn rancid, it emits a smell characteristic of rotten dairy products – this is called the butyric fermentation stage. Another wave of flies invades the remains, consisting mainly of small cheese skippers, such as *Piophila megastigmata* (Piophilidae). The common name is derived from the larvae of the cosmopolitan species *P. casei*, which attack stored cheese and ham. They have the ability to 'jump': the larva grasps the folds of the tip of the abdomen with its mouth hooks, rolls into a ring and tenses its muscles; when it releases its grip, the larva is propelled up to 15cm away. Also often present at this stage is a small, elongate, green beetle with red legs, the cosmopolitan red-legged ham beetle, *Necrobia rufipes* (Coleoptera: Cleridae), which also feeds on fats.

Final-stage carcass colonisers

The final stage of decomposition of the carcass is when it dries out, leaving only skin, fur, hooves, horns, feathers and bones. Of these, everything except bones is fed on by insects. These remains are attractive to keratin

Steve Marshall

7.86 Carrion in later stages of decomposition attracts various insects to different fractions of the remains: (**a**) carrion-feeding 'dung' beetle *Onthophagus* sp. (Scarabaeidae: Scarabaeinae); (**b**) fly maggot predator (Coleoptera: Histeridae); (**c**) *Charaxes jasius saturnus* (Lepidoptera: Nymphalidae) attracted to minerals in carrion fluids; (**d**) red-legged ham beetle, *Necrobia rufipes* (Coleoptera: Cleridae), feeds on fatty carrion exudates, especially on bones; (**e**) cheese skipper, *Piophila casei* (Diptera: Piophilidae), whose larvae feed in fat fermentates; (**f**) carrion beetle larvae (Coleoptera: Silphidae) and (**g**) adults feed on late succession fleshy remains.

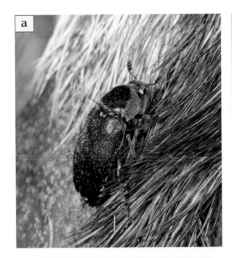

7.87 Hide beetle, *Dermestes maculatus* (Dermestidae), **(a)** adult and **(b)** larvae.

7.88 The final stage of keratin decomposition is undertaken by horn moths, *Ceratophaga* spp. (Lepidoptera: Tineidae), whose larvae tunnel into old horns and simultaneously build an external tube of silk and faeces in which they eventually pupate. **(a)** Old horns with protruding larval cases; **(b)** close view of larval tubes showing pupal exuviae at the ends; **(c)** freshly emerged horn moth, *C. vastella*.

beetles (Trogidae; see 'Keratin beetles of the Kalahari', alongside), hide and skin beetles (Dermestidae), and clothes or horn moths (Lepidoptera: Tineidae).

Hide and skin beetles, as their names imply, feed on a wide array of keratinous products. Some very small species also feed on dead insects (a few are pests in insect collections), the major component of whose exoskeleton is chitin, a similarly complex, but unrelated compound to keratin. The most familiar carrion species is the cosmopolitan *Dermestes maculatus* (fig. 7.87). Both adults and larvae feed on keratin and other dry tissue remains, although larvae live longer and feed more actively than adults.

The horn moth, *Ceratophaga vastella*, which has an unusual life style for a moth, is one of the very last species in the long line of succession from fresh carcass to hoof, bone and horn remains. The adult, which does not feed, is a yellow-brown moth with a wingspan of about 12mm, and is seldom seen. Signs of the larvae and their feeding, however, are very characteristic on old horns (fig. 7.88). The larvae tunnel into the horns and build a tough cocoon of silk and faeces that protrudes about 1cm from the horn. Pupation takes place in this tube. The mature pupa wriggles to the exit and the moth emerges there. Cast-off pupal skin protrudes from the mouth of the tube for many months after adult emergence. Old horns may have many of these tubes protruding from them and they may remain on the horns for very long periods.

Keratin beetles of the Kalahari

Africa has the richest keratin beetle (Coleoptera: Trogidae) fauna in the world – a total of about 80 species. More than half occur in southern Africa in the genera *Omorgus* and *Phoberus* (see 'Ancient keratin-feeding beetles', p. 291).

Omorgus consists of an ancient group of biologically fascinating beetles already present during the dinosaur era (fig. 7.89). Both adults and larvae are capable of digesting keratin, the complex protein of which scales, feathers, hair, horns and hooves consist; no vertebrates have the gut enzymes necessary to digest this material.

The genus is widespread in savanna areas. Some species are capable of flight, whereas others are flightless, particularly in arid savanna areas (in common with many other unrelated beetle groups). Flight-capable species can quickly cover large distances to locate ephemeral keratin sources, but while flightless species do not have such an option, they are well adapted to overcome this hurdle.

Although keratin is ephemeral, closer inspection reveals that there are numerous, albeit often small, pieces of keratinous material to be found in the form of feathers, as well as scales, fur and feather remains in carnivore faeces and raptor 'pellets' (regurgitated indigestible fragments). Keratin also weathers very slowly, so remains may lie on the ground virtually intact for years (see box, p. 255).

7.89 Keratin beetles (Trogidae): (**a**) *Omorgus* spp. are common and abundant on late-stage carcasses in savannas; (**b**) *Phoberus squamiger* is active on carcass remains under cool conditions.

The survival of flightless *Omorgus* species in the Kalahari can be attributed to this wider-than-expected availability of small keratin fragments, which serve to sustain them until they chance on sufficiently large remains to allow successful breeding. Furthermore, walking is less energy-intensive than flying, so considerably less energy is expended in finding food and mates and this saved resource can be invested in increased reproduction.

Another advantage for flightless beetles is that they are usually more convex than their winged relatives, because the thorax shortens when the flight muscles degenerate. This increased convexity increases the volume of the subelytral cavity – the space between the top of the abdomen and the underside of the elytra – into which the spiracles open. This is an adaptation to arid habitats, as the larger volume of the subelytral cavity limits the loss of respiratory water (see 'Flightless beetles', p. 139).

Carrion insects on carcasses in the Kruger National Park

Some of the most comprehensive studies of the process of decomposition and successional colonisation of a carcass under natural conditions in South Africa were done by Leo Braack (currently at the University of Pretoria) in the Kruger National Park.

The studies involved insect succession during mid-summer in the decomposition process of impala carcasses (about 60kg each). The entire process – from freshly dead to only hair, bone and horn remains – took an average of just 11 days.

A total of 227 species of arthropods (97% were insects) in 36 families utilised or visited the carcasses. Total insect numbers as well as maximum species numbers peaked on days 4 and 5 after death. The insects were predominantly in the orders Diptera and Coleoptera. Fly larvae were most numerous, feeding primarily on the soft tissue of the carcass during the early stages of decomposition. Most of these were blow flies (Calliphoridae), with more than 210,000 maggots at a carcass belonging to *Chrysomya marginalis*. Beetle predators (mainly Histeridae), feeding on the abundant fly maggots, were the next most numerous group, often with more than 20,000 individuals at a carcass.

The first-instar larvae of another calliphorid species, *C. albiceps,* fed on soft tissue of the decomposing carcass, while the older larvae (second and third instars) became facultatively predatory and fed on *C. marginalis* larvae along with the beetles. Other flies (Muscidae, Piophilidae and Sepsidae) were also present.

Beetles of the families Staphylinidae and Trogidae were present from day 1 until day 11, and beetles of the Cleridae had peaks on days 6 and 11. Dung beetles (46 species) were attracted to the rumen contents.

Parasitic wasps reached maximum abundance on day 10. The late arrival at the carcass of these fly pupal parasitoids can be explained by the abundance of pupae at this stage. About 5–6% of *C. albiceps* pupae were parasitised by two wasp species. Although *C. marginalis* numbers were higher than those of *C. albiceps*, they were not parasitised at all, possibly because *C. albiceps* pupae lie exposed in a concentrated mass near the carcass, whereas *C. marginalis* larvae disperse away from the carcass, burrow into the soil, and pupate underground.

Ants were present in high numbers throughout the process as general predators and scavengers.

The skins of the dead impala were fed on predominantly by adults and larvae of *Dermestes maculatus* (Coleoptera: Dermestidae) – numbers in excess of 3,000 were counted at a carcass. Keratin beetles (Trogidae) were present to the end.

Survival strategies of *Omorgus freyi*

In the winter of 1985, an opportunity arose for Clarke Scholtz and colleagues from the University of Pretoria to study the survival strategies of *Omorgus freyi* (fig. 7.90), a wingless keratin beetle. During this severe winter drought, about 20,000 antelope died within a few weeks in the Kgalagadi Transfrontier Park. This sudden abundance of carrion overwhelmed the vertebrate carrion feeders. Because it was winter, there were few blow flies and other carrion-feeding insects active, so hundreds of whole carcasses dried out and lay in the same place, where they remained virtually unchanged for up to four years. The carcasses provided an ideal opportunity for Scholtz and his colleagues to study the beetle's survival strategies.

As the environment dries out between rainfall events in summer, adult *O. freyi* become progressively less active and more and more of them burrow into the soil beneath the carcass. There they switch off major physiological processes and may remain in a quiescent state (see 'Dormancy', p. 44) for up to three months, until conditions become favourable for activity once more. Males store mature sperm in their testes and sperm ducts, and females stop egg development at whatever stage is current when conditions deteriorate. Larvae also burrow down into the soil.

Within hours of rain, however, the adults and larvae become active and resume their feeding and breeding activities as if there had been no interruption. This ensures that they can start to feed, mate and lay eggs immediately after conditions improve, as this favourable state may not last for long. In this way, large populations build up over the time that the carcass is undisturbed.

Eggs and pupae, however, are unable to survive dry conditions. Consequently, females only lay eggs after rain, and mature larvae only pupate when the soil is wet. The duration of these stages is short (7–10 days each) and they can usually be completed after even a small amount of rain has fallen.

The study also revealed that during periods of activity after rain, the adult beetles have two distinct activity peaks – one in the evening, and the other early in the morning. Beetle behaviour differs substantially during these two peaks.

Mating and social activities occur during the evening peak, while temperatures are still high, and the behaviour is frenetic: dozens of stridulating beetles run around; males attempt to mate with anything remotely resembling a female, including sand clods or other males; and nonreceptive females try to escape from the attentions of males. Morning activity, on the other hand, is quiet, with beetles crawling out of the ground, climbing onto a piece of suitable food, and feeding.

The explanation for the different activity peaks is simple: the beetles are dependent on an environmental temperature above about 25°C for intense activity, and as summer evening temperatures in the Kalahari are often above 30°C until about midnight, evening social activity is possible. However, with mostly clear skies at night, radiant heat loss from the soil is high, leading to cold mornings and precipitation of dew just before sunrise. These low temperatures limit early morning activity, but the dew is absorbed by the keratin, making it more attractive for the beetles and supplementing their water intake in the early morning hours.

As the autumn days start to shorten, ambient temperatures decrease and the soil becomes progressively drier. Now, male and female beetles stop producing sperm and eggs and resorb any still in their reproductive systems; the energy saved by doing this is needed for the long, irreversible 6–7-month-long winter diapause (see 'Dormancy', p. 44).

7.90 The flightless Kalahari endemic *Omorgus freyi* (Trogidae) subsists on small pieces of keratin, such as fur in pellets regurgitated by owls, and feathers.

CHAPTER 8
INDIAN OCEAN TROPICAL BELT

This region is generally known as the Indian Ocean Coastal Belt, but because of its 'coastal' association and the possible confusion that may arise with the Coastal Zone (chapter 13) we refer to it as the Indian Ocean Tropical Belt. It stretches in a narrow strip from coastal Mozambique in the north to roughly East London in the south, and is essentially a southern extension of the mainly central African tropics (known as Tropical Broadleaved Moist Forest), which gives it a strikingly tropical character (fig. 8.1). The part that falls in the Eastern Cape is known as Pondoland, while Maputaland straddles the border between northern KwaZulu-Natal and Mozambique; both are areas of particularly high plant endemicity.

 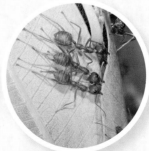

Rina de Klerk

8.1 (pp. 256–257) The Indian Ocean Tropical Belt is characterised by dense broad-leaved tree vegetation.

8.2 (left) Although the Indian Ocean Tropical Belt has similarities with the neighbouring savanna, it has distinctive tropical aspects such as lianas and epiphytes.

Rain in the Indian Ocean Tropical Belt falls mostly in summer, but as much as 40% of the total may fall during winter. The region shares many elements with the adjoining savanna, but it is distinguished by the year-round rainfall and characteristic 'tropical' vegetation – a mixture of trees, lianas and epiphytes (fig. 8.2). The narrow coastal zone that it forms along southern Africa's east coast is only a thin extension of the huge Central African tropical forest block, which is largely fragmented by savanna intrusions.

The insects encountered here reflect a mix of typical tropical and mostly widespread savanna species. Few can be considered endemic to the region, and fewer still are sufficiently well known to be considered iconic representatives of the biome, although at least two Nymphalidae butterfly species fit the definition (figs 8.3, 8.4): *Euphaedra neophron neophron* and *Sevenia boisduvali boisduvali*; *E. n. neophron* is restricted to dense forests where the butterflies fly in clearings close to the ground (fig. 8.3a). They feed only on fallen, fermenting fruit. Larvae feed on species of Sapindaceae (fig. 8.3b). *Sevenia boisduvali boisduvali* may become abundant in the biome, with mass emergences and localised migrations (fig. 8.4).

Besides the butterflies, there are four other insect groups worth mentioning. These are the subsocial colonial webspinners; weaver ants that live in nests constructed of leaves spun together with larval silk; and two blood-feeding groups of flies – mosquitoes and tsetse flies – which, although not strictly restricted to the biome, are synonymous with it, as they thrive in the humid environment typical of the region. They are vectors of serious human and livestock diseases.

André Coetzer

André Coetzer

8.3 *Euphaedra neophron neophron* (Nymphalidae), one of the few endemic butterflies restricted to tropical forests: **(a)** adult; **(b)** larva.

8.4 *Sevenia boisduvali boisduvali* (Nymphalidae): **(a)** a few adults clustering together; **(b)** a large number after a mass emergence during a localised migration.

Detritus feeders

This tropical region is home to a characteristic and important group of insects, the webspinners, which perform an important ecological role as consumers of moist detritus, tree bark, lichens and mosses.

Webspinners

Embioptera is a small order of mainly tropical and subtropical communal insects that live in colonies of related individuals. Little is known about the southern African fauna, of which only a few species have officially been named, although about 40 are known to occur in the region. They are mostly in the family Embiidae, and are robust insects 15–20mm long. Another local family, Teratembiidae, consists of small, delicate insects, 5–10mm long. The Asian family Oligotomidae is represented in southern Africa by the introduced Indian species *Oligotoma saundersii*, which is common along the tropical east coast. Species of Archembiidae, although not yet officially recorded from southern Africa, are known to occur here.

As their common name suggests, they spin mazes of often extensive silken webs covering tree stems and branches, or lining tunnels under bark or among tree roots, and live in these enclosures (fig. 8.5), where they feed on detritus, algae and lichens; the silk is thus central to colony life (see box below). The tunnels provide an environment with a stable microclimate that is relatively safe from predators and parasites, and affords protected access to food.

The silk is produced by the uniquely swollen basal segment of the foretarsus, which houses numerous silk glands with external pore openings, which extrude liquid silk that solidifies in air. By stroking the foretarsi against the substrate, silken strands adhere to it and are then stretched further. This is repeated until a fairly dense covering of silk is produced. Embioptera is the only insect order in which all nymph stages, as well as adult males and females, spin silk. Also, it is one of very few insect groups in which insects continue to spin silk throughout their lives. Furthermore, no other insects have silk glands in their tarsi – they either produce silk from labial glands in the mouth (e.g. Lepidoptera and Hymenoptera larvae) or from modified Malpighian tubules (which usually function in removing waste chemicals from the haemolymph, e.g. Neuroptera).

8.5 Webspinners (Embioptera) are most abundant in the tropical parts of southern Africa: (a) a nymph inside its silken web; (b) an adult male; (c) an adult female.

The role of silk in webspinner colonies

Silk – one of the strongest natural fibres – is central to colony life and performs many functions.
- It is used in the construction of the galleries in which the colony members live.
- It moderates the temperature and humidity in the galleries.
- It facilitates rapid communication between individuals induced by body vibration in response to threats; they communicate with other colony members by tapping on the silk sheets, a behaviour that is thought to respond mainly to a nest defence breach. Such a warning induces the individuals spread across the extensive system of silk galleries to retreat into the safety of denser silk tunnels.
- It provides a medium for covering faeces to lower the chances of fungal development in the colony; the insects usually pick up their faecal pellets with their mandibles after defecating and place them into gallery walls, where they isolate them with a covering of silk.
- It affords a degree of physical protection against predators and parasitoids. One family of wasps (Hymenoptera: Sclerogibbidae) are specialised parasitoids of only Embioptera. These small wasps (2.2–6.5mm long) are ectoparasitoids on embiopteran nymphs; males are winged and females wingless. Webspinners are also victims of spider and ant predation.

Individuals are highly modified for moving forwards and backwards equally rapidly in their silken tunnels, which are too narrow to enable the insects to turn around. The insects are slender, with a prognathous (forward-projecting) head and enlarged muscular hind femurs to aid in rapid movement. The cerci at the tip of the abdomen are highly sensitive to touch and function as navigation aids when the insect runs backwards. Males of most species are winged (fig. 8.5b), whereas females are always wingless (fig. 8.5c). The wings are also modified for life in an enclosed space – they are flaccid and fold forwards if snagged on the edge of a tunnel when the insect runs backwards. Before flight, however, the larger wing veins are pumped full of haemolymph to stiffen them.

Colonies develop from a mature female who builds a small gallery in which she lays a batch of 5–10 eggs, covering them with bark and several silk layers. Although this covering affords the eggs some protection, it hinders the emergence of the newly hatched nymphs – they can only escape with assistance from the female. She protects the eggs and young nymphs from parasites and predators for the several weeks of their development, during which she does not feed. She then continues to care for early-stage nymphs that start to expand the colony as they grow and seek new sources of food.

Parasitic wasp species appear to be the main egg and nymph predators; the female webspinner attempts to repel invading wasps by lunging at them when they enter the galleries. In experiments, the survival rate of eggs and nymphs attended by the female was much higher than those without an attendant female.

The nymph stages last 4–6 months. After maturing, the female offspring may also remain in the colony and breed, and their progeny, in turn, will continue to expand the nest until an extensive web of silk with hundreds of tunnels and silken chambers may cover the habitat.

Only nymphs and female webspinners feed; males do not feed, although they have well-developed mouthparts that are used exclusively for holding the female during copulation. Soon after maturing, males leave the natal colony to find and mate with females in nearby colonies – often their close relatives. The males die after mating or within a short while if unsuccessful in their reproductive quest. Parthenogenesis is common in the order.

Females die before their offspring have matured, and webspinners are therefore considered 'subsocial' insects. One of the requirements to qualify as truly social or 'eusocial' (such as termites, some wasps and bees), is that there must be overlapping generations of parents and offspring.

Predators

Although the region has the usual suite of insect and other arthropod predators, the dominant predatory species is without doubt the African weaver ant, a widespread tropical eastern species. These ants are chiefly arboreal and aggressively pursue, capture and dismember their prey, which, likewise, mainly occurs on the surrounding forest trees.

The woven-leaf nests of weaver ants

The distribution of the arboreal African weaver ant, *Oecophylla longinoda* (Hymenoptera: Formicidae: Formicinae – for detailed ant biology, see 'Ant biology and behaviour', p. 159), in southern Africa reaches down the coast as far south as the tip of Lake St Lucia. The ants 'weave' tree leaves together with silk produced by their larvae, which are used as 'shuttles', to form compact nest chambers in trees (see box opposite). The term weaver ant is also used for

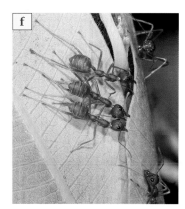

8.6 (opposite & above) The nests of weaver ants, *Oecophylla longinoda* (Formicidae: Formicinae), are formed by enclosing clumps of leaves with larval silk. Different elements of the colony are housed in separate clumps. The nests are formed around living leaves (**a**), but the ants continue to use older nest compartments (**b**). (**c**) Major and minor workers; (**d**) workers with brood; (**e**) workers preparing a leaf edge for folding; (**f**) beginning the nest-building process, workers grasp a leaf edge and pull together, rolling the edge over; (**g**) a worker holding a larva at the join between leaves and moving it back and forth like the shuttle of a loom, weaving the leaves together with larval silk.

Weaving nests

The unique method of nest construction used by weaver ants is one of the unusual attributes of this species. Workers start by inspecting leaves and in a new, potential site, tugging at the leaf margins to test their flexibility. If the leaf can be bent over, the ant is joined by more workers that bite onto the leaf margin and start to roll it over (fig. 8.6f). They are then joined by other workers that grasp onto their petiole (waist; see chapter 5, fig. 5.14, p. 162), forming chains of tugging workers. Multiple chains form on adjoining leaves and the ants start to ratchet them together. Once the leaves are drawn together, mature larvae are retrieved from the nest to 'weave' the leaves together. The larvae arch their body into a shallow S-shape while the workers hold them, antennating them on the head. The larvae then start to produce sticky silk from their labial glands and the workers move them back and forth across the leaf margins requiring stitching, like the shuttle of a weaving loom (fig. 8.6g).

two other groups, the Old World genus *Polyrhachis*, with eight southern African species, and the tropical American *Camponotus* (subgenus *Dendromyrmex*).

The genus *Oecophylla* consists of two extant species, the African *O. longinoda*, and *O. smaragdina* from southern India, Southeast Asia and northern tropical Australia (where they are known as 'green ants', because some individuals have bright green abdomens). It is an ancient genus, once more widespread, and is known from the fossils of several extinct species, mainly from Germany (of Eocene age, about 40 million years ago).

Oecophylla longinoda has several unusual and interesting biological attributes. The ants are obligate tree dwellers and their nests consist of several pockets of woven leaves (fig. 8.6) containing different stages of brood development. Nests may be extensive, often spreading over several adjoining trees, and colonies may be enormous, numbering up to 500,000 workers. There are two distinct worker castes, major and minor; major workers are 8–10mm long and minor workers are half that length. Minor workers function chiefly as brood nurses in the nests, but sometimes also harvest honeydew from bugs close to the nest.

Major workers operate mainly outside the nest, maintaining, defending and expanding it and hunting for prey; they have large, toothed mandibles with which they kill and dismember prey – mainly arthropods, but also small vertebrates. They also use their mandibles in defence, swarming over an intruder, biting and 'stinging' aggressively. Large numbers drop from branches overhead ('ant rain') onto potential intruders such as browsing mammals or inquisitive humans, crawling over and 'stinging' the victim repeatedly. This is sufficient to deter all but the most persistent entomologist!

The 'stinging' sensation is actually the result of formic acid being sprayed onto the bite wound (see 'The pugnacious ant', p. 191). All ants of the subfamily Formicinae, to which *O. longinoda* belongs, have a special glandular opening (acidopore), surrounded by a fringe of setae at the tip of the abdomen that channels and sprays the formic acid secretion outwards. More primitive ant species (see 'Matabele ants', p. 243), as well as bees and wasps, sting by inserting their modified ovipositor into the victim and injecting venom into the wound.

Colonies and new nests are established by a mated queen finding a protected site amongst leaves near the outer perimeter of a tree; this is to avoid potentially intruding into an existing colony's territory. There she lays eggs and protects them and then nurses the larvae until they mature and take over the work functions of the colony. As the colony size increases, it expands into new nest satellites constructed by the ever-increasing numbers of workers.

In virtually all ant species, except the weaver ants, the mature larvae produce silk for spinning the cocoon in which they eventually pupate. The cocoons provide protection for the pupae, and are the large, oblong, white objects that workers in a disturbed ant colony quickly gather and try to move to a protected location away from danger. However, in weaver ants, the larval silk is used for nest construction, and none remains for spinning cocoons; consequently, the pupae lie naked in the nests.

Female *O. longinoda* larvae have larger silk glands and they are used more often by workers during nest building than are male larvae. Researchers think this phenomenon supports the kin-selection hypothesis in social Hymenoptera, which states that because females are more closely related to each other (as they share the same mother and father) than they are to their brothers (with which they share only their mother – males are produced parthenogenetically from unfertilised eggs, and are haploid), they are more likely to contribute to colony needs than are males.

Blood feeders

The tropical regions of Africa are home to various blood-feeding fly parasites of mammals, including humans. Although their primary ecological role is that of feeding on the blood of various hosts, a secondary, and important role, from a human and animal health perspective, is that they carry and transmit pathogenic microorganisms to the host. These insects include mosquitoes and tsetse flies, the vectors of malaria and sleeping sickness in humans and nagana in livestock. Although nagana is viewed as a serious livestock disease with economic and social implications for rural agriculture, tsetse flies have, until recently, helped maintain some of the most pristine natural areas on the continent by preventing invasion by livestock – examples are the Zululand coast and the Okavango Delta in Botswana. These areas are now being rapidly degraded by overgrazing after the successful control of tsetse flies.

Mosquitoes and their biology

Mosquitoes (Diptera: Culicidae) are ubiquitous, well-known insects because of the nuisance value of the whining, biting, blood-sucking females. Some species are vectors of very serious human and domestic animal diseases, of which malaria is undoubtedly one of the most widespread and dangerous insect-borne human diseases across the world's tropics.

Culicidae (see 'Aquatic flies', p. 339) are divided into two subfamilies, Culicinae and Anophelinae, each with distinctive morphology and behaviour. Several genera in southern Africa, including *Culex* (figs 8.7a, b, d), *Aedes* (figs 8.7c, 8.8), *Toxorhynchites* (fig. 8.9) and *Skusea* (see box opposite), belong to Culicinae, whereas *Anopheles* (fig. 8.11) is the only genus in Anophelinae.

Females lay floating eggs, either singly, as in *Anopheles*, or in clusters ('rafts', fig. 8.7a) in most culicines. All mosquito larvae are aquatic (fig. 8.7). Culicinae larvae live in still water of various types, while those of Anophelinae live mostly in running water. The water types preferred by culicines may be divided into 'groundwater' and 'container' habitats; groundwater habitats

8.7 The mosquito life cycle: (**a**) a raft of *Culex* eggs floating on water; (**b**) *Culex* larvae; (**c**) *Aedes* pupa and larvae; (**d**) *Culex* adult emerging from the pupa at the water surface.

Skusea pembaensis and mangrove crabs

One remarkable East African mosquito species, *Skusea pembaensis* (formerly *Aedes pembaensis*), is a specialised groundwater breeder: it makes use of holes of the mangrove crab, *Neosesarmatium meinerti* (formerly *Sesarma meinerti*), in tidal mangrove estuaries. Although the detritus-feeding crab occurs in mangrove swamps along the East African coast as far south as northern KwaZulu-Natal, as well as on several Indian Ocean islands, including Madagascar, the mosquito has so far not been collected south of Maputo in Mozambique. Female mosquitoes perch in the near vicinity of the entrance to crab burrows and when a crab emerges, the mosquito attaches eggs to its carapace. The eggs hatch when submerged in the water at the bottom of the burrow after the crab returns to its burrow. There the larvae develop.

are subdivided further into permanent (ponds, lakes, dams), temporary (rain pools) or specialised (e.g. crab holes, in which *Skusea pembaensis* breeds in the northern part of the biome). Natural container habitats include rot holes in trees and rock pools, but water-filled human-made objects such as tyres and cans are favourite habitat for many species.

Some *Aedes* species, including the cosmopolitan pest *A. aegypti*, lay eggs in ephemeral pools; the eggs dry out when the pool does and may lie in the dust for years. Eventually, after rain when the pools fill up again, the eggs hatch and the larvae develop. This strategy is one of the reasons for certain sporadic disease epidemics such as Rift Valley fever in drier regions of southern Africa.

Most mosquito larvae feed on tiny organic particles suspended in the water; *Toxorhynchites* larvae, however, are predators of other mosquito and midge larvae. *Anopheles* larvae hang just below and parallel to the water surface, while culicine larvae move vertically up and down in the water. All mosquito larvae breathe atmospheric air; those of *Anopheles* breathe directly through abdominal spiracles, while culicines use a breathing tube that is connected to terminal abdominal spiracles. In *Culex* (fig. 8.7b) the breathing tube is long and slender, while in *Aedes* it is short and stout (fig. 8.7c).

Mosquito pupae are curved and active, moving vertically up and down in the water, particularly if disturbed. They also breathe at the surface, through two horn-like structures on the dorsal thorax (fig. 8.7c). Adults emerge from the pupa at the water surface (fig. 8.7d).

Adult mosquitoes are sexually dimorphic and easily separable – males have bushy, plumose antennae (see box, p. 264), whereas those of females have sparse, short hairs. In *Anopheles*, the maxillary palps of males and females are as long as the proboscis, while in the culicines, female palps are much shorter. *Anopheles* are usually dark mosquitoes with patterned wings, *Culex* are usually silvery-brown, *Aedes* are mostly small with black-and-white banded legs, and *Toxorhynchites* are almost twice the size of any other mosquito. At rest, *Anopheles* adults sit with the body at roughly a right angle to the surface, while culicines sit with the body parallel to the surface.

All adult male and female mosquitoes feed on plant juices, but prior to the eggs developing, females (except those of *Toxorhynchites*) need extra protein, which they obtain from blood sucked from a vertebrate host. Because *Toxorhynchites* (fig. 8.9) larvae feed on other insect larvae, they obtain enough protein during their development to enable the adult female to produce eggs without a blood meal, hence they feed only on plant juices.

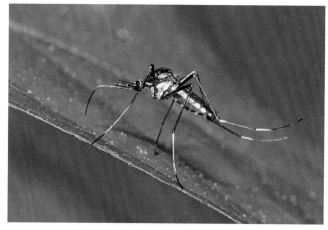

8.8 Female *Aedes* (Diptera: Culicidae) mosquitoes suck the blood of humans and other animals and may transmit disease. They are common across southern Africa but the diseases caused are sporadic.

8.9 *Toxorhynchites* mosquitoes are common in tropical areas, but do not feed on blood because their predatory larvae acquire sufficient animal protein from their food for egg development in the females.

Male mosquitoes have bushy antennae (fig. 8.10), the function of which is for hearing the sound produced by the wing beats of females in a prelude to mating. The common, familiar sound is the 'whine' produced by female mosquitoes during flight. Not only is this a highly irritating sound for a potential human victim, but it attracts males to the flying female and they then mate in flight. Different species produce species-specific wing beat frequencies that males of that species are able to distinguish from others.

In *Anopheles gambiae*, males beat their wings about 690 times per second and females about 460 times per second. The differences in frequencies are because of size differences between the sexes – males are smaller than females and beat their wings faster. Mate and species recognition are dependent on the sexes' ability to harmonise their wing beat frequencies – to do this they speed up or slow down their wing beats and shift the pitch up or down until together they produce a harmonic tone of about 1,500Hz, which neither can hear! They then mate. If the sexes belong to different species of mosquito they are unable to harmonise and, consequently, avoid mating.

8.10 A male mosquito uses his bushy antennae to hear the female's wing beat in a prelude to mating.

Anopheles gambiae (fig. 8.11) and *A. arabiensis* are the main vectors of malaria in southern Africa. The disease-causing organisms are protozoa of the genus *Plasmodium*. Although the mosquitoes are found in most parts of southern Africa, malaria is restricted to those areas where infected hosts already occur – when a mosquito feeds on an infected person, the parasite is ingested with the blood meal and transferred to another person at the next meal. So, although malaria is mainly restricted to particular areas, occasional cases are reported far from these areas – this happens when an infected mosquito is transported by human activity to the distant place where it feeds on, and infects, a human.

The yellow fever mosquito, *Aedes aegypti*, which is present in southern Africa, transmits the yellow fever virus; although common in tropical regions of countries such as Angola and northern Mozambique, it is absent in much of southern Africa. *Aedes aegypti*, along with other

species of *Aedes*, is also a vector of Rift Valley fever and the fast-spreading Oriental dengue fever, which is present in East Africa, but currently absent in southern Africa.

Culex is not responsible for any human or domestic animal diseases in southern Africa, but it hosts several viruses and nematode worms that infect people, mainly in West Africa.

Tsetse flies as carriers of disease

Tsetse flies (fig. 8.12) belong to the small family Glossinidae (Diptera), with about 22 species; and together with the Hippoboscidae, which is a much larger family, they belong to the superfamily Hippoboscoidea. The members of this superfamily have larval development analogous to foetal development in mammals, a phenomenon known as a pupiparous condition (fig. 8.12b; see 'Parasitic flies'. p. 353).

Glossinidae flies are restricted to Africa between 29°S and 14°N and are renowned throughout the continent as the vectors of the human disease sleeping sickness (African trypanosomiasis) and the livestock disease nagana. The diseases are caused by flagellated protozoans of the genus *Trypanosoma*.

Sleeping sickness is a serious, debilitating and often fatal disease that is widespread in West, East and Central Africa, as well as some northern parts of the southern African region. *Glossina palpalis* and *G. morsitans* are the main vectors of sleeping sickness and the principal disease-causing organisms they transmit are *Trypanosoma brucei gambiense* in West and west-central Africa and *T. brucei rhodesiense* in east-central Africa.

8.11 *Anopheles gambiae*, one of the vectors of malaria in southern Africa, feeding on a human. Malaria is prevalent in the tropical areas of southern Africa.

a

b

c

Rina de Klerk

8.13 Clumps of trees adjoining grassland are ideal sheltering habitat from which tsetse flies fly out in daylight to feed on grazing mammals.

8.12 (a) The tsetse fly, *Glossina austeni* (Diptera: Glossinidae), has replaced various other *Glossina* species as the main host of nagana in KwaZulu-Natal. *Glossina austeni* females give live birth to mature larvae, which pupate immediately; **(b)** the pupae are encased in the final larval exuviae. **(c)** *Glossina austeni* sucking blood from a human.

Rina de Klerk

8.14 The blue wildebeest, *Connochaetes taurinus*, is a host of the *Trypanosoma* blood parasite, which is transmitted by tsetse flies and causes nagana in cattle.

Nagana, however, is endemic to large parts of Africa, including the Maputaland region of northeastern KwaZulu-Natal and southeastern Mozambique. Periodic outbreaks claim thousands of livestock, mainly cattle, which are the agricultural mainstay of rural people in the region. Nagana in Maputaland is transmitted by *G. brevipalpis* and *G. austeni*, and the causative organisms are *T. vivax* and *T. congolense* in cattle, *T. brucei brucei* in horses, and *T. simiae* in pigs.

The flies are confined to subtropical evergreen forests and thickets, or other densely or semiforested subtropical areas, often near water courses. There they feed by day on passing mammals. They occasionally venture into open areas (fig. 8.13) adjacent to their preferred wooded habitat to suck the blood of suitable hosts (fig. 8.14). Although they feed on indigenous as well as domestic mammals, the indigenous species are immune to nagana, but nevertheless serve as reservoirs for the parasites.

Nagana in southern Africa

Before the end of the 19th century, *Glossina morsitans*, a vector of nagana, occurred in parts of the savanna along the eastern border of South Africa and Mozambique in the area roughly equivalent to the present-day Kruger National Park, and along the Limpopo valley for some distance into the interior of the country. Early European pioneers reported from about the 1830s that 'fly-disease' was killing their cattle, but as the settlers killed off the game and cleared the bush for cultivation, tsetse flies retreated into smaller and smaller enclaves. Then in 1896–1897 the rinderpest virus epizootic (epidemic) that killed an estimated five million cattle and countless millions of wild ungulates in southern Africa, killed off most of the cattle and remaining game animals in the area. This also led to the local extinction of *G. morsitans* and it has never re-established in South Africa.

The situation in Zululand, however, was that historically *G. pallidipes* was the most common vector of nagana, and although *G. brevipalpis* and *G. austeni* were present in localised areas, they were not considered to be serious disease vectors.

Nagana (the Zulu name for the disease) was known to Zulu farmers and earliest records date back to about 1840, but the flies were partially suppressed by hunting wild animals and bush clearing. In 1897, when Zululand was annexed by Britain, game preservation laws were introduced and game reserves were proclaimed, but the rinderpest epizootic kept the situation under control for a while. However, after the epizootic ended, cattle herds on farms and game numbers in the reserves slowly increased, with several localised outbreaks of nagana occurring at different times until about 1921, when farmers pressurised the Natal administration to deproclaim reserves in nagana areas, and proclaim new ones in disease-free areas.

Then, a large outbreak of nagana in 1929 saw the introduction of the legalised killing of game animals in and around iMfolozi Game Reserve, when more than 27,000 wild animals were killed. This, and the deployment of the so-called 'Harris trap', appeared to bring nagana under control. A Harris trap consists of a dark vertical sheet of animal hide (or some other material) with a one-way collecting funnel and cage at the top; the flies are attracted to the hide, walk up it into the cage, and are contained until they can be destroyed.

8.15 Hippos such as this one were not culled during the nagana control programme in Zululand, although they are one of the hosts of the disease. The red-billed oxpeckers, *Buphagus erythrorhynchus*, feeding on this hippo were also inadvertent victims of the insecticide spraying and had to re-colonise afterwards.

8.16 Lake Sibaya in KwaZulu-Natal, which is surrounded by the perfect forest habitat for tsetse fly (Glossinidae) species.

In 1942, another outbreak of the disease occurred. A second wild animal eradication programme was launched, with more than 130,000 game animals killed over the 10-year life of the programme. These included many wild animals that serve as reservoirs, such as wildebeest and zebra, but charismatic species, such as rhinos and hippos (fig. 8.15), which also serve as reservoirs, were excluded, so the programme did little to stem the disease.

During this period, and just after World War II ended in 1945, the chlorinated hydrocarbon pesticides had just been developed, and benzene hexachloride (BHC) was sprayed from the air, while the other 'miracle pesticide', dichlorodiphenyltrichloroethane (DDT) was simultaneously sprayed around human habitations. The continued use of the pesticides on a large scale eventually permanently eradicated *G. pallidipes* by 1954.

Around this time, another major agricultural development commenced in Zululand: the commercial planting of pine and eucalyptus trees in grassland areas created ideal forested conditions for tsetse fly populations to build up in areas that were previously unsuitable. Until then, little attention had been paid to the other tsetse fly species in Zululand, *G. austeni*

(fig. 8.12c) and *G. brevipalpis,* and because they have different habitat preferences (fig. 8.16) and do not occur sympatrically with *G. pallidipes,* their populations had been largely unaffected by the control measures. In 1990, another outbreak of nagana occurred. More than 20,000 cattle died. However, as this happened during a very bad drought year, it wasn't possible to distinguish between deaths caused by nagana and those brought on by the effects of drought.

Since then, control measures in South Africa have turned to environmentally friendly techniques that involve attracting the flies to traps baited with various synthetic odours that simulate cattle breath, urine and other volatile odours that animals produce naturally, where they are killed by pesticide-soaked surfaces or an electrified grid.

The environmental consequences of blanket spraying of insecticides, although never empirically measured, probably resulted in, at least, the disruption of indigenous orchid pollination (see box below). No doubt, more recent but similarly extreme measures to control tsetse flies with pesticides in the Okavango Delta in Botswana will have equally unintended and unpredictable consequences.

What happens when a system loses pollinators?

The Hluhluwe-iMfolozi Game Reserve in KwaZulu-Natal is considered to be the region in southern Africa with the most extensive, diverse and best-preserved coastal dry savanna plant communities. However, orchids (fig. 8.17), which are present in adjoining areas, are absent in the reserve. Why is this?

It has been speculated that heavy concentrations of game could have led to the destruction of the underground rhizomes of the terrestrial orchid species; this may have prevented asexual reproduction from taking place. However, it is very likely that sexual reproduction of both terrestrial and epiphytic orchids was inhibited by the accidental destruction of their insect pollinators – a result of the extensive and intensive use of the pesticides DDT and BHC for the control of tsetse flies in game reserves in 1947–1950.

Orchids are very vulnerable to disruption of the intimate relationship with their pollinator communities, most of which would have disappeared along with the tsetse flies.

We thus have a situation where an area was set aside specifically for the protection of its wildlife and accompanying environment, but as a result of a management system that was ignorant of the ecological requirements of its members, a major and obvious component was totally destroyed.

8.17 Orchids, such as this epiphytic species of *Mystacidium*, were driven to extinction in nature reserves in KwaZulu-Natal by the tsetse fly control programmes of the 1950s.

CHAPTER 9

ALBANY THICKET BIOME

The Albany Thicket Biome is a small region of dense vegetation (fig. 9.1) on the eastern seaboard of South Africa. There is much debate around what actually constitutes the biome and it is the least clearly defined of all the biomes in southern Africa, largely because it is a transition zone that has aspects of many of the surrounding biomes: Fynbos, Forest, Nama-Karoo, Grassland and Savanna. The biome boundaries are roughly the Gamtoos–Groot River basin in the south, the Kei River basin in the north, the Sundays–Great Fish River basin in the west, and in the east, the Indian Ocean.

9.1 (pp. 268–269) Bushveld with prominent cycads (Zamiaceae family) and aloes. (Photo: Rina de Klerk)

9.2 (right) Spekboom veld is a characteristic component of Albany Thicket vegetation. It is dominated by spekboom, *Portulacaria afra*.

Sue Dean

The name Albany was first used in South Africa in 1814 and is the name of the district in which the most characteristic vegetation of the biome occurs. The name was given to the district by the Governor of the Cape Colony, Sir John Cradock, in honour of the Duke of York (who had a double dukedom, being also Duke of Albany).

The vegetation of the area comprises elements of the biomes mentioned on page 269, but also has a distinctive structure: it has an average height of 2–3m and is dense, woody and spiny with many tangled vines, making a virtually impenetrable thicket in many places. Plants are mainly succulent or semisucculent; those typical of this biome are the spekboom, *Portulacaria afra* (fig. 9.2), large euphorbias, the tall *Aloe ferox* (figs 9.3a, b), and the crane flower, *Strelitzia reginae*, which is depicted on the South African 50-cent coin. A number of plant families are represented by endemic species, among them the ancient cycad families Zamiaceae (fig. 9.1) and Stangeriaceae.

Rainfall may occur at any time of the year, but has bimodal peaks in spring and autumn, and is strongly influenced by the summer rainfall regime to the north and northeast and the winter rainfall patterns to the south. However, it is unreliable and droughts are common. Temperatures along the coast are mild, with averages of 25°C in summer and 9°C in winter, but become more severe further inland, where maximum summer temperatures can be higher than 45°C and winters with heavy night-time frosts are common.

a

Jonathan Ball

b

c

9.3 (a) *Aloe ferox* is characteristic of the Albany Thicket. (b) An *A. ferox* inflorescence; (c) honey bees, *Apis mellifera*, harvesting pollen from aloe flowers.

Characteristic clumping of vegetation has been attributed to below-ground animal activity, including termites, which results in elevated levels of calcium and potassium, as well as higher organic matter and moisture levels compared to adjacent soils. The insect fauna of the biome is less well known than the plant composition, but one well-studied insect species, the flightless Addo dung beetle, *Circellium bacchus*, although not a true Albany Thicket endemic, is a familiar element of the region. Some studies have also been done on cicadas, several of which are known to be endemic to the biome. Then there are honey bees, which contribute to the pollination of aloes and other plants, as well as beetles and moths that pollinate, or are herbivorous on, cycads.

Pollinators

The high rates of endemicity of several groups of rare, threatened or unusual plant species in the biome require equivalent levels of specialised or otherwise successful pollinators to maintain healthy plant populations. Among the plants are various aloe species that provide large quantities of pollen and nectar and are primarily bird-pollinated. They are nevertheless visited by honey bees (fig. 9.3c), since they flower during winter when there is a dearth of other sources of nectar and pollen, and are an important resource. Cycads are another group of rare plants in the biome. Unlike aloes, they have an intimate relationship with specialised insect pollinators, without which their ever-dwindling numbers would decrease even further.

Honey bees as aloe pollinators

In southern Africa, aloes grow in almost all regions and in most vegetation types, often in dense stands. Although widespread, most species have small or fairly limited distribution ranges, and are often associated with only one of these vegetation regions. Many species are well adapted to arid conditions or periodic droughts in their natural environment, as their succulent leaves contain food and water reserves that help the plants survive extended periods of unfavourable conditions.

Large aloes, such as *Aloe africana* and *A. ferox* (figs 9.3a, b) are characteristic components of the Albany Thicket Biome; although *A. ferox* is not confined to the biome, it is nonetheless common in more open areas. Other large aloes are *A. pluridens*, which can grow up to 5m tall, and *A. speciosa*, which grows up to 6m. Various smaller endemic or near-endemic *Aloe* species occur in this biome (e.g. *A. lineata*, up to 2m), as well as species in the related genus *Aloiampelos* (e.g. *A. ciliaris*, *A. gracilis* and *A. tenuior*).

Most aloes have large inflorescences containing many brightly coloured tubular flowers; the flowers are usually red, orange or yellow, although those of a few species are green or white. Most species flower in winter. The flowers bear profuse quantities of pollen and are often filled with nectar at a time when other rich food sources are limited, thus providing a plentiful supply of food for many birds, insects and a few specialised mammals; certain low-growing species are pollinated exclusively by rodents.

Although the large size of individual plants and their often high population densities provide a potentially large food resource for insects, there are relatively few groups associated with them. Part of the reason might be the presence of various defensive chemicals in aloe sap: more than 130 chemical compounds have been isolated from aloes, largely from two commercial species – the introduced *Aloe vera* and *A. ferox*, the latter having been used in traditional medicine in South Africa for centuries. However, various insects have overcome some of the most toxic chemicals plants produce, so this seems an unlikely reason for insect exclusion.

Aloes, especially those with red-orange flowers, are mostly bird-pollinated. Red flowers usually exclude visits by insects because of their colour: most insects see poorly in the red colour spectrum (but see 'The Table Mountain beauty butterfly', p. 83), as their vision is adapted to colours of a shorter wavelength (blue, white, ultraviolet). The aloe flower structure (a tubular perianth with exserted anthers and stamens that block the tube and prevent insects from entering) and dilute nectar are further obstacles to insect feeding. Nevertheless, insects, mainly honey bees, frequently visit flowers of bird-pollinated *Aloe* species, but mainly to 'steal' pollen, rather than contribute to pollination success.

A study of the pollination of five common *Aloe* species in the Albany Thicket by scientists from Nelson Mandela Metropolitan University and the University of KwaZulu-Natal found that the species *A. pluridens*, *A. speciosa*, *A. africana*, *A. ferox* and *A. lineata* were self-incompatible (as are most *Aloe* species) and depended on birds and honey bees for successful pollination. In *A. africana*, *A. speciosa* and *A. ferox*, bees contributed little to successful pollination, but substantially more so in *A. pluridens* and *A. lineata*, although still less than birds. Pollen formed an important food source for the bees, as did nectar in species where it was accessible at the mouth of the flower, or where the bees had chewed a hole at its base, or when nectar was exposed by bird feeding damage. Although aloe nectar has a relatively low sugar concentration (15–18%), honey bees are able to concentrate dilute nectar by regurgitating it in small volumes and exposing it to the dry winter air during flight on their way back to the hive.

Hermann Staude

9.4 A cone of the cycad *Encephalartos ferox.*

Cycad pollination

Cycads and other gymnosperms (cone-bearing plants) once dominated the vegetation on earth. Cycads, specifically, had their origins as far back as 280 million years ago (mya) and were a pervasive element of the flora until about 65mya. Since then, they have declined in numbers and diversity worldwide, while angiosperms (flowering plants) have steadily increased and now dominate the plant landscape. Nevertheless, cycads still exist and are some of the most primitive living seed plants; they are considered to be 'living fossils' because their morphology has changed so little since their earliest beginnings.

Cycads are amongst the most threatened groups of plants worldwide because of habit disturbance and indiscriminate collecting, while the absence of successful pollination and seed set in disturbed areas has been attributed to disturbance or local extinction of insect pollinators. There are only about 240 extant cycad species in 10 genera worldwide. Two cycad genera occur in southern Africa: *Stangeria* (Stangeriaceae) has only one species, *S. eriopus,* which is endemic to coastal

KwaZulu-Natal and the Eastern Cape, including the Albany Thicket Biome; *Encephalartos* (Zamiaceae) has 28 species, 13 of which are found largely within this small biome.

All cycads are dioecious (separate male and female plants) and bear large cones (fig. 9.4) in which pollen (male plants) and ovules (female plants) are produced. The cones consist of specialised leaf structures (sporophylls) arranged spirally around an axis. All species are mainly insect-pollinated and have a highly specialised pollination system (there is possibly a small percentage of wind pollination in certain species). When male cones start to produce pollen, they physiologically raise their temperature substantially (thermogenesis) and emit a suite of insect-attracting volatile chemicals (see box below). Female cones do the same, but at different times of the day in order to lure pollen-bearing insects away from male cones. This combination of odour elicited by volatile chemicals and enhanced by thermogenic heating is an evolved strategy to attract pollinators and to increase pollination success, especially since male and female cycad plants may be separated by some distance.

As far as is known, all southern African cycads are beetle-pollinated, whereas in other parts of the world beetles and thrips (Thysanoptera) perform the function. The beetle pollinators are almost exclusively herbivores, and specific to a cycad species, whose larvae feed on cone tissue of the host cycad.

Amongst the beetles with a specialised association with cycads are some with a dual relationship – both agonistic and beneficial. The larvae feed on the cone

9.5 Various small beetles, some of which are pollinators, are associated with cycad cones, although their identities and their relationships with the host are unclear.

Temperature differences between male and female cycad cones

In a study of *Encephalartos villosus,* an eastern southern African species that also occurs in the Albany Thicket Biome, peak odour emission and temperature in female cones were around midday, while those of males were in the early evenings when ambient temperature was decreasing. The odour chemicals were similar between the sexes, although those of the males were richer and generally more complex. Male cones raised their temperature by 7–12°C above the ambient

temperature and female cones by 0.9–3°C. The maximum temperatures and volatile compound emissions in males peaked at the pollen-shedding phase, while in females they peaked at the pollen-receptive stage. Male cones have tightly packed sporophylls that separate a few days before pollen release and those of females separate soon after the males have released pollen. The main pollinators breed in cycad cone tissue, chiefly that of males.

tissue of mainly male cones, while the adults are the main pollinators. The beetles belong to several species in four families: *Porthetes* (Curculionidae), *Metacucujus* (Boganiidae), and unnamed species of Erotylidae and Languriidae (fig. 9.5). They are mostly small beetles (3–10mm long), of which some (especially *Porthetes*) are very hairy, which boosts their efficiency in carrying pollen.

The beetle pollinators are mainly attracted to the male sporophyll, where mating and egg-laying take place and where the larvae develop; they seldom feed on or damage the developing pollen. They are usually not attracted to female cones, which have higher levels of toxic chemicals. This prevents the beetles from breeding there and damaging the ovules. Only after the mature beetles emerge and the female cones produce volatiles and increase their temperature, do they become attractive to beetles carrying pollen.

Herbivores

Some of the most specialised feeding in the Albany Thicket Biome is by insects feeding on cycads. Not only are cycad leaves leathery and spiny, but all their tissues contain the toxic compounds macrozamin and cycasin, which have mutagenic and neurotoxic properties against vertebrates and general herbivorous insects. Yet some insect species have overcome these hurdles, having evolved mechanisms to avoid being poisoned. Some, in turn, use the plant toxins to protect them from their own predators; among these are various scale insects and the larvae of several highly adapted Coleoptera and Lepidoptera species. Scale insects suck leaf sap, beetle larvae develop in cone and stem tissue, and moth larvae eat leaves, or bore into cones or leaf petioles.

The larvae and adult moths of the species that have a special association with cycads are brightly coloured in combinations of yellow, orange, red and black. These colours are typically considered to be aposematic, 'warning' potential predators of the toxic nature of the insect.

Seed-feeding cycad weevils

Species of *Antliarhinus* (Coleoptera: Brentidae) are intimately associated with cycads, where their specialised morphology and behaviour contribute to their ability to breed in cycad seeds deep inside the female cones, but their larvae may destroy up to 80% of the seeds. They contribute little to pollination.

The life cycle of *Antliarhinus zamiae* (fig. 9.6) is one of the most remarkable examples of seed feeding amongst insects. The female weevils have the longest rostrum (about 20mm) relative to body length of any beetle, roughly twice the length of the body. Males have a short rostrum, less than the body length. The evolution of this extraordinary structure is directly related to the female cone structure of *Encephalartos* cycads.

The compact, protective female cone consists of many sporophylls arranged spirally around a central axis, somewhat like a pine cone. Each sporophyll carries a pair of ovules, which will later develop into seeds. The ovule contains a gametophyte, which is surrounded by two fleshy tissue layers and a hard stony layer. The ovules remain entirely concealed within the cone, except for a short period when the sporophylls separate to allow pollen entry. Not only are the ovules physically well protected, they are also very rich in toxic compounds.

How the beetles managed to lay their eggs within the gametophytes deep inside the cone tissue remained a mystery from its first report about 100 years ago; it was only when John Donaldson of the South African National Biodiversity Institute (SANBI) in Cape Town studied the phenomenon in 1995 that it was fully explained.

It had been proposed that the long rostrum was used by the female weevil to drill an oviposition hole through the protective tissues to the gametophyte and then to use it to push eggs down the tunnel to the target. What Donaldson found was that the female uses her rostrum to drill a hole between adjacent sporophylls, pushing it deep into the cone until it is totally embedded as far as the antennal sockets (a process that takes about three hours), and then withdraws the rostrum. She then turns around and telescopically extrudes and extends her ovipositor, which is the same length as the rostrum, into the hole and

9.6 **(a)** The female cycad weevil, *Antliarhinus zamiae* (Brentidae), is adapted to lay eggs in cycad seeds that lie deep inside a thick layer of cone tissue; **(b)** a male cycad weevil.

lays a batch of eggs in the gametophyte (this takes her about 30 minutes). The oviposition process is not without risk – Donaldson and others have reported that broken rostrums are often found protruding from cone tissue, the result of failed attempts to access the gametophytes.

How this remarkable oviposition process evolved can be seen by comparing rostrum length and oviposition behaviour in other species of *Antliarhinus* that use cycads. *Antliarhinus peglerae*, a stout species with a relatively shorter rostrum than *A. zamiae*, drills into and lays eggs in sporophylls in which the larvae then develop. The considerably smaller *A. signatus* female squeezes between adjacent sporophylls when they open to allow pollination, and then drills through the ovule to lay batches of eggs inside the gametophyte. *Antliarhinus zamiae* is clearly the most specialised and highly co-evolved species, resulting in the extraordinary process described above.

Looper moths feeding on cycads

The only Lepidoptera recorded to feed on cycads in Africa are members of the Geometridae. This is a large family of moths of which the larvae are characteristic loopers – the 'looping' characteristic is derived from the fact that they only have prolegs (fleshy, leg-like abdominal appendages for holding onto the substrate) on abdominal segments 6 and 10, instead of on several abdominal segments as in most other caterpillars (larvae of the cycad-feeding *Callioratis*, however, also have prolegs on abdominal segments 4 and 5, which is unique in the family). Geometrid larvae move in a series of loops: first the forebody is lifted and arched, then placed down, followed by the hind body being pulled forward and placed on the substrate next to the forebody; they do not crawl continuously as do other caterpillars. Like many moths, adults are mostly nocturnal and often cryptically coloured to provide camouflage against their diurnal resting background.

All the cycad-feeding geometrids in southern Africa have been placed in a small tribe, Diptychini, in the large subfamily Ennominae. There are three small genera and 16 species (*Zerenopsis*, with eight species, *Callioratis* with five, and *Veniliodes* with three). The tribe is restricted to Africa and is thought to have ancient origins, possibly having evolved in association with cycads over millions of years. It is characterised by several unique traits:

- an obligatory association with cycads on which larvae feed gregariously for the first three instars, after which they become solitary and usually disperse to secondary host plants;
- adults that have developed diurnal activity;
- pronounced aposematic colours in adults and larvae; and
- mating behaviour that includes aerial lek formation by males, to which females are attracted and where mating takes place.

Diptychine larval duration is relatively long for caterpillars of their size (final instars about 20–65mm long); it lasts from six weeks in tropical species to six months in temperate-zone species. Feeding larvae, can, however, suspend feeding and development when environmental temperatures drop temporarily, spinning cocoon-like silk nests that incorporate surrounding debris or frass in which they are able to rest for up to weeks at a time until temperatures rise sufficiently for their development to continue.

In southern Africa, diptychines have been recorded feeding on many cycad species. As with certain cycad species, several of the cycad moth species are very rare, and at least one, *Callioratis millari*, is possibly southern Africa's most threatened moth species.

Zerenopsis lepida (fig. 9.7) is possibly the most polyphagous of all diptychine species. It has been recorded using about 30 *Encephalartos* species, *Stangeria eriopus*, and the introduced cycad genera *Cycas* and *Dioon* as primary hosts. It is the most familiar and widespread cycad looper moth, occurring in savanna in the east and northeast of South Africa, as well as in the Drakensberg and Winterberg highlands. It is considered a pest by cycad collectors.

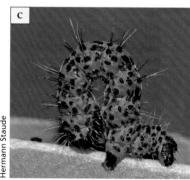

9.7 The larvae of the cycad looper moth, *Zerenopsis lepida* (Lepidoptera: Geometridae), are among the few insects that feed on cycad foliage: **(a)** adult day-flying moth; **(b)** young, gregarious larvae before they take on bright, aposematic colours; **(c)** mature larva in the 'looping' pose characteristic of most members of the family.

Under natural conditions when the host cycad is surrounded by natural vegetation, *Z. lepida* larvae, which feed in dense aggregations surrounded by web until the end of the third instar, drop in a seemingly coordinated movement from the cycad and disperse to various secondary hosts. However, when the cycad stands isolated from surrounding vegetation as in gardens, the larvae remain on the host cycad until maturity. Pupation is in the soil at the base or some distance from the host plant. Natural secondary plant hosts include several angiosperm species, such as white pear, *Apodytes dimidiata* (Icacinaceae), big num-num, *Carissa macrocarpa*, forest num-num, *C. bispinosa* (Apocynaceae), bluebush, *Diospyros lycioides*, bladder-nut, *D. whyteana* (Ebenaceae), false assegai, *Maesa lanceolata*, and dwarf false assegai, *M. alnifolia* (Maesaceae). They have also been recorded on cultivated marula, *Sclerocarya birrea* (Anacardiaceae). Although some of these plant species contain toxic compounds in their tissues, the larvae feed with impunity, illustrating their wide feeding preference and plant chemical tolerance. Adults and larger larvae are strongly aposematic.

The rare, threatened and spectacular *Callioratis millari* (fig. 9.8a) feeds on *Stangeria eriopus* (fig. 9.8b). Although the cycad host is still fairly common (albeit under conservation threat from harvesting for traditional medicine) in coastal areas of KwaZulu-Natal and the Eastern Cape, where it grows in grassland and inland forests, *C. millari* is much more restricted, and despite intensive surveys by the lepidopterist Hermann Staude, has only been recorded from three highland grassland sites, which are surrounded by coastal scarp forest or cultivated land near Eshowe in KwaZulu-Natal. The reason for its restricted habitat is thought to be the required presence of its currently unknown secondary larval host plant.

Sound and breeding in cicadas

The southern African cicada fauna (Hemiptera: Auchenorrhyncha: Cicadoidea: Cicadidae) is rich (fig. 9.9), with about 40 genera and 180 species. All of the species discussed here occur in the Eastern Cape, although some have distributions that extend beyond the province. The species are *Platypleura capensis*, *P. wahlbergi*, *Azanicada* (formerly *Platypleura*) *zuluensis*, *Pycna semiclara* and *Albanycada albigera* (Cicadinae: Platypleurini). The name of *Albanycada albigera* is derived from the Albany Thicket Biome and its host plant is *Portulacaria afra* (fig. 9.2). There are also four species of *Xosopsaltria* (Cicadettinae: Tettigonyiini) that are strict endemics to the biome.

9.8 One of southern Africa's rarest moth species, *Callioratis millari* (Geometridae), is associated with the endangered cycad *Stangeria eriopus*: (**a**) adult moth; (**b**) some of the leaves of this *Stangeria* show signs of larval feeding.

9.9 A selection of the rich southern African cicada (Cicadidae) fauna, comprising some 180 species: (**a**) *Pycna semiclara*; (**b**) *Platypleura brunea*; (**c**) *Munza* sp.; (**d**) *Melampsalta* sp.

Martin Villet of Rhodes University and his colleagues have performed the only studies of calling in southern African cicadas. In an early study on seven cicada species of the Platypleurini in coastal KwaZulu-Natal, they found that the calls were generally very loud. Smaller species, such as *Azanicada* (formerly *Platypleura*) *zuluensis* (wing length about 26mm), had quieter calls with sound pressure levels of about 93 decibels (dB) – nevertheless louder than the sound produced by the average garden lawnmower. In larger species, such as *Pycna semiclara* (wing length about 40mm), the sound pressure level of the call is about 106dB, while *Brevisana brevis*, another large species, produces the loudest insect sound known: 106.7dB at a distance of 50cm, which is equivalent to the noise made by a chainsaw!

Pycna semiclara is a large, widespread eastern and northern southern African species. Thousands of males may produce incredibly loud, synchronous calls (called choruses) in indigenous bush and forest, as well as in plantations of exotic trees. Choruses typically last about 30 minutes and are most frequently heard at dawn and dusk, although there are sporadic bursts of chorusing during the day. The cicadas begin chorusing as early as 04h00 while it is still dark, and evening choruses last until after dark. The cicadas may call from host plants on which they feed, or perch and call from nonhost plants, usually from exposed trunks and branches within the understorey but clear of the dense undergrowth. Choruses consist of 5–10 calling males, about 5m apart. Individual choruses form at least 50m apart, but neighbouring choruses often synchronise their calling activity.

Males fight with other contenders that call within 50cm. When one approaches another, they both produce an 'encounter call' and proceed to fight, clawing at each other's heads with their forelegs and flicking their wings to dislodge the opponent. When one gives up and flees, the winner reverts to the 'calling' song.

The species vary considerably in size, from about 10–50mm in body length. They feed on the sap of a wide array of different plants – on root sap as nymphs and stem sap as adults.

The often very loud sound produced by cicadas on a hot summer's day is familiar to many people. It is produced by a special vibrating membrane (tymbal, fig. 9.10) on the male's abdomen. The chorus produced by thousands of singing males of some species can be one of the most overwhelming natural sounds. It is also probably the most studied form of sound production in insects, and extensive studies have been done by Martin Villet of Rhodes University on sound (see box above), as well as on temperature control (see box, p. 278), in some South African species.

Although they are often heard, the insects themselves are seldom seen, as they are usually cryptically coloured and sit against a background that offers effective camouflage. They abruptly stop singing when approached or threatened. They see well and will move around to behind the branch or leaf they are resting on or drop to the ground when danger approaches; then, if threatened further, they fly away. Flight is fast and strong, and some species display bright colours that 'disappear' when the cicada lands, a strategy thought to confuse potential predators about where they have settled. They spend most of their life cycle – which can sometimes last many years – underground in the nymph stage.

Calling and hearing

Though only males sing, a tympanum (ear) on the abdomen allows both male and female cicadas to hear well. Males close the tympanum while singing, to avoid deafening themselves! The calls by cicada males are primarily a reproductive strategy to attract females (but see box opposite), and secondarily, a 'spacing' or 'encounter' sound to warn other males.

The sound-producing tymbals are found on the first abdominal segment, one on either side of the body of a

9.10 The sound-producing tymbal with which cicadas produce their characteristic sound is the ribbed, disc-shaped structure on the abdomen, clearly visible through the transparent wing membrane of this *Stagira* species.

male. The tymbal is characterised by a well-demarcated area of very thin cuticle supported by a thick rim of cuticle and a series of dorsolateral strengthening ribs. It is protected by a tymbal cover formed by a forward extension of the abdomen. The internal mechanism consists of a ventral, cuticular abdominal strut that attaches to the edge of the posterior rim of the tymbal. Running parallel to this are the tymbal muscles, which attach at one end to the abdominal wall via an apodeme (groove) and at the other to the tymbal itself. Behind the tymbal, and surrounding the muscle, lies an air sac (see box, p. 27), which is fed by the metathoracic spiracle.

The sound is produced myogenically in most cicadas, but in some it is neurogenic. In species that produce the sound myogenically, a single nervous impulse produces a series of muscle contractions. In those that produce it neurogenically, each nervous impulse results in a single tymbal contraction. In some species the two tymbals act synchronously; in others they alternate. The sound is produced when the tymbal muscle contracts and buckles the tymbal membrane inwards, producing a click. The muscle then relaxes and the elasticity of the cuticle returns the tymbal to its original position, producing

another click as it does so. Hundreds or thousands of clicks per second produce the sometimes continuous train of sound (e.g. *Platypleura capensis*). The frequency of these sounds differs between species, based on various attributes (e.g. body size) that determine the natural frequency of the tymbal.

Not all cicadas produce a deafening continuous chorus. Many species make use of clicks, which can be heard from their perches on branches or in flight, or produce croaking or bleating sounds. The bladder cicada, *Xosopsaltria punctata*, an endemic species from the Albany Thicket Biome, emits a repetitive frog-like grating call. The males and females are dimorphic: males are cryptically coloured and females uniformly green.

Breeding and nymph stage

When a female lands near a calling male, the male responds as it does when another male lands close by, changing its call to an encounter call, head-clawing and wing-flicking. Unreceptive females and other males respond by flying off, while receptive females sit quietly and do not react to the male's aggression. The male then falls silent and copulation takes place.

Sound parasitism of cicadas

It seems that not only female cicadas are attracted to calling males. In a fascinating report by Simon van Noort of the Iziko Museum in Cape Town, a large and beautifully coloured green lacewing, *Italochrysa neurodes* (Neuroptera: Chrysopidae, fig. 9.11a), was found to be attracted to feeding and calling *Platypleura capensis* cicadas on several occasions in the Western Cape. The only previous record of such behaviour was from 1891: in Natal, up to 16 individuals of the related *I. gigantea* were found sitting in a semicircle around the head of an unidentified calling and feeding cicada. Since Van Noort's report, other cicada species such as *Capcicada decora* (fig. 9.11b) have been found to be participants in a similar association.

Platypleura capensis suck sap mainly of bush-tick berry, *Chrysanthemoides monilifera* (Asteraceae), perching in an approximately vertical position, facing upwards, on older woody stems, against which they are well camouflaged. The lacewings sit head-to-head, very close to the feeding cicada. In one instance, when the cicada was disturbed, the lacewing appeared to feed at the puncture left by the cicada.

Adults of the European lacewing species *Italochrysa italica* feed on honeydew and pollen, as do many other chrysopids (although possibly just as many others are predatory) so the possibility that *I. neurodes* and *I. gigantea* might do the same, was considered. However, it was thought unlikely that fluids excreted by the cicadas (honeydew) were the primary attraction since these are usually sprayed away from themselves and their perches. An appealing alternative hypothesis is that the chrysopids are attracted to plant volatiles escaping from the feeding wound and that they are homing in on the sound produced by the calling cicadas.

9.11 (a) The green lacewing *Italochrysa neurodes* (Chrysopidae) is attracted to (b) calling cicadas such as this *Capcicada decora*.

Endothermy in platypleurine cicadas

In researching the platypleurine cicadas, a group that occurs widely across Africa, Martin Villet of Rhodes University and his colleagues found that most of those that they studied (11 of 12 species in six genera) warm up endothermically. This is in contrast to most other cicada groups, which regulate their body temperature ectothermically by changes in body orientation and perch selection in order to maximise exposure to the sun. Most platypleurines call from perches in the canopy, which is usually heavily shaded, and they avoid sunlit spots. Although the precise mechanism of warming up is unknown, they apparently don't use muscle vibration or wing movement as do most other endothermic insects. They do, however, produce characteristic abdominal telescoping movements while warming up, behaviour unique to endothermic cicadas. This is thought to increase ventilation and oxygen availability to muscles during warm-up.

One small species, however, is considered facultatively endothermic. *Platypleura wahlbergi* (fig. 9.12) uses exposed areas of stems and branches in sunlit patches to warm up when these are available, but is able to move to the interior branches if needed and can continue to sing at dusk and dawn by switching to endothermy to raise its body temperature.

Another equally small species is strictly ectothermic. *Albanycada albigera* calls from exposed branches of its leafy host plants (*Portulacaria afra, Euphorbia bothae, Euclea* spp.) in Albany Thicket, but only after warming up in sunlight during the day (it does not sing at dawn and dusk). Although it appears capable of warming up endothermically, other ecological factors appear to have determined that ectothermy is a better thermoregulatory strategy in its specific habitat.

So, why does endothermy occur in cicadas?

- It may decrease predation risk because they sit in shaded locations maximising the benefits of their cryptic colours.
- They can select calling sites beneath the canopy but above the undergrowth, where there is decreased scattering and absorption of sound by the vegetation.
- Calling at reduced light intensities of dusk and dawn reduces the predation pressure of birds, because of reduced foraging efficiency in dim light.
- The ability to adapt to cooler microclimates decreases competition with other species for calling sites and resources for nymphs.
- Endothermy permits calling at dawn and dusk when sound travels further in the environment, increasing the number of females likely to hear the calls.

9.12 *Platypleura wahlbergi*, one of the few cicada species capable of facultative endothermy.

Mated females lay loose batches of long, thin eggs (fig. 9.13) in slits cut in the bark of terminal twigs of the nymphal host plant or in soft dry wood; they use a series of blades on the ovipositor to cut the slits. The tiny emergent nymphs drop to the ground and burrow down to where they can start to feed by sucking xylem fluids from plant roots. These are strange-looking insects, with a typical squat, hunched shape, front legs with strongly developed spines for effective digging, and large bulbous eyes. Because of their subterranean habits, nymphs are seldom seen, but evidence is occasionally found: their last, papery, yellow-brown exuviae (moulted skin) are sometimes spotted attached to tree trunks (fig. 9.14) where they have undertaken their final moult before emerging as adults.

Duration of the nymphal development is long by insect standards, an average of 2–5 years, but the famous 13- and 17-year periodical *Magicicada* of the southeastern USA are amongst the longest-lived insects. These irrupt in synchronised emergences at 13- and 17-year intervals, during which millions of individuals suddenly appear, mate and die, only for the next generation to appear again many years later. The mass emergences of adults are hypothesised to be a strategy for overwhelming predators by their sheer numbers; far more are simultaneously present than can be consumed by the guild of predators present, with the consequence that relatively few members of the population are actually killed.

Although nymphs would appear to be fairly well protected in their subterranean habitat, they are no doubt preyed on by various small predatory mammals such as moles and mongooses. There is at least one insect family that specialises in parasitising cicada nymphs –

a

9.14 Nymphal cicada exuviae, one of the signs of the presence of these insects.

9.15 The beetle *Chameorhipis* sp. (Rhipiceridae) is a specialised parasite of cicada nymphs; the active first-instar triungulin larvae find and attach to the nymphs, then moult into a caraboid form and parasitise them.

b

9.13 Males of this cicada species, *Brevisana brevis,* produce the loudest insect sound known. Here, **(a)** a female cicada lays her eggs in slits in a grass stem; and **(b)** cicada eggs exposed.

parasitic comb beetles (Coleoptera: Rhipiceridae), with three genera and about 10 species in southern Africa (fig. 9.15). The beetles lay eggs on the plant close to the cicada egg clutch; tiny mobile larvae called triungulins emerge from the eggs (see 'Blister beetle larvae', p. 171 and box, p. 42). The triungulins attach to the cicada nymphs when these hatch and live with them in the soil where the beetle larvae parasitise them.

Dung feeders

The Addo area of the biome was proclaimed as the Addo Elephant National Park in 1931. It was covered by dense thicket vegetation and inhabited by elephant and black rhino, several antelope species such as bushbuck and kudu, as well as monkeys and baboons. Co-occurring with them, and dependent on their dung, was a large, flightless dung beetle species. The dung beetles were able to attain a large size because they were better able to utilise body energy by becoming flightless; flightlessness also gave them the ability to forage on relatively small amounts of dung in dense bush without competition from other large-winged dung beetles.

The famous Addo dung beetle

The Addo dung beetle, *Circellium bacchus* (Coleoptera: Scarabaeidae: Scarabaeinae, fig. 9.16a), is probably the best-known insect species in the Albany Thicket Biome. Although it also occurs outside the biome, almost as far west as Cape Town, it is mainly restricted to dense vegetation and is clearly of ancient 'thicket' origin, and probably evolved here. It is southern Africa's largest ball-rolling dung beetle and was one of the first beetles described from the subcontinent (in 1781). It has a number of unique biological attributes, but besides these, it has long been something of an entomological and conservation enigma (see box, p. 281).

Circellium bacchus has been demonstrated to be a relict of an ancient (Eocene) lineage that has persisted in the Albany Thicket Biome, which has apparently remained environmentally stable for millions of years. Phylogenetic studies of African dung beetles have provided very strong

Meagen Mansell

Meagen Mansell

9.16 (a) The large, flightless dung beetle *Circellium bacchus* (Scarabaeidae: Scarabaeinae) is one of the most familiar insects in the Albany Thicket. It has atypical reproductive biology for a dung beetle: **(b)** females form and roll brood balls, **(c)** which then attract males. One of a number of competing males will triumph over the others and then mate with the female.

evidence that *C. bacchus* has no close relatives, something that has been suspected for a long time and which led to its being moved backwards and forwards between the tribe of the quintessential ball-rollers (Scarabaeini) and that of the putative ancient rollers (Canthonini; see 'The earliest dung beetles', p. 290). However, recent molecular analysis suggests that it should probably be considered as being the only surviving member of a unique lineage, something comparable to the aardvark and pangolin amongst mammals.

Circellium bacchus adults range in size from 22–47mm long. The dung that they feed on also ranges extensively in size (see box opposite). Depending on the quantity of dung available for brood ball construction, the balls vary considerably in size and so does the food available for the developing larva. A small amount of dung may lead to a small brood-ball and the development of a small adult, whereas a large ball, containing a plentiful supply of food for the developing larva, results in a big individual. Adults in the Addo Elephant National Park, where elephant, buffalo and rhino dung is plentiful, are generally bigger than those in small pockets of dense habitat further west, where dung deposits are generally smaller.

Larger body size in beetles has been linked to higher body water content, which increases their capacity to resist desiccation in more arid areas, such as those in large parts of the Albany Thicket Biome.

Besides its size variation and the fact that it is the only member of an extinct evolutionary lineage with no close living relatives, *C. bacchus* also has other distinctive biological attributes: it is flightless; females form, roll and bury brood balls without the assistance of a male, and spend 4–5 months underground caring for a single offspring.

Flightlessness in insects can be attributed to various environmental factors, the most important being that the habitat should remain stable over evolutionary time. When this happens, insects can divert energy from flying, which becomes unnecessary in a stable environment replete with essential resources, and invest more in aspects such as reproduction and brood care.

Ball-rolling and brood care

In most large dung-rolling beetles, the process of forming, rolling and burying the brood ball is carried out entirely by the male, with the female following or riding on the ball. Mating takes place a few days after the male has buried the ball; he then departs from the nest, leaving the female to re-form the brood ball, lay an egg in it and remain with and care for the brood for up to several months. The evolutionary explanation for this is that the male invests a substantial amount of energy in procuring the potential brood ball, defending it against competitors, rolling it for often substantial distances, digging a burrow, sometimes in hard and unyielding soil, and then burying it. After mating, he can feed again, replenishing his fat reserves and building up energy for another reproductive effort. The female, on the other hand, only starts to expend energy once the brood ball has been buried; she requires substantial reserves for the long period of brood care that is to follow, as she does not feed during this time.

Females forming brood balls (fig. 9.16b), rolling them to a suitable burial site and burying them unaided by males (fig. 9.16c) is not only unique among ball-rolling dung beetles, but represents somewhat of an evolutionary paradox. That *C. bacchus* has reversed these roles suggests that females are more assured of successful breeding if they take over responsibility for the entire process. They roll the dung balls (sometimes tennis-ball-sized) for up to 100m, taking up to 24 hours to bury them. Being flightless (and usually with a dependable source of food) enables the females to build up and conserve sufficient energy reserves not only to roll and bury the brood ball, but to last for the 4–5 months spent caring for the brood. After emerging from the brood burrow they have to replenish their energy reserves before breeding again.

These breeding events potentially repeat during the spring and autumn rainfall peaks when soil conditions are suitable for brood-ball burial. However, females are only able to breed more than once per year under almost perfect conditions, something that probably rarely occurs. Given that the females live 3–5 years and usually produce only one, at most two, progeny per year, they are one of the insect species with the lowest lifetime fecundity.

Conservation status of *Circellium bacchus*

Based on old but unsubstantiated scientific records, it was often reported in the media and mentioned in conservation agency reports that the distribution of the flightless dung beetle *Circellium bacchus* had decreased from a subcontinent-wide range to a mere fraction in the Eastern Cape. It was also thought to be an elephant-dung specialist and that its distribution shrank together with that of elephants across southern Africa, with only a small number surviving along with the 11 elephants that made up the original population of the Addo Elephant National Park (AENP) in 1931 (fig. 9.17). These myths were perpetuated by somewhat superficial scientific studies – one of which rather fancifully linked the dung beetle's range contraction to that of the black rhino.

The perpetuation and expansion of the mystique around *C. bacchus* certainly contributed to public and scientific awareness of the species, and led in the early 1990s to a study by Clarke Scholtz and Kevin Coles of the University of Pretoria after tourists to the AENP had complained to the National Parks Board (now SANParks) about the large numbers of beetles being killed by cars driving over piles of elephant dung containing beetles. The study led to road signs being erected that 'Dung Beetles Have Right of Way', a tradition now followed by several other conservation areas in South Africa (fig. 9.18). Concerns about its putative range contraction and survival threat led to its being proclaimed an endangered species in the then Cape Province in 1992, but this was entirely an emotional decision. Several subsequent studies discovered and reported on the many unique biological aspects of this unusual species and have proved that it is not endangered, only scarce in areas with insufficient dung and a dearth of dense vegetation.

The myth of the beetles' dependence on elephant dung has also been dispelled. The beetles feed on and, if sufficient dung is available, form brood balls from virtually any available herbivore or omnivore dung. Given choices between various dung types where elephant and buffalo are present, the beetles prefer elephant dung to feed on, and the more pliable buffalo dung to roll brood balls. However, they also feed on and roll brood balls from the dung of monkeys, humans, ostriches, zebras, kudu, cattle and various small forest antelope such as duiker and bushbuck.

9.17 For years, *Circellium bacchus* was thought to be dependent on the dung of Addo elephants, which were saved from extinction by conservation efforts implemented in the 1930s. Recent research shows that the beetles eat and roll balls from almost any herbivore or omnivore dung available.

9.18 Large numbers of *Circellium bacchus* in elephant dung on roads in the Addo Elephant National Park were run over by visitors' vehicles, until the park's authorities erected road signs (**a**) warning visitors of the presence of dung beetles on the roads and (**b**) that the beetles enjoy right of way.

CHAPTER 10
FOREST BIOME

A forest consists of a multitude of different habitats subjected to large variation in local environmental conditions. In general, relative humidity remains high and temperatures are cool, but seldom cold. The vegetation is dominated by tall trees and other woody plants (fig. 10.1) and plant diversity is exceptionally high. The structural complexity of the vegetation is very variable, depending on the intensity of sunlight shining through the canopy and the amount of soil moisture locally available. An abundance of plant remains at various stages of decomposition contributes to a rich litter layer. Streams may flow through the forest creating pools, backwaters and lakes, some deeply shaded, others in sunny clearings.

10.1 (pp. 282–283) Forests occur in high-rainfall areas; the high moisture supports a rich undergrowth of plants and plant-like fungi, mosses and lichens. The latter grow on the abundant living plants and dead wood and some contribute to decomposition processes. Insects are intimately associated with many of these organisms. The forest streams have a rich endemic fauna of aquatic insects.
(Photo: Rina de Klerk)

10.2 Forest consists of tall, woody plants that form a closed canopy. The understorey varies greatly depending on the amount of sunlight filtering through, soil type and moisture availability.

10.3 Tall evergreen or semideciduous trees are the main elements of southern African forest vegetation.

10.4 (above right) Many southern African forests survive as isolated fragments surrounded by other vegetation types, in this case, fynbos.

10.5 (right) A very small montane forest pocket, possibly too small to support a significant endemic insect fauna.

From an entomological point of view, the most important indigenous forests in southern Africa are the scattered remnants of the large African evergreen Pleistocene forests (fig. 10.1) that existed 2.6 million to 12,000 years ago. They stretch along the eastern mountain chain of the continent from Ethiopia through East Africa, Malawi and Zimbabwe into South Africa, where they continue along the escarpment from the Soutpansberg in the north along the Drakensberg range, through the Eastern Cape to the Cape Peninsula. In the southern Cape, forests extend to sea level.

Southern African forests are characterised by tall evergreen or semideciduous trees (figs 10.2, 10.3), including the well-known giant or Outeniqua yellowwood, *Podocarpus falcatus*, which is the tallest indigenous tree in South African forests, up to 60m. The forest trees have largely overlapping crowns; woody climbers and epiphytes hang from the trunks, and ferns and mosses are common. The forest floor consists of detritus to a large extent. Most of the forest patches are small and are surrounded by grassland, fynbos, thicket or savanna (figs 10.4, 10.5).

The Knysna forest in the Eastern and Western Cape provinces is the largest of these fragments (about 250km²). It forms part of a larger forest area (600km²), much of which lies close to sea level. Many of the smaller forest patches along the escarpment occur at altitudes of up to about 1,800m above

sea level. Forests in the winter-rainfall area receive about 525mm of rain per annum and those in the summer-rainfall region receive above 725mm.

Conditions in the coastal forest are moderated by its proximity to the sea. The tree canopy and shrub layers further buffer the external conditions to create a more equitable microclimate inside the forest. At increasing distance from the coast and at increasing altitudes, however, small forest fragments are subject to more extreme conditions, such as periodic strong dry winds and cold to near-freezing winter temperatures.

Although the Forest Biome is the smallest in the region, covering just 0.1% of the land surface area, it is biologically unique, particularly because several relicts of once widespread insect faunas are still to be found here. Amongst them are species with limited dispersal capabilities, or those confined to the specific environment that a forest provides. These include bristletails and ancient endemic forest species, such as damp-wood termites and various beetles. The humid and sheltered forest ecosystem also hosts other invertebrate groups, some of which represent groups that are even more ancient than insects.

Forests are home to members of all the common trophic guilds – from pollinators, predators and parasites, to many different kinds of herbivores. The huge biomass of living plant material occurring in forests results in large amounts of plant litter, more so than in any other biome. This detritus sustains fungi, algae, lichens and mosses (fig. 10.6), and numerous insect species and other arthropods involved in decomposition and soil recycling processes. Detritivores include termites and various wood-boring beetles and moths, as well as earwigs, earthworms, millipedes, woodlice and mites. There are also flies that feed on fungi or spread their spores, and even highly specialised earwigs, which glean fungus growing on their rat hosts.

Insects of various trophic levels provide a multitude of potential hosts for an equally wide range of parasitoid fly and wasp species. The predatory guild includes numerous non-insect invertebrate groups such as planarian worms, velvet worms, centipedes and many arachnids – spiders, scorpions, harvestmen, whip spiders and pseudoscorpions. Insect predators include a very unusual frog-eating beetle and specialised bugs, among which are millipede assassins and spider-hunting thread assassins.

Dung and carrion feeders are also present in forests, and although they are not as apparent as in biomes with large mammals, there is a rich fauna of small, specialised species.

Since forests lie in high-rainfall areas, various aquatic habitats are usually present; these support a diverse and often endemic semiaquatic and aquatic insect fauna.

10.6 (a) A multiple-branched fruticose lichen; one of many in damp forests; (b) red berry-like reproductive bodies of the fungal partner of a forest lichen; (c) a moss, another of the important plant-like elements in damp forests, growing on a tree trunk; (d) a mushroom-like basidiomycete fungus growing on rotting wood; (e) slime mould, *Fuligo septica*; (f) mould fungi.

Ancient insect relicts

The southern African forests are home to several groups of insects from ancient lineages. It is perhaps fitting that some of these primordial species live side by side in ancient forests.

Bristletails: the oldest order

Bristletails (Archaeognatha, fig. 10.7a) are members of the most basal (primitive) order of living insects, and with their sister order, the fishmoths or silverfish (Zygentoma, fig. 10.7b; see 'Absorbing water from air', p. 148; 'Fishmoths', p. 347), they represent a lineage of flightless insects that has remained virtually unchanged since the mid-Devonian period, about 380 million years ago (mya).

The two groups share some primitive features, the most important of which are the ancestral absence of wings, ametamorphic development (see 'Ametamorphic development', p. 40) and 'external' fertilisation, in which there is no copulation during mating. They share this

10.7 (a) Bristletails (Archaeognatha) are the most primitive of all insects and thrive under cool, moist conditions. They share a number of their primitive characteristics with their more widespread and more diverse sister group, **(b)** the fishmoths (Zygentoma).

form of fertilisation with other ancient arthropods such as spiders and centipedes (see 'Spiders', p. 304).

Archaeognatha is a small group worldwide, with about 500 species, of which about 20 species in four genera (*Machilinus, Machilellus, Machiloides, Hypomachiloides*) are found in southern Africa, all in the family Meinertellidae.

Bristletails are slender, silvery-grey insects with three long 'bristles' or 'tails', a typically arched body, large compound eyes and prominent ocelli. They range in size from about 10mm to 15mm, excluding the three characteristic tails at the end of the body. The tails are sensory organs; the longer central bristle is the median dorsal appendix, with two lateral cerci. Bristletails are capable of fairly long jumps, which are produced by sudden abdominal flexing that propels the insect away in defensive leaps. The body is covered with tiny overlapping scales and the underside of the abdomen is armed with eversible vesicles, which are thought to absorb moisture from the substrate on which the insects live.

Most bristletails in southern Africa are found in cool, moist conditions in forests and on the mountain escarpment. They live amongst litter and under logs and stones. They feed on algae and lichens, which they 'chop' from the substrate with specialised mandibles.

Reproduction in Meinertellidae is unique in the Archaeognatha. In the presence of a receptive female, a male produces silken threads to which are attached sperm droplets held together by a jelly-like substance (a structure termed a spermatophore). The stalked spermatophores are attached to the substrate. During a mating 'dance', the male touches the female with his antennae and then sweeps the spermatophores into her genitalia with his antennae.

Eggs are laid in cracks and crevices in the substrate. Nymphs undergo many moults over a period of about two years, when they become adults; however, they continue moulting as adults – another primitive group characteristic. Reproduction takes place after each moult, as the lining of the genitalia consists of cuticle which is shed at moulting; this renders the reproductive organs temporarily nonfunctional. Some species lay only a single egg at a time, but adults are long-lived (two years or longer) and many eggs may be laid during the course of a lifetime.

Damp-wood termites

The small termite family commonly known as damp-wood termites (Blattodea: Termitoidae: Termopsidae) is represented by only two relict species in southern Africa. It is one of the basal Gondwana Termitoidae families with only a few groups surviving on parts of the original continents. The family is known from Early Cretaceous (146–100mya) extinct fossil genera from China and Late

Cretaceous (100–66mya) fossils from Canada and France. No fossils are known from the southern Gondwana continents where most of the extant species are currently found.

There are two genera in southern Africa, each with a single species in the region. *Porotermes planiceps* (fig. 10.8) and *Stolotermes africanus* are restricted to forested areas of the Western (*P. planiceps*) or Western and Eastern Cape (*S. africanus*).

One of the obvious morphological characteristics of termopsids is that all individuals have well-developed compound eyes – no other termites have well-developed eyes in all stages. Unlike most other termite families that have four different castes (reproductive queen and king, sterile workers, and soldiers of either sex; see 'Social structure of a termite colony', p. 70), Termopsidae have only three: the worker caste is absent and their role is fulfilled by nymphs. Almost all termite groups have a soldier caste, in most of which the soldiers are sterile males or females. In Termopsidae, however, some soldiers have functional reproductive organs, and are considered as 'soldier-like intercastes' or 'neotenic soldiers'. Nymphs are not pre-programmed to develop into a specific caste but can develop into either primary reproductives or soldiers, depending on the colony's needs. Reproductive soldiers usually have a smaller head and less well-developed mandibles than nonreproductive soldiers, and also have either male or female reproductive organs.

As their common name suggests, Termopsidae live in damp, rotting wood. They have relatively small colonies, living and feeding in the confines of a small nest in logs in contact with the soil. The only time colony members leave the nest is when alates (winged reproductive individuals) abscond to establish new colonies. This they do by flying a short distance, then settling under bark or entering holes made by beetles in wood at the appropriate state of decay. Often the result is that a founding pair establishes a new colony in close proximity to either their natal colony or to another one, which may eventually lead to conflict between adjacent colonies. This is when reproductive soldiers become important. If a colony invades another, soldiers first attempt to kill the royal pair. Battles between soldiers often lead to fatalities on both sides. If the royal pair is killed, the nymphs of the vanquished colony are accepted into the conquering colony. A dearth of soldiers in the new colony then leads to reproductive soldiers laying eggs. Should a colony be split by, for example, a branch housing some colony members breaking off the log, the satellite group of individuals can start a new colony from eggs laid by a female reproductive soldier mated with a male, and build up again slowly.

The silver-spotted ghost moth

The silver-spotted ghost moth, *Leto venus* (Lepidoptera: Hepialidae), is one of the region's largest and most spectacular moths (fig. 10.9). Females have a wingspan of up to 150mm. In 1780, the species was one of the first insects from southern Africa to be given a scientific name by the famous Swedish taxonomist Carolus Linnaeus. Leto, in Greek mythology, was a beautiful woman and the mistress of Zeus and mother of the twins Apollo and Artemis; Venus was the Roman goddess of love, beauty, sex, fertility, prosperity and victory. The first specimen from a precise locality was discovered in 1869 near Plettenberg Bay.

Hepialidae is a small, primitive family of greyish, medium-sized moths whose larvae are mostly grass-root feeders; a few species are occasional lawn pests. *Leto venus*, however, differs from all its relatives in both size and beauty, as well as in feeding behaviour. The moth's larval host plants are two species of keurboom, *Virgilia oroboides* and *V. divaricata* (Fabaceae) (see box, p. 288).

10.8 The damp-wood termite, *Porotermes planiceps* (Blattodea: Termopsidae), is an ancient southern African relict of a once much more widespread group.

Ian Thomas

10.9 *Leto venus* (Hepialidae), one of southern Africa's largest and most spectacular moths, was named after ancient Greek and Roman goddesses of beauty.

Keurboom

Ernst van Jaarsveld

10.10 (a) The keurboom, *Virgilia oroboides*. *Leto venus* larvae tunnel in trees belonging to this genus. **(b)** The trees bear profuse bunches of sweetly scented pink and mauve flowers.

Virgilia oroboides and *V. divaricata* (fig. 10.10) are small to medium-sized bushy trees with beautiful, sweetly scented mauve flowers, common at lower elevations on mountains near the coast. *Virgilia oroboides* occurs from George to the Cape Peninsula, while *V. divaricata* occurs from east of George to the Eastern Cape. The trees grow fast, reaching a maximum diameter of about 600mm and a height of 10–15m within 12–20 years, after which they die. They are typical pioneer species; seed germinates easily and the trees grow quickly in sunny, disturbed edges of forest patches and riverine bush.

Leto venus has a more restricted distribution than its host, occurring mainly in forest from Knysna to the Tsitsikamma National Park, although there are records of its natural distribution extending much further west.

The moths are nocturnal and lay many eggs on the soil, near the base of the keurboom. The larvae (fig. 10.11a) bore into the wood of living trees about 1m above the ground and expel their frass (fig. 10.11b) through external tunnel openings, which are eventually plugged by the mature larva with a mixture of sawdust and gum. Larval development is thought to last for several years, similar to that of other wood-boring insect larvae, consistent with the low nutritional quality of their diet. The pupa, which is mobile (a characteristic of Hepialidae), wriggles quickly to the mouth of the tunnel (fig. 10.11c), pushes the plug out, and protrudes just prior to adult emergence (fig. 10.11d). It has a series of abdominal ridges and protuberances that aid the wriggling motion, as well as spines and setae that anchor the pupa in its tunnel while the adult is emerging. The adult moth climbs up the tree to inflate and expand its wings after emergence. Males fly readily and strongly, beating their wings rapidly like a locust; females are larger and clumsy and do not fly well or far. Adults do not feed, and die after breeding. Ants are the principal egg and larval predators, and bats consume the adults.

The most primitive beetles: Cupedidae

The most primitive beetle suborder, Archostemata, contains only 42 living species worldwide. This is a mere fraction of a once very rich Mesozoic fauna, preserved as thousands of fossils from hundreds of species from Permian, Jurassic and Cretaceous deposits. The living species appear similar to fossil beetles that lived 250mya.

10.11 (a) *Leto venus* larvae tunnel into keurboom trunks, **(b)** expelling clumps of frass stuck together by gum extruding from the wound. **(c)** They pupate in a larval tunnel just below the bark. **(d)** The pupa wriggles to the exit and protrudes about halfway from the hole, after which the adult emerges.

Jonathan Ball

10.12 (above)
Tenomerga leucophaea
(Cupedidae), a relict
of a once abundant
and widespread beetle
fauna, is superficially
similar to the earliest
beetle fossils known.

10.13 (left) The
African red log beetle,
Prostomis africana
(Prostomidae), is the
only African member
of the family, and
another relict of a once
widespread group.

There are two species of Archostemata in southern Africa: *Tenomerga leucophaea* (Cupedidae, fig. 10.12) and *Micromalthus debilis* (Micromalthidae), which is rare and was probably introduced; it has only been found in old mine timbers.

Cupedidae is the largest family in the suborder, with 33 extant species worldwide. Adults have peculiar and typical window punctures on their elytra, with a granular elytral surface and a covering of scales. These were all present in the oldest fossil beetles known. The genus *Tenomerga* is the largest in the family, with 12 species: 10 in Asia, one in North America and *T. leucophaea* in Africa.

Besides its relatively large size (15–20mm long) and attraction to lights near forest patches, very little is known about the biology of *T. leucophaea*. The larvae of related species tunnel in rotten wood and apparently depend largely on fungi for some of their nutritional requirements. This seems likely for *T. leucophaea* as well, considering its presence in rotting wood in evergreen, damp forests where there is an abundance of decomposing tree branches and stems.

The African red log beetle

The African red log beetle, *Prostomis africana* (fig. 10.13) (Coleoptera: Prostomidae), also belongs to an ancient lineage that has a highly disjunct current distribution. The Prostomidae are closely related to the huge cosmopolitan family Tenebrionidae. There are only two extant genera with about 30 species: *Prostomis* is found in North America, Eurasia, several Pacific islands and South Africa, and *Dryocora* in Australia and New Zealand. The family

is known from a well-preserved Cretaceous (95mya) amber fossil discovered in Myanmar, as well as Tertiary (about 45mya) Baltic amber fossils from Northern Europe. *Prostomis africana* is the only African species in the family and is restricted to the Knysna forest.

Prostomis africana adults are flattened, smooth, markedly red-brown beetles, 7–10mm long, with large and prominent prognathous (forward-projecting) mandibles; males are slightly larger and have bigger mandibles than the females. Larvae and pupae of the European and North American species, *P. mandibularis*, have characteristics that are unique to the Prostomidae, so may also be found in *P. africana*. The larvae are markedly dorsoventrally flattened and have short legs armed with stout claws. They grow to about 10mm long, are pale and translucent with the gut contents clearly visible. The darkly pigmented head capsule is broad and characteristically asymmetrical: it is twice as wide as it is long, with the right side more expanded than the left. The mouthparts are distinctly prognathous and the mandibles are of different lengths. The pupa is pure white, and like the larvae and adults, strongly dorsoventrally flattened, with the large developing mandibles clearly visible.

Adults and larvae live in well-rotted, moist wood, where they probably depend largely on fungi for their food requirements. It has been speculated that the strongly prognathous mandibles and flattened bodies of the larvae are adaptations for forcing their way between fibres of decaying wood. Unlike many other characteristically flattened insects, prostomids never live under bark.

Ant-like stone-beetles

Amongst the smaller members of the forest litter fauna are species belonging to the small group of ant-like stone-beetles (Coleoptera: Staphylinidae: Scydmaeninae: Mastigini). These closely related and superficially similar genera form part of the rove beetle family, which is not only the largest beetle family, but the largest family in the animal kingdom, with about 55,000 known species worldwide. Most members of the family have an extended, flexible abdomen and hind wings that are not covered by their very short elytra. Ant-like stone-beetles, in contrast, have the abdomen completely covered by their elytra. As their common name suggests, the beetles are ant-like in size (3–5mm) and appearance.

The southern African Mastigini are represented by the endemic genera *Mastigus* and *Stenomastigus*, as well as *Palaeostigus* (fig. 10.14), which has a disjunct distribution in the Mediterranean region and southern Africa. *Mastigus* occurs mainly along the coast, north and south of Cape Town. *Stenomastigus* is distributed along the escarpment, from northern Mpumalanga to East London. *Palaeostigus* is found along the coast from East London,

10.14 The Knysna forest species of ant-like stone-beetles, *Palaeostigus micans* (Staphylinidae); the common name reflects their ant-like appearance and presence in forest litter.

10.15 Small ball-rolling dung beetles (Scarabaeidae: Scarabaeinae) that are restricted to forest pockets (the largest is 4mm long and the two smallest about 1.6mm long):
(a) *Silvaphilus oubosiensis*;
(b) *Endroedyolus paradoxus*;
(c) *Outenikwanus tomentosus*;
(d) *Nebulasilvius insularis*;
(e) *Bohepilissus nitidus*;
(f) *Aliuscanthoniola similaris*.

Christian Deschodt

through the Garden Route and as far as Lambert's Bay on the West Coast.

The current distribution of *Palaeostigus* and a Cretaceous (100mya) fossil from Myanmar suggests that the group had its origin outside of its current distribution range and that southern Africa was colonised more recently, along the eastern forested montane or coastal strip of Africa.

The earliest dung beetles

Dung beetles (Scarabaeidae: Scarabaeinae) evolved in Africa about 60mya and spread to other continents over time. The world's richest and most diverse dung beetle fauna is still found in Africa, as are relicts of both of the earliest major groups. Although there have been hypotheses proposed over the years that dung beetles may have coexisted with dinosaurs, recent molecular studies show that dung beetles evolved after the demise of the dinosaurs (65mya) and that they radiated in concert with the rise of the mammals.

Primitive dung beetles can be divided into two groups on the basis of various characters, especially their dung-moving behaviour – either 'tunnelling' or 'rolling' (see box, p. 249). Tunnellers bury dung immediately beneath the dung source, while rollers first form a ball of dung, then roll it away to be buried at some distance from the source. Some of the world's most ancient groups of rollers (Canthonini) still live in small forest fragments in southern and East Africa, while their ancient tunnelling equivalents (Dichotomiini) live in small stable rocky habitats in the western parts of southern Africa in association with hyraxes, on whose dung they depend (see 'Hyrax-associated dung beetles', p. 125).

Most African forest Canthonini are very small and flightless, probably an adaptation to the dependable environmental conditions and reliable food supply that a forest offers over millennia. Environmentally stable habitats often allow beetles to lose their ability to fly (see 'Flightless beetles', p. 139). The smaller the beetles are, the more dependable their food sources become, since even tiny amounts of dung (even that of birds and lizards) are sufficient to sustain them. The result is that some of the smallest dung beetles in the world (1.8–2.2mm) still live in the southern and eastern forests. Almost every forest fragment has some of these small beetle species, and they often differ from those in neighbouring forest remnants.

Although there are many minute dung beetles under 3mm long in southern African forests (e.g. *Bohepilissus*, *Peckolus*, *Outenikwanus*, fig. 10.15), those most likely to be encountered belong to the genus *Epirinus* (fig. 10.16), as they are sometimes abundant in suitable habitat. There are about 29 *Epirinus* species in southern Africa; all are less than 7mm long, with some species measuring a mere 2.3mm (*E. ngomae*, fig. 10.16c). They are perfect miniature ball-rolling beetles that roll balls of dung 5mm in diameter; the balls are buried, an egg is laid in each, and the larva develops inside the tiny ball.

10.16 Members of the forest dung beetle genus *Epirinus* are typical ball rollers: (a) *E. validus* and (b) *E. asper* are both montane grassland species on forest edges, and larger than (c) *E. ngomae*.

Ancient keratin-feeding beetles

Keratin is a complex protein that is the main structural element of mammal hair, fur, hooves and horns, bird feathers and reptile scales. Because of its complex linked sulphur bonds (which produce the characteristic smell of burning hair), it is indigestible to most animals. A few insect groups, however, are exceptions: the moth family Tineidae, which includes horn moths (see 'Final-stage carcass colonisers', p. 252) and clothes moths (see 'Clothes moths', p. 401), hide and skin beetles (Dermestidae; see 'Final-stage carcass colonisers', p. 252) and keratin beetles (Trogidae; see 'Final-stage carcass colonisers', p. 252; 'Keratin beetles of the Kalahari', p. 253). Of these, the keratin beetles are the most ancient (fig. 10.17), with their origins reaching back to the tropical world of the Jurassic period (200–150mya), which they shared with giant dinosaurs and the feathered *Archaeopteryx*, on whose remains they may have fed.

Amongst the ancient members of this small, cosmopolitan family (about 300 species worldwide) is a mainly southern African genus, *Phoberus* (previously known as *Trox*). It includes several small forest and montane species, of which a number are flightless (fig. 10.18). *Phoberus* is thought to have evolved in Africa at about the time that the dinosaurs were driven to extinction by large-scale worldwide climate change induced by a meteorite impact (65mya). The oldest lineages in the group live along the eastern escarpment of southern and East Africa, mostly in small protected refuges, while the more recent groups have dispersed more widely, into Karoo and savanna areas. Most members of the ancient lineages are wingless, while all of the more modern species are capable of flight.

Keratin beetles are among the last insects to arrive at a carcass, when little more than hair, skin, scales or feathers remain. These serve as food for the arriving adults and for larvae that develop from eggs laid beneath the carcass. The larvae dig vertical burrows below the carcass and drag keratin fragments into the burrow where they feed.

Like the dung beetles discussed opposite, the forest Trogidae species are small (4–6mm long) and flightless for similar reasons – moderate climatic conditions that have remained stable over millennia, and the abundance of keratin in the form of small animal remains on the forest floor; a few feathers, hairs or scales from a bird, mammal or reptile carcass are enough for the survival of adults and larvae.

10.17 The ancient family Trogidae stretches back to the time of the dinosaurs. This fossil from the lowlands formed by early movement of the East African Rift Valley is slightly more recent, about 46 million years old.

10.18 Keratin beetles (*Phoberus* spp.: Trogidae): one of very few groups of insects capable of digesting keratin. (**a**) *P. capensis*, a 5mm-long wingless relict forest species; (**b**) *P. fascicularis*, a widespread winged southern escarpment species; (**c**) *P. rowei*, a Drakensberg species; (**d**) *P. squamiger*, a widespread Highveld species.

Pollinators

Many of the forest plants are endemic to the particular forest patch in which they occur; some are relicts of the ancient forests of which they formed part, while others are more recently adapted to forest conditions. They are mostly insect-pollinated. The giant yellowwoods, *Podocarpus*, on the other hand, are wind-pollinated.

Although there have been no detailed studies of pollination in southern African forests, there is broad agreement amongst botanists and entomologists that generalist insect pollinators are probably the most important for most forest plant species. This is unlike some other biomes, where specialised pollination systems are commonly found.

Pollen and nectar are the most desirable and nutritious elements of any flower, and many species of different orders visit and feed on them, with pollination a coincidental consequence of their feeding activities. Pollen and nectar feeders include many flies, wasps, honey and solitary bees, butterflies (fig. 10.19) and numerous smaller groups of Hemiptera, Orthoptera and Thysanoptera. Many beetles, likewise, visit flowers, but they are generally less selective and some damage parts of the flower while feeding. Some beetles appear to cause little damage, while others, such as fruit or flower chafers (Scarabaeidae: Cetoniinae), obviously damage flowers while feeding (fig. 10.20). In spite of the damage caused, it is known from other biomes (see 'Monkey beetles as pollinators', p. 80; 'Protea pollination by fruit chafer beetles', p. 184) that some apparently destructive species, while feeding, simultaneously pollinate the plant and that successful pollination of some of the flowers outweighs the total damage caused.

10.19 Forest plants are mostly pollinated by generalist pollinators such as flies, butterflies and bees: (**a**) a bee-mimicking small-headed fly, *Psilodera hessei* (Acroceridae); (**b**) the African wood white butterfly, *Leptosia alcesta inalcesta* (Pieridae); (**c**) the honey bee, *Apis mellifera* (Apidae); (**d**) the solitary bee *Allodape skaifeorum* (Apidae).

10.20 Fruit and flower chafers (Scarabaeidae: Cetoniinae) are also frequent flower visitors, but since they often damage the flower in the process, it is not clear how much pollination they effect: (**a**) *Leucocelis rubra*; (**b**) *Cyrtothyrea marginalis*.

Herbivores

In view of the large quantities of living plant matter of different forms in forests, it is not surprising that herbivorous insects are abundant and diverse and that they have a wide range of feeding strategies. Katydids, including the Knysna forest endemic, *Zitsikama tessellata* (fig. 10.21a), and *Pomatonota dregii* (fig. 10.21b), feed on leaves. Other insects mine inside the leaves, some suck sap, while other specialised species feed on living tissue deep inside tree trunks. A few very small species, such as bark lice and various beetles, live under loose bark where they feed on starch in outer cambium cells. Ripe fruit is highly attractive to fruit-feeding cetoniine beetles, while fermenting fruit is visited by small beetles (Nitidulidae) and vinegar flies (Drosophilidae, fig. 10.22). However, as in most biomes, the plant-feeding guild is dominated by Lepidoptera larvae, and although snails are not insects, they are important invertebrate forest herbivores.

a

b

10.21 Foliage-feeding forest katydids (Orthoptera: Tettigoniidae): (**a**) *Zitsikama tessellata*, endemic to the Knysna forest; (**b**) although *Pomatonota dregii* is present in Knysna coastal forests, it is more common in the subtropical coastal forests of KwaZulu-Natal.

10.22 Vinegar flies, in this case *Drosophila immigrans* (Diptera: Drosophilidae), are very common around fermenting fruit and beverages that are produced by fermentation processes, such as beer and wine.

Beautiful forest butterflies and moths

Several species of butterfly, particularly the 'browns' (Nymphalidae: Satyrinae), are found most commonly in forests, where the larvae feed on grasses in forest clearings and the adults fly in sunny areas on forest edges. The common squinting bush brown, *Bicyclus anynana anynana* (figs 10.23a, b), is widespread in southern African forests; the forest beauty, *Paralethe dendrophilus albina* (fig. 10.23c), is a South African forest endemic; the rainforest brown, *Cassionympha cassius* (fig. 10.23d), occurs in coastal bush, wooded canyons in mountains of the escarpment, and forests from the Cape Peninsula to the Soutpansberg.

Another typical forest butterfly is the garden acraea, *Acraea horta* (Nymphalidae, fig. 10.24), whose larvae feed on the wild peach, *Kiggelaria africana* (Achariaceae). Although both the tree and butterfly were probably originally forest species, the tree has been planted in gardens and parks and the butterfly has followed. Both are now found across the region. Amongst the most highly specialised and geographically localised herbivorous insects are the larvae of certain butterflies, such as the Wolkberg Zulu, *Alaena margaritacea* (Lycaenidae, fig. 10.25), that feed on algae or cyanobacteria. Cyanobacteria are bacteria that photosynthesise, living amongst lichens that grow on rocks exposed to direct sunlight in a few very small forest patches on the northern escarpment.

Many moth species also live and feed in forests. The larvae feed on forest plants, while the adults of many cryptic species rest against appropriately coloured and patterned backgrounds during the day (fig. 10.26). Among these are the larvae of the hawk moths *Temnora zantus zantus* (Sphingidae, fig. 10.27a) and *T. plagiata plagiata* (fig. 10.27b), which feed on the leaves of the white pear, *Apodytes dimidiata* (Icacinaceae). This is a forest tree in southern Cape forests, but also grows in grassland margins of mid-elevation evergreen forests.

a

b

c

d

10.23 Forest satyrine butterflies (Nymphalidae: Satyrinae) are common in sunlit glades: (**a**) squinting bush brown, *Bicyclus anynana anynana*; (**b**) larvae of *B. anynana anynana*; (**c**) forest beauty, *Paralethe dendrophilus albina*; (**d**) rainforest brown, *Cassionympha cassius*.

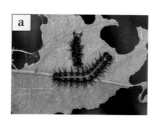

a

b

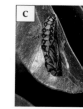

c

10.24 The garden acraea, *Acraea horta* (Nymphalidae: Heliconiinae), originally a forest species, has spread across the subcontinent and now occurs wherever its host, the wild peach, *Kiggelaria africana*, has been planted, often in gardens: (**a**) third-instar larva; (**b**) fifth-instar larva; (**c**) pupa; (**d**) adults.

d

10.25 The Wolkberg Zulu, *Alaena margaritacea* (Lycaenidae), is one of southern Africa's most localised and threatened butterflies. It occurs in small forest patches in the northern Drakensberg, where its larvae live on rocks amongst lichens: (**a**) dorsal view; (**b**) ventral colour patterns.

André Coetzer

10.26 Cryptic forest moths: (**a**) *Nyodes lutescens lutescens* (Noctuidae), common in Afromontane and riverine forests; (**b**) *Parectropis spoliataria* (Geometridae), common in Afromontane forests; (**c**) *Laelia kettlewelli* (Erebidae), endemic to southern and east coast Afromontane forests; (**d**) *Episteira confusidentata* (Geometridae), widespread in Afromontane forests; (**e**) *Acronicta transvalica* (Noctuidae), widespread across wetter parts of southern Africa; (**f**) *Psilocadia obliquata obliquata*, common in Afromontane forests across southern Africa and into tropical Africa.

10.27 (**a**) *Temnora zantus zantus* and (**b**) *T. plagiata plagiata* (Sphingidae) are amongst the larger moths found in forests. Their larvae feed on the foliage of the white pear, *Apodytes dimidiata* (Icacinaceae), a forest tree.

Terrestrial snails

Snails and slugs are soft-bodied invertebrates, usually with a spirally coiled shell, and belong to the class Gastropoda in the phylum Mollusca (fig. 10.28). There are more than 500 indigenous terrestrial snail and slug species in southern Africa, of which about 80% are endemic. In addition, 28 introduced species have become established in the region; 13 of these have been declared invasive. Introduced species are found in almost every habitat (including forests), causing extensive damage to gardens and crops, and may be a threat to forest plants.

Gastropods have a large muscular foot and a well-defined head with a mouth and two pairs of tentacles – the longer tentacles have an eye at the tip. The soft body (visceral hump) lies inside the shell and contains the internal organs. A mantle surrounds the base of the visceral hump, and secretes the material that builds the shell. All soft parts can be drawn entirely into the shell by a special muscle. (Slugs are snails that lack a shell.)

The mouth has a tongue (radula) that is attached to a large muscle, and bears many rows of teeth with which to rasp food. It is pushed out of the mouth so that the teeth are against the plant material and dragged over the plant while moving forward, scraping off particles of plant material which are then carried back into the mouth when the radula is drawn back. Some species are predatory and in these cases the radula is modified to both capture and bore into prey.

Snails move forward with the large flat muscular foot that has numerous mucous glands and cilia (tiny hairs) on its sole. A mucus trail is laid down and the cilia act upon it to propel the animal slowly forward, assisted by slow, continuous waves of muscular contraction and expansion that move over the sole of the foot, each wave moving the animal forward a small distance. The mucus trail is also used to attract mates.

Most snails are hermaphroditic – each individual produces both eggs and sperm. Mating follows a courtship ritual and copulation is reciprocal: the penis of each snail is inserted into the vagina of the other to deposit a spermatophore. After mating, each deposits one or more batches of eggs in damp places or shallow burrows. After a number of days the young emerge as minute snails resembling the adults.

Snails are mainly active at night and in damp weather. By day they hide beneath stones, logs, or in burrows or crevices, with the soft body parts drawn into the shell. A secretion of mucus covers the entrance to prevent desiccation.

Detritus feeders

Detritus is particularly abundant in forests and consists of layers of plant material at various stages of decomposition. Well-rotted, fairly dense matter occurs at the soil/detritus interface. Growing in and on the decomposed litter and more solid plant remains – such as leaves, twigs and logs – is a multitude of fungi, lichens and mosses.

The type of detritus feeders found in a specific location will vary according to the nature of the litter's components, its state of decomposition, and how wet or dry it is. The feeders ingest either the litter itself or fungi and other organisms involved in the decomposition process. The wood of fallen tree trunks provides food for termites (see 'Damp-wood termites', p. 286) and the larvae of a wide range of different beetles (figs 10.29, 10.30), as

10.28 Snails are common under moist conditions such as in forests, where many are important herbivores. Their diet needs to include matter high in calcium in order to maintain their shell, and includes (a) tree leaves and (b) lichens, using special enzymes to digest the algal component of the lichens. (c) Although common in moss beds, they do not feed on the moss itself but on algae and fungi amongst it.

10.29 Cerambycidae (Coleoptera): (a) the larva of a hardwood-boring species; (b) a spectacular adult beetle, *Hypsideroides junodi*.

10.30 The larvae of this beetle, *Atractocerus brevicornis* (Lymexylidae), bore into hardwood logs.

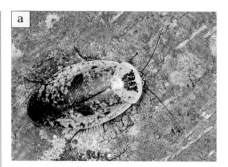

10.32 Cockroaches (Blattodea) are common and important members of the detritus community in forests: (**a**) *Gyna caffrorum*; (**b**) *Hostilia* sp.; (**c**) *Supella* sp.; (**d**) an unidentified species.

10.31 (**a**) The hardwood-boring larva and (**b**) an adult *Metahepialus* moth (Hepialidae).

well as the wood-feeding larvae of a few specialised moth species (fig. 10.31). Many different insects may be found in finer litter, on which they either feed or in which they live; the most important are cockroaches (fig. 10.32) and earwigs.

Many detritus feeders, including earthworms, millipedes, woodlice and mites, are not insects, but are so important in the forest biome that we discuss them here.

Earthworms

Earthworms belong to the class Oligochaeta in the phylum Annelida (see 'What is an insect?', p. 14). Forests contain the highest numbers of earthworms of any biome in the region. In southern Africa, 282 endemic species in three families have been recorded. There are also 44 introduced species that share most habitats with indigenous species; they have even spread to relatively undisturbed areas, including forests.

Earthworms are made up of between 115 and 200 ring-like segments, with the mouth on the first, and the anus on the last. There is no distinct head. Each segment has four pairs of tiny bristle-like setae contained in a chitinous sac inside the body wall. The setae assist in locomotion and stabilisation in the burrows in which they live. Adult earthworms are able to regenerate their segments if injured, even growing a new mouth and segments, or anus and segments.

Earthworms are found in many regions of the world, mainly in healthy, moist soils rich in humus (organic matter). They excavate the soil by forming numerous burrows, consuming soil containing decaying vegetable matter as they burrow. As the soil passes through the gut, it is enriched with microbes and the remains of digested organic matter, which improves the soil quality considerably in the process. When temperatures drop in winter, earthworms dig deeper into the soil and remain inactive until conditions become warmer. They do the same when conditions become intolerably hot and dry, rolling up into tight balls to retain moisture. When soil is moist and temperatures moderate, they lie in the upper part of their burrows during the day.

Earthworms are nocturnal, foraging and mating at night. They do not usually leave their burrows; the front part of the body is extended forward out of the burrow over the ground surface where they consume above-ground litter, while the hind end of the body remains anchored in the burrow by setae. This enables the worm to retract into the burrow quickly at any sign of danger. After flooding following heavy rains, they emerge completely from their burrows, and may be found crawling on the soil surface.

Earthworms have both male and female reproductive parts (hermaphroditic) in the same individual and they mate throughout the year, mainly in warm, moist weather. Two worms stretch out from their burrows and bring their body surfaces together, with the front ends pointing in opposite directions. In this way the reproductive receptacles are lined up – male with female in both individuals – and sperm is passed from one to the other, after which they separate. Each worm later produces cocoons, each containing several eggs, which are then fertilised with sperm. Development requires several days, and the worms hatch as tiny replicas of the adults.

Millipedes

Millipedes are arthropods and belong to the class Diplopoda (see 'What is an insect?', p. 14), represented by eight families with 67 genera and about 467 species in southern Africa; there are four introduced species.

Diplopoda are many-segmented, cylindrical arthropods that have a head and trunk (fig. 10.33). The trunk consists of segments, of which the first four form the thorax; the first thoracic segment is legless and the next three have one pair of legs each. The remaining segments make up the abdomen, and each segment has two pairs of legs. The millipede exoskeleton is strengthened with calcium and the dorsal and ventral plates are completely fused. This explains why white 'rings' often remain long after a millipede has decomposed.

The head has a pair of short, jointed antennae, a pair of eyes and mouthparts. The fused maxillae form a broad flattened plate with a pair of sensory palps and a pair of sharp, serrated mandibles used to cut up food. The antennae have tactile setae and chemoreceptors and are probably the main sensory organs; they continually touch the substrate while the animal is moving about. Some large diurnal millipede species have compound eyes, others have from a few to many ocelli, and some lack eyes altogether. However, all millipede eyes can only distinguish between light and dark.

Millipedes lack cuticular waxes and consequently have poor water retention capabilities. They have to live in moist environments; if not, they can only be active under moist conditions or at night. They also curl up in a tight coil to preserve moisture or when threatened. Most species have another form of defence: a pair of glands on each segment secretes toxic hydrogen cyanide. This repels most predators, except civets, hedgehogs, scorpions and millipede assassin bugs (see 'Millipede assassin bugs', p. 309).

Most millipedes move slowly: the legs move in pairs, seemingly in waves, with the legs on one side of the body moving in unison with those on the opposite side. This type of movement is an adaptation for the power necessary to push through humus and soil, where the millipedes search for decomposing vegetation – their main diet. They occasionally feed on plant bulbs and decomposing animal carcasses.

Reproduction is by direct sperm transfer. The genital openings (gonopores) are on the third segment in both sexes. The male, in addition, has mating legs (gonopods) on the seventh abdominal segment with which he removes the spermatophore from his gonopore, and places it in the gonopore of the female. During this process their bodies may be intertwined.

Although forests contain the highest numbers of earthworms, one of the largest earthworm species in the world, *Microchaetus skeadi*, is found in the Karoo and Eastern Cape of South Africa; specimens up to 7m long have been recorded.

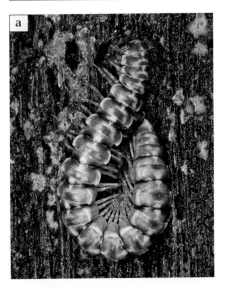

10.33 Millipedes (Diplopoda) are diverse, abundant and important detritivores in the forest: (**a**) a member of the Dalodesmidae; (**b**) *Deratogonus annulipes* (Spirostreptidae); (**c**) a pill millipede, *Sphaerotherium dorsaloides* (Sphaerotheriidae).

Females of some species dig brood chambers in moist soil in which they lay 20–300 eggs; others lay each egg separately and cover it with a clay capsule; members of a third group lay a clutch of eggs that is covered with a casing. Some species show maternal care with the female curling protectively around the batch of eggs until they hatch. Miniatures of the adult hatch within a few weeks, and these grow throughout their life (which in some species may be 10 years) by moulting. The moulting process may take up to three weeks to complete; the shed cuticle is consumed.

Millipedes are common in forests, as they require a moist environment in which to live; indeed, pill millipedes (fig. 10.33c) are rarely found elsewhere. Many species have adapted to drier environments, where they commonly inhabit the moist burrows of other animals. In the Kalahari, they are common in the burrows of rodents and the beetle *Parastizopus armaticeps* (Tenebrionidae; see 'Subsocial beetles and their nest parasites', p. 234) and feed at night.

Armadillo-like pill woodlice

Woodlice (fig. 10.34) are small crustaceans in the order Isopoda (phylum Arthropoda, class Crustacea; see 'What is an insect?', p. 14). There are around 10,000 species of Isopoda globally, of which about half are aquatic. Terrestrial woodlice make up the largest suborder (Oniscidea), with over 4,000 species, which inhabit forests, mountains, deserts and the littoral zone (see 'Common woodlice', p. 385). Two woodlouse families occur in southern Africa: common woodlice (Porcellionidae) and pill woodlice (Armadillidae).

An unusual characteristic of pill woodlice is that they can roll themselves into a tight ball (termed conglobation), which is the reason for their common name, as well as the family name. They do this when they are disturbed or threatened, and the behaviour is triggered by stimuli such as vibrations or pressure; it is a key defence mechanism and also conserves moisture.

Members of the Armadillidae are usually found in moist environments such as forests, where they live under decomposing leaf litter and in the soil. They feed on moss, algae, bark and decaying matter on the forest floor.

Mites

Mites are also arthropods, but are arachnids in the order Acari, which they share with ticks (class Arachnida; see 'What is an insect?', p. 14 and 'The life of ticks', p. 246). There are 40,000 described species of mites worldwide, with an estimated 2,500 species occurring in southern Africa; it is, however, thought that the known species are a mere fraction of the actual numbers.

Mites are found in most regions across the world from forests to deserts and polar regions to hot springs. They have diversified widely in their ways of life: some are parasites and are associated with disease, such as mange and scabies in mammals; others are predators; many are herbivores, including numerous pest species. Many more are detritus and fungus feeders and are abundant in forest soil: a small sample of leaf mould could contain hundreds of individuals belonging to several species.

All mites and ticks are covered by a tough carapace and have a fused cephalothorax and abdomen without signs of external segmentation. Adults usually have four pairs of legs, but the larvae hatch with only three pairs, followed by a few eight-legged nymphal stages. Eyes, if present, are located in various positions, depending on the species.

In mites, the mouthparts are carried in the capitulum, which usually projects from the body in a small point (the buccal cone) at the front of the body. On either side of the mouth is a pair of chelicerae for piercing, tearing and gripping food, and a pair of pedipalps; these differ widely between species. Although feeding differs greatly between groups, the general method is to ingest fluids. Pieces of solid food may be torn off using the chelicerae, then digested externally and sucked up as a fluid.

Many species reproduce by indirect sperm transfer: a male deposits a spermatophore, which is then picked up by the female; in some species, the male may place the spermatophore in the female's genital orifice with

10.34 (left) Woodlice (Crustacea: Isopoda) are members of a terrestrial group of the otherwise marine or freshwater crustaceans. This species belongs to the Porcellionidae.

10.35 (right) Although mites are abundant throughout forests and other biomes, most are so small that they are seldom seen. This red velvet mite (Trombidiidae) is about 8mm long and belongs to a group of relatively large species.

his chelicerae. In some species, the male transfers sperm directly to the female; parthenogenesis is also a common method of reproduction.

Most mites are very small – some are small enough to live in the tracheae of insects. On the other side of the spectrum, the southern African velvet mite grows to about 8mm long (fig. 10.35). Most free-living mites in forests are found on plants, in moss, on leaf litter, on rotten wood and in detritus. They are often found on larger insects, which they use for transport between suitable habitats.

Herbivorous species, such as red spider mites, have chelicerae modified into needle-like stylets that are inserted into plant cells and used to suck out plant sap. Red spider mites also construct protective webs from silk glands that open near the base of the chelicerae. Most soil mites feed on fungi, algae and decaying plant and animal material, and have mouthparts that are modified for their particular diet. Some carnivorous species, which live in forest detritus or soil, feed on nematodes, tiny arthropods (including insects) and their eggs, or even other mites.

Free-living earwigs

Earwigs are insects that belong to the small but diverse order Dermaptera. It is divided into three suborders: the free-living Forficulina, and two suborders that live on their hosts (see 'Rat-associated earwigs', p. 300).

Southern African Forficulina are divided into six families with about 50 species. All members are broadly similar in appearance – they are elongated insects with short, square, leathery forewings (tegmina) and mobile, flexible abdomens armed with abdominal pincers or forceps (cerci) (fig. 10.36). The characteristic forceps are used by winged species to tuck the broad, fan-shaped, elaborately folded membranous hind wings beneath the tegmina, in a manner unique in insects, so that they occupy very little space under the small tegmina. The forceps are also used to capture prey and in defensive displays. Winged species rarely fly.

Males are usually smaller than females and they differ slightly morphologically: the forceps of males are longer and usually scimitar-shaped, while they are short and straight in females; the abdomen of males consists of 10 segments, while females have eight segments. Females practise an advanced form of brood care (see left-hand box, p. 300).

Forficulina are nocturnal and all live in damp protected environments under logs, rocks and loose bark and in leaf litter. Some species are herbivorous, a few are predatory (capturing small invertebrates with their forceps), but most are detritivores, feeding on a wide range of plant and animal remains.

Several cosmopolitan species are found in southern Africa. The predatory river earwig, *Labidura riparia* (Labiduridae, fig. 10.36a), is common under rocks and logs on river banks and the sea shore and is thought to have colonised Africa naturally. Although harmless, they may adopt a threatening posture by bending the abdomen over the head and pointing the forceps at a perceived enemy when disturbed, while at the same time producing a foul odour. Some species are occasionally found in suburban homes.

10.36 Free-living earwigs (Dermaptera: Forficulina) are important detritivores in forests: (**a**) *Labidura riparia* (Labiduridae); (**b**) nymph (Pygidicarnidae); (**c**) *Forficula* sp. (Forficulidae); (**d**) *Echinosoma* sp. nymph (Pygidicarnidae).

Brood care in earwigs

The females of Forficulina – free-living earwigs – practise a fairly advanced form of brood care. The mated female usually digs a burrow in the soil (or sometimes uses an existing cavity), in which she lays a batch of 20–40 eggs that hatch after 2–8 days. She remains in the burrow with the eggs and the white first-instar nymphs until they moult into the second instar 4–8 days later; thereafter she and the nymphs disperse.

Brood care in the Dermaptera has apparently evolved in response to predation and pathogen pressure. Predation from birds, small mammals and terrestrial arthropods, such as hunting spiders and scorpions, is high in shallow burrows. Likewise, underground burrows in damp soil provide a fertile environment for pathogenic microbes such as fungi to develop. Maternal care of the most vulnerable stages significantly improves individual survival. The details of brood care vary between species:

- In its simplest form, the female remains with and guards the eggs against predators and cleans them of fungus; after they hatch, she guards the first-instar nymphs until they moult and disperse.
- In a slightly more complex interaction between the brood and the female, she not only guards, but also feeds the nymphs, either on regurgitated food or food harvested outside the burrow and carried in her mouth.
- The most unusual form of brood care is found in cold temperate regions of the world, such as Japan. The female, because of the short warm season, lays only one batch of eggs in her lifetime. She remains with and cares for the eggs and nymphs until the end of the first instar, after which she is eaten by the nymphs (matriphagy). Although this may seem bizarre, it is the ultimate form of altruism – the female sacrifices her body to ensure that her offspring have a rich food source before they leave the safety of the burrow.

Disturbed brooding females usually eat the eggs or young nymphs (filial cannibalism). This is assumed to be a way of recycling energy invested in the brood, which is recaptured and utilised during a subsequent attempt at breeding.

Rat-associated earwigs

Two suborders of Dermaptera are epizoic – they live nonparasitically on the external surface of other animals. The Arixeniina of Southeast Asia live in close association with insectivorous bats (Molossidae) and the African Hemimerina have an obligatory dependence on giant pouched rats (Nesomyidae).

There are two genera in the Hemimerina, both in the family Hemimeridae: *Araeomerus* from East Africa and *Hemimerus* across tropical Africa. *Hemimerus deceptus* (fig. 10.37) is the only southern African species and lives on the Gambian pouched rat, *Cricetomys gambianus* (see box below), in localised forested areas of the Soutpansberg in Limpopo province.

10.37 The epizoic earwig *Hemimerus deceptus* (Dermaptera: Hemimerina) lives on the Gambian pouched rat (also known as the African giant pouched rat), *Cricetomys gambianus*, in South Africa.

Gambian pouched rats

Gambian pouched rats are widespread across tropical West, East and southern Africa, where various *Hemimerus* species are associated with them. The rats are large (1.0–1.5kg) and live in colonies of up to 20 individuals. They are omnivorous and carry food in their cheek pouches to underground stores for later consumption. They have poor eyesight but an acute sense of smell, an attribute that has led to their being trained to detect buried land mines in war zones and tuberculosis infection in the sputum of sufferers of the disease.

Because of the obligatory dependence of *Hemimerus deceptus* on Gambian pouched rats, the conservation status of the insect is closely related to that of its host. Although widespread in sub-Saharan Africa, in South Africa the rats are restricted to forested areas of the Soutpansberg. They are threatened by habitat disturbance and the bush meat trade and are considered to be Vulnerable in South Africa.

Hemimeridae have highly modified external structures compared to other Dermaptera, which can be attributed to their specialised life style. Their adaptations include a cockroach-like body; very short, broad legs that have specialised, spiny depressions on the top of the tibia to accept the tarsus when this is folded back to hold onto the host's hair; and tarsi with large membranous pads beneath and claws at the end to assist with adhering to the host's skin. They also have reduced sclerotisation of the cuticle and straight narrow cerci, and lack wings and eyes. Unlike other Dermaptera, they give birth to live young (vivipary).

Most rodents are adept at removing parasites from themselves and each other by grooming, but these epizoic earwigs are tolerated to such an extent that substantial numbers (up to 100, but more usually about 40) live on a single rat. They roam freely on its body. For years, *Hemimerus* species were thought to be parasites, but it has been shown that they have a mutualistic relationship with their hosts instead – they feed primarily on the host's dry skin cells and on fungus. The fungi are probably pathogenic, causing hair loss and bare patches on the host's skin – the lower the numbers of earwigs on the body, the greater the numbers of bare patches. The insects' mouthparts are specialised for grazing and brushing the dead skin and fungus off their hosts, not for feeding on blood. In return for this service, they are tolerated by the rats.

Hemimerus deceptus earwigs spend their entire life cycle on host rats, where they live in colonies of mixed-age individuals. The adults are about 10mm long, with females slightly larger than males. Dispersal between individual rats occurs when the rats mate, as well as from the mother rat to her offspring in the nest. Brood care in the Hemimerina has progressed from the typical brood care of free-living Forficulina (see 'Free-living earwigs', p. 299) by the evolution of vivipary and social living, which afford substantially improved protection of offspring. A *Hemimerus* female produces about 20 nymphs per breeding cycle, 10 serially from one ovary, then, shortly thereafter, another 10. There are four nymphal stages.

Fungus feeders and spore dispersers

The large deposits of detritus and the generally high humidity in forests create ideal conditions for the growth and development of various decomposition fungi, of which there is a high diversity in southern African forests (fig. 10.38). Some of these are eaten by specialised fungus-feeding insects; however, many species that appear to feed mainly on detritus depend to a large extent on fungi in the detritus to meet their nutritional

10.38 The high humidity and abundance of dead plant matter at various stages of decay in forests create ideal conditions for the growth of a very wide diversity of fungi, and many of these have insects associated with them: (**a**) false turkey tail, *Stereum ostrea*; (**b**) funnel woodcap, *Lentinus sajor-caju*; (**c**) golden coin cap, *Cyptotrama asprata*; (**d**) jelly shell fan, *Crepidotus mollis*; (**e**) unknown; (**f**) unidentified species (Tricholomataceae).

10.39 The beetle *Chryphaeus taurus* (Tenebrionidae) on a bracket fungus.

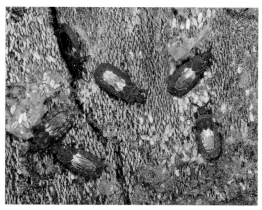

10.41 Bark or flat bugs such as this *Neuroctenus caffer* (Hemiptera: Aradidae) live under bark, where they feed on fungi.

10.42 Blow flies are attracted to the bright, carrion-like colours and odours of stinkhorn mushrooms, and spread their spores.

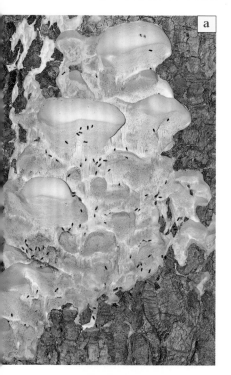

10.40 The fungus-associated fly *Mycodrosophila fracticosta* (Diptera: Drosophilidae): (a, b) Males and females congregate on a suitable fungal mass to mate; (c) females lay eggs on the fungus which serves as larval food.

needs. This association may extend to some foliage and wood feeders, which may also depend largely on fungal deposits in their food.

Many groups of beetles (fig. 10.39) and flies (fig. 10.40) have a strong association with fungi, as do the atypical bark bugs or flat bugs (Hemiptera: Aradidae, fig. 10.41), which live under bark or in cavities in rotting wood where they feed on fungi.

Blow flies attracted to foetid fungi

Fungi are not only fed on by insects – there are also some that, in turn, depend on various insects to distribute their reproductive spores. These fungi have specialised mechanisms to attract insects. Stinkhorn mushrooms (Phallaceae) produce carrion-like or dung-like odours to attract spore-dispersing insects, especially flies. Most species consist of a white stalk (receptaculum) with a sticky spore mass (gleba) carried on a terminal structure. Some species (e.g. *Aseroë rubra*, fig. 10.42) are thought to represent rotting flesh around the anus of a dead animal. Whether the flies that are attracted see it this way, is questionable, but the foetid smell undoubtedly attracts blow flies. The flies that feed on the gleba ingest spores and get them stuck to their legs, then carry the spores away from the fungus. The flies that are attracted to the fungus probably derive little benefit, although there may be some nutritional elements in the sticky fluid on which they feed.

Predators

The terrestrial invertebrate predatory guild living on plants and on the forest floor is probably shared almost equally by different invertebrate groups, including planarian worms, velvet worms, insects and a host of arachnids, all discussed in detail in this section. Aerial predators include various Neuroptera, such as silky and green lacewings, and Odonata (see 'Forest damselflies and dragonflies', pp. 316–317).

Terrestrial planarian worms

Planarian worms are flatworms, in the class Turbellaria of the phylum Platyhelminthes. Other common members of this phylum are human or other mammal parasites such as tapeworms (class Cestoda) and liver flukes (class Trematoda).

The majority of planarian worms are aquatic predators, occurring in marine and freshwater habitats. A few are terrestrial, living in moist places such as forests, where they are found under logs, in the soil, or on plants (fig. 10.43). They have a pair of eyespots (simple eyes) in the centre of the head region; these are sensitive to light but form no image. Prey is located by chemoreceptors that taste or smell. A muscular tubular pharynx (or proboscis) can be extended from the mouth, which is situated on the ventral surface near the middle of the body.

Planarian worms move by gliding over a film of mucus produced by gland cells in the epidermis. Mucus is also used in prey capture. Planarians move around slowly, searching actively for prey or insect remains. When they locate suitable prey, they grip it with the head region and glide over it, trapping it in mucus; then the tubular pharynx is extruded and enzymes are secreted onto the prey. Digestion begins externally and the resulting broth is sucked up through the pharynx into the intestine, where digestion is completed.

Planarian worms are able to regenerate lost body parts; indeed, if cut into pieces each piece will regenerate into a complete new individual. Asexual reproduction happens in a similar way – the worm breaks off its last segment, which then regenerates into a separate individual. Sexually mature worms are hermaphrodites, each bearing both testicles and ovaries. Two individuals join their posterior ends and both give and receive sperm. Eggs then develop in each individual and are shed in egg capsules. The eggs hatch weeks later into tiny, but otherwise typical, planarians.

10.43 Planarian worms (Turbellaria) are slow-moving predators of small invertebrates or their remains amongst moist detritus on the forest floor.

Velvet worms: living fossils

Velvet worms are members of the small phylum Onychophora, which has two living families, Peripatidae and Peripatopsidae. Eleven species of Peripatopsidae occur in southern Africa. Onychophorans are called 'living fossils' because they appear to have changed little since they evolved from a marine ancestor more than 530mya; evidence suggests that they became terrestrial during the Ordovician period, about 450mya. They are considered to be an evolutionary link between Annelida (see 'Earthworms', p. 296) and Arthropoda, the phylum to which insects, crustaceans, arachnids, millipedes and centipedes belong (see 'What is an insect?', p. 14).

Onychophorans have a cylindrical, soft-skinned, worm-like body with between 16 and 23 pairs of short stumpy legs, each of which ends in two hard, sclerotised claws (fig. 10.44). Adults vary in size from 5–200mm long. The head is only slightly defined and has a pair of sensory antennae, with a small simple eye at the base of each. The mouth is located on the ventral side of the head and has a pair of hidden mandibles that tear and grind food. Onychophorans

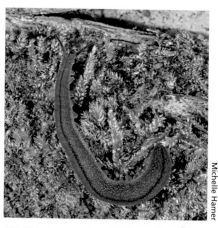

Michelle Hamer

10.44 Velvet worms belong to the ancient invertebrate phylum Onychophora. There are 11 southern African species, all in the genus *Peripatopsis*.

Traumatic copulation in velvet worms

Onychophorans – worm-like animals that have been called 'living fossils' – have a life span of up to six years. Males and females are separate individuals, with females being larger. Fertilisation takes place internally, and in most species males deposit a spermatophore (packet of sperm cells) into the genital opening of the female. Some species of *Peripatopsis*, however, reproduce using a method called traumatic copulation (see 'Bed bugs and bat bugs', p. 352; 'Vinegar flies', p. 399; 'Bed bugs', p. 403). The male sticks spermatophores onto the female's skin. Amoebocytes from the female's haemolymph collect below the spot on the inside of the body, secreting enzymes that cause the decomposition of the female's body wall, as well as the spermatophore casing (the wound heals afterwards). The sperm are released from the casing and enter the female's haemocoel and move via the haemolymph to the ovaries, where the ovary wall is penetrated and the ova are fertilised. Females of many species are fertilised only once during their lives and sperm are kept in a special reservoir where they can remain viable for long periods.

Most onychophorans are ovoviviparous, and the medium-sized eggs remain in the uterus for a gestation period of up to 15 months. The young, which resemble tiny adults, emerge from the eggs in the uterus shortly before birth. A single female can produce up to 23 offspring per year.

have an unusual way of capturing prey: they squirt sticky slime at their prey, secreted by two fleshy papillae next to their mandibles. The slime physically immobilises the prey and enables the onychophoran to inject it with saliva, which begins an external digestion process. Once some external digestion has taken place, the prey is devoured and ground up by the mandibles.

Their thin velvety skin dries out easily, so velvet worms can only live in moist environments and have to hunt at night when humidity is high. Their skin has a unique structure and is repellent to the stickiness of their slime, although in some species, spermatophores can be stuck to it during reproduction (see box, p. 303).

Spiders

Southern Africa has a rich, relatively well-studied spider fauna comprising about 2,300 species in 78 families. Spider diversity is particularly high in forests (fig. 10.45).

True spiders belong to the order Araneae of the class Arachnida, in the phylum Arthropoda (see 'What is an insect?', p. 14). The cephalothorax and abdomen are separated by a narrow 'waist', called the pedicel. They usually have eight simple eyes arranged in two rows of four pairs on the front of the cephalothorax. The chelicerae, which in some species are equipped with teeth, are modified as fangs with which venom is injected into the prey. Spiders in the suborder Araneomorphae are distinguished by having chelicerae that point forward and cross in a pinching action, whereas suborder

Mygalomorphae have chelicerae pointing straight down. The pedipalps of females are short and leg-like, while those of males are modified as copulatory organs.

In web-building spiders (mostly members of Araneomorphae) the last segment of the leg ends in three claws. Hunting spiders (mostly Mygalomorphae) have only two claws with a dense tuft of hair between them, forming a scopula; this creates adhesion, enabling the spiders to climb up smooth surfaces. Sensory setae are found on almost all parts of the body surface of most species.

All spiders have special silk glands producing silk (see box opposite) that is excreted through spinnerets, but not all spiders build webs in order to catch their prey – the more active cursorial hunting spiders do not build webs and instead capture their prey by running them down and pouncing on them. Both types of spider kill their prey with injected venom. Most species then secrete digestive juices onto the prey while chewing it with their chelicerae before sucking up the liquid mass. The cuticle of the abdomen is much thinner than that of the cephalothorax, which allows the abdomen to distend after feeding.

In most spiders, sensory perception is through setae, with which they are able to sense vibrations from the web or silk line. They can perceive the size of prospective prey caught in the web, or feel vibrations from the tapping of a prospective mate. The setae are also used in chemoreception: they can smell pheromones, and chemoreceptive hairs in the mouth are sensitive to taste. Sight is not very important in most species, but some

10.45 Spiders are the dominant arthropod predators in forests: (**a**) thyene jumping spider, *Thyene* sp. (Salticidae); (**b**) Namibia's green lynx spider, *Peucetia crucifera* (Oxyopidae); (**c**) horned bark spider, *Caerostris sexcuspidata* (Araneidae); (**d**) yellow box kite spider, *Isoxya tabulata* (Araneidae); (**e**) Thornton's red ladybird spider, *Paraplectana thorntoni* (Araneidae); (**f**) dark spitting spider, *Scytodes fusca* (Scytodidae).

Spider silk

Jenny Scholtz

Web-building spiders build webs of astonishing complexity (fig. 10.46); moreover, they are able to build such webs immediately after hatching. The web is usually replaced daily, since it loses its stickiness after a few days. The old silk is often eaten and the protein re-used in the production of new silk.

Silk is also used for various other functions by both web builders and hunting spiders, including:

- lining nests;
- encasing eggs;
- wrapping up prey;
- dispersal (using hanging threads);
- guide lines assisting them to find their way;
- drop lines to escape from predators;
- communicating (pheromones placed on silk assists members of the opposite sex to locate each other); and
- mating (males deposit sperm in a small 'sperm web').

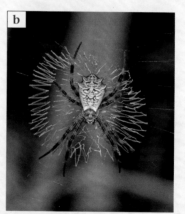

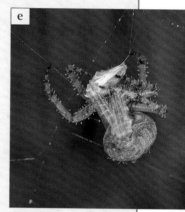

10.46 (a) *Stegodyphus dumicola*, commonly known as community nest spiders, build large communal nests which have advantages such as cooperative nest maintenance, prey capture and brood care; (b) *Argiope* sp.; (c) some spiders, like this *Nephila* sp., wrap a significant amount of silk around their prey and include bits of debris in the web to advertise its presence and prevent it from being damaged by large animals; (d) *Gasteracantha versicolor*, which commonly build their orb webs across paths at 1.8 metres from the ground; (e) *Neoscona* sp. wrapping a prey item to immobilise it.

cursorial hunting species, such as wolf spiders (Lycosidae) and jumping spiders (Salticidae), have good eyesight that helps them to catch their prey.

Male spiders are usually significantly smaller than females. Before mating, the male deposits a droplet of sperm on a small web that he has previously spun. He then dips his pedipalps into this globule until all the semen has been absorbed into special containers at the end of the pedipalps. He sets out to find a female, and after a courtship ritual (which varies greatly between species), he inserts his pedipalps into her genital openings and deposits the sperm. The female stores the sperm in seminal receptacles until she lays her eggs.

A week or two after mating, the female spins a small cup-shaped nest. The eggs are fertilised with the sperm and laid in the nest, which is covered with a layer of silk, forming an egg sac. The egg sac is then either attached to the web, hidden in a hole or burrow, stuck to the ground with silk, or dragged about with the female. The spider nymphs, which resemble the adults, hatch and remain in the egg sac until after the first moult, after which they emerge. Some females carry the nymphs on their back until they are old enough to fend for themselves. The nymphs moult many times before adulthood, when moulting ceases.

Harvestmen

Harvestmen are arachnids in the order Opiliones (see 'What is an insect?', p. 14). They are found mainly in humid environments, such as in leaf litter, on logs and tree trunks in forests, as well as in caves. Of the approximately 6,500 species of Opiliones globally, about 215 occur in southern Africa.

Harvestmen resemble daddy-long-legs spiders (Araneae: Pholcidae), as they have extremely long and slender legs (fig. 10.47); the second pair of legs is the longest and has a sensory function. The cephalothorax and abdomen are joined, not separated by a pedicel as in spiders, so the body looks like a single oval structure. The abdomen is externally segmented. The chelicerae are small, slender and claw-like, and the pedipalps are usually short and leg-like.

Their most unusual feature is the placement of their eyes on a tubercle in the centre of the cephalothorax with an eye on each side. They also have openings to defensive scent glands along the sides of the cephalothorax and secrete quinones and phenols with an acrid odour when threatened. Harvestmen are able to cast off a leg if caught by a predator; the legs do not regenerate, so these arachnids are often encountered with missing legs.

Harvestmen are mainly predatory, feeding on mites and aphids, but do sometimes scavenge. Their food is not limited to liquids – they can ingest small particles and it is therefore assumed that most digestion takes place in the midgut.

Reproduction is direct and internal insemination takes place by means of a penis. There is no courtship; copulation occurs promptly when a male and female meet. The female has an ovipositor positioned between her front legs with which she lays eggs.

Whip spiders

Yet another order of arachnids is the whip spiders (Amblypygi), of which there are only three species in southern Africa. The most common and widespread of these is *Damon variegatus* (fig. 10.48). Despite their common name, they are not closely related to spiders.

The whip spider body is extremely flattened and they are found beneath logs, bark, rocks or in leaf litter in forests. They have eight eyes, two of which are located centrally, and two groups of three eyes placed laterally. Like spiders, whip spiders have a pedicel connecting the abdomen and the cephalothorax. The end segment of their chelicerae also forms a fang-like hook, but they have no venom glands.

Whip spiders have heavy, spiny, often pincer-like pedipalps, with which prey are physically overwhelmed and held while being eaten. The first pair of legs is long and antennae-like, terminating in a very thin and flexible whip-like structure, which gives them their common name. These specialised legs have a sensory function and are often held in front of the whip spider as it moves, frequently touching the ground. They often

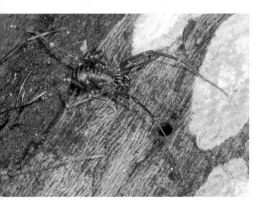

10.47 (left) Most harvestmen (Opiliones) are predators of very small invertebrates, but they may also scavenge on animal matter.

10.48 (right) Despite its intimidating appearance and rapid movement in any direction, the whip spider *Damon variegatus* (Amblypygi) is a harmless predator of small invertebrates.

10.49 Pseudoscorpions, like this (**a**) 5mm-long member of the Atemnidae (Pseudoscorpiones), live in protected environments beneath rocks, logs or bark, but are quite often seen hitching a ride on large insects, which they use as a transport method, as in (**b**).

move sideways in a crab-like manner, with one of the antenna-like legs pointed in the direction of movement. They are able to run equally rapidly sideways, forwards and backwards.

Reproduction involves elaborate courtship displays – male and female approach each other while moving their whips in stroking motions and swaying their bodies from side to side. They use spermatophores in a similar manner to that of scorpions (see 'Scorpions', p. 129). The eggs are carried by the female in an egg purse, and the hatchling nymphs are carried below her body until their first moult, and then on her back until the second moult, after which they disperse.

Pseudoscorpions

Pseudoscorpions resemble tiny scorpions and are placed in the arachnid order Pseudoscorpiones (see 'What is an insect?', p. 14). These small arachnids (3–10mm long) occur in all biomes, but are most abundant on vegetation and leaf litter in forests, where they prey on mites. There are about 2,000 species worldwide, of which 135 are found in southern Africa.

Although pseudoscorpions look like scorpions, they have a rounded abdomen without the characteristic scorpion tail (fig. 10.49). The rounded cephalothorax is not separated from the abdomen and is covered by a carapace-like rectangular shield. Their chelicerae contain spinnerets with which they produce silk to line their nests. Some species have eyes. The pedipalps are large and pincer-like and contain poison glands. They are slow-moving and can be recognised by their habit of holding their pedipalps up in front of them as they walk.

In all forms of reproductive behaviour a

spermatophore is first placed on the ground, and the female eventually moves over it and takes it into her genital opening. In some species, the male simply deposits a spermatophore on the substrate, marks it with a pheromone, and leaves it for the female to find. In others, the male spins a silk thread that leads the female to the spermatophore. The most complex type of mating behaviour involves courtship – the male makes elaborate movements with his pincers to attract the female. This is similar to the courting 'dance' of scorpions.

Some species deposit eggs in silk-lined nests, while others carry the eggs below the abdomen until they hatch. The nymphs may be fed with gland secretions during extended brood care.

Pseudoscorpions are often found attached to large insects, especially those that live under bark, such as long-horned beetles (Cerambycidae). They use the insects for transport between suitable habitats. Some are found in the nests of honey bees where they prey on mites associated with bees, and also use the bees for transport.

Centipedes

Centipedes are predatory arthropods in the class Chilopoda. The class belongs to the subphylum Myriapoda, an arthropod group that also includes millipedes (see 'Millipedes', p. 297). Centipedes occur all over the world and there are about 1,700 species globally. In southern Africa, they are represented by 10 families, 30 genera and 113 species.

Centipedes are nocturnal and usually live in humid environments such as under leaf litter or under bark or logs. They have to live in a moist environment because their spiracles cannot close and they lose water easily.

10.50 Centipedes are fast-moving, aggressive predators of any invertebrates (or occasional small vertebrates) that they can overpower: (**a**) stone centipede, *Paralamyctes spenceri*; (**b**) *Scolopendra* sp.

The bodies of centipedes are long and flattened and consist of a head and trunk (fig. 10.50). The head has a pair of very long, segmented antennae. Some species have a few ocelli that can distinguish between light and dark. In certain species there are special sensory organs at the base of the antennae, which apparently sense vibrations and monitor humidity. The mouthparts consist of mandibles that have teeth, a thick fringe of setae below the mandibles, and two pairs of maxillae. On either side of the mouth is a curved poison claw that terminates in a fang with which venom is injected into prey or enemies; these hook-like appendages are modified legs on the first trunk segment, not the head.

The trunk consists of 15 or more segments of which each, except the last two, bears a single pair of long legs. Centipedes move fast to catch their prey and are able to run rapidly both forwards and backwards. The legs on the third-last segment are the longest and are sensory or, in some species, modified into defensive pincers. Some species have glands on each segment that secrete repellent chemicals, including hydrogen cyanide and benzoic acid. Many species can shed their legs as a means of defence; the missing legs are replaced over subsequent moults. Aposematic colours are common.

Centipedes locate prey using their antennae or sensory legs, then grab and immobilise it with their poison claws, which inject venom into the body. The venom contains digestive enzymes. Soon after, the centipede rips open the prey's body using its mandibles and ingests it.

Reproduction is by indirect sperm transfer using a spermatophore. In some species, there is courtship before mating. Both sexes may be involved in palpating their opposite's posterior with the antennae; the process may last as long as an hour. The male then spins a small web with spinnerets located on the last legless segment next to his gonopore, on which he deposits a spermatophore. He then signals the female by palpating her with his antennae; she picks the spermatophore up and deposits it in her gonopore. In other species, the male simply sticks a spermatophore to the female's gonopore and the sperm migrates into the female unaided.

Females of some species practise brood care of egg masses and early instar young; others abandon eggs soon after laying them. In those that practise brood care, the mated female finds a cavity in a piece of wood or a hollow in the ground, lays the eggs, and coils herself around the egg mass. She protects them throughout the incubation period, which may take up to two months. Once the young have hatched, she remains with them until after the first or second moult.

In species that lack brood care, the female lays large sticky eggs singly and drags them around between her hind legs; grains of sand or bits of detritus stick to the eggs and camouflage them. The eggs are then dropped and left to hatch.

Ectrichodia crux

Ectrichodia crux (fig. 10.51) is a large common reduviid species found throughout much of southern Africa. The bugs feed on spirostreptid millipedes (Diplopoda: Juliforma), which produce defensive quinones, but these do not deter the bugs and it has been speculated that the bugs may even sequester some of their preys' defensive chemicals for strengthening their own defensive glandular secretions. *Ectrichodia crux* adults kill and feed singly on millipedes that are often many times their own body weight. Their bright red nymphs, however, attack and feed communally (fig. 10.51b) and it has been suggested that their collective injections of toxin are required to immobilise large prey.

10.51 The millipede assassin, *Echtrichodia crux* (Hemiptera: Reduviidae: Ectrichodiinae): **(a)** adult; **(b)** nymphs and millipede prey. All members of the subfamily prey exclusively on millipedes.

Millipede assassin bugs

Assassin bugs (Hemiptera: Heteroptera: Reduviidae) are members of a huge family of almost exclusively predatory insects. Reduviids can be distinguished from other Hemiptera by their elongated head and short curved beak or proboscis (rostrum); their head is relatively small and often tapered behind the large eyes, giving the impression of a long neck, and the short, three-segmented rostrum is curved outwards and downwards from the head, but swung forwards to attack and pierce prey. They are aposematically coloured (fig. 10.52), often red or yellow and black, or metallic blue, indicating noxiousness. Most are generalist predators, but some specialists target specific prey, including millipedes and spiders. They stalk their prey, then pounce, stab it with their short beak (rostrum) and inject it with proteolytic enzymes that immobilise and kill the animal, and also begin the digestion process. Careless handling of large reduviids may result in a very painful bite and even temporary paralysis of the area around the bite. Members of the Central and South American subfamily Triatominae suck vertebrate blood, including that of humans. They are vectors of the protozoan *Trypanosoma cruzi*, which causes Chagas disease; these protozoans are closely related to those transmitted by tsetse flies, which cause sleeping sickness in humans and nagana in livestock in Africa (see 'Tsetse flies as carriers of disease', p. 264).

Ectrichodiinae, one of the largest and most widespread of Reduviidae subfamilies, comprises about 700 species distributed in the tropics, all of which seem to be specialist predators of millipedes (see box opposite). The biology of the dozen or so southern African genera and their roughly 40 species is largely unknown, although *Ectrichodia, Glymmatophora* and *Maraenaspis* species have been recorded to prey exclusively on millipedes.

Millipede assassin bugs are nocturnal and usually prey on millipedes larger than themselves. Although millipedes are often very smooth, the bugs have an unusual adaptation to help hold onto their prey: their front and middle tibiae have specialised soft spongy areas that function as suction cups to attach and hold onto slippery, writhing prey long enough to insert their proboscis into the soft intersegmental membranes while injecting it with digestive enzymes. Paralysis is almost instantaneous – and fatal; if the bug is removed from its prey before it starts to feed, the millipede does not recover. The enzymes liquefy the prey internally and the assassin bug sucks up the resultant fluids through its proboscis using a strong pharyngeal pump.

10.52 Assassin bugs (Reduviidae) are so called because of their stealthy approach and quick strike on prey, which they stab with their characteristic mouthparts. These are in typical pose: (**a**) *Odontogonus pallidus*; (**b**) a mating pair of dimorphic *Rhynocoris erythrocnemis* – the male is on top; (**c**) *Vitumnus scenicus*. They are all brightly coloured to advertise their ability to defend themselves by 'biting'.

Thread assassin bugs

Thread assassins (Hemiptera: Heteroptera: Reduviidae: Emesinae) are atypical members of the assassin bug family – they are very slender, with long, thin, thread-like limbs, and raptorial front legs, similar to those of praying mantises (fig. 10.53). They hold their raptorial legs in front of them as they walk in a swaying motion, somewhat resembling crane flies (Diptera: Tipulidae; see 'Crane flies', p. 342; 'Crane flies and leather jackets', p. 387).

They are voracious predators and feed in the same way as millipede assassins (see above). They usually prey on small flies and gnats, but some take up residence in spiderwebs, where they either steal the insect prey caught in the web (kleptoparasitism), or prey on the spider itself. Those that prey on spiders (araneophagic) have two hunting strategies: they 'stalk' the spider slowly and then strike; or they 'lure' the spider by manipulating the web silk with their legs to simulate movement caused by snared prey before striking.

Thread assassins are nocturnal and are attracted to lights. During the day, they stay in dark, humid places, such as in holes or under rotting logs. About 45 species have been recorded in southern Africa.

10.53 Some slender thread assassins (Reduviidae: Emesinae) prey on small insects caught in spiderwebs, and also on the spiders themselves.

Frog-eating beetles

Most vertebrates are so large in comparison to insects that very few predatory insects are capable of preying on them. The few records of such interactions are usually incidental occurrences of ants preying on nestling birds or rodents, mantises attacking small lizards and birds on plants, or bugs and beetles feeding on small fish, terrapins and tadpoles in aquatic habitats (see 'Water scorpions', p. 333). Undoubtedly one of the most unusual and bizarre examples of insects feeding on vertebrates is that of a terrestrial ground beetle preying on frogs that are 5–20 times its own size – and not just occasionally. In a complete role reversal, insect-eating frogs have become the prey of specialist frog-eating beetles.

Two beetle species in southern Africa are known to be frog eaters: *Chlaenius circumscriptus* and *C. simba* (Carabidae: Licininae: Chlaeniini). *Chlaenius circumscriptus* is widespread in Europe, the Near East and across Africa; *C. simba* is restricted to southern Africa. Both are large, about 16–25mm long.

The larvae of these species, like other Carabidae larvae, are predatory (see 'Predatory ground beetles', p. 239; 'Ferocious tiger beetle larvae', p. 363), and have three instars, but are obligatory frog eaters (fig. 10.54). In the first instar they are blood-feeding ectoparasites on their frog host, in the second they feed on blood and tissue, and in the third, on tissue only. Adults eat mostly insects, but kill and eat frogs when they encounter any. Adults and larvae share the same moist habitats as their hosts.

Most beetle larvae have small antennae, but in *Chlaenius* they are well developed. The larvae also have unusual, large, double-hooked mandibles, which enable them to attach firmly to the frog's body. They have a group of six very large stemmata on each side of the head capsule (as do their tiger beetle relatives; see 'Ferocious tiger beetle larvae', p. 363), which suggests that they have reasonable vision; most other beetle larvae have small stemmata that only distinguish between light and dark.

All larval stages are sit-and-wait predators that attract approaching frogs by imitating potential prey (termed aggressive mimicry). When a frog approaches, the larva starts waving its mandibles and antennae simultaneously from side to side to attract the frog's attention. These movements increase in frequency as the frog comes closer. When the frog gets to within striking distance, it lunges at the larva, but the larva retaliates by attaching onto the frog, usually on the mouth, throat or chest.

It has been recorded that frogs occasionally successfully swallow the larvae, but that they are soon regurgitated – after which they immediately attach to the host and start feeding! In one especially bizarre case, a frog swallowed a larva, which could be seen moving in the frog's abdomen for about two hours until the frog regurgitated it; the larva promptly attached to the frog and eventually ate it.

Chlaenius species are rare examples of insects that are both parasitic and predatory in the larval stages. The blood-sucking first-instar larvae stop feeding and detach from their still-living host at the end of the instar, after which the frog probably survives. Second- and third-instar larvae always kill their prey. After feeding, the larvae moult in a sheltered site on the ground, after which a new host has to be located and attacked; this is repeated at the end of each instar. Larval and pupal duration is short for such large insects – about four weeks – during which time they feed on at least three frogs.

The adult beetle attacks amphibian prey by jumping onto its back and biting into the lower back muscles. Although the frog tries to dislodge the attacker by jumping, its movement ceases within one to two minutes, after which the beetle eats the frog, leaving only bones.

Three frog species have been recorded as beetle hosts or prey in southern Africa: the raucous toad, *Amietophrynus rangeri* (record from Port Elizabeth), the clicking stream frog, *Strongylopus grayii* (Cape Town, Knysna), and the painted reed frog, *Hyperolius marmoratus verrucosus* (George).

Colin Ralston

Colin Ralston

10.54 (a) A larva of the forest frog-eating beetle *Chlaenius* (Carabidae) attached to a painted reed frog, *Hyperolius marmoratus*, which it is slowly consuming; **(b)** larva with partially consumed frog; **(c)** adult beetle.

Aerial predators

The guild of forest aerial predators is fairly small but represented by the nocturnal adults of various unusual and endemic Neuroptera of especially the Psychopsidae (silky lacewings) and Chrysopidae (green lacewings). Adults of the Psychopsidae resemble moths (fig. 10.55a); little is known about larval behaviour but some Psychopsidae species may live and prey on small invertebrates under bark as occurs with similar species in other parts of the world. Chrysopidae larvae are free-living predators on foliage. The compound eyes of Chrysopidae adults (fig. 10.55b) are conspicuously golden in some species. Other significant aerial predators include members of the Odonata (see 'Forest damselflies and dragonflies', pp. 316–317), which are diurnal.

10.55 Moth-like silky lacewing adults (Neuroptera: Psychopsidae) such as **(a)** *Cabralis pallidus* are common predators in forests, as are green lacewing adults such as **(b)** *Apochrysa voeltzkowi*.

Parasites and parasitoids

In general, the parasites of natural insect populations are poorly known, but many disease-causing parasites such as fungi (fig. 10.56), bacteria and viruses are undoubtedly prevalent in all regions, fungi perhaps more so in humid forests than in drier regions. On the other hand, the larvae of many species of fly and wasp are well known as internal and external parasitoids that feed on and kill their hosts – usually the larvae of other insects (see 'Parasites', p. 52).

Parasitoid flies

The fly family Tachinidae has about 400 species in southern Africa (fig. 10.57). Females may lay (oviposit) their eggs directly onto the host, or, in the case of ovo-viviparous species, deposit a larva (termed larvipositing) on the host. Other species lay their eggs (or larvae) close to the host; when the eggs hatch, the mobile first instars, termed planidia, are able to find it. Planidia are the first-instar larvae of holometamorphic insects with a hypermetamorphic life stage – a type of metamorphosis in which the different larval instars have forms that are morphologically and behaviourally different (see box, p. 42; 'Blister beetle larvae', p. 171). Most tachinid flies parasitise butterfly and moth (Lepidoptera) larvae. Some species do this by laying large numbers of very small eggs on leaves that are consumed by the caterpillar; the eggs then develop inside the host. Other species stick large eggs or a young larva to a host. The parasitoid larva then penetrates the host's cuticle and develops as an endoparasite.

10.56 Fungal pathogens thrive in the humid conditions in forests. Weakened insects, such as this fly, are quickly attacked and overwhelmed.

10.57 All species of Tachinidae, the largest fly family, are parasitoids of other insects.

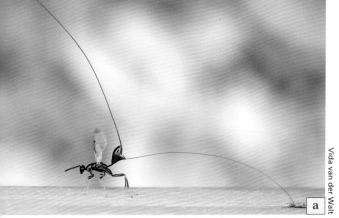

Vida van der Walt

10.58 This 5mm-long wasp, *Ecdamua macroteles* (Chalcidoidea: Torymidae), is a parasitoid of the hole-nesting wasp *Polemistus braunsii* (Crabronidae). (**a**) She extends her 20mm-long ovipositor and detects the host's nest entrance, before (**b**) inserting the full length of the ovipositor to lay an egg on the host brood deep inside the wood. The ovipositor consists of three valves, but only the central valve carries eggs; the other two valves are not used during egg-laying.

10.59 (**a**) The suspended pupa of a species of *Charops* (Ichneumonidae), whose larva parasitises (**b**) these caterpillars (Lepidoptera: Limacodidae).

Parasitic wasps

Wasps in the large families Ichneumonidae and Braconidae (Hymenoptera) are well known as parasitoids – their larvae are either endo- or ectoparasites of a wide range of hosts, killing the host in the process. The female wasps use sensilla on their long antenna to find their hosts. There are also sensilla on their ovipositors, which are used for host recognition and acceptance and to lay eggs accurately. Wasps that specialise in locating and parasitising the larvae of hole-nesting bees and wasps, as well as wood-boring beetles, have exceptionally long ovipositors (fig. 10.58). Adult ichneumonid and braconid wasps are often superficially similar and can most readily be distinguished only by the presence or absence of a particular wing vein.

There are more than 500 ichneumonid species in southern Africa. They vary in size (5–20mm long) and parasitise a wide range of hosts, although most are parasitoids of butterfly and moth larvae and pupae. Other hosts are wood-boring beetles, flies, antlions, lacewings, bees, ants and other wasps.

Members of the ichneumonid subfamily Campopleginae spin mottled brown and black pupal cocoons that hang from a long thread (fig. 10.59). The cocoon swings when even lightly touched and the colour pattern is thought to imitate bird droppings. This may offer the wasp pupa

10.60 These Braconidae wasps parasitise Lepidoptera and wood-boring beetle larvae. (**a**) *Apanteles* females lay several eggs in the host. After feeding, the larvae emerge and spin tiny pupal cocoons on the caterpillar's body wall, or (**b**) beneath the still-living larvae. (**c**) A *Serraulax* female drilling her long ovipositor through the wood surrounding a host beetle larva.

some protection against attack by hyperparasitoids (see 'Hyperparasitoids', p. 54).

Braconid wasps, of which there are several hundred species in southern Africa, are usually smaller than ichneumonids. Most species parasitise moth and butterfly larvae. A typical example is the large and widespread genus *Apanteles*, whose larvae are endoparasitoids of various Lepidoptera larvae (figs 10.60a, b). Multiple larvae feed inside the host caterpillar; they eventually emerge to pupate in characteristic small egg-shaped cocoons attached to the host, which may sometimes still be alive. Other groups in the family specialise on other hosts – an example is *Serraulax*, which parasitises the larvae of wood-boring beetles (fig. 10.60c).

Dung and carrion feeders

Southern African forests are home to mammals such as monkeys (fig. 10.61), bush pigs and various small antelope, including bushbuck and endemic duiker species. Their dung is a resource used by a host of dung feeders. The dung of smaller vertebrates, such as rodents, birds and reptiles (and even that of invertebrates), provides a range of small-sized food items for smaller insects. When these animals die, various carrion insects feed on their carcasses at different stages of decomposition (see box alongside).

The most important dung-feeding insects in forests are dung beetles (Scarabaeidae: Scarabaeinae), although the suite of groups present differs considerably from those in other biomes (see 'Dung feeders', p. 50). Many deep-forest species are very small and are relicts of ancient faunas (see 'The earliest dung beetles', p. 290). Larger and often more widespread species occur along forest margins and typically feed on larger dung deposits. These include rollers, such as species of *Sisyphus* (fig. 10.62), and tunnellers in the large genus *Onthophagus*. Dung is also used by various flies (fig. 10.63).

10.61 A samango monkey, *Cercopithecus albogularis*, one of the larger forest mammals whose dung and dead bodies provide food for numerous dung- and carrion-feeding insects.

10.62 The typical ball-rolling dung beetle *Sisyphus muricatus* (Scarabaeidae: Scarabaeinae) is a forest and highland member of a large, widespread African group.

Stages of decomposition

The different stages of decay of a decomposing carcass largely determine the types of insects it attracts (fig. 10.64). Under humid forest conditions, these stages may differ somewhat from those in other biomes, although the major groups involved are similar (see 'Carrion feeders', p. 54). The earlier decomposition stages attract flies, such as blow flies (Diptera: Calliphoridae) and flesh flies (Sarcophagidae), and beetles, such as carrion beetles (Coleoptera: Silphidae) and scavenging rove beetles (Staphylinidae). These are followed by beetles that prey on fly maggots in the carcass, for example, hister beetles (Histeridae) and other rove beetle species. The later dry stages of the carcass attract hide beetles (Dermestidae) and keratin beetles (Trogidae; see 'Ancient keratin-feeding beetles', p. 291).

10.64 Three groups of insects from different stages of the decomposition of a small carcass: (**bottom left**) a late-stage keratin beetle (Trogidae); (**lower centre**) an early-stage mature blow fly (Calliphoridae) maggot; (**top left and right**) middle-stage carrion beetles (Silphidae).

10.63 (right) Various flies quickly colonise fresh dung. Among the first are small, black, wing-waving members of the Sepsidae, such as this *Adriapontia* species.

a

b

10.65 Adult and larval carrion beetles (Coleoptera: Silphidae) are attracted to and feed on carrion under cool or forested conditions: **(a)** *Thanatophilus* sp. adult and **(b)** larva.

a

Lyndall Pereira

b

c

10.66 These mayflies (Ephemeroptera) are endemic to cool waters in southern African montane forests: **(a)** *Lithogloea harrisoni* nymph (Teloganodidae); **(b)** *Aprionyx* sp. nymph (Leptophlebiidae); **(c)** *Aprionyx* sp. adult.

Carrion beetles are common in the northern hemisphere, but are poorly represented in southern Africa: only a few species in two genera, *Thanatophilus* and *Silpha* (Silphidae: Silphinae, fig. 10.65), occur here. Both adults and larvae are free-living under carcasses and may be fairly abundant under suitable conditions. Adult beetles are grey/blue/ black and medium-sized (10–20mm long). Larvae are black and cockroach-like, with fringes of lateral plates along the length of the body. Adults mostly eat the carrion itself, while larvae eat carrion and fly maggots. Members of the silphid subfamily Necrophorinae, which occur only in the northern hemisphere, have well-developed brood care. A pair buries a small carcass (such as that of a bird or rodent) and then lives with their larvae in the surrounding soil chamber, where they feed on decomposition fluids.

Aquatic forest insects

Most of the aquatic insect species inhabiting forest streams and ponds are widespread species that occur in a variety of habitats. There are, however, some mayflies, dragonflies, damselflies and caddisflies that are predominantly associated with water bodies in forests.

Forest mayflies

Mayflies (Ephemeroptera) are one of the basal insect orders with long-lived aquatic nymphs and terrestrial adults (see 'Damselflies and dragonflies', p. 324) that live for only a few hours. There are 14 families and 105 species in southern Africa; two families contain forest-dwelling species.

Teloganodidae are endemic to the western and southern Cape, with five genera and 13 species. The nymphs of some species of *Lithogloea* (fig. 10.66a), *Nadinetella* and *Ephemerellina* are confined to forest streams, where they live in moss beds on rock faces in fast-flowing water.

Leptophlebiidae genera that are found in forests are *Aprionyx* (figs 10.66b, c), with eight southern African endemic species, and *Castanophlebia*, with two species. *Aprionyx* nymphs live under stones in moderately flowing streams or in pools associated with forests, while *Castanophlebia* nymphs prefer fast-flowing forest streams.

Forest caddisflies

Adult caddisflies (Trichoptera) are moth-like terrestrial insects with hairy wings (fig. 10.67); most are short-lived and do not feed. All caddisfly larvae are aquatic and most live in a shelter or case (see 'Caddisflies', p. 343).

The most diverse larval biology is found in the Leptoceridae, the largest family in the order. Some species build cases of pure silk; others use sand grains; while still others use carefully cut sections of plant matter. Larvae may also make cases of different materials during their development or modify the abandoned cases of other species. Some species are predatory, others are detritivores. Some species of *Leptecho* and *Athripsodes* are forest dwellers.

Pisulia austrina and four species of *Silvatares* (formerly known as *Dyschimus*; Pisuliidae, fig. 10.68a) are restricted to forested streams. These are among the larger species in the order: adults have wingspans of 20–40mm and larvae are 15–22mm long. A characteristic of this family is that larvae make triangular portable cases from dead leaves and twigs.

Goera hageni (Goeridae, figs 10.68b, c) adults have a wingspan of 10–13mm and larvae live in cool, high-lying streams. The larval cases are made from small stones, with a few larger ones attached on the sides.

Lepidostoma caffrariae (Lepidostomatidae) larvae live in forested streams among leaf litter and detritus, on which they feed. Their cases are started with fine sand grains; as the larva grows it progressively adds finely cut leaf fragments until the final case appears square when viewed end-on. Adults have a wingspan of 12–15mm.

Anisocentropus usambaricus (Calamoceratidae, fig.10.68d) larvae are found in slow-flowing streams and backwaters of forested areas. The larvae use two cut leaves of slightly different sizes to make their cases; the smaller leaf is attached beneath the larger with silk. Adults have a wingspan of 28–32mm.

10.67 A forest caddisfly adult, possibly *Athripsodes* sp. (Trichoptera: Leptoceridae).

10.68 Caddisfly larvae and pupae: (a) *Silvatares* sp. larva (Trichoptera: Pisuliidae); (b) *Goera hageni* larva (Goeridae); (c) *G. hageni* larvae and pupae; (d) *Anisocentropus usambaricus* larva (Calamoceratidae).

Ferdy de Moor

Forest damselflies and dragonflies

The ancient insect order Odonata has existed since the Permian period (299 mya). It consists of two suborders – damselflies (Zygoptera) and dragonflies (Anisoptera). All species have aquatic nymphs and strongly flying terrestrial adults; both stages are voracious predators in their particular habitats (see 'Damselflies and dragonflies', p. 324).

Although the adults of the suborders appear similar, there are some characteristics that distinguish the two groups. Damselflies are daintier with slender bodies and narrower wings that, in most species, are closed along the length of the body when perched, and their large compound eyes are typically widely separated. Dragonflies, however, appear much more robust and always perch with their wings widely spread at right angles to the body, and their eyes usually touch at the top of the head. The nymphs also differ considerably; Zygoptera are slender, swim with sinuous movements, and breathe through three long caudal gills at the end of the abdomen, while Anisoptera are squat, crawl, and breathe through internal gills situated in the rectum.

There are specialist forest species in both suborders. Damselflies are more prevalent in the southern forests, whereas dragonflies are mainly tropical species with their southernmost distribution restricted to forests of the northern escarpment of South Africa.

Forest damselflies

The queen malachite, *Ecchlorolestes nylephtha* (Synlestidae, fig. 10.69a), is a South African forest endemic restricted to southern Cape forests, where it frequents fern-lined streams under closed forest canopy. Although restricted to their habitat, populations can often be locally abundant.

The goldtail, *Allocnemis leucosticta* (Platycnemididae, fig. 10.69b), is a shade-seeking southern African endemic that is widespread along the escarpment. It is found along the margins of flowing streams and rivers in forests and well-wooded valleys. Individuals are often gregarious, with several perching together on objects close to the water.

10.69 Forest-endemic damselflies (Odonata: Zygoptera): (**a**) *Ecchlorolestes nylephtha*; (**b**) *Allocnemis leucosticta*.

10.70 Both subspecies of the damselfly *Pseudagrion hageni* (Odonata: Zygoptera) are forest endemics: (**a**) *P. h. hageni* in the southern Cape; (**b**) *P. h. tropicanum* in forests of KwaZulu-Natal, northwards to East Africa.

Hagen's sprite, *Pseudagrion hageni* (Coenagrionidae), is an eastern escarpment forest species with two subspecies. *Pseudagrion hageni hageni* is locally common in forests of the southern Cape, where it is shade-seeking along vegetated edges of flowing streams (fig. 10.70a). *Pseudagrion hageni tropicanum* occurs in forests from KwaZulu-Natal northwards to East Africa (fig. 10.70b).

Forest dragonflies

The distribution of the three forest dragonfly species in southern Africa is centred in Central and East Africa with their southern African distribution restricted to forest streams of the northern escarpment; all are rare. The forest hawker, *Zosteraeschna usambarica* (Aeshnidae, fig. 10.71a), frequents forested streams and glades in indigenous forests as well as in plantations. Jones' forestwatcher, *Notiothemis jonesi* (Libellulidae, fig. 10.71b), is restricted to pools and calm stretches of shaded forest streams. The unicorn or sable cruiser, *Phyllomacromia monoceros* (Macromidae, fig. 10.71c), is occasionally encountered along montane forest streams.

10.71 Rare southern African forest dragonflies (Odonata: Anisoptera): **(a)** *Zosteraeschna usambarica* (Aeshnidae); **(b)** *Notiothemis jonesi* (Libellulidae); **(c)** *Phyllomacromia monoceros* adult (Macromidae); **(d)** *P. monoceros* nymph hiding amongst leaf litter on the bottom of the pool – typical behaviour of Odonata under shaded conditions. **(e)** Typical habitat of these forest endemics.

CHAPTER 11
FRESHWATER HABITATS

Although less than 1% of southern Africa is covered by open water, the region has a rich aquatic and semiaquatic insect fauna in perennial standing water and running water systems, as well as on their shores. The water bodies include rivers and streams (fig. 11.1), pools in river courses, artificial impoundments across water courses and thousands of farm dams and livestock drinking troughs. They also include temporary water bodies of various sizes that hold water only during the rainy season. Ephemeral sources of water may even include the organically enriched decomposition fluids under large carcasses and effluent spills from feedlots and dairies. A few species live in brackish, others in highly saline waters inland or close to the sea.

For each of the wide range of possible aquatic habitats, insect inhabitants require special adaptations for movement, breathing and feeding. These adaptations range from special breathing structures and mouthparts, to eyes adapted for sight both in and out of water.

Some of the basal (primitive) insect orders – mayflies (Ephemeroptera), damselflies and dragonflies (Odonata) and stoneflies (Plecoptera) – are often called aquatic orders because their immature stages are wholly aquatic and mostly long-lived. The adults are free-living, terrestrial, mostly short-lived and, with the exception of Odonata, do not feed. The holometamorphic alderflies and dobsonflies (Megaloptera) and caddisflies (Trichoptera) also have aquatic immature stages and short-lived, nonfeeding, terrestrial adults. Some orders have groups with aquatic or semiaquatic immature and adult stages; these include a few grasshoppers and crickets (Orthoptera), several bugs (Heteroptera), and many flies (Diptera) and beetles (Coleoptera).

Aquatic insects may occur at various trophic levels. Herbivores, such as aquatic and semiaquatic algal grazers and plant feeders, are found amongst mayflies, caddisflies, grasshoppers and crickets. Mayfly and stonefly nymphs and caddisfly, beetle and fly larvae are often litter or detritus feeders. Aquatic predators include larval and adult beetles, alderfly and dobsonfly larvae, damselfly and dragonfly nymphs, as well as nymphs and adults of aquatic and semiaquatic bugs.

Adaptations to aquatic life

Conditions in water are very different from those experienced by terrestrial insects, and breathing and feeding under water require special adaptations.

Respiration

Water is obviously not a limiting factor for aquatic insects, but the oxygen content and pH levels of a water body may be. Daily temperature fluctuations are more moderate in large water bodies than on land; however, in shallow pools the temperature can fluctuate widely during the day. Extreme temperature variations limit the availability of oxygen in the water, because oxygen levels decrease with increasing temperature. Dissolved chemicals and decomposing organic matter may lead to eutrophication and anoxia, placing physiological stress on the respiration and osmoregulatory processes of aquatic insects. When oxygen levels drop below a certain threshold, wastes accumulate in the body and may reach toxic levels.

Aquatic insects obtain oxygen in one of two ways: directly from the atmosphere, or from air dissolved in the water.

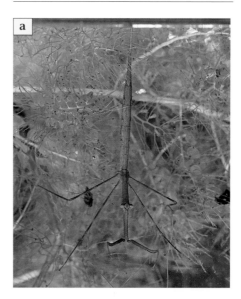

11.1 (pp. 318–319) The Olifants River in the Lowveld Savanna floods periodically and its riverbed provides a wide range of habitats for a diversity of insects.

11.2 While submerged, certain insects breathe atmospheric oxygen by means of tubes connected to the spiracles. In (a) water scorpions (Hemiptera: Nepidae) and (b) larvae of predaceous diving beetles (Coleoptera: Dytiscidae), the tube is permanently extruded. (c) The larva of the hover fly *Eristalis tenax* (Diptera: Syrphidae) can telescopically extend and withdraw its breathing tube.

Oxygen from the atmosphere

Some species breathe directly from the atmosphere while the body is submerged. This happens through a breathing tube (siphon), the tip of which is exposed through the surface film of the water. The posterior spiracles open at the end of the tube; these are usually the only functional spiracles in the insect's tracheal system. Water scorpions (Hemiptera: Nepidae, fig. 11.2a) and certain beetle larvae (fig. 11.2b) have a permanently extruded siphon. In many other groups the siphon is extendible, sometimes by as much as three times the body length of the insect, as in the larvae of the hover fly *Eristalis tenax* (fig. 11.2c). Further typical examples of breathing atmospheric oxygen are mosquito larvae and pupae (Culicidae), water beetle larvae (Dytiscidae), and giant water bug adults and nymphs (Belostomatidae).

11.3 Some insects, when they submerge, carry an air supply with them in the form of (a) an air bubble under the elytra, as in this predaceous diving beetle (Dytiscidae), or (b) a thin layer of air held by water-repellent hairs on the underside of the insect, as in some bugs.

Other insects breathe during periodic visits to the surface. They need a mechanism that prevents water from entering the spiracles when they submerge again after taking in air. Tufts of special hairs cover each spiracle during submersion. When the insect surfaces, the tufts are forced open by surface tension forces, much like the strings of a mop being forced together under water, then falling apart when it is withdrawn. In some groups the hairs around the spiracles are coated with oily, water-repellent substances.

Oxygen from aquatic plant tissues

The immature stages of several insect species obtain oxygen from the air spaces in aquatic plant tissues. These air spaces provide free air for insects capable of puncturing the plants. Certain beetles, such as the leaf beetle genera *Donasiasta* and *Donaciocrioceris* (Chrysomelidae: Donaciinae), and the larvae of the fly families Syrphidae and Ephydridae have a sharp, pointed siphon, which is often armed with teeth to penetrate plant tissues. Some Ephydridae pupae and Nepidae eggs, likewise, have a respiratory spine that is inserted into plant tissues, from which oxygen is extracted.

Air stores

Diving insects that depend on free air can only stay submerged for as long as their tracheal supply lasts, after which they must surface to replenish it. Some species augment the tracheal supply by carrying a bubble of air that is held close to the spiracles. This specialised area of the cuticle is called a plastron. The nature and position of the air supply varies among species. In water beetles, a bubble is held beneath the elytra (fig. 11.3a); when it is expended, the beetle drifts backwards and upwards to the water surface until the tip of the abdomen is exposed and replenishes it. In other beetles and some heteropteran bugs air is held in a thin layer by hydrofuge (water-repellent) hairs that cover the ventral surface of the abdomen (fig. 11.3b) adjoining the spiracles.

Air dissolved in water

Air in the tracheal system of a diving insect is at equilibrium with the atmosphere and contains about 21% oxygen, 79% nitrogen and less than 0.5% carbon dioxide. In water saturated with air, the proportion of gases changes to about 33% oxygen, 64% nitrogen and 3% carbon dioxide, as oxygen and carbon dioxide are more soluble in water than nitrogen.

In all aquatic insects there is some inward diffusion of the oxygen dissolved in the water through the cuticle, and in the larval stage of many groups this is the only form of gaseous exchange. These insects usually have a closed tracheal system in which all the spiracles are nonfunctional. In this system, oxygen from the water diffuses through the cuticle and into the tracheae, which spread it to the tissues. A few species also have haemoglobin that aids oxygen transport; it is chemically similar to that of vertebrates, but has a much higher affinity for oxygen. These insects have red haemolymph (see 'Midges, gnats, bloodworms', p. 340).

11.4 Immature stages of various aquatic orders have externally visible tracheal gills: (a) mayflies (Ephemeroptera), visible as 'hair-like' structures on the abdomen; (b) damselflies (Odonata: Zygoptera), visible as three 'tail-like' structures at the end of the abdomen; (c) dobsonflies (Megaloptera), visible as 'leg-like' structures on the abdomen.

11.5 Dragonfly nymphs as in this *Phyllomacromia monoceros* (Macromiidae) obtain oxygen from air-saturated water being drawn into the rectum when abdominal muscles contract. The lining of the rectum is provided with a fine tracheal network, which draws the oxygen into the tracheal system. Oxygen-depleted water is either slowly expelled from the rectum, or in bursts which propel the nymph forward – this is one of their defensive strategies.

Many submerged aquatic insects extract oxygen from air-saturated water using tracheal gills, which consist of a network of tracheoles just below the insect's cuticle, either widespread across the body, or in special leaf-like extensions in certain body parts, particularly the abdomen. In some aquatic immatures such as mayfly, damselfly and stonefly nymphs and dobsonfly larvae (fig. 11.4), they are externally visible, while in dragonfly nymphs they are situated inside the rectum (fig. 11.5).

As water flows, or is drawn across the gill surface, oxygen diffuses from the water into the tracheoles. This occurs as oxygen is used up in the insect's system and the proportion of nitrogen increases. This disturbs the equilibrium between the gases in the system and the gases in the water, and results in the movement of gases to restore the equilibrium. Oxygen therefore diffuses from the water into the tracheae to reduce the proportion of nitrogen in the tracheal system. As carbon dioxide is very soluble, it is quickly 'extracted' from the air in the insect's respiratory system and passed out into the water.

Feeding in aquatic habitats

In an aquatic environment, insects have to contend with nutrient dilution of their food source, which has led to the evolution of special mouthparts and food-gathering mechanisms in many groups (see box below).

Special feeding mechanisms in aquatic insects

Flowing water has led to the evolution of novel food-gathering mechanisms among aquatic insects, such as the silken nets spun by many caddisflies (Trichoptera, fig. 11.6) and some midges, gnats and bloodworms (Chironomidae) to trap food particles transported by the stream. Other examples are:

- The nymphs of certain mayflies (Ephemeroptera) have specialised organs to filter food from the water or to assist in brushing food into the mouth; these are on the front legs in brush-leg mayflies (Oligoneuridae) and on the mouthparts of stout crawlers (Trichorythidae).
- Larvae of the finger-net caddisflies (Trichoptera: Philopotamidae) have mouthparts with a wide, membranous fringe of setae that are used to brush organic particles, diatoms and minute animals from the silken trap net where they are collected, into the mouth.
- Species living in standing water, such as some mosquito larvae, generate a current around themselves with mouth brushes that stir up bacteria and organic particles which are then consumed. Chironomid larvae do the same, except that they undulate the body in pulses to generate currents.
- Herbivorous and predatory insects (fig. 11.7) have evolved sucking-type mouthparts.

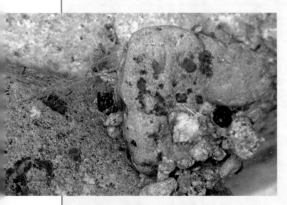

11.6 The larvae of some caddisflies (Trichoptera) spin silken nets to capture food drifting past in the current.

11.7 Feeding under water may cause dilution of food, but this is overcome by insects with piercing-sucking mouthparts, seen here in (**a**) a water scorpion (Nepidae), having captured a tadpole, and (**b**) a predaceous diving beetle larva (Dytiscidae).

Herbivores

Some aquatic herbivores feed on a variety of plants growing in the water. Others feed on algae – loose fragments, single cells, or growing on submerged rocks and other objects. Some also feed on layers of slimy organic deposits found underneath stones. The slime is a highly nutritious layer of organic precipitates consisting of polysaccharides with fungi, bacteria, algae and particulate matter woven into it.

Many caddisflies (Trichoptera) are typical grazers, for example, net-tube caddisflies (Psychomyiidae), saddle-case makers (Glossosomatidae), snail-case caddisflies (Helicopsychidae), limpet caddisflies (Petrothrincidae) and members of the Goeridae. Microcaddisflies (Hydroptilidae) suck the juice out of algal cells and Barbarochthonidae species feed on the leaves of aquatic sedges, *Scirpus* spp. Some mayfly nymphs are also typical herbivores.

Detritivores

Mosquito and chironomid larvae are common detritivores in standing water, whereas caddisfly larvae and some mayfly nymphs fill this niche in flowing water.

Primary production of green plant matter is relatively low in most aquatic ecosystems, so much of the fauna is dependent on nutrient input in the form of litter (detritus) from adjacent terrestrial systems. Detritus needs some microbial preparation before it becomes suitable as food for detritivores.

There is a fine balance between the oxygen required by the microbes to condition the detritus and that available to aquatic insects for respiration. In warmer water, the microbial processes happen more quickly and lead to a higher demand for oxygen. At the same time, the concentration of dissolved oxygen in water becomes lower as temperature increases. Unnaturally hot conditions and a large influx of litter may therefore lead to lethal anoxic conditions.

Predators

Some Odonata (particularly dragonflies), certain bugs, and members of a few beetle families dominate the predatory guild in warmer waters. In colder waters, damselflies, mayfly and stonefly nymphs, as well as alderfly, dobsonfly (Megaloptera) and caddisfly larvae are voracious predators.

11.8 Adult mayflies (Ephemeroptera): (**a**) *Afronurus* sp. (Heptageniidae); (**b**) *Afronurus oliffi*; (**c**) a subadult (Baetidae); (**d**) *Adenophlebia* sp. (Leptophlebiidae).

11.9 Mayfly nymphs (Ephemeroptera): (**a**) *Baetis harrisoni* (Baetidae); (**b**) *Aprionyx* sp. (Leptophlebiidae); (**c**) *Afronurus scotti* (Heptageniidae); (**d**) *Trichorythus* sp. (Trichorythidae).

Mayflies

Mayflies (Ephemeroptera) belong to a fairly small order with 14 families and about 105 species in southern Africa.

Mayfly adults (fig. 11.8) are free-living and terrestrial and do not feed, whereas the nymphs (fig. 11.9) of all species are aquatic and feed. Nymphs moult 20–30 times (compared to 5–9 times in most other insects) and take one to two years to complete their development. Ephemeroptera are the only insects in which a sexually immature but otherwise typical, winged

11.10 A female mayfly (Trichorythidae) with a clutch of eggs.

11.11 Dead mayflies floating on the water a few hours after synchronised emergence, mating and egg-laying.

11.12 The dragonfly nymph *Anax imperator* (Aeshnidae) showing the retracted hinged prehensile labium or 'mask' (the disc-shaped organ visible beneath the eye).

11.13 *Anax* sp. nymph with mask extended and holding tadpole prey.

adult stage (a subadult or subimago) is present. These are termed 'duns' by fishermen since the insects are often pale and largely unpigmented. They moult again soon into a sexually mature adult stage (known as the 'spinner' by fishermen).

Adults are short-lived. They often have synchronised emergence and form mating swarms in spring, hence the common name of 'mayflies' because of their activity in May in the northern hemisphere.

Females of the various groups have different oviposition behaviour (fig. 11.10):

- The female may scatter eggs on the water surface.
- She may plunge her abdomen into the water, at which point it ruptures, releasing the eggs.
- She may alight on the water or aquatic plants and then crawl into the water to lay eggs on submerged vegetation or on rocks.

Males die after mating and females die after laying eggs (fig. 11.11).

The nymphs live under stones, amongst aquatic vegetation, or burrow into the bottom substrate. They are mainly detritivores and herbivores, although some are predatory on small invertebrates. The immature stages are very sensitive to water pollution and are model indicators of the pH, oxygen levels and chemical health of the water. In healthy water bodies, they may make up the bulk of the aquatic insect fauna and are often the major prey of indigenous fish and introduced trout.

Damselflies and dragonflies

Damselflies (Zygoptera) and dragonflies (Anisoptera) are suborders of Odonata and are possibly the most familiar aquatic insects. Their often brilliant colours and dazzling aerial displays have long fascinated people. The southern African species are fairly well studied, and illustrated field guides are available. South Africa's Odonata fauna consists of approximately 98 dragonfly species in six families, and about 66 damselfly species, also in six families.

Damselflies are distinguished from dragonflies by the fact that in four of the six families the wings are closed along the length of the body when perched; in dragonflies the wings are always spread at right angles to the body. Damselfly eyes are widely separated, while those of dragonflies (in all but one of the families) touch at the top of the head. Damselflies also appear more delicate than dragonflies.

All Odonata are predators. The adults capture prey in flight – the legs are placed well forward on the thorax and are armed with long spines that form a 'basket' in which the prey is caught and then held during feeding.

There are also some differences between the two suborders in the aquatic nymph stage: Zygoptera breathe through external caudal gills (on the 'tail'), while Anisoptera have internal gills located in the rectum. Zygoptera nymphs swim with sinuous body movements, whereas Anisoptera crawl; Anisoptera occasionally suddenly propel themselves forwards by expelling water from the anus.

In all nymphs, the labium is highly modified into a specialised toothed grasping organ, known as a mask, which is hinged (fig. 11.12). Prey is captured in the teeth when the hinge is suddenly relaxed and the mask projected forwards (fig. 11.13). The mask is then retracted and the prey brought closer to the mouth, where it is consumed. Young nymphs feed on small animals, but some of the larger species may feed on prey as large as tadpoles and small fish.

a

b

c

d

e

11.14 Damselfly (Odonata: Zygoptera) nymphs breathe through external caudal gills: (**a**) *Ecchlorolestes peringueyi* (Synlestidae); (**b**) *Pseudagrion* sp. (Coenagrionidae). Dragonfly (Odonata: Anisoptera) nymphs have internal gills in the rectum: (**c**) *Pinheyschna subpupillata* (Aeshnidae); (**d**) *Paragomphus cognatus* (Gomphidae); (**e**) *Zygonyx natalensis* (Libellulidae).

a

b

11.15 Odonata males grasp the female prior to and during mating: (**a**) on the thorax in damselflies, here *Proischnura rotundipennis* (Zygoptera); and (**b**) behind the head in dragonflies, here *Anax speratus* (Anisoptera).

Some species live in mud or amongst debris and stones, while others are active crawlers amongst plants (fig. 11.14). Mature nymphs crawl onto protruding reeds, branches or rocks until just above the water surface where they moult. As soon as it can, the newly emerged adult flies to a protected situation where it can rest while its wings strengthen and harden.

Reproduction in Odonata is unique. The male has two sets of genitalia – primary and secondary – the first is on the eighth abdominal segment and the second on the underside (sternite) of the second and third abdominal segments. Before mating, the male transfers semen from his primary genitalia to the secondary genitalia by curling his abdomen around to reach the second and third sternites. He then catches hold of a female in flight using his terminal appendages. Zygoptera males grasp females on the prothorax (fig. 11.15a), while Anisoptera males clasp them on the head (fig. 11.15b). The locked males and females then fly around in this tandem position for some time until the female curls her abdomen up to lock her genitalia with his secondary genitalia (termed the 'wheel' position). Mating then takes place. After mating, the male may continue to clasp the female as a form of mate guarding to prevent her from mating again soon and possibly having his sperm removed by a subsequent male.

Most Anisoptera females oviposit directly into water by tapping the tip of the abdomen on the water surface to help withdraw the fertilised eggs from her genital pore, after which they sink. All Zygoptera and members of the anisopteran family Aeshnidae have a spiny, sheathed ovipositor with which they cut slits into aquatic plants just above or below the water surface; they lay eggs in the slits (fig. 11.16).

Damselfly and dragonfly habitats

Most natural (and many artificial) freshwater bodies will have representatives of both Zygoptera and Anisoptera, and although many of the species have a preferred habitat type, their ecological tolerances may be fairly wide. There are certain species, however, that are highly restricted habitat specialists. Adults may be found far from water, so it is mainly the habitat requirements of the nymphs that determine the species' actual ecological needs.

Finding suitable habitat for the nymphs is a multi-step process that the adult female must carry out before laying eggs. She starts by visually selecting the appropriate macrohabitat – the water body type and its associated vegetation. Then she needs to select the correct oviposition medium by using tactile structures on her ovipositor. Most Zygoptera and Aeshnidae oviposit in the tissue of aquatic plants with relatively soft tissue (fig. 11.16). Some Aeshnidae, however, such as the vagrant emperor, *Anax ephippiger*, lay their eggs in dead plant material or wet mud. All Gomphidae and most Libellulidae (both Anisoptera) lay their eggs in open water.

Michael Samways of Stellenbosch University divided the habitats of dragonflies and damselflies into seven types of water bodies with suitable surrounding vegetation.

Small, cool mountain streams, often partially shaded by adjacent indigenous vegetation are mainly found in the Drakensberg (fig. 11.17a) of KwaZulu-Natal and mountains of the Eastern and Western Cape, and are home to some of the rarest and most range-restricted damselfly species, for example, *Chlorolestes draconicus* (fig. 11.17b).

Fast-flowing rivers at lower altitudes with quiet, shaded rock pools (fig. 11.18a) are the preferred habitat of the damselfly *Phaon iridipennis* (Calopterygidae, fig. 11.18b), while several other damselflies (figs 11.18c, d), some Gomphidae (fig. 11.18d) and many skimmers and dropwings (Libellulidae, fig. 11.18e) are common along fast-flowing streams.

Slow-moving, wide waters, with an abundance of quiet reaches and pools of different kinds, surrounded by grass and reeds, or trees provide a wide range of smaller habitat types with correspondingly rich Odonata fauna.

Forested swamps (fig. 11.19a) are a specialised habitat in northeastern KwaZulu-Natal. Here, where coastal dunes prevent forested streams from reaching the sea, well-vegetated swampy areas form. They provide a habitat for southern elements of tropical African species such as *Chalcostephia flavifrons* (Libellulidae, fig. 11.19b) and *Gynacantha usambarica* (Aeshnidae, fig. 11.19c).

11.16 A female dragonfly, *Pinheyschna subpupillata* (Aeshnidae), laying eggs in a submerged aquatic plant.

11.17 (a) The Drakensberg has numerous cool, rocky streams, which are favoured by endemic damselflies. (b) Damselflies such as *Chlorolestes draconicus* (Synlestidae) inhabit cool, high-altitude streams in the Drakensberg.

Rina de Klerk

Rina de Klerk

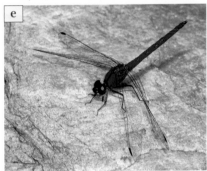

11.18 (a) Pools in fast-flowing rocky streams are favoured by species such as: **(b)** *Phaon iridipennis* (Zygoptera: Calopterygidae); **(c)** *Platycypha caligata* (Zygoptera: Chlorocyphidae); **(d)** *Paragomphus cognatus* (Anisoptera: Gomphidae); **(e)** *Trithemis furva* (Anisoptera: Libellulidae).

Rina de Klerk

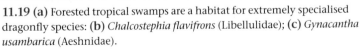

11.19 (a) Forested tropical swamps are a habitat for extremely specialised dragonfly species: **(b)** *Chalcostephia flavifrons* (Libellulidae); **(c)** *Gynacantha usambarica* (Aeshnidae).

11.20 Vegetated permanent pools and marshes on (**a**) high Western Cape mountains are inhabited by some of the rarest dragonflies in the region, such as (**b**) *Orthetrum rubens* (Libellulidae). This species was feared extinct: it was last seen in 1960, until it was rediscovered in 2016.

11.21 (**a**) Seasonal and ephemeral pools attract dragonflies such as (**b**) *Pantala flavescens* (Libellulidae). This dragonfly probably migrates over a greater distance than any other species of insect: it flies from India across the Indian Ocean to the east coast of Africa and back to recolonise the region on a yearly basis.

11.22 (**a**) Weedy ponds attract dragonfly species such as (**b**) *Crocothemis erythraea* (Libellulidae). This is one of the most widespread dragonfly species, due to its tolerance of a wide range of water conditions.

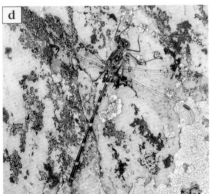

11.23 These malachite damselflies (Synlestidae) are narrow endemics restricted to South Africa: **(a)** *Chlorolestes apricans*; **(b)** *C. conspicuus*; **(c)** *C. umbratus*; **(d)** *Ecchlorolestes peringueyi*.

Still-water habitats consist of vegetated permanent pools and marshes (fig. 11.20a) and are found mainly in the central, eastern and southwestern areas that receive higher rainfall. The rare and localised dragonfly *Orthetrum rubens* (Libellulidae, fig. 11.20b) is a southwestern Cape species that lives in highland bogs.

Seasonal water bodies such as pans and vleis fill up during the rainy season and provide suitable habitat for generalist species. Whether they have dense vegetation or none strongly affects their suitability for colonisation. Even shallow, highly ephemeral pans without significant vegetation (fig. 11.21a) are readily colonised by the dragonfly *Pantala flavescens* (Libellulidae, fig. 11.21b), a widespread and common species in these habitat types. *Pantala flavescens* is almost worldwide in distribution. Individuals also migrate within Africa and between India and Africa. Much of the species' ecological success can be attributed to the fact that it breeds in temporary water bodies virtually without vegetation, often after the first summer rains. In southern Africa, individuals even disperse into the Namib Desert when conditions are favourable. The nymphs develop fast (in about 35 days), feeding voraciously on prey as large as, or larger than themselves – large larvae regularly catch tadpoles. They emerge and disperse before the pools dry up.

Artificial ponds and dams are common in urban parks and rural areas, especially on farms, and are suitable habitats for several species if they are well vegetated (fig. 11.22a). An example of a generalist species that occurs in a wide variety of habitats is the broad scarlet, *Crocothemis erythraea* (Libellulidae, fig. 11.22b). It is the most common and frequently encountered red dragonfly in southern Africa and may be found close to any grass- or sedge-lined water body, including streams, rivers, ponds, marshes and lakes. The females lay their eggs in open water and the squat nymphs live amongst debris on the bottom.

Habitat-restricted and endemic species

Several habitat-restricted species are endemic to South Africa. Most occur only in clear streams and pools in forests along the eastern escarpment (see 'Forest damselflies and dragonflies', p. 316) and in the mountains of the southwestern Cape.

Malachites (Synlestidae, fig. 11.23) are colourful, medium-sized damselflies. Most species have metallic green bodies and contrasting yellow stripes on the side of the thorax. Malachites are unusual because they perch with their wings spread, like dragonflies; the only other damselflies that do this are the seven South African species of *Lestes* (Lestidae). There are nine malachite species – two *Ecchlorolestes* species and seven *Chlorolestes* species. Of these malachites, eight are endemic to South Africa, while *C. elegans* occurs only in the mountains of Zimbabwe, Malawi and Mozambique and in the northern escarpment of South Africa.

Other damselflies with similar habitat requirements are the mauve bluet, *Proischnura polychromatica* (Coenagrionidae, fig. 11.24a), and the spesbona, *Spesbona angusta* (Platycnemididae, fig. 11.24b); both are rare and localised near Franschhoek in the Western Cape. The blue riverjack, *Metacnemis valida* (Platycnemididae, fig. 11.24c), occurs in the same type of habitat in a small area in the Eastern Cape.

Four narrowly endemic dragonflies called presbas, *Syncordulia* spp. (Synthemistidae, fig. 11.25), also occur in the Western Cape. They are restricted to areas with a specific combination of shaded, cool streams and aquatic vegetation.

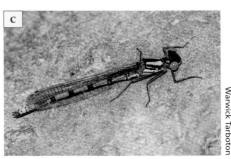

11.24 Range-restricted damselflies: **(a)** *Proischnura polychromatica* (Coenagrionidae); **(b)** *Spesbona angusta* (Platycnemididae); **(c)** *Metacnemis valida* (Platycnemididae). These damselflies, which are limited to a few localised populations and are therefore vulnerable to extinction, are restricted to small slow-flowing clean water streams or pools with emergent water plants: **(a)** and **(b)** in the Western Cape; **(c)** in the Eastern Cape.

Warwick Tarboton

11.25 Two of the four range-restricted endemic damselflies known as 'presbas' from cool, shaded streams in the Western Cape: **(a)** *Syncordulia legator*; **(b)** *S. venator*. The genus *Syncordulia* is a relict group that includes only these representatives in South Africa of a once widespread family.

Stoneflies

Stoneflies (Plecoptera) have aquatic nymphs and free-living, terrestrial adults. There are two distinctive families in southern Africa: true stoneflies (Perlidae) and southern stoneflies (Notonemouridae). Adult Perlidae (fig. 11.26a) probably do not feed, while Notonemouridae adults are thought to feed on lichens and algae close to water. Moulted exuviae of emergent adults remain on rocks surrounding the water habitat and are called 'shucks'; these are signs of the presence of stoneflies in the water (fig. 11.26b).

Adult perlids mate during daylight, on objects such as rocks and plants near the water. Fertilised eggs collect in a ball at the tip of the female's abdomen and these are released as she flies over water, dipping her abdomen periodically to release them. Perlid eggs are elaborately patterned, swelling markedly and becoming sticky when moistened. They also have an adhesive disc with which they attach to submerged objects to prevent them being swept away by the current into an unfavourable habitat. Little is known about oviposition behaviour and egg morphology in the Notonemouridae.

11.26 Stoneflies (Plecoptera: Perlidae) such as these are most common in and around sluggish streams: **(a)** an adult *Neoperla* sp.; **(b)** a 'shuck', the moulted skin of an emerged adult on a rock in the stream bed.

Notonemouridae nymphs feed on detritus, whereas immature Perlidae are predatory on small aquatic animals. They live in well-oxygenated flowing water from which they extract oxygen. Perlidae nymphs have external, tufted gills at the base of the legs and on the abdomen; notonemourid nymphs do not have external gills. Notonemourids prefer faster-flowing, cool waters, while perlids are more often found in more sluggish, turbid streams.

Crickets and grasshoppers

Crickets and grasshoppers (Orthoptera) are divided into two suborders based on various characters, including the length of their antennae (see box, pp. 118–119). They are known as long-horned grasshoppers (Ensifera) and short-horned grasshoppers (Caelifera). Two small families of the Caelifera – Tetrigidae and Tridactylidae – are typically found in saturated soils in the zone close to slow-moving or standing water. Members of both families feed on small plants and algae, they can both dive and swim well, and readily take to the water when threatened, but tridactylids can also walk on and even jump off the water surface.

11.27 Groundhoppers (Orthoptera: Tetrigidae), one of the very few groups of semiaquatic grasshoppers: (a) commonly found amongst algae on which they feed on wet soil near water bodies; or (b) on adjoining plants.

How far do pygmy mole crickets jump?

The pygmy mole cricket *Xya capensis* (Tridactylidae, fig. 11.28a) is a widespread Western Cape species, which lives in colonies in closely situated individual burrows (about 75mm apart) in saturated soil adjacent to water bodies. The habitat in a study was shared by various tiger beetle species, the adults (fig. 11.28b) and larvae (fig. 11.28c) of which (see 'Tiger beetles', p. 337; 'Ferocious tiger beetle larvae', p. 363) preyed actively on the crickets. The crickets are small (about 5.5mm long) and wingless.

Although they dig actively, their forelegs are not enlarged like those of true mole crickets (Gryllotalpidae; see 'Garden crickets and mole crickets', p. 383). The middle legs are similar in shape to the forelegs but larger, while the hind legs, especially the femora, are enormous, obscuring the abdomen when seen from the side. Average leg lengths of a sample of the crickets were: foreleg 1.5mm, middle leg 3.2mm, hind leg 6.8mm. The hind leg is 1.3mm (31%) longer than total body length.

As in other orthopterans, the pygmy mole cricket's jump is powered by rapid extension of the hind tibiae, but they are more efficient jumpers than any other recorded crickets or grasshoppers. They are also capable of jumping with propulsion from only one hind leg, and actually power about 40% of jumps in this way. However, the jumps are more powerful and cover more ground when the cricket is propelled by both legs acting in synchrony. The crickets hold their hind legs parallel to the longitudinal axis of the body when walking, keeping them 'cocked' until stimulated to jump. A cricket can jump as far as 1.4m forward – 250 times its body length – and half as high vertically. Jumping using only one leg often results in an 'unpredictable' direction with the body spinning in the air.

The study reached the conclusions that jumping is mainly a means to escape predators and, as a result of the erratic jumps, predators cannot learn to predict their direction.

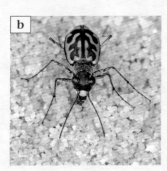

11.28 (a) The pygmy mole cricket, *Xya capensis* (Orthoptera: Tridactylidae), and its major predators: **(b)** an adult tiger beetle, *Lophyra* sp. (Carabidae: Cicindelinae) and **(c)** a tiger beetle larva removed from its burrow.

11.29 Velvet shore bugs, *Ochterus* sp. (Hemiptera: Ochteridae): (**a**) adults have large eyes and raptorial front legs, characteristics of many aquatic and semiaquatic bugs; but (**b**) nymphs are unusual because they cover themselves with sand grains, which they scoop up using their head and push onto their back with their forelegs.

11.30 Water boatman (Hemiptera: Corixidae) with the long, oar-like legs that are the origin of the group's common name.

11.31 Pygmy water boatmen (Hemiptera: Micronectidae), which, besides being considerably smaller than members of the Corixidae with which they were once grouped, are very similar to them in most respects.

Groundhoppers or grouse locusts

Groundhoppers or grouse locusts (Tetrigidae, fig. 11.27) superficially resemble small grasshoppers, but are easily distinguished by the extreme extension of the pronotum to beyond the end of the body – it covers most of the top of the thorax and abdomen. They have very reduced scale-like front wings and large fan-like hind wings. Some species fly strongly, others are wingless. Females lay eggs in batches but without a covering pod, another characteristic that distinguishes them from other Caelifera, which all lay eggs in pods.

Pygmy mole crickets

Pygmy mole crickets (Tridactylidae, fig. 11.28a) are usually small, dark brown to black crickets that jump extraordinarily well and far when threatened. To do this they use their massively enlarged hind femora, which are sometimes the same size as the abdomen. A study of one of the species, *Xya capensis*, by Malcolm Burrows of Cambridge University and Mike Picker of the University of Cape Town revealed just how disproportionately large the hind femora are, and how strongly the insects jump (see box, p. 331).

Aquatic or semiaquatic bugs

All aquatic and semiaquatic bugs (Hemiptera: Heteroptera) are predatory. The front legs of most aquatic bugs are adapted for prey capture (raptorial) (fig. 11.29). The middle and hind legs may be modified in the following ways:
- flattened with fringes of hairs, for swimming;
- long, thin and flat, for skating;
- reed-like, for walking on the water; or
- armed with powerful claws, for walking on emergent vegetation.

The species in aquatic groups breathe under water in different ways:
- from air bubbles held by a plastron, a specialised ventral structure covered in hydrofuge hairs;
- through an extensible breathing tube; or
- through a permanently extended abdominal breathing siphon.

Water boatmen

Water boatmen (Corixidae, fig. 11.30), which are active in stagnant water, will surface regularly to breathe, but in oxygen-rich water a thin layer of air envelops the hind body and functions as a plastron. The front pair of legs is usually short, but the two rear pairs are long and oar-like (hence 'water boatmen') and covered with hairs to enhance swimming. They are similar to backswimmers, but swim right side up rather than upside down.

Pygmy water boatmen

The small pygmy water boatmen (under 5mm long, fig. 11.31) were formerly considered to be a subfamily in the Corixidae, with which they share various morphological and behavioural characteristics. Current opinion, however, places them in their own family, Micronectidae. They are mostly found in stagnant or very slow-moving water with a sandy bed.

11.32 Backswimmer (Hemiptera: Notonectidae). These are unusual among aquatic insects since they respond to incoming light from above to maintain their upside-down position. If the light is artificially reversed as in a tank, the bugs flip over and try to swim right-side-up, and if left confused for long enough, drown.

Les Minter

11.33 Giant water bugs (Hemiptera: Belostomatidae) are (**a**) the largest bugs in this family and are capable of preying on vertebrates such as this young terrapin; (**b**) paternal care is rare among insects, but males of some species care for the eggs they have fertilised: the female cements the eggs to the male's back, and the male alternately submerges and raises himself out of the water to cool and oxygenate the eggs.

Backswimmers

Backswimmers (Notonectidae, fig. 11.32) swim upside down and often float just below the water surface. They breathe under water by plastron respiration – air is trapped in hair-covered grooves that are in contact with the spiracles and lie on either side of a mid-ventral keel.

Giant water bugs

Giant water bugs (Belostomatidae, fig. 11.33a) are some of the largest bugs known (up to 75mm long) and prefer standing water where they rest head-down, usually holding onto a submerged object, with the tip of the abdomen just breaking the surface. They breathe through two retractile abdominal appendages functioning as respiratory siphons. Some female belostomatids (e.g. *Hydrocyrius* and *Appasus* spp.) cement their eggs to the male's hemelytra (fig. 11.33b), a more secure substrate than an inanimate object.

Saucer bugs

Saucer bugs (Naucoridae, fig. 11.34) superficially resemble giant water bugs, but are smaller (9–14mm long), not as flattened and more adapted to crawling than to active swimming. They can be found in standing water, but (unlike giant water bugs) also occur under rocks in fast-flowing streams. Careless handling of a saucer bug often results in a painful bite.

Water scorpions

Water scorpions (Nepidae) are characterised by two nonretractile abdominal extensions that form the respiratory siphon (or 'sting' of the 'scorpion' as is sometimes mistakenly assumed). The siphon has hydrofuge hairs that are protected by glandular secretions (see box, p. 334). Some southern African species are large insects (40mm long). They are sluggish in the water, spending most of their time holding onto submerged vegetation, with the tip of the siphon protruding, waiting for passing prey. They are voracious predators of insects, tadpoles and small fish (fig. 11.35). Females lay eggs in the tissues of submerged aquatic plants. Each egg has respiratory tubes that either absorb oxygen from the water or pierce the plant tissues and breathe from the air cavities (aerenchyma) in the plant.

11.34 A saucer bug (Hemiptera: Naucoridae). These bugs are also known as creeping water bugs because of their habit of creeping among stones and debris in slow-moving or stagnant water, where they capture and prey on small crustaceans and insects.

11.35 Water scorpion (Hemiptera: Nepidae) with tadpole prey. They grab prey (often much larger than themselves) with their raptorial forelegs and pierce victims with their mouthparts, injecting paralysing enzymes.

Antibiotic glandular secretions

All bugs (Heteroptera) possess scent glands and most of these glands produce strong-smelling repellent secretions belonging to three different chemical classes: aldehydes, esters and alkanones. In nymphs, the scent glands are situated dorsally on the abdomen where they are often clearly visible; in adults they lie in the ventral metathorax (metasternum). The secretions have defensive functions in terrestrial species, but in aquatic groups a different function has evolved – that of protecting respiratory hydrofuge hairs against microbial contamination. Only adult aquatic bugs employ this system of antibiotic control of microorganisms attached to the respiratory hairs; the nymphs do not. A similar system has been recorded in water boatmen (Corixidae), saucer bugs (Naucoridae), backswimmers (Notonectidae) and pygmy backswimmers (Pleidae).

Members of the Naucoridae, Notonectidae and Pleidae do not readily produce glandular secretions when disturbed, and when they do, the secretions (mainly hydrogen peroxide) are virtually odourless. Corixidae, on the other hand, produce strong-smelling, volatile compounds with little provocation. Still, the primary function of the secretions is for coating the respiratory areas, a behaviour referred to as 'secretion-grooming'.

Pleidae, Notonectidae and Naucoridae secretion-groom outside the water. They climb onto objects just at the water surface, where they proceed to secrete chemical substances from the glands and then brush them over the hydrofuge hairs using their legs.

This behaviour varies somewhat amongst different Corixidae groups. Some species groom on land adjacent to the water bodies where they live; others climb onto a partially submerged object to groom; most swim to the water surface and then, while lying on the surface film, brush the secretions over their respiratory hairs.

In all species that have been tested, the secretions are strongly antibiotic, killing bacteria and fungi. If prevented from secretion-grooming, the respiratory hairs soon become matted by microbial attachment; the bugs lose the ability to collect air and can no longer prevent water from penetrating the respiratory system while diving, and eventually drown.

As mentioned above, nymphs do not display secretion-grooming: early-instar nymphs do not need a plastron for respiration since they obtain their oxygen by cutaneous diffusion. In older-instar nymphs, which do carry an air bubble, secretion-grooming appears to be unnecessary because microbial contaminants of the hydrofuge hairs are shed with the cuticle during moults.

Water striders

Water striders (Gerridae, fig. 11.36) are familiar insects with compact bodies and long legs, particularly the middle and hind legs. They often perch on aquatic plants such as water lily leaves. The middle legs are mostly used for rapid locomotion, while the forelegs, which are held close to the body, are used mainly for detecting insects struggling on the water surface, and prior to mating for detecting vibrations caused by other individuals.

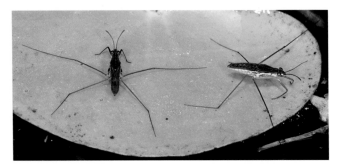

11.36 Water striders (Gerridae) are familiar long-legged insects common on urban ponds and other still water bodies.

Alderflies and dobsonflies

Megaloptera is one of the smallest insect orders in the southern African region and consists of just two families. There are fewer than 10 species of dobsonfly (Corydalidae) and only two alderfly species (Sialidae) in the region. Alderflies are rare, known only from a few localities in the Eastern and southwestern Cape and from KwaZulu-Natal. Their larvae live in still waters and sluggish streams, where they burrow into the muddy substrate.

Dobsonfly larvae are often abundant and important members of the predatory aquatic community in cool, fast-flowing streams of the escarpment from KwaZulu-Natal to the southern part of the Western Cape. Adults (fig. 11.37a) do not feed. They fly weakly and are found amongst vegetation near streams. Females lay batches of eggs attached to objects above the water surface. When the larvae (fig. 11.37b) hatch, they drop into the water below. The large larvae (up to 50mm long) are voracious predators that prey on various small aquatic animals.

11.37 Dobsonflies, *Taeniochauloides ochraceopennis* (Megaloptera): (**a**) adult; (**b**) larva.

11.38 Predaceous diving beetles (Coleoptera: Dytiscidae): (**a**) a large member of the rich southern African fauna; (**b**) a very small individual with a respiratory air bubble.

Aquatic beetles

Beetles (Coleoptera) associated with water can be divided into three groups:

- water beetles, which spend their entire life cycle in water;
- false water beetles, whose larvae develop in water, although the adults are free-living and terrestrial; and
- beetles that spend most of their lives on the shores of water bodies.

The most familiar water beetles are predaceous diving beetles (Dytiscidae) and whirligig beetles (Gyrinidae). The unrelated water scavenger beetles (Hydrophilidae) may be either true or false water beetles. Water-penny beetles (Psephenidae) are false water beetles with highly unusual larvae. Terrestrial shore beetles are mainly scavengers that feed on algae growing in damp soil or dead aquatic insects that wash out of the water, but some fast-moving predators in the Staphylinidae and Carabidae feed mainly on the many flies that frequent this habitat.

Predaceous diving beetles

Predaceous diving beetles (Dytiscidae) vary in size from 1mm to about 45mm long. There is a rich diving beetle fauna in southern Africa and they make up a large percentage of the water beetles in most types of water bodies – flowing, stagnant or brackish. Most species are uniformly yellow-brown or black (fig. 11.38a), but some have a yellow pattern against a dark background.

Adults and larvae are general predators of a variety of small animals. The larvae are sometimes called water tigers because of the prognathous (forward-projecting) mandibles in some species. Some small larvae have a curious trunk-like extension of the clypeus in addition to the mandibles, with which they grasp the tiny crustaceans (mainly ostracods) upon which they feed. The crustaceans have a round, rigid carapace, and without the three-pronged grip, it would be difficult to catch and hold the slippery prey.

The hind legs of adults are typically flattened, elongated and hairy to increase the surface area for swimming, which they do strongly. The fore- and mid-tarsi of males are broad and flattened and sometimes have suckers for attaching to a female while mating.

Many adult Dytiscidae breathe under water from an air bubble obtained at the water surface (fig. 11.38b). It is carried in the subelytral cavity between the elytra and abdomen where the spiracles open. Repeated visits to the surface to replenish the air supply may expose them to surface predators or to fast-moving surface currents, which may sweep them into less favourable habitat. Some small species have developed the ability to stay submerged for long periods, even months, without visiting the surface. They either use a permanent air-gill of tiny hairs (plastron) in which air is trapped, or they extract oxygen dissolved in the water through respiratory pores in their integument.

However, even species that are capable of staying submerged for long periods need to visit the surface periodically to groom their body surfaces with their legs to clean them of attached microorganisms and simultaneously apply antibiotic secretions. Dytiscidae produce antimicrobial substances from pygidial glands (glands at the tip of the abdomen), as well as from special subsidiary thoracic glands, which are unique to the family.

Predaceous diving beetles may be confused with superficially similar and distantly related water scavenger beetles (Hydrophilidae; see 'Water scavenger beetles', p. 338), but these have elongated maxillary palps and they alternate their legs while swimming; diving beetles swim with synchronised leg movements.

Whirligig beetles

Whirligig beetles (Gyrinidae, fig. 11.39) are possibly the most familiar water beetles because of their gregarious nature and rapid, erratic, but apparently synchronised circular movement on the water surface (see box opposite). Watching them may create the impression that this is random movement without any apparent purpose, but the position of individuals in the group, and their activity, are actually highly structured.

There are four genera of Gyrinidae in southern Africa, including the widespread and well-studied *Dineutus*. The beetles are active on the surface of many types of water bodies – from still ponds to fast-flowing streams – and groups may consist of dozens of individuals of one or more species. They dive readily when threatened. Adults prey on live insects that have fallen into the water, or they scavenge on dead insects floating on the surface. Larvae are underwater predators of small invertebrates.

Gyrinids have a suite of special behavioural, morphological, anatomical and neurological adaptations to life on the water surface. The most obvious externally visible characters are their divided eyes, tiny antennae and the exposed tip of the abdomen (pygidium). The eyes are clearly divided into sets of dorsal and ventral compound eyes: the dorsal eyes provide an aerial view and the ventral ones an underwater image. The antennae are very small, and lie flat on the water surface where they pick up surface vibrations produced by struggling insects with the Johnston's organ, a collection of sensory cells on the second segment of the antenna (pedicle) that measures the amount of movement of the terminal antennal segment (flagellum). The antennae are also used to guide males that are pursuing females by measuring wave amplitude as a function of speed and distance.

Large sensory mushroom bodies are present in the forebrain (protocerebrum) of gyrinids, something that distinguishes them from all other aquatic insects. They share this characteristic with their terrestrial relatives (e.g. Carabidae), although the bodies have completely different functions. In terrestrial insects, mushroom bodies are neurally connected to the antennae and have an olfactory function. In Gyrinidae, the bodies are connected to the optic lobes of the dorsal eyes in a complete anatomical and functional switch – sight instead of smell. The dorsal and ventral eyes, furthermore, have independent optic lobes.

11.39 Whirligig beetles of the genus *Aulonogyrus* (Gyrinidae) have complex behaviour that controls group dynamics when they swim in fast-moving groups. **(a)** Typical swarming behaviour on the water surface; **(b)** a beetle resting on the bottom on gravel with a respiratory bubble; **(c)** showing the exposed tip of the abdomen.

Interpreting group movement in whirligig beetles

Whirligig beetles are named for their habit of swimming rapidly in circles in a group, and various studies from around the world have resulted in somewhat different interpretations of the functions of this behaviour. Some claim that the group functions mainly for predator avoidance; others that hungry individuals swim on the group's periphery and well-fed ones stay in the centre, but that group structure is probably maintained by potential threats from predators; while a third viewpoint is that movement by individuals within groups is mating behaviour. Most species swim in groups (fig. 11.39a) by day, but individuals disperse at night.

Although predator avoidance is central to at least some of the hypotheses about group living, gyrinids are also well protected by several morphological and physiological defensive adaptations to avoid predation:

- hard, waxy, slippery elytra;
- dorsal and ventral eyes;
- antennae sensitive to wave movement on the water surface;
- paddle-like legs that enable them to swim fast (up to 0.5m per second); and
- pygidial defensive chemicals (gyrinidal and gyrinidione), which have been shown to have strongly repellent properties against various predators, including frogs and fish; these sesquiterpenoid aldehydes are unique to the family.

The predator-avoidance hypothesis is centred on the premise that naïve predators will eat a few gyrinids, then avoid them thereafter (because of the pygidial chemicals), associating the swirling individuals in a group as aposematic. This suggests that predation remains a risk factor for most of the time for the beetles.

Another hypothesis proposes that the position of individual beetles in a group is determined primarily by how hungry they are – hungry beetles swim on the periphery of the group where there is less competition for food, but where they are more vulnerable to predation than the individuals near the centre. As soon as they are satiated they return to a more secure position within the confines of the group.

The third hypothesis suggests that groups are mating swarms, at least for part of the time that the group is constituted, and that the dynamics of the group change as a result of interactions between males and females. Males chase females as a prelude to mating – chasing is guided by surface waves created by the female and the pursuing male, and not by vision. The waves are perceived by Johnston's organ in the male antennae. The swimming female produces stern waves high enough to guide the pursuing male, and the female can detect and measure the male's bow wave. Males swim faster than females and there are indications that females might choose a male on the basis of his swimming speed and manoeuvrability, since these are signals of his fitness assets for feeding, mating and predator avoidance. Not all chases end in copulation and some species continue to swarm long after the mating season (usually spring) is past, so mating behaviour does not fully explain group maintenance and dynamics. Consequently, the behaviour is probably explained by a combination of each of the hypotheses.

Tiger beetles

Tiger beetles (Carabidae: Cicindelinae, fig. 11.40) are long-legged, fast-running or -flying diurnal beetles characterised by large bulbous eyes and protruding mouthparts. They vary in size from about 10mm long to the largest species in the world, the southern African *Manticora*, which is 50–70mm long (see 'Predatory ground beetles', p. 239). Many are brightly or metallically coloured; others are dark brown or black. There are about 150 species in southern Africa; most are capable of flight but some are flightless. All are aggressive predators as larvae and adults.

The larvae are highly specialised (fig. 11.28c), living in vertical burrows from which they launch themselves when prey approaches. Unusually for holometamorphic insect larvae, tiger beetle larvae have well-developed stemmata (simple eyes) with good vision, so they can see their potential prey. The dorsal plate of the first thoracic segment is strongly sclerotised and shield-like, with the mandibles curving upwards and outwards past the shield. The larvae wait with their mouthparts and eyes protruding while they plug the burrow entrance with their shield. When prey approaches, the larvae launch out of their burrows, extending about two-thirds of their body out, while anchoring the last third in the burrow using hooks on the fifth abdominal segment (see 'Ferocious tiger beetle larvae', p. 363). The subdued prey is then pulled into the burrow where it is consumed.

11.40 Tiger beetles (Carabidae: Cicindelinae) are long-legged, fast-running or -flying predatory beetles and are often abundant on sand flats next to water bodies, where they prey on flies, grasshoppers and other shore-living insects: (**a**) *Chaetodera regalis*; (**b**) *Lophyridia fimbriata*; (**c**) *Lophyra brevicollis peezi*; (**d**) *Myriochila melancholica*. Unrelated groups often have broadly similar colour patterns which provide camouflage against the mottled sandy substrate of their usual habitat.

Water scavenger beetles

Water scavenger beetles (Hydrophilidae, fig. 11.41) are a large but poorly studied group in southern Africa, where about 100 species have been recorded. These vary from tiny (1mm long) to some of the largest aquatic beetles (50mm long). All have extended maxillary palps that are as long as, or longer than, the antennae – the palps function as antennae, and the antennae have adopted a respiratory function. Some species live in moist terrestrial habitats such as wet dung and decomposing plant remains, while others are more typical water beetles.

11.41 Water scavenger beetles (Hydrophilidae) vary greatly in shape and size: (**a**) a large species of *Hydrophilus*; (**b**) a small species of *Amphiops*.

11.42 Many species of rove beetles (Staphylinidae, the largest family of animals) frequent the edges of water bodies: (**a**) *Pinophilus* sp.; (**b**) *Paederus* sp.

Rove beetles

With about 55,000 described species, rove beetles (Staphylinidae, fig. 11.42) comprise the largest family of beetles – indeed of any animals – in the world. They vary in size from about 1mm to 40mm, although generally are probably less than 20mm long. Most have a very elongated body with a long flexible abdomen that is typically not covered by the elytra (but see 'Ant-like stone-beetles', p. 289). Although there is a diversity of habitat preferences, most species live in cool or damp environments such as in leaf litter, under bark and stones or in dung. There are also many feeding types amongst the species, with scavenging, algae feeding and predation being the most common. Some highly specialised species live as parasites in the nests of social insects.

Water-penny beetles

There are three species of water-penny beetles (Psephenidae, fig. 11.43) in southern Africa, one each in the genera *Afrobrianax*, *Afroeubria* and *Afropsephenoides*. The adults are typically rather featureless small brown beetles that live in damp environments close to streams and are seldom encountered. The larvae, however, are quite unlike any other beetle larvae and may be quite abundant in strongly flowing clear water. They are small, round and a coppery-brown colour, about 6–10mm in diameter, and reminiscent of the penny coins of years gone by. The round shape is produced by the lateral expansion of the sclerotised thoracic and abdominal segments under which the head, legs and gills are concealed. The strong legs hold onto the rocky substrate, while the rounded body shape acts like a suction cup, holding the body close to the rocks. The larvae attach to the underside of submerged rocks and wood by day, but move around to the exposed upper side at night where they feed on algae.

Aquatic flies

There are more aquatic or semiaquatic species in the Diptera than there are in any other order – about 20 families (some 10% of Diptera species). Some of these are familiar species, many of which are present around homes or gardens; others are vectors of human and livestock diseases.

In some of these fly families, all species have aquatic larvae, while there are several families that have species with diverse larval habitats. The aquatic larvae may occur in one or more of a range of water-body types: fresh, saline, standing, flowing, clear, richly oxygenated, or a soup of decomposing organic matter. Mosquitoes, for example, have very diverse larval and pupal habitats, and occur in most of these water bodies.

Clear, flowing, well-oxygenated water

The larvae of aquatic snipe flies, blackflies and net-winged midges occur in this pristine habitat.

Aquatic snipe flies

Aquatic snipe flies (Athericidae) are fairly large flies of which southern Africa has a very rich fauna. The larvae (fig. 11.44) live under stones in the rocky shallows of streams, where they prey on other aquatic insects. Adults are usually found close to the larval habitat.

Blackflies

Blackfly larvae (Simuliidae) live attached to rocks in shallow and moderate- to fast-flowing water (fig. 11.45). The larva spins a patch of silk on the rock and clings to it using a ring of hooks at the tip of the abdomen. It has a brush-like structure on the head that is used to filter fine organic matter from the water. The small adult females suck blood from mammals, including humans. In certain areas, such as the lower Orange River system in the Northern Cape and southern Namibia, huge numbers severely irritate people and livestock, leading to considerable economic losses. The flies are also the vector for a devastating illness in humans, onchocerciasis (river blindness), elsewhere in Africa.

Net-winged or mountain midges

Adult net-winged or mountain midges (Blephariceridae) are unremarkable small to medium-sized flies, but the larvae are interesting and adult emergence is very unusual. Larvae have deep constrictions between the segments, lateral tufted gills, and suckers on the underside (fig. 11.46); they use the suckers to attach to rocks in fast-flowing water where they graze on algae and diatoms. Just before adult emergence, the pupa floats to the water surface and explodes, launching the adult – whose wings are fully developed – into the air.

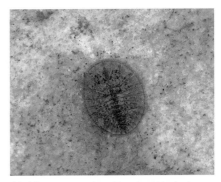

11.43 Water pennies (Psephenidae), the coin-like larvae of small beetles, live under stones in fast-flowing water.

Steve Marshall

11.44 Larva of the aquatic snipe fly (Diptera: Athericidae).

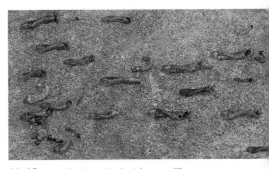

11.45 Blackfly (Simuliidae) larvae. These are often extremely numerous in shallow water flowing over rocks or cement spillways in weirs across river courses. The large numbers of emergent adults attack livestock and humans in the vicinity.

Steve Marshall

11.46 Net-winged or mountain midge (Blephariceridae) larvae live in clear, flowing, well-oxygenated water.

11.47 Larva of a phantom midge (Chaoboridae), so called because of their translucent appearance.

11.48 Mosquito (Culicidae) larvae, with unusually long diagnostic breathing siphons.

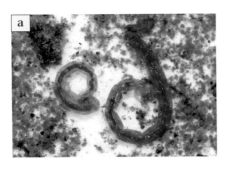

a

b

11.49 Bloodworms (Chironomidae larvae): **(a)** characteristically red larvae coloured by blood pigments; **(b)** a mature pupa already showing adult characters such as wing rudiments.

11.50 Dixidae larvae – the one on the left illustrating the typical inverted U-shaped resting position characteristic of the group.

Clean standing water

The larvae of phantom midges, mosquitoes, gnats, bloodworms and meniscus midges are found in clean standing water.

Phantom midges

Phantom midge larvae (Chaoboridae, fig. 11.47) have air sacs that provide buoyancy and give them a transparent appearance. The family is poorly represented in southern Africa, but in the northern hemisphere they are an important element of lake faunas, where the larvae and pupae move up and down in the water column in distinct day/night cycles. A unique characteristic of the larvae is that their antennae are modified into grasping organs with which they capture and crush their small insect and crustacean prey.

Mosquitoes

Most mosquitoes (Culicidae) breed in standing water, although some *Anopheles* larvae live in running water. All larvae are characterised by the presence of a terminal respiratory siphon (fig. 11.48); all pupae have a dorsal siphon. Both larvae and pupae swim by wriggling the body, usually in an up-and-down fashion. Larvae are filter feeders of organic matter. (For detailed biology, see 'Mosquitoes and their biology', p. 262.)

Midges, gnats, bloodworms

Midges, gnats and bloodworms all belong to the largest aquatic insect family, Chironomidae. The adults are mosquito-like and may be very common at lights at night near water. The larvae are found in virtually any type of water body and some are coloured red (bloodworms, fig. 11.49a) by the oxygen-carrying blood pigment haemoglobin, which allows the larvae to survive in situations with low oxygen levels.

There are two pairs of blood-filled tubes at the posterior end of the larval body, which function as gills and extract the little oxygen that there is from the water. The small larvae live in tubes of silk they spin around themselves. By making undulating body movements in the tube, they produce currents that aid in the flow of oxygen-enriched water over themselves, the oxygen of which diffuses into the 'gills'. During these intermittent periods of movement the haemoglobin is quickly saturated with oxygen and rapidly distributes it throughout the tissues during the still periods that follow movement.

The larvae of some species grow to 25mm before pupating in the silken tube. The developing adult is clearly visible: the head, legs, wings and gills (in the form of dense tufts of threads on the thorax) can be seen (fig. 11.49b). When the pupal stage is completed, the pupa wriggles from the tube and floats to the surface where the adult emerges.

Different species have diverse feeding habits, including filter-feeding and predation (see 'The stressful life of splash midges', p. 361; 'Midges', p. 409); some adults feed on nectar and/or pollen and may act as pollinators.

Meniscus midges

Meniscus midges (Dixidae) are members of a small family in southern Africa with mosquito-like adults and unusual, easily identifiable larvae (fig. 11.50). The filter-feeding larvae live at the water surface near the edges of a water body and swim in a zigzag fashion. They rest with the head and tail ends pointing downwards and the middle of the body protruding above the water surface, their bodies forming a U shape.

Saline pools

Although the larvae of some Chironomidae live in saline water, those best adapted to do so are some members of the Ephydridae, which are known as shore or brine flies.

Shore or brine flies

Some shore flies or brine flies (Ephydridae) are specialised for life in highly saline waters, either inland or close to the seashore. Elsewhere in the world some species live at the edges of hot mineral springs. The remarkable *Helaeomyia petrolei* lives in naturally occurring crude oil seeps in California, where the larvae feed on dead insects that become trapped in the oil.

The adults of the widespread genus *Octhera*, which in southern Africa is found near brackish or saline water, have enlarged raptorial forelegs, which they use to capture smaller flies at the edges of water bodies (fig. 11.51a). Males use the large legs and their inner markings to display in territorial disputes with other males and to advertise their suitability to females (fig. 11.51b).

Freshwater marshes

Marshes with shallow warm water and emergent plants develop seasonally in low-lying areas after rain; there are also permanent marshes adjacent to larger bodies of water.

Snail-killing or marsh flies

Adult snail-killing or marsh flies (Sciomyzidae) are usually active after the onset of summer rains in central and eastern parts of southern Africa, where they are attracted to grasses growing out of shallow water. This is the habitat of several groups of snails that are the prey of the fly larvae.

The female fly lays eggs on the emergent grasses and after hatching the larvae drop into the water below. The larvae have air sacs in the gut, which keep them buoyant, and a ring of hydrofuge hairs around the terminal spiracles that prevent water from entering the spiracles. These adaptations allow the larvae to hunt for their snail prey near the water surface.

Southern African species of the widespread genus *Sepedon* (fig. 11.52) prey on various species of snail, including those that are hosts of *Schistosoma mansoni* and *S. haematobium*, the parasitic blood-flukes (Trematoda) that cause schistosomiasis (bilharzia) in humans. *Sepedon neavei* has been considered for use as a biological control agent of these snails in South Africa.

Organically enriched water

Water enriched with organic matter is usually an ephemeral and localised habitat for a few specialised insects. They benefit from the high organic content but are severely restricted by the low levels of oxygen in the water – mostly used by decomposition bacteria – and need mechanisms to breathe atmospheric air.

Hover flies

The most characteristic flies associated with turbid and enriched semiliquid water sources – such as decomposition fluids under large carcasses and effluent from dairies and cattle feedlots – are hover flies (Syrphidae). Some of the most familiar species look like honey bees and are often seen on flowers. The larvae of one widespread species, *Eristalis tenax* (fig. 11.53), are known as rat-tailed maggots because of the long, tail-like respiratory tube (fig. 11.2c). Some larvae are predators of scale and aphids (see 'Predatory hover fly larvae', p. 381).

11.51 (a) Adult brine flies (Ephydridae) are abundant near suitable larval habitats. **(b)** *Octhera* adults capture smaller co-occurring flies with their raptorial forelegs. Males advertise to females with their dark, broad foretibiae.

Steve Marshall

11.52 The larvae of snail-killing flies such as *Sepedon nasuta* (Sciomyzidae) are snail predators.

11.53 The common bee-like hover fly, *Eristalis tenax* (Syrphidae), has larvae with long respiratory tubes and which live in organically enriched water.

11.54 Various *Culex* mosquito species (Culicidae) breed in temporary, contained water sources rich in organic matter.

11.55 Adult soldier fly, *Hermetia illucens* (Stratiomyidae), whose larvae are common in garden compost heaps.

11.56 Adult crane fly (Tipulidae). These long-legged, mosquito-like insects are common at lights in urban environments.

11.57 *Aedes* (Culicidae) is a large genus of mosquitoes characterised by black and white bands on the legs. Certain species are common near humans.

Mosquitoes

Two of the most common mosquito species in houses in southern Africa and in many other parts of the world belong to the large genus *Culex* (Culicidae, fig. 11.54). *Culex pipiens* prefers to breed in sewage effluent or other water rich in organic matter, while *C. quinquefasciatus* breeds in small artificial containers rich in organic matter.

Semiaquatic systems

Semiaquatic habitats are the muddy, sandy or organically enriched substrates on the edges of water bodies, or otherwise damp and humus-rich habitats.

Soldier flies

The larvae of soldier flies (Stratiomyidae) live in semiaquatic habitats. One of the most familiar species is the widespread *Hermetia illucens* (fig. 11.55); its dorsoventrally flattened and leathery larvae are often found in wet compost (see 'Black soldier flies', p. 388). There is a developing maggot-farming industry in South Africa in which the larvae are reared in farm waste as a source of livestock protein.

Crane flies

Some crane fly larvae (Tipulidae) also fall into the semiaquatic habitat category, although as one of the larger fly families, its larval habitats and habits are diverse. The larvae of some species appear leathery and are called 'leather jackets' (see 'Crane flies and leather jackets', p. 387). Some Tipulidae are important shredders of rotting leaves in streams, while a few others are considered to be root pests of various plants. The adults (fig. 11.56) are mosquito-like but have very long legs. They can be common around homes and are frequently attracted to light. Adults probably do not feed.

Temporary water sources

Pools formed after rain often dry up within a few days, yet are a habitat for certain species, of which some have the extraordinary ability to survive almost total desiccation for long periods between rainfall events.

Mosquitoes

The larvae of some species of *Aedes* (Culicidae, fig. 11.57) are adapted to developing in ephemeral pools after rain. The eggs may remain in the mud and sediments for months or even years after the pool has dried out, then hatch soon after submersion during subsequent rainfall events. *Aedes vittatus* breeds in ephemeral granite rock pools where eggs may survive 4–5 months of desiccation at temperatures of about 40°C and relative humidity as low as 5%.

Small, contained water sources

Small, temporary water bodies may occur naturally, for example as water-filled tree-holes, but can form in any number of containers, especially around human habitations.

Mosquitoes

Many species of mosquito breed in small, temporary water sources. Some are major vectors of serious human diseases, such as *Aedes aegypti*, the principal vector of yellow fever and dengue fever – the fastest-spreading mosquito-borne disease worldwide. There are also unusual species of *Aedes* that breed only in water trapped by plants. Along the east coast of southern Africa, *A. demeilloni* breeds in water that collects at the base of *Dracaena aletriformis* leaves; *A. strelitziae* uses the leaves of *Strelitzia nicolai* in the same way.

Chironomid flies

The West and Central African *Polypedilum vanderplanki* (Chironomidae) (see 'Midges, gnats, bloodworms', p. 340) is possibly the only insect that – in the larval stage – can survive body water levels as low as 8% (normal insect body water content is 80–95%) and (experimental) exposure to temperatures between –270°C and +102°C. The larvae live in small, tube-like nests in the mud of temporary pools, which often dry out. The species may occur in southern Africa.

Caddisflies

There are 19 caddisfly (Trichoptera) families in southern Africa, but many are represented by only a few species. Several species occur in forest streams (see 'Forest caddisflies', p. 315). Adults are short-lived and usually do not feed (fig. 11.58).

Both larvae (fig. 11.59) and pupae are wholly aquatic, remaining totally submerged throughout their development. Respiration in both stages is either through the integument or through nonretractile abdominal gills. Most larvae live in some sort of shelter or case; they are either predatory or feed on small organic particles in the water. Larvae can be divided into three behavioural groups based on their use of silk: net-making, case-making, and free-living species (which only construct cocoons prior to pupation). Net- and case-makers continue to add to their structures as they grow.

Net-makers spin their nets in flowing water amongst vegetation and debris, where they collect organic particles or small animal prey; the larvae retreat into the nets when threatened. Some are voracious predators, darting out of the protection of their shelters to capture prey when alerted by movement of 'alarm cords' extending from the net.

Case-makers build their cases of silk only or, more commonly, of silk with substrate materials such as sand, small pieces of stone, twigs or other debris bound into it; some are exquisitely constructed of identically sized and shaped sand grains.

Pupation takes place in a larval net or case, or a cocoon may be constructed especially for the purpose. The case is usually attached to the substrate. Pupae lie free inside the cocoon and are capable of movement that creates currents, circulating oxygenated water. In some groups the pupa lies within a closed silk cocoon that is separate from the larval case; in others, the case itself is lined with silk. The species that produce a larval net or case usually live in richly oxygenated flowing water; water flowing into the case and bathing the cocoon is sufficient for respiration through the integument. Species that occur in slow-moving water construct a special cocoon, leaving holes at each end of the case to allow currents to flow over the pupa to aid in respiration.

The pupa has well-developed mandibles, which it uses to cut its way out of the cocoon prior to adult emergence. It then either crawls along submerged objects or swims to the surface, where the adult emerges from the pupal skin and soon flies away.

11.58 Caddisfly (Trichoptera) adults: **(a)** *Chimarra* sp. (Philopotamidae) and **(b)** *Cheumatopsyche* (Hydropsychidae).

11.59 Caddisfly (Trichoptera) larvae: **(a)** *Hydroptila* sp. (Hydroptilidae) and **(b)** *Rhoizema* sp. (Sericostamatidae).

CHAPTER 12
CAVES

The environment of caves ranges from a twilight zone near the entrance (fig. 12.1) which, because of the availability of some light, has the largest diversity of fauna, through a middle darker zone, to a zone of complete darkness in the deep interior where the existence of life depends on external influences. In some regions of the world, the insect fauna of caves is very rich and contains highly specialised species, but southern Africa does not have substantial cave systems or typical specialised cave insects. For this reason, in addition to true caves we include rocky overhangs in this chapter. Large caves are usually inhabited by various mammals and birds whose dung and carcasses introduce organic matter into the system, which increases the availability of food for certain insects.

12.1 (pp. 344–345) Near cave entrances there is enough light for plant growth which gives food and shelter to a greater variety of fauna. (Photo: Jenny Scholtz)

Jenny Scholtz

12.2 True caves are deep and black-dark with temperatures constant to within a few degrees.

Ronald Cocks

12.3 Owls, such as this spotted eagle-owl, *Bubo africanus*, sometimes roost in caves and produce regurgitated pellets that provide food for detritus-feeding cave dwellers.

Caves may appear to be stable and benign environments, but the opposite is actually true: conditions for insects living in caves are mostly harsh. Although temperatures remain fairly constant, caves are often excessively dry or excessively wet – the former because rain cannot penetrate, the latter because of ground water seepage. In deep caves (fig. 12.2), there is no distinction between day and night with which insects can regulate their activity cycles, and they are often blind (see box below).

Little has been published on the cave insect fauna of southern Africa, other than the omnivorous Table Mountain cave cricket, known from wet caves and rocky overhangs on the Cape Peninsula. Yet there is a significant fauna, especially in caves in the arid western parts of the region, often directly or indirectly associated with the reptiles, birds (fig. 12.3), bats and other mammals that frequent or inhabit caves. These include scavenging spider beetles and fishmoths, predatory antlions, thread-winged lacewings and wormlions, as well as parasitic bat flies and bat bugs. All live in the dusty interior of caves and under rocky overhangs (fig. 12.4), or in association with other cave inhabitants.

Omnivores

Accumulations of organic matter from dung and wind-blown detritus, as well as the remains of birds and mammals, provide a rich food source for a variety of insect omnivores. These include endemic cave specialists such as the Table Mountain cave cricket and the Cederberg crevice katydid, but also widespread generalist species like fishmoths and spider beetles.

Types of cave dwellers

Animals that are obligate cave dwellers are termed troglobionts; those that spend at least part of their life cycle in a cave are troglophiles, while those that occasionally spend time in a cave because of some ecological requirement, such as hibernation, are termed trogloxenes. Typical troglobiont insects lack body pigmentation and are often blind, but they make up for the lack of vision with long antennae or legs armed with specialised tactile sensory structures. As happens with most attempts to compartmentalise animal biology, many individual species may be assigned to different categories at various stages of their life cycle or in particular conditions.

12.4 Ideal rocky habitat with numerous small to large sheltered cavities in which a variety of insects live.

Jenny Scholtz

Mike Picker & Charles Griffiths

a

12.6 (a) The widespread and cosmopolitan spider beetle, *Mezium americanum* (Ptinidae), lives in sheltered dry places, such as some caves, where (b) the beetles feed on dried-out bat guano.

Jonathan Ball

b

12.5 (a) The Table Mountain cave cricket, *Spelaeiacris tabulae* (Rhaphidophoridae) is found in various damp caves, such as (b) Elephant's Eye Cave near Cape Town.

b

Table Mountain cave cricket

The Table Mountain cave cricket, *Spelaeiacris tabulae* (Orthoptera: Ensifera: Rhaphidophoridae, fig. 12.5a), is a well-known Cape Peninsula insect, but in spite of this, very little has been recorded about its biology other than general information that applies to most of its relatives. A second species was recently described: *Spelaeiacris monslamiensis* was found in a cave in the Hex River Mountains of the Western Cape. These two species are the only members of the family known from Africa. The family occurs across the northern hemisphere, the tip of South America, and down the island chains that stretch from Asia to Australia and New Zealand. The cave crickets' closest relatives are from Tasmania, South America and New Zealand, indicating an ancient Gondwana lineage.

Rhaphidophoridae have various common names: cave crickets, camel crickets, hump-backed crickets and cave wetas. Most species live in damp environments, including caves (fig. 12.5b), forests and rotten logs. All are omnivorous, feeding on various forms of plant or animal remains such as the carrion or guano of bats, or are carnivorous on smaller cave invertebrates. Although *S. tabulae* is considered a 'cave' cricket, it is also found in rock crevices, in cavities under large rocks, and in damp forest environments.

Spider beetles

Spider beetles (Coleoptera: Ptinidae) are mostly very small (2–5mm) and spider-like in appearance, as their long antennae look like an extra pair of legs. They have long legs that enable them to move quite fast in the dusty places where they live. Dirt attaches to setae on their bodies, enhancing their similarity to small spiders. There are 14 genera and about 30 species in southern Africa, most of which occur in the arid western parts of the region. Some are cosmopolitan pests, found in households and grain storage facilities, where they may become very abundant in suitable food; the most familiar pest species in southern Africa is *Mezium americanum* (fig. 12.6a).

Both larvae and adults are scavengers of almost any source of dry animal and vegetable matter, including the 'refuse' in ant nests and old, dry dung lying on hot soil in direct sunlight. They have some remarkable, but as yet unknown, adaptations to survive extreme heat. Many species are found in the dung accumulations (fig. 12.6b) (middens) of mammals that frequent caves, especially rodents, hyraxes and bats. The species found in caves are mostly generalists that also occur in suitable food sources outside of caves.

Fishmoths

Fishmoths and silverfish (Zygentoma, fig. 12.7a) are superficially similar to bristletails (Archaeognatha; see 'Bristletails: the oldest order', p. 286) with which they share the evolutionary characteristic of never having developed wings over the 350 million years of their existence.

12.7 **(a)** Fishmoths (Zygentoma) are common cave inhabitants that subsist on detritus such as bat guano, where they, in turn, provide food for **(b)** six-eyed crab spiders (*Sicarius*: Sicariidae).

12.8 The spectacular Cederberg crevice katydid, *Cedarbergeniana imperfecta*. This adult female has a body length of 35mm, with a 20mm-long ovipositor.

Fishmoths and silverfish are dorsoventrally flattened, whereas bristletails are tubular, with a humped back; most species are covered in silver scales, hence the popular names. Eyes may be small or absent. Like bristletails, they have three tails, although they are all of similar length, whereas the centre tail is longer in bristletails.

Reproduction is similar to that in bristletails, but the mating process is more elaborate. The male deposits a spermatophore on the ground and, after an elaborate dance, eventually 'waltzes' the female over it. She picks up the spermatophore in the valves of her ovipositor and squeezes the sperm into her genital canal.

Zygentoma live in various dry habitats that have an abundance of food. They subsist mostly on dry organic matter high in carbohydrates. In caves, they feed on dry bat faeces, dead insects and other detritus, where they themselves form part of the food chain and are preyed upon by predators, such as six-eyed crab spiders (fig. 12.7b). Some species living in exceptionally arid environments acquire water by absorbing moisture through the rectum from air with relative humidity as low as 50% (see 'Absorbing water from air', p. 148).

Two Zygentoma families occur in southern Africa: Lepismatidae and Nicoletiidae.

Lepismatidae are the more typical fishmoths and are about 10mm long, excluding their tails. They are often seen in and around human habitation, as well as caves. The genera *Lepisma* and *Asterolepisma*, however, are small and secretive and have mostly been recorded from ant and termite nests, where they are assumed to live and feed in refuse accumulations.

Members of the Nicoletiidae are very small (2–3mm long), blind insects, which lack the scales that characterise members of the order. Most are known from the drier western parts of southern Africa. About half (eight species) of the described fauna lives in nests of the harvester termite, *Microhodotermes viator* (see 'The heuweltjie termite', p. 104). Nothing is known about their biology, but they are assumed to be detritivores, like *Lepisma* and *Asterolepisma*.

Cederberg crevice katydids

The Cederberg crevice katydid, *Cedarbergeniana imperfecta* (Tettigoniidae: Mecopodinae, fig. 12.8) is a large, very slender, orange-brown katydid, known only from specimens that live in rock crevices in a very small area of the Cederberg in the Western Cape. Adults emerge from the crevices at night to feed on the seed of grasses growing nearby. Nymphs remain in the sheltered crevices, where they probably feed on detritus until mature.

Predators

Southern African caves, particularly in the arid western regions, are home to a range of small predatory insects that prey mainly on small omnivores such as fishmoths and spider beetles, as well as on spiders (fig. 12.9) that compete with them for prey. Amongst these predators are some of the region's most specialised antlions and lacewings, as well as wormlions – the only fly larvae that excavate and live in pit-traps in the sand.

12.9 Six-eyed crab spiders, *Sicarius* (Sicariidae), are possibly some of southern Africa's most venomous spiders and are common predators of cave insects.

Pit-building antlions

Although antlion funnel-traps in dry sand are the best-known signs of antlion larvae (Neuroptera: Myrmeleontidae), and are a familiar sight to most rural children in southern Africa, most species are free-living. Of the roughly 40 antlion genera in the region, only four are typical pit-builders; they are *Cueta* (see 'Thermal refuges of antlion larvae', p. 146), *Hagenomyia, Macroleon* and the cosmopolitan genus *Myrmeleon*. Larvae of *Macroleon quinquemaculatus* (fig. 12.10a), *Myrmeleon lanceolatus* and *M. pallescens* build pits in deep sand under rocky shelters. The conical pits (fig. 12.10b) are often surrounded by trails; these are left at night by larvae from disturbed pits wandering in search of another suitable site for building a new pit.

The antlion larva is squat, with a large flattened head bearing four or five simple eyes and strong, curved, sickle-like jaws; these sometimes protrude from the base of the pit. The small thorax is flattened and has three pairs of legs, and the rounded abdomen is often armed with bristles that secure it in the base of the pit.

The conical pit is usually about 25mm deep and about 30mm in diameter. The antlion larva builds the pit by moving backwards and spiralling down just below the surface in ever-decreasing circles, all the while throwing sand to one side by jerking its head. When the pit is deep enough and steep enough, the larva buries itself in the centre of the pit and waits for suitable prey to fall into it.

Prey that falls into the pit struggles to climb up the soft, crumbly surface, and the antlion larva makes the struggle even worse by throwing up sand with jerky movements of its head. Once the prey is in reach, the larva lurches forward, seizes it in its jaws and drags it below the surface. The jaws consist of a pair of mandibles, each with a groove over which the pair of maxillae fit, thus forming a channel. Each jaw ends in a sharp point with which prey is pierced; enzymes are injected that dissolve the prey internally and the juices are sucked up through the channel. Prey typically consists of small arthropods – mostly ants, but sometimes prey even larger than the antlion.

Most of the life cycle is spent in the larval stage which, depending on the amount of food consumed, could last a few years. When ready for pupation, the larva spins a silken cocoon around itself within which it pupates. The pupal stage lasts about a month, after which the adult emerges from the pupa and cocoon and climbs to the soil surface to spread its wings before flying off.

Antlion larval physiology is unusual in that the alimentary canal is closed at the end so they do not excrete waste during their development; the excrement is stored and voided as a faecal pellet only at the end of the pupal stage. Additionally, their Malpighian tubules, which have an excretory function in most insects, are modified to produce the silk for the cocoon in which the larva pupates.

Adults (fig. 12.10c) look similar to dragonflies (Odonata), but the antennae are conspicuously clubbed and they fly clumsily with over-long wings. Adults of most species are predatory. They live for about a month, during which time they mate, lay eggs and then die.

Free-living antlions

Free-living antlion larvae (Neuroptera: Myrmeleontidae) look similar to those that live in pits, but hunt prey in a variety of habitats, such as in loose soil, plant litter and under bark and rock overhangs. Some are ambush predators, lying in wait for prey; others hunt actively. Species of four genera are known to inhabit caves in southern Africa: *Tricholeon* (fig. 12.11a), *Bankisus, Cymothales* and *Neuroleon*.

Tricholeon is a widespread southern African genus with about five species known from small caves and rock overhangs in most mountain ranges; one species is particularly common in the Drakensberg. The larvae are free-living in small, dusty recesses on well-sheltered rock ledges. *Bankisus* occurs across Africa and has seven species, of which five are southern African; their

Rina de Klerk

12.10 (a) The pit-building larva of the antlion *Macroleon quinquemaculatus* (Myrmeleontidae) digs **(b)** familiar conical depressions in the sand. After often slow development in the pit in which it eventually pupates, **(c)** a winged adult emerges, reproduces, and lives for about a month as a nocturnal predatory adult.

12.11 (a) The larvae of a few antlion genera, such as this undescribed species of *Tricholeon* (Myrmeleontidae), are free-living in dusty recesses in sheltered sites. After taking between three and seven years to develop, they pupate in the soil and adults, such as this **(b)** *T. nigripes*, emerge.

12.12 Thread-winged lacewings, such as this adult *Tjederia namaquensis* (Nemopteridae: Crocinae), are small and fragile insects that live in a surprisingly harsh environment.

larvae live in sheltered, dusty rocky recesses in caves and under buildings. *Cymothales* larvae usually live in detritus in tree-holes, but the larvae of some species also occur in similar situations to those of *Tricholeon* and *Bankisus*. Occasionally, larvae of all four genera may be found close together.

The larvae of *Tricholeon*, *Bankisus* and *Cymothales* have characteristic long dorsal setae on the thorax and the ability to open their mandibles by more than 180°. *Bankisus* larval setae are glued together, often with a pebble or a few sand grains on top – they are thought to function as 'triggers' that sense approaching prey and stimulate the larva to thrust its head towards the stimulus point to capture the prey with its sharp-pointed mandibles. The presence of the dorsal setal tuft distinguishes these genera from *Neuroleon*.

Thread-winged lacewings

There are about 60 species of Nemopteridae (Neuroptera) in southern Africa. They are divided into two subfamilies: the spoon- or paddle-winged lacewings (Nemopterinae, 50 species; see 'Ribbon- and spoon-wing lacewings', p. 106) and thread-winged lacewings (Crocinae, 10 species, fig. 12.12); all have extremely long hind wings. The southern African species represent about 60% of the world fauna. Most of the species are restricted to the arid western parts of the subcontinent.

All Neuroptera larvae are predators; some adults are pollen feeders, while all others are predatory. Thread-winged lacewing larvae live in sheltered sandy environments, such as caves and rock overhangs (see box opposite), but also in dust layers on ceilings in buildings. The adults venture beyond their sheltered habitats at dusk in search of food or to disperse.

Larvae pass through three instars in a period of one to seven years. The time it takes them to complete their development is entirely dependent on the amount of food they consume – the more food they have, the faster they develop. The mature larvae spin a spherical, pea-sized silken cocoon in the floor detritus, and then pupate.

The slender and seemingly fragile adults that emerge are morphologically and behaviourally well adapted to life in small and confined spaces, with their long white filamentous hind wings acting as tactile sensors. When they fly, the long, hair-fringed hind wings sweep back and forth, sensing proximity to the sides, back, front and bottom of their habitat, while the erect antennae prevent contact with the roof. They are even able to fly within the confines of small containers such as 350ml honey jars.

They are among very few insects that can fly and hover with the body in a vertical position, an adaptation that has enabled an elaborate mate-recognition and mating sequence. Their white hind wings play a central role in initial detection of one another in the gloomy interior of small cave habitats. When a male encounters a female, the pair continues to hover in small vertical circles with their bodies positioned vertically, and mating takes place during flight. The female then alights on the cave wall and after about 30 minutes starts to lay eggs, dropping them singly onto the soil below; she dies after egg-laying.

Two features allow thread-winged lacewings to inhabit some of the most arid and inhospitable regions of the world. The sheltered habitats in which they live provide small microclimates, shielded from wind, sun and extreme temperatures; and the extraordinary ability of the larvae to survive long periods of starvation enables them to extend their development with intermittent feeding bouts until they have fed and grown enough to pupate.

Some thread-winged lacewing (Crocinae) larvae have an extremely long neck. They were first discovered in 1833 by archaeologists excavating ancient Egyptian tombs around the great pyramids of Giza, but they had no idea of what they actually were. In 1923, adults were reared from larvae collected in tombs and it was discovered that they were actually the larvae of a thread-winged lacewing.

The first long-necked larva in southern Africa was discovered in Namibia in 1974 by entomologist Mervyn Mansell (fig. 12.13a) from Rhodes University. Shortly thereafter, he also discovered short-necked species, and after his years of detailed study, we now know that there are six species with long necks (*Tjederia* and *Laurhervasia*, fig. 12.13b) and four with short necks (*Concroce* and *Thysanocroce*, fig. 12.13c).

The 'necks' are formed by sclerotised plates (sclerites) of the first thoracic segment (prothorax) that attach to the strongly sclerotised head capsule, which is armed with large sickle-shaped mandibles. This heavily armoured body extension makes up more than half of the total body length of the larva (of about 10mm). It has evolved to enable the larva to capture and hold prey at a distance from the very soft abdomen until it is overcome by the larval digestive enzymes and stops struggling. Long necks hold a significant advantage over short necks, as the long-necked species are able to capture larger and more aggressive prey. Prey includes various small invertebrates that occur in the dusty recesses of the caves: spiders, termites, fishmoths and various beetle larvae.

12.13 **(a)** Entomologist Mervyn Mansell collecting Neuroptera under a rock overhang. Thread-winged lacewing larvae: **(b)** a long-necked *Tjederia namaquensis* larva and **(c)** a short-necked *Thysanocroce damarae* larva, both discovered by him.

Pit-building wormlions

Wormlions (Diptera: Vermileonidae) are the only fly species that construct larval pitfall traps to capture prey (see box, p. 352). There are four southern African genera: *Lampromyia*, *Namamyia*, *Vermilynx* and *Vermipardus*. Some of the most interesting species are found in the arid western parts of the region.

Wormlion larvae (fig. 12.14a) develop from eggs dropped by females (fig. 12.14b) perching on a rock above sandy soil. They build pits by throwing sand upwards using their head (fig. 12.14c). When the pit is finished, the larva lies across the base of the shaft, ventral side uppermost, where it remains in wait for prey.

Larvae are worm-like, with those of the largest species, such as those of *Vermipardus*, reaching about 20mm in length and a thickness of about 2.5mm. Their body is covered in hairs of varying length that trap fine dust grains and camouflage the larvae against their dusty background. When dug from their pit they curl into a U-shape and lie still; the grey body colour and covering of dust presumably gives them some protection against predators that might dig them out of their pits.

The head capsule is very small and can be retracted into the first body segment. The mouthparts extend forwards from the head capsule. The combination of curved mandibles, an elongated triangular labrum, large flattened maxillae and cylindrical maxillary palps makes for a very efficient killing and feeding mechanism.

Wormlions have an eversible, spiny leg-like pseudopodium on the fourth abdominal segment, which is probably used to detect prey. The larva wraps its

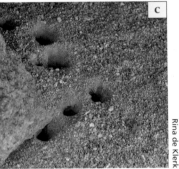

Rina de Klerk

Jenny Scholtz

12.14 (a) Wormlions are the larvae of (b) long-proboscis flies, e.g. *Vermilynx* sp. (Diptera: Vermileonidae); (c) wormlion pits in the dust of a sheltered site, such as (d).

forebody around the prey and holds it while anchoring itself in the pit using an 'abdominal comb' on the tenth abdominal segment. The comb consists of two transverse rows of spines: one row has short spines, the other has long spines. After the softer parts of the prey have been eaten, the remains are thrown out of the pit.

Pupation takes place at the bottom of the pit and the emergent adults leave the cave to feed on nectar, although it is thought that some may not feed. After feeding for a few days, they return to the cave to mate and the females drop eggs from rocky perches onto the soil below.

Parasites

Caves inhabited by bats also provide suitable habitat for their insect ectoparasites – among them bed bugs and bat bugs. Members of both groups attach intermittently to the host to feed on blood, but mostly breed in cracks and crevices in the cave interior.

Bed bugs and bat bugs

The best-known member of the blood-feeding bug family Cimicidae (Hemiptera: Heteroptera) is the bed bug, *Cimex lectularius* (see 'Bed bugs', p. 403), a cosmopolitan human parasite. The family has about 10 species in southern Africa. The widespread tropical bed bug, *Cimex hemipterus*, also feeds on humans, although it has been found near gorillas and chimpanzees, which may be its preferred hosts. In southern Africa, it occurs in northern KwaZulu-Natal. *Paracimex africanus* feeds only on birds, and all other southern African species feed on bats. The bat bug, *Stricticimex antennatus* (fig. 12.15), occurs in bat caves in southern Africa and has been recorded to feed on many different species of bat.

All cimicids feed at night or at low light intensity and have beak-like mouthparts with which they pierce the skin and suck the blood of their hosts. They usually do not remain on the host after feeding, returning to hide in cracks and crevices between feeding bouts – *S. antennatus* hides in crevices in the cave wall, and *C. lectularius* and *C. hemipterus* in cracks in the wall and floor, as well as behind skirting boards and inside bed frames. Sometimes the bugs may remain on the host – in this way new colonies of bugs are established when the host moves to a new roost or nest. For example, an abandoned mineshaft in KwaZulu-Natal had bats but no bugs in it in the mid-1950s, but by the mid-1970s there were tens of thousands of bat bugs living in the mine and feeding on the five bat species roosting there.

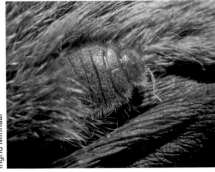

Ingrid Minnaar

12.15 Bat bugs, *Stricticimex antennatus* (Hemiptera: Cimicidae), mostly live near bat roosts in caves, but occasionally cling to a host bat.

There are five nymphal instars, of which each must take a blood meal to develop to the next stage. All stages can survive long periods without feeding, reappearing from hiding places when hosts become available. The development from egg to adult ranges from two weeks under ideal conditions of warm temperatures and abundant food supply, to more than three months when food is scarce, although adults may survive more than a year without feeding.

Reproduction is one of the most unusual and bizarre known from insects, and is termed traumatic copulation or hypodermic insemination; although a few other invertebrate species have similar reproductive systems (see 'Velvet worms: living fossils', p. 303; 'Vinegar flies', p. 399), that in the Cimicidae is the most extreme (see box below).

Parasitic flies

Hippoboscidae is a large family of blood-feeding flies that are parasites of birds and mammals. One of the unusual and distinguishing characteristics of the family is that the females are ovoviviparous and larval development is analogous to foetal development in mammals: the larva develops inside the mother in a pseudoplacenta and is fed by 'milk' produced by special glands. Only a single larva develops at a time. When it is mature, it is deposited externally and immediately pupates; in some species (Streblini), the larva has already pupated before

it is 'born'. This phenomenon is also found in tsetse flies (Glossinidae; see 'Tsetse flies as carriers of disease', p. 264).

The family consists of two subfamilies, louse flies or horse flies (Hippoboscinae) and bat flies (Nycteribiinae). All Nycteribiinae are obligatory blood-feeding bat ectoparasites and can be divided into two biologically distinct tribes – Nycteribiini and Streblini.

Louse and horse flies

Louse and horse flies (Hippoboscinae) are blood-sucking parasites that spend most of their lives on a host. They are reasonably host-specific, living either on birds, antelope, equids or carnivores. Their endemicity in the region is low, probably because of the general mobility of their hosts. The only endemic genus and species in southern Africa is the monotypic ostrich fly, *Struthiobosca struthionis*.

The species that live on birds are usually winged. *Ornithoctona laticornis* has the widest distribution and host range of any hippoboscid species in Africa; it is widespread south of the Sahara and its host range includes at least 40 genera of birds.

Amongst the mammal parasites are two common and widespread species, *Hippobosca longipennis* and *H. rufipes* (fig. 12.16). *Hippobosca longipennis* is a typical carnivore parasite and is very common on dogs in rural areas. The horse fly, *H. rufipes*, originated in southern Africa, but has now spread into Central and East Africa. Its original hosts were probably wild antelope species. It now also commonly infests cattle, horses and donkeys.

Traumatic copulation in Cimicidae

Bed and bat bugs belong to the family Cimicidae, the members of which feed on the blood of mammals. Female cimicids have fully functional external genitalia, but these are only used for laying eggs. Females (except in the New World species *Primicimex cavernis*) have a special area on the underside of the abdomen where the edge of the fifth abdominal sternite has a groove leading to a membranous area. The groove guides the male's sharp penis to this area during mating. He punctures the membrane here and ejaculates into a sac (mesospermalege) below it. Sperm are then transported to the ovaries via the haemolymph. Fertilised eggs are laid through the external genitalia as in 'normal' reproduction.

However, since the confined cracks and crevices in which Cimicidae live are polluted with their own faeces, as well as dead and decomposing bugs, males may carry potentially pathogenic bacteria that could be transmitted to the female through the haemocoel during mating. The female's

mesospermalege therefore contains phagocytic haemocytes that help to protect her against pathogens; the male's semen in turn, contains antipathogenic substances to protect his sperm against the female's immune response system and simultaneously destroys pathogenic bacteria introduced during copulation.

Females may mate multiple times, so it is advantageous for the male to establish whether she has already mated; since some fertilisation may already have taken place, the energy he invests in mating may be wasted. During copulation, a male can detect chemically with his penis whether the female already has sperm in the mesospermalege. If she does, the male will mate for a shorter time than if she were a virgin female, and produce less sperm. Studies indicate, however, that a second male will have higher fertilisation success than the first male, possibly because the phagocytes in the female's mesospermalege may have destroyed some of the first mate's sperm.

Bat flies of the Nycteribiini

In spite of their bizarre, spider-like appearance and their remarkable biology, the southern African Nycteribiini (Nycteribiinae) bat flies are poorly known. There are 10 species, some of which are found only on fruit bats, whereas others live on insectivorous bats. One species, *Basilia meridionalis*, is reported to live on both fruit-eating and insectivorous bats (see box opposite).

All Nycteribiini are flightless and have extremely modified morphology (fig. 12.17a). The thorax is dorsoventrally flattened, the legs are inserted dorsally, and the head is folded backwards to lie in a special groove on the thorax. Both males and females suck blood and live permanently on their host. It appears as if the flies are not particularly host-specific, as some species have been recorded from multiple hosts. It seems probable that fly species living on bats that share roosts with others are very likely to switch hosts readily. Bat species with specialised habitat requirements may be hosts to fly species with equally specific habitat and host preferences.

Nycteribiini females (fig. 12.17b) drop their mature larva from their position on the host, or climb off the host to deposit the larva near the roost surface, where it sticks and pupates immediately. The pupa is flat on the ventral side, which is attached to the substrate, and convex on the dorsal side. Adults emerge, climb onto a host, and mate.

Bat flies of the Streblini

Most species of Streblini bat flies (Nycteribiinae) appear to be typical winged flies, though this masks the very unusual reproductive biology of some species. As with the Nycteribiini, little is known about the southern African species; knowledge of their host associations and specificity suffers from the same lack of detailed study, attributable to poor host records and taxonomic changes to bat names. There are eight strebline species in southern Africa.

In some genera, both males and females are winged and run around on the host and they can fly actively; *Ascodipteron* species, however, have winged males (fig. 12.18a) and highly specialised females. The female emerges from the pupa as a winged fly, with a forward-projecting (prognathous) head and well-developed cutting-piercing mouthparts. Soon after finding a suitable bat host, she burrows into its skin and casts off her wings and legs.

The position on the bat is characteristic of the fly species: some burrow into the facial skin, others below the ears, yet others on the wings. Under the skin, the female encysts, leaving only the last few abdominal segments exposed for mating and excretion (fig. 12.18b). The head and thorax of the encysted female fold back completely into the greatly enlarged abdomen. The female produces a single pupa roughly every three weeks; it drops to the ground beneath the bat roost. Since the area where the adult flies emerge might be several metres from where the bats roost, the flies need wings to reach their hosts.

12.16 The blood-feeding horse fly, *Hippobosca rufipes* (Hippoboscidae: Hippoboscinae), is parasitic on various mammals, including horses.

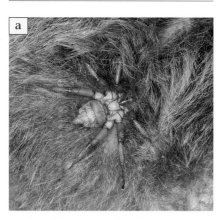

a

b

12.17 (a) The morphology of this bizarre bat fly (Hippoboscidae: Nycteribiinae: Nycteribiini) is highly modified for life on the host. Its small head is retracted into a groove on the thorax. (b) A female bat fly with her abdomen swollen with a mature larva about to be 'born'.

a

b

12.18 (a) A winged male bat fly, *Ascodipteron* sp. (Hippoboscidae: Nycteribiinae: Streblini). (b) Female *Ascodipteron* bat flies lose their wings and legs and become embedded in the skin of their host. Here, the encysted females are visible as white discs below the ear of their bat host.

The role of bats in cave ecosystems

Bats are the only large group of vertebrates that have exploited caves as a permanent shelter, and their excrement (guano) and the bodies of dead bats form a crucial part of cave ecosystem functioning. Many species form large colonies roosting and breeding only in deep caves, but there are also species that roost in rock crevices, tree hollows and in man-made structures. Some caves host colonies numbering millions of individuals; in South Africa the biggest colony of about 300,000 is found in a cave in the southern Cape, where *Miniopterus schreibersii* (fig. 12.19a) is the most abundant species, but four other species, including *Nycteris thebaica* (fig. 12.19b), also occur there. Bat diversity in southern Africa is high, with about 75 species recorded.

Bats belong to the order Chiroptera ('hand-wing') and are the only mammals capable of flight. They spend the diurnal hours roosting and breeding, coming out at night to feed. Most species are insectivores, but many feed on nectar, pollen and fruit, making these species important for pollination and seed dispersal; bat pollination occurs in more than 528 plant species from 67 plant families and 28 orders worldwide.

About two-thirds of the bat species in the world are insectivorous (fig. 12.19c) and feed on crepuscular and nocturnal flying insects located by echolocation. Sounds emitted by the bats are in the range of 20–210kHz (up to about 20kHz is audible to humans). Bats are such efficient predators that various nocturnal flying insects such as many species of moth – but also some beetles, mantises, various orthopterans as well as green lacewings – use hearing additionally, or solely, for perceiving the ultrasound frequencies emitted by echolocating hunting bats, and respond with evasive action. Nevertheless, the number of insects consumed nightly by bats is enough to make them significant regulators of insect populations; a single North American little brown bat, *Myotis lucifugus*, can consume up to 1,200 mosquito-sized insects per hour, or 5,000 per night. Although studies have not been done to substantiate the numbers of mosquitoes consumed by bats in Africa, it has been suggested that their feeding may play a role in curbing the spread of malaria in the region.

Bat guano provides the primary organic input into many cave ecosystems, especially deep caves which, being devoid of light, are also devoid of other organic matter. It supports bacteria, fungi and a host of invertebrates such as nematodes, springtails, fishmoths, cockroaches, bark lice, beetles, flies, isopods, millipedes, centipedes, harvestmen, pseudoscorpions and spiders (fig. 12.7b). Some feed on the guano, others on the bacteria and fungi present, while predators are attracted to feed on the feeders. Consequently, bats keep life functioning in these caves and their loss would result in the collapse of the ecosystem.

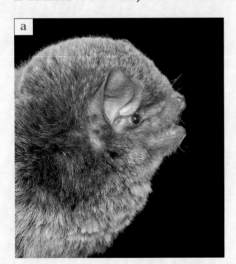  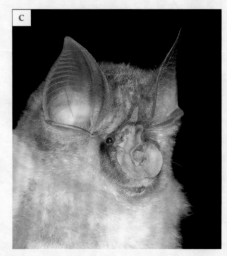

12.19 (a) Schreiber's long-fingered bat, *Miniopterus schreibersii* (Vespertilionidae), is an insectivorous, gregarious species with worldwide distribution; they are obligate cave dwellers and migrate inter-regionally. (b) Egyptian slit-faced bat, *Nycteris thebaica* (Nycteridae), is a common Africa-wide insectivorous gregarious species often with a preference for the darkest part of caves where colonies of up to hundreds may occur. (c) Bushveld horseshoe bat, *Rhinolophus simulator* (Rhinolophidae), is an insectivorous species found in small groups in caves in the bushveld regions on the eastern side of southern Africa.

CHAPTER 13
COASTAL ZONE

The shorelines of rocky intertidal areas (fig. 13.1) and sandy beaches along coasts constitute an extremely harsh and unstable environment. They are constantly pounded by waves that regularly cover them with water, transforming sandy beaches and leaving high levels of salt in the sand when they recede. Additionally, shorelines are usually exposed to strong winds and direct sunshine with high levels of ultraviolet radiation. Yet, in spite of the harsh elements, the southern African coastline is home to a wide range of marine crustaceans and a few terrestrial insect groups that have adapted to survive repeated inundation as well as highly saline and exposed conditions.

13.1 (pp. 356–357) Rocks, sand and beached seaweed provide suitable, yet harsh and ever-changing habitats for numerous invertebrates. (Photo: Anton Scholtz)

Southern African shorelines are home to a surprising variety of arthropods, but few of these are insects. The coastal zone represents a relatively simple ecosystem with its main nutrient input in the form of seaweed dumped by wave action on the sand and rocks (fig. 13.2). This provides food and protection for a host of marine detritivores, which in turn constitute the prey of various crustacean, arachnid and insect predators.

Although insects have dominated terrestrial animal life for the past 400 million years and continue to do so, they have never successfully invaded the marine environment. The reason for this has puzzled biologists for centuries and various hypotheses have been proposed to explain the apparent anomaly. Most of these hypotheses revolve around aspects of insect biology that ostensibly render their physiology, behaviour and reproduction unsuited to life in the ocean, yet many insect species have colonised large water bodies on land that are subject to similar wave action to that of the sea, are as deep, and are also as saline as seawater.

Some of the more plausible hypotheses are that:
- Six legs may render insects somewhat unstable in the ocean;
- Their respiration mechanism using trachea to distribute oxygen throughout the body is unsuitable for life in the sea;
- The absence of anything resembling a plankton stage makes dispersal at sea problematic; or
- Wings, the evolution of which was possibly one of the insects' greatest developmental triumphs, are useless in water.

Perhaps the most satisfactory explanation is simply that the oceans were already occupied by other arthropods such as crustaceans (fig. 13.3) before insects evolved into the diverse groups that we see now, and that there was insufficient ecological space for them to colonise. Some of the other biological attributes mentioned above may further have restricted their ocean invasion.

In southern African oceans, only two groups of truly marine insects occur in the deep waters of the open sea. One is the sea skater, *Halobates*, a predator of zooplankton living or floating on the water surface. The other is a group of blood-feeding lice which, in southern African waters, feed on Cape fur seals and elephant seals.

Several other groups of insects, however, live on the shoreline, either in association with living kelp and other seaweeds attached to rocks that may be totally submerged by seawater at high tide, feeding on stranded kelp and animal bodies lying on the sandy shore just above the high-tide mark, or preying on the abundant marine organisms living on the beach.

Two flies are common on the shoreline: splash midges live in the intertidal zone, feeding on living seaweeds attached to the rocks, and kelp flies feed on stranded kelp. Another intertidal insect is the parasitic wasp *Echthrodesis lamorali*, a parasitoid of spider eggs.

Adults and larvae of various generalist predatory beetles (Carabidae) roam the beaches in search of small prey. Along the south and east coast, carabid habitat overlaps in adjacent sand dunes with another insect predator, the larva of the antlion *Syngenes longicornis*.

Then, there is a diverse group of terrestrial opportunists that occasionally enter the coastal zone, mostly to feed on the remains of various marine plants and animals that wash up during high tides.

13.2 (left) Above the high-tide line, flat sandy beaches are used by a few specially adapted insect species.

13.3 (below) Insects in the intertidal zone suffer fierce competition from co-occurring crustaceans such as this semiterrestrial nocturnal predatory and scavenging juvenile pink ghost crab, *Ocypode ryderi* (Ocypodidae); adults are pink with a single white claw.

Anton Scholtz

Open sea

Two oceans lap the shores of southern Africa: the Indian Ocean with its warm Agulhas current on the eastern and southern coasts, and the Atlantic Ocean with the very cold Benguela current off the west coast. The Southern Ocean lies farther south, around Antarctica. Within these oceans, two marine insect species are found.

Sea skaters of the open sea

The sea skater, *Halobates micans* (fig. 13.4), belongs to the large group known as water striders (Hemiptera: Heteroptera: Gerridae), all of which are predators or scavengers of small insects and zooplankton living or floating on the water surface. *Halobates micans* is one of five *Halobates* species worldwide, but the only one found in southern African waters, and the only species in the genus with a cosmopolitan distribution, occurring on the Atlantic, Indian and Pacific oceans. It is limited to the warmer tropical regions and waters of these oceans, and is not found in the cold southern African Atlantic.

Although the populations from the three major oceans are morphologically indistinguishable and there is a broad contact zone between the Indian and Pacific ocean populations, each population remains genetically distinct, suggesting that speciation has already taken place, or is in the process of doing so.

The adult sea skater is small (5mm body length) with short front legs and extremely long middle and hind legs. It has large, bulbous eyes and several specialised morphological adaptations for living and moving about on the water surface.

As the insects are unable to escape direct solar radiation, the cuticle has a dark ultraviolet-absorbent cell layer that excludes the most harmful ultraviolet radiation at wavelengths of 260–320 nanometres.

The thorax is a well-sclerotised, rigid box, without any sign of wings; the prothorax is small, the mesothorax large, and the metathorax tiny. The abdomen is very short and compact, jutting from the base of the thorax.

Each pair of legs is adapted for different functions. The short, stout front legs, which support and stabilise the insect at rest, are used for grasping and holding prey, and for grooming with special comb-like structures on the tibiae. The middle and hind legs are inserted on the sides of the thorax, far from the front legs, which allows very wide movement. The slender middle legs have rows of long, prominent, silvery brush-like hairs on the tibiae and tarsi, which increase their surface area; these legs function as oars, moving in a synchronised rowing fashion to propel the insect forwards. The hind legs are used to steer the insect and to support the body when the middle legs are lifted during rowing. Sea skaters' light weight and minimal surface contact, limited only to

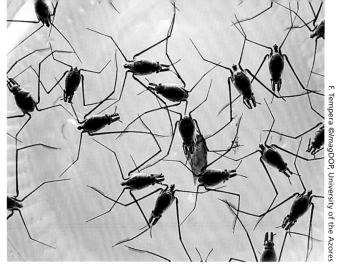

13.4 *Halobates micans* (Hemiptera: Gerridae) is one of the very few insect species that live on the open sea.

the distal parts of the legs, allows them to skate on the surface film of the water without breaking through.

The body is covered in three layers of dense setae – evenly distributed longer hairs (4,000–5,000/mm^2), underlain by a dense, carpet-like layer of shorter hairs (8,000–12,000/mm^2), on top of an even denser layer of minute microtrichia (600,000–700,000/mm^2). This setal covering keeps the sea skaters dry in wet conditions (sea spray, rain and mist) or when accidentally submerged. The hair layers also maintain an air layer around the insect that renders it buoyant when submerged, and able to resurface very quickly. As soon as it surfaces, the hydrofuge hairs repel the water, instantly leaving the insect almost completely dry. Any remaining moisture is then removed by grooming with the combs on the front tibiae.

All life stages occur on the surface of the open sea. The eggs are large (about 1.0 × 0.5mm), compared to the size of the female. To accommodate the developing eggs, her abdomen expands to twice its normal length; even her thoracic cavity is packed with them. Females lay about 10 eggs, each of which is attached to any source of floating material – feathers, pieces of plastic and wood, mollusc shells and even lumps of tar have been recorded. Suitable oviposition sites are a severely limiting factor for the insects. There is one record of about 70,000 eggs of the eastern Pacific species, *H. sobrinus*, attached to a floating 5-litre plastic bottle. The eggs were packed 15 layers deep and were estimated to have been laid by about 7,000 females over the course of a few days.

Newly hatched nymphs are feeble and their movements uncoordinated, and those hatching from submerged eggs may struggle for up to two hours to break through the water surface film. After about 30 minutes of exposure to sunshine their cuticles have tanned and they become very active. There are five nymphal instars.

Halobates micans is strictly an open-ocean species that feeds on plankton. However, adults and nymphs regularly get blown onto southern African beaches by strong on-shore winds after storms at sea.

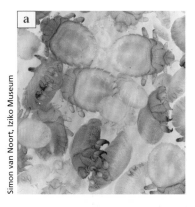

a

Simon van Noort, Iziko Museum

13.5 **(a)** Elephant seal lice, *Lepidophthirus macrorhini*, from **(b)** the sub-Antarctic elephant seal, *Mirounga leonina*. Elephant seals such as this bull with his harem and pups (in the background) on Marion Island are host to elephant seal lice, one of the most highly adapted parasitic louse species known.

b

Nico de Bruyn

Parasitic elephant seal lice

Seal parasites count amongst the few truly marine insects, with some species spending much of their life submerged in seawater, interspersed with short periods on land when the seals breed. Those that live on Antarctic seals are exposed to the most extreme environmental conditions of any insect species and may spend several months on their host submerged in near-freezing water.

Worldwide, there are five genera and 12 species of lice (Psocodea: Echinophthiriidae) that occur on marine mammals. On the southern African coast, *Proechinophthirius zumpti* is a parasite of the Cape fur seal, *Arctocephalus pusillus*, while *Lepidophthirus macrorhini* (fig. 13.5a) lives on the southern elephant seal, *Mirounga leonina* (fig. 13.5b), on various sub-Antarctic islands.

Lepidophthirus macrorhini may live for several months on their elephant seal hosts while at sea. Their life cycle is similar to that of terrestrial blood-feeding lice (see 'Head lice', p. 403), but differs in its length: it takes 30–40 days in land lice and only 21 days in seal lice. Eggs are attached to the fur of the seal, and the three nymphal stages are similar to, but smaller than the adults. Adults are 2–3mm long. All stages are covered in a dense layer of scales and flattened setae of different sizes. There is a poorly defined constriction between the thorax and abdomen, and the cuticle is thin and elastic, swelling greatly as the louse feeds on the host's blood.

The life of elephant seal lice at sea

Elephant seal lice are particularly remarkable for their ability to spend long periods on their marine hosts, often in extreme conditions. The seals spend about 85% of their lives at sea; 78% diving and only about 7% at the sea surface. Not only are the lice submerged in near-freezing water for most of the time the seals are at sea, but the seals dive for 20–30 minutes, interspersed with periods of only 2–3 minutes at the surface. While submerged, the lice's spiracles are closed by a special mechanism and they breathe by diffusion of oxygen from the water through the cuticle, made easier because the cold seawater may be saturated with oxygen up to 80%. If there are air bubbles trapped in their burrows in the skin, they open their spiracles for short periods to breathe. While the seal is briefly floating at the ocean surface, the lice breathe through their spiracles. The temperature to which they are exposed varies from about 25°C at the surface to about 4°C in deeper water. While the seals are on land, the lice behave as terrestrial insects, breathing through their spiracles.

The most extraordinary adaptation the lice have is the ability to survive the immense water pressure when the seals dive, 600–2,000m below the surface. The water pressure at these depths is about 600–2,000 times that at the surface, which places immense physical pressure on the tiny insects. At this depth, when pressure is great and the water very cold, the louse's metabolism slows down, which reduces the amount of oxygen required; as soon as the seal surfaces and lies in warmer water, the metabolism speeds up again. However, since the seals spend 20–30 minutes in dives and only 2–3 minutes near the surface, the lice need to adapt very quickly to the rapid environmental changes.

The seals come ashore twice a year for three to five weeks – once to breed and the other time to moult – and the rest of their life is spent at sea (see box above). Both periods on land occur during the warmer months between August and April. The lice breed only while the seals are on land, and complete the immature stages of the life cycle in about three weeks, moving quickly from female seals to their pups, which are the most heavily infested.

Lepidophthirus macrorhini is the only louse species that excavates a burrow in the skin of its host. Elephant seals' skin is thick, particularly the stratum corneum that bears the hairs, which are short and dense, except on the webs and hind flippers. The lice tunnel into the epidermis below the stratum corneum. This is below the layer of skin with pelage that is shed when the seal moults. The skin temperature of seals on land remains at about 30°C irrespective of air temperature. It is a degree or two warmer between the digits of the flippers, and it is here that the largest concentrations of lice are found, although they may be found all over the body.

Rocky intertidal shores

Rocky shores are a stressful environment in which to live – pounding waves, submersion in salt water for about six hours each day, as well as exposure to direct sunlight and high temperatures with highly desiccating effects.

The stressful life of splash midges

Splash midges, *Telmatogeton* spp. (Diptera: Chironomidae), are tiny, fragile midges active at low tide, when they may be seen fluttering amongst seaweeds. Their larvae are continuously exposed to the intertidal environment. Like most of their relatives (e.g. bloodworms; see 'Midges, gnats, bloodworms', p. 340; 'Midges', p. 409), they live totally or partially submerged in water.

Telmatogeton larvae live among and feed on the red seaweed *Porphyra capensis*, which grows on exposed rocks on the shore between low- and high-tide levels. The larvae prefer rocks that are only partially submerged at high tide. There they live between the seaweed fronds in tunnels they form by binding the fronds together with a viscous oral exudate. Most of the hind part of the body remains in the tunnel while the front part protrudes when the larva feeds on the fronds. The tip of the abdomen has a pseudopod and a ring of recurved spines that the larva uses to attach itself to the seaweed to lessen the chances of being displaced by wave action. The mouth has hooks that attach to the frond while the larva feeds. A thick, tough cuticular covering protects the larva against environmental extremes. Pupation takes place inside a larval tunnel, and the pupa, too, has hooks with which it attaches itself to the seaweed.

Wasps parasitic on intertidal spiders

The minute wasp *Echthrodesis lamorali* (Hymenotpera: Platygastridae: Scelioninae, figs 13.6a, b) is less than 1mm long, hairy and wingless, and is one of only five in the family Scelioninae, of which all members are parasitoids of insect or spider eggs. *Echthrodesis lamorali* is one of only three wasp species worldwide known from a marine environment and is a parasitoid of the eggs of the intertidal spider *Desis formidabilis* (Desidae). Several wasp species parasitise the submerged eggs of various freshwater insect groups, including Trichoptera (caddisflies), Dytiscidae (predaceous diving beetles), Gerridae (water striders – Hemiptera), Nepidae (water scorpions – Hemiptera) and Aeshnidae (hawkers and emperors – Odonata); these groups are discussed in chapter 11.

Desis formidabilis (fig. 13.6c) is the only species of southern African spiders in the cosmopolitan marine genus *Desis*. It is one of several species of spiders that share the intertidal zone (fig. 13.6d) on the east, southern and west coasts of southern Africa between East London in the Eastern Cape and Lüderitz in southern Namibia.

The 10mm-long spiders forage at night and nest in various cavities amongst rocks, including crevices, polychaete tube masses and beneath

13.6 The wasp *Echthrodesis lamorali* (Platygastridae) parasitises the eggs of the marine spider *Desis formidabilis* (Desidae). In spite of living in one of the harshest habitats imaginable, a tiny flightless parasitic wasp regularly traverses exposed bare coastal rocks to locate the nests and eggs of its spider host. (a) *Echthrodesis lamorali*; (b) a female wasp with eggs of (c) the spider *D. formidabilis*; (d) typical spider and wasp habitat.

limpet shells where they line the cavity and seal the entrance with a silken 'door' at high tide to prevent water from entering the submerged nest. The door is semipermeable to gases, allowing exchange of oxygen and carbon dioxide between the nest cavity and the seawater. The spiders are able to survive inundation outside of the nest because they are covered in a layer of hydrofuge (water-repellent) hairs which trap air and act as an external lung (see 'Air stores', p. 321) enabling them to breathe under water.

The unusually hairy body of *E. lamorali* is thought to trap an air layer (as in the spider), enabling it to breathe while submerged. To slow their metabolism down and to decrease their demand for oxygen, the wasps enter a quiescent state (torpor) from which they recover once the inundation ends.

Both male and female wasps are virtually wingless (tiny wing stubs are present; those of males being slightly larger than those of females) and unable to fly. Wing reduction is a common phenomenon in various parasitic Hymenoptera. In female *E. lamorali* it is probably mainly to enhance movement through the spider's web surrounding the eggs and also to facilitate movement inside the cramped space of the egg sac interior; here she lays a single egg in each of the spider's eggs. Reduced wing size undoubtedly helps to prevent both male and female wasps from being blown into unsuitable locations by the strong prevailing coastal winds.

Although the host spider is found along about 2,000km of coastline, *E. lamorali* has only been recorded along a very short stretch of coast along the Cape Peninsula, roughly where the cold Benguela and warm Agulhas currents converge. The spiders nesting in this area behave differently from those in areas where the parasitoid is absent; they construct a multicompartment egg sac inside the nest and eggs are laid in some of the compartments, but not in others. The empty compartments are thought to act as decoys since the female wasps are unable to penetrate the tough silken egg sac cover repeatedly. In areas where the wasp is absent, the spiders appear not to produce decoy empty egg compartments, each one having a clutch of eggs.

Sandy beaches

The intertidal area of sandy beaches is a harsh and unstable habitat. Wave action is the dominant force here: strong waves buffet and scour beaches away, while gentler waves deposit sand and rebuild contours.

The animals that occur here are regularly immersed in seawater, alternating with periods of direct exposure to sunlight. The instability of the sandy zone makes it impossible for seaweeds to grow here, so animals are dependent on nutrients delivered by wave action. Marine arthropods are abundant in this zone and are well adapted to the alternating wet and dry periods by burrowing into the sand, and emerging when conditions are favourable. They provide a rich source of food for small (invertebrate) and large (mostly bird) predators.

13.7 The sandy areas near the limit of the high-tide zone, where kelp and carcasses of marine animals are beached, are rich in invertebrate life.

13.8 (a) One of the most common detritus-feeding insects under stranded plant and animal remains on the West Coast is the beetle *Pachyphaleria capensis* (Tenebrionidae); (b) an aggregation of beetles close to suitable shelter and a food source.

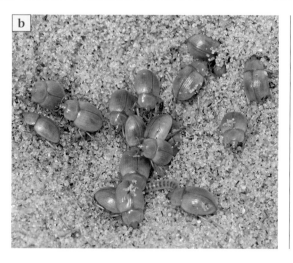

13.9 The amphipod sand-hopper *Talorchestia capensis* (Talitridae) is a crustacean that is often extremely abundant amongst kelp on West Coast beaches.

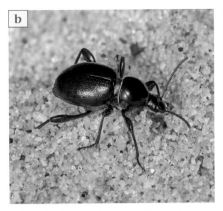

13.10 Generalist insects occasionally feed on stranded plant and animal remains: (a) a carrion-feeding blow fly, *Lucilia sericata* (Calliphoridae); (b) the beetle *Carchares macer* (Tenebrionidae).

13.11 The kelp fly, *Fucellia capensis* (Anthomyiidae), often becomes abundant, especially on the West Coast, where larvae breed in stranded kelp.

The part of sandy beaches of importance to insects is the zone at the top end of the high-tide mark (fig. 13.7). This is a fairly stable, food-rich and sheltered habitat for a variety of scavengers that feed on seaweed and animals washed up after storms. The common kelp fly, *Fucellia capensis*, is a specialised kelp feeder. Stranded kelp also provides food and shelter for less specialised scavengers. A common species in this zone is the beach ground beetle, *Pachyphaleria capensis* (Tenebrionidae, fig. 13.8), which may occur in large numbers under stranded kelp, often with the crustacean sand-hopper *Talorchestia capensis* (Talitridae, fig. 13.9). Various predatory beetles make use of the bounty of small crustaceans and insects in this zone.

Opportunistic species move into the coastal zone when conditions are favourable or food is abundant. Typical examples are blow flies (fig. 13.10a) that colonise fish, bird and mammal carcasses that are left stranded above the high-tide mark. General scavengers of plant and animal remains, such as tenebrionid beetles (fig. 13.10b), also frequently invade these high-tide edges.

Kelp flies

Adult kelp flies, *Fucellia capensis* (Diptera: Anthomyiidae, fig. 13.11), may become very abundant under certain conditions. They are occasionally numerous enough to be considered a nuisance by people living close to beaches with stranded kelp, on which the larvae feed. Adults are most abundant in early winter, when greater quantities of kelp usually wash ashore. The flies are most common along the West Coast, where the principal larval food is the sea bamboo, *Ecklonia maxima*, which is the main seaweed species washed up on beaches.

The duration of the immature stages is usually 22–28 days and appears to be linked to lunar cycles. The adults lay eggs on kelp deposited by spring tides and the life cycle is completed before the next spring tide about 28 days later. Mature larvae are about 10mm long, and the puparium (the pupa encased in the last larval cuticle) about 7mm long. Both larvae and pupae can survive inundation by seawater for several hours. The buoyant pupae may be washed out of the seaweed and are sometimes deposited in substantial numbers along the drift line, quite far from where the kelp has been stranded.

Ferocious tiger beetle larvae

Most predatory beetles found on southern African beaches are carabids that include tiger beetles (Coleoptera: Carabidae: Cicindelinae; see 'Predatory ground beetles', p. 239; 'Tiger beetles', p. 337). Like most Carabidae, both adults and larvae are predatory: adults run about searching for prey, but cicindeline larvae are sit-and-wait predators that live in burrows.

The sandy beaches in different coastal regions have been colonised by different 'pairs' of tiger beetle species that have sufficiently distinct habits to avoid competition. On the south and east coasts, *Lophyra differens* and *Habrodera capensis* (figs 13.12a, b) form a species 'pair' that avoids competition by preferring different areas of the beach – *L. differens* is found on the upper, drier dune sands some distance from the water's edge, whereas *H. capensis* is active on lower sands periodically inundated by tidal swells. *Lophyra barbifrons* and *Habrodera nilotica* (figs 13.12c–e) are another 'pair', occurring on the northern KwaZulu-Natal coastline.

On the west coast, *Eurymorpha cyanipes* (fig. 13.13) and *Platychile pallida* (fig. 13.14) form a species pair that avoids competition by being active at different times. The diurnal *E. cyanipes* occurs from Lüderitz in southern Namibia to southern Angola. *Platychile pallida* is a relatively common nocturnal species that occurs from Cape Town to Walvis Bay in central Namibia. The distribution areas of the two species overlap by about 500km. In this zone, the beetles depend on the same prey – the various small marine invertebrates and insects associated with stranded kelp.

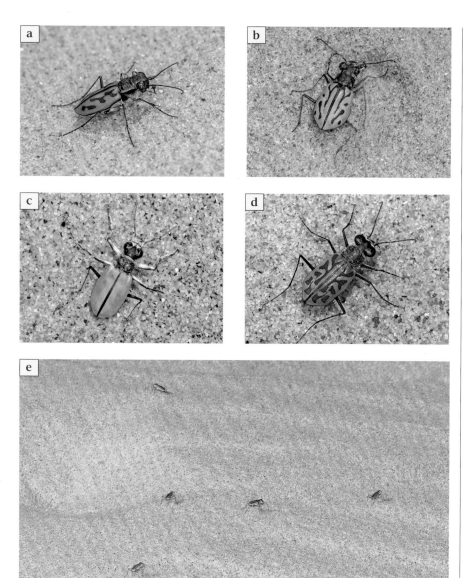

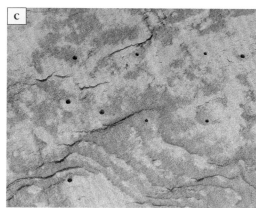

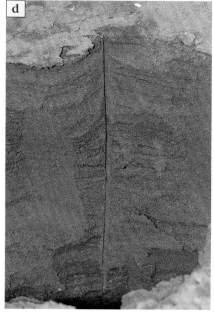

13.12 Tiger beetles are common and widespread on white sandy beaches of the east coast, where unrelated species often have similar pale and contrasting darker elytral patterns to enhance their camouflage against their background: **(a)** *Lophyra differens* and **(b)** *Habrodera capensis* make a species 'pair' from the south and east coasts, while **(c)** *L. barbifrons* and **(d, e)** *H. nilotica* are a 'pair' occurring on the northern KwaZulu-Natal coastline.

Platychile pallida and *E. cyanipes* have different evolutionary origins. *Platychile pallida* is the solitary member of a primitive lineage, while *E. cyanipes* belongs to a more derived group. The adult *P. pallida* is cryptically pale in colour, has lost the ability to fly, moves relatively slowly and has become nocturnal in an area where food is plentiful but night-time temperatures are low; these are probably all energy-saving adaptations. On the other hand, *E. cyanipes* is black and depends on sunshine to warm up, after which the beetle becomes active; it runs and flies rapidly in search of prey and to avoid predators.

Another difference between the two species is that their larvae live in different sandy strata. Those of *P. pallida* live in deep burrows (up to 1m deep) in loose sand well above the high-tide mark, while *E. cyanipes* larvae live in much shallower burrows (about 20cm deep, fig. 13.13d) in wet sand that is periodically inundated by high tides. Their behaviour at the burrows, however, is very similar.

13.13 The tiger beetle *Eurymorpha cyanipes* (Carabidae: Cicindelinae) occurs on beaches along the northern regions of the west coast of southern Africa: **(a)** adult; **(b)** larva; **(c)** burrow entrances below the high-tide zone on a beach; **(d)** exposed larval burrow in wet sand.

13.14 The common nocturnal west coast tiger beetle *Platychile pallida*: (a) adult; (b) larva.

13.15 Beach ground beetles: (a) *Acanthoscelis rugicornis*; (b) *Scarites rugosus* (Carabidae: Scaritinae).

All tiger beetle larvae are sit-and-wait predators that live in vertical burrows from which they launch themselves to capture passing prey. This is enabled by several morphological adaptations. The head and prothorax are strongly sclerotised and flattened (figs 13.13b, 13.14b) to lie flush with the burrow rim, and are used to plug the burrow entrance while the larva lies in wait. The head has upward-projecting, curved mandibles, sensory bristles and large stemmata (simple eyes). The eyes are arranged in a way that enables the larva to see in different directions and scan a wide field for approaching prey. Although insect stemmata are usually only sensitive enough to distinguish between light and dark and some movement, those of tiger beetle larvae are densely packed with photoreceptors that permit detailed focusing and depth perception.

Prey is captured in the mandibles by a backward strike of the head. This is where another special morphological adaptation comes into play. The larva has an enlarged fifth abdominal segment armed with large hooks. The structure anchors the larva when it lunges out of the burrow to capture prey and prevents it from being pulled out of the burrow in the struggle. The larva then pulls its prize into the burrow, injects it with digestive enzymes and swallows the dissolved tissues. The dry, skeletal remains are ejected from the burrow.

Nocturnal beach ground beetles

The beach ground beetle, *Acanthoscelis rugicornis* (Carabidae: Scaritinae, fig. 13.15a), is a voracious nocturnal predator that roams the sandy beaches at night and shelters under stranded seaweed during the day. Another member of the Scaritinae found on sandy beaches is the smaller *Scarites rugosus* (fig. 13.15b), which hides under dune vegetation higher up on the beach. The larvae and adults of both species are predatory: the larvae are active predators with strong legs adapted for running; adults have long legs and run around rapidly searching for prey (see 'Ground beetles', p. 127; 'Predatory ground beetles', p. 239).

Cryptic antlion larvae

Antlions (Neuroptera: Myrmeleontidae) have adapted to virtually every type of sandy habitat, including stable coastal sands above the high-tide line (see 'Thermal refuges of antlion larvae', p. 146; 'Giant lacewings and their antlion larvae', p. 237; 'Pit-building antlions', p. 349; 'Free-living antlions', p. 349). Highly cryptic *Syngenes longicornis* adults inhabit coastal forests and bush, where they rest on tree trunks and branches, well camouflaged from their own predators. The characteristic black-and-white, free-living, fast-moving, predatory larvae (fig. 13.16) are common inhabitants of dune sand above the high-tide mark at the fringes of dune vegetation where they prey on other arthropods.

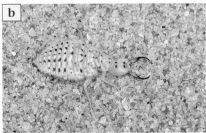

13.16 The antlion *Syngenes longicornis* (Neuroptera: Myrmeleontidae) occurs only close to the coast of the southern and eastern parts of South Africa. (a) The cryptic adult hides on tree bark or twigs in the forests or scrub-land during daytime while (b) the pale-coloured larva lives in the white coastal sand.

CHAPTER 14
URBAN ENVIRONMENT

Urban and suburban areas offer a unique suite of potential habitats that attract and support a range of different insect species. Some of these are intermittently or temporarily present as visitors from surrounding rural environs; others are permanent inhabitants that thrive in the mosaic of buildings and plants provided by human development. The habitats include buildings of various kinds, their contents and their inhabitants, home gardens, parks (fig. 14.1) and avenues of street trees. The plants in these habitats modify the environment to such an extent that lush oases with tropical forest or savanna-like conditions are created that are completely different from the surrounding natural vegetation.

14.1 (pp. 366–367) Public gardens in and around cities such as this view captured in Kirstenbosch National Botanical Garden in Cape Town provide habitat for a multitude of insects. (Photo: Alberto Ballero)

City areas usually have higher temperatures than rural environments, caused by thermal radiation off buildings and roads, and increased relative humidity due to respiration from high plant densities. The diversity of potential habitats within these modified areas provides ideal conditions for many groups of insects that are attracted to some aspect of the environment, both outside and inside buildings. Some urban areas, however, have transformed the natural environment to such an extent that insects are probably almost totally excluded (fig. 14.2).

The insects in an urban environment usually belong to two broad classes: those that live and thrive in close association with humans (termed synanthropic), their pets and homes, and those that live in the external environment of gardens, parks, or the areas on the outskirts of the city that consist of small patches with limited agricultural development where horses and other livestock are maintained. Some may become numerous enough or of sufficient nuisance value to be considered pest species.

The species that occur in gardens (fig. 14.3) and parks include flower visitors and pollinators (butterflies and honey bees); herbivores of woody plant foliage (caterpillars and chafer beetles) and lawns (mole crickets, crickets, beetles and termites); root feeders (cutworms and white grubs); and sap feeders (aphids, scale insects and other bugs) and their predators (ladybirds). There are also detritivores such as woodlice and compost insects (soldier flies, crane flies, stable flies, rhinoceros beetles and fruit chafers).

The insects that are attracted to buildings (fig. 14.4) use them for sheltered nest sites, such as under eaves (paper and potter wasps); to nest in various man-made cavities (honey bees); to bore into roof trusses (carpenter bees) or timber at ground level (termites); to breed in water-filled containers (mosquitoes); to live in accumulations of firewood (borers of various kinds); or are attracted to pet faeces (dung beetles and flies).

Insects that live indoors include species attracted to exposed food (cockroaches, Parktown prawns, various flies and ants) or stored food products like flour, meal, rice, pulses and dry pet food (fishmoths, weevils, biscuit beetles and meal moths); as well as species that feed on the human occupants themselves (mosquitoes, bed bugs and head lice) or their companion animals (fleas and stable flies). Many otherwise unobtrusive insects may be attracted to lights in and around the house at night (mantises, beetles, moths and midges).

The majority of urban insect species occur in gardens surrounding homes, or nest in or on buildings and other structures. Most people would be surprised at their numbers and diversity (see box, p. 370).

14.2 A hostile environment: a smoggy, polluted and highly disturbed industrial development with vegetation contaminated by effluent.

14.3 This well-maintained rural aloe garden, interspersed with a few other plants, is a haven for local insects.

Rina de Klerk

14.4 Urban areas include parks, gardens, homes, and their inhabitants, all of which have insects associated with them.

Although generalisations about the plant composition of most gardens are difficult to make, we have, nevertheless, assumed that the average garden would consist of at least some annual and perennial herbaceous plants, various woody shrubs and trees and, usually, an expanse of lawn grass.

Generalisations about the insects likely to occur in garden environments are also necessarily imprecise but there are certainly some that commonly occur in these environments and it is on these that we have focused.

Insects associated with garden plants

The species composition of garden plants varies tremendously in different regions and depends on numerous factors – some climatic (rainfall, temperature and the occurrence of frost), others aesthetic and determined by choice of plants and layout. Garden plants may represent virtually every group of plants, ranging in size from tiny succulents to huge hardwood trees. Some of the plants may be endemic to the immediate region, while others are indigenous to the continent, but many are likely to be introduced from other continents. Indigenous plants generally attract guilds of local insects, which may be transported with their host plants when these are distributed to gardens, or the dispersal of the host plants leads to gradual natural range extensions of their associated insects. Exotic plants are generally hosts to cosmopolitan insect species.

Chafer beetles

Leaf chafers (Coleoptera: Scarabaeidae: Melolonthinae and Rutelinae) are nocturnal brown or yellowish beetles that feed on the foliage and flowers of many garden plants, leaving typically jagged round sections cut from the margins of leaves or large flowers such as roses. Culprits are seldom seen as they feed at night, although adults are attracted to lights in and around houses at night. Amongst the Melolonthinae, *Camenta*, *Pegylus* and *Schizonycha* species are common in gardens; common Rutelinae are species of *Adoretus* and *Anomala* (fig. 14.5).

Fruit chafers, such as the common black and yellow *Pachnoda sinuata* (Scarabaeidae: Cetoniinae, fig. 14.6a), occasionally feed on flowers or ripe fruit, and should not be confused with the CMR beetle, *Hycleus tricolor* (Meloidae, fig. 14.6b), which is especially attracted to mauve flowers. Both beetle species are diurnal and brightly coloured; their bright colours serve as a warning to potential predators that they are unpalatable. Chafer larvae are amongst the most common compost insects (see 'Rhinoceros beetle and fruit chafer larvae', p. 386), whereas CMR larvae are bee and grasshopper egg parasites (see fig. 5.34, p. 172).

14.5 Chafers are common nocturnal beetles (Scarabaeidae) that feed on the foliage and flowers of garden plants: (a) *Camenta innocua* (Melolonthinae); (b) *Pegylus sommeri* (Melolonthinae); (c) *Adoretus* sp. (Rutelinae).

14.6 (a) The common garden fruit chafer, *Pachnoda sinuata* (Scarabaeidae: Cetoniinae), occasionally feeds on fruit; (b) the CMR beetle, *Hycleus tricolor* (Meloidae), sometimes feeds on garden flowers.

A lot of insects

Frank E. Lutz, the author of the book *A Lot of Insects* (1941), was an entomologist employed as curator of insects by the American Museum of Natural History. He wanted to increase the number of entomologists employed at the museum and argued that '*the more species there are in a group of animals or plants, the more difficult it is to identify any one of them*' – and since there were more than three times as many insects as all other animals put together, at least three-fourths of the staff of any zoological museum should be entomologists. He added that more species of insects either lived in or visited his 1,400m² garden in the middle of a suburban town than there were bird species in the whole of the USA and Canada together.

Although he and the museum director (with whom he was in conversation) realised that they didn't have a clue about the number of birds, Frank estimated that at least 500 different kinds of insect either made their living on, or came of their own initiative to his home lot. The director was convinced that this was an exaggeration, which prompted Frank to say '*if the Museum will agree to raise my salary by ten dollars a year for every species above five hundred that I honestly find on our lot, I shall agree to have my salary reduced by ten dollars a year for every species short of five hundred.*'

This conversation motivated him to start a record of the number of insect species in his garden plot, which he did over a four-year period and, during which, he also documented their behaviour (which constitutes the bulk of his book). During this time he recorded a total of 1,402 different species! The greatest number of species – 467 – were butterflies and moths, followed by 259 beetles, 258 flies, 167 bees, wasps and ants, and smaller numbers from many other orders.

At the same time, to prove to neighbours that having, and attracting, insects to one's garden does not result in 'an awful place', he entered his garden into the garden contest conducted by one of the New York newspapers. He received a silver medal for first place, two bronze medals for second place, and a certificate of achievement, during that period.

Since the bargain was not officially made with his director, he never did get his increase in salary (nor in staff), but he left the world with an appreciation for insects, for which many of us are grateful!

Jenny Scholtz

14.7 The larvae of large, colourful *Brachycerus* weevils (Curculionidae) feed inside the bulbs of river lilies, amaryllis and clivias. Adults may be found wandering around in gardens. (**a**) Clivias, in particular, attract (**b**) *B. labrusca*. (**c**) Plants such as this *Amaryllis belladonna* are often attacked by (**d**) *B. ornatus*.

Red-spotted lily weevils

Many parks and gardens have beds of perennial bulb plants that produce showy displays of bright flowers at certain times of the year; among these are species of *Crinum, Clivia* and other lilies and amaryllids (figs 14.7a, c). The permanence of the plants allows certain insect species to establish and maintain long-term populations on them – these include various foliage and bulb feeders, one of which is the red-spotted lily weevil.

Brachycerus (fig. 14.7b) is a sizable genus of large colourful weevils (Coleoptera: Curculionidae). At a length of about 60mm, the red-spotted lily weevil, *B. ornatus* (fig. 14.7d), is one of the largest weevils in the world. The bulb-feeding *Brachycerus* species are almost spherical, either brightly coloured in red and black, or with yellow or orange patches, or ornately tuberculate. When threatened they 'play dead' (termed thanatosis) and depend on their incredibly hard exoskeleton to protect them from predators. Feeding on toxic bulb plants imparts some level of toxicity to the beetles, hence their bright warning colours. Adults feed on young leaves and the larvae tunnel into and feed on the bulbs.

14.8 (a) The lily borer caterpillar is the larva of the moth *Brithys crini* (Noctuidae). It feeds inside the leaves and bulbs of garden bulb plants such as **(b)** river lilies, *Crinum bulbispermum*.

Lily borer moths

Besides beetles, there are also species of Lepidoptera that feed on bulbs. The larvae of the lily borer or amaryllis borer moth, *Brithys crini* (also known as *B. pancratii*, Noctuidae, fig. 14.8a), is one of these. The adult is a rather dull black moth about 15–20mm long, but the larva is strikingly banded in black and yellow. Female moths lay eggs in clusters low down on the plants and the emergent larvae tunnel into the fleshy leaves, feeding in groups, often down into the bulb. In later instars, the large larvae move out and feed on the surface of the leaves. Before pupation, they tunnel back into the plant as far as the corm or bulb, or enter the soil surrounding it, where they pupate. Populations of this species may build up to pest proportions and under certain circumstances it is considered a serious pest of river lilies, *Crinum* spp. (fig. 14.8b), *Clivia* species and other amaryllids.

Garden butterflies

The black-and-yellow citrus swallowtail, *Papilio demodocus* (Lepidoptera: Papilionidae, fig. 14.9a), is a large and striking butterfly. It occurs across the African continent, also breeding in gardens, where the adults sip nectar from a wide range of nectar-producing plants and the larvae feed on ornamental and fruit-bearing citrus trees (Rutaceae). Early-instar larvae are cryptically coloured: they are predominantly black, with white speckles and a white saddle, reminiscent of bird droppings (fig. 14.9b). In later instars, the larvae turn citrus-green with brown and white mottling (fig. 14.9c) and reddish eyespots, although they may vary somewhat. They are strongly cryptic and well camouflaged, but they have an additional and unusual defensive system – a special gland (osmeterium) that produces defensive secretions (fig. 14.9d).

14.9 (a) The citrus swallowtail butterfly, *Papilio demodocus* (Papilionidae), is a common garden inhabitant associated with ornamental and fruit-bearing citrus plants. **(b)** Young larvae are similar in colour to bird faeces, which they are thought to mimic. **(c)** Older larvae are similar to the background citrus leaves. **(d)** Larvae have a secondary defence mechanism: the osmeterium is an extensible wriggling orange gland that produces defensive secretions.

14.10 The garden acraea, *Acraea horta* (Nymphalidae: Heliconiinae), is a widespread and common garden visitor.

14.11 **(a)** A green stink bug, *Nezara viridula* (Pentatomidae); **(b)** a batch of *N. viridula* eggs; **(c)** *N. viridula* nymph.

The osmeterium is an eversible gland characteristic of all Papilionidae larvae. It is located behind the head and is everted as a forked, wriggling, red appendage when a larva is threatened. It simultaneously secretes volatile chemicals with repellent terpenoid odours that are strongly citrus-like. The secretions are thought to be mainly repellent against invertebrate predators and have been shown to be effective against some ant and mantis species, but ineffective against wasps. Their efficacy against bird predators is somewhat mixed – some bird species are apparently repelled, but others are unaffected by the odour and consume the larvae.

Another butterfly commonly seen in gardens is the garden acraea, *Acraea horta* (fig. 14.10), whose larvae are often abundant on the wild peach, *Kiggelaria africana* (see 'Beautiful forest butterflies and moths', p. 293), which is widely planted as a garden tree. Larvae may pupate on the host tree or wander off to pupate on walls.

Green stink bugs

Most Heteroptera (Hemiptera) produce repellent defensive chemicals (see box opposite) and qualify as 'stink bugs'; the name is usually used for the Pentatomidae, although another of their common names – shield bugs – is more descriptive. It refers to the large shield-shaped scutellum between the wing bases, which is usually longer than half the length of the abdomen.

A common and virtually cosmopolitan garden insect and agricultural pest in the Pentatomidae is the green vegetable stink bug, *Nezara viridula* (fig. 14.11a), thought to have originated from Africa. It feeds on the fruit, pods and seeds of a wide variety of plants – over 200 plant species in 30 families have been recorded, including vegetable, field and fruit crops, weeds and wild plants.

Although the adults are mostly green, some may be yellowish; over-wintering individuals, which hide under bark, amongst fallen leaves or in buildings, darken to brownish-green. Females lay eggs in clusters (fig. 14.11b) on the underside of leaves; after 5–20 days, depending on temperature, they hatch into bright orange nymphs, the first of five instars. These do not feed and remain clustered together near the emergence site. After moulting they change colour, turning black with white and yellow spots; they disperse a short distance and start to feed but remain together in a group. From the fourth instar, individuals start to leave the group. After the next moult the thorax turns green while the abdomen is still spotted (fig. 14.11c). The adult green colour is acquired after the final moult.

Brood care in twig-wilters

Twig-wilters (Hemiptera: Heteroptera: Coreidae) feed on the sap of young plant shoots, injecting saliva that causes wilting and die-back (fig. 14.13a). There are several familiar garden species across southern Africa and some are considered to be minor pests (figs 14.13b–e). *Carlisis wahlbergi* is one of these, but appears not to cause wilt. It is sometimes very abundant, particularly on *Gardenia* plants – there is a record of more than 9,000 individuals, weighing about 6.8kg in total, from a single bush in a Pretoria garden! It has several interesting biological characteristics: it is capable of spraying its defensive secretions for a distance of about 15cm, and females care for the eggs and young brood (this trait is also known from other Coreidae).

Carlisis wahlbergi females lay batches of eggs, which they then squat over for 7–20 days until the eggs hatch and the young nymphs have dispersed. During this time they do not leave the brood nor do they feed. The main

Stink bugs' defensive chemicals

Most people will have encountered a 'stink bug' at some stage. These are usually shield bugs (Pentatomidae), but most heteropterans readily produce defensive, volatile and repugnant chemicals when threatened.

Many brightly coloured Heteroptera produce defensive secretions, but others that are more dull-coloured also produce highly volatile and often pungent odours. Colour appears not to be involved in the defensive arsenal of these species and it is the repellent odours that perform the major defensive function. Those with bright colours, however, clearly combine aposematic colours with noxious secretions as a secondary line of defence. Others, particularly predatory groups such as assassin bugs (Reduviidae), may be brightly coloured, produce repellent secretions and also 'bite' readily, injecting proteolytic digestive enzymes into the wound. A bite by some large species causes an intense burning pain in humans that may persist for hours.

Both adults and nymphs produce the repellent secretions from special glands. In nymphs of many species, the glands are clearly visible on the top of the abdomen (fig. 14.12). When the bugs mature, the glands migrate to the lower surface of the body between the metathoracic legs. The gland reservoir may extend as far as the second abdominal segment when it is full. The discharge ducts open on the metapleura on either side of the body between the second and third pairs of legs, where there are often specialised evaporative areas that disperse the volatile fluids, which mostly contain aldehydes, esters or alkanones.

When the insects are threatened, the defensive chemicals may be secreted onto their cuticle or transferred with the tarsi to the body surface of the attacker (such as ants or parasitoids) or ejected towards the attacker. In many instances, the smell is almond-like, but when produced by thousands of individuals collectively, such as in the moist savannas of southern Africa in summer when thousands of small black burrowing bugs (Cydnidae) may be attracted to light, the smell (and taste if they land in or near food), is overwhelming and repulsive.

The gland reservoir does not have muscles like those of ground beetles, which also spray defensive chemicals (see 'Ground beetles', p. 127), but contraction of abdominal muscles increases the pressure on the haemolymph flowing around it, which, in turn, exerts pressure on the reservoir. Some species are capable of spraying these secretions up to 15cm. The contraction of the muscles also opens the discharge duct and the secretion flows onto the evaporative area.

14.12
The dorsal abdominal stink gland is visible in this *Nezara viridula* nymph.

14.13 Coreidae bugs are known as twig-wilters, because (a) the twigs of the host plant become wilted as a result of their feeding on the plant sap. Some common coreid species are: (b) *Homoeocerus* sp.; (c) *H. nigricornis*; (d) *Leptoglossus gonagra*; (e) *Elasmopoda valga*.

purpose of this vigilance appears to be to guard against attack by parasitoids and ants – the female kicks out at these insects when approached. Although this may appear to be a rather ineffectual defensive mechanism, studies have shown that eggs with a coreid female in attendance (fig. 14.14) have a significantly higher survival rate than those from which the female has been experimentally removed. They spray defensive chemicals only against vertebrate predators.

Aphids and whiteflies

Aphids (Hemiptera: Sternorrhyncha: Aphididae) occur on a very wide range of plants – from grasses to shrubs and trees (fig. 14.15). Although there are relatively few indigenous species in southern Africa, cosmopolitan species with wide food plant tolerance are common. Many species produce honeydew to which ants are attracted (see 'The Namib detritus ant', p. 153; box, pp. 218–219). Some species, for example the green peach aphid, *Myzus persicae*, have been recorded on hundreds of host plants including weeds, vegetables, agricultural crops, fruit trees and many others.

Aphids have a remarkable and complex life cycle that is completed on at least two different host plant species: a primary host and, in mid-summer, one of several possible secondary hosts.

Many aphid species (e.g. *Myzus persicae* – see box opposite) are polymorphic, differing between generations in colour, presence or absence of wings, behaviour, and in the offspring they produce (fig. 14.16). The physiological mechanisms underlying this are complex and determined by day length and temperature or by crowding of individuals, especially on summer hosts. The different life cycle strategies result in rapid population increases, which provide abundant food for numerous predators and specialist parasitoids (fig. 14.17).

Whiteflies (Hemiptera: Sternorrhyncha: Aleyrodidae, fig. 14.18) are not flies but tiny fly-like bugs. They differ from aphids and scale insects in that both males and females feed and are winged. First-instar larvae have functional legs but once they have started to feed they become immobile and remain attached to the plant by the mouthparts until they emerge as adults. Most species are coated in white, waxy dust.

14.14 A female twig-wilter, *Homoeocerus nigricornis* (Coreidae), guarding her batch of eggs. Although the eggs on the edges of the cluster may be parasitised, those in the centre usually survive.

14.15 Aphids (Hemiptera: Aphididae) vary greatly within and between species. Males (rare in southern Africa) and females are quite different; females may be winged or wingless and may also differ in colour. (a) *Neophyllaphis grobleri* nymphs with droples of honeydew; (b) *Aphis taraxacicola*; (c) *Toxoptera citricidus*; (d) *Macrosiphum euphorbiae*; (e) *Melanaphis* sp.

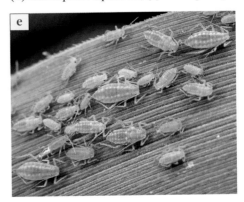

14.16 Reproduction in aphids is mostly by parthenogenetic ovovivipary (live birth) by either winged or wingless females: **(a)** *Neophyllaphis grobleri*; **(b)** *Macrosiphum euphorbiae*; **(c)** *Aphis* sp.; **(d)** winged and wingless morphs of the same generation.

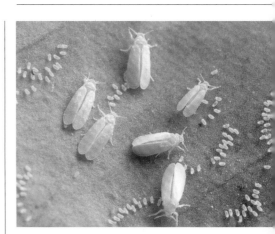

14.18 Whiteflies, in spite of their common name and fly-like appearance, are actually bugs (Hemiptera: Aleyrodidae) and are not always white. The eggs are laid in spiral patterns or arcs on the underside of leaves.

14.17 **(a)** Aphids are heavily parasitised by *Lysiphlebus* and *Aphidius* (Braconidae) wasps. **(b)** Parasitised aphids, called 'mummies', become bloated and white.

The aphid life cycle

The physiological mechanisms underlying aphid reproduction are complex. In this example of the green peach aphid, *Myzus persicae*, the eggs are laid in autumn, overwinter and hatch in spring, giving rise to:

- *fundatrices* (founders), wingless, egg-laying (oviparous) but parthenogenetic females, which produce numerous
- *fundatrigeniae*, which are a distinctive, all-female, egg-laying and parthenogenetic form that go through several spring and early-summer generations; in mid-summer they give rise to
- *migrantes*, winged females that migrate to secondary hosts where they give live birth (ovoviviparous) by parthenogenesis to the next distinctive generation
- *alienicolae*, which are also ovoviviparous and parthenogenetic and undergo several generations on the secondary host; these include some winged male and female forms that migrate to other secondary host plants and produce
- *sexuparae*, winged forms produced in autumn that return to the primary host and give rise to
- *sexuales*, wingless sexual females that mate with males that were produced by *alienicolae* on secondary hosts; they lay eggs that can overwinter, thus completing the annual life cycle.

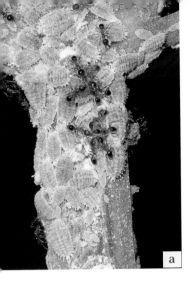

14.19 The many scale insect families are placed in the superfamily Coccoidea (Hemiptera). Most are characterised by the specific wax coating that covers the adult females and nymphs: (a) soft scale insects (Pseudococcidae); (b) brown soft scale, *Coccus hesperidum* (Coccidae); (c) *Ceroplastes* sp. (Coccidae).

Scale insects

'Scale insect' is a general term for a large number of small insect species that mostly live permanently under a covering of wax that they secrete around themselves (fig. 14.19). There are 15 families of these sap-sucking bugs (Hemiptera: Sternorrhyncha: Coccoidea) in southern Africa.

Female scale insects have greatly reduced morphology and are little more than legless, wingless but feeding and egg-laying individuals permanently covered by a wax layer. Once established, females of most species don't ever move again. Males, if present, are small, 'typical' two-winged insects; they do not feed. Reproduction is mostly parthenogenetic, although mating does take place at times.

The type of female wax covering is one of the main characters that defines the different families. The coverings may be tiny (1mm), flat and round or elongate, white or orange; larger (5mm), raised and globular, soft or hard; or appear as quite large (6–7mm) waxy sacs.

Various species of scale insects feed on any of a great diversity of plants – from tiny succulents, grasses, aloes and cycads, to many garden and crop plants and numerous indigenous and ornamental tree species. Many secrete honeydew, a characteristic that brings them into conflict with farmers, because the honeydew attracts ants, which protect the scale insects from predators and parasitoids – farmers would prefer that scale insects are controlled. Honeydew may also cover leaves and stems; various fungi such as black mould grow on the honeydew and suppress photosynthesis, which eventually results in stunted leaf growth. Some scale insect species also transmit plant pathogens to the host plant, including several major pests of fruit and crops.

Females either lay eggs (oviparous) or give live birth (ovoviviparous). The emergent nymphs, called crawlers, crawl a short distance from the female, attach to the plant and begin to cover themselves with wax (figs 14.20a, b). Some, however, are blown off the host plant and may land on another appropriate plant where they establish. The majority of crawlers are female and

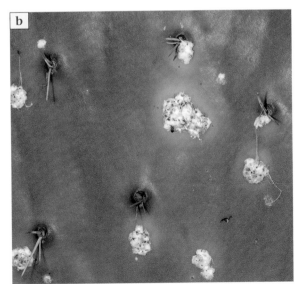
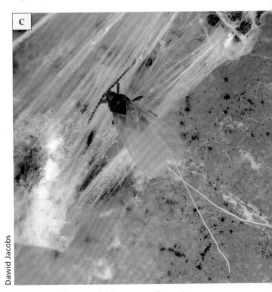

Dawid Jacobs

14.20 Prickly pear cochineal, *Dactylopius opuntiae* (Dactylopiidae), is specific to prickly pears, *Opuntia* spp.: (a, b) females are wax-covered; (c) males are tiny, fragile winged insects. Carminic acid, which is metabolically produced by this species, is the source of the commercial red food colourant, cochineal.

after attaching, they never leave the attachment site. Male nymphs eventually moult into small, winged insects that fly short distances to locate females (fig. 14.20c). Because the majority of the offspring of reproductive female scale insects establish close to their mother and siblings, they are often found in dense aggregations which may remain at one site for many months.

Giant scale (Hemiptera: Monophlebidae) are atypical members of Coccoidea in many respects (fig. 14.21). They are the largest scale insects and are mostly solitary. They also have only a light covering of wax, and unlike other scale insects, are mobile, moving readily between plants. The Australian bug, *Icerya purchasi*, is unusual: it is hermaphroditic, each individual containing both female and male reproductive organs (see box below).

14.21 Giant scales, *Monophlebus* sp. (Monophlebidae), are atypical of Coccoidea: they are large (this one is about 10 mm long), live singly, have little wax covering, and are mobile, walking around on their host plant or between host plants.

Hermaphroditic Australian bug

Insect hermaphrodites are rare, unlike their distant relatives, the earthworms (see 'Earthworms', p. 296) in which the phenomenon is the norm. Hermaphrodites are individuals that have both male and female reproductive organs and in which fertilisation occurs mainly within that individual.

The only well-studied hermaphroditic insect species found in southern Africa is the introduced Australian citrus pest *Icerya purchasi* (Hemiptera: Monophlebidae), coloquially known as the Australian bug or cottony cushion scale.

Icerya purchasi has a very characteristic appearance: individuals are small, reddish-brown insects (about 3mm long), but closely attached to them are much larger grooved, white cottony wax egg-sacs. These give females (which usually occur in groups on their host plant) the appearance of insects with a brown forebody and fluffy white hind body (fig. 14.22a). Gently poking the egg-sac with a sharp object will reveal that the sac is soft and tears easily, exposing a mass of up to 1,000 bright red eggs or recently emerged red nymphs (fig. 14.22b). The nymphs disperse (figs 14.22c, d) and settle before starting to secrete their own wax sac.

All *Icerya purchasi* 'females' are actually hermaphrodites – they have both female and male reproductive organs (ovaries and testes). Males are tiny winged red insects and are very rare. Each 'female' has diploid ovaries and haploid testes. Self-fertilisation gives rise to diploid eggs. The nymphs that emerge from these eggs are diploid, but soon after emergence haploid cells form amongst their ovaries and become testes. The occasional unfertilised egg gives rise to a male, which can fertilise 'females', but no cross-fertilisation between hermaphrodites occurs.

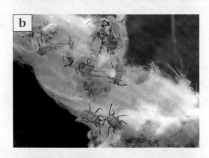

14.22 The Australian bug, *Icerya purchasi* (Hemiptera: Monophlebidae), is one of very few hermaphroditic insects. (**a**) What appears to be the insect is an egg sac (the white hind part), while the actual insect is the smaller, dark front part. (**b**) Nymphs, called 'crawlers' in scale insects, inside an opened sac. (**c, d**) Crawlers starting to settle on the host plant; like most scale insects, they produce honeydew that attracts ants.

Assassin bugs: generalist predators

Assassin bugs (Reduviidae) belong to one of the largest and most variable families of Hemiptera; the variation is reflected in the division of the family into more than 20 subfamilies of which about 13 occur in southern Africa. Most species are predators of various arthropods while New World members of the Triatominae suck human blood and transmit Chagas disease (see 'Millipede assassin bugs', p. 309). Among the groups are several that specialise on a particular type of prey (e.g. Ectrichodiinae on millipedes and some Emesinae on spiders; see 'Thread assassin bugs', p. 309) while the large often colourful Harpactorinae (e.g. *Rhinocoris segmentarius*, fig. 14.23) are generalist predators of other insects captured when they roam over flowers and shrubs; prey is frequently other Hemiptera such as Pyrrhocoridae (cotton stainers) and Lygaeidae (seed bugs) which they sometimes mimic, as well as Coccinellidae (ladybirds), which are often present.

14.23 Assassin bugs such as *Rhynocoris segmentarius* (Reduviidae) are amongst the larger general insect predators in urban areas.

Ladybirds: specialist predators

Aphid and scale insect population numbers build up quickly due to their short breeding cycles, the prolific number of progeny produced, and their small size. They attract various specialised insect predators, including ladybirds, lacewings and hover fly larvae. These are often, in turn, preyed on by larger insect predators such as assassin bugs (Reduviidae, fig. 14.23).

Ladybirds (Coleoptera: Coccinellidae) are typically highly convex, shiny beetles that may be 0.5–10mm long. The adults of some of the more familiar species are bicoloured or spotted in black and yellow or black and red-orange, although some all-black species are also fairly common (fig. 14.24). Larvae are slow-moving and tuberculate, grey-black with paler body patches, or waxy (fig. 14.25). Pupae are often brightly coloured, without a cocoon. All stages are chemically protected by synthesised blood chemicals; the bright colours of adults and pupae, especially, advertise this fact. Adults ooze yellow defensive haemolymph from leg joints when threatened (reflex bleeding).

Predatory ladybirds spend their entire life cycle in the vicinity of prey. Both adults and larvae feed on the same prey – small plant-feeding mites and insects, including aphids (Hemiptera: Aphididae), scale insects (Hemiptera: Coccoidea), whitefly (Hemiptera: Aleyrodidae) and thrips (Thysanoptera).

Some of the common species in southern Africa were deliberately introduced from various continents to control certain pest aphids and scale insects. These are now naturalised and form a characteristic element of the southern African ladybird fauna. However, one aggressive, recently introduced predatory species, the harlequin ladybird, *Harmonia axyridis* (figs 14.24b, 14.25b), has spread across South Africa in less than

14.24 Most ladybirds (Coleoptera: Coccinellidae) are predatory and are familiar insects around their aphid and scale insect prey. Both adults and larvae prey on these soft-bodied insects: (**a**) *Cheilomenes lunata*; (**b**) *Harmonia axyridis*; (**c**) *Cryptolaemus montrouzieri*; (**d**) *Exochomus* sp.

a

b

14.25 Ladybird larvae are also predators of aphids and scale insects and are invariably found with them: (a) *Cheilomenes lunata*; (b) *Harmonia axyridis*; (c) *Cryptolaemus montrouzieri*; (d) *Psyllobora variegata*.

c

d

a

b

10 years and is thought to be outcompeting indigenous species. Besides eating the same aphid prey as many southern African species, they may also turn to eating the indigenous ladybird eggs and larvae, and when food is limited, they eat those of their own species. They also frequently invade homes (fig. 14.26) at the end of the summer and have nuisance value because they secrete pungent noxious odours and stain furniture, carpets and curtains with defensive chemicals when disturbed.

Although most ladybirds are predators, members of the subfamily Epilachninae are plant feeders of various plants, including certain agricultural crops and garden vegetables. One common southern African species is the potato ladybird, *Epilachna dregei* (fig. 14.27), whose adults and larvae feed on potato leaves. Some *Epilachna* species undergo local autumn migrations where they aggregate in protected habitats, usually in high-lying areas but sometimes in houses; this and their plant-feeding habits bring some of the species into conflict with humans.

14.26 (a, b) The highly variable alien invasive ladybird *Harmonia axyridis* (Coccinellidae) overwinters in large clusters in protected situations, often in houses.

a

b

14.27 A small group of ladybirds (Epilachninae) have become plant feeders. *Epilachna dregei* feeds on potatoes in home gardens and commercial crops: (a) adult; (b) larva.

14.28 Green, brown and dusty-winged lacewings (Neuroptera) are common in gardens. Both adults and larvae are predators of small, soft-bodied arthropods such as mites, aphids and scale insects. Adults are often attracted to lights at night: (**a**) Larva of *Chrysoperla zastrowi* (Chrysopidae); (**b**) Larva of *Micromus sjoestedti* (Hemerobiidae); (**c**) *Pseudomallada* sp. (Chrysopidae); (**d**) *M. sjoestedti* (Hemerobiidae); (**e**) *M. oblongus* (Hemerobiidae); (**f**) Coniopterygidae adult.

Predatory lacewing larvae

Many urban lacewing (Neuroptera, fig. 14.28) larvae and adults share the habit of voraciously preying on mites and small, soft-bodied insects, and adults of many species are attracted to lights at night in urban environments. The common names of the three families most often encountered hint at their general appearance: green (Chrysopidae), brown (Hemerobiidae) and dusty-winged lacewings (Coniopterygidae), although all members are not necessarily green, brown or have 'dusty' wings.

There are about 25 Hemerobiidae species in southern Africa, most of which are brown and have hairy wings, and 40 species of Coniopterygidae, the body and wings of which are often covered in a powdery exudate.

The green lacewing family Chrysopidae has about 80 species in southern Africa. Its members are mostly green, but some are brown and others brightly marked in yellow and red. Green species are most commonly encountered in gardens in urban areas.

Green lacewings are delicate insects with a wingspan of about 20–30mm. Adults of some species feed on nectar and pollen, others on small insects. Eggs are laid singly on leaves or bark and are characteristically placed at the end of a long stalk; this is thought to offer protection against ants and cannibalism by siblings. The larvae are voracious predators of aphids, scale insects, moth and butterfly eggs, and mites. Larvae of a widespread southern African species, *Chrysoperla zastrowi* (formerly *Chrysopa zastrowi*), reared in the laboratory, each ate about 500 aphids during their development of 10–12 days. Chrysopid larvae may be smooth or tuberculate, while some, termed 'trash-carriers', carry the remains of their prey on their back as a form of camouflage (fig. 14.29). Pupation takes place in a spherical silken cocoon on a leaf or on bark.

Adults have hearing organs at the base of the forewing and are known to have good hearing. Sound production (which is by body vibration) and hearing are primarily for mate recognition, but some *Chrysopa* species have been shown to be able to hear the echolocation calls of hunting bats and to drop to the ground to avoid being caught.

14.29 This 'debris-' or 'trash-carrying' larva of *Pseudomallada chloris* (Chrysopidae) is one of many species in the family with the habit of covering themselves with various bits of debris from their environment. Depending on the species, the debris includes the remains of prey, their waxy flocculence and their skeletons. The purpose is probably as camouflage against other predators. Since their prey is mostly sessile, they locate it by 'sampling' various possibilities, which often include their siblings, so sampling 'trash' may save them from being cannibalised.

14.30 (a–c) Adult hover flies (Syrphidae) are common flower visitors in gardens, but they also frequent plants infested with aphids and scale insects where they lay eggs. **(d, e)** The larvae are predators of mites and soft-bodied insects.

Predatory hover fly larvae

There are more than 250 hover fly species (Diptera: Syrphidae) in southern Africa. The adults of the more common species are bee-like in size and appearance. They are regular flower visitors and feed on nectar and pollen (figs 14.30a–c). Controlled hovering flight, often in sunny patches, is common.

The larvae of many species are predators of small, soft-bodied insects such as aphids and scale insects on which they feed voraciously (figs 14.30d, e). Some species are detritus feeders. The unusual larvae of *Eristalis* species live in shallow organically enriched water and breathe through a long telescopic 'tail' that is protruded above the water surface – they are known as 'rat-tailed maggots'.

Gall wasps

Coral trees, *Erythrina* spp. (fig. 14.31), are popular garden and street trees. The beautiful red flowers that appear in late winter and early spring are also highly attractive to sunbirds and bees. The leaves of coral trees are often covered with very prominent nodules, called galls. Insect galls are abnormal growths on the leaves, stems or fruits of plants and are common in natural areas (see box, p. 49; 'Gall-forming insects', p. 120; 'Moth galls on Bushveld trees', p. 233).

Braam van Wyk

14.31 Coral trees, such as this *Erythrina lysistemon* (Fabaceae), are popular garden plants because of their beautiful red flowers in late winter and early spring. Their leaves are often disfigured by heavy infestations of gall wasps that cause galls in the leaf tissue. There are several wasp species involved: some produce galls, while others parasitise the gall formers.

14.32 *Erythrina* leaves are (**a**) often so severely galled by *Quadrastichus* spp. wasps that they (**b**) appear deformed. The galling seriously affects the leaves' ability to photosynthesise to such an extent that plants may die as a result.

Erythrina leaf galls are pea-sized and show on both the top and bottom surfaces of the leaves. They are dome-shaped and blister-like on the upper surface of the leaves, but are more elongated below, often appearing as finger-like projections. They may be so numerous that the leaves appear deformed (fig. 14.32). The trees are now planted far from their indigenous ranges and the gall-forming insects appear to have spread with the plants. The galls are caused by wasps in the genus *Quadrastichus* (Hymenoptera: Eulophidae, fig. 14.33a). They are very small – males are about 1mm and females 1.5mm long.

One species, *Q. erythrinae*, is of African (possibly East African) origin and is associated with indigenous coral trees, but is rapidly spreading around the world, attacking and often killing various *Erythrina* species. The wasp has a life cycle from egg to adult of about 20 days. Females insert the eggs into plant tissue and may lay up to about 320 eggs over an adult life span of about five to six days. Larvae emerge after a few days and their feeding induces gall formation. Heavily galled leaves curl and deform but otherwise the galls appear as separate, often adjoining, blister-like structures.

The exact nature of the community of tiny wasps emerging from *Erythrina* galls has long been a puzzle. Several species emerge from individual galls, and they belong to large families that contain both gall-forming and parasitoid members. It was only fairly recently established by entomologist Gerhard Prinsloo, working at the Agricultural Research Centre, that some species cause the galls and others are parasitoids of the gall wasps. All of these gall formers and their parasitoids belong to the same family, Eulophidae:

- *Quadrastichus gallicola*, the most common and widespread gall species in southern Africa, forms galls on the common coral tree, *Erythrina lysistemon*, Cape coral tree, *E. caffra*, and plough breaker, *E. zeyheri*;
- *Quadrastichus bardus* forms galls on the dwarf coral tree, *E. humeana*, and plough breaker, *E. zeyheri*; and
- *Quadrastichus ingens* forms galls on the broad-leaved coral tree, *E. latissima*.

The gall-forming wasps are parasitised by wasp species in the genus *Aprostocetus* (fig. 14.33b). The female parasitoid lays minute eggs in the tiny developing *Quadrastichus* larvae. The parasitic wasp species are:

- *Aprostocetus tritus* (parasitoids of *Q. gallicola* and *Q. bardus*);
- *Aprostocetus nitens* (parasitoids of *Q. gallicola* and *Q. bardus*); and
- *Aprostocetus exertus* (parasitoids of *Q. erythrinae* from galls on *E. latissima*).

The parasitoid *Eurytoma erythrinae* (Eurytomidae) has been released in the USA in an attempt to control the spread of *Q. erythrinae*.

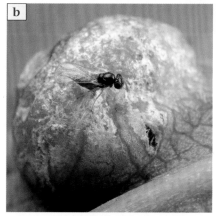

14.33 (**a**) *Quadrastichus* sp. (Eulophidae), one of the gall-forming wasps.
(**b**) *Aprostocetus* sp. (Eulophidae) parasitising a *Quadrastichus* sp. inside its gall.

Twig-boring caterpillars

Coral trees, *Erythrina* spp., are often attacked by coral tree borers in the genus *Terastia* (Lepidoptera: Crambidae, fig. 14.34). The *Terastia* larvae tunnel into young twigs, killing them in the process. *Terastia* consists of a few widespread species, all of which are associated with *Erythrina*. The taxonomy of the species, however, is unresolved and it is not clear whether different geographical regions (e.g. USA and southern Africa) share the same, or have different, species. As with the *Erythrina* gall wasps, it is quite likely that species have been spread outside of their indigenous regions by the transcontinental trade in ornamental plants.

14.34 (a) The larvae of **(b)** *Terastia* moths (Crambidae) are stem borers of *Erythrina* species. **(c)** They can cause severe die-back of twigs and branches.

Insects associated with lawns

Lawns, sports fields, golf courses and similar areas with patches of turf grass create ideal habitats for grass-living insect species, including crickets, mole crickets, termites, cutworms, lawn caterpillars and white grubs. These grassed areas are often irrigated and fertilised, leading to a dense and rich sward that offers shelter and highly nutritious plant matter.

Grass-feeding termites

The harvester termite, *Hodotermes mossambicus* (Blattodea: Termitoidae: Hodotermitidae; see 'The large harvester termite', p. 177), is a common inhabitant of natural pastures and grassy verges along roads, rather than well-maintained lawns, but it is nonetheless common in some urban areas. Since harvester termites have underground nests, they are less visible than termites that build mounds. Signs of their presence are small mounds of excavated soil near foraging burrows. The termites forage above ground at night under hot conditions, but become active during daylight in winter and on overcast days. They cut grass stems and drag pieces back to the burrow entrance, leaving bare patches of soil and accumulations of cut grass around the entrance.

Garden crickets and mole crickets

The common garden cricket, *Gryllus bimaculatus* (Orthoptera: Ensifera: Gryllidae, fig. 14.35a), and mole cricket, *Gryllotalpa africana* (Gryllotalpidae, fig. 14.35b), live in burrows in the soil, from which they emerge at night to feed on grass foliage and roots.

Males of both garden and mole crickets make loud and mostly familiar night-time garden sounds to attract females. The garden cricket produces a high-frequency chirp, either continuously or at short intervals, while the mole cricket produces a low-frequency, monotonous and continuous call.

14.35 Certain crickets become abundant in lawns, under which they live in burrows in the soil. Males produce characteristic, loud night-time calls. **(a)** The garden cricket, *Gryllus bimaculatus* (Gryllidae); **(b)** the mole cricket, *Gryllotalpa africana* (Gryllotalpidae).

Both make the sound by stridulating – rubbing the bases of the forewings against each other. The rear edge of the left wing, the plectrum, is rubbed against the lower surface of the right wing, which has a ridge of teeth, known as the file. Both males and females have hearing organs at the top of the foretibia; these are clearly visible as oval depressions. Garden crickets call above ground from near the burrow entrance, while mole crickets call from just inside the burrow.

Garden crickets are large black crickets (20–30mm long) with two characteristic yellow spots at the wing bases (*bimaculatus*, 'two-spotted'). Unlike the house cricket, *Gryllodes sigillatus* (fig. 14.68; see 'House crickets', p. 401), they seldom venture into homes. By day, they hide in burrows or other sheltered refuges under natural and man-made objects.

A variety of sounds are made by male garden crickets, each of which has a particular function. The main function is for mate attraction as a prelude to mating; a specific 'calling song' attracts females from a distance, while a 'courtship song' entices them to copulate. Loud, high-frequency chirps have a territorial and aggression function to warn other males of their presence, and they will stridulate aggressively if a contestant enters their territory. Ignoring warning calls leads to combat: males grip each other's mandibles and push forwards with their back legs.

Females mostly don't produce sound but are capable of quiet chirps. Males and females attempt to mate with several individuals of the opposite sex over a few days. Females that have mated with more than one male produce more eggs. These are laid in loose batches in moist soil and hatch after about 14 days.

The few species of mole crickets in southern Africa are represented in lawns mainly by *Gryllotalpa africana*. They are robust, fuzzy, yellow-brown, and about 30mm long, with forelimbs highly modified for burrowing – the femur and tibia are broad and stout with terminal teeth on the tibia and last two tarsal joints. Males live in permanent burrows which may be as deep as 1m.

Males modify the burrow entrance to enhance their calls. The burrow has twin entrances that converge just below ground at a constriction near a resonating chamber. When calling, the male sits with his head in the chamber and his abdomen near the fork leading to the entrances. The burrow construction amplifies the deep, buzzing sound he produces.

Females live in shallow, temporary burrows from which they emerge to feed, and in which they lay their eggs. Males are clumsy flyers and seldom leave the immediate vicinity of the burrow except to feed. Females fly readily to disperse and when attracted to a calling male; the female joins the male in his burrow to mate. They are also often attracted to lights at night.

White grubs

The white grubs in lawns are the larvae of chafer beetles (Coleoptera: Scarabaeidae: Melolonthinae and Rutelinae, fig. 14.5; see 'Chafer beetles', p. 369). They are yellow-white and C-shaped with a distinct brown head capsule (fig. 14.36). The grey colour of the abdomen is due to the accumulation of faecal material in the hindgut visible through the abdominal wall. They are similar to larvae of Dynastinae and Cetoniinae (figs 14.40a, c; see 'Rhinoceros beetle and fruit chafer larvae', p. 386). Some feed on fine roots such as those of grasses, but others feed on humus around the base of plants. These larvae are sometimes mistakenly also referred to as 'cutworms'. Common southern African species belong to the genera *Schizonycha* (Melolonthinae) and *Anomala* (Rutelinae). The adults feed on flowers and leaves.

14.36 White grubs are the larvae of beetles in the Scarabaeidae, especially Melolonthinae and Rutelinae.

Black maize beetles

The black maize beetle, *Heteronychus arator* (Coleoptera: Scarabaeidae: Dynastinae, fig. 14.37), is a shiny, black beetle (12–15mm long), which may become abundant in lawns. The adults feed on grass roots. The larvae, although typical white grubs, feed on organic matter in the soil. Adults are also frequently attracted to lights at night. This is an African species but has been introduced accidentally into Australia and New Zealand where it is known as the African black beetle; it is a serious pasture pest there.

14.37 Adults of the black maize beetle, *Heteronychus arator* (Scarabaeidae: Dynastinae), may become abundant in lawns.

Cutworms

The caterpillars known as cutworms, army worms and lawn caterpillars are moth larvae (Lepidoptera: Noctuidae). These include the black cutworm, *Agrotis ipsilon*, and various *Spodoptera* species, such as the lesser army worm, *S. exigua*, and the lawn caterpillar, *S. triturata*. They are smooth, plump, grey-green caterpillars that roll into a tight circle when threatened. The adults are fairly nondescript grey or blackish moths that may be attracted to lights at night. They do not feed, but mate, lay a fairly large number of eggs (up to 300) on grass at the soil interface and then die. The larvae live in the soil and emerge at night to feed on the grass.

Insects associated with compost and pet faeces

Many parks and gardens have a compost heap – usually an accumulation of lawn cuttings and other soft garden and household refuse in some quiet corner, in which different layers are in various stages of decomposition – and is essentially enriched detritus, which is a very rich food source for various insects, as well as for earthworms and woodlice. Amongst the larger and more noticeable insects are the larvae of rhinoceros beetles and fruit chafer beetles, as well as the larvae of crane flies, house flies and black soldier flies.

Fresh horse dung and dog faeces (which could be considered 'fresh detritus') readily attract house and blow flies, as well as various dung beetles. House flies feed on and breed in the dung, while blow flies usually only feed on fluids in the dung. Which dung beetles are present depends largely on the surrounding area, with a fairly rich fauna often present on agricultural holdings on the outskirts of cities, where horses or other livestock are kept.

Dung beetles and dog parasites

Dog faeces are a rich source of food for a number of small *Onthophagus* (Coleoptera: Scarabaeidae: Scarabaeinae; fig. 14.38) and other dung beetle species which often become intermediate hosts as part of an interesting cycle with the dog parasite *Spirocerca lupi* (Helminthes: Spirocercidae).

Dogs often eat their own and other dogs' faeces and if they accidentally ingest dung beetles infected with the parasite, they become infected. The parasites are released into the dog's mouth when the beetles are chewed. After they reach the stomach, the parasites travel along the coeliac arteries into one of the large blood vessels such as the aorta, and later move into the oesophagus. If the parasite establishes in the wall of a blood vessel it thins

14.38 Certain *Onthophagus* dung beetles, such as this *O. obtusicornis* (Scarabaeidae: Scarabaeinae), are partial to dog faeces. They may become intermediate hosts for the lethal dog parasite *Spirocerca lupi* (Helminthes: Spirocercidae).

the vessel, which may rupture, leading to the almost instantaneous death of the dog. The parasites mature in the wall of the oesophagus, causing lesions that inevitably become cancerous. While the parasites are living in the oesophagus, they release eggs into the dog's gut, which are excreted in its faeces. The cycle is completed when the egg-infested faeces are eaten by dung beetles.

Common woodlice

Woodlice are not insects but terrestrial crustaceans (Crustacea: Isopoda: Oniscidea). They belong to the largest group of crustaceans to have established permanently on land – about half of the world's isopod species live on land. Two families, common woodlice (Porcellionidae) and pill woodlice (Armadillidae; see 'Armadillo-like pill woodlice', p. 298) occur in southern Africa. *Porcellio scaber* (Porcellionidae, fig. 14.39) is a cosmopolitan species found in almost every garden in southern Africa.

Woodlice are well adapted to terrestrial life and inhabit moist environments, living under stones and bark or in leaf litter, scavenging on dead plant matter or fungi; in gardens they are most often found clustered under plant pots or bricks.

The head and body are dorsoventrally flattened, with overlapping segments that give flexibility. The head is fused with the first segment of the thorax to form the cephalon, and the remaining seven segments of the thorax each bear a pair of legs, while the abdomen is made up of six fused segments. There are two pairs of antennae on the cephalon. In woodlice, one pair is tiny and nonfunctional, while the functional pair is short and angled (all other Isopoda have two functional pairs).

14.39 Woodlice are not insects, but crustaceans. Some species, such as this *Porcellio scaber* (Crustacea: Isopoda: Porcellionidae), become very abundant in gardens, especially amongst decaying plant matter such as in compost heaps.

14.40 (a) One of the commonly encountered 'white grubs' in compost, that of a rhinoceros beetle (Scarabaeidae: Dynastinae); **(b)** adult rhinoceros beetle *Syrichthodontus*; **(c)** another of the commonly encountered white grubs, this one of the subfamily Cetoniinae – they are characterised by wriggling on their back when exposed.

Most woodlice have a pair of poorly developed compound eyes. Their mouthparts consist of a pair of maxillipeds and mandibles, and a pair of palps with sensory functions.

The cuticle is thin with no wax layer and is a primary site for evaporation, so woodlice are equipped with special sensors that are able to detect relatively slight differences in humidity in order to remain in humid habitats. They are mostly nocturnal, which is another moisture-saving adaptation. Water lost through evaporation is replaced through eating food high in moisture, drinking water, and by cutaneous absorption of water vapour.

The first five abdominal segments of aquatic isopods have a pair of branched limbs called pleopods that function as external gills for gas exchange; in most terrestrial Oniscidea the respiratory structures are situated on inner branches of the pleopods and consist of lung-like air sacs (pseudotracheae) with a spiracle. This arrangement also serves to reduce the rate of evaporation.

Woodlouse eggs may number from a few to hundreds. They are brooded in a special pouch called a marsupium, which is formed by flat plates on the underside of the female's body and is kept filled with fluid so the young can develop in an aquatic environment. They look like tiny adults upon hatching.

Rhinoceros beetle and fruit chafer larvae

The larvae of most species of rhinoceros beetles (Coleoptera: Scarabaeidae: Dynastinae, fig. 14.40a) feed on decomposing plant matter and some species may therefore become abundant in garden compost. The larvae are C-shaped grubs as thick as a finger, with a brown head capsule and a creamy-white body, with the last few abdominal segments appearing grey because of the gut contents visible through the abdominal wall.

The adult males of some species have a prominent horn on the head or thorax (fig. 14.40b); females may have a small horn. Horn size also varies amongst males based mainly on the size of the beetle – small beetles have small horns, while larger individuals have larger horns.

There are about 60 species in 20 genera in southern Africa. All are brown or black, 10–45mm long, and nocturnal; many are attracted to lights at night. Amongst the largest and most common in southern African gardens is *Oryctes boas*. The adults of most dynastine species do not feed, but a few, such as the African black maize beetle, *Heteronychus arator*, feed on grass roots and may become pests of pastures and maize (see 'Black maize beetles', p. 384).

Rhinoceros beetle larvae often co-occur in compost with fruit chafer larvae (Cetoniinae, fig. 14.40c), which are very similar in appearance. However, the way in which the two types move is distinctly different: rhinoceros beetle larvae crawl face-down, whereas fruit chafer larvae wriggle on their back. Furthermore, dynastine pupae lie naked in the compost, while cetoniine larvae pupate in an earthen cocoon.

One of the most common southern African cetoniine species found in compost is *Pachnoda sinuata*. The very characteristic black and yellow adults (fig. 14.6a) are amongst the most commonly encountered fruit chafers in southern Africa. Ripe fruit is its primary food, but it occasionally feeds on flowers (see 'Chafer beetles', p. 369). Some cetoniine flower visitors are involved in pollination (see 'Protea pollination by fruit chafer beetles', p. 184).

Crane flies and leather jackets

Crane flies (Diptera: Tipulidae) are slow-flying mosquito-like insects. They have extraordinarily long legs that are often shed as a means of escaping predation (figs 14.41a–d). Most adults feed only on nectar. Besides flitting around slowly by day, some are attracted to lights at night.

The brown, leathery larvae of crane flies are known as leather jackets. They have a simple head capsule, but the characteristic tail-end is often mistaken for a head (figs 14.41e, f). Called a spiracular disc, it has a variable number of elongated, fleshy lobes and two darkly sclerotised eye-like spiracles above the 'mouth' – which is actually the slit-like anal opening. The spiracles at the tail end protrude above the often sodden medium in which the larva lives and enable it to breathe atmospheric air. They are usually found singly in coarse compost.

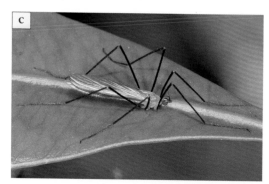

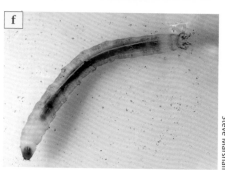

Steve Marshall

Steve Marshall

14.41 Crane fly (Tipulidae) adults (**a–d**) and larvae (**e, f**) are common in gardens. Adults are attracted to lights at night. Larvae are often abundant in rich organic matter, but are seldom noticed because of their small size. Adults frequently shed legs as a defensive strategy, so individuals (**d**) with fewer than six legs are commonly encountered.

Stable flies

The adults of the cosmopolitan stable fly, *Stomoxys calcitrans* (Diptera: Muscidae, fig. 14.42a), are grey-black and about the size of the common house fly. Both males and females feed on blood and in urban areas they suck the blood of dogs and horses (and occasionally humans). On dogs, the preferred area for feeding are the tips of the ears and unless controlled, these areas become raw and scabrous. The bites are painful and lead to severe discomfort.

The larvae are typical maggots, tapering from the tail towards the head (fig. 14.42b). There is no distinct head capsule, but close examination will reveal two sclerotised mouth hooks. The larvae are found in mixtures of rotted straw and horse dung around stables or in well-rotted compost heaps.

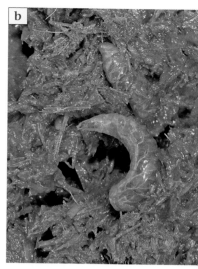

14.42 (a) Adult stable flies, *Stomoxys calcitrans* (Muscidae), are common in urban environments. They feed on the blood of dogs, horses and occasionally humans. **(b)** Larvae breed in wet, well-rotted organic matter such as dung, compost and stable waste.

14.43 Larvae of the cosmopolitan black soldier fly, *Hermetia illucens* (Stratiomyidae), are used to decompose commercial organic waste, and are then harvested to produce livestock protein feed: (**a**) larva; (**b**) adult.

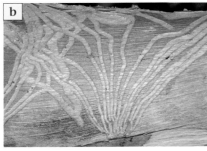

14.44 Several species of long-horned beetles (Cerambycidae) are associated with wood piles. (**a**) *Eucalyptus* wood is particularly prone to attack by introduced species of *Phoracantha*. (**b**) Typical signs of *Phoracantha* feeding just below the bark of a freshly felled *Eucalyptus* log.

Black soldier flies

The larvae of the black soldier fly, *Hermetia illucens* (Diptera: Stratiomyidae), appear leathery and are distinctly segmented (fig. 14.43a). They are often found in clusters in compost. The adult fly is wasp-like (fig. 14.43b) but harmless, with two transparent 'windows' in the base of the abdomen.

The larvae are rather catholic in their choice of food and have been recorded from a large variety of organic substances, including kitchen waste, curry-infused mango chutney, and the decomposing wax and bee remains of an old beehive. Because of their wide food acceptance, soldier fly larvae are increasingly being used commercially in different parts of the world, including South Africa, to decompose various types of organic waste. The mature larvae are then harvested, dried and milled to produce high-protein animal feed.

Insects found in wood piles

Wood is largely composed of cellulose, hemicellulose and lignin and is rich in starch and sugars, but the digestion of the tough components requires special gut enzymes or a specialised microbial gut fauna. Wood at different stages of decomposition is attractive to several insect groups – some attack freshly dead wood, others when it is already partially decomposed. Amongst the insects commonly encountered in wood piles are cockroaches, termites, wood-boring long-horned beetles, powder-post beetles and auger or false powder-post beetles, whose larvae feed on the wood. Adults of some of these species are commonly attracted to lights at night.

Long-horned beetles

Adult long-horned beetles (Coleoptera: Cerambycidae) have exceptionally long antennae, which are as long as or longer than the body. Species range from small and delicate to extraordinarily large and heavy; many are brightly coloured. Females lay eggs in cracks in wood and the hatched larvae bore into the wood. Most of their life cycle is spent in the larval stage (some up to five years) because of the poor nutritional value of the wood upon which they feed (for detailed biology, see 'Wood-boring long-horned beetles', p. 221).

Wood from gum trees, *Eucalyptus* spp., is very prone to attack by the introduced Australian cerambycids *Phoracantha recurva* and *P. semipunctata* (fig. 14.44a). Females lay eggs in cracks beneath the bark of freshly felled trees. The emergent larvae radiate out into the sapwood, leaving their tunnels clearly visible beneath the bark (fig. 14.44b).

False powder-post beetles and their kin

The large wood-boring beetle family Bostrichidae has three morphologically distinct subfamilies in southern Africa: Dinoderinae, Lyctinae and Bostrichinae.

Members of the Dinoderinae are very small and little is known about the indigenous species. The group is well known in the region, though, through two serious cosmopolitan pests: *Rhizopertha dominica*, a stored grain pest that bores into grain, and *Dinoderus minutus*, which bores into basketwork and cane furniture.

Lyctinae, likewise, are small beetles that bore into dry wood, producing fine, flour-like powder which gives them their common name powder-post beetles.

14.45 Auger beetles (Bostrichidae: Bostrichinae) are very common inhabitants of wood. Tunnelling adults and larvae produce piles of powdery dust. **(a)** *Apate terebrans*; **(b)** *Bostrychoplites cornutus*; **(c)** *Enneadesmus* sp.; **(d)** *Sinoxylon ruficorne*.

14.47 Paper wasp (Vespidae: Vespinae) larvae are fed masticated caterpillars. This female *Belonogaster* sp. has a caterpillar that she will masticate before feeding it to her larvae in the paper nest.

Bostrichinae (fig. 14.45) are known as false powder-post beetles, shot-hole or auger borers and are more familiar and better studied in southern Africa than the other subfamilies. They are common, characteristic and conspicuous members of the wood-boring community. Many are quite large (25mm long). The head is inserted under the pronotum, and the back edges of their elytra are squared off and often armed with spines, teeth or hooks. The pronotum may also be armed with spines or horns. Adults and larvae bore into living, weakened trees, or into freshly cut wood, producing fine, powdery shavings in the process (fig. 14.46a); larvae cause most of the damage. The fact that they are often the only visible signs of 'infestation' when a tree is physiologically stressed or weakened, may lead to the assumption that they are the cause of the symptoms, but these are usually the result of some disease. Suitable dry wood piles may attract hundreds of beetles that drill many tunnels (fig. 14.46b) and reduce it to a pile of dust within a few months.

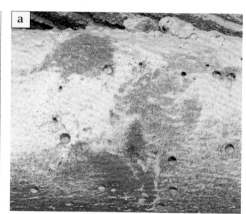

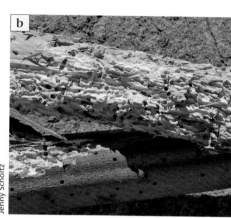

14.46 (a) Holes and powdery shaving dust from tunnelling by auger beetle larvae; **(b)** multiple holes and tunnels from a severely infested dry branch of the introduced mesquite tree, *Prosopis* sp.

Insects associated with structures

Many insects are attracted to buildings, either as support for their nests, as a shelter from the elements, or in the case of termites, to feed on the wooden components. Sometimes, it is the infrastructure associated with the building, such as the sewage system, that is the attraction.

Eusocial paper wasps

There are three genera of paper wasps (Hymenoptera: Vespidae: Polistinae) in southern Africa: large red paper wasps, *Belonogaster* (figs 14.47, 14.48a), small red paper wasps, *Polistes* (fig. 14.48b), and *Ropalidia* (fig. 14.48c). All three genera are superficially similar in appearance and construct nests of paper-like carton, which are often seen attached to walls under eaves. They are all eusocial and live in small groups that include a single egg-laying queen and a few other members of usually related individuals.

Belonogaster and *Polistes* are, no doubt, familiar to just about everyone across the region because of their irascible behaviour and willingness to attack and sting, often repeatedly, anyone who comes within metres of their nest. *Ropalidia*, on the other hand, are placid, even timid wasps and seldom respond aggressively. In the 1980s, Malcolm Keeping of the University of the Witwatersrand studied *Belonogaster petiolata* in detail. The information given here is based on his work.

14.48 Paper wasps (Vespidae: Vespinae) build their nests of papery chewed plant matter in sheltered places such as under eaves or in dense vegetation. **(a)** *Belonogaster* wasps are larger than **(b)** *Polistes* and **(c)** *Ropalidia* individuals, which are of similar size. *Belonogaster* and *Polistes* wasps are notoriously aggressive in defence of their nest, while *Ropalidia* species are much more timid.

Colony formation

Belonogaster petiolata colonies are started by a single mated female (a foundress) in mid-August, after she has overwintered for several months with her likewise inseminated sisters in a sheltered place (hibernaculum) near their natal nest (where they hatched). For the next three months, the foundress is joined by up to 16 other mated females to form multifoundress colonies. There is a high probability that they are nest mates from the previous summer; although wasps that are not nest mates are tolerated, nest mates receive preferential treatment and are accorded higher status in the hierarchy of individuals that develops.

Although the primary foundress of the colony may become the queen, this is not assured. Aggressive interactions between several foundresses lead to the dominance of the most aggressive female who then becomes queen. She maintains her dominance by various aggressive displays; this stimulates subordinates and workers to forage, which taxes them energetically and decreases the likelihood of their laying eggs. Once the queen's position is established, she remains the dominant female and her primary function is that of laying eggs.

The new nest is built (see box opposite) within 2–50cm of the foundress's natal nest. This increases the likelihood of nesting in a site already confirmed to be suitable by previous colonies and also leads to higher levels of relatedness between the subordinate foundresses and the brood of the queen, which they help rear. The subordinate females rear the first brood from which the workers, who are the queen's daughters, emerge in about mid-November. At this time, the colony consists of the queen, the subordinate foundresses and emerging workers.

Mature *B. petiolata* colonies seldom exceed 50 adults on a fist-sized nest usually comprising a maximum of about 70 cells within each of which the queen lays an egg. After hatching, the larva takes about three weeks to reach the pupal stage and then approximately 10 days before emerging as an adult.

As the number of workers increases, the subordinate foundresses leave the nest. By January, the colony consists only of the queen and her daughters. The workers assist the queen in rearing a batch of reproductive females and males, which emerge in February or March. After the reproductive females mate with the males, the males, queen and workers die. The mated females enter hibernacula to overwinter (fig. 14.49) and will form the core of foundresses that start the cycle again the following spring.

Adult dependence on larval saliva

Adults feed on nectar, but they prey on ground-living caterpillars – lawn caterpillars, *Spodoptera* spp., are a favourite in domestic gardens. The wasps masticate and feed the regurgitated caterpillars to the developing larvae in the nest, after which the adults solicit and imbibe salivary secretions from the larvae. The larval secretions contain the bulk of the protein required by adults since their primary food source is nectar, which is rich in carbohydrates but lacking in protein. Older larvae are preferred as sources of saliva, probably since they donate larger quantities than do young larvae.

Larvae need to be stimulated into producing saliva: the adult does this by antennating (stroking) the larva's head. The larva responds by rearing up to the top of the cell and exuding a large drop of clear fluid, which the adult immediately imbibes. If the larva fails to respond to antennation, the adult starts to vibrate, while at the same time producing an audible rattling sound. This is often performed simultaneously and synchronously by several females in bouts of vibration that last 20–45 seconds; larvae invariably respond by producing a drop of saliva.

Paper wasp nest construction

Belonogaster petiolata is a paper wasp with a strong presence in southern Africa. It builds its nest in trees with dense foliage (*Searsia* species are preferred in Gauteng), under the eaves of buildings, or in other protected places. Open water near the nest site is essential for successful nest building and brood rearing.

The nest consists of an exposed comb of cells suspended from a pedicel. The building material used is pulp prepared from grass fibres harvested nearby; the wasps chew the fibres into a moist ball using their mandibles.

The nest is started by the foundress: she makes a base for the attachment of the pedicel with the first ball of pulp. Subsequent loads of pulp are used to construct an initial fragile pedicel; then the base is expanded. The pedicel is strengthened by coating it with an oral secretion. When this is done, the foundress begins to build the low walls of the first cell from a saucer-like base on the tip of the pedicel. Subsequent cells are added to the first in a line moving away from the pedicel. The first eggs are laid before the cells are completed; their walls are built up later. If there are secondary foundresses,

they make pulp and assist with nest building.

The nest increases in size over time. Distinct zones show the different stages of brood development: the white-capped pupal cocoon zone is closest to the pedicel (the cells in which the first eggs were laid), followed by a larval zone, and along the outer margin, an egg zone. To add support, the wasps may attach lateral arms to the pedicel base and to the underside of the nest.

Mature larvae spin a silken cocoon, which protrudes some distance from the cell margin, and then pupate. Within a few days, workers cover the domed white caps of the cocoons with thin layers of dark pulp. Adjoining cell caps are connected by bridges of pulp. This probably conceals the bright white caps, and also reinforces the nest structure.

When the young adults emerge, their pupal cells are demolished and chewed up to make pulp, which is used to extend the rest. Cells are never re-used for brood. As the colony ages, a zone of demolished cells develops outwards from the pedicel, and in extreme cases, a bare zone or large open space may result.

14.49 (left) Wasp colonies last only one year, at the end of which surviving inseminated females from nearby colonies collect in often large numbers in sheltered overwintering aggregations.

14.50 (right) In spite of their aggression, paper wasps **(b)** are vulnerable to several parasites and predators. They are more or less powerless against **(a)** the specialist wasp parasite *Anacamptomyia* sp. (Diptera: Tachinidae) and **(b)** the predatory fruit chafer *Oplostomus fuligineus* (Cetoniinae).

Larval excretion

Larval excretory products are removed at the end of larval growth. Adults prepare the larval cell for the event a few days before the mature larva starts spinning its pupal cocoon. A worker chews a hole at the base of the larval cell and the larva starts spinning the cell capping, but does not cover the hole at the base. It then produces a meconium – a 13mm-long 'sausage' of dark matter contained in a bag – which is removed by a worker through the hole in the cell base and dumped at some distance from the nest. The larva then completes spinning its cocoon, closing the hole in the cell during the process.

Colony defence and predation

Besides the notorious aggression and willingness of *Belonogaster petiolata* females to attack and sting possible intruders, the wasps have also evolved a mechanism to protect their nest from ants. When left unattended by adults, the brood is potentially vulnerable to ant predation. The wasps rub the underside of their last abdominal segment, which oozes an ant-repellent substance, repeatedly along the long axis of the nest pedicel (the pedicel is clearly visible in fig. 14.48c).

None of the paper wasps' defences, however, appear to be effective against small flying brood parasitoids such as the wasp *Camptotypus apicalis* (Ichneumonoidea) and the fly *Anacamptomyia* sp. (Tachinidae, fig. 14.50a). The large hive beetle, *Oplostomus fuligineus* (Cetoniinae, fig. 14.50b), a predator of honey bee brood (see 'Invertebrate exploiters of honey bees', p. 77), is also a fairly common predator of wasp brood; it is strongly sclerotised and apparently impervious to the wasps' defensive attempts. Once settled on a nest it usually consumes the entire brood and destroys the nest.

Solitary potter wasps

Potter wasps (Hymenoptera: Vespidae: Eumeninae) are very diverse in Africa, with 75 genera and about 690 species, but are poorly studied. Most species need open water for successful nest building. They carry water in the crop to a 'quarry site' and use it to mix mud (fig. 14.51), which they transport to the nesting site. Some species excavate multicellular nest burrows in soil, some nest in pre-existing burrows, while the more familiar potter wasps build above-ground mud nests on rocks or under roof eaves. Species of *Afreumenes*, *Delta* (fig. 14.52a), *Eumenes* and *Pseudonortonia* build pot-shaped nests, while *Tricarinodynerus guerinii* builds characteristic curved clay turrets leading from a burrow (fig. 14.52b). Once the nest is completed, the wasp finds suitable larval prey – caterpillars are preferred – which it paralyses and deposits in the nest. The female suspends an egg from the roof of the mud cell and when the larva hatches from the egg, it drops onto the host, which it devours. After completing its development, it pupates. The adult emerges from the pupa and mud nest some time later.

Some Sphecidae wasps also build clay nests, similar to those of Eumeninae, and these may also be found on structures in urban areas (fig. 14.52c).

14.51 (above) Some potter or mason wasps (Vespidae: Eumeninae) use dampened clay to build their nests. It is collected near water, or water is collected in its crop and carried to suitable clay which is then dampened, such as this *Delta emarginatum* is doing.

14.52 (right) Some potter or mason wasps (Vespidae: Eumeninae) use clay to build characteristic nests or turrets at burrow entrances under eaves or similar sheltered situations, such as **(a)** the pot-like nest of a *Delta* spp. wasp and **(b)** the characteristic curved turret of *Tricarinodynerus guerinii*. Some sphecid wasps (Vespoidea: Sphecidae) also build clay nests such this **(c)** clay nest made by *Sceliphron quartinae*.

14.53 The honey bee, *Apis mellifera* (Hymenoptera: Apidae).

14.54 Carpenter bees are the largest bees found in gardens, where their bright colours and buzzing flight draw attention when they visit flowers for nectar and pollen. They often nest nearby in holes excavated in wood. (**a**) *Xylocopa flavorufa*; (**b**) *X. capitata*; (**c**) *X. flavicollis*; (**d**) *X. caffra*.

Honey bees and carpenter bees

Honey bees, *Apis mellifera* (Hymenoptera: Apidae: Apinae, fig. 14.53), are familiar visitors to flowers in gardens, but occasionally a whole swarm will move into a suitable hollow structure such as a post box or electricity meter box, where they might be considered something of a novelty or, alternatively, cause concern because of their potential to sting people and pets when disturbed (for detailed biology, see 'The ubiquitous honey bee', p. 74).

Carpenter bees, *Xylocopa* species (Hymenoptera: Apidae: Xylocopinae), are the largest bees found in southern African gardens – they are about 25mm long (fig. 14.54). They buzz loudly when visiting flowers, and seem to be especially attracted to mauve flowers. As their common name implies, they excavate tunnels in wood in which they live and nest. Although they prefer soft substrates such as dried *Aloe* inflorescences or wood softened by decay (dead tree branches, fig. 14.55), they are capable of tunnelling into fairly solid wood such as exposed roof trusses, usually where the wood has been weathered. The entrance burrow to the nest is about 10mm in diameter and the nest is located 15cm into the wood. The nest is a sloping tunnel about 10cm deep.

There are approximately 500 *Xylocopa* species worldwide, with 21 species in southern Africa. They have a special symbiotic relationship with mites in the genus *Dinogamasus* (see box, p. 394). Female bees have developed a special abdominal pouch (called an acarinarium) in which they carry the flightless mites from nest to nest, and although the details of the association have not been clarified, it appears that the mites depend on the bees for food and dispersal, while the bees depend on the mites to keep their brood clear of pathogenic fungi.

A female *X. caffra* in possession of a nest in the winter-rainfall Western Cape starts nesting in early summer (October to early November). She prepares the nest by cleaning it of refuse such as sawdust, broken cell partitions and faeces and while doing this, she repeatedly rubs her abdomen against the entrance to give the nest her unique odour; this improves her chances of locating the nest in strong wind. Before provisioning a cell, she licks its entire interior, and the resultant cell lining hardens into a thin cellophane-like layer. The lining is thought to be hydrophobic, protecting the cell and its contents from desiccation and excessive external humidity.

14.55 (a) *Xylocopa senior* at a nest in a hollow branch. **(b)** The inside of an abandoned *Xylocopa* nest with plant shavings and pollen remains.

Once nest preparation is completed, she prepares 'bee bread' from a mixture of nectar, pollen and glandular secretions (enough for the entire duration of larval development), provisions the bottom cell and lays a large egg, 12–14mm long. She seals the cell with a mixture of saliva and sawdust produced during nest excavation. She repeats this process six or seven times, laying successive eggs in cells stacked one on top of another, with intervals of two to three days between each event. When she has finished, she guards her nest from potential intruders or predators (such as blister beetles; see box opposite) until the new adult bees are just about to emerge; she then dies.

The eggs hatch about 14 days after they were laid. Larval development takes about three to four weeks; during this time the larvae consume all the bee bread. After the larvae have matured, they enter a nonfeeding, prepupal stage that lasts 14–15 days, and is followed by pupation. The pupae are naked, without a cocoon; the duration of the pupal stage is 36–40 days.

The bottom three or four cells are always occupied by female brood, the top cells by males. At the end of January, the first female to emerge is furthest from the nest entrance and sealed into her nest cell. She proceeds to break down the sawdust partition between her cell

Carpenter bees and their mites

Symbiosis is the interdependent relationship between two species in which both benefit from the association. The relationship between the common and widespread southern African carpenter bee, *Xylocopa caffra*, and its symbiotic mite, *Dinogamasus braunsi* (Laelapidae), was studied by S.H. Skaife in Cape Town in the 1950s and his study remains one of the most detailed of its kind. Many carpenter bee species have similar associations with *Dinogamasus* species – all of the 50 or so species of *Dinogamasus* live in association with solitary bees.

Female carpenter bees have a special abdominal pouch (acarinarium) in which the symbiotic mites are carried. The acarinarium is situated in the first abdominal segment on the dorsal surface, just above the junction of the abdomen and thorax. There are usually about 10 (but there may be 2–18) *Dinogamasus* individuals visible in the acarinarium (fig. 14.56). The mites are large (1.75mm long) and white, with brownish legs and body plates. The first and second pairs of legs have stout, blunt hairs.

When the female bee lays an egg, one or two *D. braunsi* mites climb from her abdominal pouch onto the 'bee bread' (a mixture of pollen, nectar and glandular secretions) where they are sealed in with the egg. This is repeated until her pouch is empty. The mites remain relatively inactive in the cell until the bee larva has finished feeding and enters the prepupal stage; at this time the mites begin to feed actively, swelling visibly in size. What the mites actually feed on remains contentious – some authors claim that they feed on larval exuviae, others that they clean the prepupae and pupae of fungal pathogens, yet others that they are parasitic. There is little evidence of the assumption that they are parasitic, and it is very unlikely that the bees would have evolved a special pouch to carry parasites.

When the bee larvae pupate, the mites begin to lay 0.5mm-long oval eggs (only females are known, so reproduction is parthenogenetic). Within three to four days the eggs develop into white, six-legged larvae, and then another two to three days later, into eight-legged nymphs. They appear to feed mainly on the surface of the pupae.

Four to six weeks later, when the young bees emerge from the pupal stage, the mites have matured, taking on their adult brown-and-white colour. During the bees' quiescent stage between maturing and the following spring when breeding starts, the mites wander about in the nests climbing in and out of bee pouches, but spending most of their time in them. The mites are dispersed with the female bees when these establish new nesting sites.

In addition to *D. braunsi*, very small *Sennertia* mites (0.25mm long) may also occur on *X. caffra* bees.

14.56 Many carpenter bees have a special mite pouch (acarinarium) on the first abdominal segment. The acarinarium and mites are clearly visible on this *Xylocopa caffra*.

Parasitic blister beetle larvae

Solitary bees belonging to the Apidae, Megachilidae and Andrenidae undertake careful nest preparation and remain at the nest to guard their brood, but this doesn't prevent blister beetle larvae (Meloidae) from sometimes parasitising the brood – including eggs, larvae, pollen and nectar.

Carpenter bees are targeted by the carpenter bee blister beetle, *Synhoria testacea* (fig. 14.57). These large red beetles may be found wandering around on logs and poles in the vicinity of *Xylocopa* nests. The female beetle lays eggs at the entrance of a carpenter bee nest. The newly hatched first-instar (triungulin) larvae enter the nest and parasitise the bee brood during a complex life cycle that includes hypermetamorphosis (see box, p. 42; 'Blister beetle larvae: predators of locust eggs', p. 171).

Once inside a cell in the bee's nest, the triungulin begins to feed on an egg. The first moult occurs immediately after it has consumed the egg. The second, third and fourth larval instars feed on the 'bee bread' (a mixture of pollen, nectar and glandular secretions), before reaching the

14.57 The blister beetle *Synhoria testacea* (Meloidae) is an obligatory parasite of carpenter bee nests.

Mike Picker

prepupal and pupal stages. Often more than one triungulin gains access to the cell, but only one reaches maturity: the youngest, most active larva eats those that are sluggish from eating, or already in the inactive prepupal or pupal stages. The mature adult meloid beetle emerges from the nest through the burrow entrance.

---

and each consecutive cell until she arrives at the nest entrance where she rests. Her sisters and brothers follow at intervals of two to three days, until all the young adults are clustered in a more or less quiescent state near the entrance. They remain here for a few days until they become active in mid-February. They then clean the nest of all sawdust, as well as the accumulated black faecal pellets excreted by the young adults, and remain together amicably for several months. They spend most of the time in the nest, interrupted only by short foraging forays of about 15–20 minutes every few days. During inclement weather they may remain indoors for up to several weeks.

In September, when the bees are about 10 months old, the female bees become agitated and expel the males from the nest. A short while later the females begin to show aggression towards each other, with the most aggressive one eventually expelling all her sisters. She then becomes the foundress of the next generation in her natal nest, while the other females are compelled to make new nests.

Expelled males usually group together in a suitable shelter from which they emerge in sunny weather to patrol around suitable flowers, waiting for females to arrive. Mating takes place in the air near the flowers and mated females then start breeding in about October. In winter-rainfall areas *X. caffra* produces only one generation per year, whereas in other parts of southern Africa, more than one is possible.

Moth flies in bathrooms

Moth flies (Diptera: Psychodidae) belong to a large, cosmopolitan family that is poorly studied in southern Africa. About 50 species have been recorded here, most of which belong to the subfamily Psychodinae. Moth flies are small, dark, hairy flies with a moth-like appearance, usually about 5mm long. Adults probably feed on plant liquids and larvae develop in moist, organically rich environments.

The cosmopolitan species *Clogmia albipunctata* (Psychodidae: Psychodinae, fig. 14.58) is quite commonly encountered in bathrooms and public toilets in southern Africa. The larvae live submerged in the water in drains and sewage systems, where they feed on organic particles. They are particularly resistant to soaps and other chemicals used in drains. The small thin larvae (3–4mm long) are seldom seen, but their presence in a drain system is indicated by adults in the vicinity.

14.58 The bathroom moth fly, *Clogmia albipunctata* (Diptera: Psychodidae), is a common inhabitant of bathrooms and public toilets, as the larvae breed in drains.

14.59 The rusty grain beetle, *Cryptolestes ferrugineus* (Laemophloeidae), is a serious pest in stored grain where it feeds on the embryo inside the seed.

a

b

14.60 (a) Grain weevils, *Sitophilus granarius* (Curculionidae), infest grain supplies such as garden bird seed and poultry grain. **(b)** Their presence is usually only noticed when the tiny beetles emerge from the grain kernels.

14.61 The biscuit beetle, *Stegobium paniceum* (Ptinidae), attacks a wide range of stored food products and even pharmaceutical drugs.

Insects found in stored products

Stored dry food products such as meal, flour, pasta, rice, pulses, spices, poultry feed and pet food often become infested with small insects, including beetles (figs 14.59–14.61) and meal moths, all of which are cosmopolitan insects.

Although both adults and larvae may be present, it is mostly the larvae that feed. Even though such infestations are undesirable, the insects present little health risk to humans or pets. The insects are invariably introduced into the home in one of the products when it is purchased and then their numbers build up in any of a range of suitable stored products.

Insects that feed on stored products depend primarily on the carbohydrates in the food source; their other main nutritional elements, especially protein, are synthesised from carbohydrates by mutualistic gut microbes. The insects are further adapted to survive in an excessively dry environment by obtaining their required water supplies from metabolic processes. They also have various types of spiracle-closing mechanisms and sieves that prevent the fine dust present in many stored products from entering the system.

Grain weevils

The grain weevil, *Sitophilus granarius* (Coleoptera: Curculionidae, fig. 14.60a), is a small (3–5 mm long), dark reddish-brown to black beetle with a prominent snout (rostrum) that is almost as long as the forebody. They feed on most grains but are commonly encountered in wheat (it is also sometimes called the wheat weevil), sorghum, rice and maize. Larvae that feed in small-kernel grain such as millet and sorghum, or broken kernels, develop into correspondingly small adults, while those that feed in larger kernels like those of maize, are larger. These insects are wingless and only disperse via infested grain. The larvae are grub-like but are seldom seen, as they live inside the grain kernels. An infestation is usually only noticed when numbers of the tiny beetles emerge from the infested kernels and become active (fig. 14.60b).

Biscuit beetles

The biscuit beetle, *Stegobium paniceum* (Coleoptera: Ptinidae, fig. 14.61), as its common name suggests, feeds on carbohydrates in the form of stored food such as biscuits, pasta, rice and grain. It is an atypical member of its family, as most Ptinidae are small wood-boring beetles that have a mutualistic association with wood-digesting fungi; *S. paniceum* has a mutualistic relationship with a different fungus. It is the only species in the monotypic genus *Stegobium*.

Adults are small (3.5mm long), reddish-brown beetles. They fly strongly and when they disperse, may be found throughout the house; this is often when they are first noticed. In the USA, *S. paniceum* is known as the drugstore beetle because included in its usual diet of dried food and spices is the occasional infestation of materials commonly used in medications. There are even records of the beetles consuming the highly toxic plant alkaloid strychnine.

Females lay up to 75 eggs at once, usually on foods before they are packaged. They coat the eggs with spores of a mutualistic yeast fungus that establishes in the gut after larvae have eaten the egg shell; the fungus then enables the larvae to digest the carbohydrates in their diet. The larvae are squat whitish grubs.

Indian-meal moths

The Indian-meal moth, *Plodia interpunctella* (Lepidoptera: Pyralidae), is a common pest in stored grain and dried fruit. The common name comes from the outdated term 'Indian-meal' for maize meal; the moths are not indigenous to India. Adults are 8–10mm long and usually sit with wings held tightly closed. The outer half of the forewing is coppery or grey while the basal half is yellowish; there is usually a black band in the middle. The larvae are yellowish with brown heads, about 12mm long, and live in a flimsy silk web (fig. 14.62). The silk strands are often attached to the inside of the container in which flour or meal is purchased or stored, and are often the first signs of an infestation.

Insects attracted to exposed food

Many household insects are opportunists that quickly locate and infest exposed food or food remains. Among the most noticeable insects that feed on food on tables and in dustbins are cockroaches. All household cockroaches are now widespread across the globe, but different species dominate in tropical or temperate regions. A South African endemic with cockroach-like habits (but considered by many people to be many times more repulsive) is the Parktown prawn, which occasionally intrudes into homes and feeds on exposed human or pet food.

Various fly species are attracted to different food types: house flies to many food products of vegetable and animal origin, blow flies to exposed meat, and vinegar flies to ripe fruit and sugar-rich beverages. Ants are ubiquitous across southern Africa and several species invade homes and opportunistically feed on exposed food; some species prefer sugary food, others prefer meat products, but most species will feed on virtually any remains of human or pet food.

Cockroaches

The majority of cockroach species (Blattodea: Blattoidae) in southern Africa occur in natural environments and are important detritus feeders (for detailed biology, see 'Detritivores', p. 88). Introduced cockroaches, however, are common and widespread in homes and hotel and restaurant kitchens where they feed on food scraps. They usually mate and breed in dark and protected refuges, such as behind fitted cupboards or under floorboards. All cockroaches lay eggs, usually in a protected leathery case or ootheca. Females of some species carry the extruded ootheca with them until the young cockroaches emerge.

There are four common household species in southern Africa. They are the German cockroach, *Blattella germanica* (Ectobiidae), the American cockroach, *Periplaneta americana* (although it is actually an African

14.62 The Indian-meal moth, *Plodia interpunctella* (Pyralidae), is one of the most common pest species in stored products such as meal, dried fruits and other foodstuffs. (**a**) The larvae live in a (**b**) spun web in the food source.

species; Blattidae), the Oriental cockroach, *Blatta orientalis* (also probably of African origin; Blattidae), and the Madeira cockroach, *Rhyparobia maderae* (formerly *Leucophaea maderae*, also of African origin; Blaberidae). *Blattella germanica* and *P. americana* are the most familiar and widespread; both are reddish-brown with visible wings in adults, although *Blattella germanica* does not fly well. It is small (12–15mm long), while *P. americana* is two to three times larger (25–40mm long). *Blattella germanica* females carry the ootheca for several days until the young are about to hatch; *P. americana* females drop the ootheca soon after it forms.

Even cockroaches that are capable of flight (*Blatta orientalis* is not) do not fly readily and primarily rely on speed and agility to escape predators. Their flattened bodies allow them to fit into small, narrow cracks. *Periplaneta americana* has been recorded to run faster than 5km per hour or about 50 body lengths per second, equivalent to a human running at 330km per hour! When speed fails to save them from predator attack, most cockroaches secrete defensive chemicals as a last resort. The cockroach body is covered with wax impregnated with repellent compounds that make it slippery to hold and noxious to taste. Dense aggregations of cockroaches have a characteristic smell that is produced by these compounds.

14.63 The Parktown prawn, *Libanasidus vittatus* (Orthoptera: Anostostomatidae), has become a fairly common household novelty in Gauteng.

14.64 House flies (Muscidae) and blow flies (Calliphoridae) are common in households in all regions. (**a**) House flies, *Musca domestica*, are attracted to almost all foodstuffs, while (**b**) blow flies, such as *Chrysomya chloropyga*, are mainly attracted to meat.

Parktown prawns

Over the past 30 years people living in cities in Gauteng have witnessed the increasing numbers of a fascinating – but to some, repulsive – large insect, the so-called Parktown prawn, *Libanasidus vittatus* (Orthoptera: Ensifera: Anostostomatidae, fig. 14.63). It is also known as the tusked king cricket, but 'Parktown prawn' is the name commonly used in urban environments; it was named after the suburb in Johannesburg where it was first recorded in the 1970s.

Libanasidus vittatus is a large long-horned cricket: the male body length is about 50mm, that of females about 60mm; from the tips of antennae to the hind legs, the total length is 160mm. It is bright orange with black abdominal bands and mature males have large 'tusks' on their mandibles. It was previously believed to be a subtropical Lowveld species originally described from Barberton, which became established under the lush conditions created in Gauteng city parks and gardens. However, recent studies have indicated that the Gauteng insects differ from the Lowveld species and that the Parktown prawn is quite probably a local species whose abundance has merely increased over time in the area.

Parktown prawns usually live in burrows in moist soil and are omnivorous, foraging at night on debris, insects and snails in their near environment. Sexually mature individuals wander about in search of mates – this is when they wander into homes. They are often attracted by easily accessible food scraps or pet food on the floor. When confronted by humans or curious pets, they respond violently by hissing, jumping into the air and ejecting repugnant black faecal fluids towards the perceived threat. They are also capable of giving a powerful bite with their mandibles if molested. Their bright orange colour and black-banded abdomen suggest that they are best avoided by predators, but hadeda ibises, *Bostrychia hagedash*, seem to be unperturbed by their defensive systems and relish them.

House flies

House flies, *Musca domestica* (Diptera: Muscidae, fig. 14.64a), are familiar to everyone because of their ubiquitous presence around homes in rural and urban areas. They breed readily in faeces, garbage and compost. Under warm conditions, they complete their development in 7–10 days. Females, during a lifetime of a few weeks, can lay up to 500 eggs in batches of 75–150 at a time. Their rapid development combined with prolific egg-laying contributes to the flies' abundance near suitable breeding places and food.

Although flies are widely regarded as nothing more serious than being a nuisance in urban areas, they may nevertheless transmit a wide range of human pathogens under less hygienic conditions. In deep rural areas they are important vectors of diseases such as *Salmonella*, which is a major cause of infant diarrhoea. Adult flies are mainly attracted to sweet foods, but females require a protein meal and visit meat and fish dishes before laying eggs. House flies are not disease carriers in the same sense as, for example, tsetse flies and mosquitoes, but transmit pathogens mechanically, on their feet and by regurgitating food they have previously consumed.

Blow flies

Blow flies (Diptera: Calliphoridae, fig. 14.64b) are able to locate dead animals very soon after death, and the more blood and exposed flesh available, the faster their response (see 'Blow flies: the first carcass colonisers', p. 251). The larvae (maggots) feed on flesh, while the adults feed on carcass body fluids, the liquid components of animal dung, and even on nectar. They are surprisingly common in urban areas, where they are rapidly attracted to any uncovered and exposed raw meat on which they lay their eggs, resulting in an explosion of maggots.

Vinegar flies

Vinegar flies (Diptera: Drosophilidae, figs 14.65a–d) are very small, usually red-eyed flies (2–4mm long), which are attracted to fermenting fruit or fruity fluids, including wine and beer. Larvae develop in the fungus-enriched juices of fermenting fruit. Vinegar flies are sometimes incorrectly called fruit flies in scientific literature, but true fruit flies (Tephritidae) are larger flies that attack ripening fruit (figs 14.65e, f).

Most of the common species belong to *Drosophila*, a very large genus with about 1,500 species worldwide. Several of these are closely associated with humans.

One species, the cosmopolitan *D. melanogaster*, is the best-studied insect on earth and has biological attributes that make it a popular experimental animal: it produces large numbers of offspring quickly; and the presence of mutant varieties in natural populations (e.g. different eye colours) make it suitable for genetic studies of heredity.

Drosophila species have several other interesting biological attributes. They produce a very low number of sperm, but the longest individual sperm of any animal: those of *D. bifurca* are 58mm long – in a 3mm-long fly! *Drosophila melanogaster* sperm are a much more modest 1.8mm long, but this is nevertheless 35 times longer than human sperm. The long spermatozoa are introduced into the female reproductive system in tangled coils – the female genital tract is also long and convoluted. Evolutionary theory predicts that males with the longest sperm will be preferred by females and that these have the highest chances of fertilising the eggs.

Males of several *Drosophila* species have paired genitalia, which they use during traumatic copulation: one lobe punctures the female body wall while the other introduces sperm through the wound into the female genital tract from where it moves to the ovaries. The external opening to the genital tract is only used in oviposition and not in copulation (bed bugs also practise traumatic copulation; see 'Bed bugs', p. 403; box, p. 353). Traumatic copulation in *Drosophila* is thought to be a mechanism to discourage females from mating again, thus ensuring the mated male of the paternity of the resultant offspring.

Ants

Ants (Hymenoptera: Formicidae) are possibly the most common and irritating insects that invade homes. Their nests are usually in protected places such as behind skirting or under tiles inside buildings, or they enter from subterranean nests outside. Several species are common in southern Africa. Most ants are omnivorous, although some prefer sweet substances over protein-rich food.

14.65 Vinegar flies (Drosophilidae) are often mistakenly called fruit flies (Tephritidae). Vinegar flies (**a–d**) are commonly, and often abundantly, attracted to fermenting fruit and fermented beverages such as beer and wine, while fruit flies (**e, f**) lay their eggs in developing fruit and seldom venture into houses. (**a**) *Zaprionus tuberculatus*; (**b**) *Drosophila hydei*; (**c**) *D. simulans*; (**d**) *D. punctatonervosa*; (**e**) *Dacus punctatifrons*; (**f**) *Ceratitis cosyra*.

Parasitoids of household pests

Although the numbers of certain species may be high enough in homes to warrant their 'pest' status, many urban insects are actually suppressed by a range of parasitoid wasps living among them, including:

- Fly parasitoids, such as *Tachinaephagus zealandicus* (Hymenoptera: Encyrtidae, fig. 14.66a);
- Biscuit beetle parasitoids, such as *Anisopteromalus* sp. (Pteromalidae, fig. 14.66b); and
- Vinegar fly parasitoids, such as *Pachycrepoideus vindemmiae* (Pteromalidae, fig. 14.66c).

14.66 Some urban insects are heavily parasitised by wasps, which helps to suppress their populations. (**a**) *Tachinaephagus zealandicus* (Encyrtidae), a generalist fly parasitoid, reared from *Chrysomya chloropyga* (Calliphoridae). (**b**) *Anisopteromalus* sp. (Pteromalidae), a parasitoid of the biscuit beetle, *Stegobium paniceum*. (**c**) *Pachycrepoideus vindemmiae* (Pteromalidae), a generalist fly parasitoid, reared from *Drosophila*.

House ants or big-headed ants in the genus *Pheidole* (Myrmicinae) are widespread in the region (fig. 14.67). *Pheidole* is a very large genus of very small ants, with about 1,000 species worldwide and more than 60 in southern Africa. The ants are characterised by specialised workers with large heads. These are not soldiers, but 'seed crushers', as a large proportion of their natural food consists of seeds and other items that need crushing. The workers of common species, including *P. megacephala*, are brown and about 2–3mm long. They are partial to exposed meat, but also enter kettles, taps, baths and showers in search of water.

The introduced Argentine ant, *Linepithema humile* (Dolichoderinae, fig. 2.25), is most troublesome in the Western Cape, but has spread through the region up to Gauteng. As in the common *Pheidole* species, workers are brown and 2–3mm long, but have a somewhat translucent abdomen when compared to *Pheidole*. *Pheidole* ants also have what appear to be two parts to the waist, while *L. humile* have one. The latter have a preference for sweet foods, but like most ant species, are omnivorous. *Linepithema humile* is one of the worst invasive ant species and is listed as one of the 100 worst animal invaders worldwide. This is largely due to the presence of multiple queens in the colonies, any of which can establish a new colony with a few workers; hence they are easily dispersed by humans. They are a major threat to indigenous ant species and have cascading ecological effects (see 'Seed burial by ants', p. 66).

Lepisiota (Formicinae) is an Old World genus with about 135 species worldwide and about 20 in southern

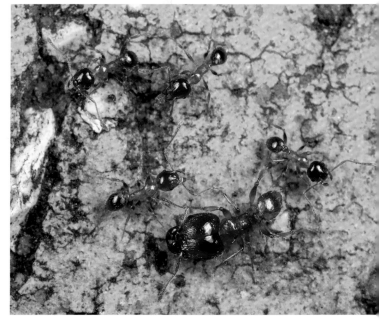

14.67 Ants are some of the most common urban insects. Many species live in gardens, and a few regularly establish in houses. These house ants, *Pheidole* sp. (Myrmicinae), have big-headed workers which are specialised to crush seed.

Africa. Like *Pheidole* and *Linepithema*, these ants are also in the 2–3mm size range, but are black instead of brown. They have a preference for sweet foods, but are omnivorous at times. The common small black ant, *Lepisiota capensis*, occurs mostly in the Western Cape. The African small black ant, *L. incisa*, may become abundant in homes in more northerly regions.

Insects that feed on textiles

Clothing, carpets and curtains made of natural fibres such as silk, cotton, mohair and wool are a food source for various moth larvae and certain crickets. The fibres consist of complex molecules that can only be digested by species that have the appropriate digestive enzymes or mutualistic gut symbionts that produce the necessary enzymes.

House crickets

The tropical house cricket, *Gryllodes sigillatus* (Orthoptera: Gryllidae), is probably of southwest Asian origin, but is now widespread in warmer parts of the world. It enters homes where it occasionally damages fabrics by feeding on fibres. The crickets do not live continuously inside houses, however, as their eggs are laid in damp soil. Urban gardens in southern Africa often support high populations and individuals may invade homes.

Gryllodes sigillatus has achieved prominence in recent years as a food source for birds, fish and reptiles in the pet trade. The main attributes that make the crickets suitable for breeding are the ease with which they can be reared, their short life cycle and a less overt tendency towards cannibalism. They also have less indigestible body chitin than other crickets because males have short wings (fig. 14.68a) and females are wingless (fig. 14.68b); this makes them more palatable and digestible.

14.68 The tropical house cricket, *Gryllodes sigillatus* (Gryllidae), breeds in moist places in soil, but adults often venture into houses. **(a)** Males have short wings; **(b)** females are wingless.

Clothes moths

Members of the Tineidae (Lepidoptera), including the clothes moth, *Tineola bisselliella*, are among very few insect species that are able to digest keratin, the main protein of wool, fur, horns and hooves (see 'Final-stage carcass colonisers', p. 252). The clothes moth is able to complete its life cycle in the home. The adults are speckled grey moths about 7–8mm long that sit with their wings closed. They shelter in dark places like cupboards by day and venture out at night to locate suitable fabrics, usually also in sheltered places, where they lay their eggs. The larvae are very small creamy-white caterpillars with a brown head capsule, and they spin a web in which they live and feed. They have a wide tolerance for food items, including dry stored products, but fabrics, particularly wool, are preferred; the adults do not feed.

Household case-bearers

Phereoeca (Tineidae) is a small tropical American moth genus consisting of about 10 species with 'case-bearing' larvae (fig. 14.69). Two of the species, *P. uterella* and *P. allutella*, are known as household case-bearers. These species are now also found outside of their indigenous ranges, having been inadvertently introduced to other warmer parts of the world. *Phereoeca uterella* is now well established in southern Africa and has become a fairly well-known curiosity in homes in many parts of the region because it has unusual and interesting biology.

Phereoeca uterella is in the same family as clothes moths (Tineidae), which shares a common ancestry and some behavioural similarities with bagworms (Psychidae). All Psychidae larvae live in self-constructed 'bags' of sticks, sand grains, thorns, grass stems or other items from their food plant or their immediate environment that are held together by silk (see 'Lichen-feeding bagworms', p. 182). Tineidae and Psychidae are sister groups in the superfamily Tineoidea.

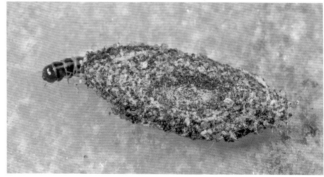

Lyle J. Buss

14.69 The household case-bearer is the larva of the moth *Phereoeca uterella* (Lepidoptera: Tineidae) and lives in a portable case. They are most often found under moist conditions, such as in bathrooms.

The larvae of household case-bearers of the genus *Phereoeca* construct a spindle-shaped casing in which they live and pupate. Construction of the case starts as soon as the larva emerges from the egg. It spins a silken arch, attached at both ends to the substrate. Below this, it progressively extends the inside into a silken tube that is lightly anchored to the arch, and open at both ends. Tiny particles of soil, plant debris, insect remains and various fibre strands are then gradually added on the outside.

When the tube is complete, the larva starts to move, dragging the tube with it. Moulting takes place inside the confines of the tube, which is extended in length and expanded in width at the middle after each moult. The tube also flattens as it increases in length and width, which allows the larva to turn around inside, enabling it to easily and safely change direction. This gives the impression that it can walk 'backwards' and 'forwards' at will. Larvae defecate inside the case and then push the faecal pellets out with their head. Likewise, after a moult, the larval exuviae are pushed out.

The main function of the case is probably for protection against predators and parasitoids, although a favourably humid microclimate is also possibly maintained in the case. Threatened larvae quickly retreat completely into the case and close a silken flap that functions as a door. The tough silk provides physical protection, while the mottled outside layer of debris camouflages the case against natural backgrounds, such as tree bark, the soil surface and similar environments.

Because of their tropical origins, household case-bearers are adapted to warm and humid environments and in southern Africa they are mostly found in the coastal and northeastern parts of the region, but they are also regularly encountered as far inland as Pretoria.

The larval case of these small, greyish, speckled moths is the species' most distinguishing characteristic, and its formation and function are the most interesting aspects of its biology (see box above). The case is flat and spindle-shaped, with the maximum size of a mature larva's case about 10–15mm long and 5–8mm wide in the middle; it often appears speckled because of the small fragments of debris attached to it. When not slowly moving, it may be mistaken for a seed.

When the larva moves, it extends its head and three dark thoracic segments from the case; these segments bear the strongly developed true legs. The abdomen, which is covered by the case, is pale, with prolegs on segments three to six and ten, each armed with well-developed crochets (hook-like structures) that anchor the larva inside the case and enable it to drag the case forward.

The larvae feed on silk produced by spiders and other insect groups, insect remains, as well as scraps of wool and hair. This occasionally brings them into conflict with humans as they damage woollen or silken household items, as do their clothes moth relatives. They are often found in bathrooms, possibly because of the larval developmental need for high humidity.

Before pupation, larvae usually drag their case up a vertical surface and attach it with silk at both ends to the substrate. They then pull the flaps closed and pupate. Just prior to adult emergence, the pupa wriggles to the top exit, pushes the flap open, and exposes its front half. The emerging moth wriggles out at eclosion and sits somewhere close while its wings inflate and expand.

Insects associated with humans and pets

Several species of blood-feeding insects may become abundant in the home under certain conditions. Mosquitoes are widespread and common across southern Africa, and familiar to everyone, while fleas are familiar to cat and dog (fig. 14.70) owners. Lice and bed bugs have been associated with humans for millennia, but their populations were largely suppressed when new-generation pesticides were introduced and used extensively to control them after the Second World War. However, since the 1980s, concern about exposure of humans to pesticides has discouraged widespread treatment. Simultaneously, parasite populations are increasing worldwide as they develop resistance to commonly used pesticides.

Kera le Roux

14.70 Dogs are popular pets that often live intimately with humans, sharing their living spaces, including (sometimes) their beds. Adult fleas are the most common external parasite on dogs, where they live on their host's skin amongst the hair. Fleas suck blood and their bites cause intense itching on dogs and humans.

Head lice

The head louse, *Pediculus capitis* (Psocodea: Pediculidae, fig. 14.71) is an obligate human parasite with a cosmopolitan distribution. It is very closely related to the human body louse, *P. humanus*, and some researchers treat them as subspecies – the head louse, *P. humanus capitis*, and the body louse, *P. humanus humanus*.

Although the two are morphologically and genetically very similar, they are ecologically distinct: the head louse occurs only among hair on the head, while the body louse is associated with hair on the upper body. Head lice do not transmit diseases, whereas body lice do. Under unhygienic conditions, typically found in refugee camps, prisons and during wars, they spread epidemic typhus, trench fever and louse-borne relapsing fever. Bites from lice may cause a localised skin reaction, called pediculosis.

A third, unrelated, louse species, *Pthirus pubis* (Pthiridae) occurs amongst pubic hair; these pubic lice are often called 'crabs'.

All of these species have specially adapted claws for holding onto the host's hair while feeding. They are specific human parasites and do not successfully transfer to other hosts such as pets. They are spread during physical contact among humans and die within a few hours if separated from a host. Head lice are periodic pests, particularly of young children in nursery and primary schools.

The three species have similar life cycles. Eggs are attached to the host's hair and are known as 'nits'. Head lice prefer the nape of the neck. Head and body louse eggs take eight to nine days to hatch; nymphs complete their development in 9–12 days, and adults live for about 30 days. Females lay about 80 eggs over a lifetime. Pubic lice have a slightly different life cycle: eggs hatch in six to eight days; nymphs develop in 10–17 days; adults also live for about 30 days. Females lay a total of about 30 eggs.

Bed bugs

Bed bugs in the genus *Cimex* (Hemiptera: Cimicidae) use their piercing and sucking mouthparts to feed on vertebrate blood. All Cimicidae, of which there are about 10 species in southern Africa, are parasites of birds, bats and humans.

Two human parasitic species are found in southern Africa: the bed bug, *Cimex lectularius* (fig. 14.72), and the tropical bed bug, *C. hemipterus*. *Cimex lectularius* is widespread and common across the world, while *C. hemipterus* occurs in warmer tropical areas. Both are obligate human parasites and they mostly bite while their human hosts are sleeping. Unlike lice, they do not live permanently on a host, but hide in dark recesses near human sleeping areas, emerging to feed at night. This they do by puncturing the host's skin and then

14.71 The head louse, *Pediculus capitis* (Psocodea: Pediculidae), is an obligate human parasite that lives on the scalp. Although it was previously kept under reasonable control by pesticides, the species is spreading and assuming greater importance because of developing resistance to commonly used pesticides.

14.72 The cosmopolitan bed bug, *Cimex lectularius* (Hemiptera: Cimicidae), is an obligate human parasite. Bed bugs hide in dark recesses near human sleeping areas and emerge to feed on blood at night.

sucking blood. They do not transmit disease, but people may have allergic reactions to bites, called cimicosis. Bed bugs may occur sporadically in homes or hotel bedrooms, from which they are easily spread in furniture, baggage or bedding from one place to another.

Female bed bugs lay 200–500 eggs over a lifetime of about nine months. Eggs hatch after some 10 days; the nymphs undergo five instars over about five weeks during their development. Both nymphs and adults feed only on blood.

All Cimicidae species have one of the most unusual and bizarre forms of reproduction known from insects, termed traumatic copulation or hypodermic insemination. Although a few other insect and invertebrate species have similar reproductive systems (see 'Vinegar flies', p. 399; 'Velvet worms: living fossils', p. 303), it reaches its most extreme form in the Cimicidae (for details, see box, p. 353).

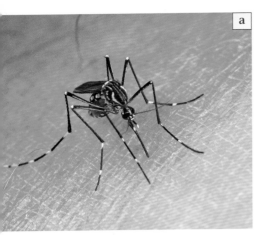

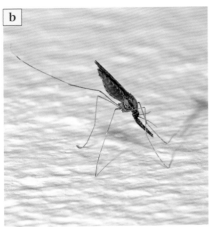

14.73 Mosquitoes are familiar to most people. (**a**) *Aedes* species breed in various water sources in urban environments and adults mostly bite outside in the late afternoon, while (**b**) *Anopheles*, some species of which are vectors of malaria, mostly breed in flowing water and bite late at night.

14.74 Many insects may be attracted to street lights and lights around buildings at night. Among them are burrowing bugs, *Aethus perosus* (Cydnidae), which may become so numerous at lights that they fall into food and drinks, to which they impart their repulsive defence compound taste.

Mosquitoes

Mosquitoes (Diptera: Culicidae) breed in water in ponds and water storage tanks, as well as in smaller containers. Because they have such short life cycles, particularly under hot conditions, even containers that hold water for only a few days are suitable breeding sites. Adults are common in urban areas in summer throughout the region. Species of *Aedes* (fig. 14.73a) and *Culex* are most common. *Aedes* species are small black mosquitoes with white bands on their legs and body; they mostly bite people out of doors in the early evenings, often on the lower legs. *Culex* mosquitoes are larger brown insects and usually bite later at night. Malaria mosquitoes in the genus *Anopheles* (fig. 14.73b) may also be common across southern Africa, although they only transmit malaria after biting an infected person (for detailed biology, see 'Mosquitoes and their biology', p. 262; 'Clean standing water', p. 340; 'Semiaquatic systems', 'Temporary water sources', 'Small, contained water sources', pp. 342–343).

Fleas

Fleas are undoubtedly the most common and irritating pests of dogs and cats, and readily switch hosts and bite humans. The most common pet flea in southern Africa is the cat flea, *Ctenocephalides felis* (Siphonaptera: Pulicidae), which is found on both dogs and cats.

When rodent numbers increase in rural and urban areas, various rodent fleas may also spread to pets and they occasionally bite humans. Amongst these are some that may transmit bubonic plague, which, proportionately, caused the worst ever catastrophe in human history and was responsible for the deaths of millions during the Black Death pandemic in the Middle Ages (around 1350). About one-third of the population of Europe died. Plague is still present in various developing countries and although there have been no serious epidemics in more than a century, its potential as a dangerous disease has not diminished.

Only adult fleas suck blood. The larvae are detritus feeders in the host's nest or pet's bed, where they feed on fragments of skin and dried blood droplets excreted by adult fleas – adults imbibe more fluids than they can digest and excrete the excess, which forms a major component of the larval diet.

Insects attracted to light

Some of the insects that live in gardens are attracted to light at night and may become numerous at outside lights or even enter homes. These commonly include mantises, midges, various bugs, moths, some beetles, and lacewings. One particularly notorious insect is the burrowing bug *Aethus perosus* (Cydnidae, fig. 14.74), which is often attracted to lights in large numbers in savanna areas; if they fall into food they render it inedible due to a repulsive defence compound.

The diversity and number of insects attracted to house lights are greatly influenced by the amount of environmental light produced by nearby street lights and well-lit business premises. Light pollution is especially disruptive of insect flight patterns where fluorescent or mercury vapour lights are used, as these produce a large amount of ultraviolet light, which is especially attractive to insects. Insect electrocutors ('bug zappers'), which use highly attractive fluorescent tubes, are used by many home owners to reduce the numbers of nocturnal insects around buildings, but they inadvertently kill many beneficial insects (and occasionally geckos attracted to fluttering insects).

Praying mantises

Praying mantises (Mantodea) are familiar insects in homes: by day they often catch flies on kitchen window sills, while at night they prey on the multitude of insects attracted to lights.

Mantodea is a small order with about 200 species in southern Africa, placed in six families: Empusidae, Hymenopodidae, Mantidae, Sibyllidae, Tarachodidae and Thespidae (fig. 14.75). Most species in the region are in the Mantidae; these are the more common, 'typical' brown and green mantises. Flower mantises (Hymenopodidae) are distinguished by their very unusual flower patterns and colours. Cone-headed mantises (Empusidae) have a characteristic cone-shaped head. Thespids are slender and have a hammer-shaped head. Only one species of Sibyllidae, *Sibylla pretosa*, is known from southern Africa.

All members of the order have the typical, fairly upright posture in which they hold their front legs together in front of their head, as if in prayer (fig. 14.76), the origin of the common name 'praying mantises'. All stages and species are voracious predators of mostly invertebrates, but some of the larger species are known to occasionally even kill and eat small vertebrates such as birds and geckos. The mantis head is very mobile, with large eyes and strongly developed mandibles. The raptorial forelegs are armed with spines on the inside of the tibia and tarsus, which close together like the teeth of a gin trap; these are used to capture and hold prey.

All mantis females lay eggs in a capsule (an ootheca), similar to that of cockroaches (see 'Cockroaches as essential detritivores', p. 88) with which mantises share an ancient ancestor. As in cockroaches, the capsule is produced by accessory reproductive glands; these secrete a liquid that is deposited onto a surface (such as a twig) in a series of successive, flattened drops that solidify in air, and between which are trapped small air pockets that make up the capsule. The result is a

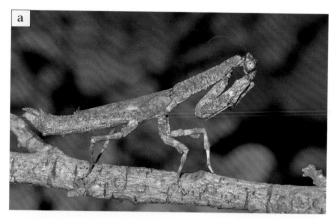

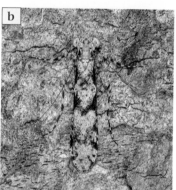

14.75 Praying mantises (Mantodea) are familiar and diverse garden insects, and some may be attracted to lights at night: (**a**) *Popa* sp. (Mantidae); (**b**) *Amorphoscelis tuberculata* (Amorphoscelidae); (**c**) *Miomantis* (Mantidae); (**d**) *Pseudoharpax* (Hymenopodidae); (**e**) *Tarachodes* (Tarachodidae); (**f**) *Hemiempusa capensis* (Empusidae).

14.76 An immature ghost mantid, *Phyllocrania paradoxa* (Hymenopodidae), illustrating the 'praying' posture.

species-specific ootheca in the form of a foam package, a translucent ball, or an elongated, flattened tube (fig. 14.77). The eggs are arranged in roughly parallel rows at the top of or inside the capsule. The ootheca is pale and soft at first, but darkens and hardens progressively into a leathery structure after a few days. As with certain cockroaches, some mantises also demonstrate simple brood care and guard the ootheca until the nymphs emerge.

The emergent pale mantis nymphs drop from the ootheca on the end of a silk strand, from which they hang suspended for a short while before separating from the silk. They darken to brown-black, irrespective of their eventual body colour. At this stage they resemble ants (fig. 14.78); this is possibly a form of mimicry to afford the tiny, fragile nymphs some protection for the first few days of their lives. They are predatory on tiny invertebrates such as mites. Their species-specific hunting strategies start developing at this early stage.

14.77 Mantis egg packets (oothecae) are formed by the female's accessory reproductive glands during egg-laying. The eggs are covered by foamy or leathery protective layers that harden and darken soon after egg-laying. The different types of oothecae are often characteristic of the species that produce them. (a) A tube-like ootheca with little covering over the eggs, but protection is enhanced by the female defending them against predators and parasitoids; (b) a translucent oothecal 'ball' of cellophane-like protective material; (c) the most common form, consisting of a dense spongy material – dark 'holes' on the side are marks that apparently mimic emergence holes of tiny wasp parasitoids, which serve to discourage 'further' parasitism.

14.78 An ant-mimicking mantis nymph.

14.79 (a) A nymph of the flower-mimicking mantis, *Pseudocreobotra wahlbergi* (Mantodea: Hymenopodidae), waiting for prey; **(b)** *P. wahlbergi* nymph with a butterfly lured to its fate.

Hunting strategies

Mantises have three different hunting strategies – ambush, cursorial and generalist:

- Ambush hunters are sit-and-wait predators that use their cryptic colours to blend into their background amongst foliage or detritus on the ground, while waiting for potential prey to approach. The spectacular flower mantises (Hymenopodidae) are patterned and coloured to resemble the flowers on which they sit and wait for flower-frequenting insects such as bees, butterflies and flies (fig. 14.79). This is called aggressive mimicry.
- Cursorial hunters frequent clear surfaces such as open ground or bare tree trunks where they use cryptic behaviour, keeping still to avoid detection, then resort to short speed bursts when they run their prey down.
- Generalist mantises use either ambush or cursorial strategies, depending on the habitat in which they find themselves.

Mating behaviour

Since mantises are solitary and predatory, encounters with other invertebrates usually result in their attempting to capture and eat them – this includes mantises smaller than themselves. As males are usually smaller and less robust than females, they fairly often end up getting eaten by the female. Consequently, males intent on approaching a female with a view to mating need to do so with the utmost caution. In contrast, females do not appear to be eaten by males. There are several published reports of female mantises eating males, in a process termed sexual cannibalism (see box, p. 408). However, there is little agreement between researchers whether the phenomenon occurs across species, whether it is part of an obligatory sexual ritual only in some species, or whether it happens only under certain circumstances. Some (possibly all) female mantises produce a sex-attractant pheromone when they are sexually receptive, so it seems unlikely that they would attract a male specifically for reproductive purposes only to eat him when he appears, and there is no evidence to suggest that the males are willing partners in the process. Nevertheless, sexual cannibalism does have potential advantages for both females and males:

- Females benefit from a post-mating nutritious meal that allows them to invest in more egg production, and males benefit indirectly, since, by getting eaten, they are likely to increase the number and viability of eggs fertilised by their sperm.
- A well-fed female is less likely to seek other mating opportunities once successfully mated, assuring the mated (albeit eaten) male of paternity of the offspring.
- There have been studies that reported that male mating efficiency improved after their heads were eaten, as there is a neural centre of copulatory inhibition situated there. This implies an evolved and not a random process and suggests that males of some species, such as *Sphodromantis* spp., at least, are ordained to be eaten.

Sexual cannibalism in mantises

Sexual cannibalism in the West African mantis species *Sphodromantis lineola* was studied by S.E. Kynaston and colleagues in the laboratory. It is a large insect (body length about 55 mm), and very similar to the common green mantis, *S. gastrica* (fig. 14.80), of east-central and southern Africa.

Males always approached females cautiously and most of them performed a prolonged courtship display after being seen by the female.

A small percentage of males used a 'sneak' approach and cautiously neared the female from behind. From a distance of 2–8cm, they leapt onto her back and initiated copulation without any courtship. If they were seen by the female during their approach, they froze until her attention wandered, whereupon they fled.

When a male openly approached a female he carried out a series of distinct antennal oscillations, abdominal movements and wing-raising from some distance until he was about 8cm away. He then raised his forelegs and swayed his body to and fro for a short time, then leapt onto the female's back and copulated. The approach and courtship display lasted between 20 and 120 minutes, with an average length of 51 minutes. This is clearly an energy-intensive and risky process for males, so the time and effort are justified by successful copulation.

It appeared as if males were unable to assess whether females were receptive or not and it was found that hungry females always ate males they encountered, whereas satiated females allowed males to perform their courtship display at fairly close quarters without interference. It would appear that acquiring food has priority over mating.

14.80 A female of the large green mantis *Sphodromantis gastrica* (Mantodea). Females of this group are known to cannibalise males under certain conditions.

Predator avoidance

Mantises are vulnerable to visual hunters such as birds during the day – their cryptic colouring helps to protect them from these diurnal predators. However, many mantises are nocturnal and fly around at night, when echolocating insectivorous bats are on the wing. As a predator avoidance mechanism, these mantises have evolved hearing that is sensitive to the ultrasound used by bats.

Mantodea is one of the few insect orders with tympanate hearing organs (ears); the others are some Hemiptera, Orthoptera, Neuroptera and Lepidoptera. Although all other hearing insects (as well as other animals) have two functional ears, mantises have only one. It is situated in a deep groove on the underside of the metathorax, between the coxae of the third pair of legs. It is tuned in to the echolocating frequencies of hunting

14.81 Only mantises with long wings capable of flight have well-developed hearing.

bats. Although the ear is not sensitive to the origin and direction of the sound, mantises react abruptly and dramatically change their flight path when sensing bat sounds. This is similar to the reaction in flying moth groups, as well as in green lacewings (Neuroptera: Chrysopidae) when they hear bat sounds.

Interestingly, only mantises with fully developed long wings capable of flight have well-developed ears (fig. 14.81); flightless individuals (mostly females) have reduced or absent ultrasonic hearing. Since many bat species hunt only flying insects, mantises that fly would be vulnerable to predation; we can assume that this selective pressure on flying mantises has led to the evolution of ultrasonic hearing.

Few mantises produce audible sound, but those that do have teeth on longitudinal veins of the metathoracic (hind) wings and stridulatory pegs on the abdominal pleura. They produce a hissing sound when they flex the abdomen up and down between the wings and rub the pegs against the ridges. The sound seems to be used only in defence, not in mating behaviour. It is combined with aggressive displays such as rearing, raising the wings and lunging at a threat.

Midges

Chironomid midges (Diptera: Chironomidae, fig. 14.82) are mosquito-like insects that are often abundant near water sources where their larvae breed. They are sometimes called nonbiting midges to distinguish them from related Ceratopogonidae and Simuliidae midges, which suck blood. The family is worldwide in distribution with an estimated 10,000–15,000 species. Although there are many species in southern Africa, the family is poorly studied, so estimates of actual numbers remain uncertain.

Midges may be attracted in large numbers to lights at night. They differ from mosquitoes in their lack of wing scales, absence of biting mouthparts and by the elongation of their foretarsi, which they hold off the ground when at rest – mosquitoes always raise their hind tarsi. Like mosquitoes, males have very plumose antennae; those of females are thread-like.

Adults often form huge mating swarms of thousands of individuals. The swarms are usually seen over or close to open water, but may also occur around a terrestrial object, such as a tree or even a car or boat. Mating swarms may form at any time of the day, but are most common at sunrise and sunset. Females ready to mate are attracted by the dancing swarms and fly into them, where they are 'picked up' by a male. The pair then drops to the ground to mate.

Most chironomid larvae live in an aquatic or semiaquatic environment, but the specific habitat of different species is as diverse as the species themselves.

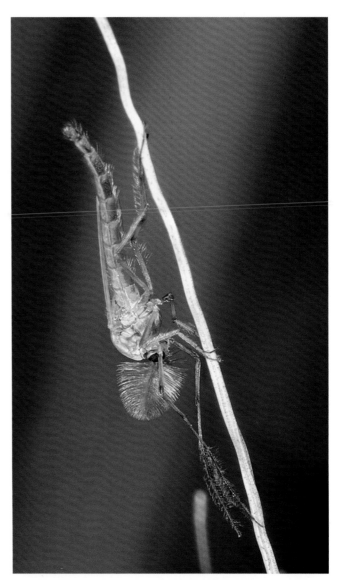

14.82 Midges (Diptera: Chironomidae) may be attracted to lights in large numbers, particularly if situated near water.

Habitats vary from seawater (see 'The stressful life of splash midges', p. 361) to highly saline water on land; it may be flowing or stagnant, richly oxygenated or heavily polluted. The larvae of some species that live in polluted water have red blood and are commonly known as bloodworms (see 'Air dissolved in water', p. 321; 'Midges, gnats, bloodworms', p. 340). Wet soil or damp detritus also harbour certain species.

One species, *Belgica antarctica*, is the largest terrestrial animal (2–6mm long) on mainland Antarctica. There are in fact three chironomid species in Antarctica. They survive the extreme conditions as a result of the evolution of various special morphological and physiological adaptations.

Chironomid larvae are an important food source for fish, frogs and aquatic insects, such as dragonfly, damselfly and aquatic bug nymphs, whereas adults are preyed on by birds, bats and dragonflies and damselflies.

APPENDIX

SOUTHERN AFRICAN INSECT ORDERS

In entomology, the order is the main classification level of importance, as it represents a group in which all members share a specific suite of major evolutionary characters. There are 28 recognised orders of insects worldwide, of which 25 occur in southern Africa. Their names and short descriptions are listed here in a phylogenetic (evolutionary) sequence – from the most primitive to the most derived. References to sections of the book that discuss members of the order are given at the end of each description.

(a) Portia widow dragonfly (Anisoptera: Libelullidae) Odonata;
(b) leprous grasshopper (Caelifera: Pyrgomorphidae) Orthoptera;
(c) earwig (Forficulina: Forficulidae) Dermaptera;
(d) barrel cockroach (Blattoidea: Blaberidae) Blattodea;
(e) boxer mantid (Hymenopodidae) Mantodea;
(f) green-winged cicada (Auchenorrhynca: Cicadidae) Hemiptera;
(g) spoon-winged lacewing (Nemopteridae) Neuroptera;
(h) eyed jewel beetle (Polyphaga: Buprestidae) Coleoptera;
(i) flesh fly (Sarcophagidae) Diptera;
(j) web-spinning caddisfly (Hydropsychidae) Trichoptera;
(k) cavorting emperor moth (Saturniidae) Lepidoptera;
(l) braconid wasp (Apocrita: Braconidae) Hymenoptera.

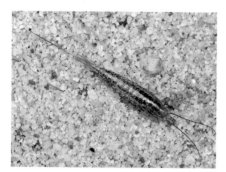

1 Bristletail (Meinertellidae)

2 Fishmoths: (a) Lepismatidae;
(b) Nicoletiidae

3 (a) Mayfly adult (Leptophlebiidae);
(b) nymph (Baetidae)

Ametamorphic orders

In the two ametamorphic orders, the nymphs that hatch from the eggs resemble tiny adults and grow without change at each successive moult, until the sexually mature adult stage is reached. They continue moulting throughout their life, although they do not increase in size.

1 Archaeognatha • Bristletails

From Greek *archaeos*, ancient, and *gnathos*, mouthparts

This is a small group of medium-sized wingless insects (up to about 10mm long) with one family, Meinertellidae, in southern Africa. It has a cylindrical body, a characteristically 'humped' thorax, and three 'tails' (cerci) at the posterior of the abdomen, with the central tail longer than the other two (fig. 1). They feed on lichens and detritus, 'chopping' bits off with their specialised mouthparts. They jump characteristically when disturbed.

Forest • **p. 286**

2 Zygentoma • Fishmoths

From Greek *zygon*, bridge, and *entoma*, insects (literally 'cut into'), as the group was considered a link between ancient wingless and modern winged groups

Fishmoths belong to two families, Lepismatidae and Nicoletiidae. They are wingless and superficially similar to the Archaeognatha (many also have three tails), but they are dorsoventrally flattened and most species are covered in silver scales, hence the common names (fig. 2a). Most are free-living detritus feeders, but some live in ant or termite nests (fig. 2b).

Desert • **p. 148**
Caves • **p. 347**

Hemimetamorphic orders

Hemimetamorphic insects undergo gradual or incomplete metamorphosis from an egg, through several instars as a nymph, and finally to the adult stage. The nymphs of most hemimetamorphic orders resemble the adults, except in orders that have aquatic immature stages.

3 Ephemeroptera • Mayflies

From Greek *ephemeros*, day-long, and *ptera*, wings

Ephemeroptera are colloquially known as mayflies because of their spring activity in the northern hemisphere. The adults are short-lived and do not feed. They are small to medium-sized (2–20mm, but usually less than 10mm), delicate, winged insects (fig. 3a) with short antennae and two or three long tails (caudal filaments). At rest their wings are held vertically. Nymphs (fig. 3b) are aquatic, with chewing mouthparts, feeding on plant or animal matter.

Forest • **p. 314**
Freshwater Habitats • **p. 323**

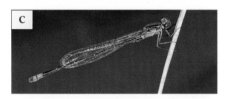

4 (a) Dragonfly (Anisoptera: Libellulidae); (b) dragonfly nymph (Anisoptera: Libellulidae); (c) damselfly (Zygoptera: Coenagrionidae); (d) damselfly nymph (Zygoptera: Lestidae)

5 Stonefly (Perlidae)

6 Webspinner male (Oligotomidae)

4 | Odonata • Dragonflies and damselflies

From Greek *odon*, toothed, referring to the insects' mandibles

These are large to very large predatory insects (wingspan 25–140mm; body length 20–100mm) in two distinct suborders: Anisoptera (dragonflies) and Zygoptera (damselflies). They have large prominent eyes, chewing mouthparts, and two pairs of long, narrow, net-veined wings; they are amongst the most robust and fast-flying insects. Their long legs are used primarily to capture prey in flight and for perching, but not for locomotion. They mate in flight in a characteristic manner. The terminal abdominal segment in the males is equipped with clasping organs which in Anisoptera are used to grab the female behind the head, while Zygoptera females are clasped around the thorax. They fly in this tandem position while mating takes place.

Adults are usually found near water bodies where they hunt for flying insects. The predatory nymphs are aquatic and have mouthparts that are modified into a grasping organ, the labial mask, for prey capture.

Although members of the suborders appear similar, there are a few distinguishing differences. Anisoptera are robust-looking and their eyes usually touch on the top of the head; they hold their wings horizontally while at rest (fig. 4a); and their nymphs have internal gills in the rectum (fig. 4b) and crawl around in the benthic layer of water bodies. Zygoptera appear quite delicate; their eyes are widely separated; most hold their wings vertically at rest (fig. 4c); and the nymphs have three external leaf-like caudal gills (fig. 4d) and swim.

Forest •	**pp. 316–317**
Freshwater Habitats •	**p. 324**

5 | Plecoptera • Stoneflies

From Greek *plekos*, plaited, and *ptera*, wings, in reference to the wing venation

This is a small order of insects with aquatic nymphs and two families in southern Africa: Perlidae (fig. 5) and Notonemouridae. The adults are cockroach-like with long antennae; they scuttle over rocks near water and rarely fly, albeit that most have two pairs of membranous wings. The large adult perlids (up to 25mm long) do not feed, although their nymphs are predatory, while the smaller notonemourid adults (5–8mm) feed on plant matter, and the nymphs on detritus.

Freshwater Habitats •	**p. 330**

6 | Embioptera • Webspinners

From Greek *embios*, lively, and *ptera*, wings (not a very informative name)

This is a small, mainly tropical, order of subsocial insects known as webspinners. They line the galleries in which they live with silk, from which they venture to feed on algae and lichens. These are small to medium-sized insects (5–25mm long), with small, slender, soft bodies and large heads and eyes (fig. 6).

Indian Ocean Tropical Belt •	**p. 259**

7 **(a)** Elegant grasshopper (Caelifera: Pyrgomorphidae); **(b)** brown tree locust (Caelifera: Acrididae); **(c)** giant cricket (Ensifera: Gryllidae); **(d)** acacia katydid (Ensifera: Tettigoniidae)

8 Stick insect (Diapheromeridae)

7 Orthoptera • Crickets and grasshoppers

From Greek *orthos*, straight, and *ptera*, wings, referring to the narrow, parallel-sided forewings

A large order that consists of several familiar and many less well-known groups. Amongst the common groups are grasshoppers, crickets, mole crickets, locusts and katydids. The order is divided into two suborders, Caelifera (mostly with antennae much shorter than the body, e.g. grasshoppers, figs 7a, b) and Ensifera (mostly species with antennae as long as or longer than, the body, e.g. crickets and katydids, figs 7c, d; see box, pp. 118–119). Most orthopterans are characteristically large-headed with strong chewing mouthparts. The femora of the hind legs are enlarged for jumping. Most are winged, with membranous hind wings folded beneath characteristic parchment-like forewings (tegmina). Many have reduced wings or are wingless. Most species are herbivorous, some are predatory, while many are omnivorous under certain conditions.

Armoured ground cricket	*Acanthoplus discoidalis*	Savanna	**p. 213**
Bladder grasshoppers	(Pneumoridae)	Succulent Karoo	**p. 115**
Cave cricket	*Spelaeiacris tabulae*	Caves	**p. 347**
Cederberg crevice katydid	*Cedarbergeniana imperfecta*	Caves	**p. 348**
Garden crickets	(Gryllidae)	Urban Environment	**p. 383**
Grasshoppers	(Lentulidae)	Fynbos	**p. 86**
Groundhoppers/grouse locusts	(Tetrigidae)	Freshwater Habitats	**p. 332**
House crickets	(Gryllidae)	Urban Environment	**p. 401**
Herbivorous katydids	(Tettigoniidae)	Succulent Karoo	**p. 119**
Mole crickets	(Gryllotalpidae)	Urban Environment	**p. 383**
Nara cricket	*Acanthoproctus diadematus*	Desert	**p. 154**
Parktown prawn	*Libanasidus vittatus*	Urban Environment	**p. 398**
Plague locusts	(Cyrtacanthacridinae and Oedipodinae)	Nama-Karoo	**p. 165**
Predatory katydid	*Clonia melanoptera*	Succulent Karoo	**p. 126**
Pygmy mole crickets	(Tridactylidae)	Freshwater Habitats	**p. 332**
Rain locust	*Lamarckiana*	Succulent Karoo	**p. 117**
Toad/stone grasshoppers	(Pamphagidae)	Succulent Karoo	**p. 117**

8 Phasmatodea • Stick insects

From Greek *phasma*, an apparition, possibly because of their good camouflage

A widespread order of mostly cryptic, stick-like insects (fig. 8). They are characterised by a very long meso- and metathorax and legs. Southern African species vary in length from about 10mm, to the longest insect species in the region, the 250mm-long *Bactrododema tiaratum*. They have antennae as long as the forelegs or much shorter, chewing mouthparts, and some have a pair of small hind wings folded under the forewings (tegmina). Many species are wingless. They move slowly and feed on plants.

Savanna	**p. 215**

a

b

9 (a) Common earwig (Forficulina: Forficulidae); (b) rat-associated earwig (Hemimerina: Hemimeridae)

10 Heelwalker (Austrophasmatidae)

a

b

9 Dermaptera • Earwigs

From Greek *derma*, skin, and *ptera*, wings, referring to the short and leathery forewings

Earwigs are small to fairly large insects (5–30mm long). There are two suborders in southern Africa: Forficulina, a large, free-living group of 'typical' earwigs (fig. 9a); and Hemimerina, with a single southern African species, which is atypical and lives as a commensal on large rats (fig. 9b). Forficulina have chewing mouthparts and are darkly sclerotised elongated insects with characteristic terminal pincers or forceps (modified cerci). Some are winged, with the forewings short and leathery. The hind wings are large, semicircular and membranous, and folded under the forewings in a unique fan-like manner. Some species are wingless.

Forest • p. 299

10 Mantophasmatodea • Heelwalkers

Concatenation of 'manto' from Mantodea and 'phasma' from Phasmatodea, referring to the similarity to these orders

These small (about 10–12mm long, fig. 10), wingless, predatory insects with chewing mouthparts are most abundant in the west of the region. The common name 'heelwalkers' refers to the way in which their terminal tarsal segments fold up, giving them the appearance of walking on their 'heels'.

Succulent Karoo • p. 126

11 Blattodea • Cockroaches and termites

From Latin *blatta*, an insect that avoids light

This order traditionally represented only the cockroaches, although it has long been known that cockroaches and termites are phylogenetically close. Today, cockroaches and termites are placed in the epifamilies Blattoidae and Termitoidae of the Blattodea. Members of both groups are equipped with chewing mouthparts. Cockroaches (figs 11a–c) feed on detritus and termites (fig. 11d) on wood.

Blattoidae are characterised by a depressed body with the head, which bears long antennae, partly hidden under the prothorax. Some members are winged (membranous hind wings held under tegmina); others are wingless. The females of some members carry the eggs attached to the hind part of the body in a hard egg packet (ootheca).

c

11 (a) Table Mountain cockroach (Blattoidae: Blaberidae); (b) American cockroach (Blattoidae: Blattidae); (c) barrel cockroaches (Blattoidae: Blaberidae)

All Termitoidae are social insects with complex behaviour, living in colonies of many thousands of individuals, in nests often housed in above-ground soil mounds (termitaria). Individuals are characterised by a soft body that has the thorax joined broadly to the abdomen, and by short antennae. Most members of a colony are wingless, although sexual males and females have two pairs of membranous wings, but only during the short reproductive period.

11 (d) Lesser fungus-growing termites
(Termitoidae: Termitidae)

12 (a) Zebra mantid (Mantidae); (b) bark
mantid (Hymenopodidae)

13 (a) Bark louse (Psocoptera: Psocidae);
(b) pig lice (Phthiraptera: Haematopinidae)

Blattodea continued from page 415

Black-mound termite	•	*Amitermes hastatus*	•	Fynbos	•	**p. 68**
Cockroaches	•	(Blattoidae)	•	Fynbos	•	**p. 88**
Damp-wood termites	•	(Termopsidae)	•	Forest	•	**p. 286**
Heuweltjie harvester termite	•	*Microhodotermes viator*	•	Succulent Karoo	•	**p. 104**
Introduced cockroaches	•	(Blattoidae)	•	Urban Environment	•	**p. 397**
Large fungus-growing termites	•	*Macrotermes* species	•	Savanna	•	**pp. 199, 236**
Lesser fungus-growing termite	•	*Odontotermes transvaalensis*	•	Grassland	•	**p. 181**
Snouted harvester termite	•	*Trinervitermes trinervoides*	•	Grassland	•	**p. 179**
Table Mountain leaproach	•	*Saltoblattella montistabularis*	•	Fynbos	•	**p. 91**

12 Mantodea • Mantises

From Greek *mantis*, prophet, referring to the manner in which the front legs are held together as if in prayer

Mantises (or praying mantises, as they are commonly known) are specialised for a predatory life. They have a triangular, mobile head with long antennae, large well-spaced eyes, and strong chewing mouthparts (**fig. 12a**). The head is attached to a slender 'neck' (the modified prothorax), which also bears the forelegs, which are modified to grasp prey and are usually held together in front of the insect, ready to strike out at prey. Some members are flightless, but those that fly have membranous hind wings folded under parchment-like forewings. They are well camouflaged, mimicking the plant habitat in which they occur, resulting in some of the common names such as 'bark' (**fig. 12b**), 'flower' or 'grass mantid'.

Eggs are laid in a frothy mass that hardens to form an egg packet (ootheca) attached to branches and twigs. The hatched nymphs of some species mimic ants (avoided by many predators) while others resemble the adults.

| Urban Environment | • | **p. 405** |

13 Psocodea • Lice

From Greek *psokhein*, to grind or gnaw – based on the old name 'Psocoptera' for a group that gnaw paper and bark

The Psocodea comprise two quite distinct groups that were, until recently, treated as separate orders, the free-living Psocoptera (book and bark lice, fig. 13a) and the Phthiraptera (parasitic lice of mammals and birds, fig. 13b).

Book and bark lice are small (2–10mm long), fragile, pale insects with slender antennae and chewing mouthparts; some have a pair of membranous wings but many are wingless. Most are detritus feeders on or under bark, where they live. The name 'book lice' is used for certain species that eat the starch binding in old books.

Parasitic lice (2–10mm long) are ectoparasites of birds and mammals, including humans. They have a short, flattened body with a small thorax and short legs. Their antennae are short and eyes reduced or absent; all are wingless. Some members have chewing mouthparts, while in others they are of the piercing-sucking type.

| Coastal Zone | • | **p. 360** |
| Urban Environment | • | **p. 403** |

a

b

c

d

14 **(a)** Cicada (Auchenorrhynca:
Cicadidae); **(b)** soft scale (Sternorrhyncha:
Pseudococcidae); **(c)** assassin bug
(Heteroptera: Reduviidae); **(d)** stink bug
(Heteroptera: Scutelleridae); **(e)** scentless
plant bug (Heteroptera: Rhopalidae);
(f) saucer bug (Heteroptera: Naucoridae)

14   Hemiptera • Bugs

From Greek *hemi*, half, and *ptera*, wings, referring to the forewings that are half hardened and half membranous

This is the largest hemimetamorphic order. It has also undergone recent changes to its classification. Traditionally it was considered to consist of two suborders, the Homoptera (a diverse group including cicadas, spittle bugs, aphids, scale insects and many more) and Heteroptera (true bugs, including stink bugs, assassin bugs, various aquatic bugs and others). However, current thinking is that the Homoptera should be divided into the suborders Auchenorrhyncha (lantern bugs, spittle bugs, cicadas and leafhoppers, fig. 14a) and the Sternorrhyncha (whiteflies, scale insects and aphids, fig. 14b).

The one characteristic that is present among all members of the order is the presence of piercing-sucking mouthparts, modified into a jointed 'beak'. All are fluid feeders, most of plant sap or body contents of arthropods, while a few suck vertebrate (including human) blood. When present, there are two pairs of wings, but many are flightless. Heteroptera (**figs 14c–f**) are the more familiar groups and have more diverse life styles, including preying on arthropods and sucking vertebrate blood.

Aphids • (Aphididae) • Urban Environment •			**p. 374**
Aquatic bugs • (Hemiptera) • Freshwater Habitats •			**p. 332**
Bat bug • *Stricticimex antennatus* • Caves •			**p. 352**
Bed bugs • *Cimex* species • Urban Environment •			**p. 403**
Cicadas • (Cicadidae) • Albany Thicket •			**p. 275**
Green stink bugs • (Pentatomidae) • Urban Environment •			**p. 372**
Mopane psyllid • *Retroacizzia mopani* • Savanna •			**p. 216**
Millipede assassins • (Ectrichodiinae) • Forest •			**p. 309**
Restio leafhoppers • (Cephalelini) • Fynbos •			**p. 87**
Scale insects • (Coccoidea) • Urban Environment •			**p. 376**
Sea skater • *Halobates micans* • Coastal Zone •			**p. 359**
Seed bugs • (Lygaeidae) • Grassland •			**p. 183**
Spittle bug • *Ptyelus grossos* • Savanna •			**p. 217**
Thread assassin bugs • (Emesinae) • Forest •			**p. 309**
Twig-wilters • (Coreidae) • Urban Environment •			**p. 372**
Welwitschia bug • *Probergrothius angolensis* • Desert •			**p. 155**

e

f

a

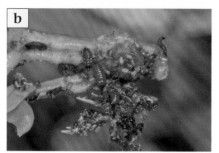

b

15 Thrips: **(a)** adults (Phlaeothripidae);
(b) gall-forming nymphs (Phlaeothripidae)

a

b

16 **(a)** Dobsonfly adult (Corydalidae);
(b) larva (Corydalidae)

a

b

17 **(a)** Antlion adult (Myrmeleontidae);
(b) green brown lacewing (Hemerobiidae)

15 · Thysanoptera · Thrips

From Greek *thysanos*, fringe, and *ptera*, wings

Thysanoptera are commonly known as 'thrips', a name derived from the largest family, Thripidae. Thrips are mostly very small (1.5–2.0mm) elongate insects with rasping, sucking mouthparts. Two pairs of wings are present in some; they are narrow with few veins, are fringed with hairs and lie flat on the body at rest (fig. 15a). Many are wingless. Most live on plants where they feed on the plant itself or form galls (fig. 15b), although some species are predatory on other small arthropods such as mites and insects, including their herbivorous relatives.

Holometamorphic orders

Holometamorphic insects develop through four stages: starting life as an egg, hatching into a larva, which, after feeding and growth accompanied by several moults, develops into a pupal stage from which the adult eventually emerges. Each stage is morphologically distinct.

16 Megaloptera · Alderflies and dobsonflies

From Greek *mega*, large, and *ptera*, wings, referring to the large hind wings

This small relict order is the most basal of the holometamorphic orders. Members are characterised by large hind wings that are wrapped around the body at rest (fig. 16a), and clumsy flight. The southern African fauna is small and restricted to mountainous areas of the escarpment. Adults are slender-bodied with long antennae and long legs; they have chewing mouthparts prolonged into a 'beak', although they do not feed. Larvae (fig. 16b) are aquatic predators. There are two families in the order, Sialidae (alderflies) and Corydalidae (dobsonflies).

Freshwater Habitats • **p. 334**

17 Neuroptera · Lacewings and antlions

From Greek *neuron*, sinew or nerve, and *ptera*, wings

Neuroptera consists of 12 families in southern Africa, the largest and most studied of which are the Myrmeleontidae, Nemopteridae, Chrysopidae and Ascalaphidae. Most adults are characterised by long antennae and two pairs of similar membranous wings (figs 17a, b), which are usually held in a roof-like manner over the body when at rest. In the Nemopteridae, however, the hind wings are modified into ribbon-, spoon- (Nemopterinae – fig. 17c) or thread-like structures (Crocinae). Adults of most groups are predatory with chewing mouthparts, but some feed on pollen and nectar.

Larvae are all predatory. Their mandibles and maxillae form piercing-sucking tubes with which they grasp and pierce their prey and inject enzymes that dissolve its tissues, which they then imbibe; some species are able to open these 'jaws' to 180°. Although most larvae live freely in soil, some are the familiar pit-building antlions (Myrmeleontidae) well known to rural children; these live at the base of conical pits built in dry sand into which their prospective prey falls to be grasped by the jaws. All larvae have the anus sealed, the waste products being stored and expelled as a white pellet (meconium) only upon emergence from the pupa.

17 (c) Spoon-winged lacewing (Nemopteridae)

Neuroptera continued from page 418

Free-living cave-dwelling antlions	(Myrmeleontidae)	Caves	**p. 349**
Giant lacewings	(Palparinae)	Savanna	**p. 237**
Green lacewings	(Chrysopidae)	Urban Environment	**p. 380**
Owlflies	(Ascalaphidae)	Fynbos	**p. 92**
Pit-building antlions	(Myrmeleontidae)	Caves	**p. 349**
Pit-building antlions	(Myrmeleontidae)	Desert	**p. 146**
Ribbon- and spoon-winged lacewings	(Nemopterinae)	Succulent Karoo	**p. 106**
Thread-winged lacewings	(Crocinae)	Caves	**p. 350**

18 Coleoptera • Beetles

From Greek *koleos*, sheath, and *ptera*, wings

Beetles are the largest order of animals, with about 390,000 named species in 175 families. And, as would be expected of such a large group, they vary tremendously in size, shape and habits. This complicates the matter of attributing any single unifying diagnostic character to its members. All have chewing mouthparts; the word 'beetle' comes from Old English *bitula*, biter, from the verb *bitan*, to bite. They also have a very hard cuticle. But the most defining characteristic is having forewings modified into hardened, rigid elytra (singular elytron), which usually cover the membranous hind wings and soft abdomen. Only the hind wings are used for flight; the elytra are usually held open at right angles to the body in flight. Many species, however, are flightless; in some of these species the elytra appear to be permanently fused. Larvae are usually grub-like with chewing mouthparts and three pairs of legs.

There are four suborders: Archostemata, Myxophaga, Adephaga and Polyphaga. Archostemata (fig. 18a) and Myxophaga are basal (primitive) and contain few species. Many familiar families, such as Carabidae (fig. 18b), Dytiscidae (fig. 18c) and Gyrinidae, are in the Adephaga. The Polyphaga (figs 18d–k) outnumber the other suborders, with about 95% of all species, with familiar families such as Scarabaeidae, Curculionidae and Tenebrionidae.

Adults and larvae occur in practically every conceivable terrestrial and freshwater environment from the equator to the poles, where they live in and feed on virtually all parts of living plants (successfully pollinating some species) and plant remains, fungi, dung and carrion. Many species are predatory. Some are highly specialised inhabitants of social insect nests, where they scavenge or prey on their host's brood.

Jonathan Ball

18 (**a**) Reticulated beetle (Archostemata: Cupedidae); (**b**) ground beetle (Adephaga: Carabidae); (**c**) predaceous water beetle (Adephaga: Dytiscidae); (**d**) dung beetle (Polyphaga: Scarabaeidae); (**e**) frantic beetle (Polyphaga: Tenebrionidae; (**f**) jewel beetle (Polyphaga: Buprestidae)

18 (g) Chequered beetle (Polyphaga: Cleridae); (h) common brentid (Polyphaga: Brentidae); (i) blister beetle (Polyphaga: Meloidae); (j) long-horned beetle (Polyphaga: Cerambycidae); (k) leaf beetle (Polyphaga: Chrysomelidae)

Coleoptera continued from page 419

Addo dung beetle	*Circellium bacchus*	Albany Thicket	**p. 279**
Ancient dung beetles	(Canthonini)	Forest	**p. 290**
Ant-like stone-beetles	(Mastigini)	Forest	**p. 289**
Aquatic beetles	(Aquatic Coleoptera)	Freshwater Habitats	**p. 335**
Auger/false powder-post beetles	(Bostrichidae)	Urban Environment	**p. 388**
Beach ground beetles	(Scaritinae)	Coastal Zone	**p. 365**
Biscuit beetle	*Stegobium paniceum*	Urban Environment	**p. 396**
Blister beetles	(Meloidae)	Nama-Karoo	**p. 171**
Blister beetles	(Meloidae)	Savanna	**p. 223**
Brush beetles	(Julodinae)	Succulent Karoo	**p. 121**
Cycad weevils	*Antliarhinus* species	Albany Thicket	**p. 273**
Darkling/toktokkie beetles	(Tenebrionidae)	Desert	**pp. 136, 144**
Darkling/toktokkie beetles	(Tenebrionidae)	Savanna	**p. 234**
Detritus dung beetles	*Pachysoma* species	Succulent Karoo	**p. 122**
Detritus dung beetles	*Pachysoma* species	Desert	**p. 150**
Dung beetles	(Scarabaeinae)	Desert	**pp. 151, 152**
Dung beetles	(Scarabaeinae)	Savanna	**p. 248**
Dung beetles	(Scarabaeinae)	Urban Environment	**p. 385**
Fruit chafers	(Cetoniinae)	Grassland	**p. 184**
Gall-forming beetles	(Anthribidae)	Succulent Karoo	**p. 120**
Ground beetles	(Carabidae)	Savanna	**p. 239**
Ground beetles	(Carabidae)	Succulent Karoo	**p. 127**
Hyrax-associated dung beetles	(Dichotomiini)	Succulent Karoo	**p. 125**
Keratin beetles	(Trogidae)	Savanna	**p. 253**
Keratin beetles	(Trogidae)	Forest	**p. 291**
Ladybirds	(Coccinellidae)	Urban Environment	**p. 378**
Leaf beetles	(Chrysomelidae)	Savanna	**p. 226**
Long-horned beetles	(Cerambycidae)	Savanna	**p. 221**
Monkey beetles	(Hopliini)	Fynbos	**p. 80**
Monkey beetles	(Hopliini)	Succulent Karoo	**p. 109**
Most primitive beetles	(Cupedidae)	Forest	**p. 288**
Predatory ground beetles	(Carabidae)	Savanna	**p. 239**
Red log beetle	*Prostomis africana*	Forest	**p. 289**
Red-spotted lily weevil	*Brachycerus ornatus*	Urban Environment	**p. 370**
Rhinoceros beetles	(Dynastinae)	Urban Environment	**p. 386**
Spider beetles	(Ptinidae)	Caves	**p. 347**
Stag beetles	*Colophon* species	Fynbos	**p. 61**
Tiger beetles	(Cicindelinae)	Coastal Zone	**p. 363**
Tiger beetles	(Cicindelinae)	Freshwater Habitats	**p. 337**
Tyrant ground beetle	*Anthia maxillosa*	Succulent Karoo	**p. 127**
Woolly chafer	*Sparrmannia flava*	Savanna	**p. 220 (box)**

19 The abdomen of a wasp parasitised by female Strepsiptera; the abdomens of a few Strepsiptera can be seen extruding from the wasp abdomen

19 Strepsiptera • Twisted-winged insects

From Greek *strepsi*, twisted, and *ptera*, wings, referring to the small forewings and large hind wings, which are 'the wrong way around' or 'twisted'

This is a small order of about 600 species worldwide with about 20 species described from southern Africa. All species are very small and show extreme sexual dimorphism. Males are free-living and winged, with functional, fan-shaped hind wings and forewings reduced to halteres. Most females are permanent, larva-like endoparasites embedded in their insect hosts with only the abdomen exposed (fig. 19); the head and thorax are fused and antennae, eyes, wings and legs are absent. Larvae are also permanently parasitic on their hosts.

20 Mecoptera • Hangingflies

From Greek *mecos*, long, and *ptera*, wings

A small order, represented in southern Africa by only the family Bittacidae (hangingflies). Elsewhere they are mostly known as scorpionflies (Panorpidae). Adult bittacids (fig. 20) are medium to large predatory insects (wingspan about 40mm), that superficially closely resemble common crane flies (Diptera: Tipulidae), but are rarely seen. Their fore- and hind legs are extremely long. The front pair are used to attach to vegetation where they hang waiting for passing prey, while the back pair of prehensile legs is used to intercept flying insects. Their biting mouthparts are prolonged into a 'beak' with which they suck the fluids from their prey. They have elaborate mating rituals where, in order to mate, the male must offer the female a gift in the form of a prey item; the male is chosen depending on the size of the gift and he mates while the female is engaged in eating the prey. Larvae live in detritus where they apparently scavenge small animal remains. They have the unique habit of ingesting soil and then spraying it from the anus over the body to provide themselves with camouflage against the background habitat.

20 Hangingfly (Bittacidae)

21 Siphonaptera • Fleas

From Greek *siphon*, pipe, referring to the sucking mouthparts, and *a-ptera*, absence of wings

Siphonaptera consist of eight families in southern Africa, one of which is the Hectopsyllidae to which the introduced atypical sand flea, *Tunga penetrans*, belongs; the females embed permanently in the soft skin of mammals (including humans) and cause intense itching. Males and females of all other families are free-living ectoparasites of birds and mammals, several species of which are familiar and common nuisance parasites of cats and dogs. They are laterally compressed, dark brown or black wingless insects (fig. 21) with long hind legs and the well-known ability to jump considerable distances. Fleas have no compound eyes and their very short antennae are recessed in grooves on the head. They have piercing-sucking mouthparts with which both males and females suck blood, and although the different species usually have a preferred host, they will feed on a wide range of birds and mammals (including humans). Some are serious disease vectors in the absence of their preferred host (e.g. plague is transmitted to humans by rat fleas). They also serve as intermediate hosts for tapeworms of dogs and cats (and via them, occasionally humans) and rodents. Only the adult stage is parasitic; larvae are detritus feeders in the host's nests or burrows.

Urban Environment • **p. 404**

21 Fleas (Pulicidae)

22 | Diptera • Flies

From Greek *di*, two, and *ptera*, wings

This large order of 'true' flies of about 100,000 described species in many suborders includes many familiar groups, some of which are not obviously typical flies, such as mosquitoes. Adult members (fig. 22) are characterised by a pair of transparent forewings, and hind wings that are reduced to knob-like halteres that function as balancing organs. Mouthparts are variable, either piercing-sucking or sponging. Larvae of most of the larger and more derived groups are typical maggots: fleshy, legless and unsclerotised, with the only distinct morphological structures being the mouth hooks (modified mandibles; e.g. blow fly maggots; see p. 251). Larvae of primitive Diptera are often aquatic and have a more or less distinct head capsule (e.g. mosquito larvae; see pp. 262, 342). Biology of members of the Diptera is incredibly diverse, possibly even more so than in the much larger Coleoptera. The order contains some of the most serious vectors of human diseases (such as malaria transmitted by mosquitoes) and those of their livestock (such as nagana transmitted by tsetse flies).

Aquatic flies	(Diptera)	Freshwater Habitats	**p. 339**	
Bat flies	(Nycteribiini)	Caves	**p. 354**	
Bat flies	(Streblini)	Caves	**p. 354**	
Bee flies	(Bombyliidae)	Succulent Karoo	**p. 110**	
Bee louse	*Braula coeca*	Fynbos	**p. 78**	
Black soldier fly	*Hermetia illucens*	Urban Environment	**p. 388**	
Blow flies	(Calliphoridae)	Savanna	**p. 251**	
Crane flies	(Tipulidae)	Urban Environment	**p. 387**	
Gall-forming fruit fly	*Tylaspis crocea*	Succulent Karoo	**p. 121**	
House flies	(Muscidae)	Urban Environment	**p. 398**	
Hover flies	(Syrphidae)	Urban Environment	**p. 381**	
Kelp fly	*Fucellia capensis*	Coastal Zone	**p. 363**	
Long-tongued flies	(Nemestrinidae and Tabanidae)	Fynbos	**p. 81**	
Louse flies	(Hippoboscidae)	Caves	**p. 353**	
Midges	(Chironomidae)	Freshwater Habitats	**p. 340**	
Midges	(Chironomidae)	Urban Environment	**p. 409**	
Mosquitoes	(Culicidae)	Indian Ocean Tropical Belt	**p. 262**	
Mosquitoes	(Culicidae)	Freshwater Habitats	**pp. 340, 342**	
Moth flies	(Psychodidae)	Urban Environment	**p. 395**	
Nasal bot flies	(Oestridae)	Grassland	**p. 193**	
Parasitoid flies	(Tachinidae)	Forest	**p. 311**	
Rhino bot flies	(Oestridae)	Savanna	**p. 245**	
Robber flies	(Asilidae)	Succulent Karoo	**p. 128**	
Splash midge	*Telmatogeton* species	Coastal Zone	**p. 361**	
Stable fly	*Stomoxys calcitrans*	Urban Environment	**p. 387**	
Tsetse flies	(Glossinidae)	Indian Ocean Tropical Belt	**p. 264**	
Vinegar flies	*Drosophila* species	Urban Environment	**p. 399**	
Wormlions	(Vermileonidae)	Caves	**p. 351**	

22 **(a)** Moth fly (Psychodomorpha: Psychodidae); **(b)** green soldier fly (Brachycera: Stratiomyidae); **(c)** long-legged fly (Brachycera: Dolichopodidae); **(d)** stilt-legged fly (Brachycera: Micropezidae); **(e)** signal fly (Brachycera: Platystomatidae)

23 Caddisfly (Leptoceridae)

23 Trichoptera • Caddisflies

From Greek *tricho*, hair, and *ptera*, wings

Adult caddisflies are small (3–25mm), soft-bodied, moth-like insects with hairy wings found most commonly near water. They have long antennae and legs (fig. 23) and only rudimentary mouthparts, as they do not feed. Larvae and pupae of this small but taxonomically diverse order are all aquatic, occurring mainly in clear, well-oxygenated, acidic waters.

Forest •	**p. 315**
Freshwater Habitats •	**p. 343**

Ian Sharpe

24 (a) Pale ranger butterfly (Hesperiidae);
(b) pirate butterfly (Nymphalidae);
(c) lunar moth adult (Saturniidae);
(d) lunar moth larva (Saturniidae)

24 Lepidoptera • Moths and butterflies

From Greek *lepidos*, scale, and *ptera*, wings

This large order comprises 150,000 species worldwide. Adults have large eyes, and wings clothed in overlapping scales, which may be dull or brilliantly coloured (figs 24a–c). Mouthparts are reduced and nonfunctional in the adults of many groups; if present, they consist of a characteristic coiled tubular haustellum (proboscis) for sucking up nectar. Butterflies are diurnal, usually rest with their wings closed and most have long, clubbed antennae. Moths are mostly nocturnal, rest with their wings spread and usually have feathered antennae.

The majority of larvae are typical caterpillars (fig. 24d) with a well-developed head capsule and chewing mouthparts. They have three pairs of thoracic legs and a variable number of fleshy abdominal protuberances (prolegs), which function as extra legs. Larvae of the greatest majority of species feed on plant tissues, but a few species are predatory.

Bagworms • (Psychidae) •	Grassland •	**p. 182**	
Bagworms • (Psychidae) •	Savanna •	**p. 227**	
Blues and coppers • (Lycaenidae) •	Fynbos •	**pp. 65, 93**	
Brown-veined white • *Belenois aurota* •	Savanna •	**p. 231**	
Citrus swallowtail • *Papilio demodocus* •	Urban Environment •	**p. 371**	
Clothes moths, case-bearers • (Tineidae) •	Urban Environment •	**p. 401**	
Cycad-feeding moths • (Diptychini) •	Albany Thicket •	**p. 274**	
Forest butterflies and moths • (Lepidoptera) •	Forest •	**p. 293**	
Gall moths • (Elachistidae and Thyrididae) •	Savanna •	**p. 233**	
Hawk moths • (Sphingidae) •	Grassland •	**p. 185**	
Horn moths • (Tineidae) •	Savanna •	**p. 253**	
Kalahari silk moth • *Gonometa postica* •	Savanna •	**p. 231**	
Karoo caterpillar • *Loxostege frustalis* •	Nama-Karoo •	**p. 170**	
Lily borer moth • *Brithys crini* •	Urban Environment •	**p. 371**	
Mopane worm • *Imbrasia belina* •	Savanna •	**p. 228**	
Noctuid moths • (Noctuidae) •	Grassland •	**p. 186**	
Processionary caterpillar • *Anaphe reticulata* •	Savanna •	**p. 229**	
Silver-spotted ghost/Keurboom moth • *Leto venus* •	Forest •	**p. 287**	
Table Mountain beauty • *Aeropetes tulbaghia* •	Fynbos •	**p. 83**	

25 | Hymenoptera • Wasps, bees and ants

From Greek *hymen*, membrane, and *ptera*, wings

This is another of the larger orders (100,000 described species) containing many familiar insect groups – including sawflies, ants, bees and wasps. It is the only order other than Blattodea (specifically Termitoidae) that has species with complex social behaviour. Most species are permanently winged (wasps and bees), but some are sexually dimorphic (winged males, wingless females in some wasps) or mostly wingless (only reproductive ants are winged). Females of many groups have the ovipositor modified for stinging, sawing or piercing. All members have chewing mouthparts, but some of these are modified for lapping or sucking.

The order is divided into two suborders – the large suborder Apocrita and the small Symphyta (sawflies – fig. 25a). Adult Symphyta lack the 'waist' common to Apocrita; the common name 'sawflies' is derived from the saw-like ovipositor. Larvae are caterpillar-like but have prolegs on all abdominal segments; most are plant feeders.

Apocrita contains the bulk of the taxa, including all the wasps, bees and ants, and is divided further into two sections, Parasitica (parasitic groups, figs 25b, c) and Aculeata (stinging groups, figs 25d, e). Adult Apocrita feed on liquids – the body fluids of their hosts in Parasitica or nectar in most Aculeata. All Parasitica larvae feed on host body tissue, while many Aculeata larvae feed on arthropod prey fed directly by the mother or cached for them by her. Many bee and wasp larvae feed on nectar and pollen provided by the mother (or their siblings in the case of social species). Ants are omnivorous.

Argentine ant	*Linepithema humile*	Fynbos	**p. 67 (box)**
Carpenter bees	(Xylocopinae)	Urban Environment	**p. 393**
Fig wasps	(Agaonidae)	Savanna	**p. 207**
Gall wasps	(Eulophidae)	Urban Environment	**p. 381**
Harvester ant	*Messor capensis*	Nama-Karoo	**p. 159**
Honey bee	*Apis mellifera*	Fynbos	**p. 74**
Honey bee	*Apis mellifera*	Albany Thicket	**p. 271**
Matabele ant	*Megaponera analis*	Savanna	**p. 243**
Mopane bees	(Meliponini)	Savanna	**p. 209**
Namib ant	*Ocymyrmex robustior*	Desert	**p. 145**
Namib detritus ant	*Camponotus detritus*	Desert	**p. 153**
Oil-collecting bees	(Melittidae)	Fynbos	**p. 84**
Paper wasps	(Polistinae)	Urban Environment	**p. 389**
Parasitic wasps	(Ichneumonoidea and Chalcidoidea)	Forest	**p. 312**
Pollen wasps	(Masarinae)	Succulent Karoo	**p. 114**
Potter wasps	(Eumeninae)	Urban Environment	**p. 392**
Pugnacious ant	*Anoplolepis custodiens*	Grassland	**p. 191**
Spider-hunting wasps	(Pompilidae)	Fynbos	**p. 84**
Spider-hunting wasps	(Pompilidae)	Grassland	**p. 186**
Spider-parasitic wasp	*Echthrodesis lamorali*	Coastal Zone	**p. 361**
Weaver ant	*Oecophylla longinoda*	Indian Ocean Tropical Belt	**p. 260**

25 **(a)** Sawfly (Symphyta: Tenthredinidae); **(b)** cuckoo wasp (Apocrita: Chrysididae); **(c)** leucospid wasp (Apocrita: Parasitica: Leucospidae); **(d)** melittid bee (Apocrita: Aculeata: Melittidae); **(e)** ants (Apocrita: Aculeata: Formicidae)

Scientific names of Appendix images

Pg.	Fig.	Species (Family) Order
410	a	*Palpopleura portia* (Libellulidae) Odonata
	b	*Phymateus leprosus* (Pyrgomorphidae) Orthoptera
	d	*Bantua* sp. (Blaberidae) Blattodea
	e	*Oxypilus* sp. (Hymenopodidae) Mantodea
	g	*Palmipenna pilicornis* (Nemopteridae) Neuroptera
	h	*Lampetis amaurotica* (Buprestidae) Coleoptera
	j	*Amphipsyche* sp. (Hydropsychidae) Trichoptera
	k	*Usta terpsichore* (Saturniidae) Lepidoptera
411	c	*Forficula* sp. (Forficulidae) Dermaptera
	f	*Stagira* sp. (Cicadidae) Hemiptera
	i	*Sarcophaga* sp. (Sarcophagidae) Diptera
	l	*Vipio* sp. (Braconidae) Hymenoptera
412	1	*Machiloides* sp. (Meinertellidae) Archaeognatha
	2a	*Ctenolepisma* sp. (Lepismatidae) Zygentoma
	2b	Nicoletiidae Zygentoma
	3a	Leptophlebiidae Ephemeroptera
	3b	*Pseudocloeon* sp. (Baetidae) Ephemeroptera
413	4a	*Tetrathemis polleni* (Libellulidae) Odonata
	4b	*Pantala flavescens* (Libellulidae) Odonata
	4c	*Pseudagrion sudanicum* (Coenagrionidae) Odonata
	4d	*Lestes* sp. (Lestidae) Odonata
	5	*Neoperla* sp. (Perlidae) Plecoptera
	6	*Oligotoma* sp. (Oligotomidae) Embioptera
414	7a	*Zonocerus elegans* (Pyrgomorphidae) Orthoptera
	7b	*Cyrtacanthacris tatarica* (Acrididae) Orthoptera
	7c	*Brachytrupes* sp. (Gryllidae) Orthoptera
	7d	*Terpnistria* sp. (Tettigoniidae) Orthoptera
	8	*Maransis* sp. (Diapheromeridae) Phasmatodea
415	9a	*Forficula* sp. (Forficulidae) Dermaptera
	9b	*Hemimerus* sp. (Hemimeridae) Dermaptera
	10	*Karoophasma botterkloofense* (Austrophasmatidae) Mantophasmatodea
	11a	*Aptera fusca* (Blaberidae) Blattodea
	11b	*Periplaneta americana* (Blattidae) Blattodea
	11c	*Bantua* sp. (Blaberidae) Blattodea
416	11d	*Odontotermes* sp. (Termitidae) Blattodea
	12a	*Omomantis zebrata* (Mantidae) Mantodea
	12b	*Oxypiloidea* sp. (Hymenopodidae) Mantodea
	13a	Psocidae Psocodea
	13b	*Haematopinus suis* (Haematopinidae) Psocodea
417	14a	*Platypleura capensis* (Cicadidae) Hemiptera
	14b	*Planococcus* sp. (Pseudococcidae) Hemiptera

Pg.	Fig.	Species (Family) Order
417	14c	*Glymmatophora* sp. (Reduviidae) Hemiptera
	14d	*Sphaerocoris annulus* (Scutelleridae) Hemiptera
	14e	*Leptocoris* sp. (Rhopalidae) Hemiptera
	14f	*Laccocoris* sp. (Naucoridae) Hemiptera
418	15a	Phlaeothripidae Thysanoptera
	15b	Phlaeothripidae Thysanoptera
	16a	*Taeniochauloides ochraceopennis* (Corydalidae) Megaloptera
	16b	*Taeniochauloides ochraceopennis* (Corydalidae) Megaloptera
	17a	*Nannoleon michaelseni* (Myrmeleontidae) Neuroptera
	17b	*Notiobiella turneri* (Hemerobiidae) Neuroptera
419	17c	*Palmipenna aeoleoptera* (Nemopteridae) Neuroptera
	18a	*Tenomerga leucophaea* (Cupedidae) Coleoptera
	18b	*Cypholoba notata* (Carabidae) Coleoptera
	18c	Dytiscidae Coleoptera
	18d	*Gymnopleurus ignitus* (Scarabaeidae) Coleoptera
	18e	*Zophosis amabilis* (Tenebrionidae) Coleoptera
	18f	*Lampetis amaurotica* (Buprestidae) Coleoptera
420	18g	*Trichodes aulicus* (Cleridae) Coleoptera
	18h	*Orphilaia vulsellata* (Brentidae) Coleoptera
	18i	*Ceroctis aliena* (Meloidae) Coleoptera
	18j	*Macrotoma* sp. (Cerambycidae) Coleoptera
	18k	Chrysomelidae Coleoptera
421	19	Stylopidae Strepsiptera
	20	*Bittacus* sp. (Bittacidae) Mecoptera
	21	*Echidnophaga* sp. (Pulicidae) Siphonaptera
422	22a	*Clogmia* sp. (Psychodidae) Diptera
	22b	*Oplodontha* sp. (Stratiomyidae) Diptera
	22c	*Condylostylus* sp. (Dolichopodidae) Diptera
	22d	*Mimegralla* sp. (Micropezidae) Diptera
	22e	*Lule* sp. (Platystomatidae) Diptera
423	23	Leptoceridae Trichoptera
	24a	*Kedestes callicles* (Hesperiidae) Lepidoptera
	24b	*Catacroptera cloanthe* (Nymphalidae) Lepidoptera
	24c	*Argema mimosae* (Saturniidae) Lepidoptera
	24d	*Argema mimosae* (Saturniidae) Lepidoptera
424	25a	*Athalia* sp. (Tenthredinidae) Hymenoptera
	25b	*Chrysis concinna* (Chrysididae) Hymenoptera
	25c	Leucospidae Hymenoptera
	25d	*Meganomia* sp. (Melittidae) Hymenoptera
	25e	*Camponotus* sp. (Formicidae) Hymenoptera

REFERENCES

Abbreviated references to chapters: pp. 426–430;
Complete references: pp. 430–437.

Quick chapter references

Chapter 1

Ahearn. 1970. The control of water loss in desert tenebrionid beetles.

Annecke & Moran. 1977. *Loxostege*.

Bateman & Fleming. 2009. There will be blood: autohaemorrhage behaviour as part of the defence repertoire of an insect.

Braack & Kryger. 2003. Insects and savanna heterogeneity. In: Du Toit, Rodgers & Biggs, eds. *The Kruger experience: ecology and maintenance of savanna heterogeneity.*

Chapman. 1969. *The insects: structure and function.*

Chown & Scholtz. 1993. Temperature regulation in the nocturnal melolonthine *Sparrmannia flava*.

Daly, Doyen & Purchell. 1998. *Introduction to insect biology and diversity.*

Gullan & Cranston. 2010. *The insects: an outline of entomology.*

Hein, Rasa & Ockenfels. 1996. Odour profile congruity …

Hickman, Roberts & Larson. 1997. *Integrated principles of zoology.*

Jones, Lawton & Shachak. 1994. Organisms as ecosystem engineers.

Meyer, Braack, Biggs & Ebersohn. 1999. Distribution and density of termite mounds …

Ruppert & Barnes. 1994. *Invertebrate zoology.*

Scholtz & Chown. 1995. Insect numbers in southern Africa.

Solomon, Berg, Martin & Villee. 1996. *Biology.*

Storer, Stebbins, Usinger & Nybakken. 1979. *General zoology.*

Triplehorn & Johnson. 2005. *Borror and DeLong's introduction to the study of insects.*

Chapter 2

Bohn, Picker, Klass & Colville. 2010. A jumping cockroach from South Africa …

Bond & Slingsby. 1984. Collapse of an ant–plant mutualism …

Davies. 1988. Leafhoppers (Homoptera: Cicadellidae) associated with the Restionaceae.

Downing & Gibbs Russell. 1981. Phytogeographic and biotic relationships of a savanna in southern Africa …

Eardley. 1987. Catalogue of Apoidea (Hymenoptera) in Africa south of the Sahara.

Gerling, Velthuis & Hefetz. 1989. Bionomics of the large carpenter bees of the genus *Xylocopa*.

Gess & Gess. 2010. *Pollen wasps and flowers in southern Africa.*

Gess & Gess. 2014. *Wasps and bees in southern Africa.*

Giliomee. 2003. Insect diversity in the Cape Floristic Region.

Goldblatt, Bernhardt & Manning. 1998. Pollination of petaloid geophytes by monkey beetles …

Heath & Claassens. 2003. Ant-association among southern African Lycaenidae.

Henning. 1983a. Biological groups within the Lycaenidae (Lepidoptera).

Henning. 1983b. Chemical communication between lycaenid larvae (Lepidoptera: Lycaenidae) and ants …

Johannsmeier. 2001. *Beekeeping in South Africa.*

Johnson. 1995. Observations of hawkmoth pollination in the South African orchid *Disa cooperi*.

Johnson. 1997. Insect pollination and floral mechanisms in South African species of *Satyrium* (Orchidaceae).

Johnson. 2005. Specialized pollination by spider-hunting wasps in the African orchid *Disa sankeyi*.

Johnson. 2010. The pollination niche and its role in the diversification and maintenance of the southern African flora.

Johnson & Bond. 1994. Red flowers and butterfly pollination in the fynbos of South Africa.

Johnson, Ellis & Dötterl. 2007. Specialization for pollination by beetles and wasps …

Johnson & Midgley. 1997. Fly pollination of *Gorteria diffusa* (Asteraceae) …

Johnson & Steiner. 1995. Long-proboscid fly pollination of two orchids in the Cape Drakensberg mountains, South Africa.

Johnson & Steiner. 1997. Long-tongued fly pollination and evolution of floral spur length in the *Disa draconis* complex (Orchidaceae).

Johnson & Steiner. 2003. Specialized pollination systems in southern Africa.

Kitching. 2003. Phylogeny of the death's head hawkmoths …

Manning. 2009. *Field guide to wild flowers of South Africa, Lesotho and Swaziland.*

Manning & Goldblatt. 1996. The *Prosoeca peringueyi* (Diptera: Nemestrinidae) pollination guild in southern Africa …

Manning & Goldblatt. 1997. The *Moegistorhynchus longirostris* (Diptera: Nemestrinidae) pollination guild …

Matenaar, Bröder, Bazelet & Hochkirch. 2014. Persisting in a windy habitat … adaptations of two endemic grasshopper species in the Cape region (South Africa).

Midgley. 1992. Why do some hopliinid beetles have large hind legs?

Midgley. 1993. Asteraceae – an evaluation of Hutchinson's beetle-daisy hypothesis.

Nalepa. 1984. Colony composition, protozoan transfer and some life history characteristics of the woodroach *Cryptocercus punctulatus* …

Nalepa & Bell. 1997. Postovulation parental investment and parental care in cockroaches.

Ollerton, Johnson, Cranmer & Kellie. 2003. The pollination ecology of an assemblage of grassland asclepiads in South Africa.

Pauw. 2006. Floral syndromes accurately predict pollination by a specialized oil-collecting bee …

Pierce, Braby, Heath, Lohman, Mathew, Rand & Travassos. 2002. The ecology and evolution of ant association in the Lycaenidae (Lepidoptera).

Shuttleworth & Johnson. 2008. Bimodal pollination by wasps and beetles in the African milkweed *Xysmalobium undulatum*.

Shuttleworth & Johnson. 2009a. A key role for floral scent in a wasp-pollination system in *Eucomis* (Hyacinthaceae).

Shuttleworth & Johnson. 2009b. Palp-faction: an African milkweed dismembers its wasp pollinators.

Shuttleworth & Johnson. 2009c. Specialized pollination in the African milkweed *Xysmalobium orbiculare* …

Shuttleworth & Johnson. 2009d. The importance of scent and nectar filters in a specialized wasp-pollination system.

Skaife. 1979. *African insect life.*

Steiner. 1998. Beetle pollination of peacock moraeas (Iridaceae) …

Switala, Sole & Scholtz. 2014. Phylogeny, historical biogeography and divergence time estimates of the genus *Colophon* …

Watmough 1973. Biology and behaviour of carpenter bees in southern Africa.

Watmough. 1983. Mortality, sex ratio and fecundity in natural populations of large carpenter bees (*Xylocopa* spp.).

Witt, Geertsema & Giliomee. 2004. The impact of an invasive ant, *Linepithema humile* …

Chapter 3

Ball. 2017. Functions of the hind wings in Nemopterinae ...

Cramer, Innes & Midgley. 2012. Hard evidence that heuweltjie earth mounds are relictual features produced by differential erosion.

Davis, Frolov & Scholtz. 2008. *The African dung beetle genera.*

Deschodt, Davis & Scholtz. 2016. A new monotypic genus, a species synonymy and nomenclatural corrections in the arid-adapted Canthonini ...

Dippenaar-Schoeman, González Reyes & Harvey. 2006. A check-list of the Solifugae (sun-spiders) of South Africa ...

Eberhard, Picker & Klass. 2011. Sympatry in Mantophasmatodea, with the description of a new species and phylogenetic considerations.

Gess & Gess. 2014. Wasps and bees in southern Africa.

Grimaldi & Engel. 2005. *Evolution of the insects.*

Holm & Dippenaar-Schoeman. 2010. *Goggo guide: the arthropods of southern Africa.*

Holter, Scholtz & Stenseng. 2009. Desert detritivory: nutritional ecology of a dung beetle (*Pachysoma glentoni*) subsisting on plant litter ...

Klass, Zompro, Kristensen & Adis. 2002. Mantophasmatodea: a new insect order with extant members in the Afrotropics.

McDonald & Van der Walt. 1992. Observations on the pollination of *Pelargonium tricolor* ...

Midgley. 1992. Why do some hopliinid beetles have large hind-legs?

Midgley. 1993. Asteraceae: an evaluation of Hutchinson's beetle-daisy hypothesis.

Midgley, Harris, Harington & Potts. 2012. Geochemical perspective on origins and consequences of heuweltjie formation in the southwestern Cape, South Africa.

Midgley, Harris, Hesse & Swift. 2002. Heuweltjie age and vegetation change based on δ13C and 14C analyses.

Moore & Picker. 1991. Heuweltjies (earth mounds) in the Clanwilliam district, Cape Province, South Africa: 4000-year-old termite nests.

Naskrecki & Bazelet. 2009. A species radiation among South African flightless spring katydids ...

Picker, Hoffman & Leverton. 2007. Density of *Microhodotermes viator* (Hodotermitidae) mounds ...

Picker & Midgley. 1996. Pollination by monkey beetles ...: flower and colour preferences.

Price & Louw. 1996. Resource manipulation through architectural modification of the host plant by a gall-forming weevil ...

Scholtz & Holm. 2014. *Insects of southern Africa.*

Scholtz, Harrison & Grebennikov. 2004. Dung beetle (*Scarabaeus* (*Pachysoma*)) biology and immature stages ...

Sole, Scholtz & Bastos. 2005. Phylogeography of the Namib Desert dung beetles *Scarabaeus* (*Pachysoma*) ...

Storer, Stebbins, Usinger & Nybakken. 1979. *General zoology.*

Terry & Whiting. 2005. Mantophasmatodea and phylogeny of the lower neopterous insects.

Van Staaden, Rieser, Ott, Pabst & Römer. 2003. Serial hearing organs in the atympanate grasshopper *Bullacris membracioides* ...

Vernon. 1999. Biogeography, endemism and diversity of animals in the Karoo. In: Dean & Milton, eds. *The Karoo: ecological patterns and processes*, pp. 57–85.

Chapter 4

Ahearn. 1970. The control of water loss in desert tenebrionid beetles.

Cloudsley-Thompson. 1977. The black desert beetle paradox.

Cloudsley-Thompson. 1979. Adaptive functions of the colors of desert animals.

Conti & Viglianisi. 2005. Ecology of the calling song of two Namibian armoured ground crickets ...

Coutchié & Crowe. 1979. Transport of water vapor by tenebrionid beetles.

Curtis. 1990. Behaviour and ecophysiology of the Namib dune ant, *Camponotus detritus* (Hymenoptera: Formicidae). In: Seely, ed. *Namib ecology* ...

Edney. 1971a. The body temperature of tenebrionid beetles in the Namib Desert ...

Edney. 1971b. Some aspects of water balance in tenebrionid beetles and a thysanuran ...

Endrödy-Younga. 1982. Dispersion and translocation of dune specialist tenebrionids in the Namib area.

Hamilton. 1971. Competition and thermoregulatory behavior of the Namib Desert tenebrionid ...

Hamilton. 1973. *Life's color code.*

Hamilton & Seely. 1976. Fog basking by the Namib Desert beetle ...

Hanrahan & Kirchner. 1994. Acoustic orientation and communication in desert tenebrionid beetles in sand dunes.

Henwood. 1975a. A field-tested thermoregulation model for two diurnal Namib Desert tenebrionid beetles.

Henwood. 1975b. Infrared transmittance as an alternative thermal strategy in the desert beetle ...

Holm & Edney. 1973. Daily activity of Namib Desert arthropods in relation to climate.

Holm & Kirsten. 1979. Pre-adaptation and speed mimicry among Namib Desert scarabaeids with orange elytra.

Holm & Scholtz. 1980. Structure and pattern of the Namib Desert dune ecosystem at Gobabeb.

Irish. 1992. The Hetrodinae (Orthoptera: Ensifera: Bradyporidae) of southern Africa: ...

Louw & Hamilton. 1972. Physiological and behavioural ecology of the ultra-psammophilous Namib Desert tenebrionid ...

Louw, Nicolson & Seely. 1986. Short Communication: respiration beneath desert sand: ...

Marsh. 1985. Thermal responses and temperature tolerance in a diurnal desert ant ...

Marsh. 1987a. Thermal responses and temperature tolerance of a desert ant-lion larva.

Marsh. 1987b. The foraging ecology of two Namib Desert harvester ant species.

McClain & Gerneke. 1990. Morphology of wax blooms on selected Namib Desert beetles ... In: Seely, ed. *Namib ecology* ...

McClain, Hanrahan & Gerneke. 1986. Extra-cuticular secretion on a Namib Desert tenebrionid ...

McClain, Praetorius, Hanrahan & Seely. 1984. Dynamics of the wax bloom of a seasonal Namib Desert tenebrionid ...

McClain, Seely, Hadley & Gray. 1985. Wax blooms in tenebrionid beetles of the Namib Desert: correlations with environment.

Nicolson. 1980. Water balance and osmoregulation in *Onymacris plana* ...

Nicolson. 1990. Water relations of the Namib tenebrionid beetles. In: Seely, ed. *Namib ecology* ...

Nørgaard & Dacke. 2010. Fog-basking behaviour and water collection efficiency in Namib Desert darkling beetles.

Prinsloo. 1990. Commentary on the insect fauna of the lower Kuiseb River, Namib Desert. In: Seely, ed. *Namib ecology* ...

Robertson. 2004. The Pyrrhocoroidea (Hemiptera–Heteroptera) of the Ethiopian region.

Robinson & Seely. 1980. Physical and biotic environments of the southern Namib dune ecosystem.

Seely, ed. 1990. *Namib ecology: 25 years of Namib research.* Transvaal Museum Monographs 7.

Seely & Hamilton. 1976. Fog catchment sand trenches constructed by tenebrionid beetles ...

Seely, Lewis, O' Brien & Suttle. 1983. Fog response of tenebrionid beetles in the Namib Desert.

Turner & Lombard. 1990. Body color and body temperature in white and black Namib Desert beetles.

Wharton. 1980. Colouration and diurnal activity patterns in some Namib Desert zophosini ...

Chapter 5

Annecke & Moran. 1977. Critical reviews of biological pest control in South Africa.

Bologna, Aloisi & Taglianti. 1990. Phoretic association of some African *Cyaneolytta* ...

Dean. 2006. Longevity and survival of colonies of *Messor capensis* ...

Dean & Yeaton. 1992. The importance of harvester ant *Messor capensis* nest mounds as germination sites ...

Dean & Yeaton. 1993a. The influence of harvester ant *Messor capensis* nest-mounds on the productivity and distribution of some plant species ...

Dean & Yeaton. 1993b. The effects of harvester ant *Messor capensis* nest-mounds on the physical and chemical properties of soils ...

Di Giulio, Aberlenc, Taglianti & Bologna. 2003. Definition and description of larval types of *Cyaneolytta* ...

Hölldobler & Wilson. 1990. *The ants.*

Skaife. 1979. *African insect life.*

Todd, Washington, Cheke & Kniveton. 2002. Brown locust outbreaks and climate variability in southern Africa.

Chapter 6

Bernays & Hamai. 1987. Head size and shape in relation to grass feeding in Acridoidea (Orthoptera).

Botha & Hewitt. 1978. Influence of diets containing green material on laboratory colonies of *Hodotermes mossambicus* ...

Cowling, Richardson & Pierce, eds. 2004. *Vegetation of southern Africa.*

Dadd. 1963. Feeding behaviour and nutrition in grasshoppers and locusts.

Heidecker & Leuthold. 1984. The organisation of collective foraging in the harvester termite ...

Hewitt, Nel & Conradie. 1969a. The role of chemicals in communication in the harvester termites ...

Hewitt, Nel & Conradie. 1969b. Preliminary studies on the control of caste formation in the harvester termite ...

Isely. 1944. Correlation between mandibular morphology and food specificity in grasshoppers.

Laker, Hewitt, Nel & Hunt. 1982a. Effects of the termite *Trinervitermes trinervoides* Sjöstedt on the organic carbon and nitrogen contents and particle size ...

Laker, Hewitt, Nel & Hunt. 1982b. Effects of the termite *Trinervitermes trinervoides* Sjöstedt on the pH ...

Leuthold, Bruinsma & Van Huis. 1976. Optical and pheromonal orientation and memory for homing distance ...

Nel & Hewitt. 1969. Effect of solar radiation on the harvester termite ...

Nel, Hewitt, Smith & Smit. 1969. The behaviour of the harvester termite ...

Nel & Malan. 1974. The distribution of the mounds of *Trinervitermes trinerviodes* [sic] ...

Smith & Yeaton. 1998. Disturbance by the mound-building termite ...

Steinke & Nel. 1989. Some effects of termitaria on veld in the Eastern Cape.

Steyn. 1954. *The pugnacious ant* (Anoplolepis custodiens *Smith*) ...

Swart, Richardson & Ferguson. 1999. Ecological factors affecting the feeding behaviour of pangolins ...

Turner. 1994. Ventilation and thermal constancy of a colony of a southern African termite ...

Willis, Skinner & Robertson. 1992. Abundance of ants and termites in the False Karoo ...

Wilson & Clark. 1977. Above ground predator defence in the harvester termite ...

Zumpt. 1965. *Myiasis in man and animals in the Old World.*

Chapter 7

Arnold. 1914. Nest-changing migrations of two species of ants.

Baker & Bry. 1987. Nutritional ecology of wool- and fur-feeding insects. In: Slansky & Rodriguez, eds. *Nutritional ecology of insects, mites, spiders, and related invertebrates.*

Barraclough. 2006. Bushels of bots: Africa's largest fly is getting a reprieve from extinction.

Bateman & Ferguson. 2004. Male mate choice in the Botswana armoured ground cricket ...

Bayliss & Fielding. 2002. Termitophagous foraging by *Pachycondyla analis* ...

Braack. 1986. Arthropods associated with carcasses in the northern Kruger National Park.

Braack. 1987. Community dynamics of carrion-attendant arthropods in tropical African woodland.

Braack & Kryger. 2003. Insects and savanna heterogeneity. In: Du Toit, Rodgers & Biggs, eds. *The Kruger experience: ecology and management of savanna heterogeneity.*

Brody, Palmer, Fox-Dobbs & Doak. 2010. Termites, vertebrate herbivores, and the fruiting success of *Acacia drepanolobium.*

Carrel, McCairel, Slagle, Doom, Brill & McCormick. 1993. Cantharidin production in a blister beetle.

Chaboo, Grobbelaar & Larsen. 2007. Faecal ecology in leaf beetles ... African arrow-poison beetles ...

Coaton. 1962. The origin and development of massive vegetated termite hills in Northern Rhodesia.

Corbara & Dejean. 2000. Adaptive behavioral flexibility of the ant *Pachycondyla analis* ...

Crewe, Peeters & Villet. 1984. Frequency distribution of worker sizes in *Megaponera foetens* (Fabricius).

Crossley. 1984. Fossil termite mounds associated with stone artifacts in Malawi ...

Crossley. 1986. Sedimentation by termites in the Malawi Rift Valley.

Dangerfield, McCarthy & Ellery. 1998. The mound-building termite *Macrotermes michaelseni* as an ecosystem engineer.

Davis, Frolov & Scholtz. 2008. *The African dung beetle genera.*

De Bruyn & Conacher. 1990. The role of termites and ants in soil modification: a review.

Fletcher & Crewe. 1981. Nest structure and thermoregulation in the stingless bee ...

Forgie, Grebennikov & Scholtz. 2002. Revision of *Sceliages* Westwood, a millipede-eating genus ...

Glover, Trump & Wateridge. 1964. Termitaria and vegetation patterns on the Loita plains of Kenya.

Gullan & Cranston. 2010. *The insects: an outline of entomology.*

Haack & Slansky. 1987. Nutritional ecology of wood-feeding insects. In: Slansky & Rodriguez, eds. *Nutritional ecology of insects* ...

Hölldobler & Wilson. 1990. *The ants.*

Jones. 1990. Termites, soil fertility and carbon cycling in dry tropical Africa: ...

Korb & Linsenmair. 2000. Ventilation of termite mounds ...

Kroon. 1999. *Lepidoptera of southern Africa: host-plants and other associations* ...

Lee & Wood. 1971. *Termites and soils.*

Levick, Asner, Kennedy-Bowdoin & Knapp. 2010. The spatial extent of termite influences on herbivore browsing in an African savanna.

Longhurst, Baker & Howse. 1979. Termite predation by *Megaponera foetens* ...

Longhurst & Howse. 1978. The use of kairomones by *Megaponera foetens* ...

Loveridge & Moe. 2004. Termitaria as browsing hotspots for African megaherbivores ...

Madder, Horak & Stoltsz. 2010. *Ticks: tick identification.*

Moritz & Crewe. 1988. Air ventilation in nests of two African stingless bees ...

Mviha, Holt, Green & Mitchell. 2003. The ecology of the armoured bush cricket ...

Nelson & Greeff. 2009. Male pollinator fig wasps ...

Nicolson, Nepi & Pacini. 2007. *Nectaries and nectar.*

Okullo & Moe. 2012. Termite activity, not grazing ...

Palmer. 2003. Spatial habitat ... an African acacia ant guild.

Palmer & Brody. 2007. Mutualism as reciprocal exploitation …

Rasa. 1990. Evidence for subsociality and division of labor in a desert tenebrionid beetle …

Rasa. 1994. Behavioural adaptations to moisture as an environmental constraint …

Rasa. 1995. Ecological factors influencing burrow location, group size and mortality …

Rasa. 1996. Interspecific association in desert tenebrionid beetles …

Rasa. 1998. Biparental investment and reproductive success …

Scholes & Walker. 2004. *An African savanna: synthesis of the Nylsvley study.*

Skaife. 1979. *African insect life.*

Tinley. 1977. *Framework of the Gorongosa ecosystem.*

Trapnell, Friend, Chamberlain & Birch. 1976. The effects of fire and termites on a Zambian woodland soil.

Turner. 2000. Architecture and morphogenesis in the mound of *Macrotermes michaelseni* …

Turner. 2001. On the mound of *Macrotermes michaelseni* …

Veldtman. 2005. *The ecology of southern African wild silk moths …*

Villet. 1990. Division of labour in the Matabele ant *Megaponera foetens* …

Waller & La Fage. 1987. *Nutritional ecology of termites.*

Watson. 1967. A termite mound in an Iron Age burial ground in Rhodesia.

Weir. 1973. Air flow, evaporation and mineral accumulation in mounds of *Macrotermes subhyalinus* …

Wood & Sands. 1978. The role of termites in ecosystems.

Young, Stubblefield & Isbell. 1996. Ants on swollen-thorn acacias …

Yusuf, Gordon, Crewe & Pirk. 2014. Prey choice and raiding behaviour of the ponerine ant *Pachycondyla analis* …

Zumpt. 1965. *Myiasis in man and animals in the Old World.*

Chapter 8

Downing & Gibbs Russell. 1981. Phytogeographic and biotic relationships of a savanna in southern Africa.

Hölldobler & Wilson. 1990. *The ants.*

Jupp. 1996. *Mosquitoes of southern Africa.*

Kappmeier, Nevill & Bagnall. 1998. Review of tsetse flies and trypanosomosis in South Africa.

Chapter 9

Botes, Johnson & Cowling. 2009. The birds and the bees: using selective exclusion to identify effective pollinators of African tree aloes.

Donaldson & Bösenberg. 1995. Life history and host range of the leopard magpie moth …

Donaldson, Nänni & Bösenberg. 1995. The role of insects in the pollination of *Encephalartos cycadifolius.*

Edge & Pringle. 1996. Notes on the natural history of the Brenton blue …

Giddy. 1974. *Cycads of South Africa.*

Sanborn, Villet & Phillips. 2004. Endothermy in African platypleurine cicadas.

Smith, Crouch & Figueiredo. 2017. *Field guide to succulents in southern Africa.*

Staude. 1996. Observations on lek behaviour and the description of male scent disseminating structures …

Staude. 2001. A revision of the genus *Callioratis* …

Staude & Sihvonen. 2014. Revision of the African geometrid genus *Zerenopsis* …

Van Wyk & Smith 2001. *Regions of floristic endemism in southern Africa …*

Chapter 10

Brusca & Brusca. 2003. *Invertebrates.*

Duke & Taylor. 1964. A note on *Leto venus* …

Forthman & Weirauch. 2012. Toxic associations: a review of the predatory behaviors of millipede assassin bugs …

Giliomee. 1985. A millipede assassinated.

Griffiths, Day & Picker. 2015. *Freshwater life.*

Grimaldi & Engel. 2005. *Evolution of the insects.*

Herbert. 2010. *The introduced terrestrial Mollusca of South Africa.*

Hickman, Roberts & Larson. 1996. *Integrated principles of zoology.*

Holm & Dippenaar-Schoeman. 2010. *Goggo guide …*

Hörnschemeyer. 2010. *Cupedidae.* http://tolweb.org/tree?group=Cupedidae

Hörnschemeyer. 2011. *Archostemata.* http://tolweb.org/tree?group=Archostemata

Janse. 1945. On the history and life-history of *Leto venus* …

Mlambo, Sole & Scholtz. 2015. A molecular phylogeny of the African Scarabaeinae (Coleoptera: Scarabaeidae). *Arthropod Systematics and Phylogeny* 73.

Myles. 1986. Reproductive soldiers in the Termopsidae.

Nxele *et al.* 2015. Studying earthworms (Annelida: Oligochaeta) in South Africa.

Picker, Griffiths & Weaving. 2002. *Field guide to insects of South Africa.*

Rehn & Rehn. 1935. A study of the genus *Hemimerus* …

Ruppert & Barnes. 1994. *Invertebrate zoology.*

Scholtz & Holm. 2014. *Insects of southern Africa.*

Skaife. 1979. *African insect life.*

Storer, Stebbins, Usinger & Nybakken. 1979. *General zoology.*

Tarboton & Tarboton. 2015. *A guide to the dragonflies and damselflies of South Africa.*

Van Wyk & Van Wyk 2013. *Field Guide to Trees of South Africa.*

Chapter 11

Bendele. 1986. Mechanosensory cues control chasing behaviour of whirligig beetles …

Benfield. 1972. A defensive secretion of *Dineutus discolor* …

Burrows & Picker. 2010. Jumping mechanisms and performance of pygmy mole crickets …

Chapman. 1969. *The insects: structure and function.*

Clausnitzer *et al.* 2012. Focus on African freshwaters: hotspots of dragonfly diversity and conservation concern.

Jupp. 1996. *Mosquitoes of southern Africa: Culicinae and Toxorhynchitinae.*

Kovac & Maschwitz. 1990. Secretion-grooming in aquatic beetles (Hydradephaga) …

Kovac & Maschwitz. 1991. The function of the metathoracic scent gland in corixid bugs …

Lin & Strausfeld. 2012. Visual inputs to the mushroom body calyces of the whirligig beetle …

Madsen. 2012. Submersion respiration in small diving beetles (Dytiscidae).

Romey. 1995. Position preferences within groups: do whirligigs select positions …

Samways. 2008. *Dragonflies and damselflies of South Africa.*

Suhling, Martens & Marais. 2009. How to enter a desert: patterns of Odonata colonisation …

Suhling, Müller & Martens. 2014. *The dragonfly larvae of Namibia (Odonata).*

Tarboton & Tarboton. 2015. *A guide to the dragonflies and damselflies of South Africa.*

Vulinec & Miller. 1989. Aggregation and predator avoidance in whirligig beetles …

Chapter 12

Allegrucci, Trewick, Fortunato, Carchini & Sbordoni. 2010. Cave crickets and cave weta …

Braack. 1989. Arthropod inhabitants of a tropical cave 'island' environment provisioned by bats.

Carchini, Di Russo & Rampini. 1991. Observations of the biology of *Spelaeiacris tabulae* …

Mansell. 2017. Biology of Nemopteridae and Myrmeleontidae.

Rampini, Di Russo & Carchini. 2010. A second species of cave Macropathinae for Africa …

Skaife. 1979. *African insect life.*

Chapter 13

Andersen & Cheng. 2004. The marine insect *Halobates* (Heteroptera: Gerridae).

Branch & Branch. 1981. *The living shores of southern Africa*.

Gess & Gess. 1981. The insect mariner. *The Naturalist* 25.

Hesse. 1934. Contributions to a knowledge of S. African Marine Clunionine-Chironomids.

Murray. 1958. Ecology of the louse *Lepidophthirus macrorhini* Enderlein 1904 on the elephant seal …

Pearson & Vogler. 2001. *Tiger beetles: the evolution, ecology, and diversity of the cicindelids*.

Stenton-Dozey & Griffiths. 1980. Growth, consumption and respiration by larvae of the kelp-fly.

Van Noort *et al*. 2014. Systematics and biology of the aberrant intertidal parasitoid wasp …

Chapter 14

Aiello. 1979. Life history and behaviour of the case-bearer *Phereoeca allutella* (Lepidoptera: Tineidae).

Annecke & Moran. 1982. *Insects and mites of cultivated plants* …

Barnes. 1975. The life history of *Chrysopa zastrowi* …

Brettschneider, Chimimba, Scholtz, Bastos & Bateman 2009. The tusked king cricket (*Libanasidus vittatus* (Kirby, 1899) Anostostomatidae) from South Africa …

Edmunds & Brunner. 1999. *Ethology of defenses against predators*.

Gess & Gess. 2014. *Wasps and bees in southern Africa*.

Holm & Dippenaar-Schoeman. 2010. *Goggo guide: the arthropods of southern Africa*.

Kamimura. 2007. Twin intromittent organs of *Drosophila* for traumatic insemination.

Keeping. 1990. *Ethology* 85 (1).

Keeping. 1990. *Journal of Insect Behavior* 3 (1).

Keeping. 1991. *Journal of the Entomological Society of Southern Africa* 54 (1).

Keeping. 1992. *Behavioural Ecology and Sociobiology* 31 (3).

Keeping. 2000. *Insectes Sociaux* 47 (2).

Keeping. 2002. *Journal of Insect Physiology* 48 (9).

Keeping & Crewe. 1983. *Journal of the Entomological Society of Southern Africa* 46 (2).

Keeping, Lipschitz & Crewe. 1986. *Journal of Chemical Ecology* 12 (3).

Kynaston, McErlain-Ward & Mill. 1994. Courtship, mating behaviour and sexual cannibalism in the praying mantis, *Sphodromantis lineola*.

Lutz. 1941. *A lot of insects*.

Prinsloo & Kelly. 2009. The tetrastichine wasps … associated with galls on *Erythrina* species …

Prinsloo & Uys. 2015. *Insects of cultivated plants and natural pastures in southern Africa*.

Skaife. 1979. *African insect life*.

Svenson & Whiting. 2004. Phylogeny of Mantodea …

Complete References

Ahearn, G.A. 1970. The control of water loss in desert tenebrionid beetles. *Journal of Experimental Biology*, 53, 573–595.

Aiello, A. 1979. Life history and behavior of the case-bearer *Phereoeca allutella* (Lepidoptera: Tineidae). *Psyche: A Journal of Entomology*, 86 (2–3), 125–136.

Allegrucci, G., Trewick, S.A., Fortunato, A., Carchini, G. & Sbordoni, V. 2010. Cave crickets and cave weta (Orthoptera, Rhaphidophoridae) from the southern end of the world: a molecular phylogeny test of biogeographical hypotheses. *Journal of Orthoptera Research*, 19 (1), 121–130.

Andersen, N.M. & Cheng, L. 2004. The marine insect *Halobates* (Heteroptera: Gerridae): Biology, adaptations, distribution and phylogeny. *Oceanography and Marine Biology*, 42, 119–180.

Annecke, D.P. & Moran, V.C. 1977. Critical reviews of biological pest control in South Africa. 1. The Karoo caterpillar, *Loxostege frustalis* Zeller (Lepidoptera: Pyralidae). *Journal of the Entomological Society of Southern Africa*, 40 (2), 127–145.

Annecke, D.P. & Moran, V.C. 1982. *Insects and mites of cultivated plants in South Africa*. Durban, South Africa: Butterworths.

Arnold, G. 1914. Nest-changing migrations of two species of ants. *Proceedings of the Rhodesia Scientific Association*, 13, 25–32.

Baker, J.E. & Bry, R.E. 1987. Nutritional ecology of wool- and fur-feeding insects. In: F.J. Slansky & J.G. Rodriguez, eds. *Nutritional ecology of insects, mites, spiders, and related invertebrates*. New York, USA: John Wiley & Sons, 815–836.

Ball, J.A. 2017. Functions of the hind wings in Nemopterinae. *In litt*.

Barnes, B.N. 1975. The life history of *Chrysopa zastrowi* Esb.-Pet. (Neuroptera: Chrysopidae). *Journal of the Entomological Society of Southern Africa*, 38 (1), 47–53.

Barraclough, D.A. 2006. Bushels of bots: Africa's largest fly is getting a reprieve from extinction. *Natural History*, 115 (5), 8–21.

Bateman, P.W. & Ferguson, J.W.H. 2004. Male mate choice in the Botswana armoured ground cricket *Acanthoplus discoidalis* (Orthoptera: Tettigoniidae; Hetrodinae). Can, and how, do males judge female mating history? *Journal of Zoology*, 262 (3), 305–309.

Bateman, P.W. & Fleming, P.A. 2009. There will be blood: autohaemorrhage behaviour as part of the defence repertoire of an insect. *Journal of Zoology*, 278 (4), 342–348.

Bayliss, J.A. & Fielding, A. 2002. Termitophagous foraging by *Pachycondyla analis* (Formicidae, Ponerinae) in a Tanzanian coastal dry forest. *Sociobiology*, 39 (1), 103–122.

Bendele, H. 1986. Mechanosensory cues control chasing behaviour of whirligig beetles (Coleoptera, Gyrinidae). *Journal of Comparative Physiology A*, 158 (3), 405–411.

Benfield, E.F. 1972. A defensive secretion of *Dineutes discolor* (Coleoptera: Gyrinidae). *Annals of the Entomological Society of America*, 65 (6), 1324–1327.

Bernays, E.A. & Hamai, J. 1987. Head size and shape in relation to grass feeding in Acridoidea (Orthoptera). *International Journal of Insect Morphology and Embryology*, 16 (5–6), 323–330.

Bohn, H., Picker, M., Klass, K. & Colville, J.F. 2010. A jumping cockroach from South Africa, *Saltoblattella montistabularis*, gen. nov., spc. nov (Blattodea: Blattellidae). *Arthropod Systematics and Phylogeny*, 68 (1), 53–69.

Bologna, M.A. 2018. Meloidae of southern Africa. *In litt*.

Bologna, M.A., Aloisi, G. & Taglianti, A.V. 1990. Phoretic association of some African *Cyaneolytta* Péringuey 1909 with carabids, and morphology of first instar larvae in Meloini (Coleoptera Meloidae). *Tropical Zoology*, 3 (2), 159–180.

Bond, W. & Slingsby, P. 1984. Collapse of an ant-plant mutalism: the Argentine ant (*Iridomyrmex humilis*) and myrmecochorous Proteaceae. *Ecology*, 65 (4), 1031–1037.

Botes, C., Johnson, S.D. & Cowling, R.M. 2009. The birds and the bees: using selective exclusion to identify effective pollinators of African tree aloes. *International Journal of Plant Sciences*, 170 (2), 151–156.

Botha, T.C. & Hewitt, P.H. 1978. Influence of diets containing green material on laboratory colonies of *Hodotermes mossambicus* (Hagen). *Phytophylactica*, 10, 93–97.

Braack, L.E.O. 1986. Arthropods associated with carcasses in the northern Kruger National Park. *South African Journal of Wildlife Research*, 16 (3), 402–409.

Braack, L.E.O. 1987. Community dynamics of carrion-attendant arthropods in tropical African woodland. *Oecologia*, 72 (3), 402–409.

Braack, L.E.O. 1989. Arthropod inhabitants of a tropical cave 'island' environment provisioned by bats. *Biological Conservation*, 48 (2), 77–84.

Braack, L.E.O. & Kryger, P. 2003. Insects and savanna heterogeneity. In: J.T. du Toit, K.H. Rodgers & H.C. Biggs, eds. *The Kruger experience: ecology and management of savanna heterogeneity*. Washington, USA: Island Press.

Branch, G., Branch, M. & Bannister, A. 1981. *The living shores of southern Africa*. Cape Town, South Africa: Struik Publishers.

Brettschneider, H., Chimimba, C., Scholtz, C., Bastos, A. & Bateman, P. 2009. The tusked king cricket, *Libanasidus vittatus* (Kirby, 1899) (Anostostomatidae), from South Africa: morphological and molecular evidence suggest two cryptic species. *Insect Systematics & Evolution*, 40 (1), 85–103.

Brody, A.K., Palmer, T.M., Fox-Dobbs, K. & Doak, D.F. 2010. Termites, vertebrate herbivores, and the fruiting success of *Acacia drepanolobium*. *Ecology*, 91 (2), 399–407.

Brusca, R.C. & Brusca, G.J. 2003. *Invertebrates*. Sunderland, Massachusetts, USA: Sinauer Associates.

Burrows, M. & Picker, M.D. 2010. Jumping mechanisms and performance of pygmy mole crickets (Orthoptera, Tridactylidae). *Journal of Experimental Biology*, 213 (14), 2386–2398.

Carchini, G., Di Russo, C. & Rampini, M. 1991. Observations on the biology of *Spelaeiacris tabulae* Peringuey (Orthoptera, Rhaphidophoridae), from the Wynberg cave (Capetown, South Africa). *International Journal of Speleology*, 20, 47–55.

Carrel, J.E., McCairel, M.H., Slagle, A.J., Doom, J.P., Brill, J. & McCormick, J.P. 1993. Cantharidin production in a blister beetle. *Experientia*, 49 (2), 171–174.

Chaboo, C.S., Grobbelaar, E. & Larsen, A. 2007. Fecal ecology in leaf beetles: novel records in the African arrow-poison beetles, *Diamphidia* Gerstaecker and *Polyclada* Chevrolat (Chrysomelidae: Galerucinae). *The Coleopterists Bulletin*, 61, 297–309.

Chapman, R.F. 1969. *The insects: structure and function*. London, UK: English Universities Press.

Chown, S.L. & Scholtz, C.H. 1993. Temperature regulation in the nocturnal melolonthine *Sparrmannia flava*. *Journal of Thermal Biology*, 18 (1), 25–33. https://doi.org/10.1016/0306-4565(93)90038-U

Clausnitzer, V., Dijkstra, K.B., Koch, R., Boudot, J., Darwall, W.R.T., Kipping, J., Samraoui, B., Samways, M.J., Simaika, J.P. & Suhling, F. 2012. Focus on African freshwaters: hotspot of dragonfly diversity and conservation concern. *Frontiers in Ecology and the Environment*, 10 (3).

Cloudsley-Thompson, J.L. 1977. The black-beetle paradox. *Entomologist's Monthly Magazine*, 113, 19–22.

Cloudsley-Thompson, J.L. 1979. Adaptive functions of the colours of desert animals. *Journal of Arid Environments*, 2, 95–104.

Coaton, W.G.H. 1962. The origin and development of massive vegetated termite hills in Northern Rhodesia. *African Wildlife*, 15, 159–166.

Conti, E. & Viglianisi, F.M. 2005. Ecology of the calling song of two Namibian armoured ground crickets, *Acanthoplus longipes* and *Acanthoproctus diadematus* (Orthoptera Tettigoniidae Hetrodinae). *Ethology, Ecology and Evolution*, 3, 261–269.

Corbara, B. & Dejean, A. 2000. Adaptive behavioral flexibility of the ant *Pachycondyla analis* (*Megaponera foetens*) (Formicidae: Ponerinae) during prey capture. *Sociobiology*, 36 (3), 465–483.

Coutchié, P.A. & Crowe, J.H. 1979. Transport of water vapor by tenebrionid beetles. *Physiological Zoology*, 52 (1), 67–87.

Cowling, R.M., Richardson, D.M. & Pierce, S.M. 2004. *Vegetation of southern Africa*. Cambridge, UK: Cambridge University Press.

Cramer, M.D., Innes, S.N. & Midgley, J. 2012. Hard evidence that heuweltjie earth mounds are relictual features produced by differential erosion. *Palaeogeography, Palaeoclimatology, Palaeoecology*, 350–352, 189–197.

Crewe, R.M., Peeters, C.P. & Villet, M. 1984. Frequency distribution of worker sizes in *Megaponera foetens* (Fabricius). *South African Journal of Zoology*, 19 (3), 247–248.

Crossley, R. 1984. Fossil termite mounds associated with stone artifacts in Malawi, Central Africa. *Palaeoecology of Africa and of the Surrounding Islands and Antarctica*, 16, 397–401.

Crossley, R. 1986. Sedimentation by termites in the Malawi Rift Valley. In: L.E. Frostick, R.W. Renaut, I. Reid & J.J. Tiercelin, eds. *Sedimentation in the African rifts*. Oxford, UK: Blackwell Scientific Publications, 191–199.

Curtis, B.A. 1990. Behaviour and ecophysiology of the Namib dune ant, *Camponotus detritus* (Hymenoptera: Formicidae). In: M.K. Seely, ed. *Namib ecology: 25 years of Namib research*. Pretoria, South Africa: Transvaal Museum Monograph No. 7. Transvaal Museum, 129–133.

Dadd, R. 1963. Feeding behaviour and nutrition in grasshoppers and locusts. *Advances in Insect Physiology*, 1, 47–109.

Daly, H.V., Doyen, J.T. & Purcell, A.H. 1998. *Introduction to insect biology and diversity*. 2nd ed. USA: Oxford University Press.

Dangerfield, J.M., McCarthy, T.S. & Ellery, W.N. 1998. The mound-building termite *Macrotermes michaelseni* as an ecosystem engineer. *Journal of Tropical Ecology*, 14 (4), 507–520.

Davies, D.M. 1988. Leafhoppers (Homoptera: Cicadellidae) associated with the Restionaceae. *Journal of the Entomological Society of Southern Africa*, 51 (1), 31–64.

Davis, A.L.V., Frolov, A.V. & Scholtz, C.H. 2008. *The African dung beetle genera*. Pretoria, South Africa: Protea Book House.

De Bruyn, L.L. & Conacher, A.J. 1990. The role of termites and ants in soil modification: a review. *Australian Journal of Soil Research*, 28 (1).

Dean, W.R.J. 2006. Longevity and survival of colonies of *Messor capensis* (Formicidae: Myrmicinae) in the Karoo, South Africa. *African Entomology*, 14 (2), 381–383.

Dean, W.R.J. & Yeaton, R.I. 1992. The importance of harvester ant *Messor capensis* nest-mounds as germination sites in the southern Karoo, South Africa. *African Journal of Ecology*, 30 (4).

Dean, W.R.J. & Yeaton, R.I. 1993a. The influence of harvester ant *Messor capensis* nest-mounds on the productivity and distribution of some plant species in the southern Karoo, South Africa. *Vegetation*, 106, 21–35.

Dean, W.R.J. & Yeaton, R.I. 1993b. The effects of harvester ant *Messor* capensis nest-mounds on the physical and chemical properties of soils in the southern Karoo, South Africa. *Journal of Arid Environments*, 25 (2), 249–260.

Deschodt, C.M., Davis, A.L. & Scholtz, C.H. 2016. A new monotypic genus, a species synonymy and nomenclatural corrections in the arid-adapted *Canthonini* (Scarabaeidae, Scarabaeinae) from the Succulent Karoo Biome of south-western Africa. *Zootaxa*, 4147 (4), 490–500.

Di Giulio, A., Aberlenc, H.P., Taglianti, A.V. & Bologna, M.A. 2003. Definition and description of larval types of *Cyaneolytta* (Coleoptera Meloidae) and new records of their phoretic association with *Carabidae* (Coleoptera). *Tropical Zoology*, 16 (2), 165–187.

Dippenaar-Schoeman, A.S., González Reyes, A.X. & Harvey, M.S. 2006. A check-list of the Solifugae (sun-spiders) of South Africa (Arachnida: Solifugae). *African Plant Protection*, 12, 70–92.

Donaldson, J.S. & Bösenberg, J.D. 1995. Life history and host range of the leopard magpie moth, *Zerenopsis leopardina* Felder (Lepidoptera: Geometridae). *African Entomology*, 3 (2), 103–110.

Donaldson, J.S., Nänni, I. & Bösenberg, J.D. 1995. The role of insects in the pollination of *Encephalartos cycadifolius*. *Proceedings of the Third International Conference on Cycad Biology*. Stellenbosch, South Africa: Cycad Society of South Africa, 423–434.

Downing, B.H. & Gibbs Russell, G.E. 1981. Phytogeographic and biotic relationships of a savanna in southern Africa: analysis of an angiosperm checklist from Acacia woodland in Zululand. *Journal of South African Botany*, 47, 721–742.

Duke, A.J. & Taylor, J.S. 1964. A note on *Leto venus* Stoll (Lepidoptera: Hepialidae). *Entomologist's Record*, 76, 189–193.

Eardley, C.D. 1987. Catalogue of Apoidea (Hymenoptera) in Africa south of the Sahara. Part 1. The genus *Xylocopa* Latreille (Anthophoridae). *Entomology Memoir*, 70, 1–20.

Eberhard, M.J.B., Picker, M.D. & Klass, K. 2011. Sympatry in Mantophasmatodea, with the description of a new species and phylogenetic considerations. *Organisms Diversity & Evolution*, 11, 43–59.

Edge, D.A. & Pringle, E.L. 1996. Notes on the natural history of the Brenton blue, *Orachrysops niobe* (Trimen) (Lepiodoptera: Lycaeniidae). *Metamorphosis*, 7 (3), 109–121.

Edmunds, M. & Brunner, D. 1999. Ethology of defenses against predators. In: F.R. Prete, H. Wells, P.H. Wells & L.E. Hurd, eds. *The praying mantids*. Baltimore, USA: Johns Hopkins University Press, 276–299.

Edney, E.B. 1971a. The body temperature of tenebrionid beetles in the Namib Desert of southern Africa. *Journal of Experimental Biology*, 55, 253–272.

Edney, E.B. 1971b. Some aspects of water balance in tenebrionid beetles and a thysanuran from the Namib Desert of southern Africa. *Physiological Zoology*, 44, 61–76.

Endrödy-Younga, S. 1982. Dispersion and translocation of dune specialist tenebrionids in the Namib area. *Cimbebasia A*, 5, 257–271.

Fletcher, D.J.C. & Crewe, R.M. 1981. Nest structure and thermoregulation in the stingless bee *Trigona (Plebeina) denoiti* Vachal (Hymenoptera: Apidae). *Journal of the Entomological Society of Southern Africa*, 44 (2), 183–196.

Forgie, S.A., Grebennikov, V.V. & Scholtz, C.H. 2002. Revision of *Sceliages* Westwood, a millipede-eating genus of southern African dung beetles (Coleoptera: Scarabaeidae). *Invertebrate Systematics*, 16 (6).

Forthman, M. & Weirauch, C. 2012. Toxic associations: a review of the predatory behaviors of millipede assassin bugs (Hemiptera: Reduviidae: Ectrichodiinae). *European Journal of Entomology*, 109, 147–153.

Gerling, D., Velthuis, H.H.W. & Hefetz, A. 1989. Bionomics of the large carpenter bees of the genus *Xylocopa*. *Annual Review of Entomology*, 34, 163–190.

Gess, F.W. & Gess, S.K. 1981. The insect mariner: *Holobates*. *The Naturalist*, 25 (1), 25–26.

Gess, S.K. & Gess, F.W. 2010. Pollen wasps and flowers in southern Africa. In: *SANBI Biodiversity Series*. Pretoria, South Africa: South African National Biodiversity Institute.

Gess, S.K. & Gess, F.W. 2014. Wasps and bees in southern Africa. In: *SANBI Biodiversity Series*. Pretoria, South Africa: South African National Biodiversity Institute.

Giddy, C. 1974. *Cycads of South Africa*. 1st ed. Johannesburg, South Africa: Purnell & Sons.

Giliomee, J.H. 1985. A millipede assassinated. *African Wildlife*, 39 (4), 149.

Giliomee, J.H. 2003. Insect diversity in the Cape Floristic Region. *African Journal of Ecology*, 41 (3).

Glover, P., Trump, E.C. & Wateridge, L.E.D. 1964. Termitaria and vegetation patterns on the Loita plains of Kenya. *Journal of Ecology*, 52 (2), 367–377.

Goldblatt, P., Bernhardt, P. & Manning, J.C. 1998. Pollination of petaloid geophytes by monkey beetles (Scarabaeidae: Rutelinae: *Hopliini*) in southern Africa. *Annals of the Missouri Botanical Garden*, 85 (2), 215–230.

Griffiths, C., Day, J.A. & Picker, M. 2015. *Freshwater life: a field guide to the plants and animals of southern Africa*. Cape Town, South Africa: Struik Nature.

Grimaldi, D. & Engel, S.M. 2005. *Evolution of the insects. In: Cambridge Evolution Series)*. New York, USA: Cambridge University Press.

Gullan, P.J. & Cranston, P.S. 2010. *The insects: an outline of entomology*. 4th ed. Oxford, England: Wiley-Blackwell.

Haack, R.A. & Slansky, J.F. 1987. Nutritional ecology of wood-feeding Coleoptera, Lepidoptera and Hymenoptera. In: J.F. Slansky & J.G. Rodriguez, eds. *Nutritional ecology of insects, mites and spiders and related invertebrates*. New York, USA: John Wiley & Sons, 449–486.

Hamilton, W.J. 1971. Competition and thermoregulatory behaviour of the Namib Desert tenebrionid beetle genus *Cardiosis*. *Ecology*, 52 (5).

Hamilton, W.J. 1973. *Life's color code*. New York, USA: McGraw-Hill.

Hamilton, W.J. & Seely, M.K. 1976. Fog basking by the Namib Desert beetle, *Onymacris unguicularis*. *Nature*, 262, 284–285.

Hanrahan, S.A. & Kirchner, W.H. 1994. Acoustic orientation and communication in desert tenebrionid beetles in sand dunes. *Ethology*, 97 (1–2), 26–32.

Heath, A. & Claassens, A.J.M. 2003. Ant-association among southern African Lycaenidae. *Journal of the Lepidopterist's Society*, 57 (1), 1–16.

Heidecker, J.L. & Leuthold, R.H. 1984. The organisation of collective foraging in the harvester termite *Hodotermes mossambicus* (Isoptera). *Behavioural Ecology and Sociobiology*, 14, 195–202.

Hein, E., Rasa, O.A.E. & Ockenfels, P. 1996. Odour profile congruity in two closely related desert tenebrionid beetles: homology as the basis for a cleptoparasitic relationship? *Chemoecology*, 7, 156–161.

Henning, S.F. 1983a. Biological groups within the Lycaenidae (Lepidoptera). *Journal of the Entomological Society of Southern Africa*, 46 (1), 65–85.

Henning, S.F. 1983b. Chemical communication between lycaenid larvae (Lepidoptera: Lycaenidae) and ants (Hymenoptera: Formicidae). *Journal of the Entomological Society of Southern Africa*, 46 (2), 341–366.

Henwood, K. 1975a. A field-tested thermoregulation model for two diurnal Namib Desert tenebrionid beetles. *Ecology*, 56 (6), 1329–1342.

Henwood, K. 1975b. Infrared transmittance as an alternative thermal strategy in the desert beetle *Onymacris plana*. *Science*, 189 (4207), 993–994.

Herbert, D.G. 2010. *The introduced terrestrial Mollusca of South Africa*. Pretoria, South Africa: South African National Biodiversity Institute.

Hesse, A.J. 1934. Contributions to a knowledge of South African marine clunionine-chironomids. *Transactions of the Royal Entomological Society of London*, 82 (1), 27–40.

Hewitt, P.H., Nel, J.J.C. & Conradie, S. 1969a. The role of chemicals in communication in the harvester termites *Hodotermes mossambicus* (Hagen) and *Trinervitermes trinervoides* (Sjöstedt). *Insectes Sociaux*, 16, 79–86.

Hewitt, P.H., Nel, J.J.C. & Conradie, S. 1969b. Preliminary studies on the control of caste formation in the harvester termite *Hodotermes mossambicus* (Hagen). *Insectes Sociaux*, 16, 159–172.

Hickman, C.P., Roberts, L.S. & Larson, A. 1997. *Integrated principles of zoology*. 10th ed. Boston, USA: McGraw-Hill.

Hölldobler, B. & Wilson, E.O. 1990. *The ants*. Cambridge, USA: Harvard University Press.

Holm, E. & Dippenaar-Schoeman, A.S. 2010. *Goggo guide: the arthropods of southern Africa*. Pretoria, South Africa: LAPA Publishers.

Holm, E. & Edney, E.B. 1973. Daily activity of Namib Desert arthropods in relation to climate. *Ecology*, 54 (1), 45–56.

Holm, E. & Kirsten, J.F. 1979. Pre-adaptation and speed mimicry among Namib Desert scarabaeids with orange elytra. *Journal of Arid Environments*, 2 (3), 263–271.

Holm, E. & Scholtz, C.H. 1980. Structure and pattern of the Namib Desert dune ecosystem at Gobabeb. *Madoqua*, 1980 (1), 3–39.

Holter, P., Scholtz, C.H. & Stenseng, L. 2009. Desert detritivory: nutritional ecology of a dung beetle (*Pachysoma glentoni*) subsisting on plant litter in arid South African sand dunes. *Journal of Arid Environments*, 73 (12), 1090–1094.

Hörnschemeyer, T. 2010. Cupedidae *Laporte* 1836 [online]. *Tree of Life Web Project*. Available from: http://tolweb.org/Cupedidae/8999/2010.12.23.

Hörnschemeyer, T. 2011. Archostemata [online]. *Tree of Life Web Project*. Available from: http://tolweb.org/Archostemata/8876/2011.03.27.

Irish, J. 1992. The Hetrodinae (Orthoptera: Ensifera: Bradyporidae) of southern Africa: systematics and phylogeny. *Researches of the National Museum*, 8 (8), 394–395.

Isely, F.B. 1944. Correlation between mandibular morphology and food specificity in grasshoppers. *Annals of the Entomological Society of America*, 37 (1), 47–67.

Janse, A.J.T. 1945. On the history and life-history of *Leto venus* Stoll. *Journal of the Entomological Society of Southern Africa*, 8 (2), 154.

Johannsmeier, M.F. 2001. *Beekeeping in South Africa*. Pretoria, South Africa: Agricultural Research Council of South Africa, Plant Protection Research Institute.

Johnson, S.D. 1995. Observations of hawkmoth pollination in the South African orchid *Disa cooperi*. *Nordic Journal of Botany*, 15 (2), 121–125.

Johnson, S.D. 1997. Insect pollination and floral mechanisms in South African species of *Satyrium* (Orchidaceae). *Plant Systematics and Evolution*, 204 (3–4), 195–206.

Johnson, S.D. 2005. Specialized pollination by spider-hunting wasps in the African orchid *Disa sankeyi*. *Plant Systematics and Evolution*, 251 (2–4), 153–160.

Johnson, S.D. 2010. The pollination niche and its role in the diversification and maintenance of the southern African flora. *Philosophical Transactions of the Royal Society B: Biological Sciences*, 365 (1539), 499–516.

Johnson, S.D. & Bond, W.J. 1994. Red flowers and butterfly pollination in the fynbos of South Africa. In: *Plant-animal interactions in Mediterranean-type ecosystems. Tasks for vegetation science*. Dordrecht, Netherlands: Springer.

Johnson, S.D., Ellis, A. & Dötterl, S. 2007. Specialization for pollination by beetles and wasps: the role of lollipop hairs and fragrance in *Satyrium microrrhynchum* (Orchidaceae). *American Journal of Botany*, 94 (1), 47–55.

Johnson, S.D. & Midgley, J.J. 1997. Fly pollination of *Gorteria diffusa* (Asteraceae), and a possible mimetic function for dark spots on the capitulum. *American Journal of Botany*, 84 (4), 429–436.

Johnson, S.D. & Steiner, K.E. 1995. Long-proboscid fly pollination of two orchids in the Cape Drakensberg mountains, South Africa. *Plant Systematics and Evolution*, 195 (3–4), 169–175.

Johnson, S.D. & Steiner, K.E. 1997. Long-tongued fly pollination and evolution of floral spur length in the *Disa draconis* complex (Orchidaceae). *Evolution*, 51 (1), 45.

Johnson, S.D. & Steiner, K.E. 2003. Specialized pollination systems in southern Africa. *South African Journal of Science*, 99 (7), 345–348.

Jones, C.G., Lawton, J.H. & Shachak, M. 1994. Organisms as ecosystem engineers. *Oikos*, 69 (3), 373–386.

Jones, J.A. 1990. Termites, soil fertility and carbon cycling in dry tropical Africa: a hypothesis. *Journal of Tropical Ecology*, 6 (3), 291–305.

Jupp, P.G. 1996. *Mosquitoes of southern Africa: Culicinae and Toxorhynchitinae*. Hartebeespoort, South Africa: Ekogilde Publishers.

Kamimura, Y. 2007. Twin intromittent organs of *Drosophila* for traumatic insemination. *Biology Letters*, 3 (4), 401–404.

Kappmeier, K., Nevill, E.M. & Bagnall, R.J. 1998. Review of tsetse flies and trypanosomosis in South Africa. *The Onderstepoort Journal of Veterinary Research*, 65 (3), 195–203.

Keeping, M.G. 1990a. Colony foundation and nestmate recognition in the social wasp, *Belonogaster petiolata*. *Ethology*, 85 (1), 1–12.

Keeping, M.G. 1990b. Rubbing behavior and morphology of Van der Vecht's gland in *Belonogaster petiolata* (Hymenoptera: Vespidae). *Journal of Insect Behavior*, 3 (1), 85–104.

Keeping, M.G. 1991. Nest construction by the social wasp, *Belonogaster petiolata* (Degeer) (Hymenoptera: Vespidae). *Journal of the Entomological Society of Southern Africa*, 54 (1), 17–28.

Keeping, M.G. 1992. Social organization and division of labour in colonies of the polistine wasp, *Belonogaster petiolata*. *Behavioral Ecology and Sociobiology*, 31 (3), 211–224.

Keeping, M.G. 2000. Morpho-physiological variability and differentiation of reproductive roles among foundresses of the primitively eusocial wasp, *Belonogaster petiolata* (Degeer) (Hymenoptera, Vespidae). *Insectes Sociaux*, 47 (2), 147–154.

Keeping, M.G. 2002. Reproductive and worker castes in the primitively eusocial wasp *Belonogaster petiolata* (DeGeer) (Hymenoptera: Vespidae): evidence for pre-imaginal differentiation. *Journal of Insect Physiology*, 48 (9), 867–879.

Keeping, M.G. & Crewe, R.M. 1983. Parasitoids, commensals and colony size in nests of *Belonogaster* (Hymenoptera: Vespidae). *Journal of the Entomological Society of Southern Africa*, 46 (2), 309–323.

Keeping, M.G., Lipschitz, D. & Crewe, R.M. 1986. Chemical mate recognition and release of male sexual behavior in polybiine wasp, *Belonogaster petiolata* (Degeer) (Hymenoptera: Vespidae). *Journal of Chemical Ecology*, 12 (3), 773–779.

Kitching, I.J. 2003. Phylogeny of the death's head hawkmoths, *Acherontia* [Laspeyres], and related genera (Lepidoptera: Sphingidae: Sphinginae: Acherontiini). *Systematic Entomology*, 28 (2), 71–88.

Klass, K.D., Zompro, O., Kristensen, N.P. & Adis, J. 2002. Mantophasmatodea: a new insect order with extant members in the Afrotropics. *Science*, 296 (5572), 1456–1459.

Korb, J. & Linsenmair, K.E. 2000. Ventilation of termite mounds: new results require a new model. *Behavioral Ecology*, 11 (5), 486–494.

Kovac, D. & Maschwitz, U. 1990. Secretion-grooming in aquatic beetles (*Hydradephaga*): a chemical protection against contamination of the hydrofuge respiratory region. *Chemoecology*, 1 (3–4), 131–138.

Kovac, D. & Maschwitz, U. 1991. The function of the metathoracic scent gland in corixid bugs (Hemiptera, Corixidae): secretion-grooming on the water surface. *Journal of Natural History*, 25 (2), 331–340.

Kroon, D.M. 1999. *Lepidoptera of southern Africa: host-plants and other associations. A catalogue*. Sasolburg, South Africa: Lepidopterists' Society of Africa.

Kynaston, S.E., McErlain-Ward, P. & Mill, P.J. 1994. Courtship, mating behaviour and sexual cannibalism in the praying mantis, *Sphodromantis lineola*. *Animal Behaviour*, 47 (3), 739–741.

Laker, M.C., Hewitt, P.H., Nel, A. & Hunt, R.P. 1982a. Effects of the termite *Trinervitermes trinervoides* Sjöstedt on the organic carbon and nitrogen contents and particle size distribution of soils. *Revue d'écologie et de biologie du sol*, 19, 27–39.

Laker, M.C., Hewitt, P.H., Nel, A. & Hunt, R.P. 1982b. Effects of the termite

Trinervitermes trinervoides Sjöstedt on the pH, electrical conductivities, cation exchange capabilities and extractable base content of soils. *Fort Hare Papers*, 7, 275–286.

Lee, K.E. & Wood, T.G. 1971. *Termites and soils*. London, UK: Academic Press Inc.

Leuthold, R.H., Bruinsma, O. & Van Huis, A. 1976. Optical and pheromonal orientation and memory for homing distance in the harvester termite *Hodotermes mossambicus* (Hagen). *Behavioral Ecology and Sociobiology*, 1 (2), 127–139.

Levick, S.R., Asner, G.P., Kennedy-Bowdoin, T. & Knapp, D.E. 2010. The spatial extent of termite influences on herbivore browsing in an African savanna. *Biological Conservation*, 143 (11), 2462–2467.

Lin, C. & Strausfeld, N.J. 2012. Visual inputs to the mushroom body calyces of the whirligig beetle *Dineutus sublineatus*: modality switching in an insect. *The Journal of Comparative Neurology*, 520 (12), 2562–2574.

Longhurst, C., Baker, R. & Howse, P.E. 1979. Termite predation by *Megaponera foetens* (FAB.) (Hymenoptera: Formicidae). *Journal of Chemical Ecology*, 5 (5), 703–719.

Longhurst, C. & Howse, P.E. 1978. The use of kairomones by *Megaponera foetens* (Fab.) (Hymenoptera: Formicidae) in the detection of its termite prey. *Animal Behaviour*, 26 (4), 1213–1218.

Louw, G.N. & Hamilton, W.J. 1972. Physiological and behavioural ecology of the ultra-psammophilous Namib Desert tenebrionid, *Lepidochora argentogrisea*. *Madoqua*, 2 (1), 87–95.

Louw, G.N., Nicolson, S.W. & Seely, M.K. 1986. Respiration beneath desert sand: carbon dioxide diffusion and respiratory patterns in a tenebrionid beetle. *Journal of Experimental Biology*, 120, 443–447.

Loveridge, J.P. & Moe, S.R. 2004. Termitaria as browsing hotspots for African megaherbivores. *Journal of Tropical Ecology*, 20, 337–343.

Lutz, F.E. 1941. *A lot of insects: entomology in a suburban garden*. New York, USA: G.P. Putnam's Sons.

Madder, M., Horak, I. & Stoltsz, H. (n.d.) Ticks: tick identification.

Madsen, B.L. 2012. Submersion respiration in small diving beetles (Dytiscidae). *International Journal of Freshwater Entomology*, 34, 57–76.

Manning, J. 2009. *Field guide to wild flowers of South Africa, Lesotho and Swaziland*. Cape Town, South Africa: Struik Nature.

Manning, J.C. & Goldblatt, P. 1996. The *Prosoeca peringueyi* (Diptera: Nemestrinidae) pollination guild in southern Africa: long-tongued flies and their tubular flowers. *Annals of the Missouri Botanical Garden*, 83 (1), 67.

Manning, J.C. & Goldblatt, P. 1997. The *Moegistorhynchus longirostris* (Diptera: Nemestrinidae) pollination guild: long-tubed flowers and a specialized long-proboscid fly pollination system in southern Africa. *Plant Systematics and Evolution*, 206 (1–4), 51–69.

Mansell, M.W. 2017. Biology of Nemopteridae and Myrmeleontidae. *In litt*.

Marsh, A.C. 1985. Thermal responses and temperature tolerance in a diurnal desert ant, *Ocymyrmex barbiger*. *Physiological Zoology*, 58 (6), 629–636.

Marsh, A.C. 1987a. Thermal responses and temperature tolerance of a desert ant-lion larva. *Journal of Thermal Biology*, 12 (4), 295–300.

Marsh, A.C. 1987b. The foraging ecology of two Namib Desert harvester ant species. *South African Journal of Zoology*, 22 (2), 130–136.

Matenaar, D., Bröder, L., Bazelet, C.S. & Hochkirch, A. 2014. Persisting in a windy habitat: population ecology and behavioral adaptations of two endemic grasshopper species in the Cape region (South Africa). *Journal of Insect Conservation*, 18 (3), 447–456.

McClain, E. & Gerneke, D. 1990. Morphology of wax blooms on selected Namib Desert beetles (Coleoptera: Tenebrionidae). In: M.K. Seely, ed. *Namib ecology: 25 years of Namib research*. Pretoria, South Africa: Transvaal Museum Monograph No. 7. Transvaal Museum, 193–202.

McClain, E., Hanrahan, S.A. & Gerneke, D. 1986. Extracuticular secretion on a Namib Desert tenebrionid, *Onymacris plana*: an indicator of aridity. *Madoqua*, 1986 (4), 363–367.

McClain, E., Praetorius, R.L., Hanrahan, S.A. & Seely, M.K. 1984. Dynamics of the wax bloom of a seasonal Namib Desert tenebrionid, *Cauricara phalangium* (Coleoptera: Adesmiini). *Oecologia*, 63 (3), 314–319.

McClain, E., Seely, M.K., Hadley, N.F. & Gray, V. 1985. Wax blooms in tenebrionid beetles of the Namib Desert: correlations with environment. *Ecology*, 66 (1), 112–118.

McDonald, D.J. & Van der Walt, J.J.A. 1992. Observations on the pollination of *Pelargonium tricolor*, section *Campylia* (Geraniaceae). *South African Journal of Botany*, 58 (5), 386–392.

Meyer, V.W., Braack, L., Biggs, H.C. & Ebersohn, C. 1999. Distribution and density of termite mounds in the northern Kruger National Park, with specific reference to those constructed by *Macrotermes* Holmgren (Isoptera: Termitidae). *African Entomology*, 7 (1), 123–130.

Midgley, J. 1992. Why do some hopliinid beetles have large hind-legs? *Journal of the Entomological Society of Southern Africa*, 55 (1), 157–159.

Midgley, J. 1993. Asteraceae – an evaluation of Hutchinson's beetle-daisy hypothesis. *African Biodiversity and Conservation*, 23.

Midgley, J.J., Harris, C., Harington, A. & Potts, A.J. 2012. Geochemical perspective on origins and consequences of heuweltjie formation in the southwestern Cape, South Africa. *South African Journal of Geology*, 115 (4), 577–588.

Midgley, J., Harris, C., Hesse, H. & Swift, A. 2002. Heuweltjie age and vegetation change based on δ13C and 14C analyses. *South African Journal of Science*, 98 (3–4), 202–204.

Mlambo, S., Sole, C.L. & Scholtz, C.H. 2015. A molecular phylogeny of the African Scarabaeinae (Coleoptera: Scarabaeidae). *Arthropod Systematics and Phylogeny*, 73 (2), 303–321.

Moore, J.M. & Picker, M.D. 1991. Heuweltjies (earth mounds) in the Clanwilliam district, Cape Province, South Africa: 4000-year-old termite nests. *Oecologia*, 86 (3), 424–432.

Moritz, R.F.A. & Crewe, R.M. 1988. Air ventilation in nests of two African stingless bees *Trigona denoiti* and *Trigona gribodoi*. *Experientia*, 44 (11–12), 1024–1027.

Murray, M.D. 1958. Ecology of the louse *Lepidophthirus macrorhini* Enderlein 1904 on the elephant seal *Mirounga leonina* (L.). *Nature*, 182, 404–405.

Mviha, P.J.Z., Holt, J., Green, S.V. & Mitchell, J. 2003. The ecology of the armoured bush cricket, *Acanthoplus discoidalis*, with reference to habitat, behaviour, oviposition site selection and egg mortality. *Proceedings of the Fourteenth Entomological Congress. Entomological Society of Southern Africa, Pretoria, 6–9 July 2003*. Hatfield, South Africa: Entomological Society of Southern Africa, 61–62.

Myles, T. 1986. Reproductive soldiers in the Termopsidae (Isoptera). *The Pan-Pacific Entomologist*, 62 (4), 293–299.

Nalepa, C.A. 1984. Colony composition, protozoan transfer and some life history characteristics of the woodroach *Cryptocercus punctulatus* Scudder (Dictyoptera: Cryptocercidae). *Behavioral Ecology and Sociobiology*, 14 (4), 273–279.

Nalepa, C.A. & Bell, W.J. 1997. Postovulation parental investment and parental care in cockroaches. In: J.C. Choe & B.J. Crespi, eds. *The evolution of social behavior in insects and arachnids*. Cambridge, UK: Cambridge University Press, 26–51.

Naskrecki, P. & Bazelet, C. 2009. A species radiation amoung South African flightless spring katydids (Orthoptera: Tettigoniidae: Phaneropterinae: *Brinckiella* Chopard). *Zootaxa*, 2056, 46–62.

Nel, J.J.C. & Hewitt, P.H. 1969. Effect of solar radiation on the harvester termite, *Hodotermes mossambicus* (Hagen). *Nature*, 223, 862–863.

Nel, J.J.C., Hewitt, P.H., Smith, L.J. & Smit, W.T. 1969. The behaviour of the harvester termite (*Hodotermes mossambicus* (Hagen)) in a laboratory colony. *Journal of the Entomological Society of Southern Africa*, 32 (1), 9–24.

Nel, J.J.C. & Malan, E.M. 1974. The distribution of the mounds of *Trinervitermes trinerviodes* [sic] in the Orange Free State. *Journal of the Entomological Society of Southern Africa*, 37 (2), 251–256.

Nelson, R.M. & Greeff, J.M. 2009. Male pollinator fig wasps (Chalcidoidea: Agaonidae) do not need an arena to fight. *African Entomology*, 17 (2), 228–231.

Nicolson, S.W. 1980. Water balance and osmoregulation in *Onymacris plana*, a tenebrionid beetle from the Namib desert. *Journal of Insect Physiology*, 26 (5), 315–320.

Nicolson, S.W. 1990. Water relations of the Namib tenebrionid beetles. In: M.K. Seely, ed. *Namib ecology: 25 years of Namib research*. Pretoria, South Africa: Transvaal Museum Monograph No. 7. Transvaal Museum, 173–178.

Nicolson, S.W., Nepi, M. & Pacini, E. 2007. *Nectaries and nectar*. Dordrecht, Netherlands: Springer.

Nørgaard, T. & Dacke, M. 2010. Fog-basking behaviour and water collection efficiency in Namib Desert darkling beetles. *Frontiers in Zoology*, 7 (1), 23.

Nxele, T.C., Lamani, S., Measey, G.J., Armstrong, A.J., Plisko, J.D., Willows-Munro, S., Janion-Scheepers, C. & Wilson, J.R.U. 2015. Studying earthworms (Annelida: Oligochaeta) in South Africa. *African Invertebrates*, 56 (3), 779–806.

Okullo, P. & Moe, S.R. 2012. Termite activity, not grazing, is the main determinant of spatial variation in savanna herbaceous vegetation. *Journal of Ecology*, 100 (1), 232–241.

Ollerton, J., Johnson, S.D., Cranmer, L. & Kellie, S. 2003. The pollination ecology of an assemblage of grassland asclepiads in South Africa. *Annals of Botany*, 92 (6), 807–834.

Palmer, T.M. 2003. Spatial habitat heterogeneity influences competition and coexistence in an African acacia ant guild. *Ecology*, 84 (11), 2843–2855.

Palmer, T.M. & Brody, A.K. 2007. Mutualism as reciprocal exploitation: African plant-ants defend foliar but not reproductive structures. *Ecology*, 88 (12), 3004–3011.

Pauw, A. 2006. Floral syndromes accurately predict pollination by a specialized oil-collecting bee (*Rediviva peringueyi*, Melittidae) in a guild of South African orchids (Coryciinae). *American Journal of Botany*, 93 (6), 917–926.

Pearson, D.L. & Vogler, A.P. 2001. *Tiger beetles: the evolution, ecology, and diversity of the cicindelids*. New York, USA: Cornell University Press.

Picker, M., Griffiths, C. & Weaving, A. 2002. *Field guide to insects of South Africa*. Cape Town, South Africa: Struik Publishers.

Picker, M.D., Hoffman, M.T. & Leverton, B. 2007. Density of *Microhodotermes viator* (Hodotermitidae) mounds in southern Africa in relation to rainfall and vegetative productivity gradients. *Journal of Zoology*, 271 (1), 37–44.

Picker, M.D. & Midgley, J.J. 1996. Pollination by monkey beetles (Coleoptera: Scarabaeidae: Hopliini): flower and colour preferences. *African Entomology*, 4 (1), 7–14.

Pierce, N.E., Braby, M.F., Heath, A., Lohman, D.J., Mathew, J., Rand, D.B. & Travassos, M.A. 2002. The ecology and evolution of ant association in the Lycaenidae (Lepidoptera). *Annual Review of Entomology*, 47 (1), 733–771.

Price, S. & Louw, S. 1996. Resource manipulation through architectural modification of the host plant by a gall-forming weevil *Urodontus scholtzi* Louw (Coleoptera: Anthribidae). *African Entomology*, 4 (2), 103–110.

Prinsloo, G.L. 1990. Commentary on the insect fauna of the lower Kuiseb River, Namib Desert. In: M.K. Seely, ed. *Namib ecology*. Pretoria, South Africa: Transvaal Museum Monograph No. 7. Transvaal Museum, 67–75.

Prinsloo, G.L. & Kelly, J.A. 2009. The tetrastichine wasps (Hymenoptera:

Chalcidoidea: Eulophidae) associated with galls on *Erythrina* species (Fabaceae) in South Africa, with the description of five new species. *Zootaxa*, 2083, 27–45.

Prinsloo, G.L. & Uys, V.M. 2015. *Insects of cultivated plants and natural pastures in southern Africa*. Hatfield, South Africa: Entomological Society of Southern Africa.

Rampini, M., Di Russo, C. & Carchini, G. 2010. A second species of cave Macropathinae for Africa (Orthoptera, Rhaphidophoridae). *Subterranean Biology*, 7, 65–68.

Rasa, O.A.E. 1990. Evidence for subsociality and division of labor in a desert tenebrionid beetle *Parastizopus armaticeps* Peringuey. *The Science of Nature*, 77 (12), 591–592.

Rasa, O.A.E. 1994. Behavioural adaptations to moisture as an environmental constraint in a nocturnal burrow-inhabiting Kalahari detritivore *Parastizopus armaticeps* Peringuey (Coleoptera: Tenebrionidae). *Koedoe*, 37 (1), 57–66.

Rasa, O.A.E. 1995. Ecological factors influencing burrow location, group size and mortality in a nocturnal fossorial Kalahari detritivore, *Parastizopus armaticeps* Peringuey (Coleoptera: Tenebrionidae). *Journal of Arid Environments*, 29 (3), 353–365.

Rasa, O.A.E. 1996. Interspecific association in desert tenebrionid beetles: a cleptoparasite does not affect the host's reproductive success, but that of its offspring. *Naturwissenschaften*, 83 (12), 575–577.

Rasa, O.A.E. 1998. Biparental investment and reproductive success in a subsocial desert beetle: the role of maternal effort. *Behavioral Ecology and Sociobiology*, 43 (2), 105–113.

Rehn, J.A.G. & Rehn, J.W.H. 1935. A study of the genus *Hemimerus* (Dermaptera, Hemimerina, Hemimeridae). *Proceedings of the Academy of Natural Sciences of Philadelphia*, 87, 457–508.

Robertson, I.A.D. 2004. The Pyrrhocoroidea (Hemiptera - Heteroptera) of the Ethiopian region. *Journal of Insect Science*, 4 (1).

Robinson, I.A. & Seely, M.K. 1980. Physical and biotic environments of the southern Namib dune ecosystem. *Journal of Arid Environments*, 3 (3), 183–203.

Romey, W.L. 1995. Position preferences within groups: do whirligigs select positions which balance feeding opportunities with predator avoidance? *Behavioral Ecology and Sociobiology*, 37 (3), 195–200.

Ruppert, E.E. & Barnes, R.D. 1994. *Invertebrate zoology*. 6th ed. Fort Worth, USA: Saunders College Publishing.

Rutherford, M.C., Mucina, L. & Powrie, L.W. 2006. Biomes and bioregions of southern Africa. In: L. Mucina & M.C. Rutherford, eds. *The vegetation of South Africa, Lesotho and Swaziland*. Pretoria, South Africa: South African National Biodiversity Institute, 30–51.

Samways, M.J. 2008. *Dragonflies and damselflies of South Africa*. Sofia, Bulgaria: Pensoft Publishers.

Sanborn, A.F., Villet, M.H. & Phillips, P.K. 2004. Endothermy in African platypleurine cicadas: the influence of body size and habitat (Hemiptera: Cicadidae). *Physiological and Biochemical Zoology*, 77 (5), 816–823.

Scholes, R.J. & Walker, B.H. 2004. *An African savanna: synthesis of the Nylsvley study*. 11th ed. Cambridge, UK: Cambridge University Press.

Scholtz, C.H. & Chown, S.L. 1995. Insects in southern Africa: how many species are there? *South African Journal of Science*, 91 (3), 124–126.

Scholtz, C.H. & Holm, E. 2014. *Insects of southern Africa*. Pretoria, South Africa: Protea Book House.

Scholtz, C.H., Harrison, J. & Grebennikov, V.V. 2004. Dung beetle (*Scarabaeus* (*Pachysoma*)) biology and immature stages: reversal to ancestral states under desert conditions (Coleoptera: Scarabaeidae). *Biological Journal of the Linnean Society*, 83 (4), 453–460.

Seely, M.K., ed. 1990. *Namib ecology: 25 years of Namib research*. Pretoria, South Africa: Transvaal Museum Monograph No. 7. Transvaal Museum.

Seely, M.K. & Hamilton, W.J. 1976. Fog catchment sand trenches constructed by tenebrionid beetles, *Lepidochora*, from the Namib Desert. *Science*, 193 (4252), 484–486.

Seely, M.K., Lewis, C.J., O'Brien, K.A. & Suttle, A.E. 1983. Fog response of tenebrionid beetles in the Namib Desert. *Journal of Arid Environments*, 6 (2), 135–143.

Shuttleworth, A. & Johnson, S.D. 2008. Bimodal pollination by wasps and beetles in the African milkweed *Xysmalobium undulatum*. *Biotropica*, 40 (5), 568–574.

Shuttleworth, A. & Johnson, S.D. 2009a. A key role for floral scent in a wasp-pollination system in *Eucomis* (Hyacinthaceae). *Annals of Botany*, 103 (5), 715–725.

Shuttleworth, A. & Johnson, S.D. 2009b. Palp-faction: an African milkweed dismembers its wasp pollinators.

Environmental Entomology, 38 (3), 741–747.

Shuttleworth, A. & Johnson, S.D. 2009c. Specialized pollination in the African milkweed *Xysmalobium orbiculare*: a key role for floral scent in the attraction of spider-hunting wasps. *Plant Systematics and Evolution*, 280 (1–2), 37–44.

Shuttleworth, A. & Johnson, S.D. 2009d. The importance of scent and nectar filters in a specialized wasp-pollination system. *Functional Ecology*, 23 (5), 931–940.

Skaife, S.H. 1979. *African insect life*. Cape Town, South Africa: C. Struik Publishers.

Smith, F.R. & Yeaton, R.I. 1998. Disturbance by the mound-building termite, *Trinervitermes trinervoides*, and vegetation patch dynamics in a semi-arid, southern African grassland. *Plant Ecology*, 137, 41–53.

Smith, G., Crouch, N.R. & Figueireda, E. 2017. *Field guide to succulents in southern Africa*. Cape Town, South Africa: Struik Nature.

Sole, C.L., Scholtz, C.H. & Bastos, A.D.S. 2004. Phylogeography of the Namib Desert dung beetles *Scarabaeus* (*Pachysoma*) MacLeay (Coleoptera: Scarabaeidae). *Journal of Biogeography*, 32 (1), 75–84.

Solomon, E.P., Berg, L.R., Martin, D.W. & Villee, C. 1996. *Biology*. 4th ed. Fort Worth, USA: Saunders College Publishing.

Staude, H.S. 1996. Observations on lek behaviour and the description of male scent disseminating structures of *Callioratis abraxas* Felder, 1874 (Lepidoptera: Geometridae). *Metamorphosis*, 7 (3), 121–126.

Staude, H.S. 2001. A revision of the genus *Callioratis* Felder (Lepidoptera: Geometridae: Diptychinae). *Metamorphosis*, 12 (4), 125–156.

Staude, H.S. & Sihvonen, P. 2014. Revision of the African geometrid genus *Zerenopsis* C. & R. Felder – moths with peculiar life histories and mating behaviours (Geometridae: Ennominae: Diptychini). *Metamorphosis*, 25, 11–55.

Steiner, K.E. 1998. Beetle pollination of peacock moraeas (Iridaceae) in South Africa. *Plant Systematics and Evolution*, 209 (1–2), 47–65.

Steinke, T.D. & Nel, L.O. 1989. Some effects of termitaria on veld in the Eastern Cape. *African Journal of Range & Forage Science*, 6 (3).

Stenton-Dozey, J. & Griffiths, C.L. 1980. Growth, consumption and respiration by larvae of the kelp-fly *Fucellia capensis* (Diptera: Anthomyiidae). *South African Journal of Zoology*, 15 (4), 280–283.

Steyn, J.J. 1954. *The pugnacious ant (Anoplolepis custodiens Smith) and its relation to the control of citrus scales at Letaba*. Pretoria, South Africa: Entomological Society of Southern Africa.

Storer, T.I., Stebbins, C., Usinger, R.L. & Nybakken, J.W. 1979. *General zoology*. 6th ed. New York, USA: McGraw-Hill.

Suhling, F., Martens, A. & Marais, E. 2009. How to enter a desert – patterns of Odonata colonisation of arid Namibia. *International Journal of Odonatology*, 12 (2), 287–308.

Suhling, F., Muller, O. & Martens, A. 2014. *The dragonfly larvae of Namibia (Odonata)*. Zeitschrift der Gesellschaft deutschsprachiger Odonatologen (GdO) e.V.

Svenson, G.J. & Whiting, M.F. 2004. Phylogeny of Mantodea based on molecular data: evolution of a charismatic predator. *Systematic Entomology*, 29 (3), 359–370.

Swart, J.M., Richardson, P.R.K. & Ferguson, J.W.H. 1999. Ecological factors affecting the feeding behaviour of pangolins (*Manis temminckii*). *Journal of Zoology*, 247 (3), 281–292.

Switala, A.K., Sole, C.L. & Scholtz, C.H. 2014. Phylogeny, historical biogeography and divergence time estimates of the genus *Colophon* Gray (Coleoptera: Lucanidae). *Invertebrate Systematics*, 28 (3), 326.

Tarboton, W. & Tarboton, M. 2015. *A guide to the dragonflies and damselflies of South Africa*. Cape Town, South Africa: Struik Publishers.

Terry, M.D. & Whiting, M.F. 2005. Mantophasmatodea and phylogeny of the lower neopterous insects. *Cladistics*, 21 (3), 240–257.

Tinley, K.L. 1977. *Framework of the Gorongosa ecosystem*. D.Sc. thesis. Pretoria, South Africa: University of Pretoria.

Todd, M.C., Washington, R., Cheke, R.A. & Kniveton, D. 2002. Brown locust outbreaks and climate variability in southern Africa. *Journal of Applied Ecology*, 39 (1), 31–42.

Trapnell, C.G., Friend, M.T., Chamberlain, G.T. & Birch, H.F. 1976. The effects of fire and termites on a Zambian woodland soil. *The Journal of Ecology*, 64 (2), 577–589.

Triplehorn, C.A. & Johnson, N.F. 2005. *Borror and DeLong's introduction to the study of insects*. 7th ed. Belmont, USA: Thompson Brooks/Cole.

Turner, J.S. 1994. Ventilation and thermal constancy of a colony of a southern African termite (*Odontotermes transvaalensis*: Macrotermitinae). *Journal of Arid Environments*, 28 (3), 231–248.

Turner, J.S. 2000. Architecture and morphogenesis in the mound of *Macrotermes michaelseni* (Sjöstedt) (Isoptera: Termitidae, Macrotermitinae) in northern Namibia. *Cimbebasia*, 16, 143–175.

Turner, J.S. 2001. On the mound of *Macrotermes michaelseni* as an organ of respiratory gas exchange. *Physiological and Biochemical Zoology*, 74 (6), 798–822.

Turner, J.S. & Lombard, A.T. 1990. Body color and body temperature in white and black Namib Desert beetles. *Journal of Arid Environments*, 19 (3), 303–315.

Van Noort, S., Masner, L., Popovici, O., Valerio, A.A., Taekul, C., Johnson, N.F., Murphy, N.P. & Austin, A.D. 2014. Systematics and biology of the aberrant intertidal parasitoid wasp *Echthrodesis lamorali* Masner (Hymenoptera: Platygastridae *s.l.*): a parasitoid of spider eggs. *Invertebrate Systematics*, 28 (1), 1.

Van Staaden, M.J., Rieser, M., Ott, S.R., Pabst, M.A. & Römer, H. 2003. Serial hearing organs in the atympanate grasshopper *Bullacris membracioides* (Orthoptera, Pneumoridae). *Journal of Comparative Neurology*, 465 (4), 579–592.

Van Wyk, A.E. & Smith, G.F. 2001. *Regions of floristic endemism in southern Africa. A review with emphasis on succulents*. Hatfield, South Africa: Umdaus Press.

Van Wyk, B. & Van Wyk, P. 2013. *Field guide to trees of southern Africa: an African perspective*. 2nd ed. Cape Town, South Africa: Struik Publishers.

Veldtman, R. 2005. *The ecology of southern African wild silk moths (Gonometa species, Lepidoptera: Lasiocampidae): consequences for their sustainable use*. Ph.D thesis. Pretoria, South Africa: University of Pretoria.

Vernon, C.J. 1999. Biogeography, endemism and diversity of animals in the Karoo. In: W.R.J. Dean & S.J. Milton, eds. *The Karoo: ecological patterns and processes*. Cambridge, UK: Cambridge University Press, 57–86.

Villet, M.H. 1990. Division of labour in the Matabele ant *Megaponera foetens* (Fabr.) (Hymenoptera Formicidae). *Ethology Ecology & Evolution*, 2 (4), 397–417.

Vulinec, K. & Miller, M.C. 1989. Aggregation and predator avoidance in whirligig beetles (Coleoptera: Gyrinidae). *Journal of the New York Entomological Society*, 97 (4), 438–447.

Waller, D.A. & La Fage, J.P. 1987. Nutritional ecology of termites. In: J.F. Slansky & J.G. Rodriguez, eds. *Nutritional ecology of insects, mites and spiders and related invertebrates*. New York, USA: John Wiley & Sons, 487–532.

Watmough, R.H. 1973. Biology and behaviour of carpenter bees in southern Africa. *Journal of the Entomological Society of Southern Africa*, 37 (2), 261–281.

Watmough, R.H. 1983. Mortality, sex ratio and fecundity in natural populations of large carpenter bees (*Xylocopa* spp.). *Journal of Animal Ecology*, 52, 111–125.

Watson, J.P. 1967. A termite mound in an Iron Age burial ground in Rhodesia. *The Journal of Ecology*, 55 (3), 663–669.

Weir, J.S. 1973. Air flow, evaporation and mineral accumulation in mounds of *Macrotermes subhyalinus* (Rambur). *The Journal of Animal Ecology*, 42 (3), 509–520.

Wharton, R.A. 1980. Colouration and diurnal activity patterns in some Namib Desert *Zophosini* (Coleoptera: Tenebrionidae). *Journal of Arid Environments*, 3, 309–317.

Willis, C.K., Skinner, J.D. & Robertson, H.G. 1992. Abundance of ants and termites in the False Karoo and their importance in the diet of the aardvark *Orycteropus afer*. *African Journal of Ecology*, 30 (4), 322–334.

Wilson, D.S. & Clark, A.B. 1977. Above ground predator defence in the harvester termite, *Hodotermes mossambicus* (Hagen). *Journal of the Entomological Society of Southern Africa*, 40, 271–282.

Witt, A.B.R., Geertsema, H. & Giliomee, J.H. 2004. The impact of an invasive ant, *Linepithema humile* (Mayr) (Hymenoptera: Formicidae), on the dispersal of the elaiosome-bearing seeds of six plant species. *African Entomology*, 12 (2), 223–230.

Witt, A.B.R. & Giliomee, J.H. 2004. The impact of an invasive ant, *Linepithema humile* (Mayr), on the dispersal of *Phylica pubescens* Aiton seeds in South Africa. *African Entomology*, 12 (2), 179–185.

Wood, T.G. & Sands, W.A. 1978. The role of termites in ecosystems. In: M.V. Brain, ed. *Production ecology of ants and termites*. Cambridge, UK: Cambridge University Press, 245–292.

Young, T.P., Stubblefield, C.H. & Isbell, L.A. 1997. Ants on swollen-thorn acacias: species coexistence in a simple system. *Oecologia*, 109 (1), 98–107.

Yusuf, A.A., Gordon, I., Crewe, R.M. & Pirk, C.W.W. 2014. Prey choice and raiding behaviour of the ponerine ant *Pachycondyla analis* (Hymenoptera: Formicidae). *Journal of Natural History*, 48 (5–6), 345–358.

Zumpt, F. 1965. *Myiasis in man and animals in the Old World: a textbook for physicians, veterinarians and zoologists*. Michigan, USA: Butterworths.

GLOSSARY

abdomen posterior section of the body of an arthropod, behind the thorax or cephalothorax

abiotic relating to the nonliving, chemical and physical parts of the environment

acephalic relating to the absence of a head capsule

aedeagus reproductive organ of male arthropods through which sperm is secreted from the testes during copulation

ametamorphic development negligible transformation, with little change other than size

amoebocytes migratory, amoeboid cells found in many invertebrates that function in excretion, assimilation, etc.

anoxic without oxygen

anterior front part of the organism

apical far from the body, for example, when referring to parts of the legs or wings

apodous without legs

basal near the body, for example, when referring to parts of the legs or wings

caeca blind sacs

campodeiform elongated, flattened, and active

caraboid Carabidae-like

caudal relating to the tail, the end part of the organism

cephalic relating to the head

cephalothorax fused head and thorax of spiders and other chelicerate arthropods

cerci terminal sensory structures

chelicerae either of a pair of appendages in front of the mouth in arachnids and some other arthropods

chitin large, structural polysaccharide made from chains of modified glucose, found in the exoskeletons of insects, cell walls of fungi, and certain hard structures in invertebrates and fish

cibarium space in front of the true mouth cavity in which the food of an insect is chewed

clypeus lower facial segment of the head

coarctate enclosed in a rigid case formed from the last larval skin

corpus adiposum fat storage organ

coxa segment of the leg of an insect nearest to its body

cuticle protective, waxy or hard layer covering the epidermis of an invertebrate

derived relating to a character not present in the ancestral form

detritus dead plant material

diffuse to move (as molecules do) from a region of high concentration to lower concentration

disjunct disjoined and distinct from one another

distal far from the body, for example, when referring to parts of the legs or wings

dorsal upper

dorsolaterally at the top of the sides

dorsoventrally extending along an axis joining the dorsal (upper) and ventral (lower) surfaces

dorsum upper surface

ecdysis process of casting off the outer cuticle

eclose to come out of the egg or pupa case

ectoparasite parasite that inhabits the skin or outgrowths of the skin of a host

elateriform wireworm-like

elytra modified, hardened forewings of beetles (Coleoptera)

endoparasite parasite that inhabits the internal organs or tissues of a host

epiphyte plant that grows on and depends on another plant for mechanical support, but not for nutrients

epizoic relating to a nonparasitic organism that grows or lives on the exterior of another organism

eruciform caterpillar-like

eusocial relating to behaviour involving cooperative brood care, overlapping generations within a colony of adults, and a division of labour into reproductive and nonreproductive groups

eversible able to protrude from an organism by being turned inside out

exarate having the legs, wings, etc, free and movable

exoskeleton hard outer structure that provides support and protection to internal organs

fat body fat storage organ

femur third segment of the leg in insects and some arthropods

flagellomeres segments of the antennal flagellum

flagellum third, compound segment of the antenna

globose having a spherical form

gonopods leg-like appendages of the external genitalia

gonopores genital openings

gymnosperm member of a group of plants that produce seeds that are not enclosed within an ovary or fruit

halteres mechanosensory flight organs

haplodiploidy sex-determination system in which females are diploid and males are haploid, as they develop from fertilised and unfertilised eggs, respectively

haustellate adapted for sucking, seen in mouthparts of certain insects

hemimetamorphic development slight transformation in the insect that hatches from the egg as a nymph that resembles the adult

hermaphrodite organism that has both male and female reproductive systems

hierarchical classification system taxonomic system used for classifying organisms from higher to lower levels

histoblast cell or group of cells capable of forming a tissue

holometamorphic development substantial transformation, with considerable differences between stages

humus organic matter

hydrofuge impervious to water

hydrostatic skeleton flexible skeleton supported by fluid pressure

hypermetamorphosis unusual type of larval development in which some or all of the larval instars have completely different forms

ileum last part of the small intestine

imaginal relating to the last stage an insect attains during its metamorphosis

instars phases between two periods of moulting during the development of invertebrate larvae

integument outer protective layer

kleptoparasite organism that steals food or prey from another organism

labium lower lip

labrum broad upper lip

lateral relating to the sides

lipoproteins class of proteins responsible for transporting lipids in blood

longitudinal relating to the axis from head to tail

mandibles jaws

mandibulate containing a pair of mouthparts that are adapted for chewing

matriphagy consumption of the mother by her offspring

maxillae upper jaws

medial situated near the median plane of the body

mesenteron middle section of the intestine in embryos or arthropods

mesothorax middle thoracic segment

metamorphosis transformation in body form and habits of individuals

metapleura sclerotised plates that make up the sides of the third thoracic segment of insects

metathorax hind thoracic segment

monotypic relating to a genus that contains a single species

moulting shedding/casting off of an outer layer and the formation of its replacement

mushroom bodies pair of structures in the brain of insects and other arthropods that play a role in olfactory learning and memory

naiad water nymph

nymph immature form of some invertebrates

obligatory capable of surviving only in a particular condition or by assuming a particular behaviour

ocelli simple eyes

oesophagus part of the alimentary canal connecting the throat to the stomach

oligopodous with a few legs

oocyte female gametocyte

ootheca egg case

osmeterium protrusible gland that secretes a foul-smelling odour as a defence mechanism

osmoregulation maintenance of an internal balance between water and dissolved materials

ostracod small aquatic crustacean of the class Ostracoda

ovarioles tubes of which insect ovaries are composed

ovary female reproductive organ in which ova/eggs are produced

oviduct tube through which an ovum/egg passes from an ovary

oviparous reproductive strategy in which the young develop outside of the body in eggs

ovipositor egg-laying tube

ovoviviparous reproductive strategy in which eggs develop within the body and live young are produced

palps pair of elongated segmented appendages near the mouth of an arthropod

papillae small, projecting body parts that appear similar to a nipple in shape

parasite organism that lives in or on host organisms and benefits by deriving nutrients at the expense of the host

parthenogenesis process in which unmated females produce offspring from unfertilised eggs

pedicel stem

pedipalps second pair of appendages attached to the cephalothorax of most arachnids

pharynx part of the alimentary canal immediately behind the mouth in invertebrates

phylogenetic relating to the evolutionary development and diversification of a group of organisms

pioneer species hardy species that are first to colonise previously disturbed ecosystems

polypodous with many legs

posterior relating to the end part of the insect

proctodeum hindgut

prothorax front thoracic segment

protocerebrum forebrain

proventriculus gizzard

proximal near the body, for example, when referring to specific parts of the legs or wings

pseudopodium temporary protrusion or retractile process of the cytoplasm of a cell

pygidial relating to the posterior body region or segment of certain invertebrates

pygidium exposed tip of the abdomen

pylorus valve connected to the duodenum that opens and closes during digestion

quiescent relating to the inactive state

rectum enlarged, thin-walled sac at the end of the intestine

relicts remnants of a once widespread species or group of organisms living in a small local area

rostrum anterior prolongation of the head in an insect

salivarium small pocket inside the oral cavity of an insect, containing the opening of the salivary duct

scape base of antenna

scarabaeiform grub-like

sclerites specialised segments consisting of solid plates

scolytoid relating to a large group of bark-boring or wood-boring beetles with a very short beak and clubbed antennae

scopula small brush-like structure

sensilla sensory receptors

setae hairs

sexually dimorphic with differences in appearance between males and females of the same species

spermatheca receptacle in which sperm is stored after mating

spermatophore protein capsule containing a mass of spermatozoa

spiracle external respiratory opening

stemmata class of simple eyes

stomodaeum foregut

stylet needle-like projection

subsocial relating to behaviour where parents care for their young for some length of time

substrate surface on which an organism lives

suctorial specialised for sucking

sympatric occurring within the same or overlapping geographical areas

tarsus final segment in the leg of an arthropod

taxonomist biologist who specialises in identifying, classifying and describing species

tegmina thickened forewings

thorax midsection of the arthropod body

tibia fourth section of the typical arthropod leg

torpor state of decreased physiological activity

tracheae tubes involved in respiration that move oxygen from spiracles to tracheoles

tracheoles tubes involved in respiration that spread oxygen throughout the body of arthropods

transverse crosswise through the longitudinal axis

triungulin in beetles, the active first instar

trochanter second segment in the leg of an insect, located between the coxa and the femur

trophallaxis liquid food exchange

tubercle small rounded projection or protuberance

tuberculate having tubercles

urticating stinging, irritating

vas deferens tube in the male reproductive system that transports sperm cells from the epididymis

venter lower surface

ventral lower

vermiform maggot-like

vivipary reproductive strategy in which embryos develop inside the body and live young are produced

vlei low-lying, marshy ground that is generally covered with water during the rainy season

INDEX

Xylocopa caffra, a carpenter bee, an important pollinator of fynbos flowers.